Do It Yourself

Microsoft® C/C++ 7

Do It Yourself

Microsoft® C/C++ 7

Jeb Long

Elizabeth Long, Consulting Editor

A Division of Prentice Hall Computer Publishing
11711 North College, Carmel, Indiana 46032 USA

This book is dedicated to my mother, Emma Long. Her strength and love have been a constant inspiration all my life.

Quotations that appear in this book were taken from these sources: *International Thesaurus of Quotations*, compiled by Rhonda Thomas Tripp. New York: Harper & Row; and *Bartlett's Familiar Quotations*, John Bartlett. Fifteenth and 125th Anniversary Edition. Boston: Little Brown and Co.

International Standard Book Number: 0-672-27390-X

Library of Congress Catalog Card Number: 92-64086

94 93 92 8 7 6 5 4 3 2 1

Interpretation of the printing code: the rightmost double-digit number is the year of the book's printing; the rightmost single-digit number, the number of the book's printing. For example, a printing code of 92-1 shows that the first printing of the book occurred in 1992.

Composed in Garamond, Univers, and MCPdigital typefaces by Prentice Hall Computer Publishing

Screen reproductions in this book were created by means of the program Collage Plus from Inner Media, Inc., Hollis, NH.

Printed in the United States of America

Publisher
Richard K. Swadley

Managing Editor
Neweleen A. Trebnik

Acquisitions Editor
Gregory Croy

Development Editors
Stacy Hiquet
Kim Logan

Production Editors
Katherine Stuart Ewing
Virginia Noble

Editorial Coordinator
Becky Freeman

Editorial Assistants
Rosemarie Graham
Lori Kelley

Technical Editor
Robert Zigon

Cover Designer
Dan Armstrong

Director of Production and Manufacturing
Jeff Valler

Production Manager
Matthew Morrill

Book Designer
Michele Laseau

Production Analyst
Mary Beth Wakefield

Proofreading/Indexing Coordinator
Joelynn Gifford

Graphics Image Specialists
Dennis Sheehan, Jerry Ellis

Production
Phil Kitchel—*Book Shepherd,*
Scott Boucher, Christine Cook,
Dennis Clay Hager, John Kane,
Carrie Keesling, Juli Pavey,
Linda Quigley, Michelle Self,
Greg Simsic, Angie Trzepacz,
Julie Walker, Kelli Widdifield,
Allan Wimmer

Indexer
Tina Trettin

About the Author

Jeb Long has more than 28 years of experience in software design and engineering at some of the most prestigious technical organizations in the country. Mr. Long has been working as an independent consultant and author since he left Ashton-Tate Corporation in 1990. While at Ashton-Tate, he was the guru of dBASE products. In that role, he was the dBASE Language Architect and was responsible for the dBASE language components for all versions of dBASE III and IV except the initial version.

Mr. Long's relationship to dBASE dates back to 1973 when, as a software engineer at the California Institute of Technology's Jet Propulsion Laboratory, he was assigned the responsibility of developing a file management program for JPL's large UNIVAC 1108 Mainframe Computer. This program, called JPLDIS, was the immediate precursor to dBASE. Later, under contract to Wayne Ratliff, Mr. Long translated and adapted the original version of dBASE II to run on the IBM PC.

In his 11 years at the Jet Propulsion Laboratory, Mr. Long was responsible for software tasks in support of our nation's planetary exploration program. Among these tasks were programs to calculate interplanetary trajectories, to process telemetry from space vehicles, and to support spacecraft tests and operations. He was actively involved in the Mariner and Viking missions to Mars.

A 1963 graduate of the University of Texas, Mr. Long now lives with his wife, Elizabeth, on a hill overlooking Los Angeles. Elizabeth has a Masters Degree in English and has worked as a technical writer at JPL. Jeb and Elizabeth have written many books and articles for technical magazines.

Overview

Contents

7 Input and Output 175

8 Operators and Expressions 209

12 Functions 305

Part III Advanced Features of C and C++

Acknowledgments

Grateful acknowledgment is extended to all the people who made this book possible with their enthusiastic support and encouragement:

The Prentice Hall Computer Publishing editorial and publishing staff. Special gratitude to Greg Croy, Stacy Hiquet, Kim Logan, Ginny Noble, Kathy Ewing, and Becky Freeman.

Robert Zigon, technical editor. Thanks for your skillful attention to technical details.

Elizabeth Long, consulting editor. Thanks for all your assistance and encouragement in developing and preparing this manuscript.

Trademark Acknowledgments

Introduction

The purpose of *Do It Yourself Microsoft C/C++ 7* is to help you learn to develop programs in the C++ language, using the Microsoft C/C++ 7 development system. Thus, the book's primary objective is to help first-time C++ language users, as well as experienced C language programmers, develop the skills necessary to program in the C++ language, using the Microsoft C/C++ 7 development system.

The organization of this book falls into four parts. Part I (Chapters 1 through 5) provides an introduction to the Microsoft C/C++ programming environment. You learn how to install and set up the development system, and you use the Microsoft Programmer's WorkBench (PWB). You are given a guided tour through the PWB menu system, and you learn how to use the development tools. Finally, you learn the basics of editing, compiling, and building an executable program with the PWB.

Parts II and III (Chapters 6 through 15) are for those who have never programmed in C or C++ or for those who want to review the C++ procedural language elements. It is here that you learn how to program in C++ by using the procedural aspects of the C++ language. These chapters are based on the theory that the best way to learn something is to use it. Provided are descriptions of the fundamental C++ language components and examples of their uses.

Part IV (Chapters 16 through 23) focuses on the object-oriented features of the C++ language. You are introduced to the fundamental concepts of an object-oriented approach to developing applications, and you learn the advantages of using object-oriented programming (OOP) to develop superior applications. You become familiar with objects, classes, abstraction, encapsulation, polymorphism, and inheritance; and you learn how to translate these concepts into practical and beneficial programming techniques. Furthermore, you learn how to use C++ to implement OOP concepts. The subject is complex. However, you are gently guided through each topic one step at a time. By the time you have completed this book, you will be able to use effectively the Microsoft C/C++ 7 development system to develop serious OOP applications.

You learn also how to test and debug applications. To help you look out for potential programming problem areas, a list of common programming pitfalls is provided. Finally, you learn how to use the Microsoft CodeView C/C++ 7 debugger to help you find insidious programming logic bugs lurking in your code.

Conventions Used in This Book

The following typographic conventions have been used to make this book easier to read and understand:

- Sample programs, program fragments, keywords, function operators, and variables appear in a special `monospace` typeface that simulates the font appearing on your computer screen.
- Words that you are asked to type appear in **`bold monospace`**.
- In format lines, placeholders (items to be substituted) appear in *`italic monospace`*.
- New terms that are introduced and words that are emphasized appear in *italics*.
- Access keys (or *hot keys*) that enable you to select menu items without using a mouse appear as bold in text (**F**ile) and as underlined characters in headings ("The File Menu").
- Filenames and program names appear in uppercase. DOS commands appear in uppercase and `monospace`. Header files appear in lowercase. Example are the `COPY` command, USEPRODS.CPP, and address.h.
- An ellipsis (. . .) used within a sample program indicates that a portion of the program has been omitted.
- The keystroke combination of Ctrl+S indicates that you should press and hold down the Ctrl key while pressing the S key. The combination Ctrl+Q, A indicates that you should press and hold down the Ctrl key while pressing the Q key. Then release both keys and press the A key.

Part I

The Microsoft C/C++ Programming Environment

Introduction to C and C++

This book can help you quickly learn to write programs in both C and C++. Examples are provided to show you how to use all the C and C++ language elements. Because you are using the Microsoft C/C++ 7 compiler, you can try out each example on your computer as you go; this reinforces what you have learned and will help you remember it. A language is difficult, if not impossible, to learn by just reading about it. You must apply the principles as you read about them. This book helps you develop both C and C++ applications that work under the MS-DOS operating system. You also learn to develop C++ applications that work in the Windows 3.1 and Microsoft DOS environments.

In This Chapter

This chapter offers some background to get you started on the road to writing C programs. The following topics are covered:

- The history of C and C++—where they came from and how the C language evolved to become C++
- Some of the advantages of programming in C and C++
- The concept of GUIs (graphical user interfaces) and how Windows was developed

Where Did C Come From?

The C language was created in 1972 by Dennis Ritchie of Bell Laboratories and was patterned after a language, called B, created by Ken Thompson. B was an adaptation of a language called BCPL, which was written by Martin Richards for use in developing the first UNIX system for the DEC PDP-7. Dennis Ritchie originally created the C language for the development of UNIX on the DEC PDP-11 computer. The original PDP-11 version of UNIX was written in assembly language but was later rewritten in C. Subsequent versions of UNIX were written also in C, and it soon replaced assembly language as the language of choice of programmers in the UNIX environment. As C became more popular, it was used for a variety of applications.

Before long, C was being written for different computers and different operating systems, and adaptations of the C language became numerous. The American National Standards Institute (ANSI)—professionals from the computer industry responsible for defining programming standards—formed a panel to standardize the C language. When a programming language is standardized, any program written in that language can be used on various computers and operating systems, and the program is said to be portable. The result of the panel's standardization of C was ANSI standard C, which is now supported by most manufacturers of C language compilers.

The Microsoft C 7 compiler is the ANSI standard C. There are many manufacturers of C compilers that operate on the IBM PC class of computers. Microsoft Corporation has been involved in developing C compilers since 1981, when the IBM PC was first introduced. Many commercial applications, especially those written for Windows and OS/2, were developed with Microsoft C compilers. The seventh version—Microsoft C/C++ 7—is presented in this book.

Advantages of C

You are probably aware of the advantages of the C language, or you wouldn't have purchased this book. Here are just a few reasons to program in C:

- C is a flexible and powerful language with commands, operators, and function libraries that can be used to write most types of computer programs.
- C is used by professional programmers who develop software for most modern computer systems, including the IBM PC and compatibles.
- You can use C to develop operating systems, compilers, real-time systems, and business applications. Microsoft Windows, OS/2, dBASE, Paradox, Microsoft Word, and FoxBase Pro are written in C, and most C compilers are written in C.
- A C program can be written for one type of computer and moved to another computer with few modifications—an attribute known as *portability*. The fact that C is portable is important. Because most modern computers have a C compiler, once you learn C, you don't have to learn a new language when you write a program for another type of computer. Nor do you have to rewrite a program so that it will work with another computer.

C is characterized by its execution speed. In the early days of computing, execution performance problems were resolved by rewriting all or a portion of a program in assembly language. The programs worked with only a certain type of computer. If a company changed computer types, it had to suffer the cost and time of rewriting programs for the new computer. These days, when you have a program written in a BASIC or dBASE interpreter that runs slowly, you can increase the speed by rewriting the program in C.

Because so many programs are written in C, many C libraries that support a variety of applications have been written by professional programmers. There are commercially available C language libraries that support database operations, graphics, text editing, communications, and so on.

In addition to programming in C, I have programmed in many languages, including FORTRAN II through V, ALGOL, COBOL, PL/I, PASCAL, BASIC, dBASE, and many flavors of assembly language. However, for the past eight years, I have spent many enjoyable hours programming in C++. It is so versatile that I can program any application I want. I suspect that you, too, will enjoy programming in C++.

During the 1980s, the C language was used predominantly by programmers for developing applications to operate under DOS. In addition, most applications that run in the Microsoft Windows 3.1 environment were compiled with the Microsoft C 6 Professional Compiler. Now that the Microsoft C/C++ 7 compiler is available, it is highly likely that programmers will develop future applications for the Windows 3.1 environment in C++. Besides including the C and C++ compilers, the Microsoft C/C++ 7 compiler system comes with a powerful development environment, the Microsoft Programmer's WorkBench (PWB). The PWB contains an integrated development environment that incorporates an editor, a compiler, a debugger, and a linker. The Microsoft C/C++ 7 compiler also contains other tools that assist you in creating dialog boxes, icons, fonts, and help screens.

The C language, like most modern computer languages, is a *procedural* or action-oriented language. In other words, the programmer concentrates during the development process on the actions that should be performed on data by a program. The programmer determines which algorithms are required for a program. Then the programmer uses the computer language to specify the algorithms as you would specify a procedure for programming a VCR. Press the green button, select the TV channel, and so on. In contrast to the procedural approach to programming is the approach that places emphasis on the data rather than the algorithm. This approach is called object-oriented programming.

Object-Oriented Programming (OOP)

Object-oriented programming (OOP) focuses on the data rather than the actions. Instead of being based on how data is manipulated, the OOP design is based on the objects being manipulated.

Traditional software engineering design methodology follows a *top-down* approach. Using this approach, you first determine the actions a program must perform. Then you break down the actions into smaller, more manageable actions, called *subprocesses*. Next you design a function to perform the actions for each subprocess, and you code and test each of these functions individually. When all the functions are operating correctly, you integrate them and test the complete system.

The object-oriented design methodology focuses on the types of data forms that are to be processed and the hierarchical structure of the various classes of data. Object-oriented programs combine data with functions and procedures. The functions and procedures, called *methods*, perform actions on the associated data to define the behavior of the data.

Data objects that share the same methods are called a *class*. A class designates what data represents an object and what actions are performed on the data. Suppose, for example, that you are designing a program to draw a circle. You could define a circle class. The data portion of the class definition contains the position (coordinates), size (radius), and color of the circle. The method portion of the class specification consists of functions and procedures used to draw the circle, move it, resize it, erase it, and so on. When you use your program to draw circles, you use the class specification to create and draw instances of the circle object. The circle object maintains the data associated with the parameters of the circle. You can use the class methods to resize the object. You can use the class methods to resize or otherwise modify any of the circle objects you have drawn.

When you design a program with the OOP approach, you first design classes that specify the objects used in the program. You determine the data elements and the methods you need in order to manipulate the data. Once you have accurately defined all the required classes, you can proceed with the task of designing the program that uses the objects associated with the classes. As you can see, this process is the reverse of top-down design because you first design the low-level elements and then proceed with the high-level program organization. The OOP design method is known as the *bottom-up* approach to program design.

The OOP approach to program development also promises that it's easier to develop reusable code with OOP than with the traditional approach. OOP also supports a technique called *polymorphism*, which allows alternative definitions for operators and functions based on the type of data being processed. Furthermore, OOP supports *inheritance*, a technique that allows a class to be created based on the characteristics of another class. The OOP approach to programming incorporates various concepts that are different from the traditional procedural programming concepts. The OOP concepts introduced here will become more apparent as you learn how to program in C++ in Part III of this book.

Where Did C++ Come From?

As you learned earlier, the C language was developed at Bell Laboratories. The C++ language was developed there also. Bjarne Stoustrup developed the C++ language in the early 1980s to operate on minicomputers that ran under the UNIX operating system. He based his new programming language on the C language because C was brief, widely available, and accepted by the programming community. The OOP components of C++ were inspired by a computer simulation language, Simula76. However, Stoustrup designed the OOP extensions to the C language in a manner that would not alter the C language elements. As a result, any operational C language program is an operational C++ program. The OOP extensions, however, make C++ an extremely powerful programming language.

Because the heritage of C++ is the C language and because so many programmers are already familiar with C, the popularity of C++ has grown considerably. For several years, companies such as Borland and Zortech have offered excellent C++ compilers that operate on IBM PCs and compatibles. The availability of these C++ compilers has added significantly to the acceptance of C++ by programmers for developing software products on microcomputers. With the release of the Microsoft C/C++ 7 compiler in 1992, Microsoft Corporation joined the growing club of software publishers that offer C++ compilers. In fact, it has been predicted by many C++ enthusiasts that the C++ language will be the predominate language of the 1990s.

C++ contains both procedural and OOP elements. Consequently, many strong OOP advocates contend that C++ is not a true OOP language, like Smalltalk or Eiffel. The OOP advocates object to C++ because they feel that programmers can be tempted to mix procedural logic with OOP logic and, as a result, will not reap the true benefits of OOP. However, other computer language experts feel that C++ offers the best of both worlds, allowing programmers to develop OOP programs while benefiting from the advantages of C.

The Graphical User Interface (GUI)

The *graphical user interface* (GUI) concept makes use of a graphical video display system. The GUI provides graphical objects, such as icons, menus, dialog boxes, push buttons, and scroll bars. You can select and manipulate these objects with a pointing device (mouse) and a keyboard. These two devices enable you to "drag" objects across the screen, choose push buttons, and move around with scroll bars. The interaction between you and the computer becomes more of a partnership rather than the give-and-take (input and output) relationship offered with the traditional keyboard-to-video-display ("glass teletype") interface. Windows 3.1 is a GUI.

Before Windows, each application running under MS-DOS had its own user interface. Every time a new software package was added, computer users had to wrestle with time-consuming and costly training. But with Windows, all programs run the same and have the same look and feel, so there is minimal retraining. This is a fundamental advantage of all GUI operating systems.

The GUI concept was pioneered in the mid-1970s at the Xerox Palo Alto Research Center (PARC) when Xerox developed a GUI for the STAR system. Apple Computer Corporation made an attempt to exploit GUI technology when it introduced the Lisa computer in 1983. The Lisa was too slow and cost too much. In January, 1984, however, Apple scored a success with the Macintosh computer, for which the GUI was built into the operating system. The Macintosh grew in popularity until it threatened to challenge the IBM PC. The Macintosh was easier to learn, and many people found it more enjoyable to use.

The success of the Macintosh sparked a renaissance in the interaction between a human and a computer. In November, 1983, Microsoft Corporation announced plans for a GUI, called Windows. Two years later, Windows 1.01 was released, and Windows 2.0 was released in November, 1987. Whereas Windows 1.01 supported only *tiled* (nonoverlapping) windows, Windows 2.0 contained changes to the user interface that allowed *cascading* (overlapping) windows.

In a joint effort in October, 1988, Microsoft and IBM released Presentation Manager for the OS/2 operating system, adding GUI features to OS/2. Meanwhile, other vendors were busy working on GUIs. Sun Microsystems, Inc., developed the NeWS GUI, Atari released its GEM GUI, and X-Windows was developed for computers running UNIX. Steve Jobs, cofounder of Apple Computer, left Apple and developed the NeXT computer with the NextStep GUI operating system.

Windows Version 3.1

Finally, in May, 1990, Microsoft released Windows version 3.0. It was significantly superior to earlier versions because it used the protected-mode operation of the Intel 80286 and 80386 microprocessors. Protected mode allows you to develop programs larger than one megabyte. Before Windows 3.0, applications developers were struggling with the 640K memory limit imposed by microcomputers running MS-DOS in Intel 8086 real-mode operation. Because Windows 3.0 ran in protected mode, applications could access a maximum of 16M of memory. In April, 1992, Microsoft released Windows 3.1, which contains many outstanding improvements over Windows 3.0, including object linking and embedding (OLE), TrueType font, support for sound, and improved performance.

Another advantage of Windows 3.1 is that it supports multitasking, enabling you to work with multiple applications at once. These applications are displayed in windows on the screen and are part of the desktop. You can easily move between applications and even exchange data. Windows was developed to run programs specifically designed to take advantage of the Windows environment. However, Windows can run most MS-DOS programs, but usually not in a window or in multitasking mode.

Windows 3.1 has given new life to the IBM PC and compatible microcomputer systems, and its success is evident with more than three million copies of Windows 3.0 and 3.1 currently in use. It is no wonder that the smart software vendors either already have a Windows 3.1 version of their products on the market or are feverishly working on one.

With all the interest in Windows 3.1 applications, the future looks good for Windows programmers. Before you become a Windows programmer, however, you have a steep learning curve to climb. It has been said that Windows is easy for users but hard for programmers. This is true. And first-time C programmers have an additional hurdle to climb. Before you attempt to program in Windows 3.1, you first must have a respectable working knowledge of the C language. This book teaches you to program in C++. Once you have learned to program in C++, you can begin using the Microsoft C/C++ 7 compiler system to develop Windows applications.

What You Have Learned

This chapter provided some background on the evolution of C and Windows. You learned the following points:

- C was developed in 1972 by Dennis Ritchie and was patterned after a language called B.
- C is powerful, flexible, and fast. C is also portable, so programs can be written for one type of computer and moved to other computers with few modifications.
- OOP, which focuses on the objects being processed rather than the actions, is a powerful new approach to software design and development methodology.
- The GUI concept was pioneered by Xerox in the mid-1970s, and GUI technology has given new life to IBM PCs and compatibles.
- C++ is composed of C with OOP extensions.

C++ Program Structure and Style

Proper words in proper places, make the true definition of a style.

—Jonathan Swift (1720)

In This Chapter

Before launching into a rigorous discussion of the various C++ language components, this chapter provides an overview of the C++ program structure. An example of a typical C++ program is presented, and the following elements are introduced:

- Variables
- Statements

- Comments
- Functions
- Compiler directives
- Programming style

You use a text editor to create and modify a C++ program, also called the *program source*. You use a compiler and linker to convert the program source to a program that can be run—an *executable program*. For additional information about the structure of a typical C++ program source, see Chapter 3, "The Programming Environment."

A Typical C++ Program

Listing 2.1 shows a typical C++ program, named TEMP.CPP, which prints a Fahrenheit-Celsius table. This sample program is referred to throughout the chapter as you learn about the individual parts of a program.

Variable Names

The smallest piece of a C++ program is the variable identifier or *variable name*. The name is chosen by the programmer and is used to define a variable or function. The name must begin with a letter or an underscore (_) and can contain as many other letters, numbers, and underscores as you want. The compiler, however, ignores all characters after the first 31. Additionally, C++ is a case-sensitive language, so upper- and lowercase letters have different values. Examples of valid variable names include the following:

```
increment
fahren
result
```

Listing 2.1. A typical C++ program (TEMP.CPP).

```
// TEMP.CPP - Prints Fahrenheit-Celsius          ← Comment
// conversion table
#include <iostream.h>                            ← Compiler declaration

#define FC (5.0 / 9.0)
float fahrtoce( float fahr );                    ← Function prototype
int main(void)                                   ← Main function
{                                                ← Definition of main()

  int lower = 0;        // Lower limit
  int upper = 100;      // Upper limit
  int increment = 10;   // Table increment
  float fahren, celsius;
  fahren = lower;
  cout << "Temperature Conversion Table\n";
  cout << "Fahrenheit.  Celsius\n";
  while ( fahren <= upper )
  {
    celsius = fahrtoce( fahren );
    cout << fahren;
    cout << "                ";
    cout << celsius;
    cout << "\n";
    fahren = fahren + increment;
    return 0;
  }
}

// fahrtoce() converts Fahrenheit to Celsius   ← Comment
float fahrtoce( float fahr )       ← fahrtoce() function
{                                  ← Definition of fahrtoce() function
    float result;
    result = FC * (fahr - 32.0);
    return result;
}
```

2

Here are some other valid names:

```
_This_is_a_valid_variable_name_99
Mary_had_a_little_lamb
```

A variable cannot have the same name as a C++ language keyword. C++ language keywords are special names used by C++, and all keywords are lowercase, as specified by the ANSI C++ 2.1 standards. New uppercase keywords were added by Microsoft, however, to support Windows 3.1 programming. C and C++ language keywords are presented in Table 2.1.

Table 2.1. The C and C++ language keywords.

__asm	__emit	__interrupt	sizeof
auto	enum	__loadds	static
__based	__export	long	__stdcall
break	extern	__near	struct
case	__far	__pascal	switch
__cdecl	__fastcall	register	__syscall
char	float	return	typedef
const	for	__saveregs	union
continue	__fortran	__segname	unsigned
default	goto	__segment	void
do	__huge	__self	volatile
double	if	short	while
else	int	signed	

The C++ language contains the following additional keywords:

asm	__finally	operator	template
class	friend	private	this
delete	inline	protected	__try
except	new	public	virtual

You also can get a list of keywords from the Microsoft Programmer's WorkBench (PWB) online help.

You learn more about variables and their uses in Chapter 6, "Data Types."

Statements

C++ code is expressed with a sequence of statements, and each statement ends with a semicolon (;). The C++ language ignores *whitespace*—blank characters (spacebands), tabs, and line breaks. TEMP.CPP shows the program statement

```
result = FC * (fahr - 32.0);
```

Practice using tabs and spaces to make your C++ program more readable.

A group of related statements can be enclosed in braces ({}) to form a *statement block* or *compound statement*. Statement blocks do not end with a semicolon. The following statements for the function `fahrtoce()` form a statement block:

```
float fahrtoce( float fahr )
{
   float result;
   result = FC * (fahr - 32.0);
   return result;
}
```

Comments

It is a good idea to add sufficient English language *comments* to your program so that you can easily recognize the purpose of a particular section of code. This helps you six months later when you return to the program to make changes. Comments also help anyone else who might have to change or maintain your program. A comment begins with two slashes (//) and extends to the end of the line. Any text following these comment introduction characters are ignored by the compiler. A comment can be alone on a line or can follow actual code. Here are some examples of comments in the typical C++ program in Listing 2.1:

```
// TEMP.CPP - Prints Fahrenheit-Celsius
// conversion table
   .
   .
   .
   int lower = 0;         // Lower limit
   int upper = 100;       // Upper limit
```

Because C++ is a superset of C, you can still use C language comments. If you are translating a C program into C++, you do not have to convert the comments.

A C language comment can appear anywhere whitespace can be used. The two-character combination of the slash and the asterisk (/*) is used to begin a comment; these two characters in reverse order (*/) end the comment. A comment can extend over one or more lines. Here is how you could code the preceding comments, using the old-fashioned C comment delimiters:

```
/* TEMP.CPP - Prints Fahrenheit-Celsius
              conversion table */
```

C++ comments are a real improvement over C comments. It is much easier to type `// comment` than `/* comment */`. Think of how many milliseconds you save by simply typing // instead of /* and */. In addition, C++ comments are not as problematic as C comments. One common error that programmers make in using comments in C is to forget to add the closing comment delimiter (*/). This problem goes away in C++ because there is no closing comment delimiter—except, of course, the end of the line.

The more complex your program, the more important it is that your code be well documented with comments. Comments are important to assist others who review or work with your program so that they can understand what it does. When you write a program, what it does may seem obvious. However, when you look at a program you wrote six months ago, it is not always easy to figure out what it does unless the program algorithms are well documented with comments.

Functions

Functions are the fundamental building blocks of a C++ (or C) program. A *function* is a block of one or more C++ statements dedicated to the performance of a specific task. A function usually returns a value to the statement that calls the function, which has the following form:

```
name( optional argument information )
{
function body
}
```

Here `name` is the name of the function and follows the same naming conventions as for any other identifier. The function name is followed first by an opening parenthesis and then by a closing parenthesis. When arguments are passed by the calling statement, a list of the arguments, separated by commas, is enclosed in the parentheses.

Following the closing parenthesis is an opening brace ({) that marks the beginning of the `function body`. It contains one or more program statements (a statement block) that perform the task delegated to the function. Following the `function body` is a closing brace (}) that marks the end of the `function body`. In other words, the opening and closing braces enclose the `function body`. Functions are discussed in detail in Chapter 12.

A special function, called `main()`, indicates the point in the program where execution begins. A program can have only one `main()` function. When a program is loaded for execution, the operating system transfers control to the first program statement after the opening brace in `main()`. The closing brace marks the end of the program.

In TEMP.CPP, information is specified inside the parentheses:

```
float fahrtoce( float fahr )
{
:
:
}
```

The argument type is sometimes declared outside the parentheses and before the opening brace, as in

```
float fahrtoce( fahr )
float fahr;
{
:
:
}
```

Calling a Function

Functions can be executed or "called" from anywhere in a program. When you call a function, you often need to pass information to it. This passed information is referred to as the *arguments of a function*. To call a function, you specify its name followed by opening and closing parentheses. A list of any required arguments, separated by commas, is enclosed within the parentheses.

TEMP.CPP calls only one function, named `fahrtoce`. The statement that calls the `fahrtoce` function looks like this:

```
celsius = fahrtoce( fahren );
```

The function call on the right side of the equation calls the Fahrenheit-to-Celsius conversion function, `fahrtoce`. The function has a single argument (a Fahrenheit temperature) and returns a value (a Celsius temperature) that is assigned to the variable `celsius`. A function can have multiple arguments. If it does, they are separated by commas. Note this example of a function with multiple arguments:

```
x_value = mfunc( arga, argb, argc );
```

Some functions have no arguments, and nothing is enclosed between the opening and closing parentheses, as shown here:

```
x_value = zfunc();
```

All C or C++ compiler manufacturers supply a library of functions that provides support for various operations. These functions are supplied to you so that you don't have to write them. You just call them when you need them.

Function Declaration Statements

A C++ program typically begins with a function declaration statement that defines the type of data a function returns. In addition, both ANSI C and C++ standards recommend that function arguments be declared with function prototypes. A *prototype* consists of the data type keyword followed by the name of a variable. The data type declaration statements for each argument are separated by commas, with the entire list of statements enclosed in parentheses. (Data types are described in detail in Chapter 6, "Data Types.") The following is the function prototype from TEMP.CPP:

```
float fahrtoce( float fahr );
```

If the function has no arguments, the keyword `void` is used in the prototype and the function declaration to indicate that arguments are not allowed. Note this example:

```
int noargsfunc( void );
```

Declaring Variables

All C++ variables must be declared before they are used. The declaration statement consists of the name of the variable preceded by the type of the data. More than one variable of the same type can be declared with one variable declaration statement. In TEMP.CPP, integer and floating-point data type variables are declared:

```
float fahren, celsius;
```

In the following function, the floating-point variable `result` is declared:

```
float result;
```

All the variables declared in TEMP.CPP are *local* variables, which can be referenced by the function in which they are declared. *External* variables can be referenced anywhere in the program. The placement of the variable declaration statement usually determines whether a variable is external or local. When a declaration statement is placed inside the braces of a function, the variable is local. When the variable declaration statement is placed outside any function in the program, the variable becomes external and can be referenced by any function in the program.

Initializing Variables

You can initialize a variable at the same time it is declared. In the following variable declaration, `lower`, `upper`, and `increment` are all declared and initialized:

```
int lower = 0;         // Lower limit
int upper = 100;       // Upper limit
int increment = 10;    // Table increment
```

#define and #include Compiler Directives

A C++ compiler translates your C++ source program into object files. Before the compiler starts compiling your source program, however, it processes lines of code beginning with the # character. These lines of code are called *compiler directives* or *preprocessor directives*. Compiler directives are not terminated with a semicolon. They are discussed in detail in Chapter 21, "Compiler Directives."

The `#define` directive used in TEMP.CPP is

```
#define FC (5.0 / 9.0)
```

This `#define` directive instructs the compiler to replace all occurrences of the symbol `FC` with `(5.0 / 9.0)` before compilation begins. A

#define directive is commonly used to define a constant used in a program. The #define makes it easier to change the value of the constant later because you have to make only one change in the code. You don't have to search the entire program to find and change each occurrence of the constant. Using #define directives to define various constants can also make your programs easier to read.

There are particular #define directives, variable declarations, and function declarations that are commonly used by programs. These elements can be placed in a source file (often called a *header file*) and inserted into the program with the #include directive. The #include instructs the compiler to read and compile the header file. TEMP.CPP includes the following #include directive:

```
#include <iostream.h>
```


iostream.h contains standard input and output declarations and definitions for input and output functions. This header file is included in TEMP.CPP because the file contains definitions used by the cout object. C++ compiler manufacturers provide many header files used with various C and C++ library functions and with C++ class libraries. In addition, header files can be created by the programmer for a particular application.

How to Display Results with C++

A computer program is not very useful if there is no way to display the results. In C you can output results with library functions, such as printf(). The printf() function can still be used in C++, but the customary method for outputing text to the screen is to use cout. In TEMP.CPP, results are displayed through the following statements:

```
cout << "Temperature Conversion Table\n";
cout << "Fahrenheit.  Celsius\n";
:
:
   cout << fahren;
   cout << "              ";
   cout << celsius;
   cout << "\n";
```

The cout statement consists of three parts:

- The cout object
- The insertion operator (<<)
- The item to display

The item to display is a constant, a variable, or an expression. In the preceding statement, the characters strung together between the double quotation marks are called a *string*. fahren and celsius are variable names.

The insertion operator (<<) is used to specify that the item to display is to be "sent to" the object cout. The direction that the angle brackets point indicates which direction the information flows. The cout object is a special object defined in the iostream.h header file and endowed with sufficient knowledge so that cout can display any type of information it is passed. If cout is passed a string, cout displays the ASCII characters in the string. If cout is passed an integer or floating-point number, cout converts that number to its ASCII character representation and displays the resulting ASCII characters.

cout is a C++ object that is a manifestation of a class definition which defines not only how data is stored but also what actions are performed on the data. The concept of an object will become clearer later in this book. At this point, you just need to understand that data—whether it is a value, an expression, or a string—is a *stream* of information (ASCII characters) that flows from the program to the display. The insertion operator (<<) is a property of cout. The information on the right side of the insertion operator is displayed by the cout object.

The strange notation \n has a special meaning in C and C++. The special symbol n is called a *newline* character. The backslash character (\) is used to denote that the next character in the string is a special character. When a newline character is encountered in a string, a carriage return/linefeed is passed to the display. This results in positioning the display cursor at the beginning of the next display line. For example, the statement

```
cout << "Fair is foul,\nand foul is fair\n  --- Shakespeare";
```

is displayed as

```
Fair is foul,
and foul is fair
  --- Shakespeare
```

Programming Style

The C++ language is a free-form language. This means that you are not restricted with respect to how you format your source programs. You can put an entire function on a line, and it should compile correctly. Note this example:

```
myfunc( int i ) { i=i*i; return i; }
```

The only guideline is that your code be readable. I knew a programmer who wrote all his programs so that they would appear on as few 132-column pages as possible. His code was impossible to read and difficult to maintain.

All the Microsoft C/C++ 7 sample programs and examples provided with the Programmer's WorkBench (PWB) online help adhere to a very readable programming style that is a standard adopted by many members of the C++ programming community. For the most part, the programming style used in this chapter's typical C++ program and in the other examples in this book conform to those guidelines. They are listed here:

1. Each sample program begins with a comment that names the program and states what it does.
2. Each statement or function is listed on its own line.
3. Variable names and function names are in lowercase.
4. Symbol constants, such as `PI = 3.1415926`, are in uppercase.
5. When a function has no arguments, the opening and closing parentheses follow the function name with no extra space, as in

   ```
   myfunc();
   ```

6. When a function takes arguments, a space appears after the opening parenthesis, before the closing parenthesis, and after commas separating arguments. Note an example:

   ```
   draw( row, col, "This is a message" );
   ```

7. Binary operators, such as + and -, are preceded and followed by a space, as in

   ```
   91 - X
   ```

8. When parentheses are used to control operator precedence, no extra spaces are included.

9. Opening and closing braces are aligned under the first character of the controlling keyword. No other elements of the statement appear on the lines containing the braces. The block underneath is indented three spaces, as shown here:

```
if ( a == b )
{
   c = e;
}
```

What You Have Learned

This chapter provided an overview of the C++ program structure. With the help of TEMP.CPP, a typical C++ program, you were introduced to the following:

- The various program components, including variable names, statements, comments, functions, declarations, and compiler directives
- The standard programming style that makes your code more readable and easier to use

The Programming Environment

Man is a tool-using animal. . . .
Without tools he is nothing,
with tools he is all.

—Thomas Carlyle
Sartor Resartus (1833)

In This Chapter

In this chapter, you learn how to turn a typical C++ program into a form that can be executed. The following topics are introduced:

- The software tools you use to develop a program
- The four phases of program development—compiling, linking, testing, and debugging

- The make utility
- Other tools used in the Microsoft C/C++ 7 programming environment

What Is the Programming Environment?

The *programming environment* is a combination of the operating system and the software (tools) used to develop a computer program. The primary tools are an *editor* (creates and modifies the source program), a *compiler* (converts a source program into an object file), and a *linker* (combines object files with the run-time library functions to build an executable program). The order in which each of these tools is used, as well as its resulting product, is illustrated in the block diagram in Figure 3.1.

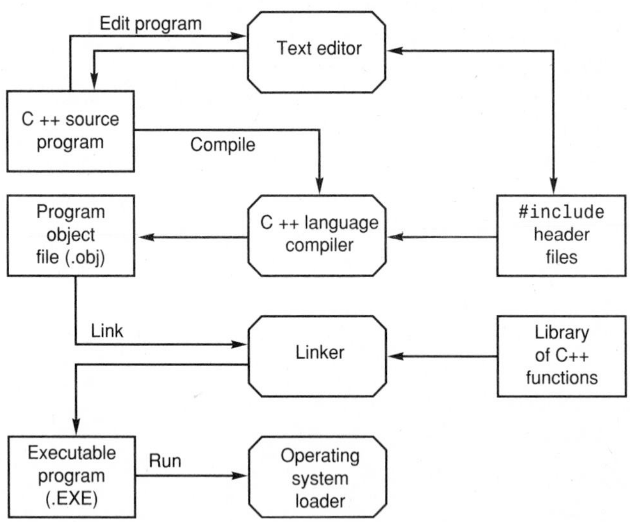

Figure 3.1. *A block diagram of the programming environment.*

Editing a Source Program

Computer programs are stored on disk as text files, called *source programs*. The filename extension of a C source program is .C. The filename extension of a C++ program is .CPP. Header files that contain `#define` directives and declarations are text files with an extension of .h.

An editor is an essential component of a programming environment. Any editor that can edit text files can edit a source program, and some editors contain specific features that simplify the editing of a C or C++ source program. You saw an example of a C++ program (TEMP.CPP) in Listing 2.1 in the preceding chapter.

Compiling a Source Program

To compile a C++ program source file, you execute a compiler that generates an object file with the same filename as the source file. However, the filename extension is set to .OBJ, so the name of the object file TEMP.CPP becomes TEMP.OBJ.

The object file contains the machine language instructions in relocatable form that cannot be run. All storage locations of variables and instructions are assigned an address relative to the beginning of the object file. The task of assigning the *absolute* (actual) addresses is delegated to the linker.

Linking a Program

The linker combines the machine language instructions in the object files with machine language instructions for the functions in the C++ function library. When the object file that you are linking is TEMP.OBJ, the instructions for the library function `printf()` and other low-level functions referenced indirectly by TEMP.OBJ will be included. The linker generates an executable program named TEMP.EXE, which you can run to produce the Fahrenheit-Celsius conversion table.

Consider a typical programming environment for the MS-DOS operating system. If the text editor is TE.EXE, the compiler is CL.EXE, and the linker is LINK.EXE, the following MS-DOS commands are used:

`C:>TE TEMP.CPP`	Creates and edits TEMP.CPP (output not shown)
`C:>CL TEMP`	Compiles TEMP.CPP and makes TEMP.OBJ
`C:>LINK TEMP`	Links TEMP.OBJ and the function library to make TEMP.EXE
`C:>TEMP`	Executes the program TEMP.EXE (output shown in Table 3.1)

Table 3.1. The Fahrenheit-Celsius conversion table.

Fahrenheit	*Celsius*
0	–18
10	–12
20	–7
30	–1
40	4
50	10
60	16
70	21
80	27
90	32
100	38

The Make Utility

In most C++ programming environments, a software tool called a *make utility* determines what files to compile and combine to create the final application. The make utility automatically executes the compiler so that any program source files that have been newly created or modified are compiled. Make then executes the linker to generate a new executable file.

Assume, for example, that your application has many source programs and that you have modified only programs XYZ.CPP and ABC.CPP. You execute the make utility, which first executes the compiler to recompile programs XYZ.CPP and ABC.CPP, and then executes the linker to build two new executable programs.

The make utility builds an executable program by following the instructions you have written in a script file. A *script file* contains commands that define which source programs are to be compiled, which header files are to be used in which source files, which object files are to be linked, and so on.

Debugging Tools

Writing a computer program is not like any other writing assignment. You can carefully design and write your computer program, proofread it, and let your friend proofread it, but it still may not work the first time you run it. A program must be syntactically perfect or it might not even compile, much less execute correctly. When you misspell a keyword or variable, specify invalid statements, forget to declare a variable, or make some other coding mistake, the compiler detects it and prints an error message indicating the problem. You can correct the error (called a *bug*) with your text editor and then recompile the program. The process of repairing bugs is called *debugging*.

When all the compiler bugs have been corrected and valid object programs have been generated, you execute the linker. The linker detects errors and prints an error message for each problem. You might have to go back and modify the source program to correct the error; then you recompile the source program and relink the object programs. When all the bugs detected by the compiler and linker have been repaired, an executable program is generated. But that's not the end. The syntax of the program may be correct, but you may have incorrectly programmed an algorithm, which causes a *logic error*.

Logic errors are harder to find. The computer does exactly what you tell it to do. When your logic is wrong, the computer precisely executes the incorrect logic with the same persistence as with correct logic. You, the programmer, must locate the abnormality and correct the problem. There are several ways to find logic bugs. You can examine the code and visually locate the problem, place print statements that display the value of certain variables at selected points in the program, or use a debugger utility.

A *debugger utility* provides insight into the internal workings of your program, speeding and simplifying the task of locating logic bugs. This utility shows you what is happening internally as it executes your program so that you can examine variables while the program executes. You can execute each line of code, tracing the logic of your program to determine which paths the program is following. You can instruct the debugger utility to execute the program until it reaches a certain location in your program, called a *breakpoint*. When a breakpoint is reached, you can examine the values of the variables. The debugger utility is discussed in greater detail in Chapter 5, "A Quick Tour of the Programmer's WorkBench (PWB)," and in Chapter 22, "Common Programming Errors."

Other Tools

Many other tools are shipped with the Microsoft C/C++ 7 compiler. Included are the following tools, which are used to assist programmers in developing programs:

- *CodeView Debugger for DOS.* An advanced debugging tool.
- *Help Compiler (HELPMAKE).* Translates source files into Microsoft help file databases.

- *Library Manager (LIB).* Creates and manages standard C libraries.
- *Browser Database Management Utility (BSCMAKE).* Builds and maintains a browser database used by the PWB source browser.
- *Resource Compiler.* Compiles a resource script file and adds it to an executable program file. A resource file contains information defining resources, such as icons, cursors, bitmaps, menus, and dialog boxes.

Additional tools are available in the Microsoft Windows programming environment, including the following:

- *Image Editor.* Creates and edits icons and cursors.
- *Dialog Editor.* Creates and modifies dialog box descriptions.
- *Font Editor.* Creates and modifies fonts.
- *CodeView for Windows.* An advanced debugging tool.
- *Profiler.* A processer that analyzes CPU time use.
- *Stress-Resource Stress Application (STRESS.EXE).* Acquires system memory resources to test a program under low-memory conditions.
- *DDE Transaction Debugger (DDESPY.EXE).* A debugging application that displays DDE transactions.
- *Windows Spy (SPY.EXE).* Displays Windows messages for debugging.
- *Multiple-Resolution Bitmap Compiler (MRBC.EXE).* Creates and modifies bitmap files with multiple bitmaps representing several resolutions of a bitmap image.
- *SDK Registration Database Editor (REGLOAD.EXE).* Adds entries to registration database.
- *Heap Walker (HEAPWALK.EXE).* A Windows applications heap-viewing tool.

The Microsoft C/C++ 7 Compiler

Microsoft Corporation has been developing high-quality C compilers for the IBM PC and compatibles since the infancy of the IBM PC. The current version, C/C++ 7, is a major new product. In addition to providing improvements to the C language development system, this version contains a comprehensive implementation of the American National Standards Institute (ANSI) C++ version 2.1 language specification. The product includes a complete interface to Microsoft Windows through C++ classes, called the Microsoft Foundation Classes/Application Frame.

The Microsoft C/C++ 7 compiler introduces innovative code-generation technology to improve the speed and size optimization of applications. The compiler offers optional *packed code* (p-code) optimization that can shrink the size of an executable program, achieving a 40–60 percent reduction in size. This technology is used in Microsoft Word, Excel, and Powerpoint applications. The execution speed of C and C++ applications can be increased by as much as 10 percent with a newly introduced optimization technique called *automatic function inlining*. In addition, a capability has been added to increase execution speed by allowing greater control over the allocation of static data.

The Programmer's WorkBench (PWB)

The Microsoft C/C++ 7 Programmer's WorkBench (PWB) is a programming environment that integrates many of the program development tools in a single software package. The PWB contains a file manager, an editor, a compiler, a linker, a make utility, a debugger, a source code browser, and an online help system (Microsoft Advisor). The PWB works under the MS-DOS operating system, which provides access to the programming tools.

Projects

The Microsoft PWB introduces the concept of projects. A *project* is a combination of all the files in an application. These *application files* include program source files, object files, executable files, and other files relating to a programming system.

A *project file* is automatically maintained by the PWB. The project file contains information regarding all the files in a project and instructions for building an executable file. A project file is similar to the make utility script file.

Projects are easier to use than most make utilities. You use menus and dialog boxes to tell the PWB which compiler and linker options, source files, libraries, and other files to use. When you are ready to build a program, you simply select a menu option.

The PWB Window

3

Figure 3.2 shows the PWB screen in which the menus for accessing each programming development tool are indicated. From the menus, you can select any of the tools to build and maintain even the most complex application in either the MS-DOS or Microsoft Windows 3.1 programming environment.

What You Have Learned

You now have learned enough fundamental C++ language development concepts to begin using the PWB and incorporating C language statements. In Chapter 4, you start learning to use the PWB.

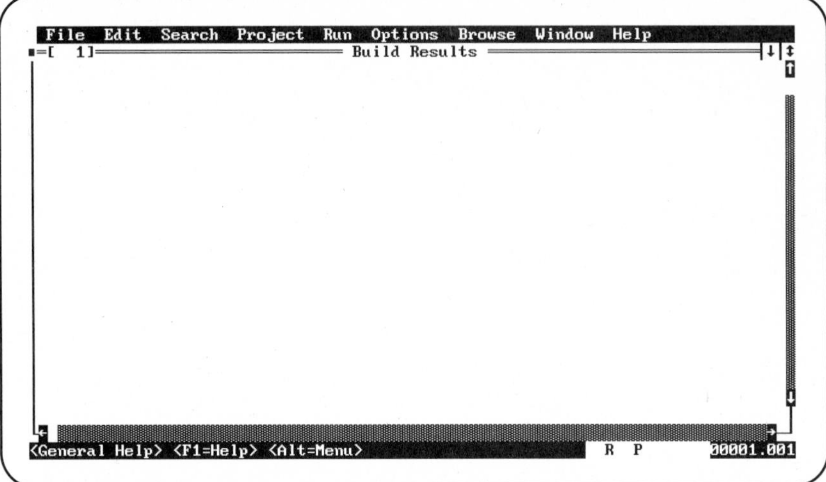

Figure 3.2. *The Programmer's WorkBench (PWB) screen.*

Before you move to the next chapter, review some of the points you have just learned:

- A programming environment consists of all the tools and utilities used to develop a computer program.
- The process of creating a source program includes compiling, linking, testing, and debugging.
- A software tool called a make utility determines what files to compile and combine in creating the final application.
- The PWB programming environment contains a file manager, an editor, a compiler, a linker, a make utility (a project), a source browser, and online help.

Getting Started

A journey of a thousand miles must begin with the first step.

—Lao-Tzu (604–531 B.C.)

In This Chapter

Now that you are familiar with the basic concepts of a programming environment, you are ready to learn to use the Microsoft C/C++ 7 Programmer's WorkBench (PWB). This chapter shows you how to do the following:

- Install Microsoft C/C++ 7
- Use the Programmer's WorkBench (PWB)
- Compile, link, and run your first C++ program
- Edit your program

In this chapter, you create your first C++ program and learn how to use the Programmer's WorkBench (PWB) for generating, compiling, linking, and executing a program.

Later, in Part II (Chapters 6 through 12), the fundamentals of the C++ language are discussed, and examples are provided. You should be able to run the examples and improve your C++ programming skills with the knowledge you gain in this chapter.

You can install the Microsoft C/C++ 7 development system from DOS or from the Windows environment. You cannot develop C or C++ applications for Windows unless you install the system from Windows. For that reason, it is recommended that you install the Microsoft C/C++ 7 system from Windows. To experience the challenge of learning to use the Microsoft C/C++ 7 tools for Windows, you must be familiar with the Windows 3.1 environment. If you are not familiar with it, study the *Microsoft Windows User's Guide* for version 3.1 and get acquainted with the Windows environment.

Hardware Requirements for the Microsoft C/C++ 7 Compiler

The Microsoft C/C++ 7 compiler system should be run under Windows 3 because the Windows development tools must run under Windows version 3 or later. Your microcomputer must be equipped with a 386 microprocessor, and you must have at least 4M of RAM to run from Windows. You should have at least 12M of available disk space on your hard drive. However, if you load the entire system with all the tools and online help, you can use as much as 35M of disk space. Your microcomputer must have a CGA, an EGA, a VGA 8514/A, a Hercules, or a compatible video graphics adapter. Microsoft recommends an EGA or a higher-resolution video adapter.

Installing Microsoft C/C++ 7

Microsoft C/C++ 7 is packaged with ten 5 1/4-inch or 3 1/2-inch diskettes or a CD-ROM disk. Insert the diskette labeled SETUP/DISK 1 into drive A. As mentioned, you can install C/C++ 7 from either DOS or Windows. If you are planning to develop applications for Windows, execute SETUP from Windows 3.1. From the Windows Program Manager **File** menu, choose the **Run** command. Type `a:setup` and either press Enter or click the OK button, as shown in Figure 4.1.

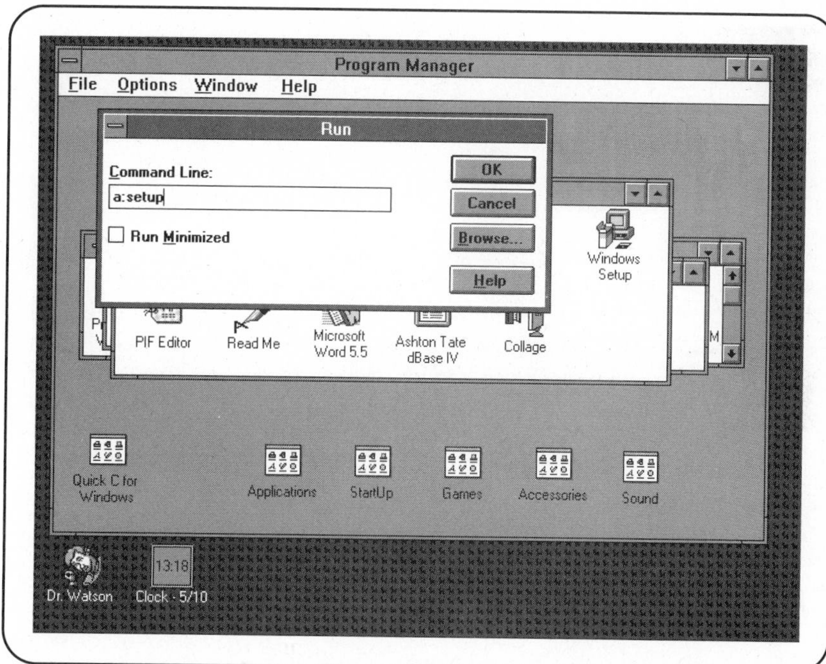

***Figure 4.1.** Executing the Microsoft C/C++ 7 SETUP program.*

When you run SETUP, several C/C++ 7 Setup dialog boxes appear. You respond to these by choosing the **C**ontinue push button. When the Installation Directory dialog box appears, you specify the base drive and directory where SETUP is to install C/C++ 7. C:\C700 is the default drive and directory. The Target Environment dialog box then appears, from which you can choose whether you want to develop applications for MS-DOS, Windows, or both environments. You should select both, which is the default.

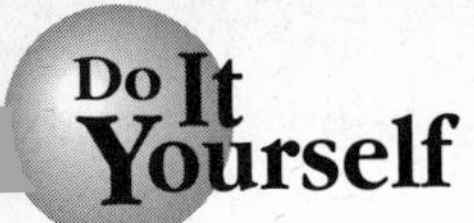

The Default or Custom Installation dialog box lets you choose whether you want the following:

- **Default Installation.** The entire C/C++ 7 compiler system is installed.
- **Custom Installation.** Selected components of the C/C++ 7 system can be installed. This option is useful if you do not have sufficient disk space to install the complete system. After you have installed C/C++ 7, you can run SETUP to modify the installation.
- **Build Additional Libraries.** If you need libraries for additional memory models, you can execute SETUP for this purpose after C/C++ 7 has already been installed.

If you select the **Default Installation** option, SETUP instructs you in loading diskettes. C/C++ 7 will be installed in the designated directory.

The Custom Installation Dialog Box

If you select **Custom Installation**, you can select which C/C++ 7 components you want installed. When you select this option, the next dialog box to appear is the Custom Installation dialog box (see Figure 4.2). You can use its menu to install C/C++ 7 initially and to modify the C/C++ 7 environment after the initial installation.

There are eight check boxes displayed on the left side of the menu. Each check box contains an `X`, which indicates that the option is selected and that the corresponding C/C++ component will be installed. The following sections describe how you should set the check boxes for the initial installation.

C/C++ 7 Compiler

The C/C++ 7 compiler contains the compilers, linkers, and other related system components for compiling source programs and building executable programs. If you are installing C/C++ 7 for the first time, this item must be installed.

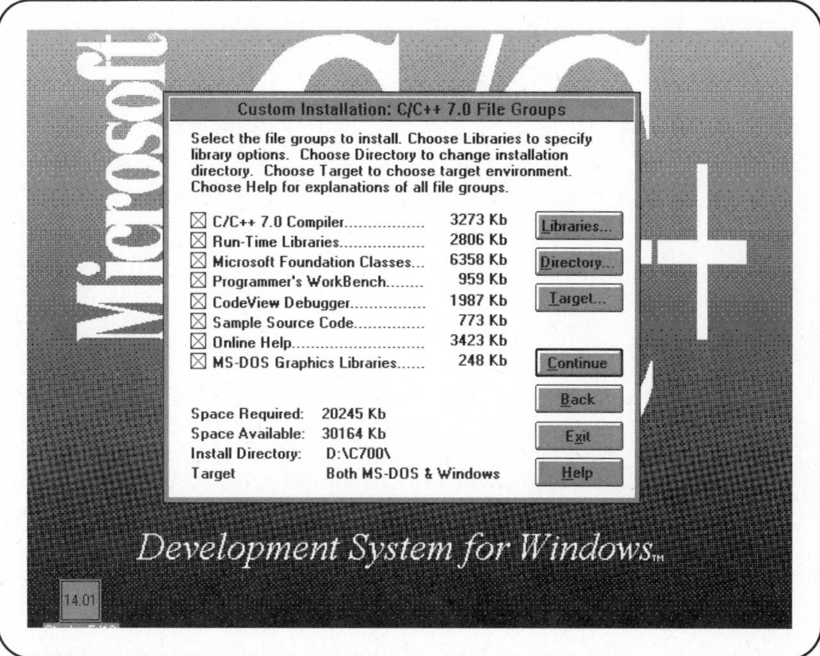

Figure 4.2. *The Custom Installation dialog box.*

Run-Time Libraries

The run-time libraries are C and C++ language libraries used with programs. These libraries must be installed. You can specify which libraries to install later if you need them.

Microsoft Foundation Classes

The Microsoft Foundation Classes library is a C++ class library used for developing nongraphic programs as well as Windows programs in C++. This class library definitely should be installed.

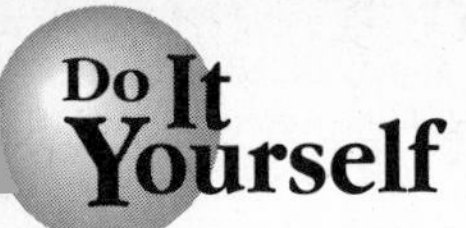

Programmer's WorkBench (PWB)

The Programmer's WorkBench (PWB) is the C/C++ 7 programming environment. You do not need this if you are going to use the compiler and linker from the DOS prompt. In this book, however, it is required that you install the PWB because it is used for creating and running the sample programs described in the text.

The MSDPMI.EXE is also loaded. MSDPMI.EXE is a DOS DPMI server that must be loaded if you are going to execute the C/C++ 7 compiler from the DOS environment. (DPMI stands for *D*OS *p*rotection *m*ode *i*nterface.) It is not used if you execute the C/C++ compiler from Windows. The C/C++ 7 compiler is a 32-bit application that runs with a 32-bit DOS extender and requires access to a DPMI server. In addition, MSDPMI.EXE must be executed before the Programmer's WorkBench is executed from DOS. This option must be installed.

CodeView Debugger

The CodeView debugger is used to debug your programs and is an important component of your debugging environment. There are actually two CodeView debuggers shipped with C/C++ 7: one operates with DOS, and the other works with the Windows 3.1 environment. The CodeView debugger should be installed.

Sample Source Code

C/C++ 7 provides a group of sample programs that are extremely helpful for learning how to program in C and C++. Although you will probably find them useful, they are not required. You can always install the sample source programs at a later date.

Online Help

The Online Help files provide assistance with the C/C++ 7 development environment, plus complete information on the C and C++ languages, Windows Applications Program Interface (API), and Microsoft C++ Foundation Classes. These help files definitely should be installed. However, they require about 4M of disk space.

MS-DOS Graphics Libraries

If you select this check box, the MS-DOS graphics libraries are installed. There exists a set of MS-DOS graphics library functions that perform coordinate conversion; line and figure drawing and filling; text, font, and image manipulation; and presentation graphics. These functions are used in MS-DOS applications. They are not used for Windows graphics programming. This dialog box provides the option of including or omitting the MS-DOS graphics libraries. If you have no need for these libraries and you want to save disk space, you can decide not to install them. Remember that you can run SETUP later and load these libraries if you ever need them. After you make your selection, choose **C**ontinue.

The Libraries Push Button

Next you select the **L**ibraries push button to choose which libraries are to be installed. The C Run-Time Customization dialog box appears (see Figure 4.3).

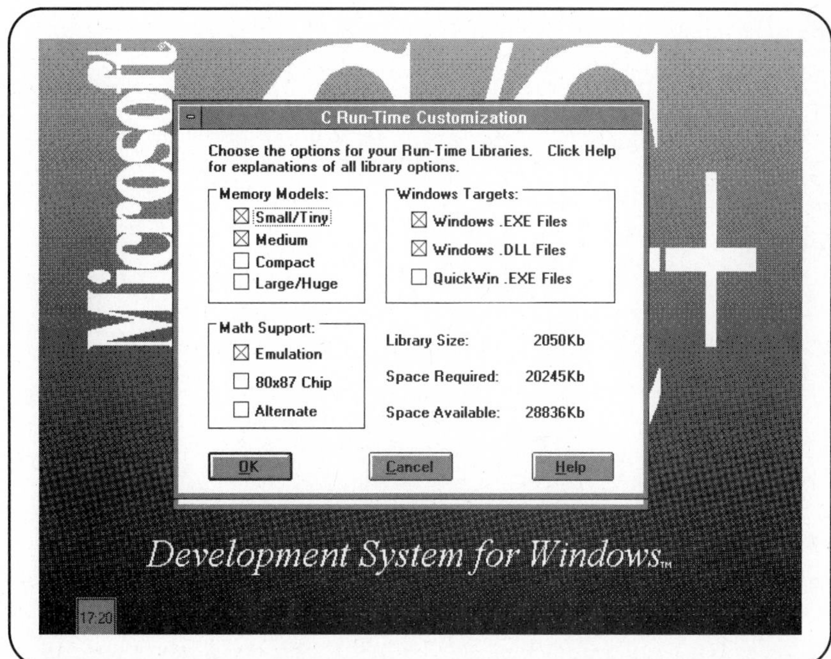

Figure 4.3. *The C Run-Time Customization dialog box.*

This dialog box contains three groups of check boxes:

- Memory Models
- Windows Targets
- Math Support

The Memory Models group pertains to the size of the address a program uses for accessing executable code or data. The address can be either 16 bits (`near`) or 32 bits (`far`), depending on the memory model (see Table 4.1). With `near` addresses, a program can access up to 65K of memory. For large programs requiring addresses of more than 65K, you use `far` addresses.

Table 4.1. C/C++ memory models.

Memory Model	*Code*	*Data*
Small/Tiny	`near`	`near`
Medium	`far`	`near`
Compact	`near`	`far`
Large/Huge	`far`	`far`

At some later time, you may want to install run-time libraries for a different memory model. You would run SETUP and select **B**uild Additional Libraries from the Default or Custom Installation dialog box. Then select only the check box for the memory model you want.

The Math Support group contains three check boxes. You select one of these run-time library math coprocessor options:

- Emulation. The program uses the 80x87 math coprocessor if it is present. Otherwise, the program uses software to emulate the coprocessor.
- 80x87 Chip. The program always uses software to emulate the 80x87 math coprocessor, even if the coprocessor is available.
- Alternate. The program uses the 80x87 math coprocessor if it is present. Otherwise, the program generates an error if the coprocessor is not present when the program is run.

The third group is Windows Targets, containing three check boxes. Here you indicate which types of libraries are needed, depending on the kind of Windows applications you are going to build with C or C++. The available options are these:

- Windows .EXE Files. Select this option if you plan to develop stand-alone applications that run under Windows 3.1.
- Windows .DLL Files. Select this option if you plan to develop dynamic linked libraries for Windows 3.1 applications.
- QuickWin .EXE Files. Select this option if you plan to develop MS-DOS applications that use standard and `iostream` input and output operations inside a window running under Windows 3.1. This is the quickest and easiest way to translate an MS-DOS program to run under Windows 3.1.

Do not choose these options if you instruct SETUP to build only MS-DOS libraries. SETUP builds a separate library for each option you select.

The Directory Push Button

Although you have already specified the drive and directory in which Microsoft C/C++ 7 is installed, you can use the **D**irectory push button to alter your selection. When you choose this push button, the Installation Directory dialog box appears, enabling you to change your original drive and directory.

The Target Push Button

You need to indicate the target environments for which you are going to develop applications. You do this by choosing the **T**arget push button, which, after a brief pause, displays the Target Environment dialog box. This dialog box contains three radio buttons:

- **M**S-DOS. Select this option if you are developing applications only for MS-DOS. If you choose this option, no Windows libraries or tools are installed. In this book, all C++ applications are written for MS-DOS.

- Windows. Select this option if you are developing applications only for Windows. If you choose this option, no MS-DOS libraries or tools are installed.
- Both MS-DOS and Windows. Select this option if you are planning to develop applications for *both* MS-DOS and Windows. If you choose this option, all Windows and MS-DOS tools and libraries are loaded, and you can use over two megabytes of disk space for the libraries. Therefore, if you plan to develop only MS-DOS applications, you can save considerable disk space by selecting the MS-DOS option.

When you finish with this dialog box, select the OK push button to return to the Custom Installation dialog box.

Completing the Installation

After you finish making selections, choose the Continue push button to begin installing the Microsoft C/C++ 7 development system.

Finally, SETUP instructs you in loading diskettes. C/C++ 7 will be installed in the designated directory. When the installation is complete, the Microsoft C/C++ 7.0 Compiler desktop is displayed (see Figure 4.4). It contains icons for the PWB, Windows CodeView, the Dialog Editor, the Image Editor, and other tools.

Modifying the Installation

Suppose that you have installed the C/C++ development system and, while developing C or C++ programs, you find that you need a different library or tool for your application. You can use SETUP to make the change.

Execute SETUP as you did for the installation. When the Default or Custom Installation dialog box appears, select the Add Additional Libraries radio button and choose the Continue push button to continue with installing the library. The Target Environment dialog box appears. Make the appropriate selections and choose the Continue push button. The Build Additional Libraries dialog box then appears. Again, make the appropriate selections, choose Continue, and follow the instructions for loading the appropriate C/C++ 7 development diskettes. Use a similar procedure to install additional Microsoft C/C++ 7 development tools.

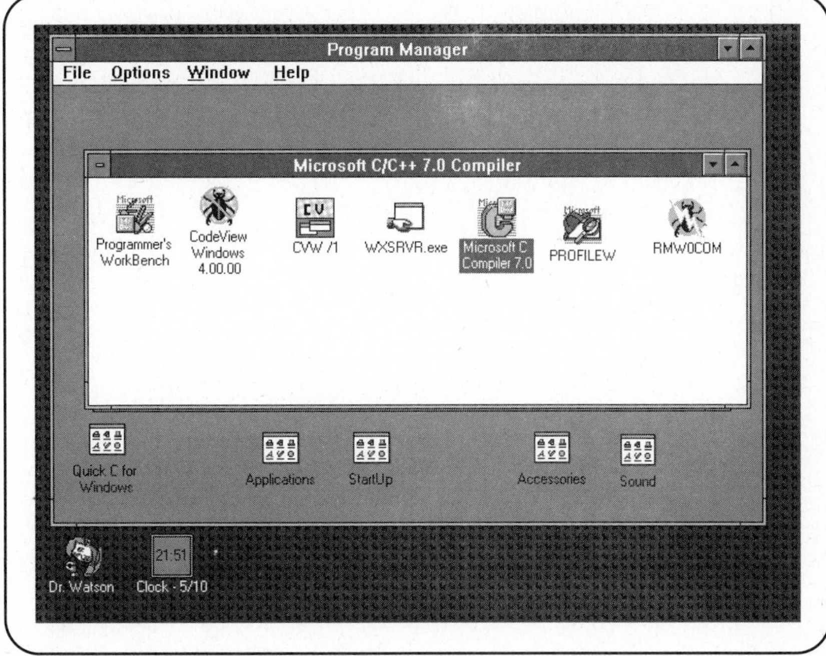

Figure 4.4. *The Microsoft C/C++ 7.0 Compiler desktop.*

Executing and Exiting the Programmer's WorkBench (PWB)

To execute the PWB from the Windows environment, double-click the Programmer's WorkBench icon from the Windows desktop. The PWB window appears (see Figure 4.5).

You also can execute the PWB from the MS-DOS prompt. However, the C/C++ 7 compiler is a 32-bit application that runs with a 32-bit DOS extender and requires a DPMI server. Before you execute the PWB, you must execute MSDPMI.EXE to start the DPMI server by typing

```
C:>msdpmi
C:>pwb
```

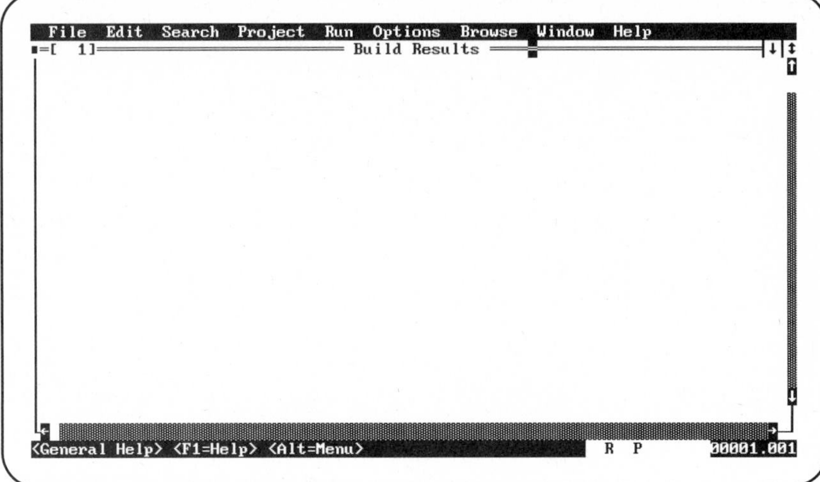

Figure 4.5. The Programmer's WorkBench (PWB) screen.

If the DPMI server is not running (that is, you did not execute MSDPMI.EXE first) when you attempt to compile, the compiler displays the run-time error `DPMI server not available`. When you exit the PWB, you can terminate the DPMI server by typing `exit` at the DOS prompt.

To exit the PWB at any time, choose the E**x**it command from the **F**ile menu. If you have executed the PWB from Windows and you want to return to Windows temporarily, you can press Alt+Esc. When you want to return to the PWB, double-click the PWB icon at the bottom of the screen or choose the S**w**itch to command from the Windows Control menu (a menu of basic Windows commands available in all Windows windows) to execute or "switch to" the PWB.

Editing Source Files

The heart of the PWB integrated development environment is the text editor. It is used to create, edit, and print your source files. Like most text editors, the PWB editor enables you to enter text, move the cursor around the window, insert or delete text, and so on. The text editor is similar to editors running in the Windows 3.1 environment in that the **F**ile and **E**dit menus have similar functions.

The PWB text editor has certain features that enhance the programming environment. The editor enables you to activate debugging breakpoints, trace program execution from the editor, and display various program elements in different colors. For example, the editor displays C language keywords in one color, comments in another, and variables in a third color. This helps you identify possible errors as you type.

Creating a New Source File

Now that you have installed the Microsoft C/C++ 7 development system, it is time to use the editor to enter your first C++ language program. First choose the **N**ew command from the **F**ile menu (see Figure 4.6). Your new file will temporarily be named Untitled.001 until you save it with a different name.

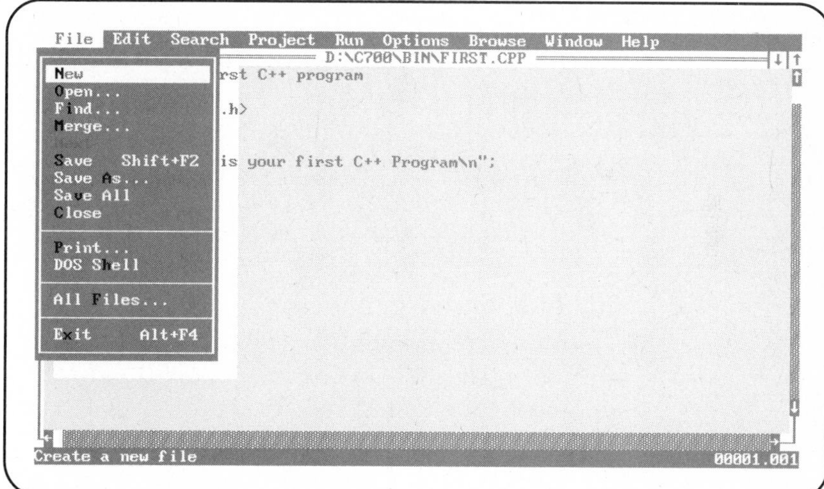

Figure 4.6. *The PWB File menu.*

Next choose the Save **A**s command from the **F**ile menu. The Save As dialog box appears (see Figure 4.7). Type `first.cpp` to name your first C++ language program. Then choose the OK push button.

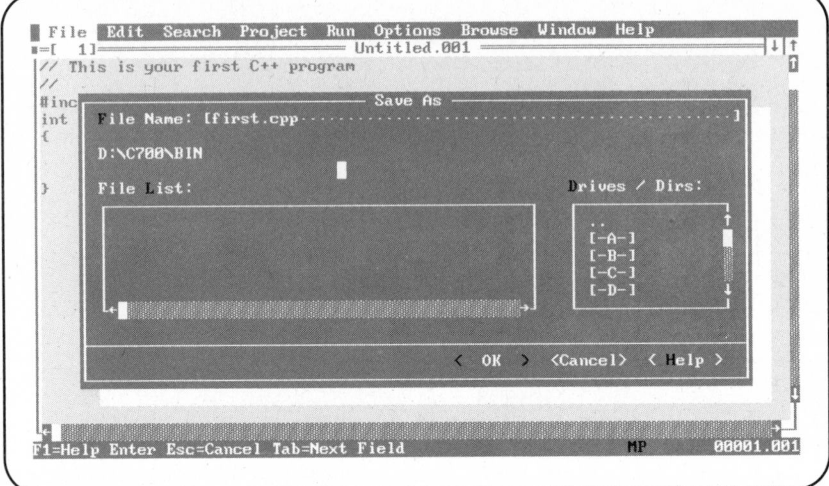

***Figure** 4.7. The Save As dialog box.*

Using the Editor

Your cursor is now positioned in the editor window, where you can type the source code for your first C++ program. The program will have a single function, `main()`, and a statement containing the `cout` object, which displays a message on the screen. Enter the text shown in Figure 4.8.

Table 4.2 shows the basic keyboard commands for performing editing operations. The PWB text editor supports special keys, such as the arrow keys and the Ctrl key. To use the Ctrl key with other keys, press and hold down the Ctrl key while pressing another key. This Ctrl+*key* combination is the same method used with the WordStar, dBASE, Borland, and Norton editors. You can use either the Ctrl+*key* combination or the alternative keystrokes. Both methods are shown in Table 4.2. All Microsoft Windows editors support these special keys. Some of the keyboard commands are supported also by **E**dit, **S**earch, or **P**roject menu commands, which are shown in parentheses in Table 4.2. The initial values for the alternative keystrokes are shown in Table 4.2. You can change the alternative keystrokes to any values you like by using the **K**ey Assignments command on the **O**ptions menu.

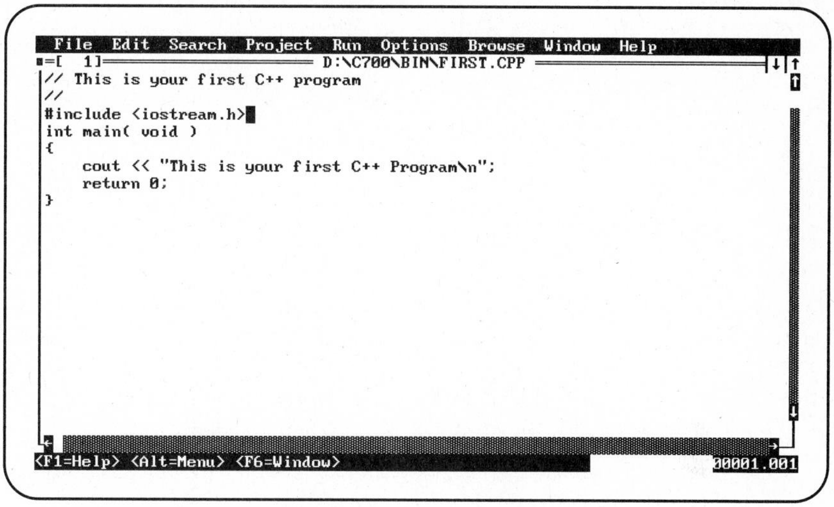

```
 File  Edit  Search  Project  Run  Options  Browse  Window  Help
=[ 1]================ D:\C700\BIN\FIRST.CPP ================
// This is your first C++ program
//
#include <iostream.h>
int main( void )
{
    cout << "This is your first C++ Program\n";
    return 0;
}

<F1=Help> <Alt=Menu> <F6=Window>                    00001.001
```

Figure 4.8. *Your first C++ program.*

Table 4.2. The text editor keyboard commands.

Keystroke Operation(s)	*Keystroke(s)*	*Alternative Keystrokes*
Move cursor one character to the left	Left arrow	Ctrl+S
Move cursor one character to the right	Right arrow	Ctrl+D
Move cursor up one line	Up arrow	Ctrl+E
Move cursor down one line	Down arrow	Ctrl+X
Move cursor one word to the left	Ctrl+Left arrow	Ctrl+A
Move cursor one word to the right	Ctrl+Right arrow	Ctrl+F
Move cursor to beginning of file	Ctrl+Home	
Move cursor to end of file	Ctrl+End	
Delete character at cursor	Delete	Ctrl+G
Delete character at the left of cursor	Backspace	Ctrl+H

continues

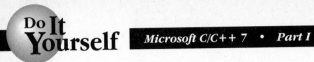

Table 4.2. continued

Keystroke Operation(s)	*Keystroke(s)*	*Alternative Keystrokes*
Delete from the cursor to the end of word	Ctrl+T	
Delete entire line and copy it to the clipboard	Ctrl+Y	
Turn insert mode on or off	Insert	Ctrl+V
Copy selected text to clipboard (**C**opy)	Ctrl+Insert	
Delete selected text and move it to the clipboard (Cu**t**)	Shift+Delete	
Place text from the clipboard at cursor location in text (**P**aste)	Shift+Insert	
Insert a blank line above current line	Ctrl+N	
Find text (F**i**nd)	Ctrl+Q, F	
Find text	Ctrl+Q, A	
Find selected text (F**i**nd)	Ctrl+F3	
Repeat last find	F3	
View next error (Ne**x**t Error)	Shift+F3	
View previous error (Pre**v**ious Error)	Shift+F4	
Scroll up one line	Ctrl+Up arrow	Ctrl+W
Scroll down one line	Ctrl+Down arrow	Ctrl+Z
Scroll up one page	PgUp	Ctrl+R
Scroll down one page	PgDn	Ctrl+C
Scroll left one window	Ctrl+PgUp	
Scroll right one window	Ctrl+PgDn	
Select character to the left of cursor	Shift+Left arrow	

Keystroke Operation(s)	*Keystroke(s)*	*Alternative Keystrokes*
Select character to the right of cursor	Shift+Right arrow	
Select word to the left of cursor	Ctrl+Shift+Left arrow	
Select word to the right of cursor	Ctrl+Shift+Right arrow	
Select current line if cursor is on column one	Shift+Down arrow	
Select line above if cursor is on column one	Shift+Up arrow	
Recover last selection	Ctrl+U	
Recover last text argument	Ctrl+O	
Set, clear, or go to last mark	Ctrl+M	
Insert literal value	Ctrl+P	
Replace pattern or text	Ctrl+L	
Display key assignment for next key	Ctrl+T	
Undo previous edit	Alt+Backspace	

When you use a mouse to select a menu item, you move the mouse pointer (an arrow-shaped cursor) to the menu item and then press and release the left mouse button. This action is referred to as *clicking* a menu item.

The mouse can be used to position the cursor, scroll and select text, and choose menu commands for editing operations. To select text, perform the following steps:

1. Place the cursor in front of the first character to be selected.
2. Press and hold down the left mouse button.
3. *Drag* (move) the cursor to the position after the last character to be included in your selection.

4. Release the mouse button.

The selected text can be copied, deleted, or moved with the editing commands in the **E**dit menu (see Figure 4.9).

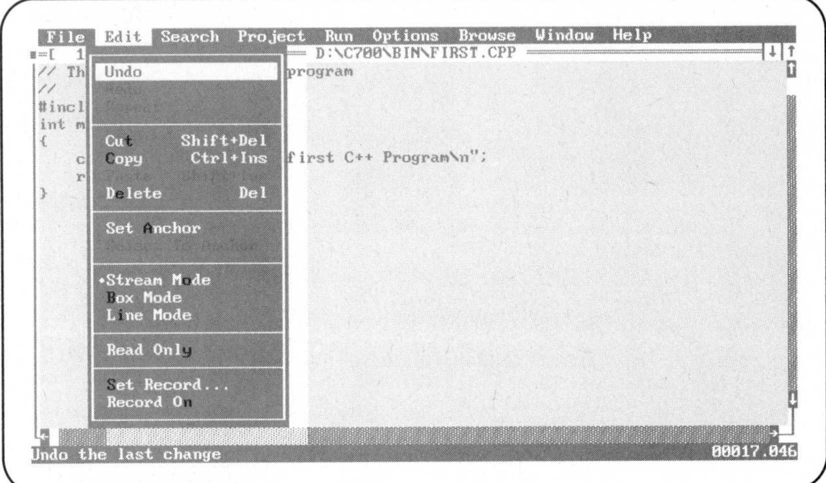

Figure 4.9. *The PWB Edit menu.*

Compiling and Linking

The Project utility automatically compiles your source programs, links objects, and generates an executable program. If you have only one module, you just choose the **B**uild command from the **P**roject menu. However, if your program consists of multiple source files, you must open a project file and add the names of all the modules associated with the application. Your first C++ program has only one source file, FIRST.CPP. Therefore, the Project utility automatically generates your project file for you.

Before you build a program, you must set the compile options. From the PWB, open the **O**ptions menu (not to be confused with the **O**ptions menu that appeared during SETUP) and choose the **L**anguage Options command. From the pull-down menu that appears, you specify which language you are using—C or C++. You should select **C++** Compiler

Options. The C++ Compiler Options dialog box appears (see Figure 4.10). It controls the program type settings for the compiler. Select the options as shown in Figure 4.10 and choose OK. Chapter 5, "A Quick Tour of the Programmer's WorkBench (PWB)," provides more information about these option settings.

```
 File  Edit  Search  Project  Run  Options  Browse  Window  Help
                       C++ Compiler Options
                          Global Options
   Memory Model        Processor          Calling Convention
   [Small·······]↓   [80286·····]↓      [C················]↓

              Warning Level
   [Level 1·······················]↓
   [ ] Make Warning Errors Fatal         < Additional Global Options...>

   Global Options: /G2 /BATCH

           (•) Debug Options      ( ) Release Options

    Debug Information          < Optimizations... >
   [Full Information··]↓
                               <     Additional Debug Options...     >
   Debug Options   : /Od /Zi /Gi$(PROJ).mdt

                        <  OK  >  <Cancel>  < Help >
F1=Help Enter Esc=Cancel Tab=Next Field                       00014.029
```

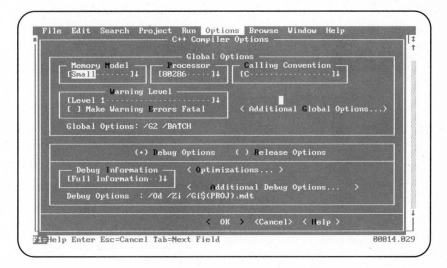

Figure 4.10. *The C++ Compiler Options dialog box.*

Now select the **B**uild command from the **P**roject menu (see Figure 4.11). This causes your program to be compiled and linked, and an executable program is created.

During the build process, an on-screen message box shows the program's progress (see Figure 4.12).

When the build is complete, a Build Operation Complete dialog box appears (see Figure 4.13). You have the option of viewing the build results, executing the program, executing CodeView to debug the program, or canceling the operation and returning to the PWB editor.

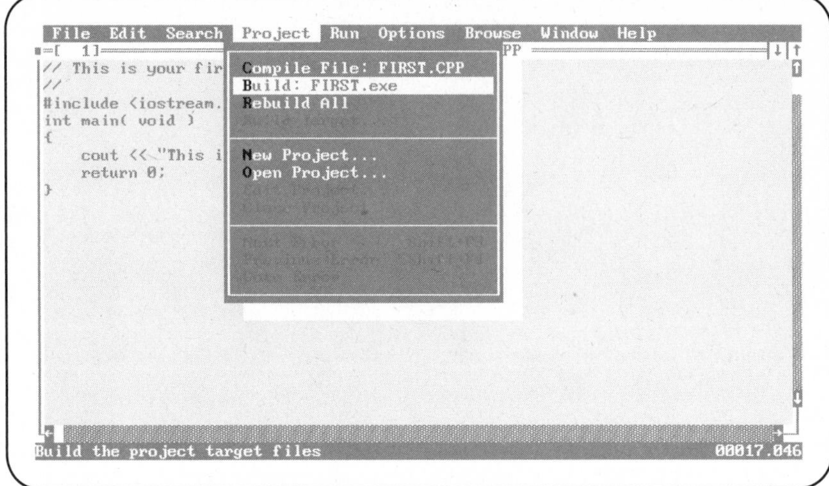

Figure 4.11. The Build command on the Project menu.

```
 File  Edit  Search  Project  Run  Options  Browse  Window  Help
=[  1]================ D:\C700\BIN\FIRST.CPP ====================
// This is your first C++ program
//
#include <iostream.h>
int main( void )
{
    cout   Rebuild all
    retur
}          NMAKE  /a /f d:\temp\PWB09973.mak all

           Press Ctrl-C to cancel current operation

Build the project target files                              100.001
```

Figure 4.12. The Build message box.

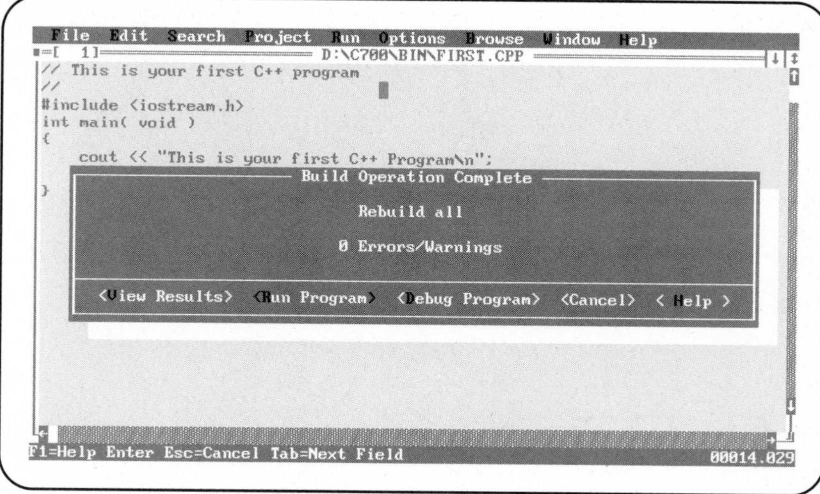

Figure 4.13. *The Build Operation Complete dialog box.*

Running Your First C++ Program

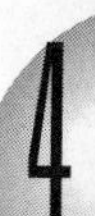

To execute your first C++ program, select the **R**un Program option from the Build Operation Complete dialog box, or select the **E**xecute command from the **R**un menu, as shown in Figure 4.14.

Your C program now executes. If the program compiles and runs correctly, the following message should be displayed:

```
This is your first C++ Program
```

You have just created your first Microsoft C++ 7 program. For an exercise, make some changes to the program, rebuild it, and execute it. Notice that the PWB will detect that changes were made and ask you what you want to do. You have the option of reexecuting the old FIRST.EXE, rebuilding FIRST.EXE, or canceling the build operation. Rebuild your program and execute the modified version.

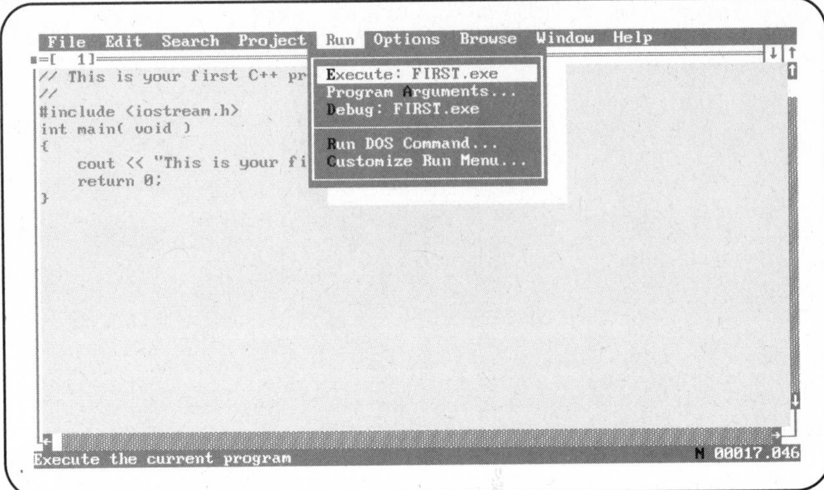

Figure 4.14. *Executing your FIRST.EXE program.*

What You Have Learned

In this chapter, you made the following strides in learning to use the Microsoft C/C++ 7 development system:

- You installed the Microsoft C/C++ 7 development system.
- You used the PWB text editor to create the source file for your first C++ program.
- You used the Project utility to compile your program, link the objects, and generate an executable file.
- You executed your first C++ program.

A Quick Tour of the Programmer's WorkBench (PWB)

Does the road wind uphill all the way?
Yes, to the very end.
Will the day's journey take the whole day?
From morn to night, my friend.

—Christina Georgina Rossetti
Up-Hill (1861)

In This Chapter

This chapter provides a quick tour of the basic elements of the PWB environment. Don't feel that you have to memorize any of the information in this chapter—you can simply scan the information for now and refer to it whenever necessary. The following topics are covered:

- The PWB screen
- The PWB menus

The PWB Screen

Figure 5.1 shows the PWB screen. The top line of the screen is the PWB *menu bar*. The bottom line of the screen is the *status bar*. Between these two lines is the work area, or workspace, which contains windows. In Figure 5.1, a single window is displayed that contains the source file for your first C++ program, FIRST.CPP.

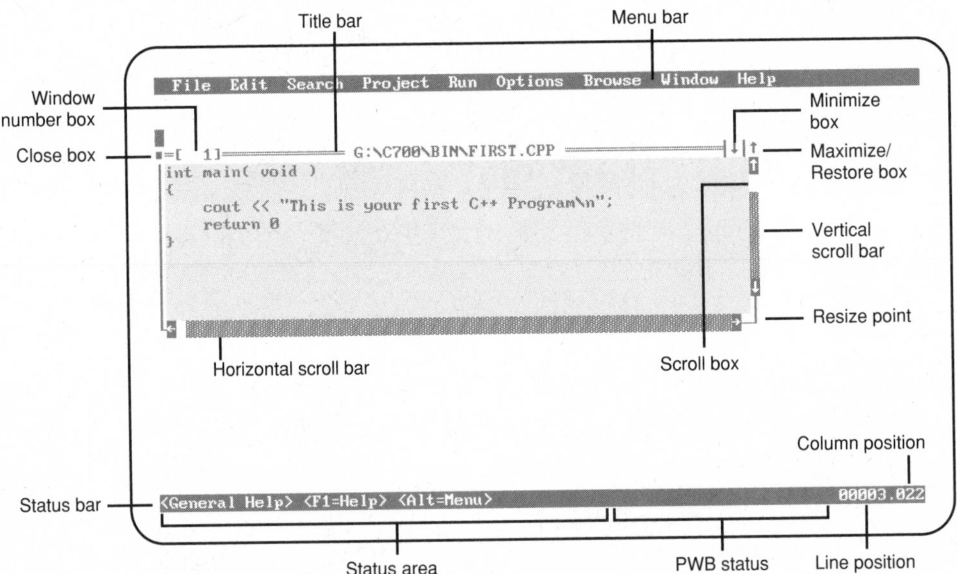

Figure 5.1. The PWB screen.

The *insertion point* is a blinking rectangular block that appears somewhere in the edit window. The insertion point, often called the text cursor, is where text is inserted when you begin typing. You can reposition the insertion point with the arrow keys, control keys (Ctrl+*letter* combinations), or mouse.

The *mouse pointer*, often called the mouse cursor, is a rectangular block that appears in the inverse color of the space where the block is located. You use the mouse pointer to select menus, reposition the insertion point, or resize and move the window.

Resizing a Window

If you place the mouse cursor on the lower-right corner of a window and then press and hold down the left mouse button while you move the mouse, you can resize the window. After you have resized the window, release the mouse button.

Moving a Window

To move the PWB window around on the screen, point the mouse at the title bar or the window border, press and hold down the left mouse button, and move the window to a new location. When you are finished repositioning the window, release the mouse button.

Elements of a Window

As noted, the work area (workspace) is located between the PWB menu bar and the status bar. This area can contain one or more windows, or none. A window can contain a source file, the results of a build, the clipboard, help information, and so on. Figure 5.1 shows a window that contains the source program FIRST.CPP. Each of the window elements is identified in that figure and described in Table 5.1.

Table 5.1. Elements of a window.

Window Element	*Description*
Close box	The close box is a small rectangle in the upper-left corner of the window. When you click the close box, the window is closed. If the window is a file and you have made changes to the file, a dialog box appears on the screen, asking whether you want to save the changes.
Window number box	Each active window is given a number. If you want to select an active window, press the Alt key and the number corresponding to the window number. For example, to select window number 3, press Alt+3. You can also select windows from the **W**indow menu.
Title bar	The title bar is at the top of the window and contains the window number and title.
Minimize box	When you click this box, the window shrinks to an icon at the bottom of the work area. The icon appears as a small box containing the window number, and the window title is displayed below the icon. If you click the icon, the box is restored to its original size.
Maximize/Restore box	When you click this box, the window is either enlarged to maximum size or restored to its original size.
Horizontal scroll bar	You use this bar to change the horizontal position of a file.
Vertical scroll bar	You use this bar to change the vertical position of a file.
Scroll box	The scroll box indicates the relative position of the display in a file or list. For example, if the scroll box is in the middle of the scroll bar, text in the middle of the file is displayed in the window.

The Status Bar

At the bottom of the PWB screen, a status bar displays information about the source file in the active window, along with general information about the environment. The status bar may contain the following elements:

- *Status area.* Information describing the currently highlighted command or menu item, as well as error messages, shortcut keys, and instructions for various operations. In Figure 5.1, the status area contains information describing how to get help and how to activate the menu bar.

- *PWB status.* At the right of the status bar are single letters used to indicate the state of the PWB. Here are the meanings of the letters:

  `A` is displayed when a meta prefix (F9) is active.

  `C` is displayed when the Caps Lock key (a toggle) is on.

  `L` is displayed when the lines being edited in the file are terminated with a linefeed character.

  `M` is displayed once the file being edited has been modified.

  `N` is displayed when the Num Lock key (a toggle) is on.

  `O` is displayed when the insert/overtype mode (a toggle) is in overtype mode.

  `P` is displayed when the contents of the window do not represent information in an actual file. Such a file is considered to be a *pseudofile*. An example is a window that shows the results of compilation and linking.

  `R` is displayed when the file is read-only or modifications are disabled (you cannot edit data in the window).

  `T` is displayed when the file being edited is temporary (not remembered between sessions).

  `X` is displayed when macro recording is turned on.

- *Line number.* The line-number position of the cursor in the active source window is displayed.

- *Column number.* The column-number position of the cursor in the active window is displayed.

The PWB Menu Bar

The PWB menu bar provides access to the command menus. The PWB menus and their commands are summarized in Table 5.2.

Table 5.2. A summary of the PWB menus.

Menu	*Operations*
File	Create, open, save, and print files and exit
Edit	Delete, add, and copy of source file text
Search	Search and replace of source file text
Project	Create, maintain, and use projects
Run	Program execution and debugging
Options	Set project, workspace, and environment
Browse	Access and display browser database
Window	Select and arrange windows
Help	Display help

You can select a menu with the keyboard or the mouse. The following sections discuss the procedures for both methods.

Using the Keyboard to Select a Menu

To open a particular menu by using the keyboard, press and hold down the Alt key and then press the highlighted letter in the menu name on the menu bar. Or just press Alt+*letter* for any menu name. When that menu drops down, simply use the left- and right-arrow keys to move to the menu you want (which will already be open).

To select a menu command, press the up- and down-arrow keys until the command is highlighted, and then press Enter to choose that command. For example, if you want to choose the **Copy** command on the **Edit** menu, press Alt+E to open the **Edit** menu. Next press the arrow keys until the **Copy** command is highlighted, and then press Enter. Alternatively, you can choose a command by pressing the highlighted letter in the command name instead of moving to that command. For example, after you open the **E**dit menu, just press the letter C to execute the **C**opy command.

Shortcut keys (key combinations) are displayed next to some of the menu commands. You can press the shortcut key combination from the main window, and the command will be executed—without first opening the appropriate menu. The shortcut keys are listed in Table 5.3. Notice that the shortcut key combination for the **S**ave command on the **F**ile menu is Shift+F2. From the PWB window, you just press and hold down the Shift key and then press the F2 function key. The **S**ave command is then executed.

Table 5.3. Shortcut keys for menu commands.

Menu	*Command*	*Shortcut Keys*
File	**S**ave	Shift+F2command
	E**x**it	Alt+F4
Edit	Cu**t**	Shift+Del
	Copy	Ctrl+Ins
	Paste	Shift+Ins
	D**e**lete	Del
	Record O**n**	Shift+Ctrl+R
Project	Ne**x**t Error	Shift+F3
	Pre**v**ious Error	Shift+F4
Browse	Ne**x**t	Ctrl+Num+
	Previous	Ctrl+Num–
Window	**C**lose	Ctrl+F4
	Move	Ctrl+F7
	Size	Ctrl+F8
	Restore	Ctrl+F5
	Minimi**z**e	Ctrl+F9
	Ma**x**imize	Ctrl+F10
	Casca**d**e	F5
	Tile	Shift+F5
	Arrange	Alt+F5
Help	Contents	Shift-F1
	Topic	F1

You may notice that some menu commands are followed by three dots (. . .). Selecting a command with three dots opens a dialog box that requires additional information. If a command is not followed by three dots, it executes immediately when you select it.

To cancel a selection or to get out of a menu at any time, just press the Esc key.

Using the keyboard to open menus is not complicated; however, the best way to feel comfortable with this method is to use it.

Using the Mouse to Select a Menu

To open a menu by using the mouse, point to the menu you want to open, and click the left mouse button. The menu drops down from the menu bar. To select a command on the menu, point to the command and click the left mouse button. If you highlight a command and then change your mind and don't want to execute it, *deselect* it by clicking anywhere on the screen—outside the opened menu.

Menu commands are usually displayed in black. When a command cannot be executed at the present time, it appears in gray and is said to be *grayed*. For example, when no source file is open, the **F**ile menu commands **M**erge, **C**lose, **S**ave, Save **A**s, and Save All are grayed because you cannot execute any of them until a file is opened.

Responding to Dialog Boxes

When you choose certain menu commands, a *dialog box* (a window that pops up to request additional information) appears on the screen, and you are expected to respond. The dialog box can be a simple Yes or No dialog box that asks you to confirm an action, or a more complicated box that contains several entry areas with buttons, check boxes, text boxes, and list boxes. When the PWB needs additional information and displays a dialog box, you can respond with the mouse, the keyboard, or a combination of both.

Figure 5.2 shows some elements that can be found in a dialog box. Elements with a particular purpose are displayed in a group and have a group title. In this example, Switch Type is a group title. The elements of the various groups are called *controls*, analogous to the controls on a television, a radio, or the dashboard of your automobile. You use the Tab key to move to the next control, and Shift+Tab to move to the preceding control.

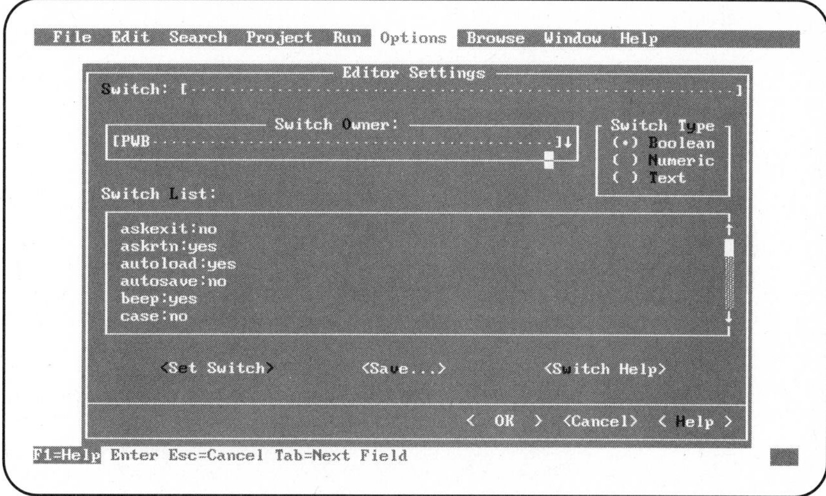

Figure 5.2. *Some of the controls in a dialog box.*

The following sections describe the dialog box controls used with the PWB and explain how to move around in a dialog box.

Text Box

A *text box* provides either a blank space for data entry or a value you can change. When a text box is active, the text cursor appears at the beginning of the text field. You can type the appropriate entry, or you can use the arrow keys or mouse to reposition the cursor within the field. You use the Backspace key to correct an error. When you type the field full of text, the field scrolls to the left as you continue typing. An example of a text box is Switch, which appears just below `Editor Settings` at the top of Figure 5.2.

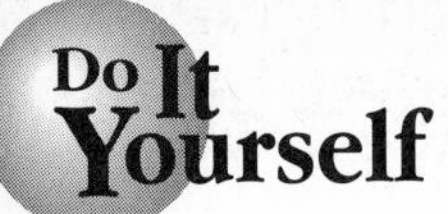

Push Button

A *push button* is a text label enclosed by two angle brackets. To "press" or choose a push button, click it with the mouse, or use the Tab or Shift+Tab keys to move to the push button and then press Enter. Examples of push buttons in Figure 5.2 are OK, Cancel, and **H**elp.

Radio Button

A *radio button* is a space enclosed by a pair of parentheses, with a text label to the right of the button. A radio button is so named because it resembles the button on an automobile radio. Just as you can select only one station at a time from an automobile radio, you can select only one radio button at a time from a group. When the button is on (selected), a "dot" appears inside the parentheses. To select a radio button, point to it with the mouse and click. Or use the arrow keys to move to the radio button and then press Enter. Alternatively, select the radio button by pressing the Alt key plus the highlighted character in the button label. Figure 5.2 shows the Switch Type group of radio buttons: **B**oolean, **N**umeric, and **T**ext. **B**oolean is selected.

List Box

A *list box* is a rectangular box that contains a vertical scroll bar and a list of items, such as filenames, from which you can make a selection. To select an item, just click the item, or use the arrow keys to highlight the item and then press Enter. Figure 5.2 shows a list box, called Switch **L**ist.

Check Box

A *check box* is a blank space enclosed by two square brackets, with a text label to the right of the check box. You use a check box to turn an option on or off. When the option is on, an X appears in the check box. When the option is off, the check box is blank. You can toggle the option on and off by pressing the spacebar, pointing to the check box and clicking, or pressing the Alt key plus the highlighted character in the text label. Examples of check boxes in Figure 5.3 are Generate **B**rowse Information and Exclude **M**acro Expanded Symbols.

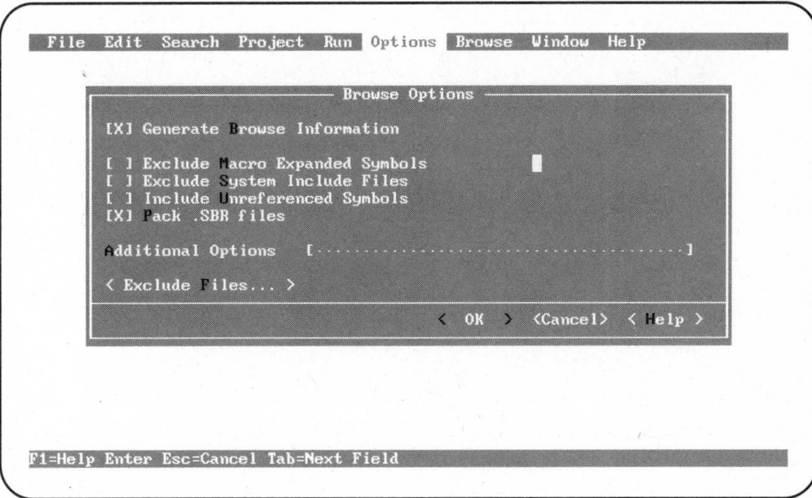

Figure 5.3. *A dialog box containing check boxes.*

The File Menu

You use the File menu to create, open, save, and print files. Figure 5.4 shows the open **File** menu. The following paragraphs describe its commands.

New

The **New** command creates a blank window named UNTITLED 1. If you create more than one blank window, the second one is named UNTITLED 2, the third one is named UNTITLED 3, and so on. When you save or close one of these windows, the Save As dialog box appears, prompting you to type or select the name of a source file.

> You cannot save a new window until you have typed something into it.

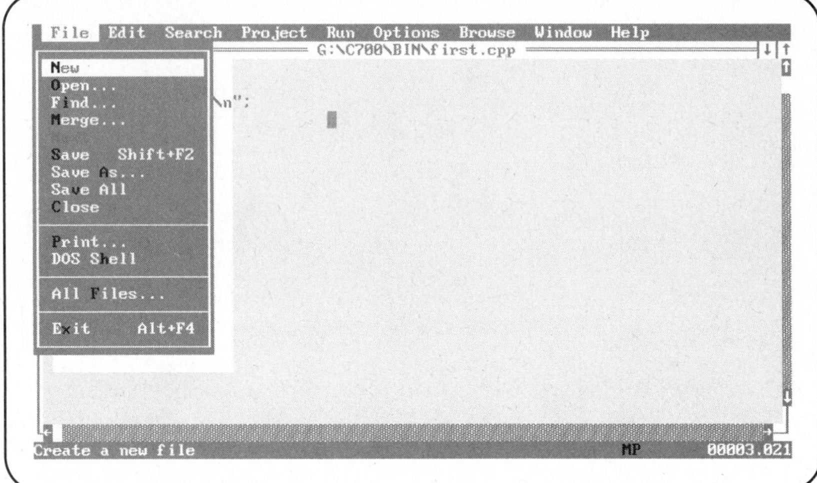

Figure 5.4. The File menu.

Open

You use the **Open** command to open an existing file. When you select this command, the Open File dialog box appears (see Figure 5.5). You can type a source filename or select a filename from the File **List** box. To select a file from the list, double-click the filename, or use the arrow keys to highlight the filename and then press Enter. Use the Tab key to move from the **File** Name text box to the **Drives**/Dirs list box.

Find

The **Find** command locates a file or a list of files in the current directory, or as a result of a recursive search operation starting with a specified directory. When you choose **Find**, the **Find** File dialog box appears. You can use radio buttons to indicate whether a recursive file search is to be performed. You can enter a filename or a wild-card specification for a list of files. Do not confuse this **Find** command with the **Find** command on the **Search** menu.

In a *recursive file search*, the specified directory and any descendant directories are searched for the specified files. Once the search operation is complete, a file list containing one file or a list of files is displayed. When you select one of the files, it is opened.

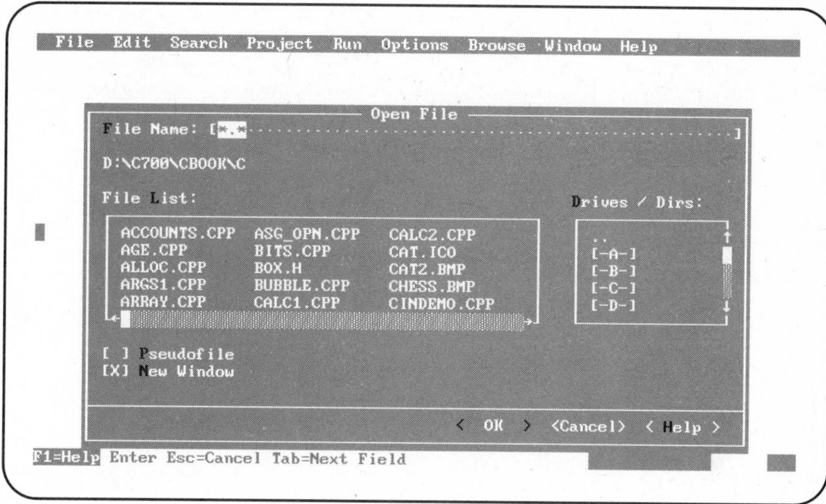

Figure 5.5. *The Open File dialog box.*

Merge

The **Merge** command adds the contents of a selected source file to the contents of a file currently open. When you select **Merge**, a dialog box appears that is identical to the one which appears when you select **Open**. When you select a file, it is merged into the current window at the insertion point (the current cursor position).

Next

You use the Next command to open the next file in the list of files specified on the PWB command line. Suppose, for example, that you execute the PWB with the following MS-DOS command:

```
C:>PWB PROG1.CPP PROG2.CPP PROG3.CPP
```

When the PWB executes, the program PROG1.CPP is displayed in a window. You can choose the **Next** command to open the file PROG2.CPP. The next time you choose the **Next** command, the file PROG3.CPP is opened.

Save

The **Save** command saves the source file in the active window. The file is saved with the filename indicated in the title bar unless the file is new (untitled). When the file is new, a file dialog box appears that prompts you to enter a new filename. If you select the name of an existing file, a dialog box appears that asks whether you want to overwrite the existing file.

Save As

The Save **As** command saves the contents of the source file in the current window to a file with a different name. When you select Save **As**, a file dialog box appears that prompts you to enter a filename. If you select the name of an existing file (or the current file), another dialog box appears, asking whether you want to overwrite the contents of the existing file.

Save All

With the Save All command, you save all the open source files. You are prompted with a file dialog box for any files that are open in a new (untitled) window. Otherwise, each file is saved with the filename indicated in its title bar.

Close

The **Close** command saves the source file in the current window and closes the window. If it is a new (untitled) window, a file dialog box appears, prompting you to enter a new filename. If you select the name of an existing file, a dialog box appears that asks whether you want to overwrite the existing file.

Print

You use the **Print** command to print the contents of all or a portion of the source file in the current window. This command also can print the contents of a list of files. When you execute **Print**, a dialog box appears. If a portion of text in the current window is highlighted, you can use the dialog box to print only that text. Otherwise, the entire source file is printed. If you choose the **Files** push button, a dialog box containing a file list appears from which you can select a list of files to be printed.

DOS Shell

The DOS **Shell** command temporarily exits the PWB so that you can execute MS-DOS commands. When you are finished and want to return to the PWB, type `exit` at the MS-DOS command.

All Files

The All **Files** command lists all open files in the PWB, including source files and pseudofiles. As mentioned earlier, a *pseudofile* is not really a file but a buffer treated as a read-only file. You cannot edit a pseudofile, but you can view its contents, which are displayed in a PWB window. Examples of pseudofiles are the the contents of help windows, results windows, and the Browser Output window.

Exit

The **Exit** command exits the PWB and returns you to either the Program Manager or MS-DOS. If any files are open and have not been saved, a dialog box appears that prompts you to save the files.

The Edit Menu

The **Edit** menu, shown in Figure 5.6, contains commands that perform text-manipulation operations. Cut, copy, paste, and delete are standard tasks for text processors. These commands operate on blocks of selected text. There are also commands for find, replace, and undo-edit tasks.

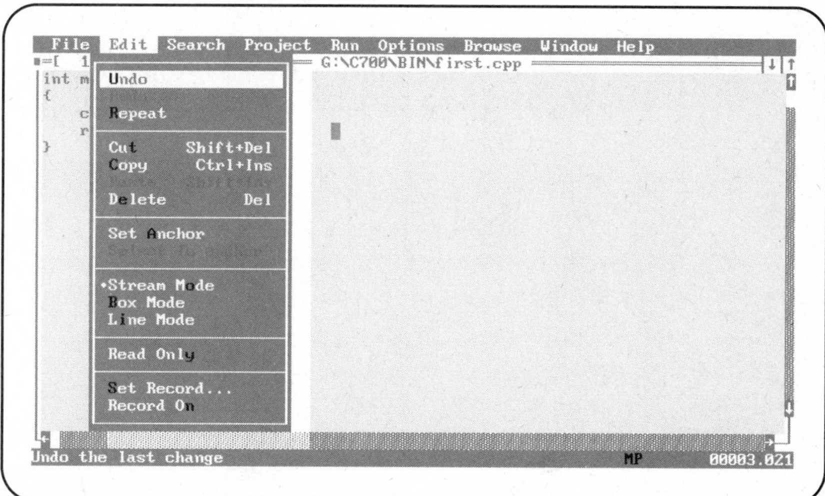

Figure 5.6. The Edit menu.

Undo

You use the **Undo** command to undo previous edit operations. You can undo the last characters typed, the last paste or copy operation, the previous text replacement, and so on.

Redo

You undo the action of the **Undo** command with the Re**d**o command. Re**d**o is grayed when no **Undo** command has been initiated.

Repeat

The **R**epeat command repeats the previous edit operation.

Cut

With the Cu**t** command, you remove selected text from the active window and place the text in the clipboard. Any text already in the clipboard is overwritten by Cu**t**. See also the discussion of the **P**aste command.

Copy

You use the **C**opy command to copy selected text from the active window to the clipboard. The original selected text is unaffected. However, the text is no longer selected.

Paste

With the **P**aste command, you can copy the contents of the clipboard into the active window (the contents appear at the cursor position). You can also paste multiple copies of the clipboard contents at different locations in the active window. Suppose that you want to move some text from one location to another. Use either the mouse or the keyboard to select the text to be moved, and execute the Cu**t** command. Poof! The text disappears. Now move the cursor to the place where you want to insert the text, and execute the **P**aste command. Presto! The text reappears at its new location.

> Remember that the clipboard contains only a *copy* of the text.

Delete

You use the Delete command to remove selected text from the active window. Delete performs the same function as the Delete (Del) key. The Undo command restores the text.

Set Anchor

The Set Anchor command saves the current cursor position. This saved position is called the *anchor*, which is useful for defining the starting point of text to be selected.

Select To Anchor

The Select To Anchor command selects text between the anchor and the insertion point. You cannot choose this command unless the anchor has been set with the Set Anchor command. You use the Select To Anchor command with the Set Anchor command to select text.

Stream Mode

The Stream Mode command changes the text-selection mode to *stream mode*, which is the normal selection mode. In stream mode, selections begin at one character in the text and extend to another character in the text. You can select any of the three text-selection modes (stream, box, or line mode) to be active at one time, and that mode will remain in effect until the end of the PWB session for all windows. The three modes are illustrated in Figure 5.7.

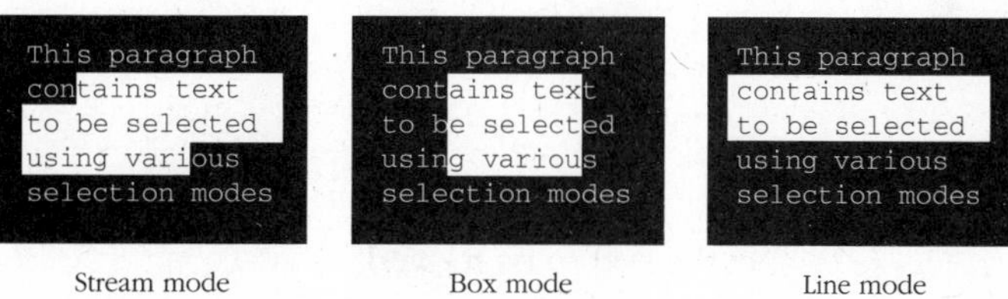

Figure 5.7. *The three text-selection modes.*

Box Mode

The Box Mode command changes the text-selection mode to *box mode*. In this mode, the selected text is inside a rectanglar selection box defined by the starting selection position and the current selection position (see Figure 5.7).

Line Mode

The Line Mode command changes the text-selection mode to *line mode*. Beginning with the line containing the insertion point, text is selected one line at a time as the selection is extended (see Figure 5.7).

Read Only

You use the Read Only command to toggle on and off the read-only status of a file in the current window. This command protects a file from accidental modification. To protect a source file from unintentionally being altered, you can set a source file to read-only status with the Read Only command. A read-only file cannot be modified by the PWB or any other editor unless the read-only setting is removed.

Set Record

The Set Record command defines a macro name and its corresponding shortcut key. At times, you may be doing a repetitive editing task that requires pressing the same sequence of keystrokes over and over. You can automate this process by creating a keyboard macro. To create a macro, first choose the **S**et Record command, and the Set Macro Record dialog box appears (see Figure 5.8).

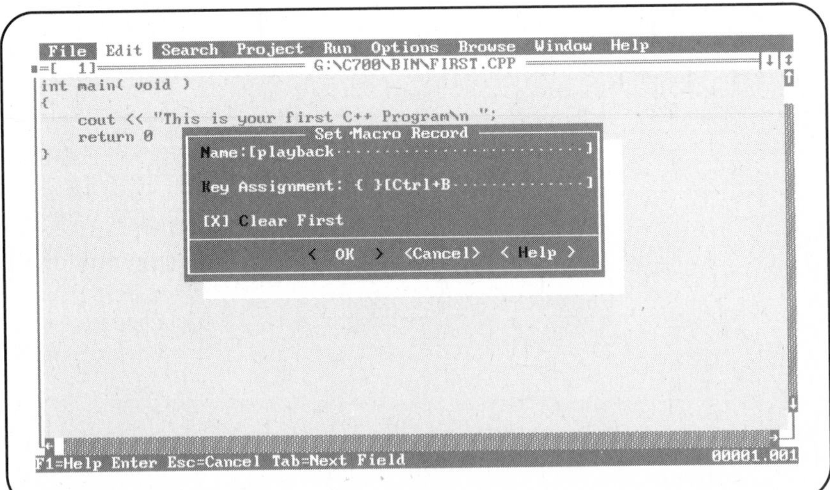

Figure 5.8. *The Set Macro Record dialog box.*

In the **N**ame text box, enter a name for the recorded macro. The default name is `playback`.

In the **K**ey Assignment text box, enter the key used to execute the macro. There are two methods for doing this. The first method is to place the cursor between the two curly braces ({}) and press the key or key combination to be assigned to the macro. The PWB then inserts the name of the key in the space between the square brackets. The second method is to type the name of the key or key combination, such as `Ctrl+B`, into the text box enclosed between two square brackets. You can assign to a macro any key (or key combination) except Tab, Shift+Tab, and Enter.

You also have the option (**C**lear First) to append the macro to an existing macro or to clear the macro buffer. If the **C**lear First check box is checked, the macro buffer is cleared before recording begins.

Once you have named the macro and assigned a key or key combination to the macro, you choose the Record O**n** command to turn the macro recording on and off. The shortcut key combination for Record O**n** is Shift+Ctrl+R.

You can open the PWB Record window to view, exit, and save the current macro recording. To edit the current recorded macro, choose the **P**WB Windows command from the **W**indow menu. A cascading PWB Windows menu appears. Choose **R**ecord, and the Record window opens. You can edit the key symbols to change the behavior of the macro. Here is an example of the Record window contents:

```
playback:= up up meta delete begline down down paste down
down "// This program was written by J Progger 20 June 2010"
```

Note that `playback` is the name of the macro.

To save a macro, choose **P**WB Windows from the **W**indow menu and choose **R**ecord. Choose the **S**ave command from the **F**ile menu. The PWB inserts the macro key assignment and definition into the TOOLS.INI file. When you exit, the PWB asks whether you want to save the TOOLS.INI file. If you allow the PWB to save TOOLS.INI, your macro becomes permanent.

5

Record On

The Record O**n** command turns the macro recording mode on and off. If the recording mode is on, an `X` appears in the PWB status portion of the status line. If the macro key is not assigned, you use the Set Macro Record dialog box. See the preceding discussion of the **S**et Record command for further information. Although not shown on the menu, the shortcut key combination for the Record O**n** command is Shift+Ctrl+R.

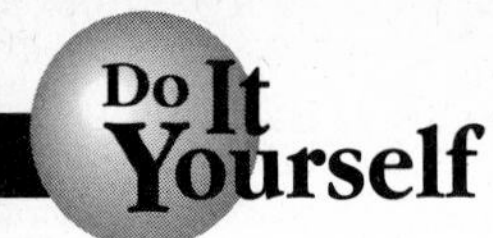

The Search Menu

Most text editors support some technique of searching for text and replacing instances of text with other text. The PWB has a powerful search-and-replace feature. In fact, a whole menu is dedicated to search and replace operations. Commands exist to search for specific text or a *regular expression* (a wild-card pattern) in one more more files, and to find and replace text in one or more files. There are also commands to go to a specified line number and to define marks and then go to them. Figure 5.9 shows the **S**earch menu. The following paragraphs describe its commands.

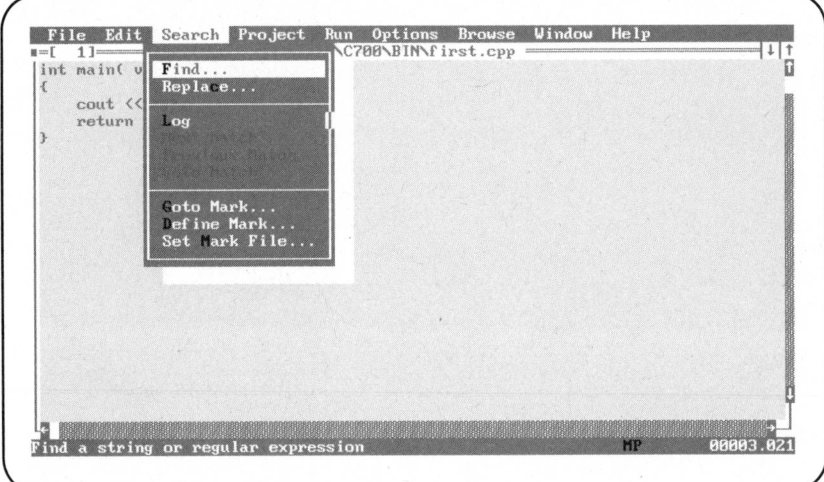

***Figure 5.9.** The Search menu.*

Find

The **F**ind command searches the active window for an occurrence of a text string. When you initiate **F**ind, a dialog box appears (see Figure 5.10). Use one of the following methods to select the string:

- Type the text string into the **F**ind Text text box.
- Select the word that is to be the search target *before* initiating the **F**ind command. When you execute **F**ind, that word appears in the text box.
- If you want to do a "logged search" over multiple files, check the **L**og Search check box and specify which files are to be searched.

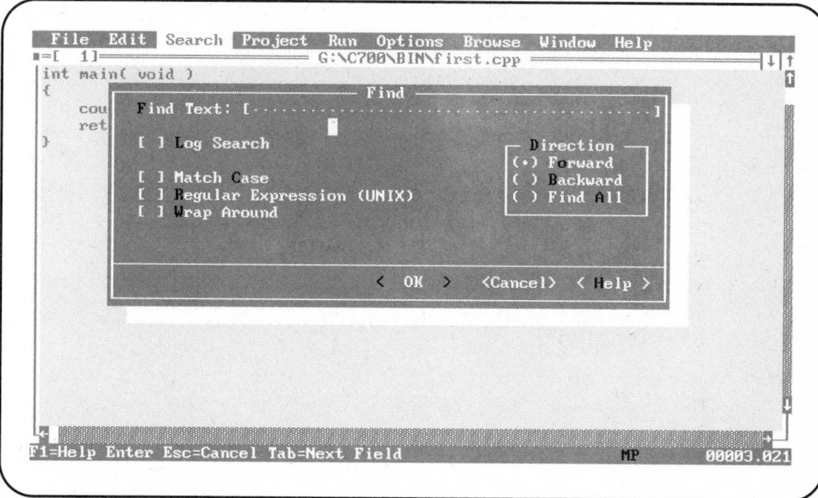

Figure 5.10. *The Find dialog box.*

After selecting the text string, you control the nature of the search by choosing the appropriate dialog box options (described in detail in the next paragraphs). Then choose the OK push button. The next occurrence of the text string is located, the cursor is positioned at that location, and the text is highlighted. Choose another **F**ind operation or press F3 or F4 to do another find. F3 finds the next occurrence of the search target, and F4 finds the previous occurrence.

If you check the **L**og Search check box, all lines containing the selected text string will be listed in the Search Results window. You can move between the logged lines by using the **N**ext Match and **P**revious Match commands from the **S**earch menu. However, the easiest way to move between the "logged" lines is to use the shortcut keys Shift+Ctrl+F3 (**N**ext Match) and Shift+Ctrl+F4 (**P**revious Match).

By default, the F**o**rward option in the **D**irection box is selected so that the search begins at the cursor and continues to the end of the file. When you select the **B**ackward option, the search begins at the cursor and continues backward to the beginning of the file. When you select the Find **A**ll option, the search begins at the beginning of the file and continues to the end of the file.

If the Wrap Around check box is checked, the search operation does not stop at the end or beginning of the file. If the direction option is Forward and the search operation reaches the end of the file, the search continues at the beginning of the file. If the search reaches the starting position and has not found the search target, the operation terminates.

Use the check boxes to control the nature of the search. By default, search operations ignore case (an uppercase `A` is equivalent to a lowercase `a`). For example, when you search for `Monkey`, the **Find** command finds `MONKEY`, `monkey`, and `Monkey`. When you want an exact match, check the Match Case check box.

By default, the **Regular Expression (UNIX)** option is turned off, and a *literal search*—which finds the source file text that matches the specified text string—is performed. When **Regular Expression (UNIX)** is turned on, Find assumes that the text string is a *regular expression*—a text string that contains special characters to match a pattern in a file. Eight characters have a special meaning when used in regular expressions (see Table 5.4).

Table 5.4. UNIX regular expression characters.

Character	*Use*
. (period)	Matches any single character
^ (caret)	Matches at the beginning of a line
$ (dollar sign)	Matches at the end of a line
* (asterisk)	Matches zero or more occurrences of the character(s) preceding the asterisk
+ (plus sign)	Matches one or more occurrences of the character(s) preceding the plus sign
[ ] (brackets)	Matches sets of the characters specified within the brackets (characters within the brackets can be other special characters)
\ (backslash)	Interprets the next character as a literal character

> You may wonder why the word *UNIX* is to the right of the **R**egular Expression check box. The PWB supports two forms of metacharacters. UNIX supports these metacharacters: `. \ [ ] : * + ^ $`. There is a non-UNIX form that supports these metacharacters: `? \ [ ] & + ^ $ @ # ( ) { }`. The UNIX form is more complicated to use. However, it is supported to provide metacharacters more familiar to UNIX gurus. Although the UNIX option is the default, you can select the non-UNIX form by changing the `unixre` switch from yes (`unixre:yes`) to no (`unixre:no`) with the Editor **S**ettings command on the **O**ptions menu.

Here are some examples of regular expressions:

`c.t` — Finds occurrences of `c` and `t` separated by any single character, such as `cat`, `c1t`, `catch`, and `catalog`, but will not locate `boat` and `car`.

`^float` — Finds occurrences of `float` located at the beginning of a line. In the following source code, `float` will be found only in line 2.

Column:

```
1234567....

int dog( float cost, int type );
float mval;
     float xval;
```

`xyz;$` — Finds occurrences of `xyz;` located at the end of the line. This type of search will locate `xyz;` in the third line only of the following example:

```
int xyz, abc;
xyz = 3;
abc = 4 * xyz;
```

5

`c*t` — Finds occurrences of `c` and `t` separated by any number of characters, such as `cat`, `coat`, `actor`, and `collection`.

`c+t` — Finds occurrences of `c` and `t` separated by one or more characters, such as `cat`, `coat`, and `collection`, but will not find `actor`.

`a[+/*-]b` — Finds all occurrences of `a` and `b` separated by any of these special characters: `+ / * -`. Notice that special characters are treated as literals when enclosed in brackets.

`a \+ b` Finds all occurrences of `a + b`, such as `a + bank`. The special character + is treated as a literal.

Replace

The Replace command searches the active window for the occurrence of a text string and replaces it with another text string. When you execute Replace, the dialog box shown in Figure 5.11 appears.

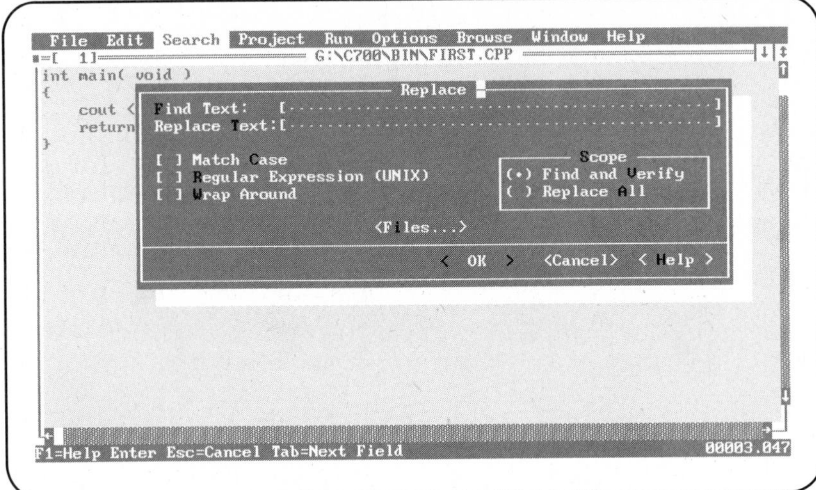

***Figure 5.11.** The Replace dialog box.*

The options in the Replace dialog box are the same as those in the Find dialog box: Match **C**ase, **R**egular Expression (UNIX), and **W**rap Around. Refer to the earlier discussion of the **F**ind command for additional information.

Usually, occurrences of the search target are replaced in the currently active window. However, you can designate that replacement operations be performed on a list of files. Just choose the F**i**les push button, and the Replace in Selected Files dialog box appears. You can select one or more files, and the search and replace operations will be performed on those files.

To replace text, execute the **R**eplace command, type the search string in the **F**ind Text text box, type the replacement string in the Replace **T**ext text box, set any required options, and either choose OK or press Enter.

The dialog box contains two radio buttons under Scope: one is Find and Verify, and the other is Replace All. If you select Replace All, all occurrences of the search string in the source file will be replaced.

When you choose Find and Verify, the first occurrence of the text is found and highlighted, and a small dialog box appears, asking whether you want to replace this occurrence. The dialog box contains the following push buttons:

Yes	Exchanges highlighted text with the replacement string
No	Finds the next occurrence of the selected string without performing the replacement
Replace All	Exchanges all occurrences of the highlighted text with the replacement string
Cancel	Cancels the replace operation and closes the dialog box
Help	Provides information about the Replace command

Log

The Log command turns the multiple-file search option on or off. See the earlier discussion of the Find command for more information regarding multiple-file search operations.

Next Match

The Next Match command positions the cursor at the next occurrence of the search target during a search operation. If the search is a multiple-file search and the file containing the search target is not open, the file will be opened and displayed in the active window. See the earlier discussion of Find for more information regarding search operations.

Previous Match

The Previous Match command positions the cursor at the previous occurrence of a search target during a search operation. If the search is a multiple-file search and the file containing the match is not open, the file will be opened, and its window becomes the current window. See the earlier discussion of Find for more information regarding search operations.

Goto Match

If the Search Results window is active, you can place the cursor on one of the match lines and choose the Goto Match command. The cursor then moves to the matched text in the corresponding file, and the window displaying the matched text is activated.

Goto Mark

The **G**oto Mark command positions the cursor at a previously *marked* position. When you choose **G**oto Mark, the Goto Mark dialog box appears. You can select which *bookmark* to address by either entering its previously defined name in the **M**ark Name text box or selecting the name from the list of bookmark names.

At times, you may want to place a bookmark at some location in one of the source files on which you are working so that later you can return to the same place in the program. Three commands in the **S**earch menu support bookmarks. You use the **D**efine Mark command to establish a bookmark, and the **G**oto Mark command to move the cursor to a bookmark. You save bookmarks in a bookmark file (.MRK) with the **S**ave command on the **F**ile menu. Finally, you create a new bookmark file or open an existing one with the Set **M**ark File command. **D**efine Mark and Set **M**ark File are described in the next two sections.

Define Mark

To establish a bookmark, move the cursor to the bookmark position and choose the **D**efine Mark command. The Define Mark dialog box appears. Type a name and press Enter. The name is used to refer to the bookmark. Notice that the Define Mark dialog box contains the following items:

- **M**ark Name. You enter the name of the bookmark into this field.
- **F**ile Name. This is the name of the file in which the bookmark resides.
- **R**ow. This is the line number of the bookmark. This field initially contains the line number of the current cursor position. You can change this number.
- **C**olumn. This is the column of the current cursor position. You can change this number.

- Add to Mark File. If this check box is checked, the bookmark is added to the bookmark file. Obviously, you can modify this check box only if a bookmark file is open. When this option is turned on and you define a bookmark, the mark is added to the file. When this option is turned off, defined bookmarks are temporary and will not be saved for future PWB sessions.

Set Mark File

The Set Mark File command opens or creates a bookmark file (.MRK). When you choose this command, the Set Mark File dialog box appears. The dialog box contains a **File Name** text box, a file list containing filenames with an extension of .MRK, and a directory list. You can enter the name of a new or existing bookmark file, or you can select the name of an existing bookmark file from the file list. Once a bookmark file is opened, you can add bookmarks to the file with the **D**efine Mark command.

The Project Menu

Projects consist of all program components and the relationships of those components. Project information is stored in a file with the .MAK filename extension and can contain the file types shown in Table 5.5.

Table 5.5. Project file types.

File Type	*Filename Extension*
C source	.C
C++ source	.CPP
Header	.H
Library	.LIB
Module definition	.DEF
Resource	.RC

The **P**roject menu commands create, maintain, and use projects that support the working environment, or workspace. The **P**roject menu is shown in Figure 5.12, and its commands are discussed in the following paragraphs.

5

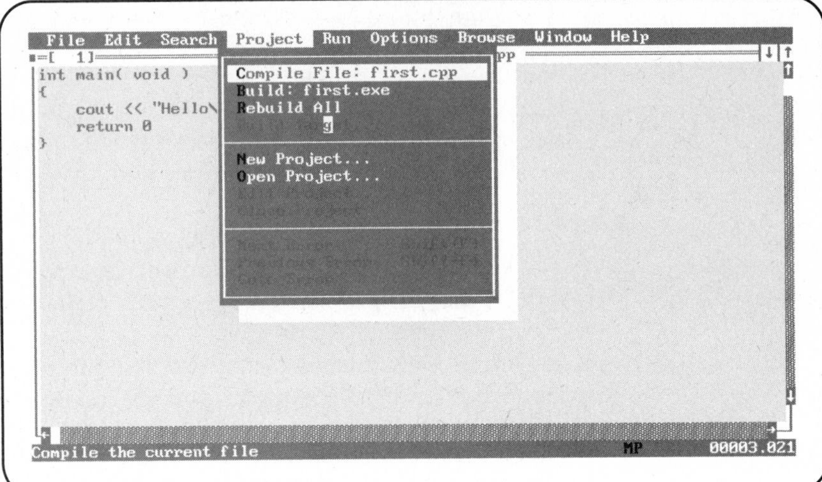

Figure 5.12. The Project menu.

Compile File

The Compile File command compiles the active source file and generates an object file. The filename of the object file has the same name as the source file except that the extension is .OBJ. Before the source file is compiled, it is saved automatically. As you learned in Chapter 3, an .OBJ file is created by the compiler and contains relocatable machine language instructions.

Build

The Build command compiles all source files that have been changed since the last compilation, and links the object files to generate a .DLL file or an .EXE file. An .EXE file is generated by the linker and is used to execute the program. When the program is a Windows program and resource files exist, the resource compiler is executed.

> The compiler and linker options must be set appropriately before **Build** is executed. You set these options by choosing Project Templates from the **Options** menu.

When a program consists of multiple source files (modules), it is called a *multimodule* program. To build a multimodule program, you must have an open project file containing a list of all associated files. The associated files include any source, header, object, resource, script, dialog script, icon, bitmap, and module-definition files required to build a program.

An open project file is not necessary for a single-module file, unless you want to save the active compiler and linker options.

A Windows program must have a modular-definition file that has a .DEF extension. If you attempt to build a Windows program without including a .DEF file in the project, a default .DEF file is usually created for you. Used to build a Windows application, a modular-definition file defines build options and specifies resources used in the application.

Rebuild All

The **R**ebuild All command compiles *all* source files in the project, links the object files, and generates a .DLL file or an .EXE file. When the program is a Windows program and there are resource files, the resource compiler is executed.

The only difference between the **B**uild and **R**ebuild All commands is that **R**ebuild All compiles *all* the source files.

Build Target

The Build **T**arget command compiles a specific target file in the project. When you choose the Build **T**arget command, the Build Target dialog box appears. It contains the **T**arget text box in which you enter the name of the target to build. In addition, the dialog box contains commands to build the specified target object (Build **T**arget) or to build the target and all its dependent objects (**R**ebuild All).

New Project

You use the **N**ew Project command to create a new project. When you execute the command, the New Project dialog box appears, prompting you to enter the name of a new project file with a .MAK filename extension (see Figure 5.13).

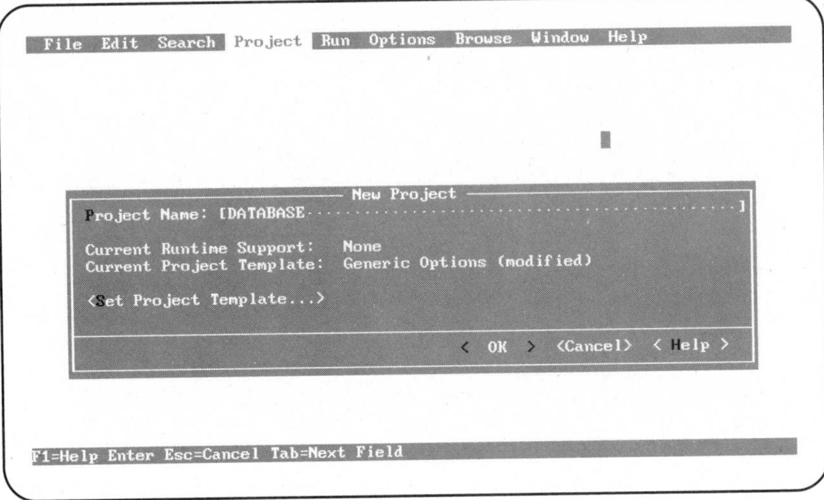

Figure 5.13. *The New Project dialog box.*

The base filename of the project file is used as the executable base filename. For example, if you name the project DATABASE.MAK, the executable filename becomes DATABASE.EXE.

Next choose **S**et Project Template, and the Set Project Template dialog box appears (see Figure 5.14). Select C++ from the Runtime **S**upport list and then select DOS EXE from the Project **T**emplates list. Finally, choose the OK push button to exit from the dialog box.

At this point, the Edit Project dialog box appears, as shown in Figure 5.15. Select a file from the File **L**ist and add the file to the project by either choosing the **A**dd/Delete push button or double-clicking the filename. Repeat the process as many times as necessary to complete the project. When you choose **S**ave List, the project file is created automatically.

Before a project is created, the compiler and linker options must be set appropriately. To do this, you choose Project **T**emplates from the **O**ptions menu.

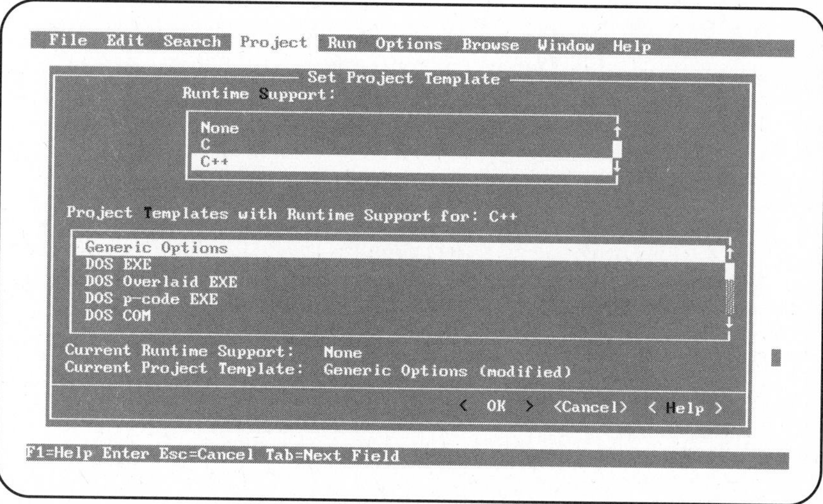

Figure 5.14. The Set Project Template dialog box.

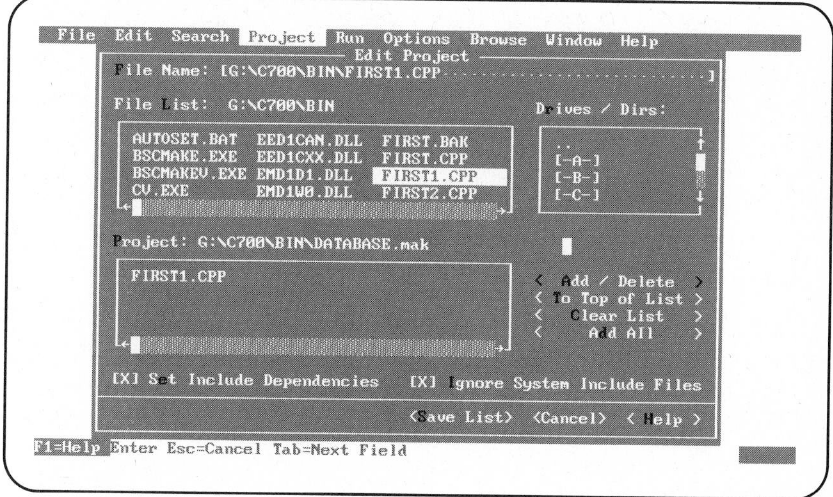

Figure 5.15. The Edit Project dialog box.

Open Project

The **O**pen Project command opens an existing project. When you execute this command, an Open Project dialog box appears that prompts you to select an existing project file from the list.

Edit Project

The Edit Project command enables you to add or delete files from the current project. When you execute Edit Project, the Edit Project dialog box appears (refer to Figure 5.15). To add a file to the project file list, select a file from the File List and either choose the Add/Delete push button or double-click the filename. To delete a file from the project file list, highlight a file in the Project list and choose Add/Delete. Repeat either process until all files are added or deleted. Then choose Save List, and the project file is changed. To remove all files from the Project list, choose the Clear List push button.

Close Project

The Close Project command saves the current project file and clears the project, leaving no project active.

Next Error and Previous Error

When you compile one or more source files and errors occur, an error window opens and displays the compilation errors. By using the Next Error and Previous Error commands, you can position the cursor on the line that contains an error in the source file. When you choose Next Error, the cursor moves to the line of code containing the next error. When you choose Previous Error, the cursor moves to the previous line of code containing an error. You can also use the shortcut keys Shift+F3 and Shift+F4 to move to the next and previous errors, respectively.

Goto Error

If the Build Results window is active, you can place the cursor on one of the errors and choose the Goto Error command. The cursor is then positioned on the line containing the error in the corresponding source file. The window that displays the text containing the error will be activated.

The Run Menu

The **Run** menu contains commands for controlling program execution and debugging operations. You can execute or debug your PWB program as you would any other program. Commands also exist to run DOS and other applications.

The **Run** menu is shown in Figure 5.16. Its commands are discussed in the following paragraphs.

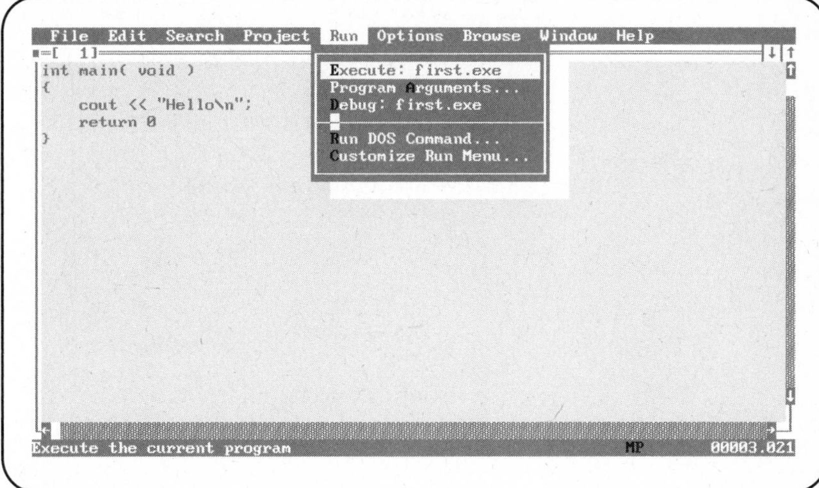

Figure 5.16. The Run menu.

Execute: *filename*.exe

The **Execute** command begins program execution, which proceeds until the program exits or crashes. The DOS prompt screen is displayed while the program is executing. When the program exits, control is returned to the PWB.

> If any of the source files have changed, a dialog box appears that asks whether the program should be rebuilt. You have the option of continuing without rebuilding, rebuilding before you continue, or canceling program execution.

Program Arguments

Many programs have program arguments that need to be specified when the program is executed or debugged. When you execute a program from MS-DOS, you specify the arguments following the processor name on the command line. Before you execute or debug a program, you can specify the program's arguments with the Program **Arguments** command. A dialog box appears that contains the **Argument** text box, where you can enter the program arguments.

Debug: *filename*.exe

The PWB executes the CodeView debugger, which is a separate application. CodeView is a *source level debugger*. This means that you can step through your source program one line at a time while executing the associated machine language program. An executable file can be built that contains debugging information. This information contains, among other things, line numbers of the source files that correspond to the machine language code to be executed. If you should modify a source file during the debugging session, the source lines usually do not correspond to the actual machine language code being executed. If you change the source code, however, you should rebuild the executable file.

You can debug executable files only when they contain debugging information. To build a debug version of the program, choose the Build Options command from the Options menu. Then choose Use Debug Options.

Run DOS Command

When you choose the Run DOS Command option from the Run menu, the Run DOS Command dialog box appears. When you enter a DOS command in the Command text box and choose the OK push button, the MS-DOS command executes. This dialog box contains a couple of options:

- You can direct the output from the executing MS-DOS command to an output file. This file can be viewed from the PWB after the MS-DOS command exits.
- You can specify that the prompt message `Strike a key when ready` be displayed when exiting from the MS-DOS command and returning to the PWB. You do this by checking the Prompt Before Returning check box.

Customize Run Menu

When you choose the Customize Run Menu command, the dialog box shown in Figure 5.17 is displayed. From within the PWB, you can add multiple MS-DOS applications. The name of each application is then added to the bottom of the Run menu, and the application can be executed from there. You can also delete an application from the menu or change the order in which applications appear in the Run menu.

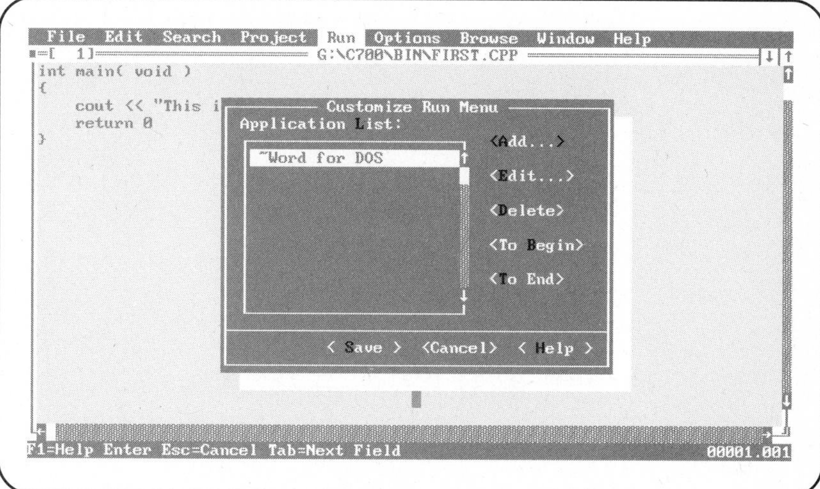

Figure 5.17. *The Customize Run Menu dialog box.*

Furthermore, you can add, delete, or reorder custom applications. To add a custom application, choose the **A**dd push button in the Customize Run Menu dialog box, and the Add Custom Run Menu Item dialog box appears (see Figure 5.18). You can edit or delete an existing custom application by choosing the **E**dit or **D**elete push button, respectively, in the Customize Run Menu dialog box. You can reorder the custom applications in the menu with the To **B**egin and **T**o End push buttons.

In the Add Custom Run Menu Item dialog box, you supply the following information, if appropriate:

- **M**enu Text. You indicate the title of the application as it will appear on the **R**un menu.
- **P**ath Name. You indicate the path of the application.
- **A**rguments. You can specify that, before an application executes, a dialog box appears to prompt you for program arguments and an output file.
- **O**utput File Name. You can direct the output from your application to an output file. You can view this file from the PWB after your application exits.
- **I**nitial Directory. This is the current directory when the application executes. (The actual directory is not changed.)

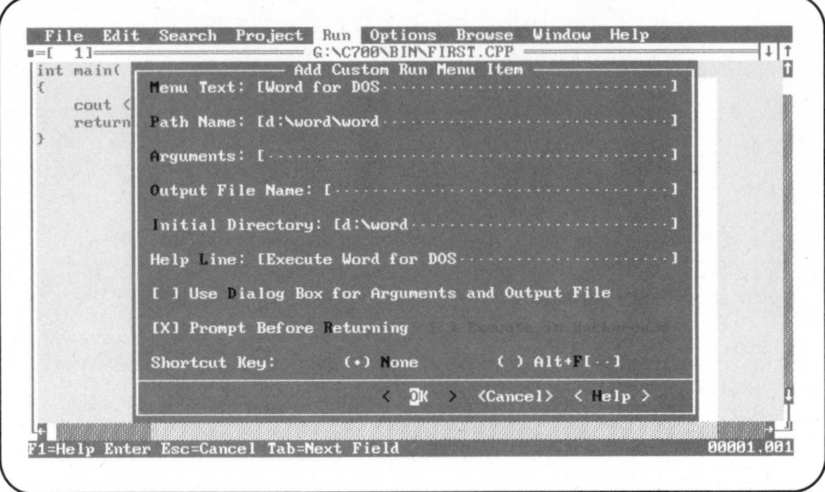

Figure 5.18. *The Add Custom Run Menu Item dialog box.*

- Help **L**ine. Here you supply the message that appears on the PWB status line when the custom application is highlighted in the **R**un menu.
- Shortcut Key. You can choose the key or key combination that becomes the shortcut key in the command label.
- You can specify that the prompt message `Strike a key when ready` be displayed when exiting from the application and returning to the PWB.

The **M**enu Text box will contain a *tilde* (~) before the character that becomes the hot key and shows in inverse video in the menu. So do not be alarmed when you see the tilde in either the **M**enu Text box or the Applications **L**ist. You can place the tilde in front of any character to make it the hot key.

In Figure 5.18, the Word for DOS application has been added. As a result, a new menu item is added to the **R**un menu, as illustrated in Figure 5.19.

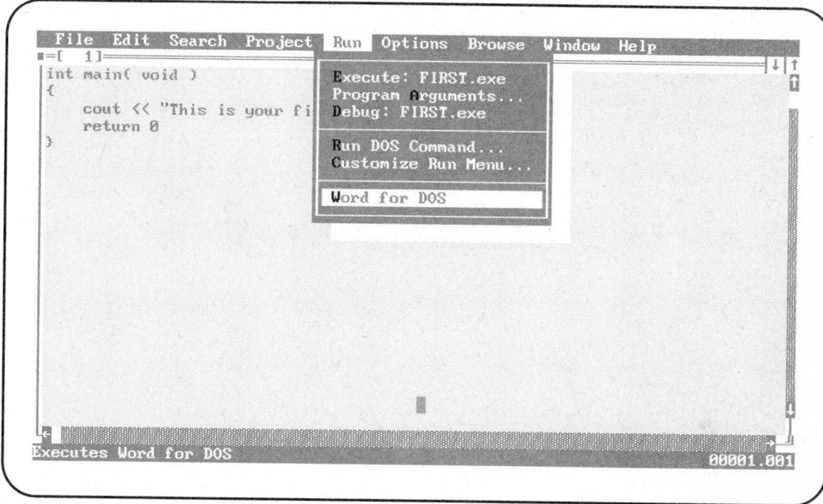

Figure 5.19. *The Run menu with the custom application Word for DOS added at the bottom.*

The Options Menu

The **O**ptions menu, shown in Figure 5.20, contains commands that customize the PWB development environment. These commands are described in the following paragraphs.

Environment Variables

When you choose the **E**nvironment Variables command, a dialog box is displayed that contains the MS-DOS environment variables (see Figure 5.21). You can view and modify the current environment variables.

Key Assignments

Suppose that you are not happy with the PWB key assignments. No problem. You can redefine the keystrokes for PWB actions by using the **K**ey Assignments command. When you choose this command, the Key Assignments dialog box appears (see Figure 5.22).

5

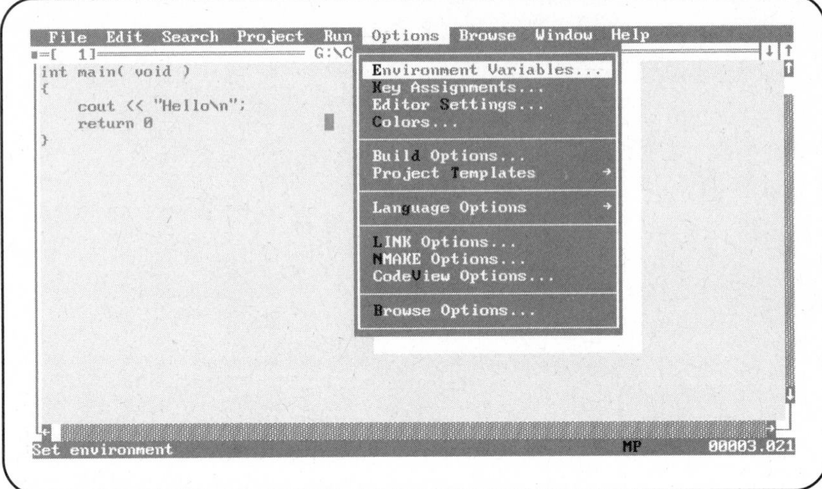

Figure 5.20. *The Options menu.*

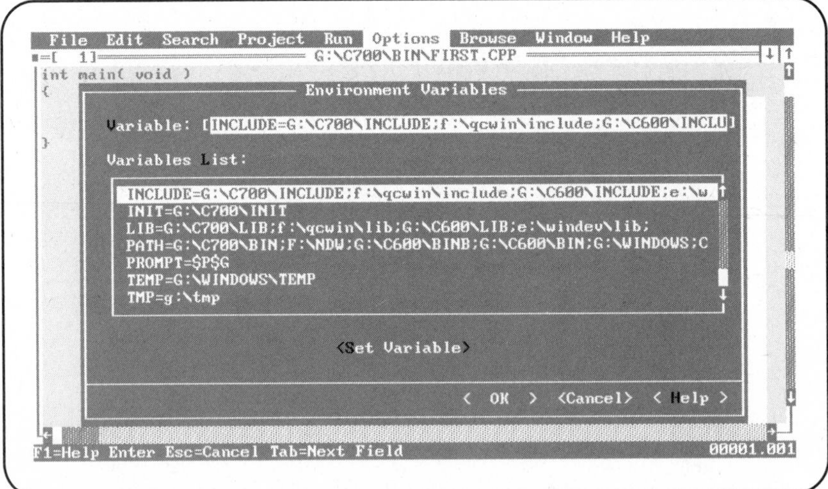

Figure 5.21. *The Environment Variables dialog box.*

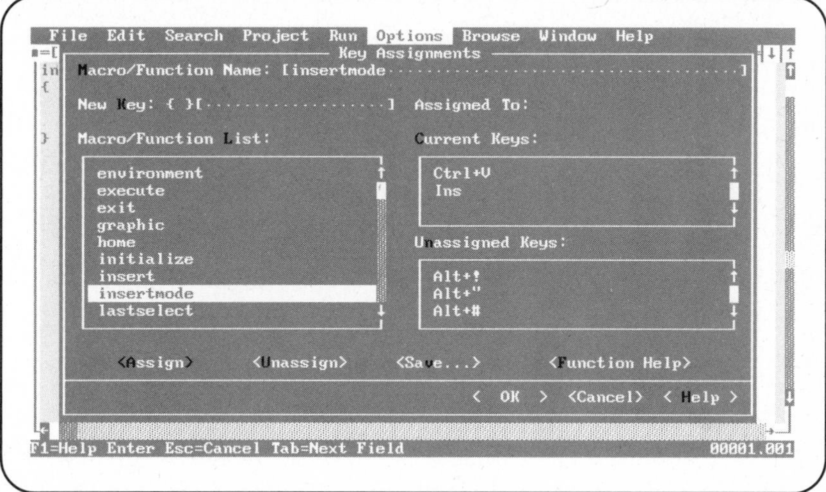

Figure 5.22. *The Key Assignments dialog box.*

To change a value, select one of the names in the Macro/Function **L**ist. The names in the list represent PWB operations or actions. For example, `begline` repositions the cursor at the beginning of the line. Any existing key assignments for the selected action are displayed in the **C**urrent Keys list. You can change a keystroke with one of three methods:

1. Type the keystroke's name within the square brackets in the New **K**ey text box.
2. Place the cursor between the curly braces in the New **K**ey field and press the new key or key combination. The key name will be placed in the New **K**ey text box.
3. Select one of the unassigned keys from the U**n**assigned Keys list.

After you have selected an action and a replacement key, choose the **A**ssign push button to assign the keystroke to the action.

You can "unassign" a keystroke from an action too. First select an action and one of its current keystroke assignments from the **C**urrent Keys list. Then choose the **U**nassign push button.

When you are finished making changes to the keyboard assignments, choose the Sa**v**e push button to save the assignments and exit.

With the Function Help push button, you can find out more information about a selected item in the Macro/Function List.

One final note should be mentioned. If you already know the key assignment, you can simply type the assignment in the Macro/Function Name text box. For example, to assign Alt+X to `exit`, type the following in the text box:

```
exit:alt+x
```

Editor Settings

A number of settings, called *switches*, control the operation of the editor. These include such functions as tab stops and initial insert mode. When you choose the Editor Settings command from the Options menu, the Editor Settings dialog box appears (see Figure 5.23).

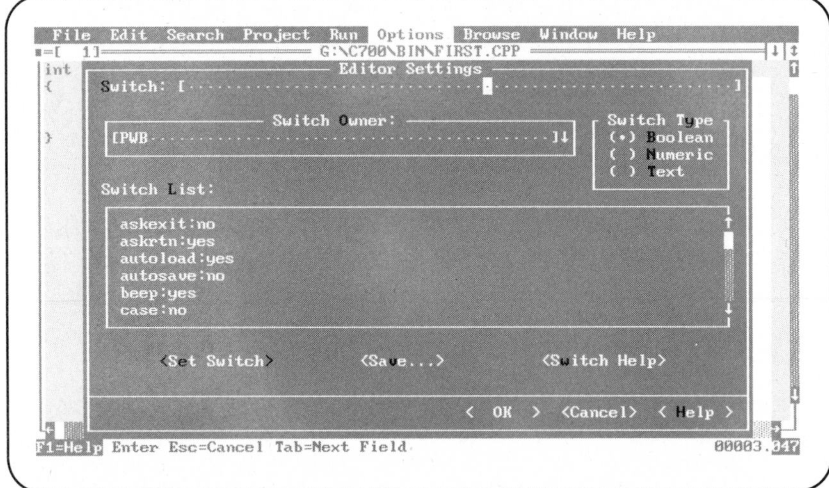

Figure 5.23. *The Editor Settings dialog box.*

The Editor Settings dialog box contains the Switch Type group of three radio buttons: Boolean, Numeric, and Text. When you select one of these radio buttons, the switches associated with that button are displayed in the Switch List. Here are the explanations of these switches:

- **B**oolean switches have binary true/false or on/off values. A Boolean switch can have a value of "yes" or 1 for on, or "no" or 0 for off. An example of a Boolean switch setting is `beep:yes`. With this setting, the bell will sound if an interface error occurred, such as the press of an invalid key. If the bell bothers you, change the setting to `beep:no`, and the bell will not sound.
- **N**umeric switches have numeric values. An example of a numeric switch is the `undocount` switch, which is the number of edit operations that can be undone. This switch is set to 30. The switch setting for a maximum number of 30 undo operations is `undocount:30`.
- **T**ext switches have text values. An example of a text switch is the `backup` switch, used to define the filename extension of a backup file. You set the extension to .BAK with the `backup:bak` switch statement.

In addition, this dialog box contains a Switch **O**wner list. You use this list to select the processor that uses the switches displayed in the Switch **L**ist. The names displayed in the Switch **O**wner list and their associated processors are shown in Table 5.6.

Table 5.6. PWB Switch Owner list.

Switch Owner	*Processor*
PWB	Switches owned by the Programmer's WorkBench
PWBC	Switches owned by the compiler and linker
PWBHELP	Switches owned by the Help processor
PWBUTIL	Switches owned by utilities
PWBBROWSE	Switches owned by the Browse processor

To change a switch setting, you select the Switch **O**wner, the Switch Type, and then the switch. The selected switch appears in the **S**witch text box at the top of the dialog box. You then make your change and choose the Set Switch push button. Continue this process until you finish changing switches.

At this point, you can exit from the Editor Settings dialog box by choosing the OK push button. The switch settings will be saved for the rest of your current PWB session. If you want the changes to be saved permanently in the TOOLS.INI file, choose the Save push button before you exit from this dialog box.

The PWB switch settings, their types, and initial values are provided in Table 5.7.

Table 5.7. PWB Owner switches.

Switch	*Type*	*Default*	*Description*
`askexit`	Boolean	`no`	Do you want a dialog box prompt before leaving the PWB?
`askrtn`	Boolean	`yes`	Do you want a dialog box prompt before returning from a shell?
`autoload`	Boolean	`yes`	Should PWB extensions be loaded automatically?
`autosave`	Boolean	`no`	Should files be saved when switching to another processor?
`backup`	Text	`bak`	Filename extension name
`beep`	Boolean	`yes`	Should audible/visible alerts be issued?
`case`	Boolean	`no`	Should letter case be significant in searches?
`cursormode`	Numeric	`2`	Block (2)/underline (1) cursor state
`dblclick`	Numeric	`10`	Double-click threshold
`deflang`	Text	`none`	Default language
`defwinstyle`	Numeric	`7`	Default window style
`editreadonly`	Boolean	`yes`	Should editing of files marked read-only on disk be allowed?

Switch	*Type*	*Default*	*Description*
`enablealtgr`	Boolean	`no`	Should Alt+G+R on non-US keyboards be enabled?
`entab`	Numeric	`8`	Tab translation mode while editing
`enterinsmode`	Boolean	`yes`	Should the PWB initially be in insert mode?
`enterlogmode`	Boolean	`no`	Should search logging initially be on?
`enterselmode`	Text	`stream`	Initial selection mode (stream, line, or box)
`envcursave`	Boolean	`yes`	Should environment variables for PWB sessions be saved?
`envprojsave`	Boolean	`yes`	Should environment variables for projects be saved?
`factor`	Text	`%50 10`	Autorepeat factor
`fastfunc`	Text		Functions for fast autorepeat, including the arrow keys (see Table 5.8)
`filetab`	Numeric	`8`	Width of tab characters in the file
`friction`	Numeric	`40`	Delay between repetitions of fast functions
`height`	Numeric	`25`	Height of the display
`hike`	Numeric	`4`	Window adjustment factor
`hscroll`	Numeric	`10`	Horizontal scrolling factor
`infodialog`	Numeric	`0f`	Set of information dialogs displayed
`keepmem`	Numeric	`2048`	XMS/EMS memory kept during shell and compile

continues

5

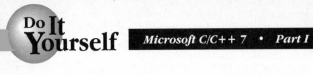

Table 5.7. continued

Switch	*Type*	*Default*	*Description*
`lastproject`	Boolean	`no`	Should the last project on startup be set?
`markfile`	Text	`none`	Name of current mark file
`mousemode`	Numeric	`1`	Mouse configuration (disabled = `0` or swapped buttons = `2`)
`msgdialog`	Boolean	`yes`	Should a dialog box for build results be displayed?
`msgflush`	Boolean	`yes`	Should only one set of build results be saved?
`newwindow`	Boolean	`yes`	Should a new window be created when opening a file?
`noise`	Numeric	`50`	Line-counting interval
`printcmd`	Text		Command for printing files
`readonly`	Text		Command for saving disk read-only files
`realtabs`	Boolean	`yes`	Preserve tab characters in the file
`restorelayout`	Boolean	`yes`	Restore the window layout when a project is set
`rmargin`	Numeric	`78`	Right margin for word wrap
`savescreen`	Boolean	`yes`	Should the operating system screen be preserved?
`searchdialog`	Boolean	`yes`	Should a dialog box for search results be displayed?

Switch	*Type*	*Default*	*Description*
`searchflush`	Boolean	`yes`	Should one set of search results be kept?
`searchwrap`	Boolean	`no`	Should searches wrap around the end of the file?
`shortnames`	Boolean	`yes`	Should access to loaded files by base name be allowed?
`showbuild`			Display progress of build
`softcr`	Boolean	`yes`	Should automatic indenting be performed?
`tabalign`	Boolean	`no`	Should the cursor in tab fields be aligned?
`tabdisp`	Numeric	`32`	Character for displaying tab characters
`tabstops`	Text	`4`	Variable tab stops
`tilemode`	Numeric	`0`	Window tiling style
`timersave`	Numeric	`0`	Timer interval for saving files
`tmpsav`	Numeric	`20`	Number of files kept in file history
`traildisp`	Numeric	`0`	Character for displaying trailing spaces
`traillines`	Boolean	`no`	Should trailing lines be preserved?
`traillinesdisp`	Numeric	`32`	Character for displaying trailing lines
`trailspace`	Boolean	`no`	Should trailing spaces be preserved?
`undelcount`	Numeric	`32768`	Maximum number of file backups

continues

5

Table 5.7. continued

Switch	*Type*	*Default*	*Description*
`undocount`	Numeric	`32`	Maximum number of edits per file to undo
`unixre`	Boolean	`yes`	Should UNIX regular expression syntax be used?
`vscroll`	Numeric	`1`	Vertical scrolling factor
`width`	Numeric	`80`	Width of the display
`word`	Text	`[a-zA-Z 0-9_$]`	Definition of a word
`wordwrap`	Boolean	`no`	Should word wraps be performed as lines are entered?

Table 5.8. Defaults for the `fastfunc` switch.

Switch	*Type*	*Default*	*Description*
`fastfunc`	Text	`down on`	Down arrow
	Text	`left on`	Left arrow
	Text	`mlines on`	Scroll down number of lines
	Text	`mpage on`	Page up one screen (PgUp)
	Text	`mpara on`	Move to beginning of paragraph
	Text	`mword on`	Move to beginning of word
	Text	`plines on`	Scroll up number of lines
	Text	`ppage on`	Page down one screen (PgDn)

Switch	*Type*	*Default*	*Description*
	Text	`ppara on`	Move to next paragraph
	Text	`pword on`	Move to end of word
	Text	`right on`	Right arrow
	Text	`up on`	Up arrow

The PWBC library switches are established by SETUP and specify which libraries have been installed. They are used by the PWB to specify the appropriate library names at link time. The switches and their corresponding library names are presented in Table 5.9. The syntax of a library switch can have one of the following forms:

```
switch= none
switch= explicit
switch= default
```

Table 5.9. PCB Owner switches.

Switch	*Library*
`doslibs`	DOS (real mode) libraries
`winlibs`	Windows libraries
`windlllibs`	Windows DLL libraries
`os2libs`	OS/2 (protected mode) libraries
`dlllibs`	OS/2 DLL libraries
`mtlibs`	OS/2 multithread libraries

5

Colors

You use the **Colors** command to modify the color of any component of the PWB interface. When you choose **Colors**, the **Colors** dialog box appears (see Figure 5.24). To change a color, choose an interface component from the **Color** list. Then select the foreground and background colors.

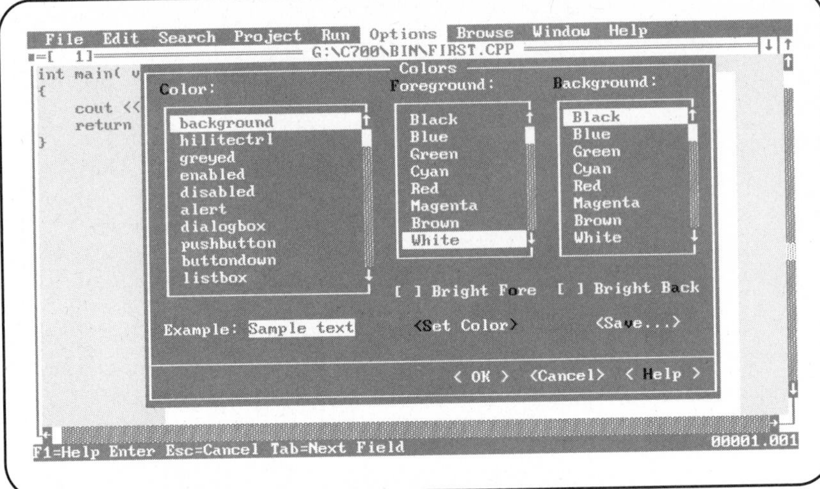

Figure 5.24. The Colors dialog box.

When you highlight one of the elements in the **F**oreground or **B**ackground list, the `Sample text` message at the bottom of the dialog box changes to the display color of that element. When you change the color, the message changes to reflect the new color (foreground or background) of the interface component. Each component has a foreground color and a background color.

Next choose the **S**et color push button to save the color setting. Continue this process until you are finished changing color settings. At this point, you can exit from the Editor Settings by choosing the OK push button, and the switch settings will be saved for the rest of the current PWB session. If you want the changes to be saved permanently in the TOOLS.INI file, choose the Sa**v**e push button before you exit from the Color dialog box.

You can use the Bright F**o**re and Bright B**a**ck push buttons to set the bright foreground and bright background color attributes, respectively.

When you are finished changing the colors of elements, choose OK to exit. Pressing Cancel discards all your changes and exits the dialog box.

Buil<u>d</u> Options

The Buil**d** Options command specifies whether the program is compiled and linked using the debug options. When you execute this command, the Build Options dialog box appears. It contains two radio buttons—Use **D**ebug Options and Use **R**elease Options. If you are going to use the CodeView debugger (which is recommended), select the Use Debug Options radio button. When you have completely tested and debugged a program and are ready to release it to your user, select the Use Release Options radio button. When a program is built using the release options, the debugging information is not present in the executable file, making the file considerably smaller and enabling it to run faster.

This dialog box contains also the Build Directory text box. You use it to specify the directory where the project is to be built. This directory will contain the object file and executables produced by the build operation.

When you change any of the options in this dialog box, you should recompile and relink all your source programs by choosing Rebuild All from the Project menu.

Project Templates

The PWB is a generalized programming environment with no prior knowledge of the specific environment in which it operates. The PWB does not know which compiler, linker, libraries, or other tools it needs to create an executable application. All the necessary information to create an application is contained in what is called a *project template*. A *template* is a language-independent blueprint used by the Project Manager to create and maintain a project make file. Although you can create your own custom project template, Microsoft provides project templates for almost all language and library configurations; these templates will probably serve all your needs.

When you choose the Project Templates command, a cascading menu appears, as shown in Figure 5.25. (Notice the right-pointing arrow at the right side of the menu. The arrow indicates that this menu contains a cascading menu.) This cascading menu provides the options to set parameters in existing project templates or to create and maintain custom templates.

Before compiling a file, you must specify a project template. The PWB uses the information in the template to perform the required build actions.

Suppose, for example, that you want to build a DOS application. The information about the compiler and linker is included in the DOS EXE project template. If you wanted to build a Windows application, there would be information relating to additional tools, such as the resource compiler. That information is included only in the Windows project templates (Windows EXE).

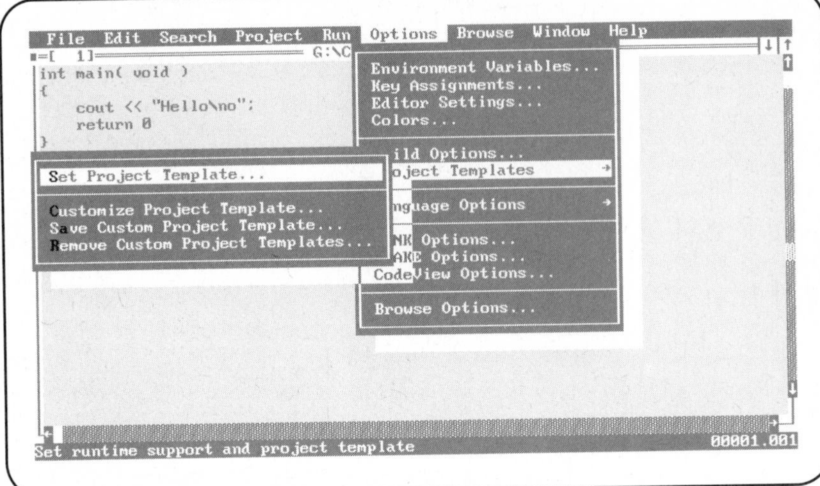

Figure 5.25. *The Project Templates cascading menu.*

You will need to choose the **S**et Project Template command to set the run-time support and project template before you build either the current project or a single-module program without opening a project. You should use this command also when you want to change the run-time support or template for an open project.

When you choose **S**et Project Template, the Set Project Template dialog box appears, as shown in Figure 5.26. This dialog appears also when you choose the **S**et Project Template push button from the New Project dialog box. (Recall that the New Project dialog box appears when you choose **N**ew Project from the **P**roject menu.)

In the Set Project Template dialog box, the Runtime **S**upport list specifies which language run-time support is to be included in the project. You should choose C++.

With a run-time support of `None`, the PWB makes no assumptions about the target environment and does not designate run-time libraries or object files. If you select `None`, you will have to add files explicitly to your project.

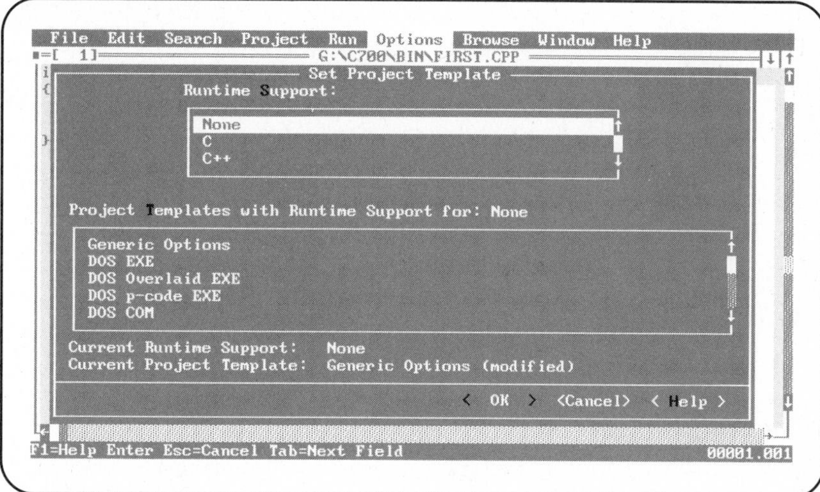

Figure 5.26. *The Set Project Template dialog box.*

When you select C++, the project template list title appears as

```
Project Templates with Runtime Support for: C++
```

The available templates with the run-time support for C++ are displayed in the list. Because you are going to be creating MS-DOS C++ applications, you should choose the DOS EXE template from the list.

Do not choose the Generic Options template. If you do, the PWB makes no assumptions about the target environment or type of target project, and supplies only the most generic options available for the compiler or utility. These options are usually the default options assumed by the compiler or utility.

After you have made your choices, the fields at the bottom of the screen appear as

```
Current Runtime Support: C++
```

```
Current Project Template: DOS EXE
```

If you have changed the language or utility options or have customized the template, the PWB displays `(modified)` after the template name DOS EXE.

Now take a closer look at four of the program types. You should choose the Windows EXE program type when you are running under Windows 3.1 and are using Windows 3.1 API functions or Microsoft C++ Foundation Classes. Windows EXE is the appropriate choice when you are going to run a program only under Windows 3.1 (not DOS) and you need the full graphical Windows interface.

Select the Windows DLL (dynamic linked library) program type when you want to divide the functionality of a program into modular parts or call a library from more than one program. Windows DLL contains DLL functions that are made accessible to a Windows executable file (.EXE). The DLL functions are not loaded into the executable file but are instead loaded into memory when a Windows .EXE file is run. In other words, the Windows .EXE file can access functions in the Windows .DLL file.

The QuickWin program type contains executable files that run only under Windows in a window that imitates the DOS environment. You can use standard C language and C++ `iostream` screen output and keyboard input library functions. However, the program will run only under Windows.

The DOS EXE program type can be executed from the DOS prompt or the PWB.

Language Options

When you select the Language Options command from the **O**ptions menu, a cascading menu appears. The cascading menu contains two items: **C** Compiler Options and C**+**+ Compiler Options. When you select C++ Compiler Options, the C++ Compiler Options dialog box appears, as shown in Figure 5.27.

The C++ Compiler Options dialog box contains various options used with the CL compiler:

- Choose the appropriate memory model from the Memory **M**odel drop-down list. (The memory models are discussed in the section "The Custom Installation Dialog Box" in Chapter 4.) For the sample programs presented in the following chapters, choose the Small memory model.
- Use the **P**rocessor drop-down list to generate the appropriate compiler switches that designate which processor the program can operate on. If your application is to run on only 80286, 80386, or 80486 computers, choose 80286. Otherwise, choose 8086. If you choose 80286, the 80286 processor-specific instruction will be used, and the program will not run on a computer with an 8086 microprocessor.

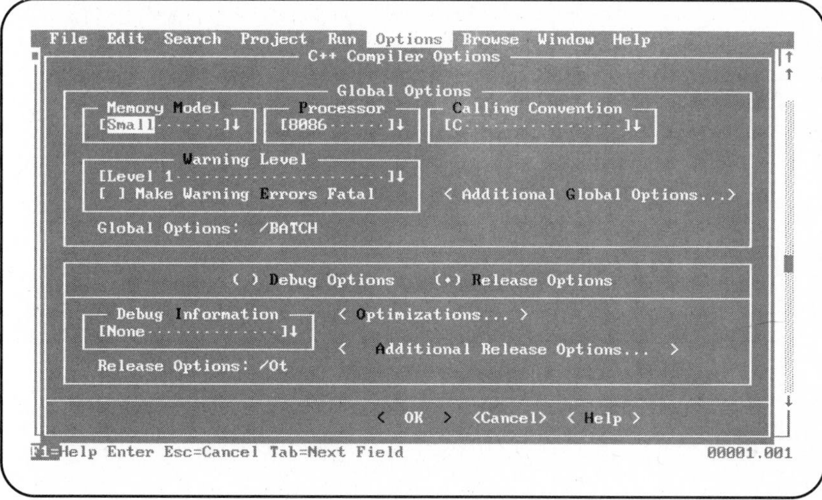

Figure 5.27. *The C++ Compiler Options dialog box.*

- Choose C from the **C**alling Convention drop-down list. This means that the compiler will generate code for function calls that conform to ANSI C conventions.
- From the **W**arning Level drop-down list, select Level 0 through 5 to determine the importance given to each level of warning message the compiler produces. Level 3 is recommended. Table 5.10 explains the warning levels.

Table 5.10. CL compiler warning messages.

Warning Levels	*Description*
0	No warning messages are displayed.
1	Displays only severe warning messages.
2	Displays Level 1 messages, plus intermediate-level warning messages.
3	Displays Levels 1–2 messages, plus warning messages relating to missing function prototype messages.

continues

Table 5.10. continued

Warning Levels	*Description*
4	Displays Levels 1–3 messages plus *lint*-like messages such as ANSI violations. Lint is a UNIX processor used to process C programs and print ANSI violations as well as other C programming standard inconsistencies.
5	Displays Levels 1–4 messages. However, the compiler treats a warning condition like an error condition; the compiler returns a nonzero return code that suspends further processing. You choose this level with the Make Warning **E**rrors Fatal check box.

- The Additional **G**lobal Options push button opens another dialog box from which you can set other compiler options.
- The Global Options item simply displays all global options, including those selected in the Additional Global Options dialog box.
- **D**ebug Options and **R**elease Options are two radio buttons for toggling between debug and release options. This choice does not change the current type of build set in the Build Options dialog box. This choice is used for compiling individual source files so that they do not contain debugging information.
- The Debug **I**nformation drop-down list allows you to select no debugging (None), minimal debugging information (Line Numbers Only), or full debugging information (Full Information) in the compiled source files.

  The Line Numbers Only option causes the compiler to produce an object file that contains only public symbols and line numbers. (Full Information contains source line numbers.) You use this option when you want to reduce memory usage while running the CodeView debugger.

  The Full Information option causes the compiler to produce an object file that contains full symbolic debugging information for the CodeView debugger. This symbolic information is a map of your source code and is used by the debugger. The information includes variable names, variable name types, function names, function return types, and the number and name of all the program's segments.

- When you choose the **O**ptimizations push button, the Optimization dialog box appears. Here you can set compiler optimization options.
- When you choose the **A**dditional Release Options push button, a dialog box appears that enables you to to set additional release options.

LINK Options

When you choose the **L**INK Options command from the **O**ptions menu, the LINK options dialog appears (see Figure 5.28). You use this dialog box to control how the PWB links your program.

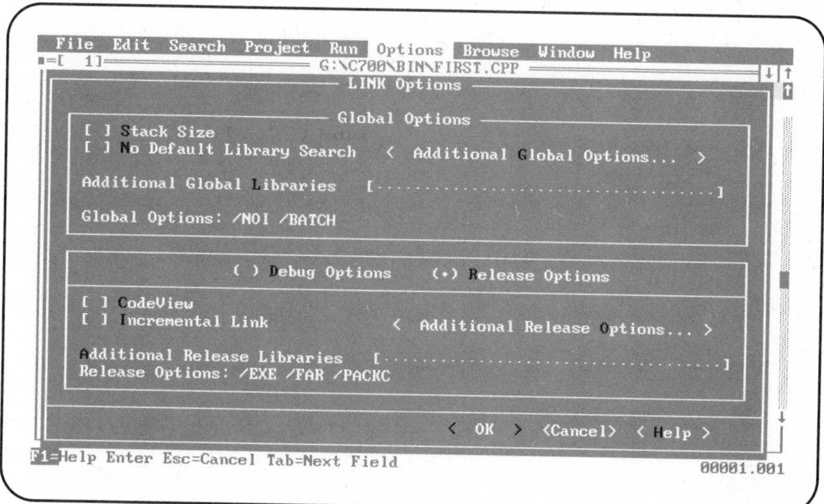

***Figure 5.28.** The LINK Options dialog box.*

The elements in the LINK Options dialog box correspond to the command-line options specified with the LINK processor:

- Stack Size. You can use the default stack size of 2048 bytes, or you can enter a positive even number up to 65534, which will define the stack size. You must not specify a stack size for a DLL.

- No Default Library Search. If you check this check box, all default libraries named in object files are ignored. Usually, this check box should not be checked.
- Additional Global Options. When you choose this push button, a dialog box appears. You can set additional LINK options for all builds, such as ignoring the case for global variables and external functions.
- Additional Global Libraries. When you choose this push button, a dialog box appears in which you can specify additional libraries for resolving references.
- Debug Options and Release Options. You use these two radio buttons to toggle between debug and release linking options. This choice does not change the debug/release option for a build.
- CodeView. If this check box is checked, debugging information will be added to the executable file by the linker. Then you can use CodeView to debug the program.
- Incremental Link. This check box does nothing because incremental linking is not supported.
- Additional Release Options. This push button opens a dialog box for setting release (rather than debug) build options.
- Additional Release Libraries. This push button opens a dialog box for specifying additional libraries for resolving references.

NMAKE Options

When you choose NMAKE Options, the NMAKE Options dialog box appears (see Figure 5.29). This dialog box offers options that control the building of your project.

The options in the NMAKE Options dialog box are equivalent to the NMAKE utility command-line options. The dialog box elements consist of the following:

- Error Significance. This element contains three radio buttons which designate the action that NMAKE is to perform when a command returns an error. The options and associated actions are these:

  Halt on Any Errors — Any command error halts the build.

Continue Building — Build only targets that are Unrelated Targets unrelated to targets in error. on Error

Ignore All Errors — Continue processing until an effort has been made to build all targets.

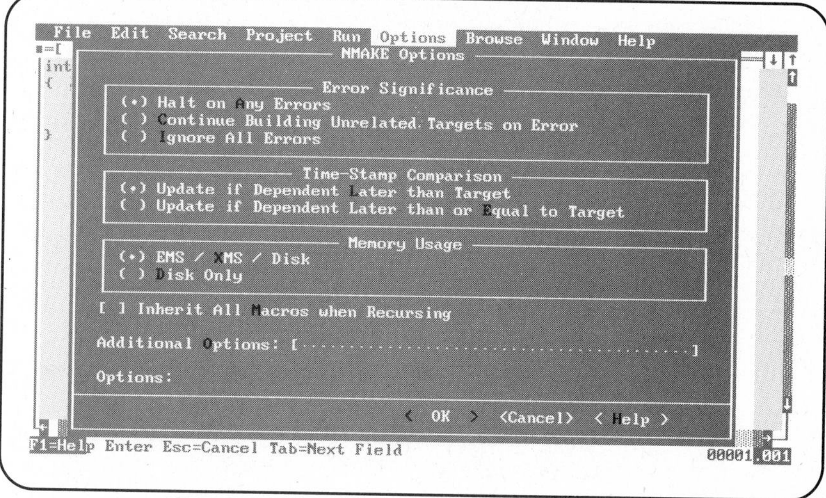

Figure 5.29. *The NMAKE Options dialog box.*

- Time-Stamp Comparison. This element contains two radio buttons. Note that a *time-stamp* is the date and time a file was created or last modified. One option instructs NMAKE to update a target if the time-stamp of any of its dependent components is later than the target's time-stamp. The second option is the same as the first option except that NMAKE is instructed to re-create the target if its time-stamp is the same as any of its dependents.
- Memory Usage. This element contains two radio buttons for designating which swap-memory method NMAKE will use.
- Inherit All **M**acros when Recursing. You use this check box to designate whether macros should be inherited by recursive NMAKE calls. You usually will not need this option.
- Additional **O**ptions. In this text field, you can supply additional NMAKE options that are used rarely and therefore not handled in this dialog box.

CodeView Options

When you choose the CodeView Options command from the **O**ptions menu, the CodeView Options dialog box appears (see Figure 5.30).

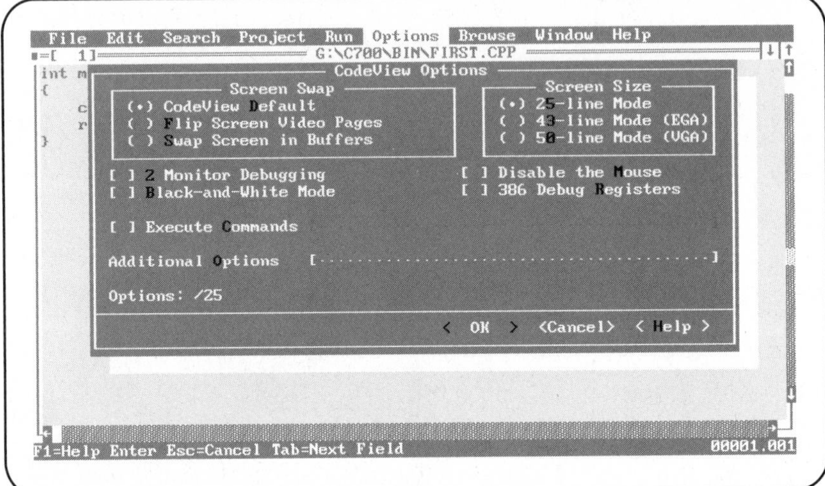

Figure 5.30. *The CodeView Options dialog box.*

This dialog box contains options that control the CodeView debugger operations:

- Screen Swap. Use these radio buttons to select the screen-exchange method. The options are CodeView **D**efault, **F**lip Screen Video Pages, and **S**wap Screen in Buffers.
- Screen Size. Use these radio buttons to select the size of the CodeView display. The options are **25**-line Mode, **43**-line Mode (EGA), and **50**-line Mode (VGA).
- **2** Monitor Debugging. The CodeView display appears on the second monitor if you check this check box.
- **B**lack-and-White Mode. Check this check box if CodeView displays on a monochrome display device.
- Disable the **M**ouse. Check this check box if the mouse is disabled in CodeView.
- 386 Debug **R**egisters. Check this box if the computer processor is an 80386. This allows the use of special debugging registers.

- Execute **C**ommands. Use this text box to specify command-window commands to execute at startup.
- Additional **O**ptions. Use this text box to specify additional CodeView command-line options.

Browse Options

The **B**rowse Options command on the **O**ptions menu enables you to specify what information is contained in the browser database when it is built. When you select **B**rowse Options, the Browse Options dialog box appears (see Figure 5.31). Once the options are established, you can rebuild the current project, and the browser database will be built. The Browse database is discussed in more detail in the next section.

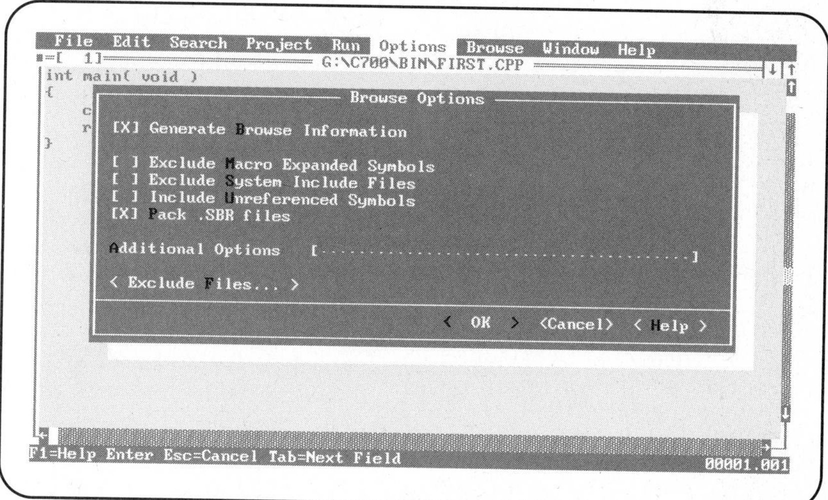

***Figure 5.31.** The Browse Options dialog box.*

You check the Generate **B**rowse Information check box to indicate that you want the browser database to be generated the next time the project is built. Until you turn on this check box, none of the other options in the dialog box can be executed. When this check box is turned off, no browser database is built along with the project.

Browser information for each module is placed in an .SBR file by the compiler, and then BSCMAKE combines the .SBR files into a single browser database (.BSC file). The database has the same base name as the project.

If the Exclude **M**acro Expanded Symbols check box is checked, symbols used in the body of macros are excluded from the list of references for each macro invocation. If this check box is not checked, the symbols used in the body of expanded macros are referenced everywhere the macros are used.

If the Exclude **S**ystem Include Files check box is checked, the information defined and used in system files is excluded. If this check box is not checked, the system include file information is included in the reference.

> Any include files delimited with angle brackets are considered system include files. In addition, any include files found in the INCLUDE environment variable path are considered to be system include files.

If the Include **U**nreferenced Symbols check box is checked, unreferenced symbols are included in the database. This allows you to find unused items by specifying the Used By query in the View Relationship dialog box (accessed through the **B**rowse menu) or the **L**ist References command (also on the **B**rowse menu). You can save disk space and speed up query operations if this check box is not checked and the unreferenced symbols are excluded.

If the **P**ack .SBR files check box is checked, after the browser database (.SBR) file is created, the SBRPACK utility is run by the compiler. SBRPACK removes unreferenced items and duplicate information from the browser database. If the **P**ack .SBR files check box is not checked, the browser database is not packed, and the compiler does not execute SBRPACK.

You cannot check both **P**ack .SBR files and Include **U**nreferenced Symbols because they are mutually exclusive.

You use the **A**dditional Options text box to specify any other BSCMAKE utility command-line options not included in the Browse Options dialog box.

If you choose the Exclude **F**iles push button, the Browse Exclude Files List dialog box appears. Choose this button to select files that are to be excluded from the browser database.

The Browse Menu

The *source browser* performs sophisticated searches for program symbols and components in your source program system. This is accomplished through the use of a database showing relationships of program symbols. You can quickly locate all occurrences of a program symbol in all the source files in a project. The source browser can also produce *call trees* and complex queries that allow you to view the definition and usage relationships of program variables, functions, and classes. All of this power is available to you through the **B**rowse menu commands.

The source browser uses symbolic and reference information generated by the compiler and stored in a file called a *browser database*.

The **B**rowse menu, shown in Figure 5.32, contains commands to access and display the browser database. These commands are discussed in the following paragraphs.

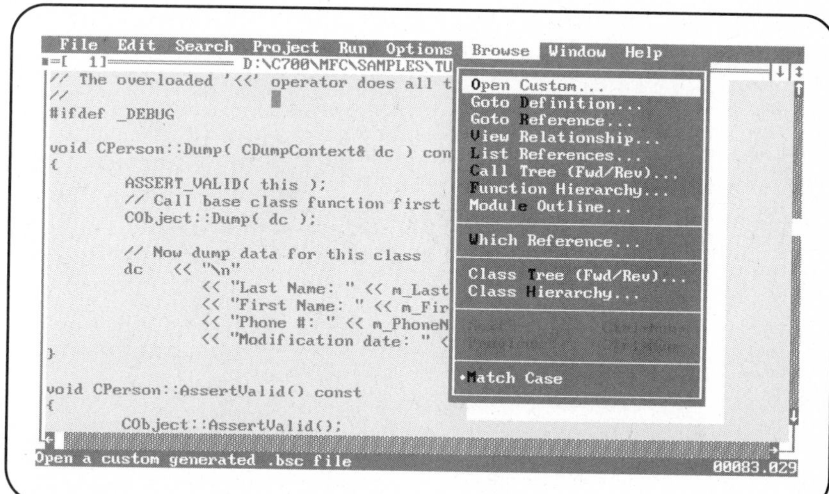

***Figure 5.32.** The Browse menu.*

Open Custom

The browser database associated with a project is called the *default browser database* because it is the one that is opened when you open a project. Although a browser database is usually built as a result of a project build, you can create a custom database apart from the project build process.

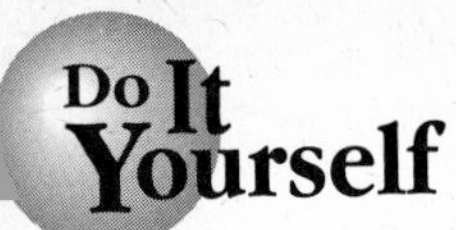

You can use the Open Custom command to open another browser database, called a *custom browser database*. You can also select the default browser database and save the name of the current custom browser database in the TOOLS.INI file. When you select Open Custom, the Custom Database Management dialog box appears, containing the following push buttons:

Use Custom Database	When you choose this push button, the Select Browser Database dialog box appears. You can either select the name of a custom browser database (.BSC) from the list or type the name into the File Name box. The custom browser database becomes the current browser database.
Use Default Database	When you choose this push button, the database for the current project is selected. If there is no active project, the current browser database is closed, and no further processing takes place.
Save Custom Database	When you choose this push button, the name of the current browser database is saved in the TOOLS.INI PWB initialization file. If you want to remove the name of a browser database file from the TOOLS.INI file, you can set the `browdbase` text switch (owned by PWBBROWSE) through the Editor Settings command on the Options menu.

Goto Definition

If you want to know where a symbol is defined, place the cursor on that symbol and choose the Goto Definition command. The symbol can be the name of a function, a variable, a constant, and so on. The Goto Definition dialog box appears with the symbol in the Name text box and highlighted in the Names list box (see Figure 5.33). The Defined in list box contains the name of the file in which the symbol is defined, as well as the line number in that file. You can double-click the filename in the Defined in list, and the file containing the definition of the symbol is opened for editing, with the symbol definition highlighted.

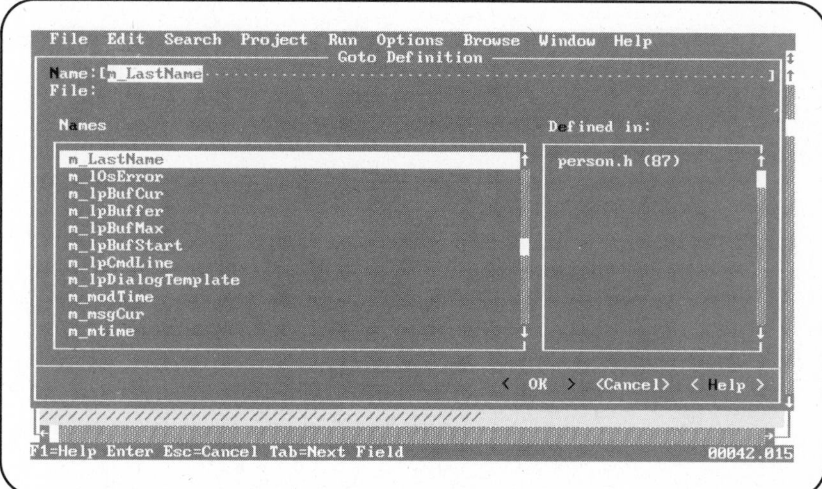

Figure 5.33. *The Goto Definition dialog box.*

If you like, you can select another name in the N**a**mes list, and the file or files in which the symbol is defined are displayed in the D**e**fined in list. In Figure 5.33, the variable `m_LastName` is selected. Notice that it is defined in the person.h header file.

Goto Reference

If you want to know every place in a program system where a symbol is referenced, put the cursor on that symbol and choose the Goto **R**eference command. The symbol can be the name of a function, a variable, a constant, a class, and so on. The Goto Reference dialog box appears with the symbol in the **N**ame text box and highlighted in the N**a**mes list. The R**e**ferenced in list box contains the names of all the files that reference the symbol, as well as the line numbers. You can double-click the name in the R**e**ferenced in list, and the file containing the reference to the symbol is opened for editing, with the line containing the reference highlighted.

You can select any other name in the N**a**mes list, and the files that reference that symbol are displayed in the R**e**ferenced in list.

Figure 5.34 shows the Goto Reference dialog box. The variable `m_LastName` is selected. It is referenced at various locations in the files person.h and PERSON.CPP.

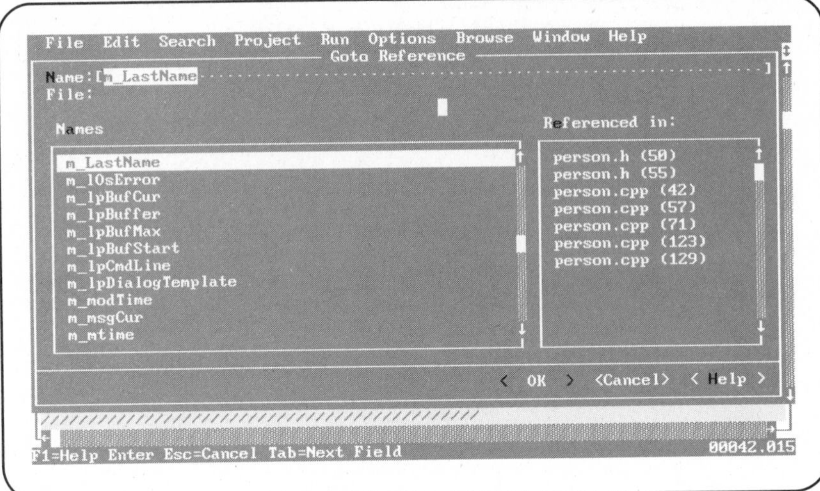

Figure 5.34. *The Goto Reference dialog box.*

View Relationship

The **V**iew Relationship command on the **B**rowse menu provides a means of viewing the relationships of various program objects in a browser database. When you choose this command, the View Relationship dialog box is displayed (see Figure 5.35).

As you can see, the View Relationship dialog box provides many ways to query the various relationships of the objects. You can view a query, or you can save it for examination or use in program documentation.

There are several ways to use this command. You can place the cursor on a name and choose the command. You can choose the command first and then type the name of the object into the **N**ame text box or select an object from the **L**ist box. Regardless of how you select a name, you can choose a query option to display some relationship between the selected name and other objects.

To filter the results of a query, you can check or uncheck the **S**how check boxes that correspond to the object types to be included in the query results. The object types are functions, classes, types, variables, and macros. For example, if the **V**ars check box is the only one checked, only variable type objects will be included in the query results.

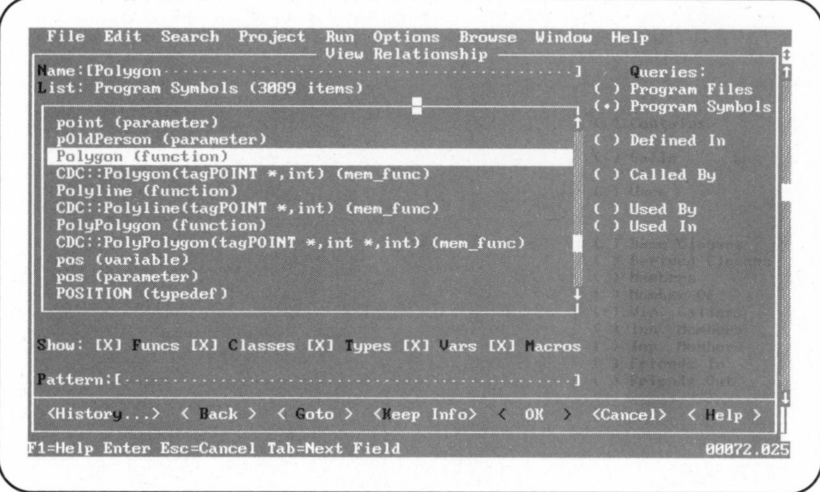

Figure 5.35. *The View Relationship dialog box.*

You can filter objects also by specifying a regular expression (see the discussion of **Find** on the **Search** menu) in the **Pattern** text box. For example, if you type x in the **Pattern** text box, only objects that contain the letter *x* will be included in the query results.

Under **Queries** is a list of radio buttons. You choose a type of query from this list by double-clicking the radio button or by selecting the button and then choosing the OK push button. The query results appear in the **List** box, and the object of the query appears to the right of the list box title. Brief descriptions of the types of queries are provided in Table 5.11.

Table 5.11. Types of View Relationship queries.

Types of Queries	*Contents of Results*
Program Files	All project source files
Program Symbols	All browser database symbol names
Contains	Names defined in the selected source file
Defined In	Source files that define the selected name

continues

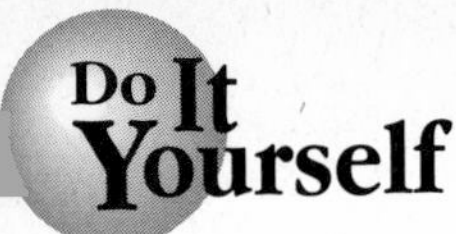

Table 5.11. continued

Types of Queries	*Contents of Results*
Calls	Functions and macros called by the selected function
Called By	Functions and macros that call the selected function
Uses	Symbol names used by the selected function
Used By	Objects that reference the selected name
Used In	Files that reference the selected name
Base Classes	The selected class's base classes
Derived Classes	Classes derived from the selected class
Members	The selected class's members
Member Of	Classes of which the selected name is a member
Vir. Callers	Classes that may do a virtual call to the selected function
Inh. Members	The inherited members of the selected class
Imp. Members	Implemented members of the selected class
Friends In	Classes that declare the selected class as a friend
Friends Out	Classes declared as friends by the selected class

You can try different queries until you are satisfied with the results. Then you press the **K**eep Info push button to close the dialog box and display the query results in the Browser Output window. You can press the Cancel push button to abandon the queries and close the dialog box. The Histor**y** push button is used to select a previous query. The **G**oto push button is used to close the dialog box and position the cursor at the line (in the source file) containing the definition of the name shown in the **N**ame box.

List References

With the **List References** command, you can obtain a cross-reference list of project objects to examine or use in a program document. When you choose **List References**, the List References dialog box appears. It consists of check boxes for each of the following object types: functions, variables, types, macros, and classes.

Initially, all five check boxes are selected. You can unselect any objects that you don't want included in the reference list. Then choose the OK push button and wait until the reference list is completed. The results are displayed in the Browser Output window. A sample page of the results is presented in Listing 5.1.

Listing 5.1. An example of a browser reference list.

```
FUNCTION                                    CALLED BY LIST
--------                                    --------------
   CArchive::CArchive(CArchive const &): (CArchive)
   CArchive::CArchive(CFile *,unsigned int,int,void *):
                                            (CArchive)
                    CDataBase::ReadDataBase(CFile *)
                   CDataBase::WriteDataBase(CFile *)
   CArchiveException::CArchiveException(int):
                                            (CArchiveException)
   CBitmap::CBitmap():                      (CBitmap)
   CBrush::CBrush(int,unsigned long):       (CBrush)
   CBrush::CBrush(unsigned long):           (CBrush)
   CBrush::CBrush(CBitmap *):               (CBrush)
   CBrush::CBrush():                        (CBrush)
                                            CMainWindow::OnPaint()
   CButton::CButton():                      (CButton)
   CByteArray::CByteArray():                (CByteArray)
   CClassInit::CClassInit(CRuntimeClass *):
                                            (CClassInit)
   CClientDC::CClientDC(CWnd *):            (CClientDC)
   CComboBox::CComboBox():                  (CComboBox)
   CDataBase::CDataBase():                  (CDataBase)
                                            CMainWindow::CMainWindow()
```

5

Call Tree (Fwd/Rev)

You display a function call tree by choosing the **C**all Tree (Fwd/Rev) command and selecting a function or module from the lists in the Display Tree dialog box. Note the following elements and how they are used:

- You use the **N**ame text box to type the name of a module or function for which a call tree is displayed. If you select a name from one of the lists, the name will be placed in this text box.
- The **M**odules list box displays modules in the project. You can select one of these modules, and a call tree will be drawn for all functions in that module.
- The **F**unctions list box displays functions in the project if no module is selected. If a module is selected, this list displays functions in the selected module. You can select one of these functions, and a call tree will be drawn for the selected functions.
- If the **R**everse Tree check box is turned on, the call tree display shows a tree of callers of the selected function. If this option is turned off (unchecked), the call tree display shows a tree of calls, starting with the selected function.

Figure 5.36 shows the Browser Output window displaying a call tree. The call tree shows the hierarchy of function calls. Sometimes a question mark (`?`) appears to the right of a function name. The question mark indicates that the name is called but that the function is not defined anywhere in the project. Such functions are usually system library functions or functions defined in a source module excluded from the project. A number enclosed in square brackets indicates how many times the function is called by the calling function. Notice that `[2]` appears to the right of the `DoSave()` function. An ellipsis (`...`) indicates that the name is expanded elsewhere in the output.

The **C**all Tree command generates substantial output that can be most useful for program documentation. But you will discover that other **B**rowse menu commands provide better real-time, interactive information. For example, when you want to know what function calls another function or what function a function calls, you can get the answer through the **F**unction Hierarchy command.

```
 File  Edit  Search  Project  Run  Options  Browse  Window  Help
=[  2]================= Browser Output ==========================
 CMainWindow::Save(int)
 ├─CString::CString()?
 ├─CExceptionLink::CExceptionLink(CExceptionLink * &)
 ├─Catch?
 ├─CDataBase::DoSave(char const *)[2]
 │ ├─CString::CString(char const *)?
 │ ├─CFile::GetStatus(char const *,CFileStatus &)?
 │ ├─CFile::CFile(char const *,unsigned int)?
 │ ├─CDataBase::WriteDataBase(CFile *)
 │ │ ├─CArchive::CArchive(CFile *,unsigned int,int,void *)?
 │ │ ├─CExceptionLink::CExceptionLink(CExceptionLink * &)...
 │ │ ├─Catch?
 │ │ ├─CObject::IsKindOf(CRuntimeClass const *)?
 │ │ ├─CArchive::Close()[2]?
 │ │ ├─CExceptionContext::ThrowLast()?
 │ │ ├─CExceptionContext::Throw(CException *)?
 │ │ ├─CExceptionContext::Cleanup()?
 │ │ ├─CExceptionLink::~CExceptionLink()?
 │ │ └─CArchive::~CArchive()?
 │ ├─CPersonList::SetDirty(int)
 │ ├─CFile::Close()[2]?
<F1=Help> <Alt=Menu> <F6=Window>                    R  P        00002.004
```

Figure 5.36. *An example of a call tree.*

Function Hierarchy

With the Function Hierarchy command, you can browse through the project function call tree. When you choose this command, the Function Hierarchy dialog box appears (see Figure 5.37). You can type a function name in the Func. Name text box, or you can select a function from the Functions list. You then choose the OK push button. The functions that call the specified function are displayed in the Called By list, and the functions called by the specified function are displayed in the Calls list. The Uses list displays objects used by the specified function.

In addition, you can double-click any function in any of the functions lists, and that function becomes the selected function. In Figure 5.37, the function `CFindDialog` (in class `CFindDialog`) is called by function `OnFind`. The functions `CModalDialog` and `CString` are called by the function `CFindDialog`.

Module Outline

Another command that is useful for documenting programs is Module Outline. When you choose this command, the Outline dialog box appears, containing a list of the modules in the project (see Figure 5.38). You can enter a filename or wild-card specification (such as `*.*`) in the File Name text box. You can also select a single file in the File List box. The specified file or files will be outlined. You can selectively turn on or off the Show only check boxes to designate which objects to include in the outline. The objects are Functions, Variables, Types, Macros, and Classes.

```
 File  Edit  Search  Project  Run  Options  Browse  Window  Help
                        Function Hierarchy
Func. Name  [CFindDialog::CFindDialog(CWnd *)...................]
Functions:                 Called By:                Calls:

 CFindDialog::CFindDi   CMainWindow::OnFind()   CModalDialog::CModalDi
 CFont::CFont()                                 CString::CString()
 CFrameWnd::CFrameWnd
 CGdiObject::CGdiObje

Uses:

  pParentWnd
  CModalDialog::CModalDialog(char const *,CWnd *)
  CString::CString()

<History...>  < Back >  < Goto >  <Keep Info>  <  OK  > <Cancel>  < Help >
F1=Help Enter Esc=Cancel Tab=Next Field                  R  P      00002.001
```

Figure 5.37. The Function Hierarchy dialog box.

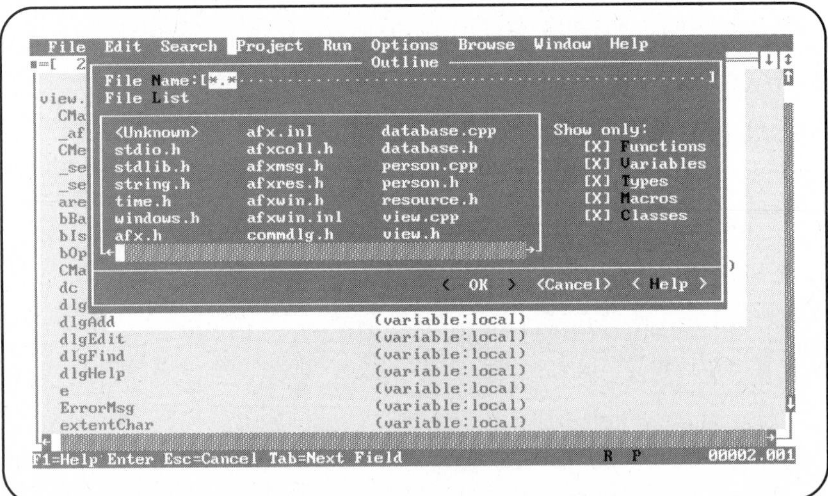

Figure 5.38. The Outline dialog box.

Listing 5.2 shows a portion of an outline for the file VIEW.CPP. The left column contains the object name, and the right column contains the corresponding type.

Listing 5.2. Sample output of a module outline for VIEW.CPP.

```
view.cpp
  CMainWindow::CMainWindow()       (mem_func:public)
 _afxExLink                        (variable:local)
 _setargv                          (function:public)
 _setenvp                          (function:public)
  area                             (variable:local)
  bBack                            (variable:local)
  bIsNamed                         (parameter)
  CMainWindow::GetMessageMap()     (mem_func:virtual:protected)
  CTheApp::InitInstance()          (mem_func:public:virtual)
  CMainWindow::InvalidateLine()    (mem_func:private)
  location                         (parameter)
```

Which Reference

Sometimes a member function is used outside the context of its definition. Place the cursor on the function name in the file window and choose the Which Reference command to display the Which Reference dialog box. Likely references are shown in the Possible Referands list. You can select one of the likely referands and choose the Goto Def push button (or double-click one of the likely referands), and the Goto Definition dialog box appears. Or you can choose the GoTo Ref push button, and the Goto Reference dialog appears. (See the earlier descriptions of the Goto Definition and Goto Reference commands.)

Class Tree (Fwd/Rev)

You can display a *class inheritance tree* with the Class Tree (Fwd/Rev) command and select a class or module from the lists in the Display Tree dialog box. For a description of the elements in the Display Tree dialog box, refer to the earlier discussion of the Call Tree (Fwd/Rev) command.

The class tree uses the same annotations as the call tree. A question mark (?) appearing to the right of a name indicates that the name is not defined anywhere in the project. A number enclosed in square brackets, such as [2], indicates how many times the name is used by the calling function. An ellipsis (...) indicates that the name is expanded elsewhere in the output.

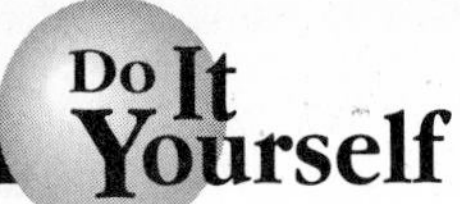

Class Hierarchy

With the Class Hierarchy command, you browse through the class inheritance project tree for the current project. When you choose this command, the Class Hierarchy dialog box appears (see Figure 5.39). You can type a class name in the Class Name text box, or you can select a class from the Classes list. You then choose the OK push button or double-click a class name in the list. Information relating to the class is displayed in the various lists. The Base Classes list contains the base classes of the selected class. The Derived Class list shows classes derived from the selected class. The Members list shows the members of the selected class.

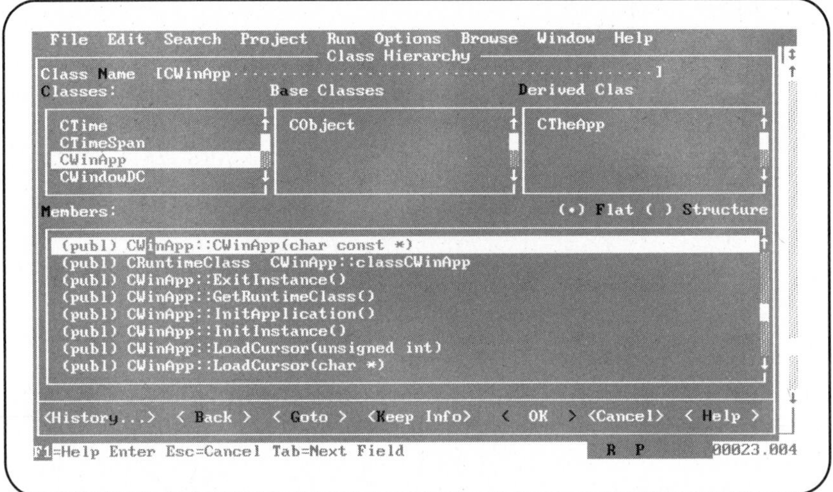

Figure 5.39. The Class Hierarchy dialog box.

In addition, you can double-click any name in the Classes, Base Classes, and Derived Class lists. Information is then displayed relating to the newly selected class.

Next/Previous

Suppose that you choose the Goto Reference command, select an object, and go to the line of code in a module in the current project where that object is referenced. You can go to the next or previous reference to that object by choosing the Next or Previous command.

Similarly, after you have used Goto Definition to go to a place in a module in the current project where an object is defined, you can use the

Next or **Previous** command to go to the next or previous location where the object is defined.

Match Case

The **Match** Case command toggles on and off the case sensitivity of the browser queries. If the case sensitivity is on when two names are compared, their cases must match *exactly* before they are considered a match. If the case sensitivity is toggled off, case is ignored when two names are compared. A bullet appears to the left of the command when case sensitivity is toggled on.

The Window Menu

You use the commands in the **Window** menu, shown in Figure 5.40, to specify window arrangement and to open PWB development environment windows. The **Window** menu commands are described in the following paragraphs.

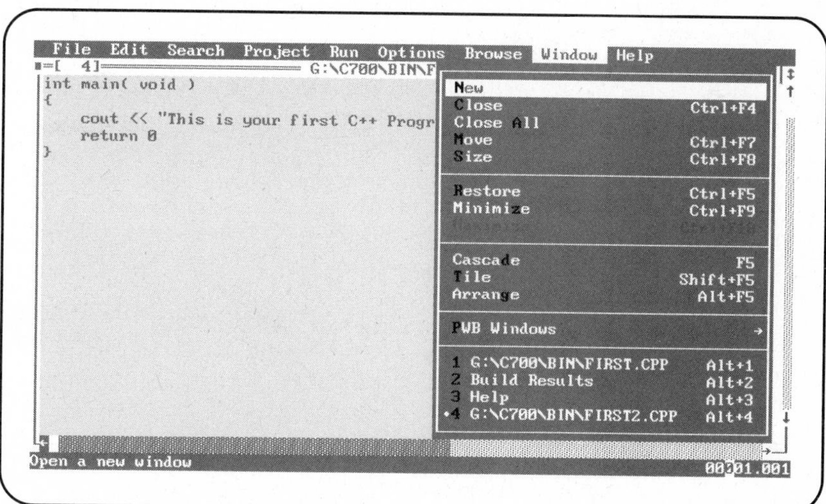

Figure 5.40. *The Window menu.*

New

The **N**ew command opens a new window, fills it with the contents of the active window, and makes the new window the active window.

Close

The **C**lose command closes the active window.

Close All

The Close **A**ll command closes all open windows.

Move

With the **M**ove command, you can move the active window to a new position by using the arrow keys. When you are satisfied with the new position, press the Enter key to terminate the move operation. If you press the Esc key, the operation is abandoned, and the window reverts to its original location.

Size

When you choose the **S**ize command, you can resize the active window by using the arrow keys. When you are finished resizing the window, press the Enter key. If you press the Esc key, the resize operation is abandoned, and the window reverts to its original size. For the resize operation, the arrow keys do the following:

Left arrow	Makes the window narrower
Right arrow	Makes the window wider
Up arrow	Reduces the window height
Down arrow	Increases the window height

During the resize operation, the top and left borders of the window remain stationary.

Restore

When a window is displayed as an icon (minimized), you restore the window to its original size by double-clicking the icon or by selecting the icon and then selecting the **R**estore command.

Minimize

When you choose the Minimi**z**e command, the active window is minimized to an icon. Remember that an *icon* is a small box with the window identification number in it. Its title is displayed below the icon.

Maximize

When you choose the Maximize command, the active window (or icon) expands to fill the screen.

Cascade

The Cascade command arranges open windows in a cascading (or overlapping) view, as shown in Figure 5.41.

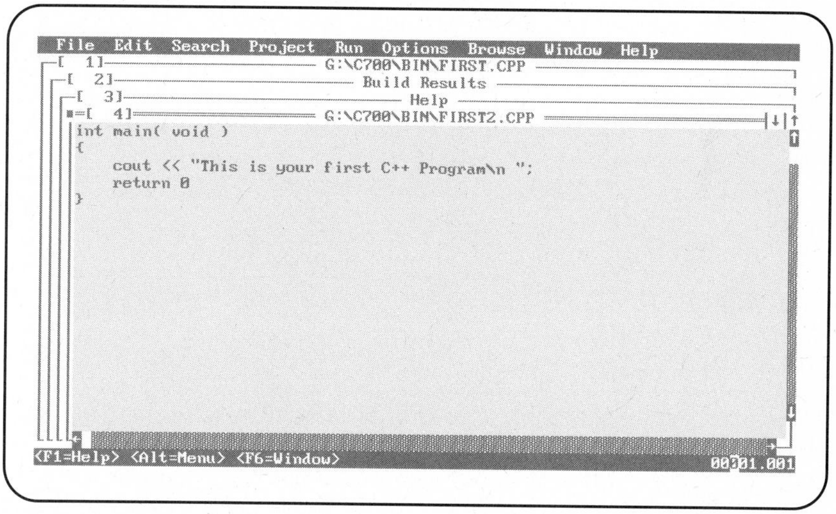

Figure 5.41. *Window arrangement with the Cascade command.*

Tile

The Tile command arranges open windows in a side-by-side (tiled) pattern, as shown in Figure 5.42.

Arrange

The Arrange command rearranges open and unminimized windows in a configuration that permits you to view simultaneously the help, Build Results, Search Results, and source windows. Only open windows are displayed. If a help window is open, it appears in the upper part of the screen. The remaining windows are displayed in the center of the screen and are cascaded.

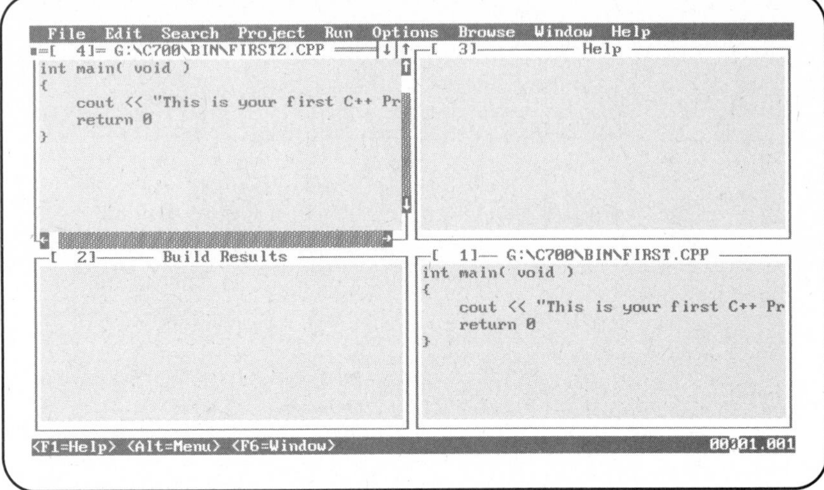

***Figure 5.42.** Window arrangement with the Tile command.*

PWB Windows

A number of windows, used by the PWB, are described in Table 5.12. Initially, these windows are inactive but are activated as they are used. If you choose the **PWB** Windows command, a submenu appears, listing the windows in Table 5.12. When you choose one of the windows, it is displayed.

Table 5.12. The PWB windows.

Window	*Description*
Build Results	Shows compiler and linker output
Search Results	Shows results of logged search
Print Results	Shows results of redirected printed output
Record	Shows or allows editing of keystrokes for current recorded macro
Clipboard	Shows current contents of clipboard
Help	Most recent help window
Browser Output	Shows results of browser database query or list

The names of open source files are also listed in the **W**indow menu. The PWB can have many windows open at one time, and the **W**indow menu can hold a maximum of five source file names. When more than five files are open, only four names are displayed, and the All **W**indows command is displayed in the menu below the last file name. When you choose the All **W**indows command, a file list appears, containing all open windows.

A bullet appears to the left of the active window's name in the **W**indow menu.

The Help Menu

The PWB online Help system provides help for the PWB development environment, as well as references to the C/C++ Language, the run-time library, the Microsoft Foundation Classes library, and the Windows API library. The final menu on the menu bar is the **H**elp menu, which provides you with online assistance (see Figure 5.43).

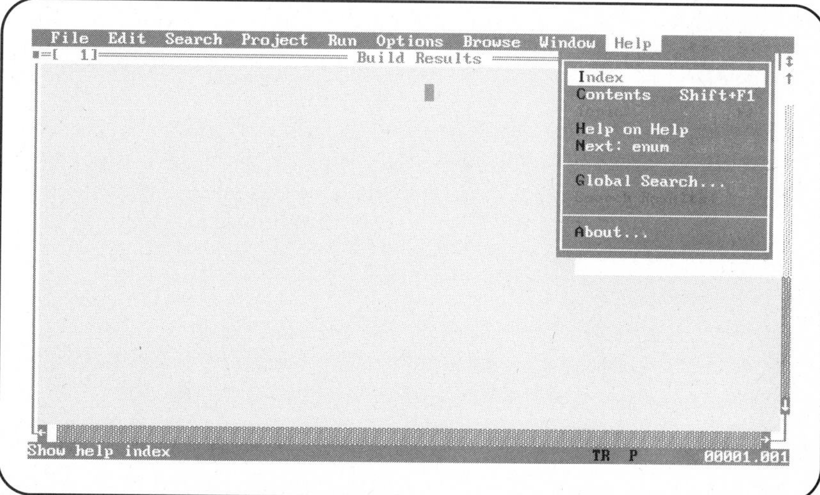

Figure 5.43. *The Help menu.*

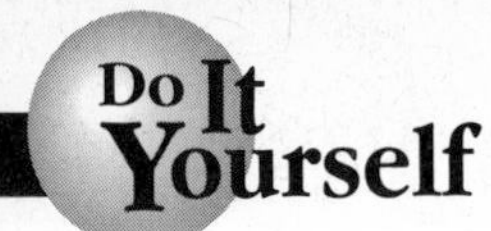

The **Index** command provides an index of help topics. The **Contents** command provides a table of contents of the help topics. With either of these commands, you can get help on various PWB and Microsoft C/C++ system elements. The **Global Search** command displays a search dialog box. Notice that the table of contents shown in Figure 5.44 has a title of Help: Microsoft Advisor. The Microsoft Advisor is the name of the Help system.

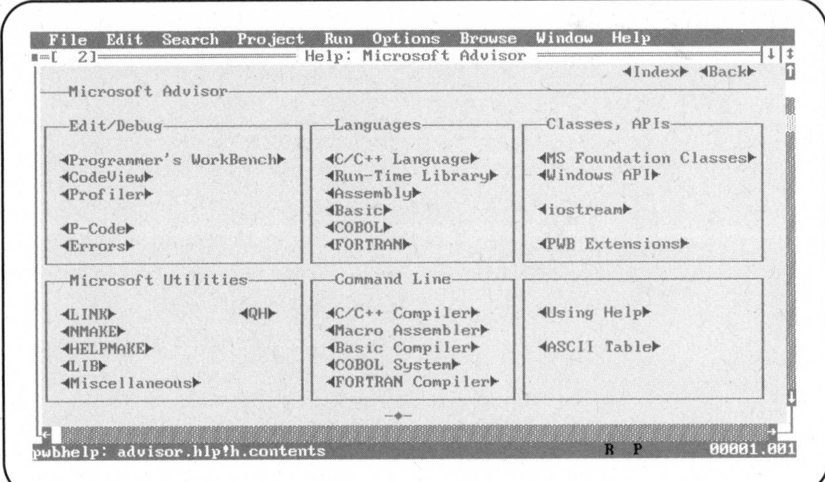

Figure 5.44. *The Microsoft Advisor window.*

The Microsoft Advisor Help system contains a hierarchy of help windows connected by links. There are two types of links in the Help system: links to topic identifiers (surrounded by triangles) and links to language keywords and functions (not surrounded by triangles). When you point the mouse at a link, and either double-click the link or press the right mouse button, a help window appears corresponding to that link.

The online Help system is divided into help topics. Figure 5.44 shows a Contents help window that contains links to various topics. A topic identifier (a link) is surrounded by triangle characters. When you select any of the topic identifiers (Programmer's WorkBench, C/C++ Language, and so on), a screen appears that describes the topic. For example, if you select the C/C++ Language topic, a C/C++ Language topic screen appears that contains C/C++ language topic links. When you select one of the links, a help window appears like the one shown in Figure 5.45. If you want more detailed information, you can select one of the language element links. Most of the help windows also have links to the help index (Index), help contents (Contents), and previous help screen (Back).

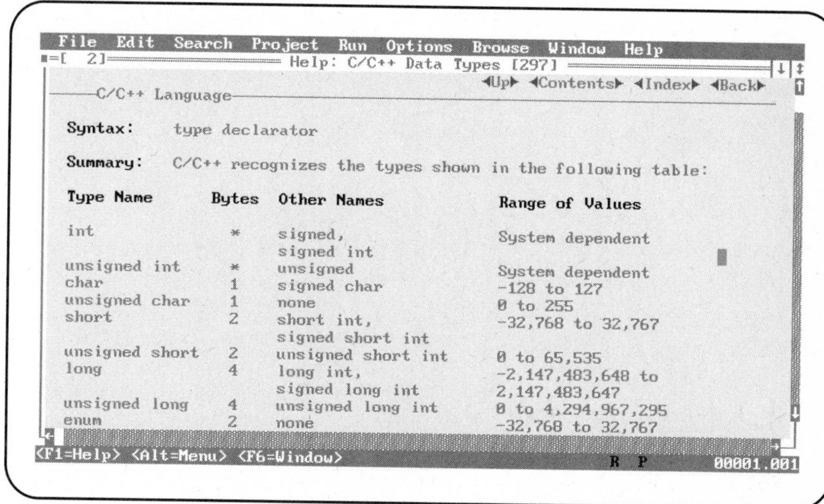

Figure 5.45. *A typical PWB help window.*

Help can be obtained in various ways. You can choose the **C**ontents or **I**ndex command from the **H**elp menu, position the cursor on a language element in a source file and press F1, press F1 while a menu command is highlighted, or choose the **H**elp push button in a dialog box. In addition, you can obtain help for a language element (or a highlighted menu command) on which the cursor is positioned by pressing the right mouse button.

What You Have Learned

In this chapter, you received a whirlwind tour of the PWB development environment and its menu system. Specifically, you learned about the following topics:

- The parts of the PWB screen
- The various menus on the menu bar—**F**ile, **E**dit, **S**earch, **P**roject, **R**un, **O**ptions, **B**rowse, **W**indow, and **H**elp
- How to create and query the PWB browser database

Whenever you have questions about the environment, refer to this chapter or access the PWB online Help system for information.

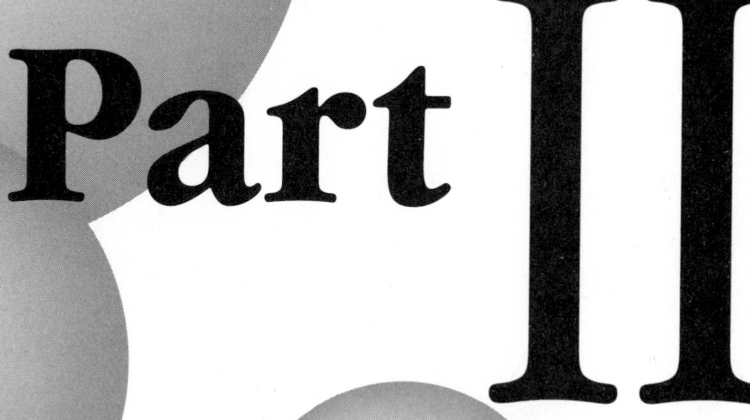

Part II

The Basics of C and C++

Data Types

God created the integer; man created everything else.

—Kronnecker (1823–1891)

In This Chapter

In this chapter, you start looking in greater detail at the basic data types supported by the C++ language. The chapter focuses on the following topics:

- Variables
- Constants
- Arrays

Variables and Constants

To refer to an item of information stored in the memory of a computer, you use a *variable* (so named because its corresponding value in memory changes). Every variable has an associated *identifier* (its name) and data type. You are responsible for *declaring* the variable—giving it a name and specifying what type of data it is. You must declare a variable before you use it. When the variable is loaded into memory, it has a location, called a *memory address*, and a value.

As noted in Chapter 2, a variable identifier or name must begin with either a letter or an underscore (_) and can contain any number of letters, numbers, and underscores. The compiler, however, ignores all but the first 247 characters. C++ is a case-sensitive language, which means that it recognizes upper- and lowercase values as being different. Choosing variable names that suggest what the variables are used for is essential, making it easier to remember what the variables do. The underscore can be used also to make longer variables more readable. Here are some examples of valid names:

```
increment
pressure
Temperature
Volume
result
Gross_national_product
Flag_used_to_indicate_that_image_is_a_bitmap
```

A Microsoft C++ language name can be any length. However, only the first 31 characters are significant; the Microsoft C/C++ 7 compiler ignores the rest of the characters.

Many Microsoft C/C++ 7 system variables and library run-time names begin with an underscore (_). To avoid possible conflict, do not use an underscore to begin the names of your variables.

You learned in Chapter 2 that a variable cannot have the same name as a C++ language keyword. C++ language *keywords* are special names used by C++; they are all lowercase, as specified by the ANSI C++ standards. Microsoft added new uppercase keywords, however, to support Windows 3.1 programming. The C and C++ language keywords are listed in Table 2.1. You can get a list of keywords also from the Microsoft C/C++7 online help.

Before using a variable, you can give it an initial value, or you may want to assign a fixed value to a variable as you use it. These initial and fixed values are called *constants* because their values never change. Each data item in a C++ program is either a variable or a constant.

Variable Types

The concept of associating a data type with a variable is common to all high-level languages. The C++ language has four basic data types: character, integer, floating point, and double. Data for each type uses a different amount of memory: *character* uses one byte; *integer* uses two; *floating point* uses four bytes; and *double* uses eight bytes. These types are illustrated in Figure 6.1, where each block depicts a single eight-bit byte of memory.

Type	Bytes
character	☐
integer	☐☐
floating point	☐☐☐☐
double	☐☐☐☐☐☐☐☐

***Figure 6.1.** The memory sizes of different variable types.*

A data type must be associated with a data item because the computer needs to know what type of data it is dealing with. For example, when you have the computer multiply two variables, it needs to know what the variable data types are so that it knows which algorithm to use for the multiplication operation.

Integer Variables

An integer variable holds whole numbers, or *integers*, with no decimal places. An integer variable can have a range of values from –32,768 to 32,767. You can figure this out for yourself, knowing that an integer is stored in two 8-bit bytes of memory. In these 16 bits, the high-order bit is the *sign* bit, and the low-order 15 bits are used for the number. The largest possible positive number would be $(2^{15})-1$, or 32,767.

Here are some examples of integer values:

```
-33
4556
91
0
32000
```

Integers are often used for counting the number of times a loop executes or as an index to an array. (Arrays are discussed later in this chapter.) Note the basic format for an integer-type declaration statement:

```
int identifier;
```

`identifier` is the name of the variable. You can declare several variables with a single `int` statement, as in this example:

```
int  counter, age, day;
int  i, j, k;
```

Two additional type specifiers—*short* and *long*—are used to define an integer variable. The short (`int`) type is a two-byte integer; the long type declares a four-byte integer.

The C++ language supports two special type specifiers—*signed* and *unsigned*. Signed integers can have positive or negative values. Unsigned integers have a zero or positive value and extend the range of the largest possible positive number. In the declaration statement, the specifiers (the keywords `signed` and `unsigned`) are placed before the `int`, `long`, or `short` keywords, as in the following examples:

```
unsigned int cost;
unsigned long large_number;
```

There is no sign bit in these examples. The variable `cost` can range from 0 to 65,535. The variable `large_number` can range from 0 to 4,294,967,295 or $(2^{32})-1$.

You can initialize any type of variable when you declare it, using an equal sign to separate the name from the constant value. (Constants are discussed later in this chapter.) In the following example, the variable `int_value` is declared to be an integer variable and is initialized to 33:

```
int int_value = 33;
```

You can also declare and initialize multiple variables with a single declaration statement, as in

```
int value1 = 51, value2 = 15, value3 = 66;
```

Table 6.1 lists various forms of integer variable types and their range of values. The system header file limits.h contains `#define` statements for limits. You can refer to this file if you are curious.

The C++ language works on many types of computers with different architectures. For computers that support Intel 8086, 80286, 80386, and 80486 (and beyond), integer variables use two bytes of memory, and the low-order part of the integer is stored first. However, for certain mini- and mainframe computers, such as the VAX minicomputer, the hardware architecture uses a four-byte C++ language integer, and the high-order part of the integer is stored first. If you are going to write a program to be used on other computers, you should consider these factors in your design.

> Use the C++ language `short` type rather than `int` because `short` declares a two-byte integer variable on all byte-oriented computers. This book, written for Microsoft C/C++ 7, focuses on the C++ language for MS-DOS and Windows.

Floating-Point Variables

A floating-point number is a number with a decimal, such as 3.45 or 234456.789. This type of number is called *floating point* because the decimal point can move, depending on the calculation. For example, when you multiply two numbers with a single decimal place (3.2×5.6), the result is a number with two decimal places (17.92). Any decimal number can be expressed also as a single digit, followed by a fraction and a power of 10. For example, 1234567.89 can be expressed as 0.23456789×10^7. Floating-point numbers are stored in memory in this form, referred to as *scientific notation* or *exponential* form. Figure 6.2 shows the number's three parts: the sign, the mantissa, and the exponent.

Table 6.1. Integer variable types.

Type	*Range of Values* *From*	*To*	*Comment*
`int`	–32768	32767	A signed integer
`short int`	–2768	32767	Same as `int`
`short`	–32768	32767	Same as `int`
`signed int`	–32768	32767	Same as `int`
`signed short`	–32768	32767	Same as `int`
`signed short int`	–32768	32767	Same as `int`
`unsigned int`	0	65535	No sign
`unsigned short`	0	65535	Same as `unsigned int`
`unsigned short int`	0	65535	Same as `unsigned int`
`long`	–2147483648	2147483647	A signed long integer
`long int`	–2147483648	2147483647	Same as `long`
`signed long`	–2147483648	2147483647	Same as `long`
`signed long int`	–2147483648	2147483647	Same as `long`
`unsigned long`	0	4294967295	An unsigned long integer
`unsigned long int`	0	4294967295	Same as `unsigned long`

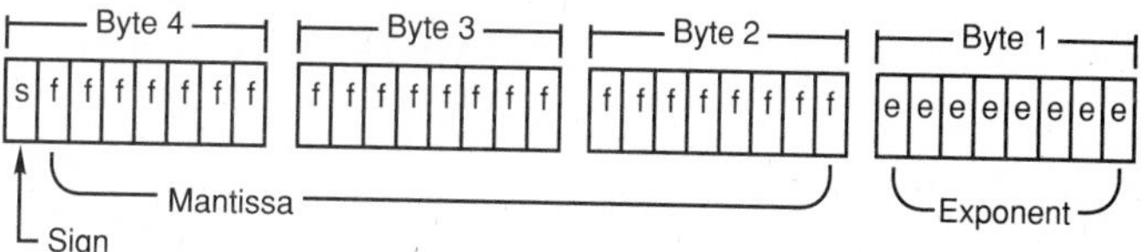

***Figure 6.2.** Storing an exponential number in memory.*

The *mantissa* is the fractional part of the number. Note that in scientific notation, 0.23456789×10^7 would be expressed as 0.23456789E+07.

The C++ language supports three types of floating-point numbers: `float`, `double`, and `long double`. A `float` type number can have a range of values from about 3.4E–38 to 3.4E+38, with a precision of 7 digits. A `double` type number, called a *double-precision* floating-point number, can have a range of values from about 1.7E–308 to 1.7E+308, with 15-digit precision. A `long double` type number can have a precision of about 1.2E–4932 to 1.2E+4932, with about 19-digit precision.

A floating-point number can never represent a number like 1/3 more accurately than the number of digits of precision it supports. For example, 1/3 for a `float` type would be accurate to 7 digits: .3333333.

Here are some examples of floating-point numbers:

```
3.44
-17.33
3.14159265359
3.45E+9
```

The following statements are used to declare floating-point numbers:

```
float identifier;
double identifier;
long double identifier;
```

`identifier` is the name of the variable. You can declare several variables with a single floating-point number declaration, as in

```
float  temperature, pressure, volume;
double x, y, z;
```

Usually, a `float` type floating-point number provides adequate significance for most calculations. However, if you are doing astronomical calculations, you probably will need additional significance and perhaps a larger exponent. You may even need `long double` floating-point variables. In addition, the mathematical functions—such as the `sin`, `cosine`, and `exp` functions—require `double` floating-point arguments.

The 8087 family of coprocessors supports 80-bit (`long double`) floating-point numbers. If your computer has a coprocessor, most calculations are performed at approximately the same speed for all three data types. However, without a coprocessor, calculations involving `float` data type numbers are performed faster than corresponding calculations involving `double` data type numbers, and much faster than corresponding calculations involving `long double` data type numbers.

Character Variables

A character variable uses a single 8-bit byte of memory to represent all 256 ASCII characters, or a single-byte integer number that ranges from –128 to 127. For example, the ASCII code for the letter A is 65. (The complete ASCII character set is provided in Appendix A.) The declaration statement used to specify a character type variable is

```
char identifier;
```

where *identifier* is the name of the variable. You also can declare several variables with a single `char` statement, as in

```
char  age, sex;       char  i, j, k;
unsigned char hour;
```

Notice that the type specifier `unsigned` can be used also with a `char` type. This type specifier is used to extend the range of a positive integer from 0 to 255. The variable `hour` can be zero or any positive value up to 255.

Constants

Constants are values that remain the same throughout the execution of a program. Constants can have any data type—integer, floating point, character, or double—but the data type is determined by how the constant is specified and used rather than by a declaration. The three categories of constants—numbers, characters, and strings—are discussed in the following sections.

Numeric Constants

Numeric constants can be decimal integers, decimal floating point, hexadecimal, or octals.

The computer interprets decimal numbers without a decimal point as integers, and decimal numbers without a minus sign (–) as positive numbers. A signed integer constant can range from –32768 to +32767; an unsigned integer constant can range from 0 to 65535. To specify that a decimal integer constant is unsigned, you can supply the suffix `U` (in either upper- or lowercase). When you want an integer constant to be data type long, specify an upper- or lowercase `L` suffix. Following are some examples of integer variables:

```
23
77u
987U
-345
34889991
1L
```

Any decimal number constant is a floating-point constant when one of the following applies:

- The constant contains a decimal point.
- The constant is followed by an exponent, preceded by an upper- or lowercase `E`.
- The constant has an upper- or lowercase `F` suffix.

A floating-point constant with an upper- or lowercase L suffix is a long double constant. Which of the numeric constants in the following list is a long double?

```
75.1
3.4E3
333.555e-5
1.0L
-.43213f
```

If you answered 1.0L, you are correct. The other numbers are floating-point constants.

Hexadecimal numbers are base 16. Hexadecimal digits can be any of the following characters:

```
0-9   A   B   C   D   E   F
```

When hexadecimal digits are the letters A through F, they can be either upper- or lowercase. You specify a hexadecimal constant by using the prefix 0x or 0X (0 is a zero). The U and L suffixes can be specified with hexadecimal constants. Here are some examples of hexadecimal numbers:

```
0x3fff
0xef
0XFF
0x7111
```

Octal numbers are base 8. Octal digits can range from 0 to 7. Octal constants are specified with a zero prefix and have a U or an L suffix. Note some examples of octal constants:

```
033
063
0777L
0377
```

Hexadecimal and octal numbers are a good way to represent values in a digital computer because they correspond to the binary patterns used by computers to represent numbers internally. Such numbers are normally used to represent addresses and status values. For a byte-oriented (eight-bit) computer, hexadecimal numbers are more useful because each hexadecimal digit represents one-half byte, or four bits (sometimes called a *nibble*). Table 6.2 shows each hexadecimal digit and its corresponding binary, decimal, and octal values.

Table 6.2. Hexadecimal digits and their binary, decimal, and octal values.

Hexadecimal	*Binary*	*Decimal*	*Octal*
0	0000	0	00
1	0001	1	01
2	0010	2	02
3	0011	3	03
4	0100	4	04
5	0101	5	05
6	0110	6	06
7	0111	7	07
8	1000	8	10
9	1001	9	11
A	1010	10	12
B	1011	11	13
C	1100	12	14
D	1101	13	15
E	1110	14	16
F	1111	15	17

A 16-bit (`near`) address can be represented with 4 hexadecimal digits. A 16-bit address can range in value from 0 to FFFF (65,757 decimal). In the 80x86 microprocessor, there are various 8- and 16-bit registers and I/O ports. A program may need to test a certain bit in a register. By convention, the bits for a 16-bit word are numbered from right to left, beginning with number 0. Bits are numbered from 0 to 15. The low-order bit is bit 0, the next bit is bit 1, and so on. Usually, you use hexadecimal numbers when working directly with registers. For example, you can use the following statement to test a 16-bit `status` value to see whether the high-order bit (bit 15) is set to 1:

```
if ( status & 0x8000 )
     cout << "bit 15 is set to 1\n";
```

The logical AND operator (&) returns a zero value if bit 15 is zero. Otherwise, the message is displayed.

Table 6.3 gives examples of numeric constants for the various data types.

Table 6.3. Examples of numeric constants for the data types.

Constant	*Type*
`127`	Decimal integer
`255L`	Long integer
`333u`	Unsigned integer
`15.33`	Floating point
`33e5f`	Floating point
`33e+3L`	Long double
`-.444`	Floating point
`0x7f`	Hexadecimal integer (127)
`0xffful`	Hexadecimal long unsigned integer
`0177`	Octal integer (127)
`0177L`	Octal long integer

Character Constants

A *character constant* is used to specify a single ASCII character. The constant is specified as a character enclosed in single quotation marks (such as `'A'`). The character is represented in memory by the appropriate ASCII code; for example, the letter *A* is represented in memory as 65. This method is fine for printable ASCII characters such as letters and numbers, but you cannot enter a tab or carriage return in your C++ code. To solve this problem, the C++ language supports *escape sequences*, which are special two-character sequences for specifying control codes that begin with a backslash (\) character (see Table 6.4).

Table 6.4. Escape sequences.

Sequence	*Character*
`\a`	Bell (supported on MS-DOS only)
`\b`	Backspace
`\f`	Form feed (supported on MS-DOS only)
`\n`	Newline
`\r`	Carriage return (ASCII 13)
`\t`	Tab (supported on MS-DOS only)
`\v`	Vertical tab (supported on MS-DOS only)
`\'`	Single quotation mark
`\"`	Double quotation mark
`\0`	Null (ASCII 0)

Although the escape sequences shown in Table 6.4 do not support all possible nonprintable ASCII codes, you can specify a backslash character (\) followed by a hexadecimal or an octal representation of the ASCII value in the form `'\xhh'` or `'\ooo'`, where *hh* is two hexadecimal numbers and *ooo* is an octal number. Note two examples:

`o'\x0e'`	Hexadecimal character
`'\025'`	Octal character

Here are examples of character constants:

`'z'`	Contains letter `z`
`'w'`	Contains letter `w`
`'\n'`	Contains newline character
`'\xff'`	Contains hexadecimal value
`'\255'`	Contains decimal value

String Constants

A *string constant* consists of a sequence of characters enclosed in double quotation marks, such as `"hello"`. String constants, which are stored in data memory and whose memory addresses can be stored with the program instructions, are different from other constants because other constants are stored with the program instructions and have no data memory location. In addition, the compiler stores an ASCII zero (`\0`) after the last character of the string constant. Figure 6.3 shows the string constant `"hello"` represented in memory.

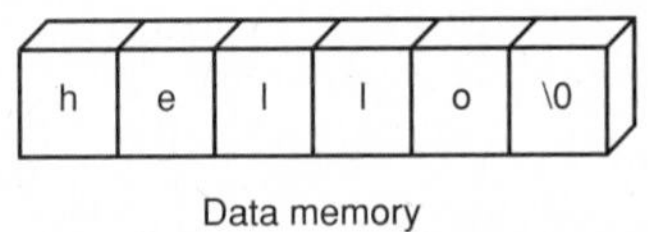

Figure 6.3. *Memory representation of the string constant* `"hello"`.

A type of string constant used occasionally by C++ programmers is called a *null string*. It is specified as `""` and stored in memory as a single null character, `\0`.

String Concatenation

If you have a string that is too long to place on a single line and still be readable, you can *concatenate* (join) two strings into one string. To do this, you just specify two quoted strings separated by whitespace characters (spaces, tabs, or newlines). In the example

```
my_string = "This is a string that does not fit on a si"
        "ngle line very well because it is too long.";
```

the string variable is assigned a string that contains the two quoted strings concatenated into one. No spaces, newlines, or null characters are inserted in the middle of the word `single`. The only character that is inserted into the resulting string is a null character following the period—at the end of the string.

Symbolic Constants

Before you consider symbolic constants, you should know that the use of a `#define` statement to specify a symbolic constant is an antiquated remnant of the C language. C++ uses the `const` qualifier to provide a superior, more powerful technique for creating constants. It is discussed in the next section. `#define` statements are used predominantly in include files that are shared by both the C and C++ languages.

A *symbolic constant* is a name used in place of another kind of constant. The name is defined by the programmer, using a `#define` compiler directive that equates the name with an existing constant. In the example

```
#define DAYS_IN_YEAR 365
```

the `#define` compiler directive instructs the compiler to replace in the program all occurrences of the symbol `DAYS_IN_YEAR` with 365 before compilation begins. The `#define` directive makes later changes to the value of a constant easier because you have to make only one change in the code, instead of searching throughout the program to find and change each instance of the constant. In addition, using a `#define` directive to define various constants can make your programs easier to read.

Customarily, symbolic constants are in uppercase so that you can easily distinguish them from other program elements.

The const Qualifier

You have already been introduced to the benefits of using symbolic constants in the place of constants. In C++ the `const` qualifier can be used to modify a declaration and initialization of a variable, and the variable becomes a constant. Note this example:

```
const double PI = 3.1415926;   // PI is a symbolic constant
```

Everywhere the variable `PI` is used, the compiler replaces it with the constant `3.1415926`. You never can change the value of a symbolic constant. In fact, the compiler displays an error if it detects an attempt to assign a new value to a symbolic constant. The syntax of a statement that uses a `const` qualifier is

```
const type name = value;
```

If you omit the *type*, `int` type is assumed. The *value* must be a constant expression. There is a convention that the *name* of a symbolic constant must begin with a lowercase `k` letter. Other conventions dictate that the first letter of the name of a symbolic constant should be capitalized. In this book, however, symbolic constants are usually in uppercase (like `#define` constants) to distinguish them from variable names.

A symbolic constant can be used anywhere you can use a constant expression. Here is an example of a constant being used as the size of an array:

```
// Use of const qualifier
void main()
{
    const int BUFSIZE = 42;  // Symbolic constant declared
    int index;
    char buffer[ BUFSIZE ];  // Use it as array size
    index = BUFSIZE
    :
}
```

One of the interesting features of constants defined with `const` is that you can use them in a header file that is included in several files, just as you do with `#define` statements. You cannot do this with variables.

Although `const` does the same thing as `#define`, there are several advantages of using the `const` qualifier instead of the `#define` statement:

- A constant defined with `const` uses the same scoping rules as any other variable, and you therefore can limit the scope of the constant's definition to a file, function, or block.
- You can specify the type of a constant defined with `const`. `#define` constants have no explicit type.
- Constants defined with `const` can be accessed by using a symbolic debugger, whereas `#define` constants cannot.

The bottom line is that good C++ programmers use `const` instead of `#define`.

The C language also supports the `const` qualifier. However, `const` works differently in C than in C++. In C a variable declaration modified by the `const` qualifier behaves like a normal variable, except that it becomes read-only after it is initialized, and it takes up memory space. You cannot change the value of a read-only variable. In other words, you cannot assign a new value to it.

In C++ the `const` qualifier works more like the `#define` statement. When a declaration is modified with a `const` qualifier, it must be initialized with a constant expression, and the compiler replaces its symbolic name with a constant. In addition, it does not take up memory space.

6

Examples of Variable and Constant Types

The sample program TYPES.CPP, shown in Listing 6.1, demonstrates how type statements are used to declare and initialize different data types.

Listing 6.1. The source listing for TYPES.CPP.

```
// TYPES.CPP - Demonstrates the use of data type declarations
#define FVAL  12.34567f
#include <iostream.h>
void main()
{
     const int int_const        = 99;
     int  number                = int_const+1;
     char character             = 'A';
     unsigned char nosign_char = 200;
     unsigned int nosign        = 60000;
     short number1              = -33;
     float decimal              = FVAL;
     double bigger_decimal      = 31.2321;
     cout << "Constant integer number = " << int_const << "\n";
     cout << "Integer constant        = " << 98 << "\n";
     cout << "Integer number          = " << number << "\n";
```

continues

Listing 6.1. continued

```
    cout << "Character type variable = " << character << "\n";
    cout << "Unsigned 8-bit number   = "
         << 0+nosign_char << "\n";
    cout << "Unsigned integer number = " << nosign << "\n";
    cout << "Another integer number  = " << number1 << "\n";
    cout << "Floating point number   = " << decimal << "\n";
    cout << "Double-precision floating-point number = "
         << bigger_decimal << "\n";
}
```

Again, the cout function is used without further explanation. You have probably observed that the cout object seems to know what type of data it is passed and formats it accordingly. Furthermore, you may have figured out that zero is added to the unsigned eight-bit integer; otherwise, cout would interpret it as a char and print its ASCII representation of the number. If you have reached these conclusions, you are correct; if you haven't, don't worry. Chapter 7, "Input and Ouput," discusses the cout object in detail.

Notice that the last message argument of the cout statement is a string constant containing \n (an escape sequence that represents a newline). \n, the last character output by cout, causes the display to end the current line and move the cursor to the beginning of the next line so that each message is printed on a separate line.

Now type TYPES.CPP into a PWB source file window, build the program, and then run it, using the knowledge you gained from Chapter 2, "C++ Program Structure and Style." The results should look something like those in Listing 6.2.

Listing 6.2. The output from the execution of TYPES.EXE.

```
Constant integer number = 99
Integer constant        = 98
Integer number          = 100
Character type variable = A
Unsigned 8-bit number   = -33
Unsigned integer number = 60000
Another integer number  = -33
Floating point number   = 12.3457
Double-precision floating-point number = 31.2321
```

Arrays

Now that you have learned about a variable that has a single value (this variable is sometimes called a *scaler*), it is time to learn about an *aggregate data type*, a type of data that contains more than one item. An array is an example of an aggregate data type.

6

What Are Arrays?

In C++ a variable that has multiple values of the same data type and that can be used to store and manipulate a list of like items is referred to as an *array*. For example, an array can contain the age of each member of a group of people, the high temperature for each day of the month, or the number of people in each of the 50 states. Each array item is called an *element*. Almost all high-level languages—such as BASIC, Pascal, FORTRAN, and Ada—support arrays.

Declaring Arrays

As with any type of variable, you must declare an array before you use it. You can declare an array by placing a *subscript* (a number enclosed in square brackets) after the identifier in the declaration statement. The subscript specifies the number of elements in the array. For example, the following statement declares an array named x that contains 10 elements:

```
char x[10];
```

When you initialize an array, the size of the array can be determined automatically by the initialization constants. These constants are separated by commas and enclosed in braces, as in the following example:

```
int  i[] = { 3,4,5 };             // Declare 3-element array
char c[] = { 'L','i','o','n' };  // Declare 4-element array
```

The array i has three elements, and the array c has four. Character arrays can be initialized with a string constant, as in

```
char s[] = { "Elephant" };
```

where the character array `s` is declared. It is allotted nine characters, eight of which are required to hold `"Elephant"`; the ninth character is required to hold a null character (`\0`) that terminates the string. Array elements are stored sequentially in computer memory (see Figure 6.4).

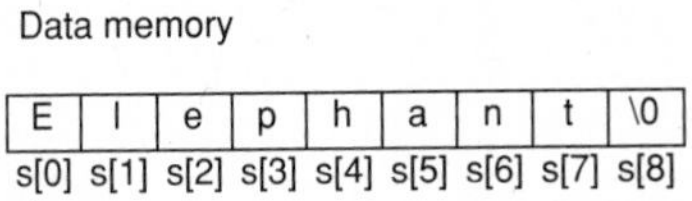

Data memory

E	l	e	p	h	a	n	t	\0
s[0]	s[1]	s[2]	s[3]	s[4]	s[5]	s[6]	s[7]	s[8]

Figure 6.4. The storage of an array.

In Figure 6.4, each box represents a byte of memory in which one character is stored. The index subscripts range from 0 for the first array element to 8, which refers to the ninth array element. You can refer to an element in an array by specifying its subscript. For example, to print the fifth element in the sample array, `s`, use the statement

```
cout << "The fifth character in array s contains: " << s[4];
```

and the letter `h` is displayed.

An array of characters is called a *string*. Although a string is not a formal data type, strings are used regularly in programs. You can use a string array the same way you use a string constant. Consider these statements:

```
char msg[] = {"Hello, world\n"};
cout << msg;                    // Print a string array
cout << "Hello, world";         // Print a string constant
```

Both `cout` statements generate the same output:

```
Hello, world
Hello, world
```

An array can be any data type, but different data types require different amounts of memory. For example, each element of an `int` type array requires two bytes of memory. Consider the following array declaration statements for different data types:

```
char   a[] = { "Cat" };
int    b[] = { 3, 11, 43 };
float  c[] = { 29.5, 14.5, 23.9 };
double d[] = { 3.3, 45.55, 14.1 };
```

Figure 6.5 illustrates how these array elements are stored in memory. Each small square denotes a byte of memory space.

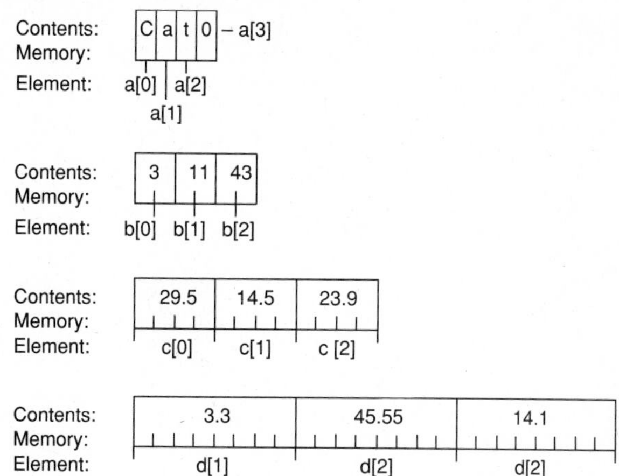

Figure 6.5. Array elements stored in memory.

ARRAY.CPP, the program in Listing 6.3, demonstrates the use of an integer array with three elements and shows how the elements are stored in memory.

Listing 6.3. The source listing for ARRAY.CPP.

```
// ARRAY.CPP - Shows how variables can be visible to two
// source files
#include <iostream.h>
extern void parray( int param[], int ind );
main()
{
     int vector[] = { 3000, 453, 211 };
     char cc[] = { 'a', 'b', 'c', '\0' };

     cout << cc;
     parray( vector, 0 );
     parray( vector, 1 );
     parray( vector, 2 );
     return 0;
}
void parray( int aray[], int ind )
{
     cout << "vector[" << ind;
```

continues

Listing 6.3. continued

```
    cout << "] = " << aray[ind];
    cout << " Address= " << &aray[ind] << "\n";
    return;
}
```

This program demonstrates how to pass an array as an argument to a function, as well as how to use a subscript with an array to address an array element. The function prints the value of an array element, the array subscript, and the address of the array element. When you run this program, you should get these results:

```
vector[0] = 3000   Address= 0x0C96
vector[1] = 453    Address= 0x0C98
vector[2] = 211    Address= 0x0C9A
```

Ordinarily, you do not need to know the address of an array element. The address is displayed here so that you can see how arrays are stored in memory. The *address-of* operator (&) is used to retrieve the address of an array element for display.

If you are familiar with BASIC or Pascal, you are accustomed to having the program check the validity of an array subscript. The C++ language does *not* check the validity of a subscript. If, for example, you declare an array to have 6 elements and then use a subscript with 99 or any other invalid value, no error is detected. As far as the C++ compiler is concerned, the following statements are correct:

```
int  l_array[6];
l_array[99]= 1;
l_array[-999]= 3;
```

> The programmer is responsible for using valid subscripts.

Multidimensional Arrays

You have learned about one-dimensional arrays with only one subscript. The C++ language also supports arrays with two or more dimensions. You declare a multidimensional array by specifying a pair of square brackets for each dimension. Here is an example of a declaration statement for a two-dimensional integer array:

```
int matrix[4][2];
```

The first subscript, [4], indicates the size of the first dimension; the second subscript, [2], indicates the size of the second dimension.

The array elements are stored in memory so that the subscript closest to the array name is the slowest. In Table 6.5, the `matrix` array has two subscripts. The left subscript is closest to the name and is therefore slower than the other subscript.

Table 6.5. An array with two subscripts.

Element	*Relative Memory Location*
matrix[0][0]	0
matrix[0][1]	2
matrix[1][0]	4
matrix[1][1]	6
matrix[2][0]	8
matrix[2][1]	10
matrix[3][0]	12
matrix[3][1]	14

You can initialize a multidimensional array when you declare it. The initialization consists of a list of constants, separated by commas and enclosed in braces, as in

```
int ary[2][3] = { 81, 82, 83, 91, 92, 93 };
```

If you do not want to initialize all the elements for one or more of the dimensions, you can use nested braces. They also make the initialization more readable:

```
int ary[2][3] = { {81, 82, 83}, {91, 92, 93} };
```

In either case, the array is initialized in this way:

Element	Value
ary[0][0]	81
ary[0][1]	82
ary[0][2]	83
ary[1][0]	91
ary[1][1]	92
ary[1][2]	93

Visibility of a Variable

A goal of C++ programmers is to make each function as self-contained as possible. You pass the function some information, and the function returns the results. In C++, as in most computer languages, a variable can be referenced only from within a function, thus making it easier to isolate a function from external intervention.

Sometimes a variable must be visible to all functions. You can reference variables from all functions in your program or from any function in any of several source files.

The place in the program at which you declare a variable determines which part of your program can access (see) that variable. A variable that precedes any specified functions is *external* and can be accessed from (is visible to) all functions in the program. A variable declared inside a function is *local* and can be accessed (is visible) only in that function.

Local Variables

Whenever you declare a variable inside a function, it becomes a *local* variable and can be referenced only inside the function. The variable cannot be referenced from other functions in the program. In SEE.CPP, the program in Listing 6.4, you can reference the variable `loc_value` from the function `main()` but not from the function `wrong()`.

Listing 6.4. The source listing for SEE.CPP.

```
// SEE.CPP - Shows how local variables are visible only to
// main()
#include <iostream.h>
void wrong( void );
main()
{
     int loc_value = 10;    // loc_value is local to main()
     wrong();
     return 0;
}
void wrong( void )
{
     int a_value;
     a_value = loc_value;  // Compiler error
     cout << "a_value " << a_value << "\n";
     return;
}
```

When this program is compiled, the following error appears in the Build Results window:

```
see.cpp(13) : error C2065: 'loc_val' : undeclared identifier
```

Because `loc_value` was declared inside the function `main()` and is local to `main()`, `loc_value` cannot be referenced by any other function. You can fix the error by making `loc_value` external, as shown in the next section, or by passing `loc_value` as an argument to the function `wrong()`. The corrected program is shown in Listing 6.5.

Listing 6.5. The source listing for SEE1.CPP.

```
// SEE1.CPP - Shows how local variables are visible only to
// main()
#include <iostream.h>
void wrong( int i );
main()
{
     int loc_value = 10;    // loc_value is local to main()
     wrong( loc_value );
```

continues

Listing 6.5. continued

```
     return 0;
}
void wrong( int i )
{
     int a_value;            // a_value is local to wrong
     a_value = i;            // No compiler error
     cout << "a_value " << a_value << "\n";
     return;
}
```

Now `loc_value` is passed as an argument in the function `wrong()`. Perhaps you should change the name of the function from `wrong()` to `right()`, because no compiler error occurs. Create a new source file (SEE1.CPP) by typing the source code for SEE1.CPP. Then compile, link, and execute the program with the **E**xecute command from the **R**un menu to confirm that `a_value = 10` is displayed in the output window.

You may wonder why typing and running these trivial C++ programs is important. It's simple. You need the experience. Before beginning programmers get used to the feel of writing a C++ program, they trip over many stumbling blocks. These errors can be simple typos, using a parenthesis instead of a brace (or the reverse), or forgetting to terminate a statement with a semicolon. The possibilities for errors are numerous. You are better off stumbling around while you work with simple programs than later, while working with more complex ones.

Generally, you declare a local variable at the top of a function, and the variable is visible to every function in the program. But if you declare a variable later in the program, the variable is visible only to the lines of code that follow the declaration. This procedure can be used to reduce a variable's visibility in a program and to put the declaration of a variable close to where it is used. The rule is that you must declare a variable before you use it. In the following example, the variable `answer` is declared right before it is used:

```
#include <iostream.h>
void main()
{
     cout << "Press any key";
     char answer;
     cin >> answer
     cout << "\nYou have pressed this key " << answer
}
```

In a C program, you usually place variable declarations at the beginning of a block or function. However, in C++ you can declare a variable anywhere in the code just as long as you declare the variable before you use it.

6

When a function is called, the memory space for all local variables associated with the function is allotted automatically, and initialization of any variables occurs. Consider the SEE1.CPP program. When the function `main()` is called, memory space is allocated for the variable `loc_value`, and it is initialized to 10. When the function returns, the memory is returned to the system, and the local variables disappear.

You cannot depend on the value of a local memory variable being retained for multiple calls of a function.

In some languages, local variables are called *automatic variables* because they are created automatically when a function is called, and they evaporate (are released) when the function returns. Although you can specify an `auto` keyword before the declaration of a local variable in the C++ language, no one ever uses this keyword because it is redundant.

Local variables reduce memory usage because they disappear when a function returns. Technically speaking, local variables are stored in the stack. The *stack* is a memory area in which data items are stored and retrieved in first-in-last-out order. The function return instruction and local memory are placed on the stack when a function is called and are removed from the stack when the function returns.

To extend the lifetime of a local variable, declare it as `static` by preceding the local variable declaration statement with the `static` keyword, as in this example:

```
static int a_value = 10;
```

The `static` local variable exists from the time the program executes until it exits, but is visible only to the local function. In Listing 6.6, the program LIVELONG.CPP demonstrates how `static` local variables are used. The `main()` function calls the function `add_one()` three times. The variable `static_value` exists for the duration of the program. The variable `local_value`, an automatic variable, is created when `add_one()` is called and exits when the function returns.

Listing 6.6. The source listing for LIVELONG.CPP.

```
// LIVELONG.CPP - Demonstrates use of static local variables
#include <iostream.h>
void add_one( void );
main()
{
     add_one();
     add_one();
     add_one();
     return 0;
}
void add_one ()
{
     static int static_value =0;
     int local_value =0;
     static_value = static_value + 1;
     local_value  = local_value + 1;
     cout << "static_value = " << static_value << "\n";
     cout << "local_value = " << local_value << "\n";
     return;
}
```

From the results shown in Listing 6.7, you can see that the value of the variable `static_value` is initialized when the program executes and is incremented each time the function `add_one()` is called. `static_value` exists throughout the execution of LIVELONG.EXE. The local variable, `local_value`, is created and initialized whenever `main()` calls `add_one()` but disappears when `add_one()` returns.

Listing 6.7. The results of executing LIVELONG.EXE.

```
static_value = 1
local_value = 1
static_value = 2
local_value = 1
static_value = 3
local_value = 1
```

External Variables

When you place a variable declaration statement outside all functions, that variable (referred to as an *external* variable) is visible to all functions that follow in the source file. When you declare a variable at the beginning of a program, before the first function, all functions in that program can access the variable.

In the example in Listing 6.8, the declaration for the variable `x_value` appears before the functions `main()` and `sample()` and is therefore external (visible) to both functions.

Listing 6.8. The source listing for SEE2.CPP.

```
// SEE2.CPP - Shows how external variables are used
#include <iostream.h>
void sample( void );
int x_value = 10;  // x_value is external to main() and sample()
main()
{
     cout << "x_value " << x_value << "\n";
     sample();
     return 0;
}
void sample( void )
{
     int a_value;
     a_value = x_value;
     cout << "a_value " << a_value << "\n";
     return;
}
```

If you move the declaration for `x_value` between the functions `main()` and `sample()` and then recompile, a compilation error should occur in `main()`:

```
see2.cpp(14) : error C2065: 'x_value' : undeclared identifier
```

The error occurs because external variables are visible only to functions that follow the external variable declaration statement. The compiler processes the source file line by line, and until the compiler reaches a variable declaration, it considers the variable to be undeclared.

When a program executes, memory is allocated for all external variables until the program exits. In other words, external variables last for the life of the program.

Thus far, you have looked at a program with a single source file. Small programs can have many functions in a single source file. When a program grows too large to edit and maintain, it takes too long to compile. Large programs usually are broken into several source files. You recompile only the source files that change.

An external variable declared at the beginning of one source file and referenced by functions in other source files is sometimes called a *global* variable. To declare the global variable to be external, specify the `extern` keyword at the beginning of the variable declaration statement of the function in which the variable is referenced, as in this example:

```
extern int x_value;
```

The declaration should be placed at the beginning of each function that references the external variable.

To illustrate the use of the `extern` keyword, consider a program consisting of two source files, ONE.CPP (Listing 6.9) and TWO.CPP (Listing 6.10). Declarations for the external variables `blue` and `green` are placed at the top of ONE.CPP and in the function `second()`.

Listing 6.9. The source listing for ONE.CPP.

```
// ONE.CPP - Shows how variables can be visible to two source
// files
#include <iostream.h>
extern void second( void );
int blue = 1, green = 2;
main()
{
      second();
      return 0;
}
```

Listing 6.10. The source listing for TWO.CPP.

```
// TWO.CPP - Shows how to use extern keyword
#include <iostream.h>
```

```
void wrong( int p );
int loc_val = 10;
void second ( void )
{
     extern int blue, green; // blue and green declared
                             // in ONE.CPP
     cout << "blue = " << blue << " green = " << green << "\n";
     return;
}
```


This is the first time you have executed a program with multiple source files. Because more than one source file is involved, a PWB project is not created automatically when you first build a file. Here are the steps you must follow to create a project (.MAK) file:

1. Choose the **N**ew Project command from the **P**roject menu.
2. The New Project dialog box appears. Type `one` into the **P**roject Name text box. Skip step 3 if the Current Runtime Support and Current Project Template fields show the following:

   ```
   Current Runtime Support: C++

   Current Project Template: DOS EXE
   ```

3. Choose the **S**et Project Template push button. When the Set Project Template dialog box appears, select C++ from the Runtime Support List and select DOS EXE from the Project Template list. Then choose OK, and the New Project dialog box reappears.
4. Choose OK to exit from the New Project dialog box.
5. The Edit Project dialog box appears. Double-click the files ONE.CPP and TWO.CPP in the File **L**ist. (You can also select a file from the File **L**ist and choose the **A**dd/Delete push button to accomplish the same results.) The **P**roject List should now contain ONE.CPP and TWO.CPP. Then choose the **S**ave List push button to complete the project-creation process.
6. From the **P**roject menu, choose the **B**uild command to compile and link ONE.EXE.
7. When the build has successfully completed, choose the **R**un Program push button to execute ONE.EXE.

Here is what the output looks like as a result of executing ONE.EXE:

```
blue = 1 green = 2
```

The variables `blue` and `green` are declared and initialized in ONE.CPP and are declared as external variables in TWO.CPP. The two variables have a global scope.

If you have any questions relating to the build process, consult the discussion of the **Project** menu commands in Chapter 5 or the PWB online help.

Static Variables

When you declare an external variable in one file, the variable is visible to functions in all other source files. If you do not want an external variable to be visible to functions outside the source file in which the variable is declared, specify the `static` keyword with the external variable declaration statement. For example, in the program SEE3.CPP in Listing 6.11, the external variable `x_value` is visible only to `main()` and `sample()` and cannot be referenced from functions in other source files.

Listing 6.11. The source listing for SEE3.CPP.

```
// SEE3.CPP - Shows how to use static keyword
#include <iostream.h>
void sample( void );
static int x_value = 10;    // x_value is external to main()
                            // and sample()

main()
{
     cout << "x_value " << x_value << "\n";
     sample();
     return 0;
}
void sample( void )
{
     static int a_value;
     a_value = x_value;    // Compiler error
     cout << "a_value " << a_value << "\n";
     return;
}
```

As you learned earlier, you can declare a local variable as a `static` variable by preceding the local variable declaration statement with the `static` keyword. An example is the declaration for the local variable `a_value` in the function `sample()`.

The Scope Resolution Operator (::)

If you have a local variable and a global variable with the same name, the local variable takes precedence. That is, if you reference the name, the local variable is used. However, you can instruct the compiler to reference the global instance of the variable instead of the local instance by prefixing the variable name with the scope resolution operator (`::`). For example, assume that a variable named `doodle` has a global declaration and a local declaration. The following statement refers to the instance of `doodle` that has a global scope:

```
Yankee = ::doodle;
```

Listing 6.12 displays the source listing for the program SEE4.CPP. In this example, two variables named `x_value` are declared and initialized. The first instance of `x_value` is declared before the function begins and is consequently a global variable. It is initialized to 10. The second instance is declared within the function `main()` and, as a result, is a local variable. It is initialized to 20. Both instances are displayed.

Listing 6.12. The source listing for SEE4.CPP.

```
// SEE4.CPP - Shows how to use the scope resolution operator
#include <iostream.h>
void wrong( void );
int x_value = 10;
main()
{
     int x_value = 20;
     cout << "local x_value  = " << x_value << "\n";
     cout << "global x_value = " << ::x_value << "\n";
     return 0;
}
```

Here are the results of executing SEE4.EXE:

```
local x_value  = 20
global x_value = 10
```

> The scope resolution operator (::) is not supported in the C language.

What You Have Learned

Take a moment to review the topics covered in this chapter:

- How to specify and use variables and constants
- The four types of variables (`int`, `char`, `float`, and `double`) and how to declare and initialize them
- How to declare and initialize arrays
- How to use the global operator to designate that you want a global variable instead of a local variable but with the same name
- Numeric, character, string, and symbolic constants
- The visibility and lifetime of local and external variables, and the use of the `static`, `extern`, and `const` keywords

7

Input and Output

Nature, which gave us two eyes to see, and two ears to hear, has given us but one tongue to speak.

—Jonathan Swift
A Critical Essay Upon the Facilities of the Mind (1707)

In This Chapter

In this chapter, you learn about input, output, and header files. The following topics are covered:

- Screen output (the `cout` object)
- Keyboard input (the `cin` object)
- C language I/O functions
- The iostream.h header file

This chapter shows you how to do keyboard, screen, and printer input and output (I/O). You *input* information from the keyboard, and you *output* information to the screen or printer. Unlike other computer languages, the C language has no I/O commands; C uses library functions to perform input and output. Functions such as `printf()`, `puts()`, and `putc()` output information. Functions such as `scanf()`, `gets()`, and `getc()` input information.

Like C, the C++ language has no built-in I/O commands. All C++ compilers come with an object-oriented I/O package, referred to as the *iostream classes*. These are standardized classes of all classes because they were designed and developed by the individuals who developed the C++ language—the authors of C++.

There exists a problem. You need to know how to do I/O operations, but you have not yet been introduced to classes, derived classes, multiple inheritance, function overloading, virtual functions, and all the other object-oriented concepts. You will not learn these concepts until much later in the book. However, you still need to know how to do I/O. The greatest computer program ever written that possesses the most elegant solution to the most complex problem is probably useless unless it can report results. You must be able to interface with your computer programs. You need to input data and output results in order to work with the sample programs in this book. Almost all these programs contain I/O statements. In this chapter, you learn how to use the C++ I/O capabilities without getting into the details of how they work.

This chapter focuses on the way I/O is done with C and C++ programs using MS-DOS. When you start programming in Windows, you will discover that the methodology is entirely different. Before you can program in Windows, however, you must develop a strong working knowledge of C++.

Streams and Redirection

In the C and C++ languages, input data and output data are often referred to as the *input stream* and the *output stream*, respectively. The concept is that input flows in a stream into the program, no matter what the source, and output flows in a stream out of the program and can be directed to an output device (the screen, a printer, or a modem).

As you probably are aware, an MS-DOS output stream can be *redirected* to another device or *piped* to another program. For example, the following MS-DOS statement pipes the standard output stream from the MS-DOS `DIR` command to the `SORT` command:

```
DIR ¦ SORT > MYDIR.TXT
```

Output from the `SORT` command is redirected to the file MYDIR.TXT. The file created by this procedure contains a sorted directory.

The standard input stream can be redirected to receive input from other devices. In the MS-DOS command

```
SORT < NAMES > SRTNAMES
```

the input stream to `SORT` comes from the file NAMES. The output stream from SORT is directed to the file SRTNAMES.

The capabilities for doing I/O in C++ are based on the concept of `iostream` classes. Streams of bytes flow into and out of what is called a *stream object*. You can visualize a stream object as an intelligent file that is a source or destination for a stream of bytes. This pseudofile can be a keyboard, video display, printer, or disk file. For example, a stream of characters originating from the keyboard flows out of the `cin` object and into the program. Like the C language functions, the `iostream` classes interface between this specialized file and a program.

You learn about classes later in this book. However, for the sake of this discussion, a *class* can be characterized as a user-defined data type (`int` is a built-in data type) that contains data and functions which enable you to define the state, attributes, and behavior of an object. The `iostream` classes provide the definition of stream objects.

The five standard I/O streams shown in Table 7.1 are used in MS-DOS. Screen output is always directed to the `cout` object, and keyboard input comes from the device `cin`.

Table 7.1. Standard I/O streams.

Stream Object	*Meaning*	*Device*
`cin`	Standard input device	Keyboard
`cout`	Standard output device	Screen
`cerr`	Standard error channel	Screen
`clog`	Standard error channel	Screen

C++ Screen Output

No matter how magnificent a program you write, if it has no way to output information, the program is probably of little use. This section discusses the technique used by C++ for directing output to the screen.

The cout Object and the Insertion Operator (<<)

The most common method of directing output to the screen is to use the `cout` object. More rigorously stated, the output stream that is passed to the `cout` object is directed to the standard output stream, which is usually the screen. For example, the string `I am a string` is directed to the screen with the following statement:

```
cout << "I am a string";
```

If you are a C programmer, you may recognize the two angle brackets (<<) as the bitwise operator. The << operator is still a bitwise operator in C++ and is discussed in Chapter 13, "More Operators." However, for `ostream` operations, this operator is called the *insertion operator*. When the `ostream` class is declared, the << operator is redefined to serve additional duty as the insertion operator through a process called *overloading*. Do not worry about this concept; overloading is discussed in detail later in this book. What is important at this point is that the insertion operator (<<) was chosen for output because it visually suggests a flow of data from right to left. You can visualize the string `I am a string` flowing from the program to the `cout` object. The operator is called the insertion operator because it *inserts* data into an output stream. Figure 7.1 illustrates the flow of data from a C++ program to the CRT (screen).

The << insertion operator*i* is defined for all the C++ basic data types: `char`, `unsigned char`, `signed char`, `short`, `unsigned short`, `int`, `unsigned int`, `long`, `unsigned long`, `float`, `double`, and `long double`. What the insertion operator does is to convert the data to the right of << to a `char` string—the type expected by the `cout` object. For example, the following integer value, `i_val`, is converted to the string `33` and passed to the `cout` object:

```
int i_val = 33;
cout << i_val;
```

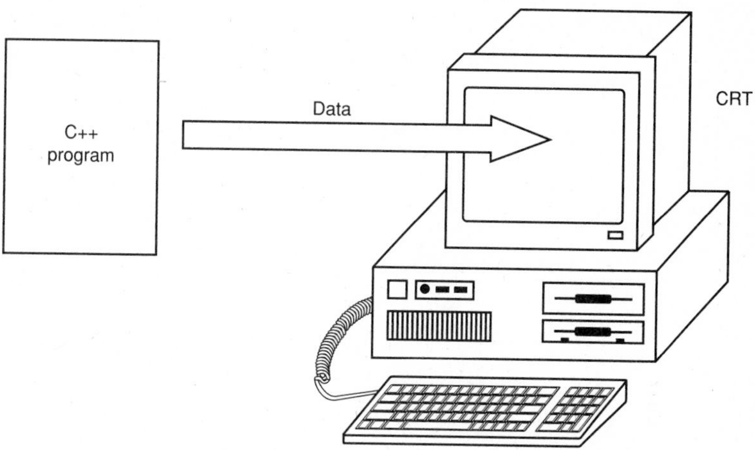

Figure 7.1. *Data flowing from a C++ program to the CRT.*

The value `33` is displayed. The phrase "passed to the `cout` object" means that the data object is passed to an output function.

Concatenated Output

In the preceding example, `cout << i_val;` is an expression, just as `3 + 4` is an expression. When `3 + 4` is evaluated, the integer operands 3 and 4 are added together. The result of the evaluation is an integer 7. When the expression `cout << i_val` is evaluated, the integer `i_val` is converted and passed to the output stream, and the expression evaluates to a `cout` object. This is nice because it allows you to concatenate output. Thus, you can output several data objects with a single expression. To understand what is happening here, consider the following simple expression:

```
x = 3 + 4 + 5;
```

The program evaluates this expression from left to right. First the program adds 3 and 4, and the resulting expression becomes

```
x = 7 + 5;
```

Then the program adds 7, which is the result of the first step, to 5. The resulting integer, 12, is converted to the same type as the variable `x`, if necessary, and `x` is assigned the resulting value.

Now consider the following expression:

```
cout << "Mars is "
     << miles/100000
     << " million miles from the earth\n";
```

The program evaluates this expression from left to right. First it converts and passes the string `Mars is` to the `cout` object (which outputs it to the screen). The result of this evaluation is a `cout` object. The resulting expression becomes

```
cout << miles/1000000
     << " million miles from the earth\n";
```

The next expression, `cout << miles`, is evaluated. The expression `miles/1000000` is then evaluated, converted, and passed to the `cout` object. Again, the `cout` object is returned, and the resulting expression becomes

```
cout << "million miles from the earth\n";
```

Finally, `million miles from the earth` is displayed, and the evaluation is complete.

From a practical point of view, each insertion operator sends one data item (a constant, an expression, or a variable) to the output stream, and you can concatenate data items of different data types in a single `cout` expression.

The put( ) and write( ) Member Functions

As mentioned earlier, classes define data and functions. A class function is called a *method* or a member function. The `ostream` class provides the `put()` method to insert a single *character* into the output stream. You use the `write()` method to insert a *string* into the output stream. Both methods return a `cout` object. The following statements output two characters to the output stream:

```
cout.put( 'W' );
char letter = 'e'
cout.put( letter );
```

The period that separates the object `cout` from the function `put()` is the member operator (.). You learn about the member operator when you read about structures and classes in Chapters 15 and 16.

Notice that the argument of put() is a char. The following statement inserts three characters, CAT, into the output stream:

```
cout.put( 'C' ).put( 65 ).put( 'T' );
```

Although the second put() contains an integer constant value, the integer is interpreted as an ASCII code for the letter A, which is displayed.

The write() method has two arguments. The first argument is a string. The second argument is an int value used to specify the number of characters in the string to display. In the following example, the first three characters of the string are inserted into the output stream:

```
cout.write( "Catalog", 3 );
```

This statement displays Cat. The write() function displays as many characters as you specify with the second argument. If you specify a number larger than the number of characters in the string, the function displays whatever resides in memory following the string.

Here are other examples that illustrate the use of the put() and write() methods:

```
cout.write( "Seize the Day", 13) << "\n";
cout.put( 65) << "pril showers\n";
cout.put( 'H' ).write( "ello", 4 ) << " folks\n";
```

Here is what is displayed:

```
Seize the Day
April showers
Hello folks
```

Formatting Output

If you do not instruct the insertion operator to do special output formatting, it determines how the output is formatted when it converts a data item to a stream of characters for output. Table 7.2 describes how the insertion operator formats output for various data types.

Table 7.2. `ostream` default output conversion for data types.

Type	*Type of Output Conversion*
`char`	Single printable characters are displayed one column wide. Display control characters, such as the newline and tab characters, can cause more characters to be output.
Integer	Any integer types (such as `int`, `short`, and `long`) are displayed as decimal numbers wide enough to contain the number and a minus sign if the integer is negative.
`float`	Floating-point numbers are displayed with six decimal digits of precision. Trailing zeros are not displayed. If the value of the number is large or very small, a two-digit exponent (three digits for `double`) prefixed by the letter `E` is displayed. Again, the display is wide enough to contain all decimal digits and, if present, a minus sign and/or an exponent.
String	The width of the display equals the length of the string.

The following lines of code are examples of `cout` statements containing different data types:

```
cout << "ABCDEFG#";                         // Output string
char letter = 'A';
cout << letter;

float f_val = 123.456789012,  big_val = 1234567890.123;
cout << f_val    << '*\n';                  // Output float
cout << big_val << '*\n';                   // Output big number

int i_val = 987, i_neg_val = -987;
cout << i_val << i_neg_val << '\n';        // Output integers
```

The output from these `cout` statements is

```
ABCDEFG#A123.456789*
1.23457e+009*
987-987
```

Some of the numbers are intentionally displayed on the same line, and an asterisk is placed at the end of the line to show that each value fills the field.

Numeric Base Format and Manipulators

Within the `ostream` class are parameters that control the output display format. Without getting into the details of how classes work, the following paragraphs describe how you can control the output format by changing these parameters.

By default, integers are displayed as decimals (base-10 numbers). You can change the default so that integers are displayed in base 10, base 16, or base 8 by calling the function `dec()`, `hex()`, or `oct()`, respectively. These functions are called *manipulators* because they manipulate the format state of an object. You can change the format state of the `cout` object to display integer base-16 numbers with the following function call:

```
hex( cout );
```

However, you usually call these functions by using this form:

```
cout << hex;
```

Once the base state is set, it remains in effect until it is changed. Consider the following example:

```
// MANIP.CPP - Demonstrates manipulators that change the
// number base
#include <iostream.h>
#include <iomanip.h>    // Must be included when manipulators
                        // are used
void main()
{
   cout << "Hex value of "   << 33 << " (decimal) is "
        << hex << 33 << "\n";
   cout << "Octal value of " << 33 << " (hex) is "
        << oct << 33 << "\n";
   cout << dec;         // Set it back to decimal base
}
```

Here are the results:

```
Hex value of 33 (decimal) is 21
Octal value of 21 (hex) is 41
```

In this example, the decimal value 33 is displayed as a hex value (21). The number base of the display state remains hexadecimal until it is changed to octal. Then the octal representation of the number is displayed (41). The last statement changes the display state back to decimal.

Specifying the Width of Display Fields

The `setw()` manipulator provides a convenient way of setting the width of the display format. `setw()` has a single integer argument, which specifies the width of the display field. Here is an example of the use of the `setw()` manipulator for displaying a field eight characters wide:

```
cout << "12345678901234567890\n";
cout << setw( 8 ) << "Hello";
cout << "Folks\n";
```

This is what is displayed:

```
12345678901234567890
   HelloFolks
```

Notice that the field in which `Hello` is displayed is eight characters wide, and `Hello` is right-aligned in the field. Listing 7.1 shows more examples of the use of the `setw()` manipulator.

Listing 7.1. The source listing for WIDTH.CPP.

```
// WIDTH.CPP - Demonstrates setw() manipulator
#include <iostream.h>
#include <iomanip.h>    // Must be included when manipulators
                        // are used
void main()
{
   cout << setw(10) << "A"  << setw(10) << "B"     << "\n";
   cout << setw(10) << 1    << setw(10) << 9.99    << "\n";
   cout << setw(10) << 10   << setw(10) << 99.99   << "\n";
   cout << setw(10) << 100  << setw(10) << 999.99  << "\n";
   cout << setw(10) << 1000 << setw(10) << 9999.99 << "\n";
}
```

Here is this program's output:

```
         A          B
         1       9.99
        10      99.99
       100     999.99
      1000    9999.99
```

In this example, the `setw()` manipulator is used to specify a width of 10 for each display field. The data items are displayed right-aligned in the fields. You need to specify `<< setw()` before each field output expression because the width reverts to the original width format after a data item has been output. When you use manipulators, you must include the iomanip.h header file and, of course, the iostream.h header file.

There are also `ostream` class member functions you can use to alter the format state. Again, you just need to memorize the syntax for now, because the syntax does not seem logical unless you know more about structures or classes. These functions are member functions of a class, which means that you must prefix the function call with the object name and a period (`cout.`) in order to call the function.

You can use the `width()` member function to alter the width of the display field. For example, to change the width of the display field, you specify the width function, as in this example:

```
cout << "12345678901234567890\n";
cout.width(5);
cout << "ABC" << "DEF" << "GHI" << "\n";
```

Here is the output from the three preceding lines of code:

```
12345678901234567890
  ABCDEFGHI
```

`ABC` displays right-aligned in a field five characters wide. Notice that the `width()` member function reverts to its original mode after one data item is printed. This is also true of the `setw()` manipulator.

Setting the Fill Character

Whenever you set the width of a display field wider than the width of the data, the extra space is filled with blank characters. This is the default state. You can change the fill character by using the `fill()` member function. For example, suppose that you want the fill character to be an asterisk (*). The following code shows you how to do this:

```
cout << "12345678901234567890\n";
cout.width(15);
cout.fill( '*' );
cout << "Go for it\n";
float x=99.95;
cout.width(15);
cout << x;
```

Here is what is displayed:

```
12345678901234567890
******Go for it
**********99.95
```

Obviously, the extra space in the field is filled with asterisks. However, did you notice that unlike the `setw()` manipulator and the `width()` member function, the `fill()` function remains in effect until it is changed?

Setting Floating-Point Display Precision

If you display a floating-point number, up to six digits of precision are displayed, by default. Trailing zeros to the right of the decimal point are removed. You can change the number of digits of precision from six to some other value with the `setprecision()` manipulator. It has a single integer argument (*i*) that specifies the number of significant digits to be displayed. The form is

```
cout << setprecision( int i );
```

Listing 7.2 shows the source listing for the program PRECISIO.CPP, which demonstrates how to use `setprecision()`.

Listing 7.2. The source listing for PRECISIO.CPP.

```
// PRECISIO.CPP - Demonstrates setprecision() manipulator
// function, which sets the number of decimal places
#include <iostream.h>
#include <iomanip.h>
void main()
{
   float value = 314.15926;
   cout << setprecision(2)
        << value << "\n"
```

```
        << setprecision(3) // 3 significant digits
        << value << "\n"
        << setprecision(4) // 4 significant digits
        << value << "\n"
        << setprecision(5) // 5 significant digits
        << value << "\n"
        << value << "\n";
}
```

Here is this program's output:

```
3.1e+002
314
314.2
314.16
314.16
```

In the first place, if the number of significant digits is less than the number of digits on the left of the decimal point, the results are displayed in scientific notation. Furthermore, when the precision is reduced, the value is rounded rather than truncated. Notice also that once the precision is set, it remains in effect until it is changed.

You can also use the `precision()` member function to set the precision. For example, the following statement sets the precision to 3 for subsequent output:

```
cout.precision( 3 );
```

Field Alignment and Other Format Controls

You use the `setiosflags()` manipulator to specify whether a data item is left- or right-aligned in a field. By default, values are right-aligned in a field. The following statement turns on the right-alignment option:

```
cout << setiosflags( ios::left );
```

The mysterious form of the argument of the `setiosflags()` manipulator is not explained until later in the book. For now, have faith and just use it as it appears. Once the left-alignment mode has been established, it will remain in effect until you turn it off. You can turn it off with this statement:

```
cout << resetiosflags( ios::left );
```

This manipulator turns off the left-alignment flag, and subsequent output is right-aligned in the display field. There are other modes of operation that you can alter with the `setiosflags()` and `resetiosflags()` manipulators. These are presented in Table 7.3. In the table, a mode is established with the `setiosflags()` manipulator and reset with the `resetiosflags()` manipulator.

Table 7.3. Arguments for the `setiosflags()` and `resetiosflags()` manipulators.

Argument	*Turned On*	*Turned Off (Default)*
`ios::left`	Left-align.	Right-align.
`ios::internal`	Left-align the sign for a decimal number and right-align the number.	Right-align the sign and number.
`ios::scientific`	Use scientific notation. Example: `1.2345e+003`	See *Note*.
`ios::fixed`	Use fixed-point notation. Example: `1234.5`	See *Note*.
`ios::showbase`	Display C++ base as a prefix. Examples: `044` (octal number) `0x2ea7` (hex number)	Do not display base as a prefix. Example: `2ae7`
`ios::showpoint`	Always display trailing decimal point and zeros. Example: `345.00`	Omit trailing zeros and decimal point. Example: `345`
`ios::uppercase`	Display uppercase letters for hex output. Example: `3AEF`	Display lowercase letters for hex output. Example: `3aef`

Note: If either the `ios::fixed` or the `ios:scientific` flag is set, the number of digits to the right of the decimal is determined by the precision. If neither flag is set, the precision determines the total number of significant digits. In that case, if the number of significant digits to the left of the decimal point is less than the precision, the results are displayed in scientific notation.

Listing 7.3 presents the source listing for SETIOS.CPP, a program that shows the use of the `setiosflags()` and `resetiosflags()` manipulators to alter the display format. The output shown in Listing 7.4 should be self-explanatory. All that needs to be said is that once an option is set with the `setiosflags()` manipulator, the option remains set permanently until it is reset with the `resetiosflags()` manipulator.

Listing 7.3. The source listing for SETIOS.CPP.

```
// SETIOS.CPP - Demonstrates setiosflags() and resetiosflags()
// manipulators
#include <iostream.h>
#include <iomanip.h>
void main()
{
      float value = -314.3333333333;
      cout << "Left-align number in the field\n*"
           << setiosflags( ios::left )      // Left-align
           << setw(10) << value
           << resetiosflags( ios::left )    // Right-align
           << "*\n";

      cout << "\nRight-align number "
           << "in the field (default mode)\n*";
      cout << setw(10) << value
           << "*\n";

      cout << "\nLeft-align sign; right-align number\n*"
           << setiosflags( ios::internal )     // Left-align sign
           << setw(10) << value
           << "*\n";

      cout << "\nNormal number display "
           << "(show that internal flag is reset)\n*";
      cout << resetiosflags( ios::internal ) // Normal sign
                                             // display
           << setw(10) << value
           << "*\n";

      cout << "\nScientific notation\n*"
```

continues

Listing 7.3. continued

```
     << setiosflags( ios::scientific )  // Set scientific
                                        // notation
     << setw(10) << value
     << resetiosflags( ios::scientific )
     << "*\n";

cout << "Fixed-point decimal display mode\n*"
     << setiosflags( ios::fixed )
     << setw(10) << value
     << resetiosflags( ios::fixed )
     << "*\n";

float f_val = 310.0;
cout << "Show trailing zeros and decimal point\n*"
     << setiosflags( ios::showpoint )   // Set to show
                                        // trailing zeros
     << setw(10) << f_val
     << resetiosflags( ios::showpoint )
     << "*\nDo not show trailing period and zeros\n*"
     << setw(10) << f_val
     << "*\n";

int i_value = 55555;
cout << "\nShow base for hex and octal values\n"
     << setiosflags( ios::showbase )   // Set octal and hex
                                       // base display
     << hex << i_value
     << "        "
     << oct << i_value
     << resetiosflags( ios::showbase )
     << "\nDon't show base for hex and octal values\n"
     << hex << i_value
     << "        "
     << oct << i_value
     << "\n";

cout << "\nShow hex alphabetic characters in uppercase\n"
     << setiosflags( ios::uppercase )  // Set uppercase
                                       // text display
```

```
            << hex << i_value
            << resetiosflags( ios::uppercase )
            << "\n";
}
```

Listing 7.4. The output from the execution of SETIOS.EXE.

```
Left-align number in the field
*-314.333  *

Right-align number in the field (default mode)
*  -314.333*

Left-align sign; right-align number
*-  314.333*

Normal number display (show that internal flag is reset)
*  -314.333*

Scientific notation
*-3.143333e+002*
Fixed-point decimal display mode
*-314.333333*
Show trailing zeros and decimal point
*   310.000*
Do not show trailing period and zeros
*       310*

Show base for hex and octal values
0xd903       0154403
Don't show base for hex and octal values
d903         154403

Show hex alphabetic characters in uppercase
D903
```

C++ Keyboard Input

In most cases, you need to communicate with your program. You do this through the keyboard. When you type, you generate an input stream. As with output, C++ uses an object-oriented approach to input. The `cin` object extracts characters from the input stream, converts it to whatever data type is designated by the input statement, and stores it in the designated memory location. Here is an example of a C++ input statement:

```
int value;      // Value to receive input
cin >> value;   // Input an integer value from input stream
```

If you are a C programmer, you may recognize the two angle brackets (>>) as the bitwise operator. This is still a bitwise operator in C++. However, for `iostream` operations, this operator is called the *extraction operator*. The >> operator is redefined when the `istream` class is declared so that >> can perform the additional duty of extraction operator. The extraction operator is used with the `cin` object to input data from the keyboard. The >> operator is easy to remember because it suggests a flow of data from left to right. You can visualize typed input data flowing into the input stream, into the `cin` object, and then into a designated variable in the program. The operator is called the extraction operator because it *extracts* data from the input stream. Figure 7.2 illustrates the flow of data from the keyboard into a C++ program.

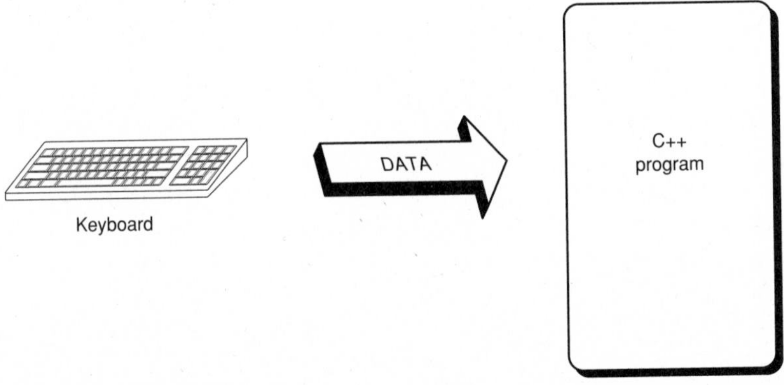

Figure 7.2. *Data flowing from the keyboard into a C++ program.*

Like the insertion operator, the extraction operator is defined for all the C++ basic data types: char, unsigned char, signed char, short, unsigned short, int, unsigned int, long, unsigned long, float, double, long double, strings, and pointers. The extraction operator converts the data from the input stream to the data type expected by the variable receiving the data.

The program INP1.CPP, shown in Listing 7.5, uses cin to input an integer value, i_val, from the keyboard and then displays it.

Listing 7.5. The source listing for INP1.CPP.

```
// INP1.CPP - Inputs a number using cin object
#include <iostream.h>
void main()
{
     int i_val;
     cout << "Enter a number: ";
     cin >> i_val;
     cout << "\nYou have entered " << i_val << ".\n";
}
```

Here is the dialog between the user and the computer:

```
Enter a number: 3456<Enter>
You have entered 3456.
```

INP1.EXE displays the prompt Enter a number:. The user enters 3456 followed by a carriage return (an Enter keystroke). The cin object extracts the characters from the input stream, converts them to an integer, and assigns i_val the value of 3456. The value is displayed to demonstrate that i_val was assigned the correct value.

> The notation **<Enter>** is used to represent a press of the Enter key. This notation appears as a reminder in the early chapters of this book but not in later chapters.

The extraction operator's operand (in this case, i_val) must be a reference to a variable. The operator stores the converted value at the address of the reference. In this example, the operator assigns the input value to i_val.

The extraction operator acts like the insertion operator in that >> returns its associated object type when it is finished handling the input value. As a result, you can input multiple values with a single statement, just as you can output several items with a `cout` statement. When you enter multiple values, you separate the items with whitespace characters. Remember that whitespace characters consist of spaces, tabs, and newlines. The program CINDEMO.CPP, shown in Listing 7.6, demonstrates the use of the `cin` object to input multiple variables.

Listing 7.6. The source listing for CINDEMO.CPP.

```
// CINDEMO.CPP - Demonstrates C++ keyboard input
#include <iostream.h>
void main()
{
     cout << "\nEnter a name, age, and salary: \n";
     char name[30];
     int  age;
     float salary;

     cin >> name >> age >> salary;
     cout << "\nName:    "
       << name
       << "\nAge:     "
       << age
       << "\nSalary: "
       << salary
       << "\n";
}
```

Here is the dialog between the user and the program CINDEMO.EXE:

```
Enter a name, age, and salary:
Alfred 34 29875<Enter>
Name:   Alfred
Age:    34
Salary: 29875
```

CINDEMO.EXE prompts the user to enter a name, an age, and a salary. The user types these items, separating them with a space, and terminates the line by pressing Enter. The keystrokes go into a buffer, and when the Enter key is pressed, the entire line is sent to the program. Therefore, the `cin` statement is not executed until the Enter key is pressed. At that time, the `cin` statement processes the input line. The string `Alfred` is stored in the first six elements of the array `name`. A null character (`\0`) is stored in the seventh element. This forms a null-terminated string, as illustrated here:

Array Element	*Contents*
`name[0]`	`'A'`
`name[1]`	`'l'`
`name[2]`	`'f'`
`name[3]`	`'r'`
`name[4]`	`'e'`
`name[5]`	`'d'`
`name[6]`	`'\0'`
`name[7]`	Unused
⋮	
`name[19]`	Unused

The second value, `34`, is stored in the integer variable `age`, and the third value, `29875`, is stored in the variable `salary`. What do you think would happen if the user entered something other than a number for the age? For example, suppose that `3A` was input for the age. The program would assign a zero value to `age` and would stop processing the input line. The variable `salary` would not be assigned a value at all. It is always a good idea to test input data to see whether it is valid before you proceed.

Input Stream Manipulators

You can use many of the manipulators you use with the C++ output functions with the input functions. The ones that are most useful are `hex`, `oct`, and `dec`. For example, the following statements demonstrate how you can input hexadecimal values:

```
int i_value;
cin << hex << i_value;
```

To enter the hexadecimal equivalent of the decimal number 10, you can enter `a`, `A`, `0A`, `0xA`, `0XA`, `0Xa`, or `0xa`.

In addition, you can use setprecision() to specify the number of significant digits you want to process.

C++ get( ) and getline( ) Member Functions

The get() member function reads a single character or a line of data from the keyboard. get() does not format data from the input stream as the extractor operator does. get() simply extracts one character or a sequence of characters from the input stream. There are three forms of the get() function, as illustrated in the following example:

```
char ch;
cin.get( ch );       // Read a single character

char line[80];       // Array to receive input
cin.get( line, 80 ) // Read characters into buffer 'line'
                     // until newline is encountered or
                     // 79 characters have been read


char line[80];
char term= 'A'
cin.get( line, 80, term ); // Read characters into buffer 'line'
                     // until termination character 'A' is
                     // encountered or 79 characters have been
                     // read
```

When you call the get() member function, the system stores keystrokes in the input stream until the Enter key is pressed. At that time, the system returns to the program, and the get() function extracts one or more characters from the input stream. If more characters exist in the input stream, they will be extracted by the next call to get(). For example, consider the following lines of code:

```
char ch, line[8];
cin.get( ch );         // Input a single character
cin.get( line, 8 );    // Input a string of up to 7 characters
cout << "ch =" << ch << "\n";
cout << "line =" << line << "\n";
```

Suppose that this code executes and you enter the following:

Concentration<Enter>

After you press the Enter key, the following output is displayed:

```
ch =C
line =oncentr
```

The first `get()` call extracts the character `C` from the input stream and stores it in `ch`. The second `get()` call extracts seven characters, `oncentr`, from the input stream and stores them in the first seven elements of the array `line`. It also stores a null value (`\0`) in the eighth element of `line`. Note that `get()` always extracts one less character than is specified, because a null byte is stored at the end of the string. Finally, the contents of both variables are displayed. Note that the characters `ation` remain in the input stream.

7

If you want to discard any characters remaining in the input stream, use the following statement:

```
cin.seekg( 0L, ios::end );  // Clear input stream
```

The `seekg()` member function is discussed in detail in Chapter 20, "File Input and Output."

The third form of `get()` allows you to specify the terminator character. For example, the following little program inputs characters from the input stream until the letter `g` is reached:

```
// A little program that demonstrates use of the input terminator
#include <iostream.h>
void main()
{
     char line[80];
     get( line, 80, 'g' );
     cout << line << "'\n";
}
```

If you type

Thank you for nothing, Mr. Jones.<Enter>

the little program responds with

```
Thank you for nothin'
```

The rest of the characters stay in the input stream, including the terminator character. In this case, `g, Mr. Jones.` remains in the input stream.

The `getline()` member function is similar to the two- or three-argument `get()` function except that the member function terminator character for `getline()` is extracted from the input stream and discarded.

In the preceding "little program," if `getline()` were used instead of `get()`, the `g` would be removed from the input stream and discarded. Otherwise, both functions operate the same. Here are some examples:

```
char line[80]
cin.getline( line, 80 );   // Extract up to 79 characters from
                           // input stream with '\n' terminator
cin.getline( line, 80, 'g' ); // Extract up to 79 characters
                        // from input stream with 'g' terminator
```

C Language Screen Output

Although C++ uses object-oriented techniques for I/O, C++ still supports the `printf()` function and other standard I/O functions. In the C language, the most common library function used to direct output to the screen is `printf()`, which always outputs data to the screen. More rigorously stated, the output stream generated by `printf()` is directed to the `stdout` device, which usually is the screen. Printing a message shows the simplest form of the `printf()` function:

```
printf( "This is a simple message\n" );
```

The `printf()` function argument `"This is a simple message\n"` is called the *format string*, which is always the first argument of the `printf()` function. The `\n` code at the end of the string is an escape sequence that represents a newline character. The newline character instructs the program to end the current line and reposition the display cursor at the beginning of the next line.

The printf( ) Function

The `printf()` function can display the value of one or more variables, as illustrated in the following examples:

```
int a = 3, b = 41.22, c = 'x';
printf( "The value of a is %d\n", a );
printf( "a = %d\nb = %f\nc = %c\n", a, b, c );
```

Here is the output from these `printf()` functions:

```
The value of a is 3
a = 3
b = 41.22
c = x
```

In the preceding example, the *format string* contains text, newline escape sequences, and format specifiers. *A format specifier* consists of a percent character (`%`) followed by a letter indicating what kind of conversion is performed when an associated argument is output (see Table 7.4). The format string is followed by zero or more arguments (variables to be output), each of which has a corresponding format specifier.

7

Table 7.4. Format specifiers.

Format Specifier	*Description*
`%c`	Prints a single character
`%d`	Prints a signed decimal integer
`%e`	Scientific notation, such as `3.2123e+04`
`%E`	Scientific notation, such as `3.2123E+04`
`%f`	Prints a floating-point number
`%g`	`%e` or `%f` format (whichever is shorter)
`%i`	Same as `%d`
`%n`	Prints character count
`%o`	Prints any type in octal format
`%p`	Prints a pointer (see Chapter 11)
`%s`	Prints a character string
`%u`	Prints an unsigned decimal integer
`%x`	Prints any type in hexadecimal format with the lowercase letters a–f, such as `3fe4`
`%X`	Prints any type in hexadecimal format with the uppercase letters A–F, such as `3FE4`

As noted, the first character in a format specifier is `%`. It is followed by a letter that is referred to as the *specifier type*. You can insert optional specification information between the percent sign and the specifier type. The following information may be included:

- Three specification flags

-	Left-aligns value in field
+	Always prints the sign
0 (zero)	Forces leading zeros to print

- Width of field printed
- Precision of printed field

The syntax of a complex format specifier is

```
%FW.PTD
```

where `F` is the specification flag, `W` is the width of the field, `.P` is the precision, `T` is the type, and `D` is the type specifier. Table 7.5 shows examples of complex format specifiers.

Table 7.5. Examples of complex format specifiers.

Specifier	*Example*	*Description*
`%6d`	`1234`	Displays decimal integer, width of 6
`%12.2f`	`1234567.77`	Displays floating-point value, width of 12, precision of 2
`%s`	`hello`	Displays string
`%7s`	`hello`	Displays string right-aligned in field 7 characters wide
`%-7`	`hello`	Displays string left-aligned in field 7 characters wide
`%6.2s`	`he`	Displays string, width of 6, precision of 2 (first 2 characters are displayed)
`%0d`	`000003`	Displays decimal with zero fill
`%04d`	`0003`	Displays decimal with zero fill
`%+d`	`+3`	Displays decimal and forces sign

Specifier	*Example*	*Description*
%c	X	Displays a character
%x	3b4f	Displays in hexadecimal
%X	3B4F	Displays in hexadecimal
%o	377	Displays in octal

Floating-point format (%f) defaults to six digits of precision, even when double-precision floating-point numbers are displayed.

The width of a field specifier designates a print field's width. For all variable types, values are right-aligned in the field. For string functions, the precision specifiers designate the number of characters displayed, from the left of the string.

FORMATS.CPP, the program in Listing 7.7, illustrates the use of format specifiers. Type FORMATS.CPP and run it.

Listing 7.7. The source listing for FORMATS.CPP.

```
// FORMATS.CPP - Demonstrates the use of printf() format
// specifiers
#include <stdio.h>
void main()
{
     char letter = 'x', *string = "hello world";
     int i_value = 234, hex_value = 0x10,
         oct_value = 010, dec_value = 10;
     double dou_value = 251.7366;
  // Display integer values
     printf( "%d    %+d    %06d    %X    %x    %o\n\n",
      i_value, i_value, i_value, i_value, i_value, i_value );

  // Display characters
     printf( "%10c%5c\n\n", letter, letter );

  // Display strings
     printf( "%25s\n%25.5s\n\n", string, string );
     printf( "%-25s\n%-25.5s\n\n", string, string );
```

continues

Listing 7.7. continued

```
  // Display real numbers
     printf( "%f    %.2f    %e    %E\n\n",
             dou_value, dou_value, dou_value, dou_value );

  // Display in hexadecimal, octal, and decimal radixes
     printf( "%i    %i    %i\n\n",
             hex_value, oct_value, dec_value );
}
```

Listing 7.8 shows the results of running FORMATS.EXE. Experiment with different format specifiers until you become familiar with their use.

Listing 7.8. The results of running FORMATS.EXE.

```
234    +234    000234    EA    ea    352


         x    x


              hello world
                    hello


hello world
hello


251.736600    251.74    2.517366e+002    2.517366E+002


16    8    10
```

In the first line in Listing 7.8, the integer variable `i_value` is displayed, using the different format specifiers, as shown here:

Specifier	*Display*	*Meaning*
%d	234	Decimal integer
%+d	+234	Decimal integer with forced plus sign
%06d	000234	Decimal integer six characters wide and zero filled
%X	EA	Hexadecimal radix

`%x`	`ea`	Hexadecimal radix
`%o`	`352`	Octal radix

The other variables displayed in Listing 7.8 illustrate the use of the `%c`, `%s`, `%f`, `%e`, and `%i` formats.

In the declaration for `string`, an asterisk (`*`) preceding the identifier declares `string` to be a *pointer* to the string `hello world`. The variable `string` contains the memory address of `hello world`. At this time, you do not need to be concerned with pointers. They are discussed in Chapter 11, "Advanced Data Structures."

The puts( ) Function

You use the `puts()` function to output a string to the screen. This function automatically appends a newline to the output stream, displaying the message and positioning the display cursor at the beginning of the next line. For example, the commands

```
printf( "Hello, " );
puts( "This is a message" );
puts( "This is another message" );
```

display these two lines:

```
Hello, This is a message
This is another message
```

Notice that `printf()` does not output a newline escape sequence.

C Language Keyboard Input

Having learned about output with the MS-DOS user interface, you are now ready to learn how to provide the computer with input from the keyboard. Several functions in the C library are dedicated to keyboard input. This section shows the use of the `scanf()`, `gets()`, and `getchar()` keyboard-input functions.

The scanf( ) Function

The most popular keyboard-input function is `scanf()`. When your program is ready to input data, you call the `scanf()` function, which instructs the computer to pause and wait for keyboard input. `scanf()` scans the keyboard, saving any characters you type until you press Enter. Then `scanf()` returns to your program so that you can process the data you have just typed. Consider the following program:

```
// KEYIN.CPP - Demonstrates the use of scanf()
#include <stdio.h>
void main()
{
     int number;
     printf( "Enter a number: " );
     scanf( "%d", &number );
     printf( "You have entered the number %d\n", number );
}
```

Look carefully at this program, which prompts you to enter a number, waits for you to enter it, and then displays the number.

Notice that you need the standard I/O include file, stdio.h, used for all the examples thus far. Both the `printf()` and `scanf()` functions use this file; `scanf()` is slightly more complicated than `printf()` because you must supply a format string with a format specifier that designates what type of data you are entering. The format specifiers used by `scanf()` are the same as those used by `printf()`. In the preceding program, the format string `%d` denotes that the input you type must be an integer value. Finally, you must pass to `scanf()` the address of the variable to input. To do this, you preface the variable name with an ampersand (`&`). The ampersand is the *address-of operator*.

To enter more than one item with a single `scanf()` statement, you must supply a format specifier for each variable, as in this example:

```
int value_1, value_2;
scanf( "%d %d", &value_1, &value_2 );
```

When you type the two numbers, separate them with one or more blank spaces and press Enter after the last number, as in

```
123  456<Enter>
```

The gets( ) Function

You use the `gets()` function to read a string variable from the keyboard without any formatting control. The `gets()` function has one argument, a character-array variable. In the example

```
char string[80];
gets( string );
```

you type a string and then press Enter. The `gets()` function returns to your program so that you can process the data you have just typed.

The getchar( ) Function

The `getchar()` function accepts a single character from the input stream. When your program is ready, you input a character and call `getchar()`. This function instructs the computer to pause and wait for keyboard input. Press any key and then press Enter; the `getchar()` function returns the character you typed to your program. The following program, ONEKEY.CPP, illustrates the use of the `getchar()` function:

```
// ONEKEY.CPP - Illustrates use of the getchar() function
#include <stdio.h>
void main()
{
     int c;
     puts( "Enter any key and press Enter" );
     c = getchar();
     printf( "\nYou have typed the %c key\n", c );
     return;
}
```

Using the scanf( ) and gets( ) Functions

The following program, KEYIN2.CPP, demonstrates the use of `scanf()` and `gets()` to input integer, floating-point, and string variables:

```
// KEYIN2.CPP - Illustrates use of scanf() and get() to input
// data from keyboard
#include <stdio.h>
void main()
{
     int result, integer;
     float fp;

     // string is an array of 81 elements
     char string[81];

     // Input an integer number
     printf( "Enter an integer and a floating-point number: ");
     scanf( "%d %f", &integer, &fp );
     printf( "%d + %f = %f\n\n", integer, fp, integer + fp );

     // Read a word into variable string
     printf( "Enter a word: " );
     scanf( "%s", string );
     printf( "%s\n", string );

     // Clear the rest of the string out of the input buffer
     // and read the entire string with the gets() function

     fflush( stdin );

     printf( "Enter a sentence with gets: " );
     gets( string );
     printf( "%s\n", string );
}
```

When KEYIN2.EXE executes, the following message is printed:

```
Enter an integer and a floating-point number:
```

Then the following `scanf()` function executes to accept your response:

```
scanf( "%d &f", &integer, %fp );
```

Type an integer, press the spacebar at least once, and type a floating-point number. For example, if you type `234 99.345`, the computer displays

```
234 + 99.345 = 333.345
Enter a word:
```

and the following `scanf()` function executes to accept your response:

```
scanf( "%s", string );
```

The `scanf()` function accepts input until it encounters a whitespace character (blank, Tab, or newline). If you want to enter a sentence, such as `Hello, Computer`, the function accepts only `Hello,`. You must execute `scanf()` a second time for it to accept the second word, `Computer`.

KEYIN2.CPP also demonstrates the use of the `gets()` function to enter a string containing blank spaces, such as `Hello, Computer`. The `gets()` function is the easiest way to input information that contains spaces and tabs.

The C Language Standard I/O Header File (stdio.h)

As you may have noticed, the first C language statement in every sample program in this book has been a compiler-directive include statement:

```
#include <stdio.h>  // Standard I/O file
```

This statement instructs the compiler to process the contents of the include file, stdio.h, as it would any source file. After that, the compiler continues processing the line of code following the include statement. The stdio.h file contains definitions of `printf()`, `scanf()`, and other standard input and output functions.

An include file, also called a ***header file*** or ***.h file***, contains function prototypes, definitions of constants needed by functions, macro define statements, and other information a program needs. The program may not use all the information in the header file but only what it needs, ignoring the rest.

Many other library header files are used with run-time library functions. In addition, programmer-defined header files contain program-specific definitions. In almost all cases, programs begin with at least one `#include` statement.

What You Have Learned

In this chapter, you learned about the fundamental C and C++ language keyboard and screen I/O functions used only for MS-DOS programs.

The following C++ I/O `iostream` operations were discussed:

```
cout << value;
cin >> variable;
```

You learned also about these C++ manipulators:

```
cout << setw( int i )
cout << hex
cout << oct
cout << dec
cout << setprecision( int i )
cout << setiosflags( long flag )
cout << resetiosflags( long flag )
```

The following C++ member functions were covered:

```
cout.width( int i );
cout.fill( char ch );
cout.precision( int i );
cout.put( char ch );
cout.write( string, int i );
cin.get( [char c] )
cin.get( string, int i [, char term] )
cin.getline( string, int [, char term] );
cin.seekg( long displacement, long origin );
```

Finally, you learned about these standard C I/O functions:

```
int printf( format string [, argument]... );
int scanf( format string [, argument]... );
int putchar( int c );
int getchar();
int puts ( string );
int gets ( string );
```

Operators and Expressions

Of every noble work the silent part is best,
Of all expression that which cannot be expressed.

—William Wetmore Story (1819–1895)
The Unexpressed

In This Chapter

This chapter covers operators and expressions. You learn about the following operators:

- Arithmetic
- Relational
- Logical
- Assignment

- Increment and decrement
- Address
- Comma

Variables and constants are basic data objects. When used in an expression, they are called *operands*. An *operator* specifies how an operand or operands are manipulated in an expression.

In C, C++, Pascal, BASIC, and many other languages, an *expression* consists of one of the following:

- A single operand (a constant, variable, or function)
- Operands combined with operators (and usually with other operands)

Here is an example that illustrates the terms *operator* and *operand*. Given that

A. + is an operator

B. 3 and 4 are constant operands

then 3 + 4 is an expression.

Binary operators (such as +) have two operands. *Unary* operators affect only one operand; for example, the unary operator ++ increments an operand. The C++ language has a *ternary* (three-part) operator also, called the conditional operator (?:), which operates with three operands. The conditional operator is discussed in detail in Chapter 13, "More Operators."

Like C, C++ is a compact language, with less than 40 easy-to-remember operators. Some of the operators can be used in more than one way; for example, the ampersand (&) can be part of three different operators.

Arithmetic Operators

The C++ language *arithmetic* operators are similar to arithmetic operators in most computer languages. Arithmetic operators are listed in Table 8.1.

Table 8.1. Arithmetic operators.

Operator	*Description*
+	Addition
-	Subtraction
*	Multiplication
/	Division
%	Modulus (remainder after division)

All these operators are *binary* operators because they operate on two operands, as in these examples:

```
answer = a + 3;
answer = a * 4;
answer = x / 3;
```

As mentioned earlier, an expression can be an operand and can be combined with an operator to form a larger expression. Note this example:

```
answer = 3 + 4 - 2 * 6 / 3 + a;
```

Precedence of operators is discussed later in this chapter. You can use parentheses to group expressions in order to get the proper results. For example, the result of the preceding equation is different from that of a similar equation:

```
answer  = ( 3 + 4 - 2 ) * 6 / ( 3 + 1 );
```

The minus sign operator (-) can be used as a unary operator because it can operate on a single operand. The minus sign changes the sign of a value, as in

```
answer = -x;
```

The only uncommon arithmetic operator is the modulus operator (%), which divides the second operand into the first. The result is the remainder. In the example

```
remainder = 16 % 3;
```

the variable `remainder` is assigned the value of 1.

Relational Operators

Relational operators, listed in Table 8.2, evaluate the relationship between two operands. The result of the evaluation is an integer with a value of 1 (true) or 0 (false).

Table 8.2. Relational operators.

Operator	*Description*	*Example*	*Result*
`<`	Less than	`1 < 2`	1
`<=`	Less than or equal to	`1 <= 2`	1
`>`	Greater than	`1 > 2`	0
`>=`	Greater than or equal to	`1 >= 2`	0
`==`	Equal	`1 == 2`	0
`!=`	Not equal	`1 != 2`	1

In WHATAGE.CPP, the program in Listing 8.1, an `if-else` statement is used to illustrate the use of relational operators. (For a detailed discussion of `if-else` statements, see Chapter 9, "Making Decisions.") In WHATAGE.CPP, if the relational expression `( age < 40 )` is true, the first `cout` statement is displayed; otherwise, the second `cout` statement is displayed.

Listing 8.1. The source listing for WHATAGE.CPP.

```
// WHATAGE.CPP - Illustrates the use of relational operators
#include <iostream.h>
void main()
{
  int age;
  cout << "How old are you? ";
  cin >> age;
  if ( age < 40 )
      cout << "\nYou are not old enough to be President "
           << "of the U.S.";
```

```
    else
        cout << "\nYou can be President of the U.S.!!!";
}
```

If the number you enter for the integer variable `age` is less than 40, the relational expression is true, and the program tells you that you are not old enough to be President. Sorry!

Logical Operators

You use the `&&` and `||` *logical* operators to combine two relational expressions to form a compound relational expression. For example, the following condition is true if the variable `c` is an uppercase letter:

```
c >= 'A' || c <= 'Z'
```

Logical operators are listed in Table 8.3.

Table 8.3. Logical operators.

Operator	*Description*	*Example*
`&&`	Logical AND	`a < b && c > d`
`||`	Logical OR	`a < b || c > d`
`!`	Logical NOT	`! a < b`

The `&&` and `||` operators are binary operators; they take two operands. If both of the `&&` operator's operands are true, the result is true. In the example

```
result = ( a < b ) && ( c > d );
```

`result` is true (equals 1) if `a` is less than `b`, and `c` is greater than `d`. If `a` is greater than or equal to `b`, or if `b` or `c` is less than or equal to `d`, the condition is false (equals 0).

Although the two operations (relational expressions) are enclosed in parentheses, the parentheses are not necessary because the precedence of logical operators is lower than that of relational operators. In other words, the computer evaluates the expression in the following order:

1. `temp1 = a < b;`
2. `temp2 = c > d;`
3. `result = temp1 && temp2;`

In more complex expressions, you may need to use parentheses (for grouping) to tell the computer the order in which each *subexpression*, or part of the expression, is to be evaluated. For example, the computer evaluates the expression

```
result = a < b && c > d || e == f && g != h;
```

in the following order:

1. `temp1 = a < b;`
2. `temp2 = c > d;`
3. `temp3 = e == f;`
4. `temp4 = g != h;`
5. `temp5 = temp1 && temp2;`
6. `temp6 = temp3 && temp4;`
7. `result = temp5 || temp6;`

This may not be what you intended, however. To ensure that the computer evaluates the expression correctly, use parentheses, as in

```
result = (a < b && c > d ) || (e == f && g != h);
```

Using parentheses also makes complicated expressions more readable.

The logical NOT operator (`!`) is a unary operator; it takes one operand. This operator produces a true (1) value if the operand is false, and a false (zero) value if the operand is true. In the example

```
result = ! (a < b);
```

the variable `result` is false (equals 0) if `(a < b)` evaluates to true.

C++ recognizes any nonzero number as a true value. Programmers commonly use the `!` operator to test a number for a nonzero value. In the following example, the `!` operator is used to test for a zero value to prevent a zero-divide error:

```
if (!x)
   cout << "Zero divide error";
else
   y = z/x;    // Do divide if x is not equal to zero
```

Assignment Operators

The *assignment* operators have already been used in many of the examples in this book. The simple assignment operator (=) stores the value of an operand to another value. The choice of an equal sign as the simple assignment operator is the same in most computer languages.

The C++ language supports a special form of assignment operator that combines any arithmetic operator with the = assignment operator. Computers have a machine language instruction that adds a value to a variable. For example, the instruction to add 3 to X is equivalent to X = X + 3 in most computer languages. In the C++ language, the add-to assignment operator (+=) closely resembles the operation performed by the computer. In other words, the line

```
X += a - b;
```

is equivalent to

```
X = X + a - b;
```

Similar assignment operators exist for other arithmetic operators. Table 8.4 lists the assignment operators.

Table 8.4. Assignment operators.

Operator	*Description*	*Example*	*Equivalent*
=	Assignment	x = y	x = y
+=	Addition	x += y	x = x + y
-=	Subtraction	x -= y	x = x - y
*=	Multiplication	x *= y	x = x * y
/=	Division	x /= y	x = x / y
%=	Modulus	x %= y	x = x % y

8

ASG_OPN.CPP, the program in Listing 8.2, illustrates the use of each assignment operator.

Listing 8.2. The source listing for ASG_OPN.CPP.

```
// ASG_OPN.CPP - Shows the use of assignment operators
#include <iostream.h>
main()
{
     int val;
     val = 7;      // Basic assignment operator
     cout << "Illustrate usage of assignment operators\n\n";
     cout << "Initial value of val: " << val << "\n";
     val += 3;     // Add 3 to val
     cout << "val += 3;  New val=  " << val << "\n";
     val -= 2;     // Subtract 3 from val
     cout << "val -= 2;  New val=  " << val << "\n";
     val *= 4;     // Replace val with 3 multiplied by val
     cout << "val *= 4;  New val=  " << val << "\n";
     val /= 2;     // Replace val with val divided by 2
     cout << "val /= 2;  New val=  " << val << "\n";
     val %= 4;     // Replace val with remainder of val / 4
     cout << "val %= 4 New val=  " << val << "\n";
     return 0;
}
```

Here is the output from ASG_OPN.CPP:

```
Illustrate usage of assignment operators

Initial value of val: 7
val += 3;  New val=  10
val -= 2;  New val=  8
val *= 4;  New val=  32
val /= 2;  New val=  16
val %= 4 New val=  0
```

Increment and Decrement Operators

Like the assignment operators, the *increment* and *decrement* operators resemble machine language instructions that increment and decrement registers. These two operators, listed in Table 8.5, are unique to the C++ language. They are extremely helpful, and C++ programmers use them extensively. As their names imply, the increment operator (++) increases an operand, and the decrement operator (--) decreases an operand.

Table 8.5. Increment and decrement operators.

Operator	*Description*	*Example*	*Equivalent*
++	Increment	`val++;`	`val = val + 1;`
		`++val;`	`val = val + 1;`
--	Decrement	`val--;`	`val = val - 1;`
		`--val;`	`val = val - 1;`

An increment or decrement operator that precedes an operand is a *prefix* operator:

```
++val;
```

An increment or decrement operator that follows an operand is a *postfix* operator:

```
val++;
```

A prefix operator increments (or decrements) the operand *before* it is used in an expression. In the example

```
val = 31;
y = ++val;
```

the variable `val` is incremented before it is stored to the variable `y`. Therefore, both `y` and `val` equal 32.

A postfix operator, however, increments (or decrements) the operand *after* it is used in an expression. In the example

```
val = 31;
y = val++;
```

the variable `val` is incremented after it is stored to the variable `y`. Therefore, after execution, `val` equals 32, and `y` equals 31. Consider the following statements:

```
// INCRE1.CPP - Example of increment and decrement operators
#include <iostream.h>
void main()
{
int val1, val2, val3;
  val1 = 4;
  val2 = 5;
  val3 = val1++ + --val2;
  cout << " val1: " << val1
       << " val2: " << val2
       << " val3: " << val3;
}
```

The output from INCRE1.CPP is

```
val1: 5 val2: 4 val3: 8
```

Do you understand why `val3` equals 8? If you do, good. An explanation is still necessary. Here is equivalent code that yields the same results:

```
// INCRE2.CPP - Example of increment and decrement operators
#include <iostream.h>
void main()
{
  int val1, val2, val3;
  val1 = 4;
  val2 = 5;
  val2--;              // val2 becomes 4
  val3 = val1 + val2;  // val3 becomes (4+4 = 8)
  val1++; // val1 is incremented after it is used
  cout << " val1: " << val1 << "\n";
  cout << " val2: " << val2 << "\n";
  cout << " val3: " << val3 << "\n";
}
```

At times, you may not be sure how some language elements will execute. One such example is the program INCRE1.CPP. When you have any uncertainties about how a statement will execute, rewrite it (and avoid any unwelcome surprises). INCRE2.CPP is the better C++ code because there are no uncertainties about how it executes.

Address Operators

The C++ language provides two operators for referencing addresses—the *address-of* and *indirection* operators (see Table 8.6).

Table 8.6. Address operators.

Operator	*Description*
&	The address-of operand
*	The contents of the address-of operand (indirection)

The first is the address-of operator (&), which gives the address of an operand. For example, `&value` yields the address of the variable `value`. The operand must have an address; it cannot be a constant or an expression like `(x + 1)`.

As you may recall, the & operator was used with an argument to the `scanf()` function. In the example

```
int  val;
scanf("%d", &val);
```

the argument `&val` is the address of the variable `val`. You provide the address of the variable to `scanf()` so that the function knows where to store the input data. If you forget to prefix the & operator to the operand `val`, anything can happen. The outcome is unpredictable. The only fairly certain result is that `val` will not be set to the correct value.

Whenever you need to pass a reference to a variable to a function, you need to pass the address of that variable. If you pass just the variable, only the value is passed.

The indirection operator (*) produces the value at the memory location designated by the operand. In the example

```
x     = 3;
addr = &x;        // addr is the address of variable x
val  = *addr;     // val is equal to 3
*addr = 4;        // x is set to 4 using * operator
```

addr contains the address of x, and val is assigned the contents of the address of addr. As a result, val is set to 3, using the indirection operator. The final statement demonstrates how to use the indirection operator to set the value of the variable x to 4.

The indirection operator is used in the declaration of a pointer variable to retrieve data pointed to by the pointer variable. Pointer variables are introduced in Chapter 11, "Advanced Data Structures."

The Comma Operator

In the C++ language, the comma (,) has two purposes: it is used as a separator and as an operator. You have seen commas used to separate items in a list, such as a list of variables in a declaration statement, and to separate function arguments. In the following examples, the comma is used as a separator:

```
int x = 3, y = 4, z = 9;
int ary[3] = { 9, 3, 42 };
xfunc( x, y, z );
```

By using the comma as an operator, you can paste together two C++ language statements, forming a single statement. Consider these statements:

```
green = 1;
blue  = 2;
orange++;
```

They can be pasted together with comma operators, forming the following single statement:

```
green = 1, blue = 2, orange++;
```

Generally, the preceding statement does not conform to good programming standards. Remember the rule "One line per statement." Although someone may argue that this pasted-together statement is a single statement, experienced programmers seldom use the comma operator except in for loops (see Chapter 10, "Loops"). It is good practice to avoid language constructs that are rarely used.

Operator Overloading

Do not let the diatribe in this section distract you from the main points in this chapter. Later in this book, you learn about a concept called *operator overloading*. An overloaded operator performs a specific operation depending on the context of its associated operands. In C++ the process of using the same operator for multiple operations is known as overloading. You can overload an operator to support a user-defined class.

You get a preview of the concept of overloading by examining the nature of some operators, such as arithmetic operators. In C++, arithmetic operators are actually overloaded. This means that there exists a different built-in function for an arithmetic operator depending on the data type. For example, there is one internal function used for multiplying two `int` data types, another for `float` data types, and a third for `double` data types. Operators are also overloaded for mixed-mode arithmetic. Table 8.7 presents some of the overloading of the multiplication operator.

8

Table 8.7. Built-in C++ language overloading for the multiplication operator (*).

Expression	*Operation*
`10 * 10`	`int` multiply
`10L * 10L`	`long` multiply
`10.0f * 10.0f`	`float` multiply
`10.0L * 10.0L`	`long double` multiply
`10 * 10L`	convert `int` to `long`, then `long` multiply
`10 * 10f`	Convert `int` to `float`, then `float` multiply
`10 * 10.0L`	Convert `int` to `long double`, then `long double` multiply

If that is not enough, the * operator also serves as the *indirection* operator.

All arithmetic operators and many other operators are overloaded by the C++ language.

lvalues and rvalues

Now consider the following simple assignment statement in C++:

```
x = y + 3;
```

The expression on the equation's left, the variable name x, represents a single storage location in memory and is referred to as an *lvalue* (for *l*efthand *value*). Generally, an lvalue is defined as any expression that refers to a memory location. The value to the left of any C++ language assignment statement must be an lvalue; other C++ language constructs must be lvalues as well. The address-of operator, for example, can be used only with an lvalue operand, as in

```
addr = &value;
```

lvalues can be on the left; however, they are used whenever you need to refer to a variable that must have a memory address. The increment and decrement operators also require lvalue operands.

Any expression that is not an lvalue is an *rvalue*. Consider the expression on the right side of the following assignment statement:

```
int x, y;
x = y + 3;
```

Because the expression y + 3 is not associated with a memory location, it is an rvalue. Constants are rvalues. An rvalue cannot go on the left side of an assignment statement.

Attempting to specify an rvalue when an lvalue is required results in an error. If the operand of an address-of operator is an rvalue, as in

```
addr = &(y + z);
```

the compiler displays this error message:

```
error C2102 '&' requires lvalue
```

Precedence

The C++ language has *precedence rules* that control the order in which expression elements are evaluated when expressions have more than one operand. The following three rules designate the order of evaluation:

1. The operator with the highest precedence is evaluated first.
2. When two operators have the same precedence, the expression is evaluated from left to right.
3. You can change the order of evaluation by enclosing a subexpression (part of an expression) in parentheses. Subexpressions enclosed in parentheses are evaluated first.

Table 8.8 defines the precedence (by level) of C++ language operators. Operators with the highest precedence (level 20) are listed first. All operators in a precedence level have equal precedence. *Associativity* (also called *binding*) is the property that defines the order in which operands are grouped with their associated operator. There are two types of associativity: right to left (the compiler begins with the right side and works left) and left to right (the compiler begins with the left side and works right).

8

Table 8.8. Precedence of operators.

Level and Operator	*Name or Meaning*	*Associativity*	*Type*
Level 20			
::	Scope resolution	None	Primary
::	Global	None	Primary
[]	Array element	Left to right	Primary
()	Function call	Left to right	Primary
()	Conversion	None	
.	Structure or union member	Left to right	Primary
->	Pointer to structure member	Left to right	Primary

continues

Table 8.8. continued

Level and Operator	*Name or Meaning*	*Associativity*	*Type*
Level 19			
`++`	Postincrement	None	Unary
`--`	Postdecrement	None	Unary
Level 18			
`++`	Preincrement	None	Unary
`--`	Predecrement	None	Unary
Level 17			
`new`	Allocate object	None	Allocation
Level 16			
`delete`	Deallocate object	None	Allocation
Level 15			
`!`	Logical NOT	None	Unary
`~`	Bitwise complement	None	Unary
`-`	Arithmetic negation	None	Unary
`+`	Unary plus	None	Unary
`&`	Address	None	Unary
`*`	Indirection	None	Unary
`:>`	Base operator	None	Unary
`sizeof`	Size in bytes	None	Unary
(type)	Type cast	Right to left	Unary
Level 14			
`.*`	Apply pointer to	Left to right	Class
`->*`	Dereference pointer to	Left to right	Class

Level and Operator	*Name or Meaning*	*Associativity*	*Type*
Level 13			
*	Multiplication	Left to right	Arithmetic
/	Division	Left to right	Arithmetic
%	Remainder	Left to right	Arithmetic
Level 12			
+	Addition	Left to right	Arithmetic
-	Subtraction	Left to right	Arithmetic
Level 11			
<<	Left-shift	Left to right	Shift
>>	Right-shift	Left to right	Shift
Level 10			
<	Less than	Left to right	Relational
<=	Less than or equal to	Left to right	Relational
>	Greater than	Left to right	Relational
>=	Greater than or equal to	Left to right	Relational
Level 9			
==	Equality	Left to right	Relational
!=	Inequality	Left to right	Relational
Level 8			
&	Bitwise AND	Left to right	Bitwise
Level 7			
^	Bitwise exclusive OR	Left to right	Bitwise

continues

Table 8.8. continued

Level and Operator	*Name or Meaning*	*Associativity*	*Type*
Level 6			
`¦`	Bitwise inclusive OR	Left to right	Bitwise
Level 5			
`&&`	Logical AND	Left to right	Logical
Level 4			
`¦¦`	Logical OR	Left to right	Logical
Level 3			
`e1?e2:e3`	Conditional tional	Right to left	Condi-
Level 2			
`=`	Simple assignment	Right to left	Assignment
`*=`	Multiplication assignment	Right to left	Assignment
`/=`	Division assignment	Right to left	Assignment
`%=`	Modulus assignment	Right to left	Assignment
`+=`	Addition assignment	Right to left	Assignment
`-=`	Subtraction assignment	Right to left	Assignment
`<<=`	Left-shift assignment	Right to left	Assignment
`>>=`	Right-shift assignment	Right to left	Assignment
`&=`	Bitwise AND assignment	Right to left	Assignment
`^=`	Bitwise exclusive OR assignment	Right to left	Assignment
`¦=`	Bitwise inclusive OR assignment	Right to left	Assignment

Level and Operator	Name or Meaning	Associativity	Type
Level 1			
,	Comma	Left to right	Comma

If a group of the world's most inspired computer science scholars were delegated the task of specifying the precedence of operators for a language, they would do well to come up with a list as good as the one specified by the authors of the C++ language.

The C++ language evaluation order is similar to that of other high-level languages. Learn the basic rules; as you gain experience with C++, operator precedence will become second nature to you.

The only precedence levels you may find difficult to master are the bitwise operators. These operators are awkward; you probably will want to group them with parentheses. For information about bitwise operators, see Chapter 13, "More Operators."

Operators in Level 20 have the highest precedence, and parentheses are the strongest of all operators. You can use parentheses to make sure that expressions are processed correctly. Consider the following line of code:

```
y = 4 + 3 * 12;
```

The `3 * 12` is evaluated first (the `*` is higher than the `+`), and then `4` is added to the result. If you want `4 + 3` to be evaluated first, use parentheses, as in

```
y = (4 + 3) * 12;
```

It is logical that unary operators are the next strongest. In the example

```
x = -x + y;
```

you expect `-x` to be evaluated first. If the precedence of unary operators were lower than that of arithmetic operators, the expression would be executed as

```
x = -(x + y);
```

That is not what you expect, though. It would not be natural.

The precedence of arithmetic operators is higher than that of relational operators. In the example

```
x + 5 < y - 4
```

you expect the computer to evaluate `(x + 5)` and `(y - 4)` before evaluating the `<` operator.

And the precedence level of relational operators is higher than that of logical operators. In the line

```
a < 3 && a > 1
```

`(a < 3)` and `(a > 1)` are evaluated before the `&&` operator.

Because the assignment operators are lower than other operators, the right side of an equation must be evaluated before the assignment operation can occur.

At the lowest precedence level is the comma operator, which is used to paste statements together.

Although the precedence table may seem intimidating at first, all you need to remember are the following levels:

1. Primary
2. Unary
3. Arithmetic (with `*`, `/`, and `%` the highest)
4. Relational
5. Logical
6. Conditional
7. Assignment

If you memorize these levels, you will not experience any precedence-related grief.

What You Have Learned

In this chapter, you learned about C++ language operators and expressions. Specifically, you learned the order in which operators are evaluated and how to use the following types of operators:

- Arithmetic (*, /, %, +, and -)
- Relational (==, !=, <, <=, >, and >=)
- Logical (&&, || and !)
- Assignment (=, *=, /=, %=, +=, -=, <<=, >>=, &=, ^=, and |=)
- Increment and decrement (++ and --)
- Address (& and *)
- Comma (,)

To learn more about other operators, see Chapter 13, "More Operators."

Making Decisions

I was a-trembling because I'd got to decide forever betwixt two things, and I knowed it. I studied for a minute, sort of holding my breath, and then says to myself, "All right, then, I'll go to hell."

—Mark Twain
Adventures of Huckleberry Finn (1884)

In This Chapter

All computers provide some capability for making a decision based on a condition. Conditional processing has always been fundamental to computers. If you have any experience with any computer language, you know what the `if` statement does. This chapter explores the conditional statements supported by the C++ language and describes how to use the following C++ language conditional-statement keywords:

- `if`
- `else`
- `switch`
- `break`
- `default`

Statements and Blocks

Statements are the building blocks of a C++ language program. A statement can be an expression or a keyword (such as `return`) followed by a semicolon. Or a *null statement*, which contains only a semicolon, may be appropriate. Here are some examples of expression statements:

```
i = 7;
j = sqrt(1.0 - pow( x , 2 );
myfunc( a, b );
x++;
j += 3;
```

Statements can be combined to form a *block*, or *compound statement*, enclosed in a pair of braces. Blocks and compound statements are synonyms. Note this example:

```
{
i++;
temp = t[i];
s[i] = t[i];
t[i] = temp;
}
```

In a *null compound statement*, the braces (`{}`) enclose no statements at all. In the following example, the function `dummy()` contains a null counpound statement:

```
void dummy()
{}
```

Incidentally, `dummy()` is a "do nothing" function.

All statements in a function are compound statements, as you can see from the following example:

```
void main()
{
     cout << "Pick a number: ";
     int i;
     cin >> i;
     cout << "\nYou picked number " << i << "\n";
     return;
}
```

You now know what a compound statement is. You learn more about this topic later in this chapter.

Conditional Statements

Conditional statements—an essential part of any programming language—control the flow of execution, based on a condition. In plain English, here is an example of a conditional statement:

```
If it does not rain,
     we can have a picnic.
```

If it does not rain, the have-a-picnic procedure is executed. Conversely, if it rains, we don't have a picnic. The C++ language has two conditional statements: `if` and `if-else`.

9

if

If a condition is true (it evaluates to a true, nonzero value), the `if` statement executes a statement. If the condition is false (it evaluates to a false, zero value), the statement is not executed. In the example

```
if ( divisor != 0 )
     answer = numerator/division;
```

the variable `answer` is computed if `divisor` is not equal to zero. Otherwise, the statement is skipped.

Here is the syntax of the if statement:

```
if ( expression )
     statement-body
```

The `if` keyword is followed by an *expression* enclosed in parentheses. The *expression* is evaluated; if the *expression* yields a nonzero number, the *statement-body* (either a single or a compound statement) is executed. Otherwise, the *statement-body* is skipped.

Listing 9.1 shows the program IFDEMO.CPP. Now it is time to execute the PWB and create the IFDEMO program. First choose the **O**pen command from the **F**ile menu and type the code lines in IFDEMO.CPP. Then choose the **E**xecute command from the **R**un menu to build and execute IFDEMO.EXE. You will modify IFDEMO.CPP as you learn more about conditional statements.

Listing 9.1. The source listing for IFDEMO.CPP.

```
// IFDEMO.CPP - Illustrates use of if statement
#include <iostream.h>
void main()
{
     int number;
     cout << "Type a number and press Enter:";
     cin >> number;
     if ( number == 7 )
          cout << "\nThe winning number has been entered.\n";
     return;
}
```

The IFDEMO.CPP program illustrates how to use the `if` statement and outputs a message prompting you to enter a number. The statement that inputs your number is

```
cin >> number;
```

When you type a number, `cin` starts to scan the keyboard for keystrokes, reading numbers until you press the Enter key. Then the number is stored in the variable `number`.

Consider the following `if` statement:

```
if ( number == 7 )
     cout << "\nThe winning number has been entered.\n";
```

The expression `( number == 7 )` is evaluated and yields a 1 (true) if `number` equals 7; otherwise, the expression yields a 0 (false). When the `if` condition is true, the `cout` statement is executed; otherwise, it is skipped. Listing 9.2 shows an example of a dialog that occurs when IFDEMO.EXE is executed.

Listing 9.2. A dialog from the execution of IFDEMO.EXE.

```
Type a number and press Enter: 7<Enter>
The winning number has been entered.
```

You can execute more than one statement when a condition is true by using a compound statement, or block. (Remember that blocks are enclosed in braces.) The program IFDEMO1.CPP shows how to use a block with the `if` statement (see Listing 9.3). This program inputs the cost of an automobile. If you enter more than `30000.00`, IFDEMO1.CPP computes and displays the tax.

Listing 9.3. The source listing for IFDEMO1.CPP.

```
// IFDEMO1.CPP - Illustrates use of conditional statements
#include <iostream.h>
void main()
{
     float cost, tax;
     cout << "Type the cost of an automobile and press Enter: ";
     cin >> cost;
     if ( cost > 30000 )
     {
          tax = .1f * cost;
          cout << "For an automobile costing " <<  cost << "\n";
          cout << "the federal tax is: "<< tax << "\n";
     }
     return;
}
```

At this time, execute the PWB to create IFDEMO1.CPP. Open the source file (IFDEMO.CPP). Then choose Save **As** from the **File** menu to save the file, renaming it IFDEMO1.CPP. Edit the source file so that the code looks like that in Listing 9.3. Next choose **Execute** from the **Run** menu to build and execute the program IFDEMO1.EXE. If you make any errors, correct them; then rebuild and execute the program. When IFDEMO1.EXE executes successfully, a prompt asks you to enter the cost of an automobile. If the cost is greater than $30,000, your program computes and displays the tax.

Listing 9.4 shows a sample dialog resulting from the execution of IFDEMO1.EXE.

Listing 9.4. A dialog from the execution of IFDEMO1.EXE.

```
Type the cost of an automobile and press Enter: 37875<Enter>
For an automobile costing 37875
the federal tax is: 3787.5
```

A compound statement can include more than one `if` statement. When one `if` statement is inside another, they are referred to as *nested* `if` statements. Listing 9.5 presents the source listing for IFDEMO2.CPP, which illustrates nested `if` statements.

Listing 9.5. The source listing for IFDEMO2.CPP.

```
// IFDEMO2.CPP - Illustrates use of nested if statements
#include <iostream.h>
void main()
{
     float cost, tax;
     cout << "Type the cost of an automobile and press Enter: ";
     cin >> cost;
     if ( cost > 30000.f )
     {
          tax = .1f * cost;
          cout << "For an automobile costing " << cost << "\n";
          cout << "the federal tax is: " << tax << "\n";
          if ( cost > 50000.f )
               cout << " That car costs a lot of money!!!\n";
     }
     return;
}
```

To create the example shown in Listing 9.5, perform the following steps:

1. Choose **Open** from the **File** menu to open the IFDEMO1.CPP source file.
2. Choose Save **As** from the **File** menu and name the file IFDEMO2.CPP.
3. Add changes to the code.
4. Choose **Execute** from the **Run** menu to compile, link, and execute the IFDEMO2.EXE program.

A sample dialog from the execution of IFDEMO2.EXE is shown in Listing 9.6.

Listing 9.6. A dialog from the execution of IFDEMO2.EXE.

```
Type the cost of an automobile and press Enter: 88765<Enter>
For an automobile costing 88765
the federal tax is: 8876.5
That car costs a lot of money!!!
```

Listing 9.7 presents another example that illustrates indented nested statements.

Listing 9.7. The source listing for NESTEDIF.CPP.

```
// NESTEDIF.CPP - Illustrates nested if statements that are
// indented
#include <iostream.h>
void main()
{
     int i;
     cout << "Enter a number:";
     cin >> i;
     if ( i < 100 )
     {
          cout << "The number is less than 100\n";
          if ( i < 75 )
          {
```

continues

Listing 9.7. continued

```
                cout << "The number is less than 75\n";
                if ( i < 50 )
                {
                     cout << "The number is less than 50\n";
                     if ( i < 25 )
                        cout << "The number is less than 25\n";
                }
          }
     }
     return;
}
```

The primary purpose of this sample code is to illustrate nesting. The `cin` statement reads your input. If the number that you enter is greater than or equal to 100, the program exits without displaying any output. If the number is less than 100, the following statement is displayed:

```
The number is less than 100
```

Then the second `if` statement is executed. If the number is less than 75, the following message is displayed:

```
The number is less than 75
```

This process continues until the `if` condition evaluates to a false value. For example, if the variable `number` equals 99, only the message `The number is less than 100` is displayed.

if-else

This section shows you how to use the `else` keyword with the `if` statement. The syntax for this form of `if` is

```
if ( condition )
     statement1
[else
     statement2]
```

If the *`condition`* evaluation yields a true (nonzero) value, *`statement1`* is executed; if the evaluation yields a false (zero) value, *`statement2`* is executed. Note this example:

```
if ( value > 3 )
     cout << "Value is a positive number.\n";
else
     cout << "Value equals zero or is a negative number.\n";
```

Square brackets are used in the syntax description to indicate that a language element is optional. In this case, you can have an `if` statement without the `else` part of the statement. You don't type the brackets; they are not part of the syntax.

If the condition `(value > 3)` evaluates to true, the first `cout` statement is displayed. Alternatively, if the condition is false, the second `cout` statement is displayed.

The program IFDEMO3.CPP, shown in Listing 9.8, illustrates the use of the `if-else` statement. Listing 9.9 shows the results of executing IFDEMO3.EXE. To generate this program, choose **O**pen from the **F**ile menu to open the source file IFDEMO2.CPP, which you generated in the last section. Now add the `else` part of the `if-else` statement. Then choose Save **A**s from the **F**ile menu and name the file IFDEMO3.CPP. Next build and execute IFDEMO3.EXE. Notice that if the value you enter for the variable `cost` is greater than $30,000, the block of code following the condition is executed. If `cost` is less than $30,000, the statement following the `else` keyword is executed.

9

Listing 9.8. The source listing for IFDEMO3.CPP.

```
// IFDEMO3.CPP - Illustrates use of the if-else statement
#include <iostream.h>
void main()
{
     float cost, tax;
     cout << "Type the cost of an automobile and press Enter: ";
     cin >> cost;
     if ( cost > 30000.f )
     {
          tax = .1f * cost;
          cout << "For an automobile costing " << cost << "\n";
          cout << "the federal tax is: " << tax     << "\n";
```

continues

Listing 9.8. continued

```
        if ( cost > 50000.f )
            cout << " That car costs a lot of money!!!\n";
    }
    else
        cout << "You do not have to pay extra taxes\n";
    return;
}
```

Listing 9.9. A dialog from the execution of IFDEMO3.EXE.

```
Type the cost of an automobile and press Enter: 8795<Enter>
You do not have to pay extra taxes
```

Now you can improvise, changing IFDEMO3.CPP by creating your own `if` and `if-else` statements. Continue working with the program until you are sure that you understand how the `if-else` statement operates.

Nesting `if-else` statements carefully is important. When one `if` statement is nested inside another, follow the rule of enclosing the nested `if` statement in braces. The following example illustrates what can go wrong:

```
// The wrong way to nest ifs
if ( value < 3 )
    cout << "Value is less than 3\n";
    if ( value == 2 )
        cout << "Value is equal to 2\n";
else
    cout << "Value is greater than or equal to 3\n";
```

Can you find what is wrong with this example? The problem is that the compiler matches the `else` keyword with the second (nested) `if` statement, causing the wrong messages to be displayed. If `value` equals 1, the messages `Value is less than 3` and `Value is greater than or equal to 3` are displayed.

Here is the correct source code:

```
// The correct way to nest ifs
if ( value < 3 )
{
```

```
        cout << "Value is less than 3\n";
        if ( value == 2 )
            cout << "Value is equal to 2\n";
}
else
        cout << "Value is greater than or equal to 3\n";
```

The braces correct the problem, indicating clearly that the `else` keyword belongs with the first `if` statement.

Remember that indenting code lines and using white space to improve readability are for the benefit of the programmer. The compiler ignores all white space.

Some programming style standards require the use of braces with all `if` statements because braces are thought to do the following:

- Improve readability
- Reduce the chances of making errors
- Reduce maintenance costs

Note the following example:

```
if ( value == 3 )
{
        cout << "Value equals 3";
}
else
{
        cout << "Value is not equal to 3";
}
```

The switch Statement

When you have many choices, the use of nested `if-else` statements can be quite involved and complicated. The problem is that each `if` statement lets you have only one action for each condition.

Suppose, for example, that you are developing an editor. Somewhere in your program, you would have code for processing each keystroke:

```
if ( key == LEFTARROW )
    move_left( vector );
else
    if ( key == RIGHTARROW )
        move_right( vector );
    else
        if ( key == UPARROW )
            move_up( vector );
        else
            if ( key == DOWNARROW )
                move_down( vector );
            else
                ... many more if-else statements ...
```

Using `if` statements for this type of application can be awkward. In this example, you could have so many `if` statements that the indentation makes the logic difficult to read and hard to maintain. The logic gets so involved that debugging becomes tedious. In addition, speed performance can suffer if you need to process many `if` statements. The C++ language `switch` statement provides an excellent solution to this kind of problem.

The `switch` statement tests a single expression that can have multiple values. Different statement blocks can be executed for each of the expression's values. In addition, you can use the `default` statement to execute a statement block for all other values with no `case` label. The syntax for the `switch` statement is

```
switch ( expression )
{
    case const:
        statements
        break;
    case const:
        statements
        break;
    :
    default:
        statements
        break;
}
```

The `expression` is enclosed in parentheses and can be any expression that evaluates to a constant, such as

```
switch ( choice )
```

Following the expression is a compound statement (block) enclosed in braces. The block is divided into groups of statements. Each group of statements begins with a *case label statement* that consists of the `case` keyword, a constant value (`const`), and a colon (:), as in the following example:

```
case 1:
```

Each `case` label constant must have a unique value and be the same type as the `switch` expression.

Any number of statements follow the `case` label. When the value of the `switch` expression corresponds to the value of the `case` label constant, the associated group of statements is executed. If the last statement in a group is a `break` statement, the action is complete, and the program exits the `switch` statement. If the `break` statement is omitted, execution flows through to the next group of statements, regardless of the value of the next `case` label. Generally, the `break` keyword is omitted when you want to execute the same action for two or more `case` labels.

The *default label* is a special `case` label. Statements following the `default` label are executed if none of the `case` label constants match the value of the `switch` expression. The syntax of the default label consists of the `default` keyword followed by a colon (:).

SWITCH3.CPP, the program in Listing 9.10, illustrates the use of the `switch` statement. When the program displays a menu of three items, you type `1`, `2`, or `3` and then press the Enter key. Your input is stored in the variable `choice`. The `switch` statement executes the statements associated with the `case` label that corresponds to the value of `choice`. If you type a number other than `1`, `2`, or `3`, the `cout` statements corresponding to the `default` `case` label are executed.

Listing 9.10. The source listing for SWITCH3.CPP.

```
// SWITCH3.CPP - Illustrates use of conditional statements
#include <iostream.h>
#include <time.h>
main()
```

continues

Listing 9.10. continued

```
{
     int choice;
     char work_buffer[9];
     cout << "     Menu (Enter a number 1-3)\n\n"
          << " 1 - Date\n"
          << " 2 - Time \n"
          << " 3 - Tomorrow's high Temperature \n";
     cin >> choice;
     switch ( choice )
     {
          case 1: // Display date
               _strdate( work_buffer );
               cout << "The date is "
                    << work_buffer
                    << "\n";
               break;
          case 2: // Display local time
               _strtime( work_buffer );
               cout << "The time is "
                    << work_buffer
                    << "\n";
               break;
          case 3:
               cout << "How would I know?"
                    << " I am just a computer.\n";
               break;
          default:
               cout << "You can type only 1-3. You typed "
                    << choice
                    << "\n";
               break;
     }
     return 0;
}
```

Listing 9.11 shows an example of output generated by the execution of SWITCH3.EXE. As the output indicates, `2` was input to the variable `choice`. The `case` label constant equaling 2 is at the beginning of a group of statements that display the time, and this group of statements is executed, as you can tell from the output.

Listing 9.11. A dialog from the execution of SWITCH3.EXE.

```
         Menu (Enter a number 1-3)

 1 - Date
 2 - Time
 3 - Tomorrow's high Temperature
2<Enter>
The time is 22:01:17
```

What You Have Learned

Conditional processing is a fundamental computer operation. Some of the conditional statements presented in this chapter, therefore, will be useful.

In this chapter, you gained more C++ programming experience as you generated and executed sample programs with decision-making statements. You learned the following:

- How the `if`, `if-else`, and `switch` statements are used to make decisions
- How to use the `case`, `default`, and `break` keywords with conditional statements

9

Loops

One must separate from anything that forces one to repeat No again and again.

—Friedrich Wilhelm Nietzsche
Ecce Homo (1888)

In This Chapter

In the last chapter, you discovered that you can control or change the flow of execution by branching over groups of statements. Looping is another essential programming operation common to and supported by all computer languages. C and C++ use looping statements similar to those used in such languages as BASIC, FORTRAN, and Pascal.

In this chapter, you learn how to perform looping operations with the following statements:

- `while`
- `do-while`
- `for`

This chapter also shows you how to use the `break` and `continue` statements to support these operations.

If you have never used a computer language, the simple diagram in Figure 10.1 should help you understand the looping process. This diagram represents a basic iteration activity with which you are familiar—getting out of bed in the morning.

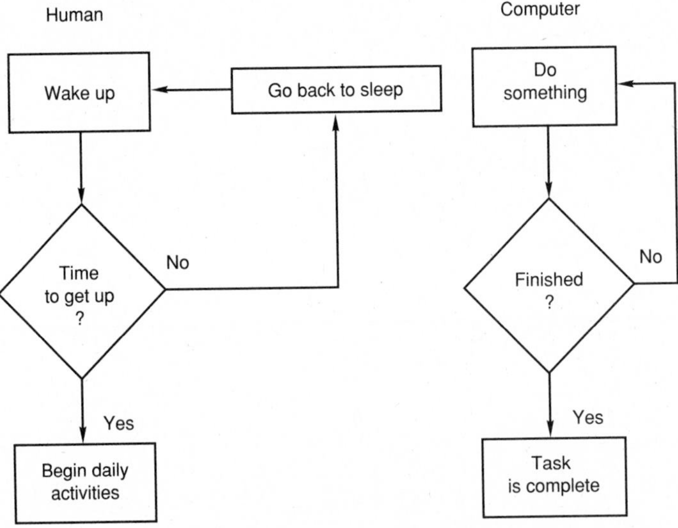

Figure 10.1. *A diagram illustrating the looping process.*

The while Statement

The simplest looping statement in the C++ language is `while`, which executes statements in a loop as long as a condition is true. The syntax of the `while` statement is

```
while ( expression )
{
     statements
}
```

The compound statement (*statements*) executes as long as the *expression*, which is evaluated first, evaluates to a true (nonzero) value. As soon as the *expression* evaluates to a false value, the loop exits. If the *expression* evaluates to false the first time, the *statements* are never executed. This process is what makes the `while` statement different from a `do-while` looping statement. The flow chart in Figure 10.2 illustrates how the `while` statement executes.

WHILE1.CPP, the program in Listing 10.1, shows the use of the `while` statement. First create a new file window. Then type the source file WHILE1.CPP, build and execute WHILE1.EXE, and enter the number of times to execute the `while` loop. The expression `( i <= number )` evaluates to true as long as the variable `i` is less than or equal to the value of `number`. While the expression is true, the message prints. As you can see from Listing 10.2, a message is displayed each time the loop is executed.

Listing 10.1. The source listing for WHILE1.CPP.

```
// WHILE1.CPP - Illustrates use of while statement
#include <iostream.h>
void main()
{
     int number;
     cout << "Enter number of times to execute the loop: ";
     cin >> number;
     int i=1;
     while ( i <= number )
     {
          cout << "Loop has executed " << i << "\n";
          i++;
```

10

continues

Listing 10.1. continued

```
    }
    return;
}
```

Listing 10.2. A dialog resulting from the execution of WHILE1.EXE.

```
Enter number of times to execute the loop: 6<Enter>
Loop has executed 1
Loop has executed 2
Loop has executed 3
Loop has executed 4
Loop has executed 5
Loop has executed 6
```

WHILE2.CPP, the program in Listing 10.3, shows how to use `while` to convert the lowercase characters in a sentence to uppercase. WHILE2.CPP loops through the sentence, one character at a time, until encountering the null character at the end of the string. This character causes the test—`( sentence[i] != '/0' )`—to equal zero and fail, and `while` to exit.

Listing 10.3. The source listing for WHILE2.CPP.

```
// WHILE2.CPP - Illustrates use of while statement
#include <iostream.h>
void main()
{
    char sentence[80];
    int i;
    cout << "Enter a sentence:\n";
    cin.get( sentence, 80 );            // Input string
    i=0;
    while ( sentence[i] != '\0' )
    {
        if ( sentence[i] >= 'a' && sentence[i] <= 'z' )
            sentence[i] -= 'a' - 'A';   // Make character
                                        // uppercase

        i++;
    }
    cout << "\n" << sentence << "\n";
    return;
}
```

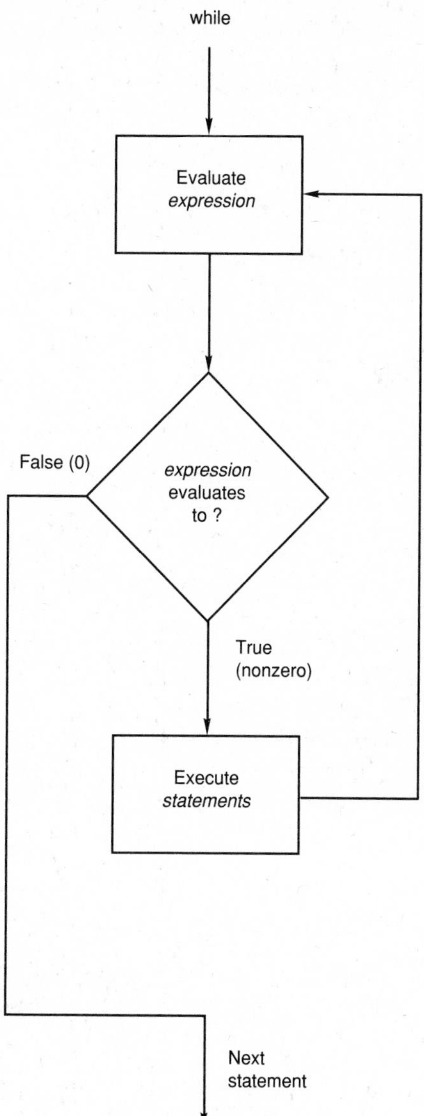

Figure 10.2. The* `while` *statement flow chart.

Do you know why the `get()` member function was used instead of the `cin` object to input the string? As you probably remember, the `cin` statement reads a token (word) for each extraction operation. In contrast, `get()` reads the entire string. This program was designed to read the entire sentence. The following dialog results from executing WHILE2.EXE:

```
Enter a sentence:
Now is the moment<Enter>
NOW IS THE MOMENT
```

Notice that the array `sentence` is input by the `cin.get()` member function. The character string in the array is translated to uppercase and displayed. You could use the `upper()` library function, which converts a character to uppercase. Reinventing the wheel, even when it makes for a more interesting and instructive example, is not recommended. Using available library functions whenever possible is good practice.

> Knowing the difference between a *string constant* and a *character constant* is important. The former uses double quotation marks; the latter uses single quotation marks. WHILE2.CPP uses the following character constants:
>
> `'\0'` (null character)
> `'a'`
> `'A'`
>
> An example of a single-character string constant is `"W"`.

Listing 10.4 presents a sample program, PAYMENT.CPP, that illustrates the use of the `while` statement. The `while` in PAYMENT.CPP executes as long as you enter a nonzero value. PAYMENT.CPP computes a loan payment, but you must provide the principal. If you enter a value of zero for the principal, the program exits. The annual interest rate is 10 percent, the term of the loan is 30 years, and payments are made monthly.

Listing 10.4. The source listing for PAYMENT.CPP.

```
// PAYMENT.CPP - Demonstrates principal computations
#include <iostream.h>
#include <iomanip.h>
#include <math.h>
```

```
const float One = 1.0;
float pmt( float principal, float interest_rate, int period );
float getfloat( char *msg );
main()
{
     float principal, yearly_rate, payment;
     int years = 30;              // Term of loan
     while( (principal =
            getfloat( "Enter loan principal: " )) != 0 )
     {
          yearly_rate = .10f;   // Yearly interest rate
          payment = pmt( principal, yearly_rate/12, years*12 );
          cout << setiosflags( ios::fixed )
               << setprecision( 2 )
               << "For a principal of         $"
               <<   setw(12) << principal << "\n"
               << "Term of the loan             "
               <<    years
               <<   " Years\n"
               << "The annual interest rate is "
               <<   yearly_rate*100
               <<   " %\n\n"
               << "The payment is:            $"
               <<   setw( 12 ) << payment << "\n";
     }
     return 0;
}

// getfloat() inputs float type number from keyboard
float getfloat( char *message )
{
     float value;
     cout << message;
     cin >> value;
     return value;
}
// Compute payment given principal, interest rate, and period
float pmt( float principal, float interest_rate, int period )
{
     float result;
     result = (principal*interest_rate)/
```

continues

10

Listing 10.4. continued

```
        ((One - (pow( (One + interest_rate), -period ))));
    return result;
}
/////////////////////// End of PAYMENT.CPP //////////////////////
```

Listing 10.5 shows a sample dialog from the execution of PAYMENT.EXE.

Listing 10.5. The results of executing PAYMENT.EXE.

```
Enter loan principal: 100000<Enter>
For a principal of         $    100000.00
Term of the loan            30 Years
The annual interest rate is 10.00 %

The payment is:            $       877.57
Enter loan principal: 0<Enter>
```

The following `while` statement expression evaluates to true as long as you enter a nonzero value for the principal:

```
while ( (principal = getfloat( "Enter loan principal:" )) != 0 )
{
        }
```

As long as the expression evaluates to true, the program computes and displays the value of the payment; otherwise, the `while` statement exits the program PAYMENT.EXE. Therefore, if you want to exit PAYMENT.EXE, just enter a zero value when you are prompted to enter a principal.

The `getfloat()` function displays a prompt message and uses the `cin` object to input the value of a `float` type number. `getfloat()` returns the value of the `float` type number to the calling number.

The `pmt()` function computes the `float` type value of the monthly payment given the principal, monthly interest rate (`yearly_rate/12`), and number of payments (`years*12`). Here is the statement that calls the `pmt()` function:

```
payment = pmt( principal, yearly_rate/12, years*12 );
```

The do-while Statement

The `do-while` statement is similar to the `while` statement except that the expression is tested *after* the statement block is executed (whereas the `while` statement performs the test *before* the statement block is executed). The syntax of the `do-while` statement is

```
do
{
     statements
} while ( expression );
```

The *`statements`* are executed, and then the *`expression`* is evaluated. (Notice that a semicolon follows the *`expression`*.) If the *`expression`* evaluates to a true (nonzero) value, the *`statements`* are executed again. This process is repeated until the *`expression`* evaluates to a false (zero) value, at which time the `do-while` statement exits. The `do-while` always executes the statements at least one time.

Figure 10.3 illustrates how the `do-while` statement operates.

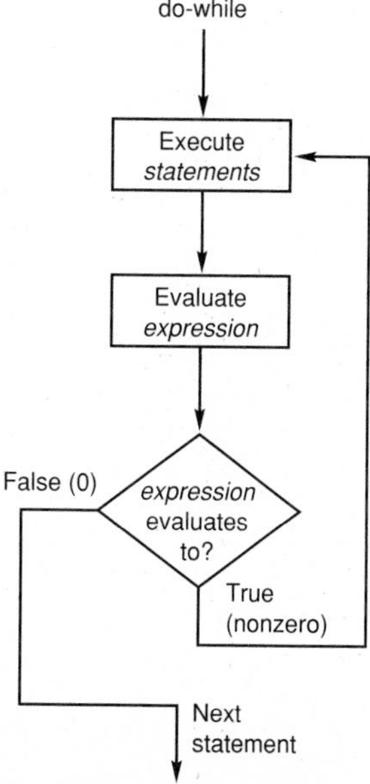

***Figure 10.3.** The* `do-while` *statement flow chart.*

10

You can use a do-while statement whenever you need to execute statements until some event occurs and is then tested by a while expression. When the expression evaluates to a false (0) value, the do-while statement exits.

As noted earlier, if the expression evaluates to a true (nonzero) value the first time it is evaluated, the do-while and while statements work as they do in DOWHILE1.CPP in Listing 10.6. If the expression evaluates to a false (0) value the first time it is evaluated, the do-while statement executes the statement block once. The while statement, however, would not execute the statement block at all, as shown in DOWHILE2.CPP in Listing 10.7.

Listing 10.6. The source listing for DOWHILE1.CPP.

```
// DOWHILE1.CPP - Illustrates use of while and do-while
// statements
#include <iostream.h>
void main()
{
     int i = 1;
     while ( i < 5 )    // "while" example
     {
          cout << "while loop " << i << "\n";
          i++;
     }
     i = 1;
     do                     // "do while" example
     {
          cout << "do while loop " << i << "\n";
          i++;
     } while ( i < 5 );

     return;
}
```

When DOWHILE1.EXE is executed, the following output is displayed:

```
while loop 1
while loop 2
while loop 3
```

```
while loop 4
do while loop 1
do while loop 2
do while loop 3
do while loop 4
```

Listing 10.7. The source listing for DOWHILE2.CPP.

```
// DOWHILE2.CPP - Illustrates use of while and do while
// statements
#include <iostream.h>
void main()
{
     int i = 5;
     while ( i < 5 )    // "while" example
     {
          cout << "while loop " << i << "\n";
          i++;
     }
     i = 5;
     do                 // "do while" example
     {
          cout << "do while loop " << i << "\n";
          i++;
     } while ( i < 5 );

     return;
}
```

When DOWHILE2.EXE is executed, the following output is displayed:

```
do while loop 5
```

Notice that the first output statement does not execute. In other words, the `while loop` message is not displayed. However, the `do-while` output statement executes once, and the `do while loop 5` message is displayed.

The for Statement

The third looping statement supported by the C++ language is the `for` statement, which has a counterpart in other high-level languages, such as FORTRAN, BASIC, and Pascal. Like the `do-while` statement, the `for` statement loops through an expression as long as the expression evaluates to a true (nonzero) value. The syntax of the `for` statement is

```
for ( expression1; expression2; expression3 )
     statement block
```

Following the `for` keyword are three expressions enclosed in parentheses and separated by semicolons. The *`statement block`* contains zero or more statements that are executed during the looping process.

The *`expression1`* statement sets initial values before the `for` loop is processed and executes only once. If you want to initialize more than one value, you can use the comma operator to paste statements together to form a single statement expression (such as `i=1, j=3, k=4`). When you do not have to initialize, omit *`expression1`*. However, you must not omit the semicolon (;) that separates *`expression1`* from *`expression2`*.

`expression2` is tested before each iteration of the loop. The loop repeats as long as *`expression2`* evaluates to a true (nonzero) value. When *`expression2`* is omitted, no test is performed, and the `for` statement executes forever. (Well, not forever. When you read about the `break` keyword, you'll see that there are other ways to exit a `for` statement.)

`expression3` is executed after the *`statement block`* is executed and before the next test is performed. Usually, this expression is used to increment values in the loop. As with *`expression1`*, you can use the comma operator to paste statements together to form a single statement. When you have no values to increment, you can omit *`expression3`*.

Figure 10.4 illustrates how the `for` statement works.

Here is a typical application of the `for` statement:

```
#include <iostream.h>
main()
{
     for ( int i = 100 ; i > 0 ; i -= 20 )
          cout << " i = " << i << "\n";
}
```

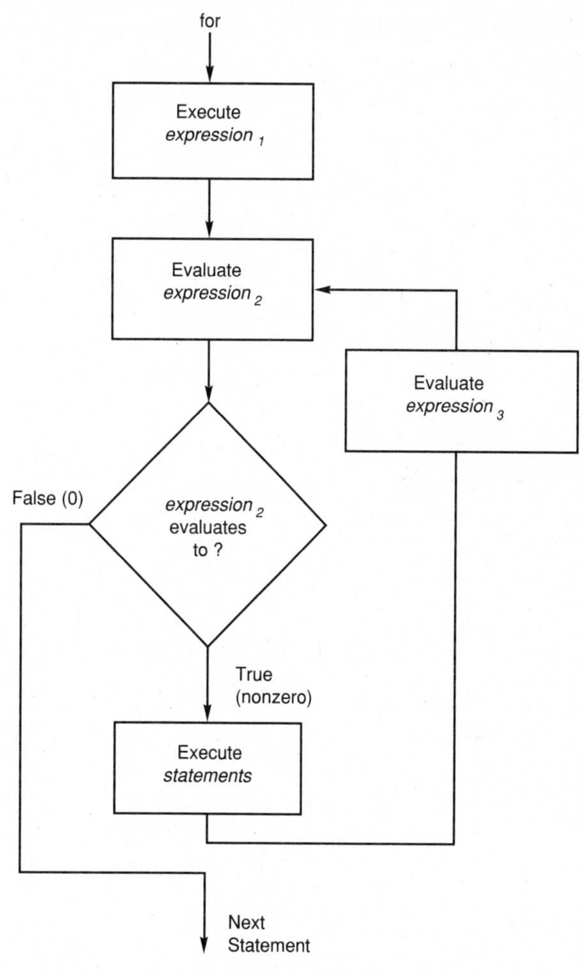

Figure 10.4. The `for` statement flow chart.

10

In this example, the integer variable `i` is set initially to 100. The test `i > 0` evaluates to true (1). The message `i = 100` is displayed, and then `i` is decremented by 20. This `for` statement processes until the variable is no longer greater than zero. Here is the output:

```
i = 100
i = 80
i = 60
i = 40
i = 20
```

In this example, *expression1* consists of the declaration of the integer variable i. This is a distinguishing factor between C++ and C. In C this would be illegal. A declaration must appear at the beginning of a block or function, or before the first executable statement of a file. In C++ you can place a declaration anywhere you want. The only restriction is that you must declare a variable before you use it.

The preceding example shows the use of a for statement with a statement block consisting of a single statement. The following example shows for used with a statement block consisting of a null statement:

```
main()
{
     int  ary[10];
     for ( int i = 0 ; i < 10 ; ary[i] = 0, i++ ) ;
}
```

This example initializes the elements of an array to zero. You can rewrite the first example so that it also initializes the elements of an array to zero. The new version, which illustrates how to omit the first and third arguments, looks like this:

```
main()
{
     int i = 0;
     int  ary[10];
     for ( ; i < 10 ; )
     {
          ary[i] = 0;
          i++;
     }
}
```

In the preceding program, the for statement can be replaced by a while statement, as in

```
main()
{
     int  i = 0;
     int  ary[10];
     while ( i < 10 )
     {
```

```
            ary[i] = 0;
            i++;
        }
}
```

You can also omit all three `for` statement arguments and still perform the same operation:

```
main()
{
        int i = 0;
        int  ary[10];
        for (;;)            // All three arguments are omitted
        {
            ary[i] = 0;
            i++;
            if ( i == 10 )
                break;  // This statement exits the for loop
        }
}
```

You have just seen four sample programs that perform the same task. Most programmers reserve the first and third `for` expressions for initializing and incrementing indexes, respectively, and would program the preceding example in this way:

```
main()
{
        int  ary[10];
        for ( int i = 0 ; i < 10 ; i++ )
            ary[i] = 0;
}
```

You can nest `for` statements as demonstrated in the examples. BUBBLE.CPP, the program in Listing 10.8, sorts a table of values, using one `for` statement nested inside another.

10

Listing 10.8. The source listing for BUBBLE.CPP.

```
// BUBBLE.CPP - Does bubble sort and illustrates nested
// for statements
#include <iostream.h>
#include <iomanip.h>
```

continues

Listing 10.8. continued

```
void main()
{
     int table[10] = { 9, 23, 1, 91, 8, 34, 12, 19, 3, 18 };
     for ( int i = 1; i < 10; i++ )      // Outer "for"
     {
          int test = 0;
          for ( int j = 0; j < 9; j++ )  // Inner "for"
               if ( table[i] < table[j] )
               {
                    int temp;
                    temp = table[i];     // Permute values
                    table[i] = table[j];
                    table[j] = temp;
                    test = 1;
               }
               if ( test == 0 )
                    break;
     }
     cout << "Sorted table: ";
     for ( i = 0; i < 10; i++ )
          cout << setw( 3 ) << table[i];
     return;
}
```

BUBBLE.CPP sorts the values in the array in ascending order. The 10-element integer array, `table`, is declared and initialized with 10 constants, selected solely to demonstrate the sorting operation. The integer variables `i` and `j` are used to index elements of `table`. Here is the output resulting from the execution of BUBBLE.EXE:

```
Sorted table: 1  3  8  9 12 18 19 23 34 91
```

The processing steps are illustrated by the flow diagram shown in Figure 10.5.

As an exercise, try different sequences of numbers for the `table` array to ensure that your program sorts correctly. Then modify BUBBLE.CPP to input 10 numbers from the keyboard. You should use a `cin` statement inside a `for` loop.

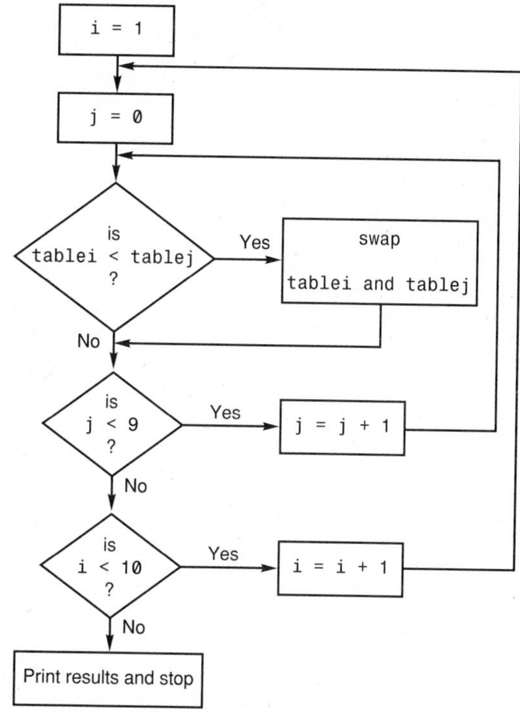

Figure 10.5. The bubble sort flow diagram.

The break Statement

You have already learned how to use the `break` statement with the `switch` statement to terminate a case. The `break` statement can be used also with the `while`, `do-while`, and `for` looping statements to break out of a loop. A programmer sometimes needs to escape from a loop, and the only convenient way to break out is to use a `break` statement. In the following example, each array element is tested until either the end of the string is encountered or the character `@` is found. In either case, the `break` statement is used to exit the loop.

```
for ( i = 0 ; ; i++ )           // Execute loop forever
{   // Look for an @ sign in string
     if ( s[i] == '\0' )        // End of string
```

```
            break;
    if ( s[i] == '@' )
            break;
}
```

The `break` statement exits only one loop. When you use a `break` statement in the inner loop of a nested loop, the statement exits that loop and executes the next statement in the outer loop.

Instead of using `break` in this example, experienced programmers would specify the looping condition in the loop test, as in

```
for ( i = 0 ; s[i] != '\0' &&  s[i] != '@'  ; i++ )
    ;
```

Under certain circumstances, you cannot escape from a loop without using a `break` statement. But try to structure your programs to reduce the frequency with which you use `break` statements. You may be wondering, "Why not use `break` all the time?" Sometimes `break` is just simpler to use than anything else. Suppose that you have been given a complicated program to maintain and the program has a bug. When you can look at the loop test to figure out why the program exits before it is supposed to, the bug is easier to find if the cause isn't a `break` statement buried deep in snarly logic, intermixed with multiple nested loops. This kind of catastrophe creates experienced programmers. After you have been burned a few times by a misplaced `break` statement, you will be more cautious about how and when to use the `break` statement in a loop.

Do not be discouraged from ever using `break`. With `switch` statements, you can use as many `break` statements as you need.

The continue Statement

The `continue` statement skips over the remaining statements in a loop and transfers control to the next iteration of the loop. In `for` loops, `continue` skips to the part of the loop that evaluates *`expression3`* (refer to Figure 10.4). In `for-while` and `do-while` loops, `continue` skips to the test. In the example

```
for ( i = 0; i < 4; i++ )
{
```

```
    if ( i != 2 )
        continue;
    cout << "i = " << i <<"\n";
}
```

the program displays only one line: `i = 2`. When `i` is equal to 0, 1, and 3, the `continue` statement skips over the `cout` statement.

As with the `break` statement, you should use the `continue` statement only when there is no other alternative. For example, the preceding example could be rewritten as

```
for ( i = 0; i < 4; i++ )
{
    if ( i == 2 )
        cout << "i = " << i <<"\n";
}
```

The goto Statement

Professional programmers seldom use the `goto` statement. I have programmed in C++ for eight years and managed large software projects with code bases of hundreds of thousands of lines of C++ code. I have never used the `goto` statement in C++ code and have discouraged other programmers from using this statement because its use can cause many undesirable side effects. By carefully and intelligently analyzing the problem you are trying to solve, you almost always can eliminate any need for the `goto` statement. The circumstances in which you have no alternative but to use `goto` are rare and infrequent.

10

The syntax of the `goto` statement is

```
    goto label;
    :
label: statement
```

where *`label`* is an identification name. Control is transferred to another statement in the same function, prefixed with the same label followed by a colon, as in this example:

```
for ( i = 0; eof() ; i++ )
{
```

```
                  :
                  for ( j = 0; j < size ; j++ )
                  {
                        :
                        if ( error == get_a_record( vector ) )
                              goto errorlab;
                        :
                  }
            }
            :
errorlab: printf( " A really bad error occurred " );
            fix_error();
            :
```

What You Have Learned

This chapter introduced you to the following three looping statements:

- `while`—initiates the `while` loop and tests the loop condition before executing the statement block.
- `do-while`—initiates the `do-while` loop and tests the loop condition after executing the statement block.
- `for`—initiates the `for` loop, initializes variables, tests the condition, and increments variables. The condition is tested after the statement block is executed.

You learned also how and when to use the `break`, `continue`, and `goto` keywords to support looping statements.

Advanced Data Structures

The greater our knowledge increases, the greater our ignorance unfolds.

—John F. Kennedy

In This Chapter

In Chapter 6, "Data Types," you learned about the basic data types (`char`, `int`, `float`, and `double`) and arrays. In this chapter, you learn about other data types and related topics:

- Basics of pointers
- Basics of structures
- The enumerated data type

- Register variables
- typedefs
- Data conversion
- Type casting

If you ask C programmers, "What was the hardest thing to learn about the C language?" most of them will tell you that learning to use pointers was difficult. C++ programmers have other areas that are difficult to grasp, such as classes and inheritance. However, pointers still rank at the top of the "hardest things to learn" list. For this reason, the discussion of pointers in this book is divided between two chapters. This chapter covers the basics of pointers, establishing enough of a foundation that you can start using them. Chapter 14, "Pointers," discusses pointers in more detail.

Pointers

A *pointer* is a variable that contains the address of another variable. The variable is called a pointer because it *points to* another variable. For example, consider POINT.CPP in Listing 11.1.

Listing 11.1. The source listing for POINT.CPP.

```
// POINT.CPP - Illustrates a pointer to a basic variable
#include <iostream.h>
main()
{
     int x = 143;
     int y;
     int *point;      // This is your first pointer declaration
     point = &x;      // Store the address of x to the pointer
                      // point
     y = *point;      // Store contents of address "pointed to"
     cout << "(1) x     = " << x      << "\n";
     cout << "(2) y     = " << y      << "\n";
     cout << "(3) point = " << (int) point  << "\n";
}
```

First, variables x and y are declared as int data types, and x is initialized to 143. The variable point is a pointer to an int type variable.

As you may recall, a variable of type char takes one byte of memory, and a variable of type int takes two bytes of memory. A pointer takes enough memory to hold an address. You don't have to worry about the size of the pointer because the compiler takes care of the size for you. For this discussion, it is assumed that an address takes two bytes.

The PWB default setting is for the *small memory model*. In the small model, addresses can range from 0 bytes to 64K. The small model can contain one 64K data segment and one 64K code segment. For other memory models, the address can be 4 bytes. (See the section "The Custom Installation Dialog Box" in Chapter 4 for more about memory models.)

Figure 11.1 shows a representation of the data memory.

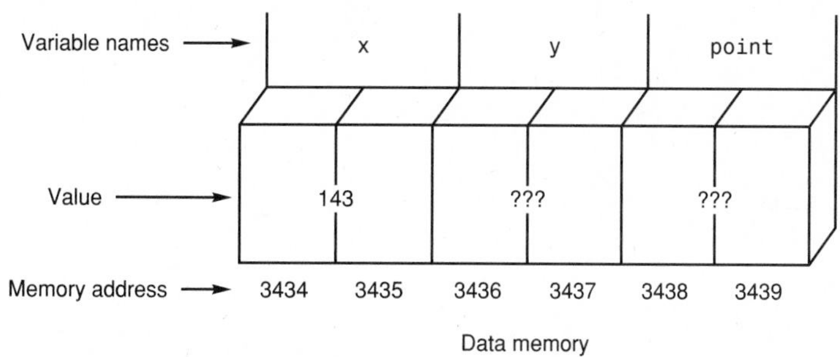

Figure 11.1. *A representation of the data memory.*

First the address-of (&) operator is used to set the value of point to the address of variable x:

```
point = &x;
```

Figure 11.2 shows the results of this action. (Remember that the address-of operator can be applied only to lvalues.)

Next the indirection operator (*) is used as a prefix to the variable point:

```
y = *point;
```

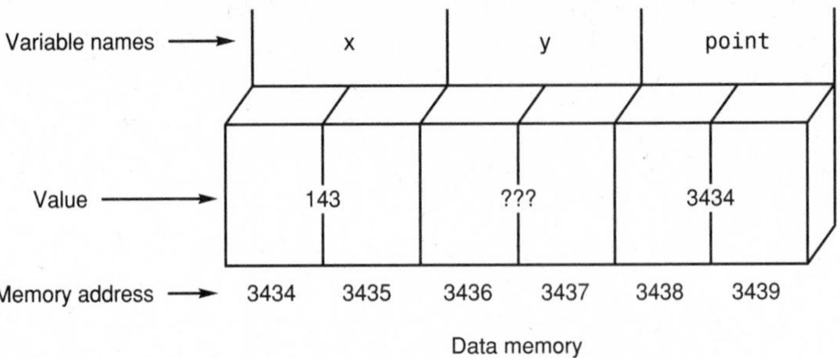

Figure 11.2. The data memory with a value for `point`.

This statement stores the contents of the address pointed to by `point` to variable `y`. Because `point` contains the address of `x`, 143 is stored to variable `y` (see Figure 11.3).

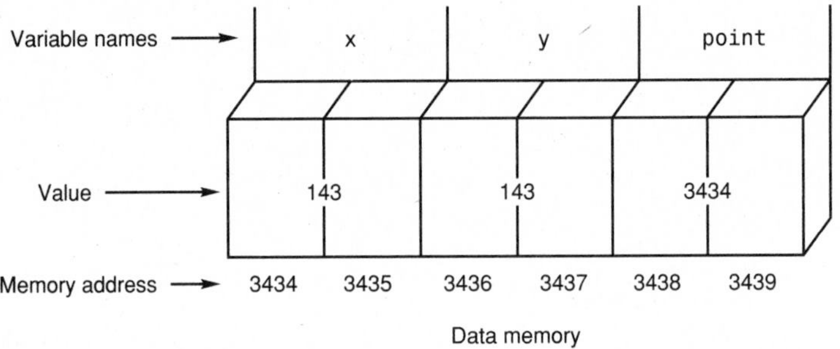

Figure 11.3. The data memory representation of variables `x`, `y`, ***and*** `point`.

Now POINT.CPP displays the contents of `x`, `y`, and `point`. The output from the program is

```
(1) x     = 143
(2) y     = 143
(3) point = 3434
```

These results show that `y` and `x` have the same value and that `point` contains the address of `x`.

Declaring a Pointer

The fundamental rule regarding a variable in the C++ language is that *you must declare a variable before you can use it*. Pointers are no exception; they, too, must be declared before they can be used. Pointers are declared with the data type they will point to. In the declarations

```
int  *ptr1;
char *ptr2;
unsigned int *ptr3;
float *ptr4;
double *ptr5;
```

the indirection operator (*) prefixes the pointer declarations.

Because it is important that you understand the meaning of the data type keywords used in declarations, Table 11.1 lists the types of data that these previously declared pointers point to.

Table 11.1. Variable pointers.

Variable	*Type of Data Pointed To*
`ptr1`	`int`
`ptr2`	`char`
`ptr3`	`unsigned int`
`ptr4`	`float`
`ptr5`	`double`

Each of these pointers still uses two bytes of memory, and the contents are undefined until you assign them a value (see Figure 11.4).

You can declare several variables of the same type in a single declaration statement. This means that you can declare pointers, arrays, and basic variables in the same declaration statement. For example, in the statement

```
int value, *ptr, table[3];
```

`value` is an integer variable, `ptr` is a pointer to an integer variable, and `table` is an array.

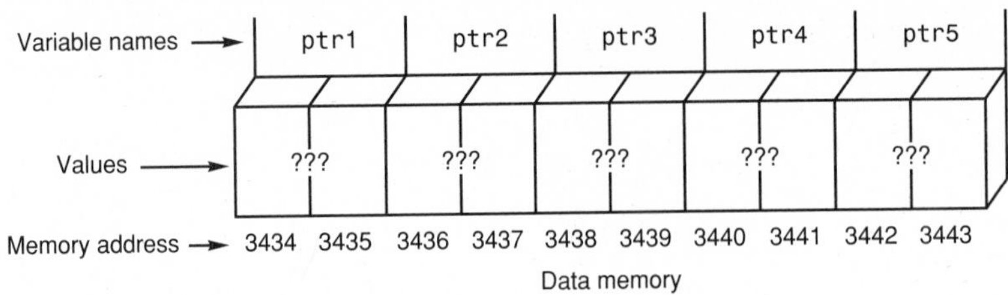

***Figure 11.4.** The data memory with several variables.*

Using a Pointer

Now that you know how to declare a pointer, focus your attention on using pointers. Here is the number-one rule: *Never use a pointer unless it has been initialized with the address of another variable.* As indicated earlier, you can initialize a pointer by using the address-of operator (&).

In the example

```
int  i, *ptr1, *ptr2, table[3];
char c, *ptr3, *ptr4, s[6] = {"Jello"};
unsigned int ui, *ptr5;
float rate, *ptr6;
double velocity, *ptr7;
```

the declaration statements define the following pointers:

Pointer	*Points To*
ptr1	Integer variable
ptr2	Integer variable
ptr3	Character variable
ptr4	Character variable
ptr5	Unsigned integer variable
ptr6	float variable
ptr7	double variable

Now each of these pointers is initialized:

```
ptr1 = &i;           // Point to variable i
ptr2 = &table[0];    // Point to first element of integer array
ptr3 = &c;           // Point to character variable c
ptr4 = &s[0];        // Point to first element of array s
ptr5 = &ui;
ptr6 = &rate;
ptr7 = &velocity
```


The following sample lines of code illustrate the two ways to assign a value to the nonpointer variables listed. You can assign a variable a value, or you can use the indirection operator (*) with a pointer to assign a value to the variable pointed to.

```
i = 91;
*ptr1 = 91;

table[0] = 211;
table[1] = 212;
table[2] = 213;
*ptr2    = 211;         // Store value to table[0]
*(ptr2 + 1) = 212;      // Store value to table[1]
*(ptr2 + 2) = 213;      // Store value to table[2]

c = 'a';
*ptr3 = 'a';

s[0] = 'J';
*ptr4 = 'J';

ui =    244;
*ptr5 = 244;

rate = 18.23;
*ptr6 = 18.23;
velocity = 12.3432541123L
*ptr7    = 12.3432541123L
```

Figure 11.5 illustrates these pointers and the variables to which they point. The figure shows the initialized values and the values of the pointers. For example, the pointer `ptr1` points to integer variable `i`. The pointer `ptr1` contains the address of variable `i`, which is 3011.

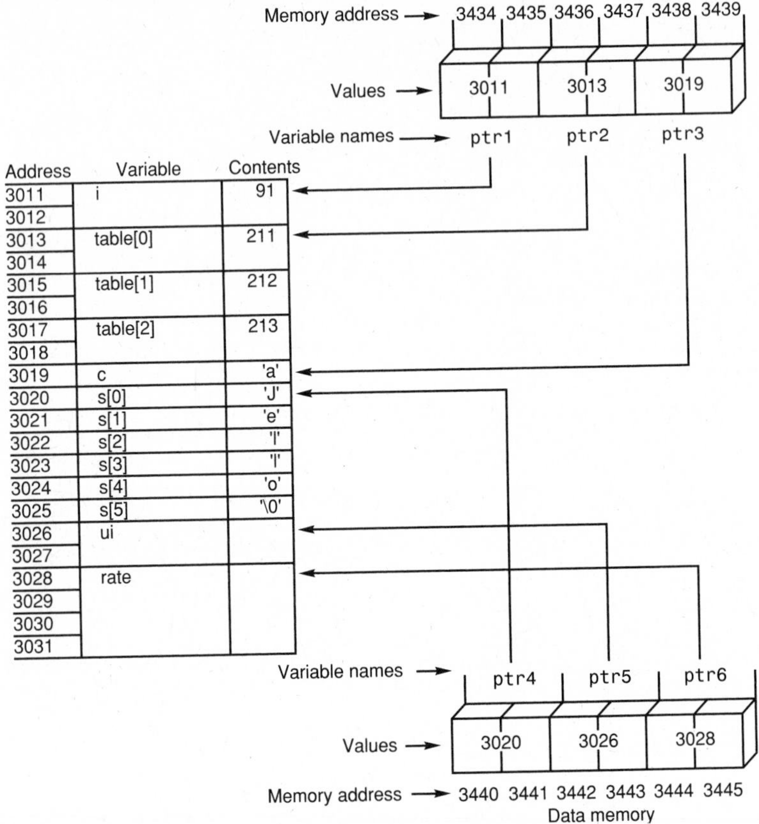

***Figure 11.5.** Storage of pointers and basic variables.*

Pointers also can be initialized when they are declared. You equate the name of the pointer with the address-of operator of an existing variable. The variable must already have been declared. In the example

```
int i;
char s[] = {"Jello"};
char *ptr4 = s;
int *ptr1 = &i;
```

note that `i` is declared before the pointer variable `ptr1`.

You can initialize a pointer to point to the first element of an array by just referencing the name of the array without the subscript. For example, `ptr4` could be initialized as

```
ptr4 = s;
```

Arrays are like pointers because an array name that appears as a function argument (without a subscript) is treated as the address of the first element of the array. Some function arguments must be the address of a variable. When you need to specify the address of an argument, you can specify the name of an array (without the subscript) as an argument. For example, the following statements are equivalent:

```
cout << "%s" << s        << "\n";        // Print Jello
cout << "%s" << &s[0]    << "\n";        // Also print Jello
ptr4 = s;
cout << ptr4             << "\n";        // Also display Jello
```

To state the obvious, the same is true for integer arrays. The following statements are equivalent:

```
ptr2 = table;
ptr2 = &table[0];
```

As you have learned, you can pass the address of the first element of an array by specifying either the name of the array (without the subscript) or a pointer to the first element of the array. For example, given the declaration

```
char *ptr, array[] = {"Jello"};
ptr = array;
```

you can use any of the following statements to pass the address of the variable `array`:

```
myfunc( ptr );
myfunc( array );
myfunc( &array[0] );
```

In the function being called, the argument can be declared as either an array or a pointer. For example, you can use either

```
void myfunc( char *ptr1 )
{
      :
}
```

or

```
void myfunc( char ary[] )
{
      :
}
```

In the second version, the array size is omitted from the array declaration because no storage is allocated for the array by the function. Memory is reserved when the array is declared in the calling program. You can include the size of the array if the size is needed to enhance readability, but the compiler ignores the size. The compiler converts `ary` to a pointer to a `char` type variable (`char *ary;`).

Pointer Arithmetic

You can use arithmetic, increment, and decrement operators with pointers. An important point to know is that you increment a pointer by the size of the variable to which it points.

To understand this process, consider the pointers `ptr2` and `ptr4` used in the preceding examples. The pointer variable `ptr2` points to an `int` type array named `table`, and the pointer variable `ptr4` points to a `char` type array named `s`:

```
ptr2 = table;
ptr4 = s;
```

Increment the pointers of these variables in this way:

```
ptr2++;
ptr4++;
```

Now `ptr2` points to the second element of array `table`, and `ptr4` points to the second element of array `s`. `ptr2` was incremented by two bytes; `ptr4`, by one byte.

Now display the current values of the two pointers:

```
cout << "The second element in table is: " << *ptr2  << "\n"
cout << "The second character is: "        << *ptr4  << "\n";
```

The output is

```
The second element in table is: 212
The second character is: e
```

Figure 11.6 illustrates the value of `ptr4` after the increment statement.

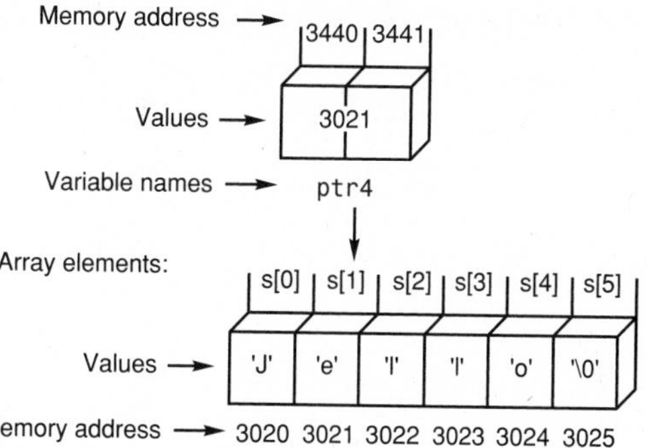

Figure 11.6. The value of* `ptr4` *after the increment statement.

You can use the `cout` statement to print the string that `ptr4` points to, as illustrated in POINT1.CPP:

```
// POINT1.CPP - Illustrates how pointers increment
#include <iostream.h>
void main()
{
     char *ptr4, s[] = {"Jello"};
     for ( ptr4 = s; *ptr4; ptr4++ )
          cout << ptr4 << "\n";
     return;
}
```

First the pointer `ptr4` is initialized to point to the first element of array `s`:

```
ptr4 = s;
```

With each iteration of the `for` loop, the program displays the string pointed to by `ptr4` with the following statement:

```
cout << ptr4  << "\n";
```

The program increments `ptr4` to point to the next character. When the program reaches the null terminator character (`'\0'`), the `for` loop test fails, and the loop exits. The output from POINT1.CPP looks like this:

```
Jello
ello
llo
lo
o
```

Type the preceding block of code (source file POINT1.CPP) and execute the program to confirm that you are able to display the same results.

ANSI Feature Used in Examples

C++ compilers that were generated before the C ANSI standards were established required that arrays initialized in a declaration statement must be *static*. The arrays must be declared outside the function, or the declaration must be preceded by the `static` keyword. The ANSI standards enable automatic arrays to be initialized as well. Microsoft C/C++ 7 supports this convention, and it is therefore used in this book. Be warned, however, that older C and C++ compilers might not compile these sample programs. The chances are rare that you would ever use a compiler that did not support the ANSI standards. However, if you do, you can add a `static` keyword in front of declaration statements that initialize an array. In POINT1.CPP, you initialize the automatic array, `table`, inside the function with the following statement:

```
char s[] = {"Jello"};
```

POINT2.CPP demonstrates another relationship between arrays and pointers:

```
// POINT2.CPP - Illustrates pointer arithmetic
#include <iostream.h>
void main()
{
     char *ptr, message[] = {"Hey, There"};
     int  i;
     i=3.0;
     ptr = message;
     for ( i = 0; message[i] != '\0'; i++ )
     {
          cout << *(ptr + i);
          cout << message[i];
     }
     cout << "\n";
     return;
}
```

The purpose of POINT2.CPP is to show that `message[i]` is the same as `*(ptr + i)`. In POINT2.CPP, `ptr` initially points to `message[0]`. The integer variable `i` is used as an integer for the array `message` and is added to the pointer. As for loop increments, each character is printed twice:

```
HHeeyy,,  TThheerree
```


TRIM.CPP, the program in Listing 11.2, demonstrates the use of pointers and pointer arithmetic to trim the blanks from the end of the character string.

Listing 11.2. The TRIM.CPP source file.

```
// TRIM.CPP - Trims blank from character string
#include <iostream.h>
#include <string.h>
int trim( char *string );
void main()
{
     char message[] = {"This is a character string.        "};
     int  i;
     cout << message << "<--\n";
     i = trim( message );
     cout << "Length of trimmed string is: " << i << "\n";
     cout << message << "<--\n";
}
int trim( char *string )
{
     int len;
     char *ptr;
     len = strlen( string ); // Return length of string
     ptr = string + len - 1; // Pointer points to last character
     while ( len > 0 && *ptr == ' ' )
     {
          *ptr = '\0';      // Replace space with null terminator
          ptr--;
          len--;
     }
     return len;
}
```

The results of executing TRIM.EXE are shown in Listing 11.3.

Listing 11.3. The results of executing TRIM.EXE.

```
This is a character string.       <--
Length of trimmed string is: 27
This is a character string.<--
```

In TRIM.CPP, the `main()` function calls the function `trim()` and passes `main()` the character string argument, `message`, which contains a sentence padded with blanks:

```
"This is a character string.      "
                                   ↑
                                  ptr
```

`trim()` calls the library function `strlen()` to get the length of the string. Pointer arithmetic is then used to point `ptr` (the pointer variable) one character past the last nonblank character of the string.

The `while` loop performs a test before executing the statement block. As long as the integer variable `len` is greater than zero and `ptr` points to a blank character, the statement block executes repeatedly. The statement block contains the following three statements:

```
*ptr = '\0';  // Replace blank character with null terminator
len--;        // Reduce character counter
ptr--;        // Move pointer backward one character
```

The first statement replaces the blank character in the string with a null terminator character. The integer variable `len` is decremented by one in the second statement. The pointer variable `ptr` is decremented by one in the third statement, repositioning the pointer back one character.

As soon as a nonblank character is encountered or `ptr` reaches the beginning of the string, the `while` loop exits, and the length of the trimmed string is returned to the function `main()`. The term *trimmed* refers to a string that has all the blank characters on the right of the string removed. `main()` displays the trimmed string and its length.

The fundamentals of pointers have been explained in this chapter. If you do not grasp the techniques presented here, you should write some programs using pointers. With what you have learned in this chapter, you should be able to write useful applications. For more information about pointers, see Chapter 14, "Pointers."

> It is the C++ programmer's responsibility *never* to overrun the boundaries of an array when using a pointer or an index. *The compiler does not check pointer references.* If your pointer wanders outside the boundaries of an array or is not initialized, you can wipe out (corrupt) other parts of your program or the operating system. The results can be devastating.

Structures

Arrays are great for working with a group of items that have the same data type, but arrays are not helpful if you have a group of items with different data types. Arrays work fine, for example, if you have a list of temperatures, but are not helpful if you have a customer information list containing such items as name, age, address, account number, charges, and so on. Even though you could have a different array for each item, you still would have to deal with all those arrays. The best solution for this type of problem is to use a structure data type.

Declaring Structures

A *structure*, another aggregate data type supported by the C++ language, is a collection of items of different data types combined in a single language construct. Each item in the collection is called a *member* and can be a different data type variable. The structure has a name called a *tag*. Each member is declared just like any other variable. That is, the member consists of a name preceded by a data type. Suppose, for example, that you have a structure whose members describe a box. Here is the template for the structure:

```
struct  box
     {
     int  height;           // Height of box
     int  width;            // Width of box
     int  depth;            // Depth of box
```

```
unsigned char row;     // Row of top-left corner of box
unsigned char column;  // Column of top-left corner
char color;            // Color of box
char *title;           // Title displayed on box
};
```

The keyword `struct` is followed by the tag name `box`. When you are ready to declare a variable to use the structure template, you specify the tag name, `box`, with the declaration statement

```
box b;
```

This statement declares one instance, `b`, of the structure `box`. Although the template exists only to define the structure of the instances of a structure variable and uses no memory, each instance (such as `b`) takes memory space.

> If you are familiar with the C language, you have probably noticed that in C++, once you have defined a structure template, you do not have to use the `struct` keyword when you declare a structure variable. If you are like me, you will exuberantly cheer this extension. As for all the C++ extensions to C, you do not have to go through your old C programs and remove the `struct` keywords from declarations. However, when you write new code, omit `struct` with structure variable declarations. For those of you that are not familiar with C and haven't the foggiest idea what I am talking about in this paragraph, here are two examples of a variable declaration for a predefined structure template:
>
> ```
> struct box a, *ptr; // struct keyword required in C
>
> box a, *ptr;        // struct keyword not needed in C++
> ```

Essentially, the structure tag name `box` becomes a data type and can be used just like any other data type. For example, the code

```
box b, c, *ptr;
```

defines two instances (`b` and `c`) of the structure `box`. How much space do you think the structures require? Add it up:

Item	*Size of Item*
`int height;`	2
`int width;`	2
`int depth;`	2
`unsigned char row;`	1
`unsigned char column;`	1
`char color;`	1
`char *title;`	2 (pointer takes 2 bytes)
	11

Does each instance take 11 bytes of memory? Not quite! The pointer variable `ptr` takes the same space as any other pointer. For all the sample programs in this book, the C/C++ 7 compiler and linker memory model options are set to the small model in the PWB. For the small model, a pointer uses two bytes of memory. However, the address of the member title must begin on an even byte. An extra byte is added to the structure to fill the unused space. Therefore, there is a hole in the structure, making the correct number 12. When you need to know the size of a structure, use the `sizeof` operator. For example, the output for the following statement is `12`:

```
cout << sizeof(b)  << "\n";
```

You can include the structure template and the declaration of a structure variable with the same statement, as in

```
struct  box
    {
    int  height;            // Height of box
    int  width;             // Width of box
    int  depth;             // Depth of box
    unsigned char row;      // Row of top-left corner of box
    unsigned char column;   // Column of top-left corner
    char color;             // Color of box
    char *title;            // Title displayed on box
    } b, c;
```

but this process is used only when you have *local* instances of a structure (instances that occur in one place). Under these circumstances, you do not even have to give the structure a tag name. Note the following example:

```
struct
     {
     int  height;           // Height of box
     int  width;            // Width of box
     int  depth;            // Depth of box
     unsigned char row;     // Row of top-left corner of box
     unsigned char column;  // Column of top-left corner
     char color;            // Color of box
     char *title;           // Title displayed on box
     } b, c, *ptr;
```

Most programmers put structure templates into include files. Here is an example of an include file, box.h, containing the structure template `box`:

```
// box.h - Defines a box
struct  box
     {
     int  height;
     int  width;
     int  depth;
     unsigned char row;
     unsigned char column;
     char color;
     char *title;
     };
```

You can include this file in your source program by using the following `#include` statement:

```
#include "box.h"
```

Then declare structure `box` variables with the following statement:

```
box b, c, *ptr;
```

Later in this chapter, the section "The typedef Keyword" discusses the use of `typedef` for declaring a structure—currently the most popular method for declaring structures.

Initializing Structures

You initialize structures the same way you initialize arrays. You separate structure variable names from the list of initialization constants by using an equal sign and enclosing the initialization constants in braces. Note an example:

```
char titleb[] = {"Box B"};
box b = { 29, 25, 18, 3, 20, 'W', titleb };
```


Referencing Structure Members

After you have declared a structure variable, you can reference the members of the structure by specifying the structure name and the member name, separated by the *member operator*. The member operator is a period (.). For example, you can use the following statements to assign values to the structure variable b:

```
box b, *ptr
char titleb[] = {"Box B"};
b.height = 29;
b.width  = b.height -5;
b.depth  = b.height -11;
b.row    = 3;
b.CPPolumn = 20;
b.CPPolor  = 'W'
b.title  = titleb;
ptr = &b;
```

Notice that the pointer ptr is also initialized to point to the structure variable b. You can reference the structure members by using the *pointer-to* operator (->)—formed by a hyphen followed by a right-angle bracket—which separates the pointer name from the member name. Here is an example:

```
ptr->column = 20;
```

Because ptr points to b, the preceding statement has the same result as

```
b.CPPolumn = 20;
```

Figure 11.7 illustrates the memory usage of the structure variable b and demonstrates how each member is stored.

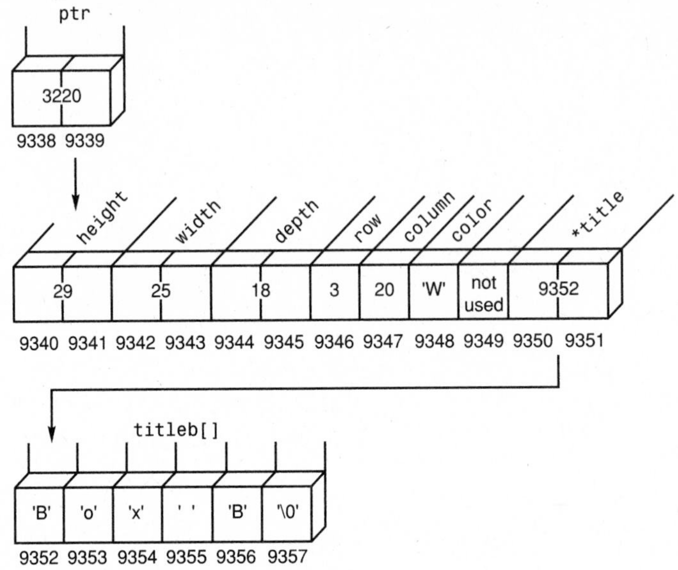

Figure 11.7. *An example of structure memory usage.*

STRUCT1.CPP, shown in Listing 11.4, demonstrates the declaration and initialization of the structure `box`. The results of executing STRUCT1.EXE are shown in Listing 11.5. This program also demonstrates the use of a pointer to a structure.

The `int` enclosed in parentheses is an example of type casting. *Type casting* explicitly converts an expression to a different data type. In this example, address values and `unsigned int` values are converted to `int` values. Type casting is discussed later in this chapter.

Listing 11.4. The source listing for STRUCT1.CPP.

```
// STRUCT1.CPP - Illustrates use of structure
#include <iostream.h>
#include "box.h"
main()
{
     char *titleb = { "Box B" };
     char *aamsg  = { " at Address : " };
     box b = { 29, 25, 18, 3, 20, 'W', titleb };
     box *ptr;
     cout << " b.height " << b.height
          << aamsg << (int) &b.height << "\n";
```

```
        cout << " b.width  " << b.width
             << aamsg << (int) &b.width << "\n";
        cout << " b.depth  " << b.depth
             << aamsg << (int) &b.depth << "\n";
        cout << " b.row    " << (int) b.row
             << aamsg << (int) &b.row << "\n";
        cout << " b.column " << (int) b.column
             << aamsg << (int) &b.column << "\n";
        cout << " b.color  " << b.color
             << aamsg << (int) &b.color << "\n";
        cout << " b.title  " << b.title
             << aamsg << (int) &b.title << "\n";
        ptr = &b;
        cout << " ptr->height " << ptr->height
             << aamsg << (int) &ptr->height << "\n";
        cout << " ptr->width  " << ptr->width
             << aamsg << (int) &ptr->width << "\n";

        return 0;
}
```

Listing 11.5. The results of executing STRUCT1.EXE.

```
b.height 29 at Address : 9340
b.width  25 at Address : 9342
b.depth  18 at Address : 9344
b.row    3 at Address : 9346
b.column 20 at Address : 9347
b.color  W at Address : 9348
b.title  Box B at Address : 9350
ptr->height 29 at Address : 9340
ptr->width  25 at Address : 9342
```

The addresses displayed in Listing 11.5 are sample addresses. Your addresses may differ depending on the compiler configuration.

Now you know what a structure is, how to declare and initialize it, and how to use members of a structure. You know enough to begin working with C++ language structures. Type the source file STRUCT1.CPP and the header file box.h and execute STRUCT1.EXE. Then make your own modifications to STRUCT1.CPP and rerun it. Chapter 15, "Structures and Unions," covers other topics relating to structures.

The typedef Keyword

You can create your own data type by using the typedef statement. The syntax is like that of a variable declaration preceded with the typedef keyword. However, the typedef statement does not operate like a variable declaration. The variable name becomes a synonym for the data type. In the following example, UCHAR becomes a synonym for unsigned char:

```
typedef unsigned char UCHAR;
```

Whenever you want to declare an unsigned char variable, you can use UCHAR in place of unsigned char to declare the variable. For example, the following declarations are synonymous:

```
UCHAR uc_value;
unsigned char uc_value
```

The variable uc_value is declared as an unsigned char data type variable.

By convention, the variable in a typedef statement is in uppercase so that it can be distinguished from other program elements. typedef statements are often placed in include files and shared by many source programs. Note that a typedef definition must be specified before it is used in a declaration. Here are examples of typedef statements:

```
typedef unsigned long DLONG;
typedef unsigned int WORD;
typedef unsigned short USHORT;
typedef char *CPOINT;
```

The following examples use the previously defined typedefs:

```
DLONG     dog, cat, mouse;    // All three animals are declared
                              // as unsigned long integers
WORD      Jello, *ptr         // Jello is unsigned int
                              // ptr is pointer to unsigned int

USHORT    i, j, k             // unsigned short variables
```

Compilers that do not support ANSI standards do not necessarily support unsigned short data types. If you write a large program, always use USHORT to declare unsigned short. Then, if you move your program to a computer with a non-ANSI compiler, all you have to do to get the entire program system to compile is to change the `typedef` statement for `USHORT` to `unsigned int` in one header file.

In the following statement, `msg1` and `msg2` become pointers to a character data type:

```
CPOINT msg1, msg2;
```

The `typedef` statement expands the preceding statement to

```
char *msg1, *msg2;
```

The `CPOINT` example shows how the directive expansion processing for `typedef` differs from that for `#define`. If you were to attempt to define `CPOINT` with a `#define` directive, the preceding statement would fail. For example, in the `#define` directive

```
#define CPOINT char*
```

the `#define` statement expands `CPOINT msg1, msg2;` to

```
char *msg1, msg2;
```

The variable `msg2` is not declared as a character pointer, as intended.

Register Variables

If you precede a `short` integer variable declaration with the `register` keyword, the variable is stored in a processor register rather than in an addressable memory location. Therefore, you cannot use the address-of operator (`&`) with a register variable.

Ordinarily, a variable maintained in a processor register is manipulated faster. For example, if a variable that is used frequently for such operations as a loop counter is maintained in a processor register, the program runs faster.

If you select the Global Register Allocation option, the compiler automatically makes use of registers to speed up the execution of a program whenever possible. In fact, if this option is specified, the compiler may disregard the `register` keyword if it determines through an analysis of the code that some other variable should use the register for improved optimization.

C programmers often declare unnamed structures in a typedef statement. Consider this example:

```
typedef struct                  // Declare unnamed structure
                                // and provide it with
    {                           // the typedef name BOX
    int  height;                // Height of box
    int  width;                 // Width of box
    int  depth;                 // Depth of box
    unsigned char row;          // Row of top-left corner of box
    unsigned char column;       // Column of top-left corner
    char color;                 // Color of box
    char *title;                // Title displayed on box
    } BOX;
```

The typedef name is then used to declare the unnamed structure variables, as in

```
BOX  small, medium, large, *ptr;
```

You can still use the typedef for this purpose in C++. However, because you do not need the struct keyword when you declare a structure name by using an existing struct tag name in C++, there is no benefit in using the typedef for this purpose. Furthermore, in C++ there is a distinction between a typedef name and types declared with struct, class, union, and enum. A typedef name cannot be used as a reference to a structure, class, or union for advanced C++ operations, which are discussed later in this book (such as inheritance, constructors, and destructors).

You can set the Global Register Allocation option by choosing the **O**ptimizations push button from the C++ Compiler Options dialog box. You open this dialog box by choosing the Language Options command from the **O**ptions menu.

Two processor registers are available at any one time. You can declare only two variables as register variables. If you declare more, the compiler treats the extra register variables as nonregister variables. In other words, the variables will be stored in addressable memory.

Here is an example of a variable declared with the `register` keyword:

```
register int counter;
```

The Enumerated Data Type

11

The *enumerated* data type designates a group of named integer constants. The `enum` keyword is used to declare an enumerated data type or *enumeration*. The syntax is

```
enum name
{
     symbol-list
}
```

where *name* is the name of the enumerated variable declared. *symbol-list* is a list of enumerated types that are assigned values when the enumerated variable is declared and can have an initialization value. If there is no initialization value, the first type is assigned a value of 0, the second type is assigned a value of 1, and so on. For example, the following code declares the enumerated variable and types:

```
enum color
{
     red, blue, green
};

enumerated type     value assigned
  red                   0
  blue                  1
  green                 2
```

You can assign enumerated types to a specified value also, as in

```
enum color
{
     red = 2, blue = 1, green = 4, yellow, green
};
```

In this case, the constants `yellow` and `green` are set to 5 and 6, respectively. In other words, if a constant in the enumeration definition is assigned an integer, the next constant is assigned a value that is one greater, and so on. To declare an int type variable to one of the enum values, you use the following enumeration statement:

```
color sky = blue
```

The integer value sky is assigned a value of 1.

Enumerated types are not used much because you can use the const qualifier (described in Chapter 6, "Data Types") for the same purpose, as in this example:

```
const  red     = 2
const  blue    = 1
const  green   = 4

int sky = blue;
```

The only difference between enumerations in C and C++ is that in C you need to prefix an enumeration statement with the enum keyword. Note the following example:

```
enum sky = red;   // C requires the enum keyword
sky = red;        // enum keyword is not used in C++
```

Data Conversion

In the C++ language, you can mix data types in expressions. The compiler processes expressions by breaking them into subexpressions according to the precedence rules (see Chapter 8, "Operators and Expressions"). A *subexpression* consists of an operator and one or two operands. For example, the following subexpression contains an operator (+) and two operands (x and 45.0):

```
int  x  = 3;
x + 45.0
```

Before the compiler generates code for the operator (+), it generates code to convert x to a temporary float data type variable, and then generates code that adds together the two float data type numbers. The compiler does this to make sure that two variables of the same type are added together.

Whenever the types differ, the compiler always converts one of the operands so that both have the same type before the operation is performed. The compiler decides which operand to convert, based on a hierarchy of data types (see Figure 11.8). The compiler converts the lower-level data type to the higher-level data type.

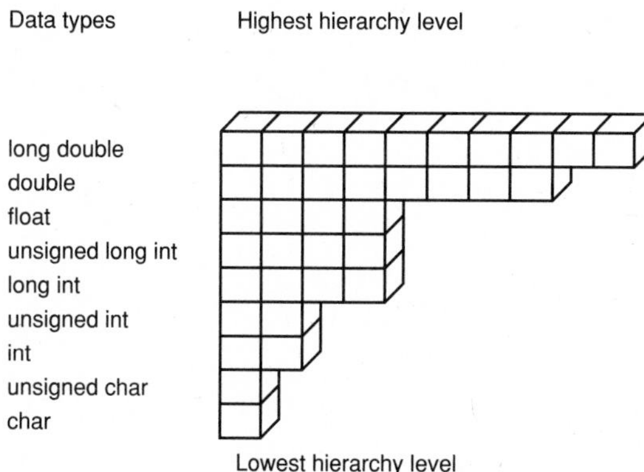

Figure 11.8. *The hierarchy of data types.*

In the following example, `char` is converted to an `int`. Then the results are converted to a `float` and added to a `float`. Finally, the `float` results are converted to a `double` and assigned to a `double` (`z`):

```
char c   = 4;
int  val = 3;
double z;
z = c * val + 32.1
```

As noted, lower-level values are always converted to higher-level values; a `char` type value is converted to an `int`, a `signed int` to an `unsigned int`, and so on. When a lower-level value is converted to a higher-level value, it is said to be *promoted*. When you assign a higher-level value to a lower-level type variable, it is said to be *demoted*. The example

```
float x;
x = 34.3L+3.0L
```

results in a `double`, `35.3L`, and is demoted and stored in the `float` as `35.3f`.

A promotion conversion seldom causes problems because a value is converted to a wider value. When you do a demotion, however, you can get the wrong results if the value being demoted is too large to fit in the smaller data-type variable. In the example

```
int i_val = 999;
char s_val;
s_val = i_val;
```

`s_val` is set to –25 when the assignment statement is executed. This happens because the range of values you can store in an 8-bit character is from –128 to 127, and 999 is larger than 127. You simply cannot put the contents of a full 2-byte `int` into a 1-byte `char`.

When the Compiler Warning Level option is set to 4 or higher in the C++ Compiler Options dialog box (refer to the discussion of the **O**ptions menu in Chapter 5), the compiler displays the following message:

```
convert1.cpp(7) : warning C4135: conversion between
                  different integral types
```

Note that the program does not execute when the warning message is displayed, although you can still execute the program. Listing 11.6 shows the program CONVERT1.CPP. A hexadecimal representation of `i_val` and `s_val` is also displayed. Notice that the high-order portion of `i_val` was simply discarded during the demotion. You can fix this problem by declaring `s_val` as an `int`.

Listing 11.6. The source listing for CONVERT1.CPP.

```
// CONVERT1.CPP - Illustrates data conversion
#include <iostream.h>
main()
{
     char    s_val;
     int     i_val = 999;
     s_val = i_val;
     cout << "s_val = "
          << (int) s_val << "\n";
     cout << "s_val (hex form) =   "
          << hex << (int) s_val << "\n";
     cout << "i_val (hex form) = "
          << hex << i_val << "\n";
     return 0;
}
```

Listing 11.7 shows the results of executing CONVERT1.EXE.

Listing 11.7. The results of executing CONVERT1.EXE.

```
s_val = -25
s_val (hex form) =   ffe7
i_val (hex form) = 3e7
```

As you can see, keeping the compiler warning level set to 2 or higher is a good idea. This setting provides a means of monitoring automatic conversions to alert you to potential problems.

Conversions take time. Your program will run faster if you avoid a conversion by not mixing data types. For example, suppose that you increment a heavily used loop counter, `i`:

```
int i;
for ( i = 0.0L; i < 99.0L; i = i + 1.0L )
      ⋮
```

Your program will run slower because you increment the counter with a `double float` value for each loop. The test expression also requires promoting `i` to a `double float` before the test. The loop runs faster without the useless conversions, as shown in the following example:

```
int i;
for ( i = 0; i < 99; i++ )
      ⋮
```

Although the preceding example may seem obvious, I have seen programs that performed poorly because of unnecessary conversions.

Unsigned types can hold larger numbers than signed ones. For instance, values in an `unsigned char` can range from 0 to 255, whereas a `signed char` can hold values from –128 to 127. Although both `char` types take 1 byte of memory, the high-order (leftmost) bit of a `char` is used as a sign bit; only 7 bits are used for the number. An `unsigned char` uses all 8 bits for the number. This is true also for the `signed` and `unsigned int` and `long`. As a result, an `unsigned char`, `int`, or `long` is a higher level than a `char`, `int`, or `long`, respectively.

Automatic conversions are usually quiet and invisible. They rarely cause abnormal results, although you may want to avoid automatic conversions under certain circumstances. You can specify conversions manually by using *type casting* when you need to mix data types.

Type Casting

You can convert a value explicitly to a different data type by using a technique called *casting*, which is performed with a C++ language *cast* construct. To cast an expression, you specify the target type enclosed in parentheses immediately before the expression. In the example

```
cat = (float) 9;
```

the constant 9 is converted to a `float` data type, and the floating-point value 9.0f is assigned to `cat`. Cast converts any data type specified to the target type. Here are examples of type casting:

```
int i =  3;
char c = 4;
float f;
f = (float) 3 / 4       // Value of .75 assigned to f
f = (float) (3 / 4 )   // Value of 0 assigned to f
f = 3.3;
i = c * (int) f         // Value of 12 returned to i
```

For the first assignment statement, the value of 3 is explicitly defined to a `float` by the cast `(float)`; 4 is converted automatically to a `float`, and 3.0 is divided by 4.0. The result, .75, is assigned to `f`. In the second assignment statement, the integer division of `3 / 4` is performed, yielding an `int` zero that the cast converts to a `float`. In the last statement, the `int`, cast manually, converts the `float` variable `f` to an `int` 3; the `char` variable `c` is converted automatically to an `int` 4; and the result, an `int` 12, is stored to `i`.

When you cast a variable, the value of the variable is not affected because the cast affects only the value the variable yields. In the preceding example, after the cast, the variable `f` is still a `float` data type value with a value of 3.3. The cast effectively creates a temporary variable that has the data type of the cast element and contains the converted value; this temporary variable is used in the expression.

In the following example, the `int` value of 3 is converted to a `float` value of 3.0f and saved internally in a temporary variable, which is used in the expression:

```
x = (float) 3 * 4.0f     // Before cast
       ↓
x = 3.0f * 4.0f          // After cast
```

The Free Store—Memory Allocation Operators

In Chapter 6, "Data Types," you learned how automatic and `static` variables are stored. In review, `static` variables are stored in the program data segment, and automatic (or local) variables are stored in the stack. Memory for `static` variables is allocated when a program is compiled. There is a third place where variables are stored. In C this place in memory is called the *heap*. In C++ it is called the *free store*. You can allocate space in the free store for a variable when you need it, and dispose of the variable (or free up the memory used by the variable) at any time.

A variable allocated from the free store has a lifetime that you determine. It can be allocated in one function and deallocated in another function. Recall that an automatic variable lives as long as a function or block is executing. A `static` variable lives as long as the program executes.

In the C language, you can allocate memory with the `malloc()` library function and free the memory with the `free()` function. The C++ language also provides this capability, using the `new` operator to allocate memory for a data object from the free store. You provide the `new` operator with a data object type, and the operator automatically allocates the correct amount of memory you need and then returns the address of the block of memory allocated. You assign the returned address to a pointer and use the pointer to access the data object. You use the `delete` operator to deallocate the data object that has been allocated with the `new` operator.

The new Operator

The `new` operator allocates a block of memory that is the size of the specified data object type. The data object can be an `int`, a `float`, a structure, an array, or any other data type. The `new` operator function returns the address of the allocated block of memory, and the address is assigned to a pointer. You use the pointer to reference the memory block. Now consider several examples that illustrate the use of the `new` operator.

```
int *ptr_i = new int;
*ptr_i = 3 * 7;
```

Here the new operator allocates a memory block large enough to hold one int variable, and returns the address of that block. The block is assigned to the pointer ptr_i. Then the new int data object is assigned a value of 21.

```
char  *ptr_c = new char [50];
strcpy( ptr_c, "Only the educated are free -- Epictetus");
```

In the preceding example, the pointer ptr_c is assigned the address of a block of memory large enough to hold an array of 50 characters. The strcpy() function copies a string (second argument) to the memory block pointed to by the ptr_c pointer. Do you think that the quotation makes much sense in modern times? Maybe things were different in ancient Greece.

```
float *ptr_f = new float;
*ptr_f = 2399.0;
```

Here the pointer ptr_f is assigned the address of a block of memory large enough to hold a float data object. The pointer is then assigned a value.

```
struct *dog;                     // Define structure dog template
{
     char breed[20];
     float height;
     char color[20];
     int age;
};
dog   *dog_ptr = new dog;        // Allocate structure of type dog
strcpy( dog_ptr->breed, "German Shepherd" );
dog_ptr->height = 30;
dog_ptr->age = 12;
```

In the preceding example, the new operator allocates a block of memory large enough to hold an instance of the structure dog. The address of the memory block is returned and assigned to the pointer, and the elements of the structure are then assigned values. The following statement allocates enough memory to hold an array of structures of type dog:

```
dog *dog_ptr = new dog [5];
```

In reality, you rarely allocate space for a single value. It requires more memory to allocate a small data object than to declare it as a `static` variable. Usually, you use the `new` operator to allocate strings, arrays, and structures. Memory allocation is most useful when you have a program in which either the number of array elements or the number of instances of a structure (or both) are determined while the application is executing. It is a more efficient use of valuable memory resources to allocate these data objects as they are needed during program execution, instead of attempting to declare the maximum number and size of objects you will ever need when you write the program. If the size of an array is designated at the time a program is compiled, the array is said to be a *static* array. If you create an array during the execution of a program, the array is a *dynamic* array.

Here are the general forms for allocating data objects with the `new` operator:

```
type *pointer = new type                  // Not for arrays
type *pointer = new type [dimensions]     // For arrays
```

The first form is for basic data types and structures, and the second form is for arrays. The *`type`* item is specified twice, and both must be the same data type. The first instance of *`type`* defines the data type of the pointer. The second instance defines the data type of the object. The *`pointer`* field is the name of the pointer that is assigned the address of the data object, or `NULL` if the memory allocation operation fails. In the second form, the *`pointer`* is assigned the address of the memory block large enough to hold an array with *`dimensions`* elements.

The free store is not an inexhaustible supply of memory. If the `new` operator runs out of memory, it returns a `NULL` pointer. It is the responsibility of the programmer *always* to test the pointer to ensure that it is valid before the pointer is assigned a value. For example, suppose that you want to allocate an array of 5,000 integers, as in the following example:

```
int  *ptr_arr = new int [5000];
if ( ptr_arr == NULL )
     {
     cout << "You have run out of memory!\n";
     return -1;  // Take some kind of recovery action
     }
for ( int i = 0; i < 5000; i++ )
     ptr_arr[i] = setarray( i );
⋮
```

There is another way. Suppose that you have a way to recover when you run out of free store memory. For instance, maybe you can swap (write) some allocated memory blocks to disk and free up some memory in the free store. You can write a function that recovers from the "out of memory" condition, and pass the address of that function to the library function `_set_new_handler()`. If your program runs out of memory, your function will be called. If your function is able to recover, it returns a nonzero value, and the `new` function tries again to allocate the memory block. If your function cannot recover, it should return a zero value. The following program fragment demonstrates the use of `_set_new_handler()`:

```
#include <iostream.h>
#include <new.h>   // Header file is used with _set_new_handler
void main()
{
     // Establish function called if new operator fails
     _set_new_handler( OutOfMemory );
     :
     // If the following statement fails, OutOfMemory is called
     char *ptr new char [20000];
     :
     return;
}
int OutOfMemory( size_t size )
{
     cout << "Insufficient memory. Recovery will be attempted\n";
     // Attempt recovery
     :
     if ( i_recovered )
          return 1; // Recovery was successful, retry allocation
     else
          return 0; // Recovery was unsuccessful
}
```

The first thing that happens in the function `main()` is that `_set_new_handler()` is called to define the error-recovery function to be `OutOfMemory()`. Later in the program, a memory block large enough to contain a 20,000-character array is allocated. If there is not enough memory, the `OutOfMemory()` function is called. It returns a flag that indicates whether the memory allocation operation should be retried.

An example of allocating memory for an array of structures is presented in Listing 11.8. The program ALLOC.CPP defines a structure template, `dog`. Then the program uses the `new` operator to allocate enough space to hold an array of three dog structures. The address of the memory block is stored in the pointer pdog. After checking to see whether the block of memory was successfully allocated, ALLOC.CPP assigns values to members of each structure element. The strcpy() library function is used to copy a string constant into the character array members breed and color of the structure dog. Note that the header file string.h is included. It is required because it contains the prototypes for strcpy() and other string-manipulation functions. Finally, the program displays the contents of all three structure elements of the array pdog (see Listing 11.9).

Listing 11.8. The source listing for ALLOC.CPP.

```
// ALLOC.CPP - Illustrates the use of the new operator
#include <iostream.h>
#include <string.h>
struct dog
{
     char breed[30];
     int    height;
     char   color[20];
     int    age;
};

void main()
{
     dog *pdog =  new dog [3];
     if ( pdog == NULL )
          cout << "You ran out of memory!!!!\n";
     else
     {
          strcpy( pdog[0].breed, "Fox Terrier" );
          strcpy( pdog[0].color, "Black & White" );
          pdog[0].height = 15;
          pdog[0].age    = 3;
          strcpy( pdog[1].breed, "Chihuahua" );
          strcpy( pdog[1].color, "Tan" );
          pdog[1].height = 6;
          pdog[1].age    = 5;
          strcpy( pdog[2].breed, "Labrador Retriever" );
          strcpy( pdog[2].color, "Golden" );
          pdog[2].height = 24;
```

continues

Listing 11.8. continued

```
            pdog[2].age       = 7;
            for ( int i=0; i < 3; i++ )
            {
                cout << "Breed:  " << pdog[i].breed  << "\n"
                     << "Color:  " << pdog[i].color  << "\n"
                     << "Height: " << pdog[i].height << "\n"
                     << "Age:    " << pdog[i].age    << "\n\n";
            }
      }
}
```

Listing 11.9. The results of executing ALLOC.EXE.

```
Breed:  Fox Terrier
Color:  Black & White
Height: 15
Age:    3

Breed:  Chihuahua
Color:  Tan
Height: 6
Age:    5

Breed:  Labrador Retriever
Color:  Golden
Height: 24
Age:    7
```

The delete Operator

When you are finished using a block of memory, you can dispose of it with the `delete` operator. The deleted memory block is returned to the free store so that more memory will be available for allocating other memory blocks. Here is an example that allocates an array and calls the `delete` operator to deallocate it:

```
dog *pdog =  new dog [3];     // Allocate pdog
if ( pdog == NULL )
     cout << "You ran out of memory!!!!\n";
else
{
      :                       // Use pdog
      delete pdog;            // Deallocate pdog
}
```


As you can see from the example, the syntax of the `delete` operate is pretty simple. Once a memory block has been deallocated, the pointer is no longer valid, and you must not reference it again until you have reassigned it some other valid address.

What You Have Learned

In this chapter, you learned enough about two powerful elements of the C++ language—pointers and structures—to do basic operations and write useful programs. To extend your knowledge of pointers and structures, you must write programs. When you try to use pointers, you will discover what you do *not* know. After you have time to get comfortable with the basics, Chapters 14 and 15 introduce you to the advanced features of pointers and structures. Specifically, you learned the following:

- How to use enumerated data types
- How and when to use register variables
- How to declare and use `typedefs`
- How the C++ compiler automatically converts values from one data type to another
- How to explicitly designate data conversion with type casting
- How to allocate memory dynamically

12

Functions

Function n. *A device for mapping a domain of unknown arguments into a range of inaccessible results.*

—Kelly-Bootle
The Devil's DP Dictionary (1981)

In This Chapter

You already know what a function is and that functions are the building blocks of a C++ program. Although you have been using functions since you encountered your first C++ program, you may not fully understand them. This chapter's detailed discussion of functions should help. The following topics are covered:

- The `main()` function
- The anatomy of a function
- How to call a function
- Prototypes
- Function visibility for multiple source files
- Recursion
- Scope
- Inline functions
- Function polymorphism
- Reference variables
- Libraries of functions

The main() Function

As you know, all C++ programs have a `main()` function. When the operating system executes a program, `main()` is the first function executed. When `main()` exits, the program is finished.

When `main()` is called by the operating system, the function is passed two arguments. Ordinarily, the variable names `argv` and `argc` are used as arguments to `main()`, but there is nothing magic about the names—you can call these arguments anything. Note that the arguments are omitted from the `main()` function declaration in all the examples thus far in this book because the arguments are not used.

As you know, when you execute an MS-DOS or UNIX program, you specify arguments on the command line. In the example

```
C:>COPY OLDFILE NEWFILE
```

`OLDFILE` and `NEWFILE` are the command-line arguments. The program ARGS1.CPP, shown in Listing 12.1, demonstrates how to retrieve the command-line arguments.

Listing 12.1. The source listing for ARGS1.CPP.

```
// ARGS1.CPP - Illustrates how to retrieve command-line
// arguments
#include <iostream.h>
main( int argc, char *argv[] )
{
     for ( int i = 0; i < argc ; i++ )
          cout << argv[i] << "\n";
     return 0;
}
```


Once you build ARGS1.EXE, you can exit from the PWB and execute ARGS1.EXE from the DOS command line. The program displays whatever command-line arguments you specify.

When ARGS1.EXE executes, the operating system passes the two items to your program as arguments to `main()`. The first argument, `argc`, is an `int` variable that contains the number of command-line arguments. The second argument, `argv`, is an array of `char` pointers. The first `argv` element, `argv[0]`, points to a string containing the program's drive and path. Each of the remaining `argv` elements points to a command-line argument. Note the following sample dialog:

```
D:>ARGS1 Once upon a midnight dreary
Once
upon
a
midnight
dreary
```

As you can see, when the message `Once upon a midnight dreary` is typed after the program name, the program displays each command-line argument on a separate line.

You can exit a program and return to the operating system by returning from the `main()` function or calling the `exit()` function. In either case, you can return to the operation an integer value that represents the DOS error code. If you call `exit()`, you pass the error code as the argument. An error code of zero means that the program is exiting normally without errors; a nonzero error code denotes an error condition. The following `main()` functions are equivalent:

```
int main()
{
      :
      return 0;
}

void main()
{
      :
      exit( 0 );
}
```

The following example illustrates how to return an error code to MS-DOS when you exit:

```
int main()
{
      :
      if ( error )
            return 1;   // Return error code of 1
      return 0;         // Normal return
}
```

Anatomy of a Function

This section takes a closer look at the elements of a function. The syntax of a function contains nine elements, some of which are optional. The *function header* consists of the following elements:

1. Return type
2. Function name
3. (
4. Argument list (optional)
5.)

   The other elements in a function are these:

6. Argument declaration (can be in argument list)

7. {
8. Function body (optional)
9. }

Here is an example of a function header:

```
int myfunc( int arg1, char arg2, char *arg3 )
```

C++ requires that you include argument declarations in the argument list, as shown in the preceding example. The argument list specifies the type and a name for each argument. If there are no arguments, the `void` keyword should be used.

The elements of a function are described in the following sections.

Return Type

If the function does not return an `int` value, you must specify the return data type, as in

```
char *func1() {...}     // Return a pointer to a char
float func2() {...}     // Return a float
int  *func3() {...}     // Return a pointer to an int
char *func4[]() {...}   // Return a pointer to a char array
```

If the function does not return a value, you must specify the `void` keyword, which is considered a special data type. Although Microsoft C/C++ 7 supports `void`, earlier C++ compilers did not. If a function did not return a value, either `int` or no type was used. If you compile your program on an older compiler, be sure to add an include file with a `#define` statement that equates `void` to `int`.

Function Name

A function name must begin with a letter or an underscore (_) and can contain as many other letters, numbers, or underscores as you want. The compiler, however, ignores all but the first 247 characters. C++ is a case-sensitive language, which means that it recognizes upper- and lowercase values as being different. This sensitivity also applies to function names.

Argument List and Argument Declarations

As you already know, a function can have no arguments or several. The argument list is a comma-delimited list of argument declarations. If a function has no arguments, the `void` keyword is specified in place of the argument list. Having argument declarations in the function argument list and using the `void` keyword are supported by C and required by C++.

Arguments in a function call statement are referred to as *actual* arguments, whereas those in the called function's argument list are referred to as *formal* arguments. Formal arguments are sometimes called *parameters*.

The rules for argument declarations are similar to the rules for variable declarations except for the following restrictions:

- A `char` data type is converted to an `int` data type.
- A `short` data type is converted to an `int` data type.
- A `float` data type is converted to a `double` data type.
- A formal argument declared as an array is converted to a pointer to the same data type as the array. Note these examples:

  `char x[]` is converted to `char *x`.

  `int x[]` is converted to `int *x`.
- A formal argument declared as a function is converted to a pointer to a function.
- You cannot initialize an argument declaration except in a prototype, as shown later in this chapter.

Function Body

In the function body, all statements are enclosed in a pair of braces ({}). Function and variable declarations are the only C++ language statements allowed outside the braces. The body of the function contains a statement block, which consists of zero or more statements. For example, the following function contains no statements:

```
dummy()
{
}
```

When developing complex computer programs, programmers often approach implementation from the *top down*. The *high-level* functions are implemented first, and the *low-level* functions consist of a `return` statement only. In other words, the low-level functions are empty (also called *stubs*), as in the following example:

```
void reports() {}
```

The functionality is added later in the implementation process. The code that prints reports will be added to the function `reports()` when the programmer reaches the point in the development process when it is time to develop the code for reporting.

In an object-oriented design, you use a *bottom-up* approach. First you determine all the low-level objects. You write them, test them, and debug them. Then you write the high-level program to use the pretested objects.

Functions come after the main loop in your program.

Return Values

A function can return a single value. An expression containing this value is specified with the `return` statement, as in

```
return (value+99);
```

The return value can be any data type except a function or an array. You can return multiple values by returning a pointer to a structure or an array. The return value must conform to the same rules that apply to either side of an assignment operator. For example, you cannot return an `int` value if the return type is a pointer. However, if you return an `int` and the return type is a `float`, automatic conversion is performed correctly. See the section "Data Conversion" in Chapter 11 for a discussion of automatic conversion.

A function can have any number of return statements. As soon as the program encounters any of the return statements, it returns to the calling statement; if there is no return statement, the program returns when it encounters the closing brace.

If there is no return statement or no expression follows the return statement, the return value is undefined and can contain any garbage value. If you intend for a function to return no value, the return type should be a void, as in

```
void func1( void )
{
        cout << "This function returns no values";
}
```

The calling program does not have to use a return value; if the calling program ignores it, the return value is discarded.

Although many programmers always enclose the return statement expression in parentheses, the parentheses are optional. (They may be needed to make a complex expression easier to read.) Programmers probably got into the habit of using parentheses from early C++ language books that advocated their use.

Calling a Function

Any expression can hold a *function call* that redirects program control to a named function. A function that receives program control executes the code and returns.

Using a Return Value

Unless a function's return type is void, a value is always returned. This return value effectively replaces the function call in the expression, as in

```
int  i;
i = fcn()*2;
```

If `fcn()` returns 3, the expression becomes `3*2`, and `i` is assigned the value of 6.

Functions with No Arguments

You can call a function and not use the value it returns. In the example

```
fcn();
```

the return value is discarded. Because `fcn()` has no arguments, it is the simplest form of the function call. To indicate that the function call has no arguments, a `void` keyword is placed in the parentheses of both the function prototype and the function declaration (see Figure 12.1).

12

```
void fcn(void ); // Prototype
main ()
{
     fcn(); // Function call
     ...
}
void fcn( void ) // Function declaration
{
     cout << "Hello from function fcn\n";
} // No return is needed
  // Right brace acts as "return"
```

Figure 12.1. *A sample function with no arguments.*

Passing Arguments

As you know, in a function call the function name is followed by a pair of parentheses that can contain an argument list. Here is an example:

```
#include <iostream.h>
void count_down( int num, char*message );
main()
{
     cout << "Count down from 3\n";
     count_down( 3, " num equals " );
}
```

```
void count_down( int num, char *message )
{
     while ( num > 0 )
     {
          cout << message << num--;
     }
}
```

Here the function count_down() is called and passed two arguments—the constant value 3 and the address of a string. The function assigns a value of 3 to the local variable num and assigns the address of a string to the local character pointer message. The num is used as a while loop counter. The function prints the string pointed to by the message and the value of num. Then the function decrements the value of num, repeating the loop until the value of num equals zero and count_down() returns. The output is

```
Count down from 3
 num equals 3
 num equals 2
 num equals 1
```

> Variables declared in a function are called *local variables*.

If you look at the output statement in count_down(), you'll notice that count_down() passes the following arguments to the cout object:

message (the value of the pointer)

num (the value of the local variable)

Some computer languages pass arguments *by reference*. This means that they pass the address of an argument (a pointer) to the called function. The called function can change the value of the argument.

The C++ language passes an argument to a function *by value*. An invisible temporary variable is created, assigned the value of the argument, and passed to the called function. The function can change the value of the variable to anything; the value of the original argument will not be changed. When the program returns, the temporary variable is discarded automatically. If you want a function to change the value of an argument (which must be an *lvalue*), you must pass a pointer to the function.

PASSER.CPP, the program in Listing 12.2, illustrates how arguments are passed by value and by reference:

Listing 12.2. The source listing for PASSER.CPP.

```
// PASSER.CPP - Illustrates "pass by value" and "pass by
// reference"
#include <iostream.h>
void fcn( int num, int *n, char c, char *pc,
          char a, char ary[] );
void main()
{
     int i_val = 3, j_val = 9;
     char c_val = 'A',  c1_val = 'B', ary[] = "ABC", *ptr;
     ptr = &c1_val;
     fcn ( i_val, &j_val, c_val, ptr, ary[0], ary );
     cout << "i_val  = " << i_val  << " was not changed\n";
     cout << "c_val  = " << c_val  << " was not changed\n";
     cout << "c1_val = " << c1_val << " was changed\n";
     cout << "ary[2] = " << ary[2] << " was changed\n";
     cout << "ary[0] = " << ary[0] << " was not changed\n";
}
//   num        - Passed by value
//   *n         - Passed by reference
//   c          - Passed by value
//   *pc        - Passed by reference
//   a          - Passed by value
//   ary        - Passed by reference

void fcn( int num , int *n, char c, char *pc,
          char a, char ary[] )
{

     num = 99;
     *n = 99;
     c = 'Y';
     *pc = 'X';
     a = 3;
     ary[2] = 'Z';
}
```

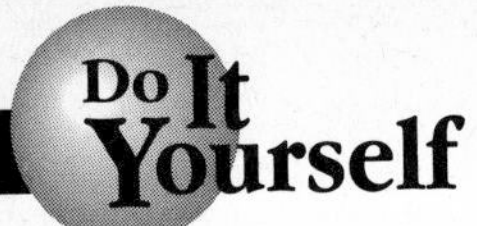

When you execute PASSER.EXE, you get the following output:

```
i_val   = 3 was not changed
c_val   = A was not changed
c1_val = X was changed
ary[2]  = Z was changed
ary[0]  = A was not changed
```

Notice that PASSER.CPP changed none of the variables that were passed by value.

The following *prototype statement* is placed near the beginning of the program, PASSER.CPP, before any function:

```
void fcn( int num, int *n, char c, char *pc,
          char a, char ary[] )
```

Prototypes are discussed in the next section. Using prototypes when you develop programs is required in C++, and there is a good reason for this. In C programs, if you do not use prototypes, your function arguments can be converted automatically and quietly. This can cause a problem if you specify the wrong argument. The error can go undetected. All data types smaller than an `int` (`char` and unsigned `char`) are converted to `int`, whereas `float` arguments are converted to `double`. If the formal arguments in the called function are assigned as a `char`, they are quietly converted back to a `char` from an `int`. The following example illustrates data conversion when arguments are passed:

```
int main()   /* C program that does not use a prototype */
{
     char c = 2;
     int  i = 3;
     fcn( c, i );
     :
}
void fcn( char ch, int ival );
{
     :
}
```

Before the function `fcn()` is called, the `char` type variable `c` is converted to an `int`. After `fcn()` is called, the passed `int` value is converted back to the received `char` type for the formal argument `ch`. The `int` variable `i` is passed without any conversion. As long as the data types of the actual arguments in the function call match their corresponding formal arguments in the called function, the arguments are passed correctly. Automatic conversions can affect the efficiency of your programs, however. Unless you are considering not using prototypes in a C program, this discussion is purely academic because C++ requires prototypes and argument declarations.

Prototypes

Function prototypes contain the same information as the function header except that prototypes are terminated with a semicolon. Specifically, a prototype consists of the following elements: a return type followed by the function name, an argument list enclosed in parentheses, and a semicolon.

Prototypes are usually placed at the beginning of a program, before the first function definition. The compiler uses prototypes to validate that the number and data types of actual arguments in the function call are the same as the number and types of formal arguments in the called function. If an inconsistency is detected, an error message is displayed. Without prototypes, a bug can occur if an argument with an incorrect data type is passed to a function. In a complex program, this type of bug is sometimes difficult to track down. Type checking eliminates this class of bug.

Type checking is an action performed by the compiler. The compiler knows what types of arguments are passed once it has processed a prototype statement. Then, when a function call statement is encountered, the compiler confirms that the type of each argument in the function call is the same type as that of the corresponding argument in the prototype. If they are not the same, the compiler generates an error message.

Prototyping was introduced into the C++ language by Bjarne Stroustrup of AT&T as part of his creation, the C++ language. The American National Standards Institute (ANSI) committee thought prototypes were such a good idea that it adopted the C++ prototyping and function argument declarations in its specifications for the C language. This ANSI syntax is optional in C so that it will be compatible with the old-style C, which did not support prototyping and function argument declarations. When you write C programs, either style is acceptable. However, if you ever write more C programs, I recommend that you always use the ANSI form, especially if you plan to upgrade your C program to C++ (because C++ requires that arguments be prototyped).

The argument list contains data type information for each argument. An example of a prototype is

```
int cruncher( int a, char b, float c, double d, char *e );
```

The compiler uses only the data type information. The argument names have no meaning and are not even required. The purpose of the names is to make the type declarations easier to read and write. Some programmers make a copy of the function header statement, place the copy at the beginning of the program, and add a semicolon. The preceding statement can be written also as

```
int cruncher( int, char, float, double, char * );
```

Automatic argument conversion is no longer needed. Because your program does not need to perform data conversion, its performance will be improved.

Prototypes without Parameters

If a function has no arguments, use the `void` keyword as the argument list in the prototype. Note the following example:

```
int sample( void );
```

Prototypes with an Unspecified Number of Parameters

A special form of prototype for such functions as `printf()` and `scanf()`, which have an unspecified number of arguments, uses the *ellipsis token* (...). In the examples

```
int  sample( int a, ... );
int  printf( constant char *format, ... );
int  scanf( constant char *format, ...);
```

the ellipsis token indicates the existence of an unspecified number of additional arguments. This token is used in a prototype whenever you have a varying number of arguments, as you do with the `printf()` function.

Prototypes with Default Function Arguments

Arguments in a function prototype can contain a default value specification. The form of the default value is just like the form of a variable declaration that is initialized. The default value must be a constant expression, as in

```
char fcn( int arg1 = 1, char c = 'A', float f_val = 33.4f );
```

When you omit an argument from the function, the compiler uses the default value. If you provide an argument, the compiler uses the argument you provide. You can call `fcn()` with any of the following statements:

```
fcn( 9, "Z", 91.2 );   // Override all three defaults
fcn( 18, "X" );        // Override first two defaults
fcn( 42 );             // Override first default
fcn();                 // Use all three default arguments
```

12

The preceding function call statements are equivalent to the following function calls:

```
fcn( 9,  "Z", 91.2 );
fcn( 18, "X", 33.4 );
fcn( 42, "A", 33.4 );
fcn( 1,  "A", 33.4 );
```

However, you cannot omit an argument unless you omit all the arguments to its right. For example, the following function call is wrong:

```
fcn( , "Z", 88.8 );  // Wrong, didn't omit arguments to the right
```

You have to be careful and place any arguments that have default values on the right side of a function.

Function Visibility in Multiple Source Files

Thus far, all but one of the examples you have encountered have only one source file. Large programs are easier to work with when they are divided into multiple source files, each containing one or more functions for a particular segment of program logic. When you divide a large program into smaller ones, the only source files you have to recompile are those that have been changed. Compile time is reduced because small source files compile faster than large ones. Large source files are difficult to maintain and edit; printing them is a slow process that uses excessive amounts of paper.

When you have more than one source file, you must be able to reference a function in one source file from a function in another source file. Unlike variables, functions are external by default. For readability, however, you can use the `extern` keyword with a function prototype and header.

You may want to restrict the visibility of a function, making it visible only to other functions in a source file. One reason for doing this is to reduce the possibility of having two functions with the same name. Another reason is to reduce the number of external references and speed up the linking process.

You can make a function invisible outside a source file by using the `static` keyword with the function header and function prototype statement. Listing 12.3 shows the source listings for the programs NUMOUT.CPP and POUT.CPP. The function `pout()` is visible outside POUT.CPP and is referenced from the function `numout()` in NUMOUT.CPP. However, `numout()` is visible only to functions inside NUMOUT.CPP because this function is declared with the `static` keyword.

Listing 12.3. The source listings for NUMOUT.CPP and POUT.CPP.

```
// NUMOUT.CPP - Illustrates recursion
#include <iostream.h>
static void numout( int n );
extern void pout( int c );
main( )
{
      int number = 42;
      while ( number > 0 )
      {
            cout << "\nEnter a number: ";
            cin >> number;
            numout( number );
      }
      return 0;
}
static void numout( int num )
{
      int remainder;
      if ( (remainder = num / 10) != 0 )
```

```
        numout( remainder );
    pout( num );
}
// POUT.CPP - Prints low-order digit of number
#include <iostream.h>
void pout (int i)
{
    cout << (char) (i % 10 + '0');
}
```

Here is a sample dialog resulting from running NUMOUT.EXE:

```
Enter a number: 349
349
Enter a number: 672
672
Enter a number: 0
```


Recursion

A *recursive function* is one that calls itself directly or indirectly. Recursion is an acceptable operation in C++ and can be helpful. The function `numout()`, shown in Listing 12.3, is an example of a recursive function; it prints a positive integer, one character at a time. Whenever `numout()` is called, it gets a different set of local (automatic) variables.

Figure 12.2 illustrates recursive calls to `numout()`. The example in this figure shows what happens after you type `349` in response to the prompt `Enter a number:`.

The function `pout()` uses the modulus (remainder) operator `(i % 10)` to extract the low-order digit from the `int` variable `i` and adds this digit to an ASCII digit 0. This yields an ASCII digit ranging from 0 to 9. The function prints the low-order digit.

You can always implement a loop to perform the same operation as a recursive call. Although a recursive program can be more compact and readable than a loop, such a program is frequently harder to understand.

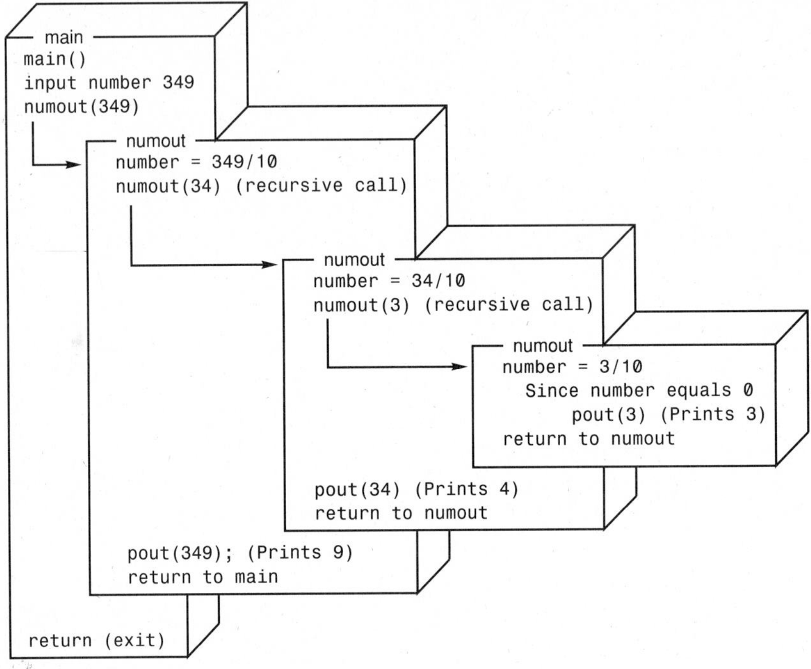

Figure 12.2. *An example of recursive calls.*

The drawback of using recursive calls is that they can use a great deal of memory. Whenever a recursive call is made, a block of memory is required to hold a complete set of automatic variables.

Scope

This section summarizes the rules for visibility, or *scope*, of functions and variables. Your program environment is divided into four types of scope: program, source file, function, and block. You can designate a variable to be associated with any of these scope types. Such a variable is invisible outside its scope and can be accessed only in its scope.

Generally, the declaration statement's position in the program determines the scope. The storage class specifiers—`static`, `extern`, `auto`, and `register`—can affect the scope. The following program fragment illustrates each scope type:

```
int i;          // Program scope
static int j;   // File scope
fcn( int k )    // fcn is program scope
                // k is block scope
{
     int m;     // Block scope
     goto label;
     :
label:          // Function scope
     :
}
```


In a function or variable declaration statement, storage type specifier keywords precede the type keyword. Table 12.1 illustrates the effect of positioning a variable declaration and applying storage class specifiers to the scope type of a variable.

Table 12.1. Scope types.

Placement of Specifier	*Storage Type Specifier* `auto`	`register`	`static`	`extern`	*None**
Out of function	NA**	NA	File	Program	Program
In function	Block	Block	Block	Block	Block
Function argument	Block	Block	NA	NA	Block

**None (no storage type specifier)*

***NA (not allowed)*

Program Scope

Variables that have *program scope* can be referenced by any function in the entire program; such variables are called *global* variables. To make a variable global, simply declare the variable at the beginning of a program, outside any functions.

Source File Scope

A variable that is declared outside any functions and whose declaration contains the `static` keyword has *source file scope*. Variables with this scope can be referenced from the point in the program at which they are declared to the end of the source file. If a source file has more than one function, all functions following the declaration of the variable can reference the variable. In the following example, `i` has source file scope:

```
static int i;
void fcn( void )
{
:
}
```

Function Scope

A variable that has *function scope* can be referenced from anywhere in the function. `goto` labels have only function scope; they can appear anywhere in a function but are invisible outside the function. You can use the same label names in different functions without a conflict.

Block Scope

A variable that has *block scope* can be referenced from anywhere—from the point in a block at which the variable is declared to the end of the block. Local variables declared inside a function have block scope; they are invisible outside the block. In the following example, `i` is a local variable:

```
fcn( void )
{
     int i;
     for ( i = 0, i < 10; i++ )
          cout << "i = " << i << "\n";
}
```

A local variable declared in a nested block is visible only inside that block. Note the following example:

```
fcn( int j )
{
     if ( j > 3 )
     {
          int i;
          for ( i=0 ; i < 20 ; i++ );
               func2( i );
     }
     // i is no longer visible
};
```


Inline Functions

The C++ language supports *inline functions* that are used to speed up your program. The difference between a normal function and an inline function is evident in the way the compiler incorporates each into the program.

A normal function is a distinct block of code called from within another function. The compiler generates code to place the return address on the stack. The return address is the address of the statement following an instruction that calls the function. Then the compiler generates code that places any function arguments on the stack as required. Finally, the compiler generates a call instruction that transfers control to the function.

For an inline function, the compiler actually inserts the code for the inline function at the point in the program where the function is called. This makes the program run faster because it does not have to execute the code associated with calling a function. However, each instance of the inline function can take up as much memory as required to hold the entire function. This increases the size of the program even though it runs faster. If you call an inline function 10 times in a program, the compiler inserts 10 copies of the function in the program. If the function is 1K, it would increase the size of your program by 10,000 bytes! If you call the same function as a normal function 10 times and the calling code overhead is 20 bytes, the function requires only 1,200 bytes.

To create an inline function, all you do is preface the function declaration with the `inline` keyword and place it in the source file before it is called. INLINE.CPP, the program in Listing 12.4, illustrates the use of an inline function that reverses two characters in a string.

Listing 12.4. The source listing for INLINE.CPP.

```
// INLINE.CPP - Illustrates how to use inline functions
#include <iostream.h>
#include <string.h>  // Contains prototype for strlen()

// Note: the inline function must appear in the file above
// any places in the program where the function is called
inline void reverse( char s[] )
{
     int len;
     len = strlen( s );     // Return length of string
     for ( int i = 0; i < len; i = i + 2 )
     {
          char temp;
          temp   = s[i+1];
          s[i+1] = s[i];
          s[i]   = temp;
     }
}
void main()
{
     char s[] = { "abcdefgh" };
     reverse( s );  // Reverse characters
     cout << s << "\n";
     reverse( s );  // Put characters in original order
     cout << s << "\n";
}
```

When you build and execute INLINE.EXE, here is what is displayed:

```
badcfehg
abcdefgh
```

If you are going to use an inline function in several files, you can put it in a header file and include it in all the source files in which it is used.

Function Polymorphism (Function Overloading)

12

Now things are going to start getting a little weird. The term *polymorphism* conjures images of a creature that has several forms—like a werewolf. Certain chemical substances that can crystallize in different forms are called *polymorphic*. In C++, *function polymorphism*, or *function overloading*, allows you to use multiple functions with the same name but different argument lists. The argument list is different if it has an argument with a different data type, if it has a different number of arguments, or both. The argument list is called the function's *signature*. Function overloading is illustrated in POLYFUNC.CPP, the program in Listing 12.5, which contains a set of functions named `whattype()` with different signatures.

Listing 12.5. The source listing for POLYFUNC.CPP.

```
// POLYFUNC.CPP - Illustrates function overloading
#include <iostream.h>
void whattype( int i );      // Prototypes for overloaded
void whattype( char *s );    // function name whattype
void whattype( float f );
void whattype( char );
void whattype( int i, int j );

void main()
{
     whattype( 1 );
     whattype( "String" );
     whattype( 3.44f );
     whattype( 'A' );
     whattype( 3, 4 );
}
void whattype( int i )          // Function instance 1
{
     cout << i << " is an integer.\n";
}
```

continues

Listing 12.5. continued

```
void whattype( char *s )        // Function instance 2
{
     cout << s << " is a string.\n";
}
void whattype( float f )        // Function instance 3
{
     cout << f << " is a float.\n";
}
void whattype( char c )         // Function instance 4
{
     cout << c << " is a character.\n";
}
void whattype( int i, int j )  // Function instance 5
{
     cout << i << " and " << j << " are 2 integers.\n";
}
```

The compiler determines which of the `whattype()` functions you actually call, based on the argument in the prototype. For example, the compiler generates code to call function instance 3 if you pass the function a `float` data type.

Here are the results from executing POLYFUNC.EXE:

```
1 is an integer.
String is a string.
3.44 is a float.
A is a character.
3 and 4 are 2 integers.
```

Do not overuse overloaded functions. An overloaded function name should contain a family of functions that perform basically the same task, such as doing the same operation on different data types. You should never overload a function name for unrelated operations.

Under certain circumstances, you might want to consider using default function arguments instead of function overloading. Look at the following functions, which can have the same name but either two or three arguments:

```
copystring( char *str1, char * str2, int n );
copystring( char *str1, char *str2 );
```

You can implement `copystring()` by either overloading the name or using a default argument. Listing 12.6 illustrates how to implement `copystring()` with function overloading. Listing 12.7 shows how to accomplish the same thing but with default arguments. The advantage of using default arguments is that you have to write only a single function, which requires less memory and time to develop.

Listing 12.6. The source listing for COPYSTR1.CPP.

```
// COPYSTR1.CPP - Illustrates function overloading
#include <iostream.h>
void copystring( char *destination, char *source );
void copystring( char *destination, char *source, int count );
void main()
{
    char *string = {"Criticism is easy, art is hard"};
    char str[50];
    copystring( str, string );
    cout << str << "\n";
    copystring( str, string, 17 );
    cout << str << "\n";
}
void copystring( char *destination, char *source )
{
    char *s, *d;
    d = destination;
    s = source;
    for ( ; *s != '\0' ; s++, d++ )
        *d = *s;
    *d = '\0';
}
void copystring( char *destination, char *source, int count )
{
    char *s, *d;
    d = destination;
    s = source;
    for ( int i=0 ; *s != '\0' && i < count  ; s++, d++, i++ )
        *d = *s;
    *d = '\0';
}
```

Listing 12.7. The source listing for COPYSTR2.CPP.

```
// COPYSTR2.CPP - Illustrates use of default function arguments
#include <iostream.h>
void copystring( char *destination, char *source,
                 int count = 32767 );
void main()
{
    char *string = {"Criticism is easy, art is hard"};
    char str[50];
    copystring( str, string );
    cout << str << "\n";
    copystring( str, string, 17 );
    cout << str << "\n";
}
// Function copystring: copy source string to destination
// string. If count is specified, transfer only count
// characters. Function assumes that number of characters to
// transfer < 32767.
void copystring( char *destination, char *source, int count )
{
    char *s, *d;
    d = destination;
    s = source;
    for ( int i=0 ; *s != '\0' && i < count  ; s++, d++, i++ )
        *d = *s;
    *d = '\0';
}
```

Reference Variables

A *reference variable* is another name for a predefined variable that is used primarily to pass a formal argument to a function or to return a value back from the function. Reference variables are an extension to the C language—compliments of C++. As you recall, when you pass a variable to a function, the program passes a copy of the variable to the function. You can pass a pointer to the variable if you want to change its value in the function, or you can use a reference variable as the argument for the function. This is especially convenient if the variable is a large structure and you want to modify members of a structure in the called function. Furthermore, as you will learn later in this book, reference variables are indispensable when you design a class. Before jumping into a discussion of how to use reference variables, consider their properties.

Creating Reference Variables

In Chapter 8, you were introduced to the address-of operator (&), which referenced the address of an operand. You used this operator to pass an argument by reference, as in the following example:

```
int x;
fcn( &x );  // Argument x is passed by reference
```

The variable x is passed by reference. You can change its value in the function if you like. C++ uses the ampersand (&) in the declaration of reference variables. This ampersand's use is similar to that of the address-of operator because the English word *reference* can refer to both uses. Beyond that, the usage differs. For example, to make automobile an alternative (or alias) name for car, use the following statements:

```
int car;
int &automobile = car;
```

In this statement, the symbol & is not used at all like the address-of operator, but is part of the data type identifier. The term int & means a reference to an int, just as int * means a pointer to an int. From this point on, you can use either automobile or car to refer to car.

A reference variable cannot exist unless it is initialized to a variable to which it refers. However, you can declare and initialize a reference variable in one file and access it in another file by declaring it with the extern keyword. Suppose, for example, that the reference variable automobile is declared and initialized in one file, as shown in the preceding example. automobile can be referenced in another file with the following statement:

```
extern int &automobile;
```

The reference variable automobile still refers to the variable car.

REFER1.CPP, the program in Listing 12.8, illustrates how a variable and its reference can be used interchangeably.

Listing 12.8. The source listing for REFER1.CPP.

```
// REFER1.CPP - Demonstrates interchangeability between
// variable and its alternate name (reference)
#include <iostream.h>
void main()
{
     int actualvalue = 3;
     int &alternatevalue = actualvalue;

     cout << "Actual value = " << actualvalue;
     cout << ", alias  = " << alternatevalue << "\n";

     actualvalue = 99;         // Change the actual value
     cout << "Actual value = " << actualvalue;
     cout << ", alias  = " << alternatevalue << "\n";

     alternatevalue = 901;     // Change its alias
     cout << "Actual value = " << actualvalue;
     cout << ", alias  = " << alternatevalue << "\n";
}
```

The following statement declares the reference variable `alternatevalue` to be of type `int &`, which means that it is a reference to the `int` variable:

```
int &alternatevalue = actualvalue;
```

Here are the results of executing REFER1.EXE:

```
Actual value = 3, alias  = 3
Actual value = 99, alias  = 99
Actual value = 901, alias  = 901
```

Notice that `actualvalue` and `alternatevalue` are interchangeable. It does not matter which name you assign a value to. Both names refer to the same memory address.

Using Reference Variables as Function Parameters

As mentioned earlier, the predominant use for reference variables is to pass arguments by reference to a function. When you pass a variable to a function, the variable is passed by value. This means that a copy of the variable is made and passed on the stack to the function. The function can change the value of the copy, but the value of the original variable is not changed. You can get around this by passing a pointer to a variable as the argument to a function. Then you can make changes to the value of the variable in the function. You can also pass a reference variable to the function and make changes to the value of the variable within the function. When a reference variable is used as a function argument, you must declare it as an `int &` type variable in the function prototype and declaration. Consider the following example:

```
void fcn( int & );
void main()
{
     int x;
     int &rx = x;
     fcn( rx );
}
fcn( int &y )
{
     y = y*3;
}
```

Note that when you refer to a reference variable, you treat it as a normal variable. Note also that with reference variables, you do not have to use the dereference notation that you use with pointers.

REFER2.CPP, shown in Listing 12.9, illustrates what happens if you pass a variable, a pointer to the variable, and a reference variable to a function.

Listing 12.9. The source listing for REFER2.CPP.

```
// REFER2.CPP - Demonstrates use of a reference variable to
// pass a variable by reference (the address of the variable)
// to a function
#include <iostream.h>
void addtwo1( int i );     // Pass argument by value
void addtwo2( int &j );    // Pass argument using reference var.
void addtwo3( int *k );    // Pass argument using pointer
void main()
{
```

continues

Listing 12.9. continued

```
     int actualvalue = 3;
     int &alternatevalue = actualvalue;

     cout << "Actual value = " << actualvalue;
     cout << ", alias  = " << alternatevalue << "\n";

     addtwo1( actualvalue );     // Pass argument by value
     cout << "Actual value = " << actualvalue;
     cout << ", alias  = " << alternatevalue << "\n";

     addtwo2( alternatevalue ); // Use reference
     cout << "Actual value = " << actualvalue;
     cout << ", alias  = " << alternatevalue << "\n";

     addtwo3( &actualvalue );    // Pass argument by reference
                                 // using pointer
     cout << "Actual value = " << actualvalue;
     cout << ", alias  = "  << alternatevalue << "\n";
}
void addtwo1( int i )            // Pass argument by value
{
     i = i + 2;
}
void addtwo2( int &i )  // Pass argument using reference var.
{
     i = i + 2;
}
void addtwo3( int *i )  // Pass argument using pointer
{
     *i = *i + 2;
}
```

The value of the variable `actualvalue` is not changed when it is passed as an argument to the function `addtwo1()`, because the variable is passed by value. However, when its reference variable, `alternatevalue`, is passed to the `addtwo2()` function, its value is incremented by two. The value of `actualvalue` is also incremented by two when a pointer (`&actualvalue`) is passed to the function `addtwo3()`. The following results of executing REFER2.EXE display the value of `actualvalue` (and its reference) after each function is called:

```
Actual value = 3, alias  = 3
Actual value = 3, alias  = 3
Actual value = 5, alias  = 5
Actual value = 7, alias  = 7
```

Pointers and References

References are similar to pointers in that you can refer to the associated variables. However, you need the dereferencing notation when you use a pointer. Note the following examples:


```
int var;           // Declare int variable
int &rvar = var;   // Declare reference variable (refers to var)
int *ptr = &var;   // Declare pointer (to var)
var  = 3;          // Assign value to var
rvar = 3;          // Assign value to var using reference
*ptr = 3;          // Assign value to var using pointer
```

You cannot manipulate a reference variable as you can a pointer. You cannot point to, modify, or assign a value to the actual reference variable. You cannot do any "pointer type arithmetic" on a reference variable. If you try to do any of these operations on a reference variable, the operation will be performed on the variable to which the reference variable refers. In the preceding example, if you use

```
ptr++;
rvar++;
```

the address to which the pointer points will be incremented, and the value of the variable `var` will be incremented.

Using References to Return Values

You can use references to return a value from a function, as illustrated in REFER3.CPP in Listing 12.10.

Listing 12.10. The source listing for REFER3.CPP.

```
// REFER3.CPP - Demonstrates use of a function returning
// a reference to an int variable
#include <iostream.h>

int i_val = 3;          // Global int variable
int &func( void )       // Note that addtwo() returns a
                        // reference to int
{
    return i_val;       // Returns reference to i_val
}
void main()
{
     int i;
     i = func();        // i is initialized to i_val (3)
     cout << "i     = " << i    << "\n";
     cout << "func()= " << func() << "\n";
     func() = 5;        // Because func() is an alias for i_val,
                        // it can be an lvalue (on the left side
                        // of the equal sign)
     cout << "func()= " << func() << "\n";
     cout << "i_val = " << i_val  << "\n";
}
```

In this example, the function `func()` returns the global value `i_val`. For this reason, the function effectively behaves as an alias for `i_val`. Because `func()` is a reference to a variable, the function can even be placed on the left side of an equal sign. The statement

```
func() = 5;
```

is legal and actually assigns a new value (5) to `i_val`.

Here are the results of executing REFER3.EXE:

```
i     = 3
func()= 3
func()= 5
i_val = 5
```

This is a "do nothing" example to demonstrate how references are used to return a value from a function. Later, you will learn that returning a reference from a function is extremely useful with structures and classes.

You should use reference variables only for passing arguments to a function or returning a reference from a function. For any other operation, you should use the variable and not its associated reference variable.

Using References with a Structure

Reference variables are much more useful when you use them to reference a structure or a class than when you use them with basic data types. References are used for structures the same way they are used for basic data type variables. You just prefix the reference variable name with an ampersand (&), as in the following example:


```
struct animal
{
    char name[20];
    char type[20];
    int  number;
}
animal dog;      // Declare a struct type animal variable
animal &aref;    // Declare a reference to a struct type animal
                 // variable
```

Here `aref` is a reference variable to an `animal` structure.

REFER4.CPP, the program in Listing 12.11, demonstrates how a reference to a structure can be passed to a function, `display()`, and how `display()` returns a reference to a structure. Because `display()` returns a reference to the structure `zoo`, `display()` can be used also as an argument, as shown in the program. The function `display()` displays members of a `zoo` type structure and increments the `displaycnt` member.

Listing 12.11. The source listing for REFER4.CPP.

```
// REFER4.CPP - Demonstrates how to use a reference variable
// with a structure, how to pass a reference to a structure,
// and how a function returns a reference to a structure
#include <iostream.h>

struct zoo    // Structure template for structure zoo
{
```

continues

Listing 12.11. continued

```
    char name[20];
    char type[20];
    int  displaycnt;
    int  age;
};
zoo &display( zoo & animal ); // Note: prototype returns
                              // reference
void main()
{
     zoo monkey =
     {
          "Hillard",
          "Capuchin monkey",
          0,
          4
     };
     zoo tiger =
     {
          "Howard",
          "Siberian tiger",
          0,
          6
     };
     zoo what =
     {
          "none",
          "Empty cage",
          0,
          0
     };

display( monkey );     // Use structure as an argument     (1)
cout << "Monkey was displayed (2) \n\n";
display( display( tiger ) );   // Use display as argument  (2)
cout << "Tiger was displayed  (2) \n\n";
display( what ) = monkey;      // Return tiger to what     (3)
cout << "What was displayed?  (3) \n\n";
display (what);                // Display what's in what   (4)
}
// Display: displays zoo animal and increments show count
zoo &display( zoo &animal )
```

```
{
     cout << "Name of animal:     " << animal.name << "\n";
     cout << " Type of animal:    " << animal.type << "\n";
     cout << " Age:               " << animal.age  << "\n";
     cout << " # times displayed: "
          << animal.displaycnt++  << "\n";
return animal;
}
```

Listing 12.12 show the results of executing REFER4.EXE.

Listing 12.12. The results of executing REFER4.EXE.

```
Name of animal:     Hillard
 Type of animal:    Capuchin monkey
 Age:               4
 # times displayed: 0
Monkey was displayed (1)

Name of animal:     Howard
 Type of animal:    Siberian tiger
 Age:               6
 # times displayed: 0

Name of animal:     Howard
 Type of animal:    Siberian tiger
 Age:               6
 # times displayed: 1
Tiger was displayed (2)

Name of animal:     none
 Type of animal:    Empty cage
 Age:               0
 # times displayed: 0
What was displayed? (3)

Name of animal:     Hillard
 Type of animal:    Capuchin monkey
 Age:               4
 # times displayed: 1
```

The program first illustrates passing an argument to the function display(), which is a reference to a structure:

```
display( monkey );      // Use structure as an argument     (1)
```

The type zoo structure variable monkey is passed to display(). The name animal becomes an alias name for monkey. animal members are displayed, which means that monkey members are displayed as shown in Listing 12.12. The structure member animal.displaycnt is incremented. In reality, however, monkey.displaycnt is incremented. The returned structure zoo reference is ignored.

The program next calls the display() function with the display() function as its argument:

```
display( display( tiger ) );  // Use display as argument  (2)
```

This statement essentially calls the function twice. The first time, the tiger members are displayed, and a reference to tiger is returned. Then the expression reduces to

```
display( animal );    // animal is a reference to tiger
```

The tiger members are displayed a second time, as shown in Listing 12.12. A function that returns a reference is actually an alternative name for a variable that is referred to.

Now it is time to examine something different. The next call to display() is on the left side of the equal sign!

```
display( what ) = monkey;      // Return tiger to what      (3)
```

Notice what is happening. First the program evaluates the function display(). It displays the members of structure what and increments displaycnt. Then the program returns the structure what. The expression becomes

```
what = monkey;
```

In C++ you can assign the contents of one structure or class to another. The contents of structure what are replaced with the contents of structure monkey. The display() function is again called, and the new contents of what are displayed:

```
Name of animal:      Hillard
 Type of animal:     Capuchin monkey
 Age:                4
 # times displayed: 1
```

Notice that `what` contains the contents of `monkey`.

> In C++ you can assign a value, structure, or class to a function only if the function returns a reference to a variable.

Libraries of Functions

All versions of the C++ language come with a run-time library of functions that provides support for frequently used operations. Some of these library functions have been used in sample programs earlier in this book.

The Microsoft C/C++ run-time library contains about 400 standard functions. Table 12.2 lists the categories of functions included in the MS-DOS run-time library.

Table 12.2. Categories of Microsoft C/C++ 7 run-time library functions.

Function Category	*Description*
Buffer manipulation	Manipulates areas of memory
Character classification	Tests individual characters
Data conversion	Converts strings and numbers
File handling	Performs file and directory operations
I/O (streams)	Processes stream I/O
I/O (low-level)	Processes low-level I/O
I/O (console and port)	Processes console and port I/O
Internationalization	Changes time and other items for international formats
Math	Performs common math manipulations
Memory allocation	Allocates, frees, and reallocates memory

continues

Table 12.2. continued

Function Category	*Description*
Process control	System process-control operations
Searching and sorting	Performs binary and linear searches and sorting
String manipulation	Processes null-terminated strings
Time	Converts system time formats
Variable-length arguments	Processes functions with a variable number of arguments

In C++ programs, files with the .h extension are known as ***header*** files or *include* files; they contain such statements as run-time library function prototypes, definitions of constants, and structures needed by run-time library functions. The `#include` preprocessor directive instructs the compiler to replace the `#include` directive with the contents of the specified file, as in the following example:

```
#include <iostream.h>    // C++ I/O stream header file
```

Table 12.3 lists the Microsoft C/C++ 7 run-time header files and their contents.

Table 12.3. The Microsoft C/C++ 7 header files.

Filename	*Major Contents*
assert.h	Definition of the `assert` debugging macro
bios.h	BIOS service function declarations and support
conio.h	Console and port I/O routine declarations
ctype.h	Character-classification macros
direct.h	Disk directory control function declarations
dos.h	Function declarations for MS-DOS interface
errno.h	System-wide error number (`errno`) variable definitions
fcntl.h	Flags used in `_open()` and `_sopen()` functions

Filename	Major Contents
float.h	Constants needed by math functions
io.h	File handling and low-level I/O
limits.h	Ranges of integers and character types
locale.h	Contains structure definitions, values for functions, and macros used by localization functions
malloc.h	Memory-allocation function declarations
math.h	Floating-point math routines
memory.h	Buffer-manipulation routines
process.h	Process-control function declarations and definitions
search.h	Searching and sorting function declarations
setjmp.h	`setjmp()` and `longjmp()` function declarations and definitions
share.h	Flags used in `_sopen()` function
signal.h	Constants used by `signal()` function
stdarg.h	Macros for variable-length argument-list functions
stddef.h	Commonly used data types and values
iostream.h	Standard C++ I/O header file
stdlib.h	Commonly used library function declarations and definitions
string.h	String-manipulation function declarations and definitions
time.h	General `time()` function declarations and definitions
varargs.h	Variable-length argument-list function declarations and definitions
vmemory.h	Virtual memory allocation functions
sys\locking.h	Flags used by locking function

continues

12

Table 12.3. continued

Filename	*Major Contents*
sys\stat.h	File-status structures and function declarations and definitions
sys\timeb.h	`time()` function declarations and definitions
sys\types.h	Types returned by system-level call for file and time information
sys\utime.h	Definitions and declarations for `_utime()` function

The following header files are used for Windows programming:

Filename	*Major Contents*
custcntl.h	Custom control library
dde.h	DDE window messages and structures
drivint.h	Printer driver initialization
windows.h	Windows API

What You Have Learned

This chapter discussed the elements of functions and showed ways to use functions. You learned the following:

- How to call functions
- Why and how to use prototypes
- How to use recursive functions
- How to overload function names
- How to use reference variables

Part III

Advanced Features of C and C++

More Operators

To most people nothing is more troublesome than the effort of thinking.

—James Bryce
Studies in History and Jurisprudence (1901)

In This Chapter

So far, you have learned about the basic elements of the C++ language, and you can write some useful C++ programs. There are still some topics you haven't encountered, and there is more to learn about pointers and structures. These topics and many others are explored in Chapters 13 through 15, and in Part IV, "C++ Object-Oriented Features."

In this chapter, you are introduced to more operators. Although they are not used as frequently as the operators discussed in Chapter 8, these operators are important elements of the C++ language. In this chapter, you learn more about the following:

- Bitwise logical operators
- Conditional operators
- The `sizeof` operator

Bitwise Operators

A byte of memory consists of eight bits. Each bit can have a value of 0 or 1. Using *bitwise logical* operators, you can manipulate data at the bit level or compare the bit sequence of two integer operands (see Table 13.1). The operands used as examples in this table are two `int` data type variables, `a` and `b`.

Table 13.1. Bitwise logical operators.

Operator	*Symbol*	*Example*	*Result*
Right-shift	`>>`	`a >> b`	`a` is shifted `b` bits to the right.
Left-shift	`<<`	`a << b`	`a` is shifted `b` bits to the left.
Bitwise AND	`&`	`a & b`	`a` is bitwise ANDed with `b`.
Bitwise OR (inclusive OR)	`¦`	`a ¦ b`	`a` is bitwise ORed with `b`.
Bitwise XOR (exclusive OR)	`^`	`a ^ b`	`a` is bitwise exclusive ORed with `b`.
Bitwise	`~`	`~a`	The bitwise complement of a complement.

All the bitwise operations are similar to the low-level assembly language instructions.

Shift Operators

You can use *shift* operators to shift `int`, `char`, or `long` expressions a specified number of bits to the right or left. In the following example, the `int i` is shifted four bits to the right and displayed:

```
int i = 0x30;
cout << "i = "
     << hex
     << i               // Display int values in hex
     << " i >> 4 = "
     << (i >> 4)        // Shift i 4 bits to the right
     << "\n";
```

The results are

```
i = 0030  i >> 4 = 0003
```

The hexadecimal, binary, and decimal representations of the operand and the resulting value of the preceding example are shown here:

Hex Value	*Binary Value*	*Decimal*
0030	00000000 00110000	24
0003	00000000 00000011	3

Note that shifting a number to the right is equivalent to dividing that number by a power of 2. Similarly, shifting a number to the left is equivalent to multiplying that number by a power of 2. In other words, `a >> b` is equivalent to `a / 2b`; and `a << b` is equivalent to `a * 2b`. As a consequence, the shift operators provide a fast way to multiply or divide an integer by a power of 2.

As you shift an integer to the left, the rightmost bits are filled with zeros. As you shift a positive integer to the right, the leftmost bits are filled with zeros. And as you shift a negative integer to the right, the leftmost bits are filled with ones. For example, the expression

```
-16 >> 2
```

yields –4. Here are the binary representations of the numbers in this expression:

–16	11111111 11110000
–16 >> 2	11111111 11111100

Now that you are working with bitwise operators, you need to understand binary numbers. When you are trying to figure out what a bitwise operation is doing, you usually display a value as a hexadecimal number. A byte (eight bits) is two hexadecimal numbers; a hexadecimal number (four bits) can be converted easily to a binary number. After converting a hexadecimal digit to a binary number, you can look at each bit. Table 13.2 shows a conversion table with the binary value for the value of each hexadecimal number.

Table 13.2. The binary conversion table.

Decimal	*Hexadecimal*	*Binary*
0	0	0000
1	1	0001
2	2	0010
3	3	0011
4	4	0100
5	5	0101
6	6	0110
7	7	0111
8	8	1000
9	9	1001
10	A	1010
11	B	1011
12	C	1100
13	D	1101
14	E	1110
15	F	1111

To give you an idea of how to use this table, the hexadecimal number `0xEAB3` converts to the following binary values:

E	A	B	3
1110	1010	1011	0011

Notice that the hexadecimal number `E` converts to the binary number 1110, `A` converts to 1010, `B` converts to 1011, and `3` converts to 0011.

Logical Bitwise Operators

The bitwise AND (`&`) and OR (`|`) operators are similar to the logical operators `&&` and `||`, except that AND and OR operate on every bit in the operand. The bitwise AND (`&`) and OR (`|`) operators compare each bit in the left operand with the corresponding bit in the right operand. The result is an `int`, a `char`, or a `long` value, with each bit set according to the results of either ANDing or ORing the corresponding bits in the two operands. The bitwise exclusive OR (`^`) operator sets a bit to one if the corresponding bits in the operands are different, or to zero if the corresponding bits are the same. The results of comparing the bits are determined by the logical AND, OR, and XOR rules shown in Table 13.3.

Table 13.3. Rules for comparing bits with logical bitwise operators.

Operand	*Values of Bit*			
Left operand	0	1	0	1
Right operand	0	1	1	0
Result of bitwise AND	0	1	0	0
Result of bitwise OR	0	1	1	1
Result of bitwise exclusive OR	0	0	1	1

The bitwise complement operator (`~`) is a unary operator (it operates on one operand) that takes the *ones complement* of the operand. A ones complement operation reverses the sense of all the bits in the operand. This involves changing the value of each one bit to a zero, and each zero bit to a one. For example, the expression `~9` evaluates to –10. The binary representations of 9 and 10 are 00001001 and 11110110, respectively.

The complement operator (~) is distinguished from the arithmetic minus operator (-) in that the minus operator takes the *twos complement* of an operand, which is the reverse of the sense of all the bits in the operand, and adds one.

Table 13.4 shows examples of bitwise logical operations. The binary representation of the numbers is provided to help you understand the operations.

Table 13.4. Examples of bitwise logical operations.

		Binary Values		
Expression	*Result*	*Left*	*Right*	*Result*
`255 & 7`	7	1111 1111	0000 0111	0000 0111
`255 ¦ 7`	255	1111 1111	0000 0111	1111 1111
`255 ^ 7`	248	1111 1111	0000 0111	1111 1000
`~2`	–3	0000 0010	N/A	1111 1101

At times, programmers like to compact information and save memory by *packing* logical-type information into a single `int` data value. Suppose, for example, that you have the following eight binary-type pieces of information about a person:

1. Male or Female
2. Married: Yes or No
3. Children: Yes or No
4. U.S. Citizen: Yes or No
5. Veteran: Yes or No
6. Employed: Yes or No
7. Retired: Yes or No
8. College Degree: Yes or No

You can store all this information in a single byte of memory, with a zero representing one state and a one representing the other state. In the example in Listing 13.1, a `typedef` structure defines the structure type, or *tag*, named `PEOPLE`. `PEOPLE` has three members:

- The person's name, stored in a `char` array (`name`)
- An `int` variable (`age`) that represents the person's age
- An `int` variable (`personal_info`) that contains the packed information about the person

In this listing, an array of structures is declared with three elements, each of which is a structure of type `PEOPLE`. The array is initialized with data. Another array of strings contains titles for the display of personal information.

Listing 13.1. The source listing for PEOPLE.CPP.

```
// PEOPLE.CPP - Illustrates use of arrays of structures
// and bitwise operations
#include <iostream.h>
void show_status( char *label, int info, int bit,
                  char *s1, char *s2 );
struct people
     {
          char name[20];
          int age;
          int personal_info;
     };
void main( void )
{
     char c = 'x';
     int i, j;
     people pdata[3] =
     {
          { "Joe Smith",   32, 95  },
          { "Mary Jones",  49, 254 },
          { "Sam Houston", 92, 1 }
     };
     char *title[] =
     {
          {"Sex"},
          {"Married"},
          {"Children"},
```

continues

13

Listing 13.1. continued

```
          {"US Citizen"},
          {"Veteran"},
          {"Employed"},
          {"Retired"},
          {"College Degree"},
     };
     while (c != '0')
     {
          cout << "\nEnter the first letter of "
               << "a name or 0 to exit: ";
          cin >> c;
          for ( i=0; i<3; i++ )
          {
               if ( pdata[i].name[0] == c )
               {
                    cout << "\n          Personal Data\n";
                    cout << "Name: "
                         << pdata[i].name
                         << "                   Age "
                         << pdata[i].age << "\n";
                    show_status( title[0],
                       pdata[i].personal_info,
                       0, "Male", "Female" );
                    for ( j = 1; j<7; j++ )
                    {
                         show_status( title[j],
                            pdata[i].personal_info,
                            j, "Yes", "No" );
                    }
               }
          }
     };
}
void show_status( char *label, int info, int bit,
                  char *s1, char *s0 )
{
     char *s;
          // Shift bit number to rightmost bit position
```

```
        // AND test it
    if ( (info >> bit) & 1 )
        s = s1;        // Print s1 message if bit is 1
    else
        s = s0;        // Print s0 message if bit is 0
    cout << label << ": " << s <<  "\n";
}
```

The personal information is packed in the eight low-order bits of the `int` variable `pdata[i].personal_info`. The function `show_status()` displays one of two messages, based on the value of the specified bit. For example, if the low-order bit is 0, the person is female; if the low-order bit is 1, the person is male. Figure 13.1 shows the meaning of each bit.

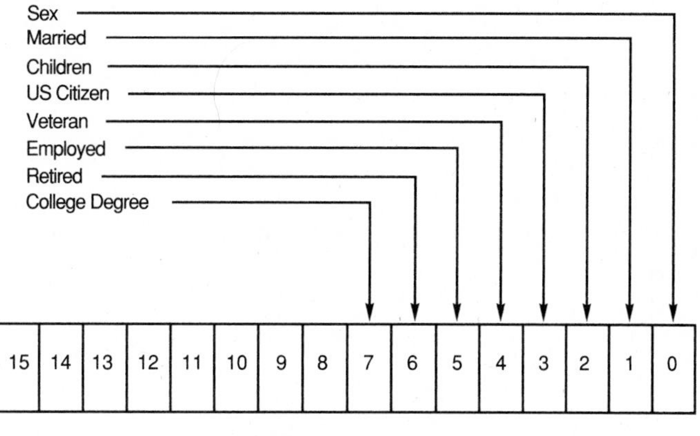

Figure 13.1. *Bit usage in PEOPLE.CPP.*

To examine one of the status bits, this program shifts the local variable (formal argument) `info` to the right until it is in the low-order position (bit 0). Then the program ANDs the shifted value with 1. If the bit is 1, the program prints `Yes`; otherwise, the program prints `No`. In the sample printout shown in Listing 13.2, the `info` integer for Mary Jones is the binary number 0000 1111 1110 (254 decimal or 0xFE hexadecimal). All values except her sex bit are one; her sex bit (zero) indicates that she is female.

Listing 13.2. Output from executing PEOPLE.EXE.

```
Enter the first letter of a name or 0 to exit: M
          Personal Data
Name: Mary Jones       Age 49
 Sex: Female
 Married: Yes
 Children: Yes
 US Citizen: Yes
 Veteran: Yes
 Employed: Yes
 Retired: Yes
Enter the first letter of a name or 0 to exit: 0
```

This example contains a couple of constructs that deserve additional comment. Consider the following `typedef` definition for the structure-type `PEOPLE`, and the declaration and initialization of the three-element array. Each element is a structure of type `PEOPLE`:

```
struct PEOPLE
     {
          char name[20];
          int age;
          int personal_info;
     };
PEOPLE pdata[3] =
     {
          { "Joe Smith",   32, 95  },
          { "Mary Jones",  49, 254 },
          { "Sam Houston", 92, 1 }
     };
```

Figure 13.2 illustrates how the three elements in the array `pdata` are stored in memory.

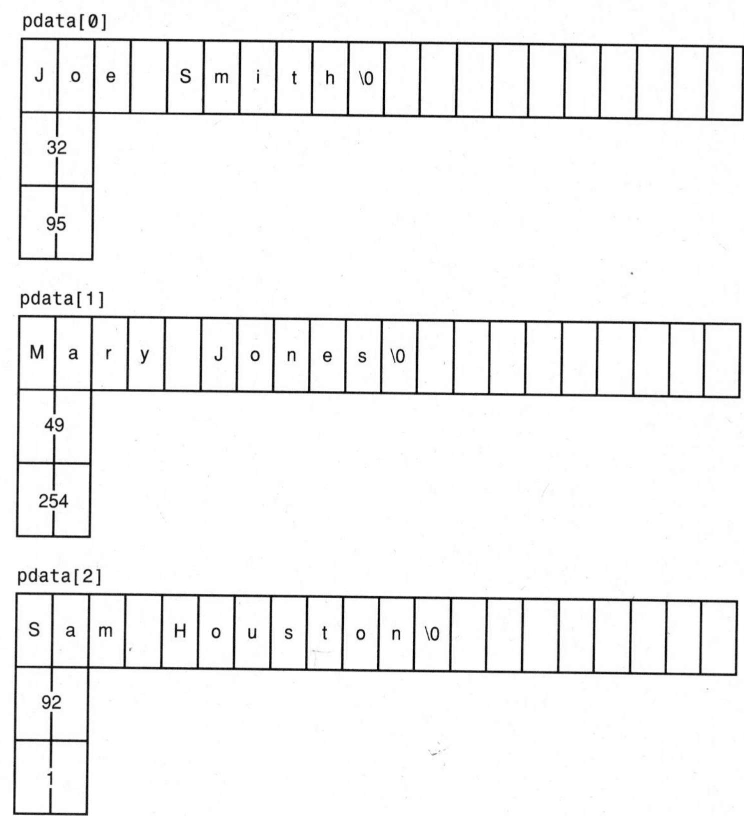

Figure 13.2. *The three elements in the array* `pdata` *stored in memory.*

13

Conditional Operator

The conditional operator—the only operator with three operands—is called a *ternary* operator. Although referred to by some people as an abbreviated form of the `if-else` statement, this operator is more than that; it can be inside an expression. The conditional operator has two symbols: ? and :. Its form is

results = *expression*$_1$? *expression*$_2$: *expression*$_3$

If `expression`$_1$ evaluates to a nonzero value, the results are assigned the value of `expression`$_2$. Otherwise, the value of `expression`$_3$ is assigned o `results`. `expression`$_1$ and `expression`$_2$ must evaluate to a scalar-type variable and can be any data type.

Consider the following `if-else` program fragment:

```
if j > 0
     x=3;
else
     x=4;
```

The conditional operator can be used to do the same thing:

```
x = j > 0 ? 3 : 4;
```

In both cases, if `j > 0`, `x` is set to 3. Otherwise, `x` is set to 4.

Some programmers discourage the use of conditional operators because they believe that code containing conditional operators is difficult to read. For example, the statement

```
if ( a<b && d>3 )
     x = 34.5L * sqrt( ( 1.0L - y*y ) / 2 );
else
     x = 42.0L * zulu( ( z * z )/321.234 );
```

is more readable than

```
x = a<b && d>3 ? 34.5L * sqrt( ( 1.0L - y*y ) / 2 ) :
   42.0L * zulu( ( z * z )/321.234 );
```

The conditional operator can be helpful at times, however. For instance, you can reduce the size of the program

```
if ( a > b )
     cout << "Value = " <<  a;
else
     cout << "Value = " <<  b;
```

by using the following statement:

```
cout << "Value = " << (a > b) ? a : b;
```

You eliminate two output statements and a duplicate format string.

The sizeof Operator

As you may recall from the discussion in Chapter 11, "Advanced Data Structures," the `sizeof` operator determines the size of a structure. The `sizeof` operator can have an expression or a data type argument, as shown in the following examples:

```
int x;
result = sizeof(x);
result = sizeof(100+99);
result = sizeof(int);
```

For all three of these examples, the variable `result` is assigned a value of 2, the size of an `int`. Here are other examples:

```
char message[] = { "Now is the time" };
result = sizeof(message);     // result = 15, length of string
result = sizeof(char);        // result = 1, char data type size
result = sizeof(int);         // result = 2, int data type size
result = sizeof(float);       // result = 4, float data type size
result = sizeof(double);      // result = 8, double data type size
result = sizeof(long double); // result = 10, long double data
                              // type size
```

Generally, you use the `sizeof` operator to find the size of a structure or array (refer to the section "Structures" in Chapter 11).

13

What You Have Learned

This chapter examined operators in more detail. You learned the following:

- How to use the bitwise logical operators to set and clear individual bits in a variable
- How to use the conditional operator effectively
- That the conditional operator is the only C++ language operator with three operands
- How to use the `sizeof` operator

14

Pointers

All things are difficult before they are easy.

—Thomas Fuller, M.D.
Gnomologia (1732)

In This Chapter

I have been told that learning to use pointers is like learning to ride a bicycle. I'm not so sure. In getting to the point where you fully understand pointers, you will encounter many plateaus—you'll reach a particular level of understanding, stabilize there for a while, and then move on to learn additional information.

A simple pointer to a string is easy to understand, but complex pointers can get pretty challenging. Don't panic—the more you use pointers, the clearer they become. This chapter covers the following topics:

- Declaring and using pointers
- String constants
- Advanced techniques in using arrays and pointers
- Calling pointers as function arguments
- Pointers to pointers, functions, and structures
- Memory allocation and pointers

Declaring Pointers

The discussion of pointers begins with a review of a pointer declaration statement. You can have a pointer point to just about any type of object, including the following:

- Scalar variables
- Arrays
- Structures
- Elements of an array
- Another pointer
- Arrays of pointers
- Dynamically allocated memory blocks
- Functions

As you know, you declare a pointer variable by preceding its name with an asterisk (*). Here are some examples of pointers of varied complexity:

```
int  *ptr1;        // Pointer to an int data type
long *ptr2;        // Pointer to a long data type
char *ptr3;        // Pointer to a char data type
char *ptr4 = {"Don't Panic"};
                   // Pointer to a string
int  **ptr5;       // Pointer to a pointer that points to
                   // an int data type
int  *ptr6[];      // Arrays of pointers to int
```

```
int  (*ptr7)[];      // Pointer to an array of int elements
int  *(*ptr8)[]      // Pointer to an array of pointers to int
PEOPLE *ptr9;        // Pointer to structure type PEOPLE (from
                     // Chapter 13)
char *ptr10();       // Function that returns a pointer to a char
char (*ptr11)();     // Pointer to a function that return a char
char (*ptr11[])(); // Array of pointers to functions
                     // returning char
```

In the C++ language, declarations can get rather complicated. Sometimes it is difficult to figure out what is being declared because complex declarations are not readable. Whenever possible, try to simplify a pointer declaration by using intermediate declarations. You also can use `typedef` statements to simplify (hide) complex declarations.

The syntax of a pointer usually makes complex declarations harder to understand. The problem is that the pointer operator (*) is placed to the left of a variable, whereas the array operator for a subscript (`[]`) and the function operator (`()`) follow the variable, as in this example:

```
int   *(*difficult[3])();
```

Here are four rules (to commit to memory) that will help you understand complex declarations:

1. Array operators (`[]`) and function operators (`()`) have a higher precedence than the pointer operator (*).
2. Array and function operators are grouped from left to right. *Grouping* operators refers to the process of binding or attaching an operator to an operand. When you group from left to right, you bind the leftmost operator to the operand first.
3. Pointer operators are grouped from right to left.
4. Parentheses can be used to change the precedence order.

To decipher a complex declaration, start with the variable name and add each part of the declaration, beginning with the operators closest to the variable name. Add the function and array operators on the right side of the variable name first because they have a higher precedence. Then add the pointer operator on the left of the variable name. Parentheses used for grouping override other precedences. Here is a simple example:

```
int *simple[5]
```

The following should help you understand the preceding declaration:

`simple` is a variable name.

`simple[5]` is an array.

`*simple[5]` is an array of pointers.

`int *simple[5]` is an array of pointers to `int` variables.

Table 14.1 summarizes the precedence levels for declarations. To help you decipher a declaration, the *Description* column provides English language replacements for the operators shown in the first column. Use the *Level* column to determine which operator to specify first. The *Placement* column indicates on which side of the variable the operator is placed.

Table 14.1. Precedence levels for declarations.

Operator	*Description*	*Level*	*Placement*
`[]`	Array of	1	After variable
`()`	Function returning	1	After variable
`*`	Pointer to	2	Before variable
type	Data type	3	Before variable

There will be more discussion of operator precedence later in this chapter. The use of pointers is discussed in the following sections, starting with a review of simple pointers.

Simple Pointers

Simple pointers are pointers that point to basic data types. In the lines

```
int  *ptr1;        // Point to an int data type
long *ptr2;        // Point to a long data type
char *ptr3;        // Point to a char data type
```

`ptr1`, `ptr2`, and `ptr3` are pointers that point to scalar variables. Each of these pointers can be initialized in the declaration statement as long as the object to which the pointer points has already been declared. Here are some examples:

```
char c_val = 3;
char *ptr1 = &c_val
int i_val  = 99;    // int type variable
long l_val = 878;
long *ptr3 = &l_val;
```

Note that you also can assign a pointer the address of the object it points to by using the address-of operator (`&`):

```
int *ptr2 = &i_val;
```

Figure 14.1 illustrates how pointers and the variables to which they point are stored in memory. Notice that the value of each pointer is also the address of the variable to which it points.

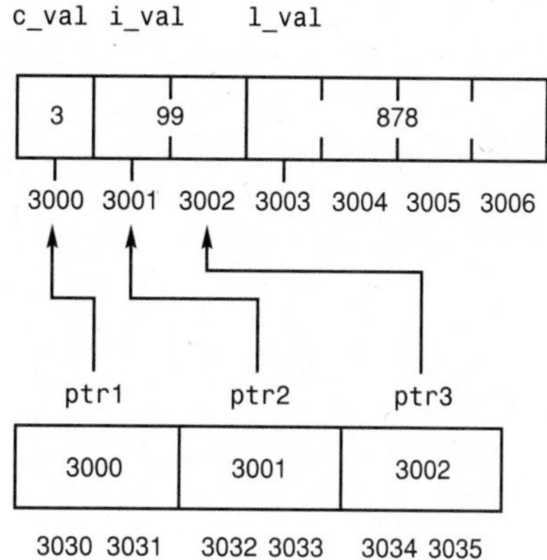

Figure 14.1. *Memory storage of pointers and basic variables.*

14

The data type of the object must be the same as the pointer data type. C++ strictly enforces type rules. If the types differ, the compiler displays the error message `Indirection to different types`. In C you get a warning message, and if you do not take corrective action, pointer arithmetic might not work correctly. In C++ you must repair the indirection error before you are allowed to proceed. There are circumstances in which it is acceptable to initialize a pointer to point to a different type of variable. If this is your intention, use a *cast*. For example, in C you can cast any type pointer to point to another type:

```
extern char *myfunc( int i );  /* C code */
int  *ptr;
char *cptr;
cptr = myfunc (20);
ptr = (int *)myfunc( 25 );
```

In the preceding example, the function `myfunc()` returns a pointer to a `char` in both cases. However, for the assignment of `ptr`, you must type cast the returned pointer to be a pointer to an `int`. Casting eliminates the error message and signals other programmers of your intentions.

In C++ the only way that you can declare a pointer so that it will point to any data type is to declare the pointer as a `void *` pointer. However, you must explicitly type cast the `void *` pointer. In addition, a pointer of any other data type can be explicitly type cast to `void`. Note this example:

```
extern void *myfunc( void *i );  // C++ code
int  *ptr;
char *cptr;
cptr = (char *)myfunc ( (int*)20 );
ptr = (int *)myfunc( (char*)"Message" );
```

String Constants

In the next example, the pointer `ptr4` points to a string constant. The declaration statement creates a string constant (`"Don't  Panic"`) and initializes `ptr4` with the address of the string:

```
char *ptr4 = {"Don't Panic"};
```

Figure 14.2 illustrates how the pointer and string constant are stored in memory. The value of the pointer equals the address of the string constant.

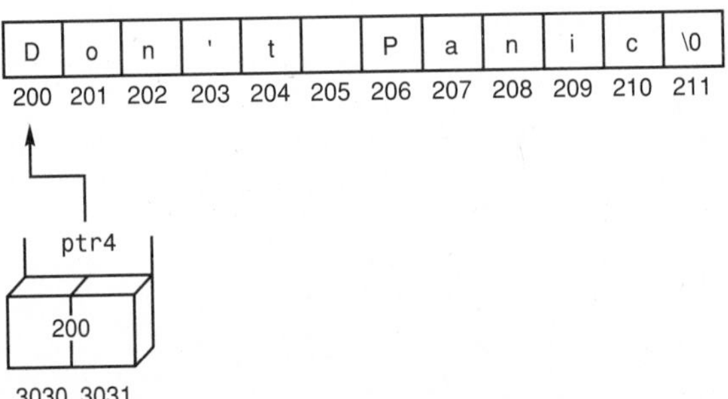

***Figure 14.2.** Memory storage of a pointer and string constant in memory.*

A Pointer to a Pointer

A pointer can point to another pointer variable. This concept is used frequently in complex C++ programs. To declare a pointer to a pointer, precede the variable with two asterisks (**).

In the following example, ptr4 is a pointer to a pointer:

```
int i_val = 99;
int *ptr1 = &i_val;
int **ptr4 = &ptr1;
```

ptr1 and ptr4 are both pointers. ptr1 points to the int variable i_val. ptr4 contains the address of ptr1. The memory storage resulting from these declarations is illustrated in Figure 14.3.

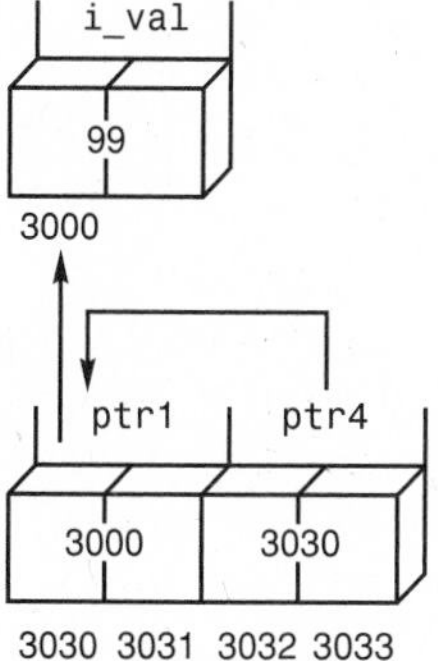

Figure 14.3. *Memory storage of a pointer to a pointer.*

You can assign values to i_val with any of the following statements:

```
i_val = 89;
*ptr1 = 90;     // Assign 90 to i_val
**ptr4 = 91     // Assign 91 to i_val
```

The next example (in Listing 14.1) also shows a pointer to a pointer. Suppose that you want a function which, given a customer's account number, finds the name of the customer. You want the function to return a pointer that points to the customer's name, or a null pointer if the function cannot find the name.

14

A *null pointer* is a pointer that does not point to any valid object A null pointer is assigned a value of zero and is used frequently in C++ programs. Note the following example:

```
int *ptr = (int*) 0; // ptr is a null pointer
```

Never use a null pointer to reference a value. Use null pointers only in a conditional test to determine if a pointer has been initialized. In the example

```
if ( ptr )
   cout << "Value of variable pointed to by ptr is "
        << *ptr << "\n";
```

the test prints a value only if the pointer is valid and is not a null pointer.

Null pointers are used most frequently in programs with arrays of pointers.

In the source file ACCOUNT.CPP in Listing 14.1, the variable `customers` is an array of pointers to string constants. When declared, this variable is initialized with five elements. Each element is a pointer to a string constant containing a customer's name. `accno` is an array of integers representing account numbers. The array elements are initialized to contain five account numbers corresponding to the customer names, plus a sixth value of zero.

Listing 14.1. The source listing for ACCOUNT.CPP.

```
// ACCOUNT.CPP - Illustrates pointer to a pointer
#include <iostream.h>
char     *get_cust( int ac, char **cust, int *acct );
int main()
{
     char *customers[] =
          {
               "Jones, Jerry",
               "Doe, Mary",
               "Smith, Bob",
               "Yeltsin, Boris",
               "Gorbachev, Mikhail"
          };
```

```
     int accno[]  = { 2211, 2222, 9123, 2345, 3333, 0 };
     int account = 1;
     char  *nameptr;
     while ( account )       // Repeat until user enters 0
     {
          cout << "Enter an account number or 0 to exit: ";
          cin  >> account;         // Input account no.
          nameptr = get_cust ( account, customers, accno );
          if ( nameptr )
               cout << "Customer is: " << nameptr << "\n";
          else
           cout << "Account number was not found. Try again\n";
     }
     return 0;
}
char *get_cust( int ac, char **cust, int *acct )
{
          while ( *acct )   // Last member of acct is zero
          {
               if ( ac == *acct )
                    return *cust;  // Return pointer to customer
               *cust++;      // Point to next customer
               acct++;       // Point to next account number
          }
          return '\0';    // Customer was not found
                          // Note: NULL is defined in iostream.h
}
```

Sample output from ACCOUNT.EXE is provided in Listing 14.2.

Listing 14.2. Sample output from ACCOUNT.EXE.

```
Enter an account number or 0 to exit: 2222
Customer is: Doe, Mary
Enter an account number or 0 to exit: 2345
Customer is: Yeltsin, Boris
Enter an account number or 0 to exit: 8888
Account number was not found. Try again
Enter an account number or 0 to exit: 0
Account number was not found. Try again
(program exits)
```

14

Take a close look at ACCOUNT.CPP. You are prompted to enter an account number. If the number you enter is zero, the program exits. If the number is anything other than zero, the function `get_cust()` is called, and three arguments are passed. The first argument is an `int` value that contains the account number (your response). The second argument is a pointer to a pointer. Specifically, it is an array of pointers, and each pointer points to a constant string. Remember, however, that an array is a pointer, and you can use either a subscript or pointer notation to access the same aggregate variable. An array of pointers, therefore, can be represented as a pointer to a pointer. Figure 14.4 illustrates the memory storage of the aggregate variable `customers`.

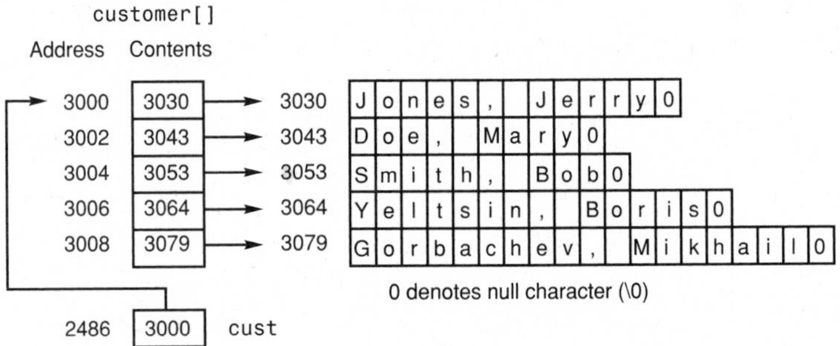

Figure 14.4. Memory storage of the aggregate variable `customers`.

The third argument is an array of integer values and is represented as a pointer to an `int`. Again, `int *acct` is the same as `int acct[]`. Now step through the function `get_cust()`. It begins with a `while` loop:

```
while ( *acct )
```

This statement continues looping as long as the `int` value in the array is not zero. The sixth item in the table is zero, and the other items in the table are account numbers. The next statement compares the user-supplied account number, `ac`, to the account number pointed to by `acct`. Initially, `acct` points to the first account number, which is 2211. Because `ac` equals 2222 in the first example, the `if` test fails. Now consider the next two statements:

```
*cust++;     // Point to next customer
acct++;      // Point to next account number
```

Initially, `cust` points to the first element in the array. Then `cust` is incremented to point to the second element in the array. `acct` is incremented to point to the second account number (2222). Next the `while` loop executes. This time, `*acct` equals `ac` and returns the pointer to `main()`. If `ac` does not match any values in `acct`, a null pointer is returned to `main()`.

The function main() tests the pointer to see if get_cust() returned a valid pointer. If it did, the customer name is displayed; otherwise, the Not found message is displayed.

More on Arrays and Pointers

The relationship between arrays and pointers is discussed in this section. To start, examine the declaration examples involving pointers and arrays, which are found also at the beginning of this chapter:

```
int  *ptr6[];     // Arrays of pointers to int
int  (*ptr7)[];   // Pointer to an array of int elements
int  *(*ptr8)[]   // Pointer to an array of pointers to int
```

In the first example, ptr6 is an array of pointers to int variables, not a pointer to an array of int variables. All you have to do, therefore, is apply the precedence rules. The array operator ([]) has higher precedence than the pointer operator (*). The example

```
static int i=3, j = 99, k = 5, l = 42;
int *ptr6[] = { &i, &j, &k, &l };
```

shows the declaration and initialization of the array of pointers. The array elements are pointers to the int variables i, j, k, and l. Figure 14.5 illustrates how these objects are stored in memory. Notice that the int variables are static because you can't use the address-of operator with an automatic variable as a static initializer.

The second pointer, ptr7, is a pointer to an array. Parentheses are used to override the higher precedence of the array operator. The array contains int values:

```
int ary[] = { 1, 3, 5 };
int *ptr7 = ary;
```

In Figure 14.6, the pointer ptr7 points to the array ary.

The third pointer, ptr8, is a pointer to an array of pointers that point to int variables. Here is how you can decipher ptr8:

ptr8 is a variable name.

(*ptr8) is a pointer to a variable name.

`(*ptr8)[]` is a pointer to an array.

`*(*ptr8)[]` is a pointer to an array of pointers to `int` variables.

`int *(*ptr8)[]` is a pointer to an array of `int` variables.

Note an example of the use of `ptr8`:

```
static int i=3, j = 99, k = 5, l = 42;
int *ary[] = { &i, &j, &k, &l };
int  *(*ptr8)[] = &ary;
cout << "i = " << ***ptr8
     << " j = " << **(*ptr8+1)
     << " k = " << **(*ptr8+2)  << "\n";
```

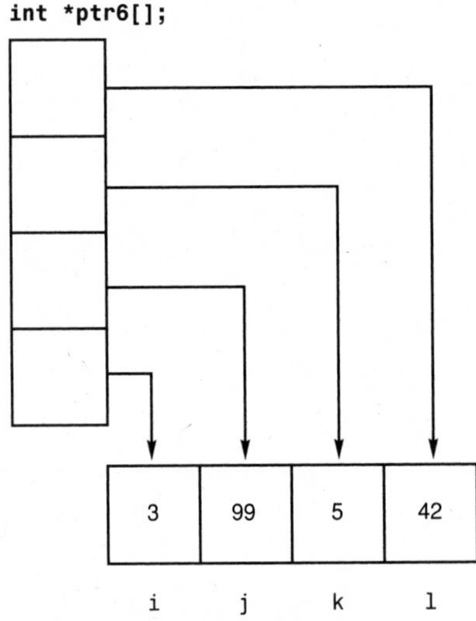

Figure 14.5. Memory storage of `*ptr6[]`.

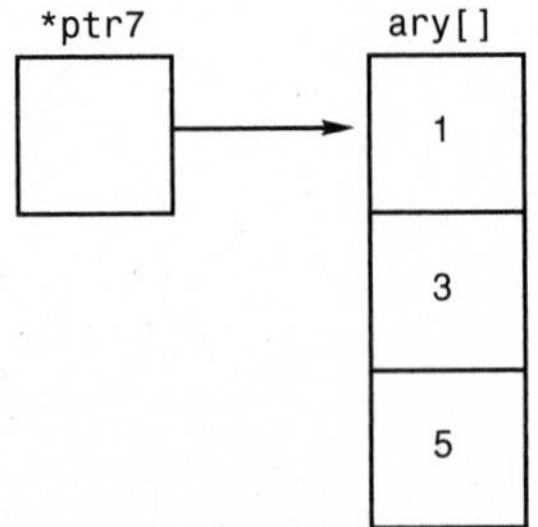

Figure 14.6. Memory storage of `*ptr7[]`.

The output statement displays the following:

```
i = 3  j = 99  k = 5
```

This example shows the declaration and initialization of the array of pointers and also of a pointer to the array. The array elements are pointers to the `int` variables `i`, `j`, `k`, and `l`. Figure 14.7 illustrates how these objects are stored in memory. Notice that the `int` variables are declared as `static`.

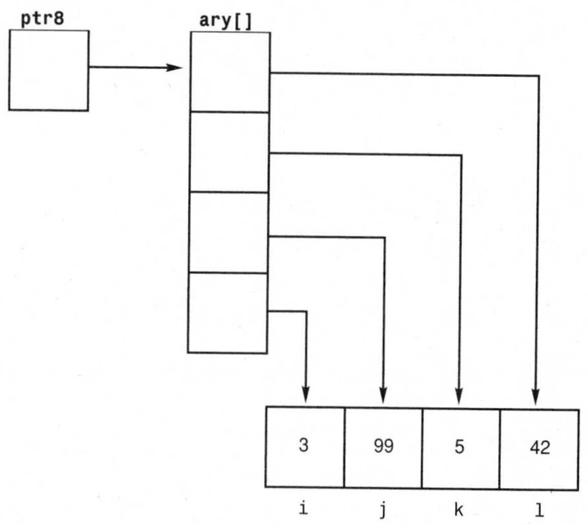

Figure 14.7. *Memory storage of* `*(*ptr8)[]`.

14

Using Pointers as Function Arguments

Although the use of pointers as function arguments was previously discussed, this topic is worth repeating because it is important. As you know, a function can return only a single scalar value. Frequently, you want a function to compute and return more than one value, or you want a function to modify the variables you pass as arguments. When you pass a variable to a function (pass by value), you cannot change the value of that variable. However, if you pass a pointer to a variable to a function (pass by reference), you can change the value of the variable.

When a variable is local to one function, you can make the variable visible to another function by passing it as an argument. You can pass a pointer to a local variable as an argument and change the variable in the other function. In the following example, the address of `i` is passed to `func()`, and `j` is passed by value:

```
int i, j;
i = 3;
j = 2;
func( &i, j );
:
int func( int *s, int t )
{
     *s = 4;
     t = 5;
}
```

When you return from the function `func()`, `i` equals 4, and `j` still equals 2 because `j` was passed by value.

Passing an array name to a function is the same as passing a pointer to the array. You can change any of the elements in the array. When you pass an element to a function, however, the element is passed by value. In the example

```
int ary[] = { 1, 2, 3 };
func( ary[1], ary[2] );
```

both the elements `ary[1]` and `ary[2]` are passed by value.

Pointers to Functions

As indicated earlier, pointers can point to functions. Function pointers are an extremely useful feature of the C++ language because they provide another technique for calling a function based on conditions.

Some of the run-time library functions, such as `qsort()`, require you to pass an argument that consists of a pointer to a function. You must pass to `qsort()` a function pointer that points to a function you supply. The `compare()` function compares two objects and returns a value indicating their relationship.

Before getting more involved in the discussion of function pointers, you should know more about how function declarations are handled by the compiler. First consider the declaration of an array:

```
int array[5];
```

The array name is a pointer to the first element in the array. The compiler places the array name in a list of pointers. Then the compiler reserves memory space for five integers and assigns the address of the first element to the corresponding pointer. A function name is treated in a similar manner. The name becomes a pointer to the function, and the memory address of the function is assigned to the function pointer. The declaration statements for a function and for an array are similar:

```
int fcn( void );
int array[5];
```

Both an array pointer and a function pointer point to some fixed memory address. The array pointer points to its first array element. The function pointer points to the first computer instruction that is executed when the function is executed. It is illegal to change either pointer; you won't get an error message, but your program just won't run properly.

Declarations

You can declare a function pointer that can be used to point to a function. Here is an example:

```
int (*fptr)();
```

Remember the precedence rules. If you do not include the parentheses, you will declare a function that returns a pointer to an integer. The preceding example is a pointer that points to a function which returns an `int` value. You must declare the pointer as a prototype before you use it. The example

```
int *(*fptr)( int x, int y );
```

shows a function pointer that points to a function which returns a pointer to an `int`. The function will have two `int` arguments.

The data type returned by the function must agree with the data type of the function being pointed to.

Assigning Function Pointers

To assign a function to the function pointer, you assign the name of the function to the function pointer. This is analogous to assigning an array name to a pointer. In the following example, the function pointer `fptr` is assigned the address of the run-time library function `strlen()`:

```
extern int strlen( char *s);
int (*fptr)( char *s );      // Declare function pointer
main()
{
     fptr = strlen;          // Assign address of strlen
     :
}
```

It is illegal to place parentheses after the function name, as in

```
fptr = strlen;    // Correct
fptr = strlen();  // Wrong --- Error
fptr = &strlen(); // Wrong --- Error
fptr = &strlen;   // Wrong, but you might get away with it
```

Using a Function Pointer to Call a Function

In Microsoft C/C++ 7 and any other C++ compiler that supports the ANSI standard C and C++ languages, you use the name of the function pointer as you would use a function name. For example, you can use the following statement to call the function pointer assigned in the preceding example:

```
len = fptr(s);
```

With older C compilers, when you made the call by using a function pointer, you had to dereference the function pointer, as in

```
len = (*fptr)(s);
```

> The phrase *to dereference a pointer* means to convert a pointer to the value to which it points.

Both forms of the statement will operate correctly with Microsoft C/C++ 7. The second form, however, is better because it is portable—it will compile and operate correctly for all C and C++ language compilers. Here is a simple example:

```
extern int strlen( char *s );
int (*fptr)( char *s ); // Declare function pointer
main()
{
     char *poe = { "as I pondered weak and weary" };
     int len;
     fptr = strlen;      // Assign address of strlen
     len = fptr( poe );
     cout << "The length of the message is " << len  << "\n";
}
```

The address of the run-time library function `strlen()` is assigned to the function pointer `fptr`. Next `fptr` is called. Because `fptr` points to `strlen()`, `strlen()` is called and returns the length of the string `poe`.

Function Pointers Used as Function Arguments

It is common to develop a generalized function that can be used for many different applications. Certain algorithms used by the generalized function might differ from application to application. Suppose that you have a program to sort a table of values. You want to sort a table of strings in ascending order in one part of your program, and sort a table of numbers in descending order in another part of the program. One solution is to duplicate the function for each application and add to each copy whatever specialized code is required. A better way of solving this problem, however, is to pass the generalized function an argument that is a pointer pointing to a user-defined function. You can write a customized user-defined function for each application.

To pass the name of a function as a function argument, just specify the name of the function as the argument. Suppose that you want to pass the myfunc() function to the yourfunc() function. Use the following statements:

```
void yourfunc( int (*f)() ); // Prototype for yourfunc()
int myfunc( int i );         // Prototype for myfunc()
main()
{
     :
     yourfunc( myfunc );
}
int myfunc( int i )
{
     return 3-i;
}
```

In the called function, you declare the passed function as a function pointer:

```
void yourfunc( void (*f)() )
{
:
     j = f( 3 );
:
}
```

The Microsoft C/C++ run-time library function qsort() is an example of such a generalized function. It uses the *quicksort* algorithm to sort an array of any data type. You must supply a function to compare the relationships of array elements. In the example in Listing 14.3, the compare() function is passed to qsort(). The compare() function compares entries from the array table and returns a negative number if arg1 is less than arg2. compare() returns a zero if they are equal, or a positive number if arg1 is greater than arg2.

Listing 14.3. The source listing for SORT1.CPP.

```
// SORT1.CPP - Sorts using run-time library quicksort algorithm
#include <iostream.h>
#include <search.h>    // Header file with prototype for qsort()
int compare( const void *arg1, const void *arg2 );
void main()
{
     int i, j, temp, test;
     int table[10] = { 9, 23, 1, 91, 8, 34, 12, 19, 3, 18 };
```

```
 // Sort table using quicksort algorithm (from run-time library)
     qsort( (void *)table, (size_t)10, sizeof( int ), compare );

     cout << "Sorted table: \n";
     for ( i = 0; i < 10; i++)
          cout << " " << table[i];
     return;
}

// Compare two elements of array table
int compare( const void *arg1, const void *arg2 )
{
     return *(int*)arg1 - *(int*)arg2;
}
```

Here is the output from this program:

```
Sorted table: 1 3 8 9 12 18 19 23 34 91
```

The `qsort()` function parameters are the following:

`(void *)table`	Array containing values to sort
`(size_t)10`	Number of elements of array
`sizeof(int)`	Size in bytes of each array element
`compare`	Name of the function that compares two array elements

14

Arrays of Function Pointers

Certain applications require that you have numerous functions called *based numerous conditions*. One way to implement such an application is to use a `switch` statement with many `case` statements (see the section "The switch Statement" in Chapter 9, "Making Decisions"). Another solution is to use an array of function pointers. You can select a function from the list and call it.

Now consider the declaration for an array of function pointers returning `int` values:

`func` is the name of an object.

func[] is an array.

(*func[]) is an array of pointers.

(*func[])() is an array of pointers to functions.

int (*func[])() is an array of pointers to functions that return int variables.

You can assign the address of the functions to the array, providing the functions have already been declared. Here is an example:

```
int func1( int i, int j);
int func2( int i, int j);
int (*func[])() = { func1, func2 };
```

The func2() function can be called with the following statement:

```
i = func[1]( j, k );
```

Listing 14.4 shows the use of an array of function pointers. CALC1.CPP is a simple calculator program that can add, subtract, multiply, or divide numbers. You type a simple expression (such as 45*23), and the program displays an answer. The program uses a table of operators, operators[], and a corresponding array of pointers to functions, func. The program searches for the operator and calls the appropriate function to perform the operation.

Listing 14.4. The source listing for CALC1.CPP.

```
// CALC1.CPP - Illustrates pointers to functions
#include <iostream.h>
float add( float x, float y );
float sub( float x, float y );
float mult( float x, float y );
float div( float x, float y );
float (*f)( float x, float y );
void main()
{
     char sign, operators[] = { '+', '-', '*', '/' };
     float     (*func[])( float, float )=
               { add, sub, mult, div };
     int tokens, i;
     float x, y, z;
     char image[80];

     cout << "          Calculator\nExpression: ";
```

```
    cin >> x >> sign >> y;
    for ( i=0; i < 4; i++ )         // Look for operator
        {
         if ( sign == operators[i] ) // Is it +, -, *, or /?
         {
              f = func[i];
              z = f( x, y );
              cout << "\n"  << x
                   << " "   << sign
                   << " "   << y
                   << " = " << z;
              break;
        }
    }
}
float add( float x, float y )
{
    return x + y;
}
float sub( float x, float y )
{
    return x - y;
}
float mult( float x, float y )
{
    return x * y;
}
float div( float x, float y )
{
    return x / y;
}
```

14

Pointers to Structures

A pointer also can point to a structure. You can declare a pointer to a structure just as you declare a pointer to any other object. Consider this structure definition:

```
struct people      // Declare the template
```

```
{
    char name[20];
    int age;
    int height;
    int weight;
};
people person =     // Create a structure
{
    "Smith, Joe", 72, 180
};

people *p;          // Create a structure pointer
p = &person;
```

You declare a structure pointer just as you declare any other structure variable: by specifying a pointer (the name preceded by an asterisk) instead of the structure variable name.

When you reference a structure member by using the structure name, you specify the structure and member name separated by a period (.). For example, to reference the name of a person, use `person.name`.

When you reference a structure member by using the structure pointer, you specify the structure and member name separated by a two-character *pointer-to-member operator*. This operator is a hyphen followed by a right-angle bracket (->). To reference the name of a person with a structure pointer, use `p->name`.

In the example shown in Listing 14.5, an array of structures, `beings`, is declared and initialized. A structure pointer, `p`, is initialized to point to the first element of the structure array. The members of each element are displayed. Notice that when you increment the structure pointer (`p`), it moves to the beginning of the next element of the array.

Listing 14.5. The source listing for PEOPLE1.CPP.

```
// PEOPLE1.CPP - Illustrates use of structure pointer
#include <iostream.h>

struct people                // Declare the template
{
    char name[20];
    int age;
    int height;
```

```
    int weight;
};
void show_person( people *ptr );
void main()
{
    int     i;
    people beings[] =       // Create structure
    {
        { "Smith, Joe",  34, 72, 180 },
        { "Jones, Mary", 39, 64, 140 },
        { "Newton, Fig", 91, 70, 200 },
    };
    people *p;              // Create a structure pointer
    p = beings;
    for ( i = 0; i < 3; i++ , p++ )
        show_person( p );
}
void show_person( people *ptr )
{
    cout << "Name: "     << ptr->name
         << "  Age: "    << ptr->age
         << "  Height: " << ptr->height
         << "  Weight: " << ptr->weight << "\n";
}
```

When PEOPLE1.EXE executes, the following output is displayed:

```
Name: Smith, Joe  Age: 34  Height: 72  Weight: 180
Name: Jones, Mary  Age: 39  Height: 64  Weight: 140
Name: Newton, Fig  Age: 91  Height: 70  Weight: 200
```

Figure 14.8 illustrates the memory storage used by the structure `beings`.

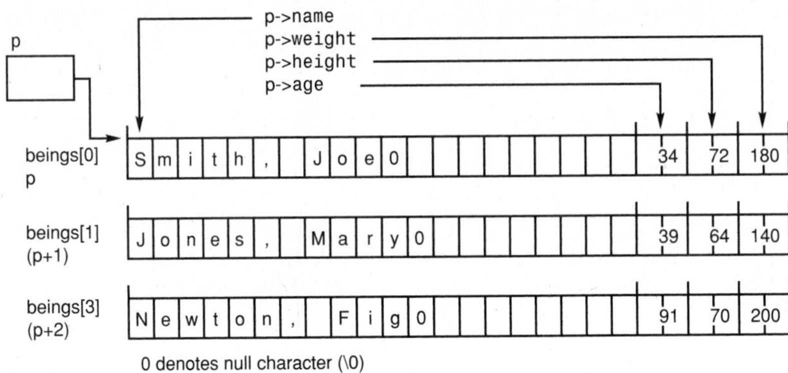

Figure 14.8. Memory storage of the structure array `beings`.

What You Have Learned

In this chapter, you learned more about pointers—but don't panic if you are still uncomfortable with them. As you gain more experience in writing C++ programs, you will rapidly learn to use pointers and start wondering how you got by without them. The following topics were covered:

- The four rules to assist you in deciphering complex pointers
- How to declare, initialize, and use four types of pointers—string constants, pointers that point to pointers, pointers that point to functions, and pointers that point to structures
- The distinction and interaction between arrays and pointers
- How to pass a pointer to a function as a function argument
- How to use arrays of function pointers

Structures and Unions

If a little knowledge is dangerous, where is the man who has so much as to be out of danger?

—Thomas Henry Huxley
"On Elemental Instruction in Physiology" (1877)

In This Chapter

In this chapter, you learn about unions, and you plunge into the study of the advanced features of structures. Specifically, this chapter covers the following topics:

- Declaring and initializing structures
- Using structures
- Arrays of structures

- Structures of structures
- Linked lists
- Bit fields
- Unions

What Is a Structure?

Although you are already familiar with structures, you should review some terminology. You know that a *structure* is an *aggregate* data type—a collection of items of different data types combined into a single language construct. Each item in a structure is called a *member*, and each member can be a different data type variable. Structures, therefore, are great for working with a group of items that have different data types.

Declaring Structures

You know that before you use a structure, you must declare the template for the structure. Here is a sample template:

```
struct  CUBE
{
     int  height;          // Height of cube
     char *title;          // Title of cube
     int  weight;          // Weight of cube

};
```

The keyword `struct` is followed by the tag name `CUBE`. When you are ready to declare a variable to use the structure template, specify the tag name `CUBE` with the following declaration statement:

```
CUBE b;
```

This declares one instance, `b`, of the structure `CUBE`. The template exists only to define the structure of instances of a structure variable. Each instance takes memory space, but the template uses no memory. Each instance can be used like any other data type. Note this example:

```
box b, c, *ptr;
```

> In the C language, you are required to prefix a structure variable declaration with a struct keyword, as in
>
> ```
> struct box b. c. *ptr;
> ```
>
> For compatibility in C++, you can preface a structure variable declaration with a `struct` keyword. However, it is not needed, and I recommend that you omit it.

Initializing Structures

You already know about initializing structures. To review, note the following example:

```
char titleb[] = {"Cube B"};
CUBE b = { 29, titleb, 250 };
```

The members of the structure variable `b` are initialized to the following values:

```
height  29 inches
title   "Cube B"
weight  250 pounds
```

15

Referencing Structure Members

You also know how to reference the members of a structure variable. You reference a structure member by specifying the structure variable and member name separated by the member operator (`.`) . If you declare a pointer to a structure, you can reference the structure members with the pointer-to operator (->), which separates the pointer name from the member name. The following statements illustrate how to reference structure members:

```
CUBE b, *ptr
char titleb[] = {"Box B"};
b.height = 29;
b.title  = titleb;
ptr = &b;
ptr->height = 20;
```

Arrays of Structures

You have already been introduced to arrays of structures. You declare an array of structures by preceding the array name with the structure `typedef` name. Note that the `typedef` name will be used from now on, as in the following example:

```
CUBE ary[3];
```

You can initialize `ary` like this:

```
CUBE ary[] =
{
     { 29, "Cube A", 250 },
     { 3,  "Cube B", 12  },
     { 10, "Cube C", 15  }
};
```

Notice the use of braces to group the initialization of the members for each array element. Now you can use this array like any other array. Listing 15.1 shows a simple example of the use of an array of structures. You first declare the structure with the `CUBE` structure tag name. You then declare and initialize an array of structures, `ary`, and declare a pointer, `ptr`. CUBE1.CPP illustrates how you can reference the members of `ary` by either indexing the array or using a pointer to the structure. The members of each element are displayed twice, the first time with array indexing and the second time with the pointer.

Listing 15.1. The source listing for CUBE1.CPP.

```
// CUBE1.CPP - Illustrates arrays of structures
#include <iostream.h>
#include <iomanip.h>
struct CUBE
{
     int  height;
     char *title;
     int  weight;
};
void main()
{
     int i;
     CUBE ary[3] =
     {
          { 29, " Cube A ", 250 },
          { 3, " Cube B ", 12 },
          { 10, " Cube C ", 15 }
     };
     CUBE *ptr;
     ptr = ary;
     cout << "size of CUBE is "
          << sizeof( CUBE ) << "\n";
     cout << " Height Weight Title\n";

     for ( i = 0; i< 3; i++, ptr++ )
          {
          cout << setw( 6 ) << ary[i].height
               << setw( 7 ) << ary[i].weight
               << ary[i].title  << "\n";

          cout << setw( 6 ) << ptr->height
               << setw( 7 ) << ptr->weight
               << ptr->title     << "\n";

          }
}
```

Remember that the `setw()` manipulator sets the width of the display.

The output in Listing 15.2 shows that the members of the array are referenced correctly. The listing displays also the size of the array element as six bytes—two bytes for each of the `int` variables, `height` and `weight`, and two bytes for the `char *` pointer, `title`. Figure 15.1 illustrates `ary` stored in memory.

Listing 15.2. Output from executing CUBE1.EXE.

```
size of CUBE is 6
 Height Weight Title
    29     250    Cube A
    29     250    Cube A
     3      12    Cube B
     3      12    Cube B
    10      15    Cube C
    10      15    Cube C
```

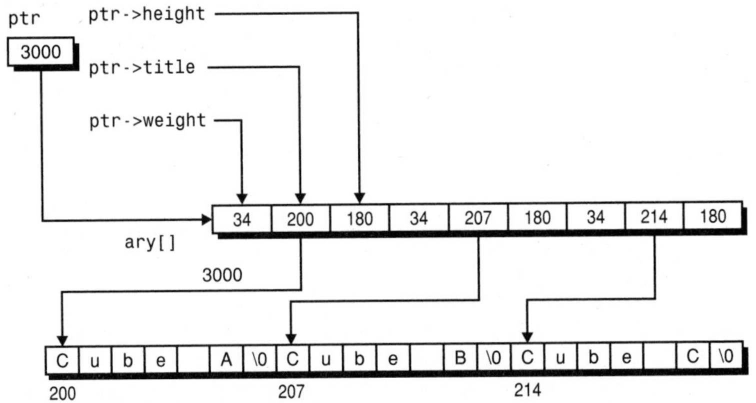

Figure 15.1. Memory storage of the structure array `ary[]`.

Refer to Listing 14.3 in Chapter 14, "Pointers," for another example of the use of arrays of structures.

Structures as Function Arguments

You can pass a structure as a function argument in two ways. You can either pass the structure (by value) or pass a pointer to the structure (by reference). Note this example:

```
CUBE cube;
:
func1( cube );    // Pass by value
func2( &cube );   // Pass by reference
```

If you pass a structure by value, a copy of the structure is made, and that copy is passed to the called function. If the structure is large, this method can be inefficient and can temporarily use too much memory. If the function makes any changes to the structure, those changes will be lost.

You usually want to pass a pointer to the structure. This method passes only the address of the structure to the function. The method is efficient and enables you to change the values in the structure.

You must declare the structure in the called function. If you pass the structure itself, you use the following function declaration:

```
int func1( CUBE cube );
{
:
}
```

If you pass a pointer to the structure, you use this function declaration:

```
func2( CUBE *cube );
{
:
}
```

Note that passing an entire structure to a function is a feature supported by most modern compilers and the ANSI standards. The passing of an entire structure, however, is not supported in the original C language specification.

15

Returning Structures

You can program a function to return a pointer to a structure or to return an entire structure to the calling program. The function declaration statement return type must agree with the actual value returned. The structure or structure pointer returned must be a `static` data type. You usually want to return a pointer to a structure, as in this example:

```
CUBE func3( void );    // Prototypes
CUBE *func4( void );
main()
{
     CUBE cube, *cube1;
     :
     cube = func3();  // Entire function is assigned to cube
     cube1 = func4(); // Pointer cube1 is assigned
     :
}
CUBE func3( void )
{
     static CUBE c;
     :
     return c;        // Entire structure is returned
}
CUBE func4( void )
{
     static CUBE c;
     :
     return &c;       // Return the address of a structure
}
```

> Returning the entire contents of a structure is not an efficient way to handle data. It is usually better to return a pointer to a structure.

Returning the entire structure is supported only by compilers that comply with ANSI standard C, such as Microsoft C/C++ 7.

In the preceding example, you may have noticed this strange assignment statement:

```
cube = func3();  // Entire function is assigned to cube
```

This statement transfers the contents of the structure on the right side of the equal sign to the structure variable on the left side. This assignment statement is supported only by compilers that comply with ANSI standard C.

Using Nested Structures

You can have any data type as a member of a structure. You can even have a structure as a member of another structure. Such a structure is called a *nested structure*. Here is an example:

```
typedef struct
{
     int  height;
     char *title;
     int  weight;
     struct
     {
          int     x;
          int     y;
          int     z;
     } location;
} CUBE1;
```

The structure `location` consists of three members: `x`, `y`, and `z`. Now declare a structure variable for this nested structure:

```
CUBE1 cube;
```

You can reference the members of `cube` with the following:

```
cube.height
cube.title
cube.weight
cube.location.x
cube.location.y
cube.location.z
```

Notice that the innermost structure tag name is used to reference its members. Now use a `typedef` to declare the innermost structure of the nested structures:

15

```
typedef struct
{
     int     x;
     int     y;
     int     z;
} COORDS;

typedef struct
{
     int  height;
     char *title;
     int  weight;
     COORDS location;
} CUBE1;
```

When you initialize nested structures, the members of the innermost structure must be enclosed in braces, as in

```
CUBE1 cube =
{
     29, "Cube A", 200, { 3, 4, 5 }
};
```

There is no limit to how deep you can nest structures. However, if the structure gets too complex, it will not be manageable or readable.

Be aware of one restriction: you cannot declare an undeclared structure as a member of another structure. Thus, a structure must be declared before it can be used as a member of another structure. You can declare a member of a structure to be a pointer to a structure that has not yet been declared. This rule enables you to have a *self-referencing structure*—a structure with a member that is a pointer to an instance of itself. Here is an example:

```
typedef struct cube2
{
     int  height;
     char *title;
     int  weight;
     struct cube2 *cube2;
} CUBE2;
```

Because you are allowed to declare a pointer to an undeclared structure, the compiler enables you to have a pointer that points to an instance of structure CUBE2. The fourth member is a pointer that points to an instance of structure CUBE2. This enables you to create *linked lists*, which are described later in this chapter.

Using the Assignment Statement with Structures

In C++ you can assign the contents of one structure variable to another as simply as you can assign the contents of one int to another int. CUBE2.CPP, the program in Listing 15.3, demonstrates how simple it is to transfer the contents of the structure cube1 to cube2. The output from executing CUBE2.EXE is shown in Listing 15.4.

Listing 15.3. The source listing for CUBE2.CPP.

```
// CUBE2.CPP - Illustrates structure assignment operation
#include <iostream.h>
#include <iomanip.h>
struct CUBE
{
     int height;
     char *title;
     int  weight;
};
void main()
{
     CUBE cube1 = { 29, " Cube A ", 250 };
     CUBE cube2;

     cout << "Height Weight Title\n";

     cube2 = cube1;     // Assign contents of structure cube1
                        // to cube2
     cout << setw( 6 ) << cube1.height
          << setw( 7 ) << cube1.weight
          << cube1.title << "\n";
```

continues

15

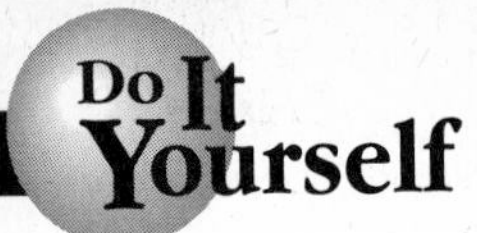

Listing 15.3. continued

```
    cout << setw( 6 ) << cube2.height
         << setw( 7 ) << cube2.weight
         << cube2.title << "\n";

}
```

Listing 15.4. Output from executing CUBE2.EXE.

```
Height Weight Title
   29    250 Cube A
   29    250 Cube A
```

Linked Lists

Sometimes when you are developing a program, factors prevent you from knowing how many data objects you should declare. The number depends on how many objects the user of your program specifies. You can plan for a maximum number of data objects. If you need to process a list of names and addresses, you can declare an array of structures with as many elements as required to handle any unforeseen situation. In the worst-case scenario, however, this method could use all your memory—leaving none for other data and functionality.

A common way to avoid this problem is to allocate memory for each data object when it is created. You can use the C++ memory allocation operator, `new`, to allocate a memory block. (Refer to the section "The Free Store—Memory Allocation Operators" in Chapter 11 for more information about the `new` and `delete` operators.) The structure containing each data object can be maintained in a *linked list*. To construct a linked list, you declare a pointer as a member of the structure. This pointer is used as a link to the next instance of a data object. Figure 15.2 illustrates a group of data objects linked with pointers.

Each pointer points to the beginning of the next data object. This is a simple *one-way* linked list because the linkage flows in one direction. You can have a *two-way* linked list with two pointers, one pointing to the next data object and the other pointing to the preceding data object.

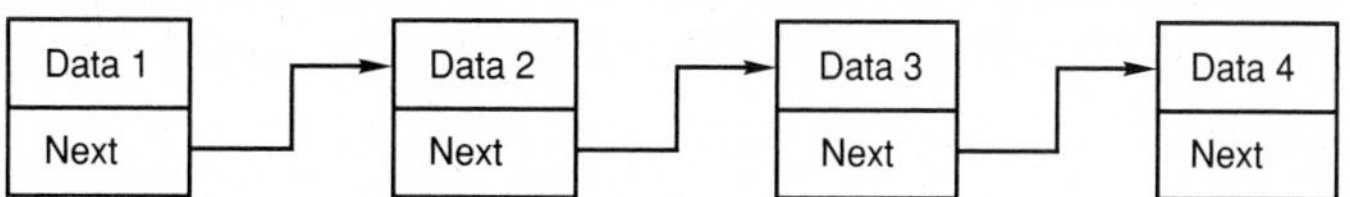

Figure 15.2. *An example of a linked list.*

Linked List Application

In this chapter, you develop a simple address book application. Before you begin programming, however, you need to do some planning. Your development effort consists of the following three steps:

1. Analysis
2. Design
3. Implementation

Analysis

To begin your analysis, first state what you want the program to do. That's pretty easy for this application—the program will maintain and display a list of names, phone numbers, addresses, and ages. Your program should perform the following steps:

1. Input new address data.
2. Delete existing address data.
3. Change existing address data.
4. View address data.
5. Save data in a file.
6. Read data from a disk file.

Next determine the information you want to include in each entry:

- Name
- Phone number

- Address
- City
- State (two-letter abbreviation)
- ZIP code
- Age

Design

After you have determined what you want the application to do, it is time to begin designing the program.

You want to maintain the data in a one-way linked list. First define the data structure. The address book data will be stored in an instance of structure ADDRESS. Its structure will be declared and placed in a header file named address.h. The structure is

```
typedef struct address
{
     char name[20];
     char phone[15];
     char address[23];
     char city[14];
     char state[3];
     char zip[14];
     int  age;
     void *next      // One-way linked list pointer
} ADDRESS;
```

Now analyze the program logic. First write out, in English, what the program will do. Your program should perform the following steps:

1. Read the data file if it exists.
2. Display current data entry.
3. Display a command-line prompt.
4. Pause while you enter a command.
5. Depending on the command, execute one of the following:

   A. Add an entry. Create an instance of the data structure and add it to the linked list.

B. Change current entry.

C. Delete current entry.

D. Display next entry.

E. Display previous entry.

F. Display help (list commands).

G. Write data into file and exit.

6. Repeat step 2.

This is just an overview of the design. You could add more levels of detail to modularize the logic further. This overview is sufficient for your purposes because additional detail would make the design too difficult to follow. In practice, you should add as much detail as needed to root out all logic paths. For now, continue with the process of determining which functions you will need.

Now create functions for each command, as well as functions that perform low-level modular tasks. For example, you need a function to add a new instance of a data object to the linked list, which also can be used by the file-read logic and the `A` (Add an entry) command. You can use a top-down approach to designing the program.

Next decide what functions you need for linked list management. Your program must be able to perform the following functions:

- Add a new link
- Delete an existing link
- Go to the next link
- Go to the previous link
- Get the current link

Then place these functions in a source file separate from the rest of the application. This hides the linked list management operations from the rest of the application. You now have the following functions to support these operations:

`add_link()`	Add object to the end of the linked list
`delete_link()`	Remove object from the linked list
`go_next()`	Position pointer at the next object in the list
`go_previous()`	Position pointer at the previous object in the list

15

`go_top()`	Position pointer to first link in list
`tail()`	Get last link in the list

Each of these functions will return the pointer or a `NULL` value.

Now you need a group of functions that support your application:

`main()`	Main control loop
`add_object()`	Input an object from the user
`change_object()`	Edit the existing object
`get_command()`	Input a command from the user and return the command number
`help()`	Display help
`display()`	Display the current item in the list
`readfile()`	Read the data file
`writefile()`	Write the data file

Each command for the address book application is a single character that you enter to perform an operation:

`A`	*A*dd an entry
`C`	*C*hange current entry
`D`	*D*elete current entry
`N`	Go to *N*ext entry
`P`	Go to *P*revious entry
`H`	Display *H*elp
`X`	Write out data and e*X*it

Implementation

The program consists of two source files, LINKLIST.CPP and ADDRESS.CPP, and one header file, address.h. The header file is presented in Listing 15.5 and contains the `typedef` declaration for the structure `ADDRESS` (the name and address data). The address.h file also contains prototypes for functions used in the program. Many of the functions return a pointer to an instance of structure ADDRESS. The typedef declaration contains the name and address data and a one-way pointer, next, which points to the instance of a structure variable.

Listing 15.5. The source listing for the address.h header file.

```
// address.h - Address book header file

struct ADDRESS
{
     char     name[20];
     char     phone[15];
     char     address[23];
     char     city[14];
     char     state[3];
     char     zip[14];
     int      age;
     void     *next; // One-way linked list pointer
};

ADDRESS *add_object( void );
void change_object( ADDRESS *ptr );
int get_command( void );
void help( void );
void display( ADDRESS *ptr );
void readfile( void );
void writefile( void );
void get_string( char *message, char *item , int maxsize );
void get_input( ADDRESS *p );
void get_string( char *message, char *item , int maxsize );

// Linked list management utilities
ADDRESS *add_link( void );
ADDRESS *delete_link( void );
ADDRESS *go_next( void );
ADDRESS *go_previous( void );
ADDRESS *go_top( void );
```

Listing 15.6, presented later, is the source listing of ADDRESS.CPP, which contains the main control operations plus functions dedicated

15

specifically to the maintenance of the address book. There are two functions for reading and writing a file.

ADDRESS.CPP calls the `get_command()` function to prompt the user to enter a single-character command. The function returns a command number (a number from 0 to 6 that corresponds to the command). A `switch` statement is used to redirect program control to the code for the selected operation. The function `add_object()` calls `add_link()` to allocate a memory block for a data object. The data object is an instance of the structure variable `ADDRESS`. The structure pointer variable `current` points to the current data object. It is used whenever you want to display or edit an address book entry. `add_object()` then prompts the user to enter the name and address information with the help of the function `get_input()`.

The function `get_input()` calls `get_string()` for each character array data item in the structure. `get_string()` was devised in a process called *generalization*. Instead of repeating a code segment for each item input, you can create a generalized function that handles input for all the items. `get_string()` is generalized even further so that it can also be used for changing data. `get_input()` and `get_string()`, therefore, are used also with the function `change_object()`, which is called by `main()` to change a data object. `get_string()` can be used whenever you want to input or edit a character array.

The functions `add_link()`, `delete_link()`, `go_next()`, and `go_previous()` are part of the simple linked list management system. `delete_link()` deletes the current data object from the linked list. `go_next()` and `go_previous()` move to the next and previous data objects in the linked list, respectively. These functions return a pointer to the new current data object.

The function `display()` outputs the name, phone number, address, city, state, ZIP, and age fields from the current data object. The function `help()` displays a list and description of each command.

You are already familiar with the run-time library functions used in ADDRESS.CPP. The only one that requires some comment is `toupper()`, which converts each lowercase character to an uppercase character.

`toupper()` is implemented in Microsoft C/C++ 7 as a macro (`#define`) statement and as a function. If you include the header file ctype.h, its macro form is used. If ctype.h is not included, `toupper()` is treated as a function, and its prototype is in the stdlib.h header file. The macro form looks like the following:

```
#define toupper(c) ( c & 2 ? c - 'a'+'A' : c )
```

This expansion is efficient but will not work correctly if the argument is a function such as `getchar()`. When the macro expansion is performed, `toupper()` calls `getchar()` twice. Therefore

```
char = toupper( getchar() );
```

will expand to

```
char = getchar() & 2 : getchar()-'a'+'A' : getchar();
```

The same side effect occurs with `tolower()`. The solution is to use the function form of `toupper()` and `tolower()`. Do not include ctype.h in your application. However, if you use a scalar variable as the argument, the macro form of `toupper()` works fine.

Listing 15.6. The source listing for ADDRESS.CPP.

```
// ADDRESS.CPP - Simple address book application that
// illustrates how to build a one-way linked list of
// structure instances
#include <iostream.h>  // Needed for screen I/O
#include <fstream.h>   // Needed for file I/O
#include <io.h>        // ios: manipulators
#include <fcntl.h>

#include <string.h>
#include <ctype.h>
#include "address.h"
ADDRESS *current = 0;  // Current pointer
void main()
{
     int     cmd;
     readfile();        // Read address book file
```

continues

15

Listing 15.6. continued

```
    help();             // Display commands
    while ( 1 )         // Loop forever
    {
        cmd = get_command();     // Input command from user
        switch ( cmd )
        {
            case 0:     // A - Add a record
                current = add_object();
                break;
            case 1:     // C - Change entry
                change_object( current );
                break;
            case 2:     // D - Delete an entry
                current = delete_link();
                break;
            case 3:     // N - Display Next entry
                current = go_next();
                break;
            case 4:     // P - Display Previous entry
                current = go_previous();
                break;
            case 5:     // H - Help
                help();
                break;
            case 6:     // X - Write data and eXit
                writefile();
                return;
            default:
                break;
        }
        display( current );
    }
}
//*********************************************************
// add_object() - Adds an address book entry
ADDRESS *add_object( void )
{
    ADDRESS *p;
    p = add_link();
    cout << "\nEnter new address book entry\n";
```

```
     get_input( p );
     return p;
}
//*******************************************************
// get_input() - Enters data for one entry from keyboard
void get_input( ADDRESS *p )
{
     cin.seekg( 0L, ios::end ); // Empty input stream
     get_string( "name", p->name, 20 );
     get_string( "phone number", p->phone, 15 );
     get_string( "address", p->address, 23 );
     get_string( "city", p->city, 13 );
     get_string( "state", p->state, 3 );
     get_string( "ZIP code", p->zip, 14 );
     cout << "\nEnter age: ";
     cin.seekg( 0L, ios::end ); // Empty input stream
     cin >> p->age;
}
//*******************************************************
// get_string() - Inputs string data item
void get_string( char *message, char *item , int maxsize )
{
     char ch;
     char s[80];
     if ( strlen( item ) > 0 )
     {
          cout << "\nCurrent value for " << message
               << " is: " << item
               << ". Change it (Y/N)?: ";
          cin.seekg( 0L, ios::end );        // Empty input stream
          cin >> ch;
          if ( ch != 'Y' && ch != 'y' )     // Not Y, y
               return;
     }
     cout << "\nEnter " << message << ": "; // Display prompt
     cin.seekg( 0L, ios::end ); // Empty input stream
     cin.get( s, 80 );          // Input string
     s[maxsize-1] = '\0';       // Truncate if max size exceeded
     strcpy( item, s );         // Copy string 's' to input item
     return;
}
```

15

continues

Listing 15.6. continued

```
//*****************************************************
// change_object() - Changes existing address book entry
void change_object( ADDRESS *ptr )
{
     cout << "\nEdit address book entry\n";
     get_input( ptr );
}

//*****************************************************
// get_command() - Inputs command letter from keyboard
int get_command( )
{
     int ch, cmdno;
     char s[80];
     char  cmds[] = {"ACDNPHX"};
     cout << "\nEnter a command (A, C, D, N, P, H, or X): ";
     cin.seekg( 0L, ios::end ); // Empty input stream
     cin >> s;                  // Get character from keyboard
     ch = s[0];
     ch = toupper( (int)s[0] );
     for ( cmdno = 0; cmds[cmdno] && ch != cmds[cmdno]
                 ; cmdno++ );
     return cmdno;
}
//*****************************************************
// help() - Lists program command help
void help( void )
{
     cout << "   ADDRESS BOOK HELP\n";
     cout << " Enter one of the following commands\n";
     cout << "     A - Add an entry\n";
     cout << "     C - Change an entry\n";
     cout << "     D - Delete an entry\n";
     cout << "     N - Display Next entry\n";
     cout << "     P - Display Previous entry\n";
     cout << "     H - Help\n";
     cout << "     X - Write data and eXit\n\n";
}
//*****************************************************
// display() - Displays an address book entry
void display( ADDRESS *ptr )
```

```
{
      if ( ptr == NULL )
           cout << "Nothing to display\n";
      else
      {
           cout << ptr->name << "\n";
           cout << ptr->address  << "\n";
           cout << ptr->city
                << ", "      << ptr->state
                << " "       << ptr->zip   << "\n"
                << "Phone: " << ptr->phone << "\n"
                << "Age:   " << ptr->age   << "\n";
      }
}
//**************************************************************
// readfile() - Reads address book entries from file ADDRESS.DAT
void readfile( void )
{

      int     size = 1, count = 0;
      ADDRESS *p;
      ifstream fis( "ADDRESS.DAT", ios::binary | ios::nocreate );
      if ( ! fis )
           cout << "Address Book File is not available\n";
      else
      {
           while ( 1 )                 // Read forever
           {
                p = add_link();
                if ( !fis.read( (char*)p, sizeof( ADDRESS ) ))
                     break;            // Exit on end of file
                count++;
                p->next = 0;           // Always last link
           }
           current = delete_link(); // Delete empty link
           cout << "Address Book contains " << count
                << " entries\n";
           fis.close();
      }
}
```

15

continues

Listing 15.6. continued

```
//************************************************************
// writefile() - Writes address book entries to file ADDRESS.DAT
void writefile( void )
{

     int     count = 0;
     ADDRESS *p, *plast = NULL;
     ofstream ofs( "ADDRESS.DAT", ios::binary );
     if ( !ofs )
          cout << "Unable to write Address Book File\n";
     else
     {
          p = go_top();
          while ( plast != p && p != NULL )
          {
               ofs.write( (char*)p, sizeof( ADDRESS ) );
               plast = p;
               p = go_next();
               count++;
          }
          ofs.close ();
          cout << count << " entries written to "
               << "Address Book File\n";
     }
}
```

The last two functions in ADDRESS.CPP are used for disk input and output. When ADDRESS.EXE executes, `readfile()` reads address book entries from the file ADDRESS.DAT if it exists. When you choose the `X` command, the program writes any existing address book entries to ADDRESS.DAT and exits. Chapter 20, "File Input and Output," provides a detailed description of C++ file I/O operations. If you are curious, here is a brief introduction to the file I/O operations used in the functions `readfile()` and `writefile()`.

Before you open a file to read or write, you must first open a file. You do this by creating an `ifstream` (read) or `ofstream` (write) data object and passing it the name of the file plus any file open mode options. For example, if you want to open an existing file named ADDRESS.DAT, you enter the following statement:

```
ifstream fis( "ADDRESS.DAT", ios::binary ¦ ios::nocreate );
```

`ifstream` is a data type. The item `fis` is the name you give the data object instance that is declared as type `ifstream`. The associated arguments are passed to a function, called a *constructor*, which opens the file. The arguments consist of the filename and two file modes that are ORed together. The file mode `ios::binary` indicates that the file should be read in binary mode. The file mode `ios:nocreate` tells the constructor not to create the file if the file does not exist. You use the item name for subsequent file read operations. In the example

```
char buf[20];
fis.read( buf, 20 );
fis.close();
```

the function `fis.read()` reads 20 bytes from the file input stream, and `fis.close()` closes the file. Output is handled similarly.

Listing 15.7 presents the source listing for LINKLIST.CPP. It contains the address book linked-list functions and constructs and maintains a linked list. LINKLIST.CPP is a self-contained program designed to hide the details of the linked list manipulation from the client (calling) functions. The functions in LINKLIST.CPP always return to the calling program a pointer to the data object. This program was designed specifically as an instructional tool for the address book application, but the program could be generalized to be independent of the structure type.

Listing 15.7. The source listing for LINKLIST.CPP.

```
// LINKLIST.CPP - Illustrates linked list utility functions
#include <iostream.h>
#include <stdlib.h>
#include <string.h>
#include "address.h"
ADDRESS *tail( void );
int compare( const void *s1, const void *s2 );
static ADDRESS *head = NULL;       // head points to first object
static ADDRESS *current = NULL;    // current points to current
                                   // object

//*************************************************************
// add_link() - Allocates memory block for object and links
// it in list
```

continues

15

Listing 15.7. continued

```
ADDRESS *add_link( void )
 // add_link adds a link to the linked list
{
     ADDRESS *p;
     p = tail();  // Point to last object in linked list
     current = new ADDRESS;         // Allocate memory block
     memset( (char*)current, 0, sizeof( ADDRESS) );
     if ( current == NULL )
          return NULL;
     if ( p == NULL )
          head = current;
     else
          p->next = current;
     return current;
}
//*********************************************************
// tail() - Positions to last linked list object
     ADDRESS *tail( void )
{
     ADDRESS *p, *plast;
     p = head;
     plast = p;
     while ( p != NULL )
     {
          plast = p;
          p = (ADDRESS *)p->next;
     }
     return plast;
}
//****************************************************
// delete_link() - Removes memory block from linked list
ADDRESS *delete_link()
{
     ADDRESS *ptr, *pdelete;
     if ( current == NULL )        // Is list empty?
          return NULL;
     pdelete = current;            // Link to delete
     if ( head == current )        // Is current link first link?
     {
          head = (ADDRESS *)current->next;   // Point to second
                                             // link (or NULL)
```

```
          current = head;
     }
     else
     {
          ptr = (ADDRESS *)pdelete->next; // Next link (or NULL)
          current = go_previous();        // Get previous link
          if ( current != NULL )
               current->next = ptr;     // Link last link to next
     }
     free( pdelete );                   // Free memory block
     return current;
}
//****************************************************
// go_next() - Positions pointer to next link in linked list
ADDRESS *go_next()
{
     ADDRESS *p;
     if ( current != NULL && current->next != NULL )
          current =  (ADDRESS *)current->next;
     return current;
}
//****************************************************
// go_previous() - Positions pointer to previous link
ADDRESS *go_previous()
{
     ADDRESS *p, *plast;
     if ( head == NULL )
        return NULL;
     for ( p = head, plast = p;
           p != current && p != NULL;
           plast = p, p = (ADDRESS *) p->next );
     current = plast;
     return plast;
}
//****************************************************
// go_top() - Positions to header
ADDRESS *go_top()
{
     current = head;
     return current;
}
```

15

The LINKLIST.CPP source file contains the add_link(), delete_link(), go_next(), and go_previous() functions that are called from the address book application. These functions return a pointer of type ADDRESS to the current data object. Two static structure pointers to type ADDRESS, named head and current, are declared at the beginning of LINKLIST.CPP. These pointers maintain the state of the linked list. The structure pointer head points to the first data object in the linked list. The structure pointer current points to the data object in the linked list that is considered the current or active data object. One of the members of the structure ADDRESS, named next, is a structure pointer of type ADDRESS. next contains the address of the next data object in the linked list, or a NULL value if the current data object is at the end of the linked list. These structure pointers are illustrated in Figure 15.3.

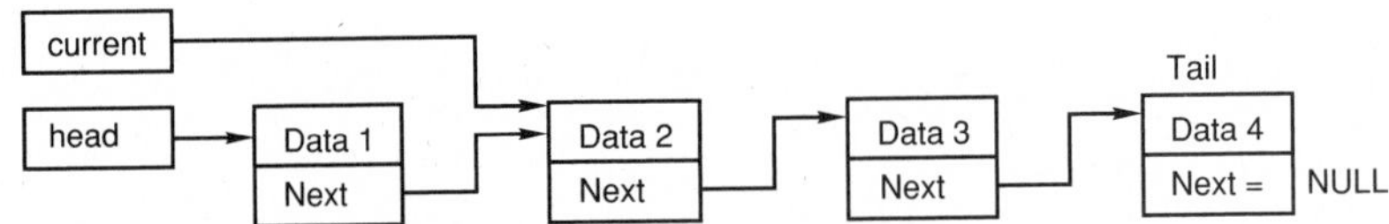

Figure 15.3. The linked list variables and data objects.

The function add_link() creates a new data object and adds it to the linked list. First add_link() calls the run-time library function calloc() to allocate a memory block and initialize its contents to zero. The memory block is the size of the ADDRESS type structure. If there is not enough memory available to allocate a block of memory, calloc() returns a NULL pointer, and add_link() displays an error message and calls exit() to exit ADDRESS.EXE. Be sure to save your data before you exit. If you cannot allocate any more memory, you cannot continue. This drastic action was contrived to illustrate that you must confirm that the pointers returned from new are valid before you use them.

Then add_link() calls the function tail() to locate the tail (end) of the linked list. add_link() assigns the address of the new data object to the ADDRESS structure pointer next. If the linked list is empty, the ADDRESS pointer head is assigned the address of the new data object. Finally, add_link() returns an ADDRESS structure pointer to the calling program.

The function go_next() points current to the next link in the linked list. go_next() then uses the ADDRESS structure pointer next in the current data object to determine the address of the next link in the linked list:

```
current = (ADDRESS*)next->current;
```

go_next() returns the value of current to the calling program. If the current data object is the tail of the linked list, current is unchanged.

The function go_previous() is more complicated. Because this is a one-way linked list, there is no pointer pointing to the previous link. The program traverses the linked list, starting with the structure pointer head, until it reaches the data object that precedes the current data object. A pointer that points to the previous data object is returned to the calling program.

The function delete_link() removes a link from the linked list. If this function is the first link in the chain, it assigns the address of the second data object in the linked list to the ADDRESS structure pointer head:

```
head = (ADDRESS*)current->next;
```

If this function is at the end of the linked list, it locates the previous data object, previous, and assigns a NULL value to its next structure pointer:

```
current = go_previous()
current->next = NULL;
```

If the current data object is in the middle of the linked list, delete_link() links the previous data object to the next data object:

```
current->next = ptr->next;
```

Finally, delete_link() calls the run-time library function free() to release the memory used by the data object. Then delete_link() returns the address of the previous data object to the calling program.

Because this program has multiple source files, you should create a project file (using the **N**ew Project command on the **P**roject menu) and include the source files ADDRESS.CPP and LINKLIST.CPP, as well as the header.h file. Next select C++ and DOS EXE from the Set Project Template dialog box. Then, whenever you modify any of the files and select the **B**uild: address.exe command from the **P**roject menu or select any execution mode, only those files that are affected by changes are recompiled. Listing 15.8 illustrates a sample dialog resulting from executing the instructive but primitive program ADDRESS.EXE. User response is in boldface print.

15

Listing 15.8. A dialog from the execution of ADDRESS.EXE.

```
  ADDRESS BOOK HELP
Enter one of the following commands
       A - Add an entry
       C - Change an entry
       D - Delete an entry
       N - Display Next entry
       P - Display Previous entry
       H - Help
       X - Write data and eXit

Enter a command (A, C, D, N, P, H, or X): a

Enter new address book entry
Enter name: David Jones
Enter phone number: 2443 Seaside Dr.
Enter address: 2443 Seaside Drive

Enter city: Oceanside
Enter state: CA
Enter ZIP code: 55512

Enter age: 5

David Jones
2443 Seaside Drive
Oceanside, CA 55512
Phone: 2443 Seaside D
Age:   5

Enter a command (A, C, D, N, P, H, or X): c

Edit address book entry
Current value for name is: David Jones. Change it (Y/N)?: n
Current value for phone number is: 2443 Seaside D.
Change it (Y/N)?: y
Enter phone number: (602)555-4545
Current value for address is: 2443 Seaside Drive.
Change it (Y/N)?: n
Current value for city is: Oceanside. Change it (Y/N)?: n
Current value for state is: CA. Change it (Y/N)?: n
```

```
Current value for ZIP code is: 55512. Change it (Y/N)?: n
Enter age: 9

David Jones
2443 Seaside Drive
Oceanside, CA 55512
Phone: (602)555-4545
Age:   9

Enter a command (A, C, D, N, P, H, or X): h
   ADDRESS BOOK HELP
 Enter one of the following commands
        A - Add an entry
        C - Change an entry
        D - Delete an entry
        N - Display Next entry
        P - Display Previous entry
        H - Help
        X - Write data and eXit
```

Review the preceding program. It was created to illustrate the following:

- Using pointers to structures
- Dynamically allocating structures
- Using nested structures
- Constructing a header file
- Constructing and maintaining linked lists

Bit Fields

Usually, a `char` (8 bits) is the smallest data type variable you can manipulate. However, there is a special type of structure, called a *bit-field structure*, that contains members with only bit-field data types. In Microsoft C/C++ 7, a bit field can contain from 1 to 16 bits and is handled the same as an `unsigned int` data type. A bit-field base data type—which can be an `int`, an `unsigned` int, or a signed int—is declared the same as any other structure. However, it is best to declare the type as unsigned. The following statement is used to declare a bit-field structure with a tag SCODE:

```
struct SCODE
{
      unsigned  ch : 8;
      unsigned  mcode : 1;
      unsigned  xcode : 3;
      unsigned  ycode : 2;
} codes[29];
```

The colon (:) to the right of the variable name tells the compiler that the member is a bit field. The number to the right of the colon shows the number of bits in the bit field. ch is 8 bits wide, mcode is 1 bit wide, and so on. Figure 15.4 shows how the bit-field structure SCODE is stored in memory.

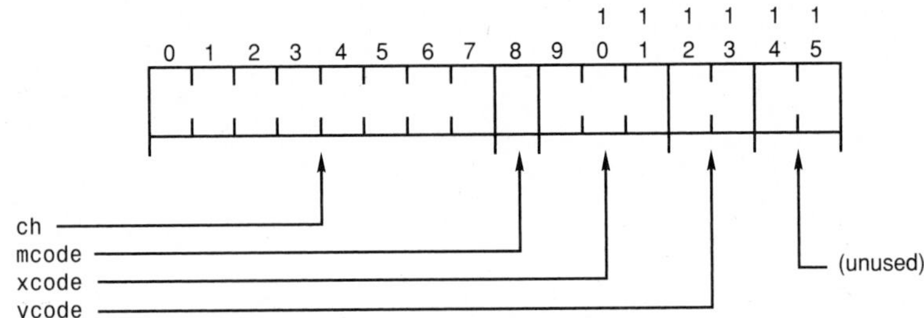

***Figure 15.4. Memory storage of the bit-field structure* SCODE.**

You reference bit fields as you would any other structure member. Note the following example:

```
codes[3]->xcode = 3;
if ( codes[0]->xcode >3 )
     codes[0]->xcode = 7;
```

In the first statement, xcode (stored in bits 10 through 12) is assigned a value of 3 for the fourth element of codes[]. In the second statement, if the xcode member of the first array is greater than 3, the xcode member is stored a value of 7.

The size of a number that can be stored in a bit-field member depends on the width of the bit field. A two-bit bit field can contain a number ranging from 0 to 3. If you attempt to store a value larger than a bit field can hold, the high-order bits will be discarded. This is illustrated in BITS.CPP in

Listing 15.9. Listing 15.10 presents the output from BITS.EXE. The integer variable `i` varies in a `for` loop from 0 to 9. Its value is assigned to each of the bit-field members, and the value is displayed each time the loop repeats.

Listing 15.9. The source listing for BITS.CPP.

```
// BITS.CPP - Illustrates bit fields
#include <iostream.h>
int main()
{
     static int i;
     struct bit
     {
          unsigned bit1 : 1;
          unsigned bit2 : 2;
          unsigned bit3 : 3;
     };
     bit     bits;
     for ( i = 0 ; i < 9 ; i++ )
          {
          bits.bit1 = i;
          bits.bit2 = i;
          bits.bit3 = i;
          cout << "bit1 " << bits.bit1
               << "  bit2 " << bits.bit2
               << "  bit3 " << bits.bit3 << "\n";
          }
     return 0;
}
```

15

Listing 15.10. Output from the execution of BITS.EXE.

```
bit1 0  bit2 0  bit3 0
bit1 1  bit2 1  bit3 1
bit1 0  bit2 2  bit3 2
bit1 1  bit2 3  bit3 3
bit1 0  bit2 0  bit3 4
bit1 1  bit2 1  bit3 5
bit1 0  bit2 2  bit3 6
bit1 1  bit2 3  bit3 7
bit1 0  bit2 0  bit3 0
```

Bit-field structures are not used frequently. When you need to do bit-level manipulation, however, they are vital.

What Is a Union?

A *union* is a variable whose syntax is similar to that of a structure except that a union's members overlay each other in memory, sharing the same memory space. Although a `union` statement is used infrequently, it is helpful for certain types of applications. For example, consider the following declaration:

```
typedef union
{
     int     a;
     char    b;
       struct
     {
          char x;
          char y;
     } c;
     float   d;
     long    e;
} UNION;

UNION sample;
```

The amount of memory reserved for a union is equal to the width of the largest variable. The storage in memory of the union variable `sample` is represented in Figure 15.5. This figure illustrates how all the union members—`a`, `b`, `c`, `d`, and `e`—share the same memory space. The union variable `sample` uses four bytes of memory, which is determined by the size of its widest members, `d` and `e`.

You can assign any of the union members with the same notation used with structures, as in this example:

```
sample.b = 'A'         // Member b is a char
sample.c.x = 'Z';      // Member c is a structure with 2 members
sample.c.y = 'Y';
sample.d = 34.33;      // d is a float
```

```
sample.e = 88773;      // e is a long int
sample.a = 34;         // Member a is an int
```

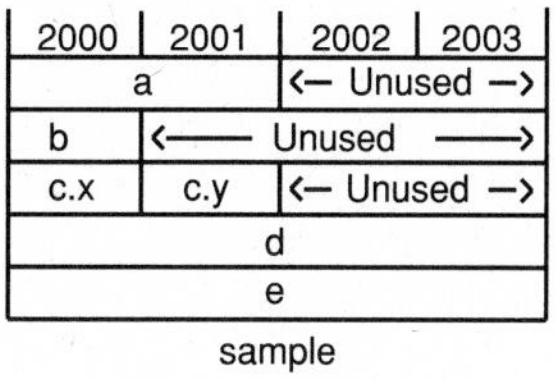

2000	2001	2002	2003
a		<— Unused —>	
b	<—— Unused ——>		
c.x	c.y	<— Unused —>	
d			
e			

sample

Figure 15.5. *Memory storage of the union* `sample`.

Whenever you store one union member, it overwrites any other member that is assigned. After the preceding statements have executed, the memory space occupied by the union variable `sample` contains whatever bit configuration is created by overlaying 34 with 88773. Writing over memory values is a rather poor example of the use of a union. Now consider another example.

Suppose that you want a database for your corporate resources, and you want to include all types of resources in the same structure. The resources are employees, facilities, and equipment. Each type of resource requires different information. You can use a union to share space in the structure among various information types. For example, a float `wages` member might be associated with an employee, an integer `square_feet` member might be associated with a facility, and a float `cost` member might be associated with a piece of equipment.

Listing 15.11 presents the UNION1.CPP program, which declares a three-element array named `res`. Each element is a structure of type `RESOURCE`. One of the members of the structure is a union consisting of three members: `wages`, `square_feet`, and `cost`. The structure member `type` defines the type of resource:

`type`	*Meaning*	*Corresponding Union Member*
`P`	People resources	`res[i].info.wages`
`E`	Equipment resources	`res[i].info.cost`
`F`	Facility resources	`res[i].info.square_feet`

ANSI standard C enables you to initialize a union. The initializer constant, however, must refer to the first union member. Because `square_root` is an `int` data type, its value is established by an assignment statement.

Listing 15.11. The source listing for UNION1.CPP.

```
// UNION1.CPP - Illustrates use of unions
#include <iostream.h>
int main()
{
     struct RESOURCE
     {
          char *item;
          char type;  // Type of resource
          union
          {
               float   wages;
               int     square_feet;
               float   cost;
          } info;
     };

     RESOURCE res[]      =
     {
          { "Joe Smith", 'P', 30000.0f },
          { "Building E", 'F', 0 },
          { "Table",      'E', 341.11f}
     };
     res[1].info.square_feet = 32000;
     for ( int i = 0; i < 3; i++ )
     {
          switch ( res[i].type )
          {
               case 'P':      // People resources
                    cout << "Employee name: "
                         << res[i].item
                         << " Wages: "
                         << res[i].info.wages << "\n";
                    break;
               case 'E':      // Equipment resources
                    cout << "Equipment:      "
                         << res[i].item
                         << "      Cost: "
                         << res[i].info.cost << "\n";
                    break;
               case 'F':      // Facility resources
```

```
                    cout << "Facilities:    "
                         << res[i].item
                         << "    Square feet: "
                         << res[i].info.square_feet << "\n";
                    break;
          }
     }
     return 0;
}
```

A switch statement tests the resource type and directs control to the appropriate output statement. Output from the execution of UNION1.EXE appears in Listing 15.12.

Listing 15.12. Output from executing UNION1.EXE.

```
Employee name: Joe Smith Wages: 30000.00
Facilities:   Building E   Square feet: 32000
Equipment:     Table           Cost: 341.11
```

What You Have Learned

In this chapter, you learned more about structures and also about union statements. Specifically, you learned the following:

- How to declare and initialize structures
- How to use structures
- How to use arrays of structures
- What linked lists are and how to create and use them
- How to use bit fields
- What unions are and how to use them

15

Part IV

C++ Object-Oriented Features

Classes

It could probably be shown by facts and figures that there is no distinctly native American criminal class except Congress.

—Mark Twain
Pudd'nhead Wilson's New Calendar (1894)

In This Chapter

In earlier chapters, you learned about the procedural aspects of the C++ language, and you can write some useful C++ programs. The theory behind this approach is that most people who intend to learn C++ probably have had some experience with procedural languages like BASIC, dBASE, C, or Pascal. Now you are going to learn about C++ features that will help you develop applications through an object-oriented approach. The object-oriented topics are explored in Part IV, "C++ Object-Oriented Features," which includes Chapters 16 through 23.

In this chapter, you are introduced to objects and classes. Classes are important elements of the C++ language. Specifically, this chapter covers the following topics:

- What OOP is all about
- What abstraction is
- What classes are good for
- How to declare classes
- What constructors and destructors are
- How to use classes
- How to use arrays of objects

Object-Oriented Programming (OOP)

As you have learned, *object-oriented programming* (OOP) is an approach to programming that focuses on the data rather than the actions. Instead of designing a system based on how data is manipulated, OOP design is based on the objects being manipulated. Object-oriented programming involves several concepts:

- *Abstraction* facilitates the development of large and complex programs.
- *Encapsulation* makes it easier to maintain a programming system.
- *Class hierarchies* make a program easier to modify and extend.

The following paragraphs introduce you to these concepts. They will become more meaningful as you familiarize yourself with C++ object-oriented features.

Abstraction is a design process in which you focus on the essential characteristics of an application and ignore the details. The higher the level of a programming language, the higher is the abstraction. For example, a program written in the BASIC language has a higher level of abstraction than a program written in assembly language because an assembly language program requires more detailed instructions for performing operations on a computer. Object-oriented languages have an even higher level of abstraction than procedural languages.

Encapsulation is a technique that lets you hide the internal operations and data of a class object from the procedure that interfaces with the class. This technique supports and enforces abstraction because external procedures can access only relevant properties of a class.

Class hierarchies are another important feature of OOP. C++ enables you to define a class that is a subtype or special category of some other class by deriving the class from another class. Several classes can be derived from a *base class*. A base class is said to be a *generalization* of a group of classes. A class that is derived from a base class is said to be a *specialization* of some other class. The advantage of having a hierarchy of classes is that classes in the hierarchy can share code and other properties. When one class derives properties from another class, the first class is said to *inherit* properties from the second class. Class inheritance is another important property of OOP.

Object-oriented programs combine data with functions and procedures. Functions and procedures, called *methods*, perform actions on the associated data to define its behavior. Using object-oriented design methodology, you concentrate on the types of data forms to be processed. You then identify the classes and determine their relationships. Finally, you arrange the classes in a hierarchical structure.

The Object-Oriented Advantage

Before OOP became accepted as the new wave, software engineering design methodology was based on an approach called *top-down* design. Using this technique, you determine the step-by-step procedure a program must perform. Then you break down the actions into smaller, more manageable actions, called *subprocesses*. Next you design a function to perform the actions for each subprocess. You code and test each of these functions individually. When all the functions are operating correctly, you integrate them and test the complete system.

You used the top-down approach in Chapter 15 for the design of the address book application. First you determined the necessary processing steps—such as reading a file, displaying the current entry, displaying a command-line prompt, and so on. Then you determined the functions required for each operation to be performed. For example, you determined that you needed functions for the following tasks:

Task	*Function*
Provide overall control	`main()`
Add a new link	`add_link()`
Delete an existing link	`delete_link()`
Go to the next link	`go_next()`
Go to the previous link	`go_previous()`

In the implementation process, the main program was written, and each of the functions were added as the development proceeded.

In contrast, object-oriented design focuses on the types of data forms that are to be processed and the hierarchical structure of the various classes of data. Object-oriented programs combine data with functions. As noted earlier, methods (functions and procedures) perform actions on the associated data to define the data's behavior. Data objects that share the same methods are called a class. A *class* designates what data represents an object and what actions are performed on the data.

Suppose that you want to use the OOP approach to design the address book application in Chapter 15. First you figure out what *object* you will be operating on. That's pretty easy—the object is an address book entry. It will be your basic data type, which represents the name and address of a person, along with other information such as city, state, ZIP code, phone number, and age.

Next you determine the methods required to handle the new data type. You need a method to input new data into this object. You need another method to modify an object, and another method for displaying data in the object. Furthermore, you need a method for destroying an obsolete data object. The bottom line is that you will be focusing on the object as a user sees it. You need to decide what information is needed in order to describe the object, and you need to think about how the user will interface with the object.

Using an object-oriented approach, you define an address book entry class. The data portion of the class definition contains information in an address book entry. The method portion of the class specification consists of functions and procedures used to create, destroy, modify or display, and otherwise operate on the address book object. You use the class methods to manipulate data associated with the instance of an address book class.

When you design a program with the OOP approach, you first design classes that specify the objects used in the program. You determine the data elements and the methods you need to manipulate the data. Once you have accurately defined all the required classes, you can proceed with the task of designing a program that uses the objects associated with the classes. This process is the reverse of top-down design because, with OOP, you first design the low-level elements and then proceed with the high-level program organization.

Data Types

When you declare a structure, you create a new data type. Suppose, for example, that you want a structure that defines weather statistics. First you define the structure template:

```
struct weather
{
     float high_temperature;
     float low_temperature;
     float inches_rain;
     float barometric_pressure;
     float relative_humidity;
     int wind_direction;      // 0=N 1=NE 2=E 3=SE
                              // 4=S 5=SW 6=W 7=NW
     float wind_velocity;
};
```

Then you declare a `weather` data type variable and initialize it:

```
weather today = { 77.8, 64.1, 0.0, 31.2, 41.2, 2, 15.3 };
```

If you are going to display today's weather with the C language run-time library `printf()` function, you cannot simply pass the structure to `printf()`. You need to write a procedure to display the weather, as in this example:

```
void printweather( weather today );
void main()
{
     printweather( today );
}
void printweather( weather today )
```

```
{
    char *direction[] =
    { "North", "Northeast", "East", "Southeast",
      "South", "Southwest", "West", "Northwest" };

    printf( "  Today's Weather\n" );
    printf( "Temperature (Degrees Farenheit)\n" );
    printf( "  High:  %6.2f Low:  %6.2f \n" ,
                today.high_temperature,
                today.low_temperature );
    printf( "Rain %6.2f (inches)\n",
                today.inches_rain );
    printf( "Relative humidity:  %6.2f\n",
                today.relative_humidity );
    printf( "Barometric pressure  %6.2f (inches mercury)\n",
            today.Barometric_pressure);
    printf( "Wind-  direction: %s\n",
                direction[today.wind_direction] );
    printf( "       velocity:  %6.2f (miles per hour)\n",
                today.wind_velocity   );
}
```

The preceding program formats the display of today's weather statistics. Here is the program's output:

```
  Today's Weather
Temperature (Degrees Fahrenheit)
  High:  77.80 Low:  64.10
Rain   0.00 (inches)
Relative humidity:  41.20
Barometric pressure  31.20 (inches mercury)
Wind-  direction: East
       velocity:   15.30 (miles per hour)
```

If you want to do any other operation, such as change the data, you will need to write another function. There is nothing built into a structure definition to verify that the data assigned to structure members is correct. For a large application, you might create many functions that use `weather` structure variables. Any invalid data that some function might insert in the structure can affect some or all of the functions that use the type `weather` variables. And if you decide that you need to change the structure, you will probably have to go to all the functions and make some kind of change. As you can see, when a structure that is used by many functions is changed, it can cause reverberations throughout a whole system of functions. This can be a programmer's nightmare. A single change can break the whole program in many places.

It is possible to write a program in C that will get around some of these problems. A set of specialized functions can be written to maintain a structure, validate data entry, and properly display members of the structure. These functions can perform conversions, such as converting temperatures from Fahrenheit to Centigrade. Rules are established that require all other functions in the program to call the structure-maintenance functions before accessing or making any changes to the data in the structure.

As long as all programmers follow the rules and never directly access data in the structure, the structure and its associated functions can be modified without affecting the rest of the application. However, as often happens, time constraints, laziness, or an unforeseen circumstance may cause a programmer to violate the rules and directly modify the structure variable. As a result, the program becomes difficult to maintain. In the next section, you examine an improved method of creating user-defined data types—compliments of C++.

The C++ Class

C++ offers a technique for creating new and safe user-defined data types—because the language provides the means to restrict access to data. This language element is called a *class*. By declaring a class, you can define both the data for a user-defined data type and the functions that operate on the data.

Declaring a Class

When you declare a class, you can declare both the data and the functions. Otherwise, a class declaration is similar to a structure. Here is an example of a declaration for a class that describes weather statistics:

```
// Weather class
class Weather
```

```
{
public;
     Weather( float, float, float,     // Constructor
              float, float, int, float );
     void Display();                   // Display weather
     ~Weather();                       // Destructor
private;
     float high_temperature;     // Weather statistics data
     float low_temperature;
     float inches_rain;
     float barometric_pressure;
     float relative_humidity;
     int wind_direction;         // 0=N 1=NE 2=E 3=SE
                                 // 4=S 5=SW 6=W 7=NW
     float wind_velocity;
};
```

In the preceding example, the data members of the class `Weather` are declared. These data items make up the weather statistics data. Three functions for `Weather` are declared also: `Weather()`, `Display()`, and `~Weather()`. These functions are called *member functions*. The member function declarations are specified as prototypes.

Declaring and Defining Member Functions

You place the member functions after the class declaration. Listing 16.1 presents the declaration of the class named `Weather` and its member functions, which are placed in a header file named weather.h.

Listing 16.1. The source listing for the weather.h header file.

```
// weather.h - Weather class
class Weather
{
public:
     Weather( float, float, float,     // Constructor
              float, float, int, float );
     void Display();                   // Display weather
     ~Weather();                       // Destructor
private:
```

```
     float high_temperature;     // Weather statistics data
     float low_temperature;
     float inches_rain;
     float barometric_pressure;
     float relative_humidity;
     int wind_direction;         // 0=N 1=NE 2=E 3=SE
                                 // 4=S 5=SW 6=W 7=NW
     float wind_velocity;
     int range( int, int, int );
     float range( float, float, float );
};
// Utility programs for member functions
// Note: function name range is overloaded
int Weather::range( int low, int high, int value )
{
     return  (value < low) ? low :
             (value > high) ? high : value;
}
float Weather::range( float low, float high, float value )
{
     return  (value < low) ? low :
             (value > high) ? high : value;
}
// The constructor that is called when a variable is declared
Weather::Weather( float thi,  // High temperature
         float tlo,           // Low temperature
         float rain,          // Inches of rain
         float bp,            // Barometric pressure
         float rh,            // Relative humidity
         int wd,              // Wind direction
         float wv )           // Wind velocity
{
     high_temperature    = thi;    // Weather statistics data
     low_temperature     = tlo;
     inches_rain         = range( 0.0, 20.0, rain );
     barometric_pressure = range( 27.0, 32.0, bp );
     relative_humidity   = range( 0.0, 100.0, rh );
     wind_direction      = range( 0, 7, wd );
     wind_velocity       = range( 0.0, 200.0, wv );
     cout << "Constructor was called\n";
}
```

continues

Listing 16.1. continued

```
// Function displays weather statistics
void Weather::Display()
{
     char *direction[] =
     { "North", "Northeast", "East", "Southeast",
       "South", "Southwest", "West", "Northwest" };
     cout << "  Weather statistics\n"
          << "Temperature (Degrees Fahrenheit)\n"
          << "  High: " << high_temperature
          << "  Low: "  << low_temperature  << "\n"
          << "Rain "    << inches_rain << " (inches)\n"
          << "Relative humidity: "
          << relative_humidity << "\n"
          << "Barometric pressure "
          << barometric_pressure
          << " (inches mercury)\n"
          << "Wind-  direction: "
          <<    direction[wind_direction] << "\n"
          << "        velocity:  "
          << wind_velocity << "(miles per hour)\n";
}
float Weather::Temperature_range()
{
     return high_temperature - low_temperature
}
Weather::~Weather()    // Return type is not allowed
                       // for destructor
{
    cout << "Destructor was called\n";
}
```

The `Display()` member function looks like any other function. However, the other two functions, `Weather()` and `~Weather()`, are called the *constructor* and *destructor*, respectively, and they have the same name as the class. All three function names are prefixed with the class name followed by the scope resolution operator (`::`), indicating that the function is a member function of the class, as in

```
Weather::Display();
```

A member function name has *class scope*, which means that the lifetime of the member function exists as long as an object declared for the class exists. Furthermore, a member function can reference member data for an object. The function prototype appears inside the declaration of the class `Weather`. Functions that are not a constructor or destructor are required to have a return type, and their general definition form is

```
return-type class-name::function-name( argument-list )
{
   :
}
```

The member function name can be overloaded. You can declare other functions with the same name but a different signature. If you declare a member function in one class, you can have other functions with the same name and signature outside the class or in another class. Remember that a *signature* is the parameter list. If, for two functions with the same name, the number of parameters, the type of parameters, or both differ, their signatures are different.

Constructors and Destructors

A *constructor* is automatically called when an instance of a class is created. The constructor performs any required initialization of the instance of a class. As shown in an earlier example, a constructor can be used also to validate data. A constructor does not have a return type, and the general form of the constructor is

```
class-name::class-name( argument-list )
{
   :
}
```

A *destructor* is automatically called when an instance of a class is destroyed. Notice that a destructor has the same name as the class except that the destructor is prefixed with the tilde (~). The general form of a destructor is

```
class-name::~class-name( argument-list )
{
   :
}
```

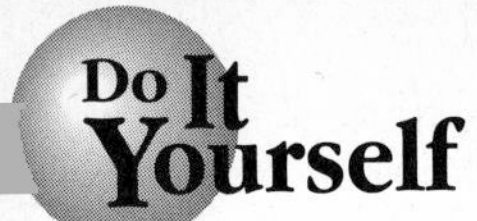

public and private Labels

There are two types of sections in a class definition: a *private* section and a *public* section. All class members are declared in one of the two sections. Each is preceded with either a `private` label or a `public` label, as in the following example:

```
class Apple
{
private:
     // Private members are declared here
     int hidden_data;
     int hidden_function();
public:
     // Public members are declared here
     int fcn1();
     int fcn2();
private:
     int another_private
};
```

The public or private mode is initiated with a `public` or `private` label, respectively, and continues either until another label is encountered or until the end of the class definition. You can have as many public or private sections as you like. However, for readability, it is customary to put all private members in one group and all public members in another group.

The default mode for a class definition is private. This means that if you do not have a label at the beginning of the class definition, members are given private visibility until a `public` label is encountered. Note an example:

```
class Pear
{
     int count;  // Private by default
public:
     int fcn();  // Public method
}
```

Again, for readability, it is best to precede each section with a label. Wouldn't it improve the appearance of the preceding code if a `private` label were placed before the declaration of the variable `count`?

Members in the private section can be accessed only from member functions or *friend functions*. Friend functions are functions shared by multiple classes and are discussed in Chapter 18, "More on Using Classes." You communicate with a class by calling one of the functions in the public section; the public member functions are called the *public interface* for a class. Data in the private section is hidden from the rest of the program. Hidden data is one of the important features of OOP.

In the `Weather` class example, the weather statistics data members (temperatures, barometric pressure, and so on) are declared in the private section and can be accessed by member functions only.

C++ enables you to specify public and private sections for `struct` definitions. However, for `struct` definitions, public mode is the default mode. This is the opposite from the `class` definition for which private mode is the default. Note an example:

```
struct mystruct
{
     // Public mode--public members are declared
     :
private:
     // Private members are declared
     :
public:
     // More public members are declared
     :
};
```

Using a Class

After you have defined a class and written its associated member functions, you can declare an instance of that class the same way you declare any other variable. The only difference is that you do not call it a "variable." You call it an "object."

The class declaration for `Weather` and associated member functions were placed in a header file called weather.h, presented earlier in Listing 16.1. A simple program that uses the class `Weather` is shown in Listing 16.2.

Listing 16.2. The source listing for WEATHER.CPP.

```
// WEATHER.CPP - Illustrates use of a class object
#include <iostream.h>
#include "weather.h"
void main()
{
     Weather Today( 77.8, 64.1, 0.0, 31.2, 41.2, 2, 15.3 );
     Weather Yesterday( 67.3, 45.3, .5, 29.2, 84.0, 4, 11.1 );
     cout << "\n Display today's Weather\n";
     Today.Display();
     cout << "\n Display Yesterday's Weather\n";
     Yesterday.Display();
}
```

In WEATHER.CPP, two instances of the `Weather` class are declared: `Today` and `Yesterday`. The parameters define the weather data (temperature, rainfall, and so on). The constructor is called to establish the values of the private data members. Listing 16.3 shows the results of executing WEATHER.EXE.

Listing 16.3. Results of executing WEATHER.EXE.

```
Constructor was called
Constructor was called

 Display today's Weather
  Weather statistics
Temperature (Degrees Fahrenheit)
  High: 77.8  Low: 64.1
Rain 0 (inches)
Relative humidity: 41.2
Barometric pressure 31.2 (inches mercury)
Wind-  direction: East
       velocity:  15.3(miles per hour)

 Display Yesterday's Weather
```

```
  Weather statistics
Temperature (Degrees Fahrenheit)
  High: 67.3  Low: 45.3
Rain 0.5 (inches)
Relative humidity: 84
Barometric pressure 29.2 (inches mercury)
Wind-  direction: South
       velocity:  11.1(miles per hour)
Destructor was called
Destructor was called
```


The `Display()` member function is called to display the weather for `Today` and `Yesterday` with the statements

```
Today.Display();  // Display member data for object Today
Yesterday.Display();
```

Notice that you preface the member function with the name of the object you want to display. The member operator (.) separates the name of the object from the name of the member function. In other words, you reference the member function just as you reference any member of a structure.

Remember that the member function uses the data members of the object used to reference the member function. You refer to a member variable within the member function `Display()` by its name with no other qualifier. The variable `relative_humidity` is a member of the `Weather` class and is referred to in `Display()` in a way similar to this:

```
cout << "Relative humidity: " << relative_humidity << "\n"
```

When you call `Today.Display()`, the value of `relative_humidity` is displayed for the object named `Today`. As the `Weather` class is currently defined, you cannot reference `relative_humidity` from outside the member function.

The Creation and Destruction of Objects

When a variable is declared, the constructor `Weather` is called, which tests the range of parameters and stores a value in the private members of the object. The constructor also displays a message indicating that it was called.

As you can see from the results in Listing 16.3, the constructor was called twice, resulting in the creation of two instances of the `Weather` class: `Today` and `Yesterday`.

As you may remember, when a variable (object) is declared inside a function, it is an automatic variable and exists until the function returns to the calling function. Then the variable no longer exists—it is destroyed. But when an object for a class is destroyed, the destructor is automatically called. The last two lines in Listing 16.3 are displayed when the class `Weather` destructor is automatically called to destroy the `Today` and `Yesterday` objects. The destructor is automatically called right before `main()` exits.

Global variables exist for the life of a program. Similarly, when a class object is a global object, it exists from the time it is declared to the time the program exits. When a global object is declared, the constructor is automatically called. Right before the program exits, the destructor is automatically called. In the example in Listing 16.3, the destructor really performs no useful task—but then, it is just an example. Usually, you use a destructor to perform cleanup operations or for such operations as saving an object to a file.

You are not required to provide a constructor or destructor. If you do not provide a constructor, no constructor is called when an object is declared. If you do not provide a destructor, no destructor is called right before an object is destroyed.

More on Member Functions

Now return your attention to member functions. You call a member function just as you would reference a member in a structure. The member function name is prefixed with the object name followed by the member operator (`.`):

```
object name.member function name( argument list );
```

With this technique, you can reference public member functions only. Private member functions are referenced by other member functions. For example, the member function `range()` is private. It is called by the constructor (refer to Listing 16.1). `range()` is also referenced directly—its name is not preceded with the object name.

You can use a pointer or a reference to an object to call a method (member function), as illustrated in the following example:

```
Weather LastTuesday( 66.2, 52.2, 1.1, 30.2, 40.2, 6, 5.1 );
Weather *Oneday = &LastTuesday;  // Oneday is a pointer
Weather &ADay   = LastTuesday;   // ADay is a reference

LastTuesday.Display(); // Use object name to display weather
Oneday->Display();     // Display weather using pointer
ADay.Display();        // Display weather using reference
```


Access Functions

If you place a variable declaration that is a member of a class in a public section of the class definition, the variable can be accessed from any function in the program. In other words, the variable can be referenced from outside the class. For example, the variable `WhatEver` can be placed in the public section of the class `Weather` definition. `WhatEver` can be referenced from the main program. For example, the following statement in the main program can be used to assign a new value to the data member `WhatEver` for the object `Today`:

```
Today.WhatEver = -99999;
```

This technique may seem simple enough. But it is a bad technique because it can increase the likelihood of errors in the program and make it difficult to maintain. When a variable can be changed outside the member functions, you can no longer guarantee the validity of objects. Any function in the program system can change the variable. Furthermore, the representation of the data member is revealed to the whole program. If you change its representation, you will have to make changes throughout the program.

It is much better programming practice to use *access functions* to assign a value to a data member of an object instead of allowing a data value to be public. An access function is used also to fetch the value of a data member of an object. An access function is a member function whose sole purpose is to access private data members. For example, declare the variable `WhatEver` as a private member. Then add to the `Weather` class an access function that fetches the value of `WhatEver`. Add another access function that stores a new valid value in `WhatEver`. Here is the code you might use:

```
// GetWhatEver is an access function to fetch value of WhatEver
int Weather::GetWhatEver( void );
```

```
{
     return WhatEver;
}
// SetWhatEver is an access function to store value to WhatEver
void Weather::SetWhatEver( int we );
{
     WhatEver = Range( 1, 31, we );
}
```

You can access the value of WhatEver for the Today object from anywhere in the program, as shown in the following example:

```
int savevalue;
savevalue = Today.GetWhatEver();
Today.SetWhatEver( 19 );
```

When you use access functions to access class data and declare the data private, you hide the representation of your class. Using this technique, called *encapsulation,* you can change the internal processing in a class without affecting the rest of a program. Encapsulation is an important feature of OOP.

The Default Constructor

When you declare a class object, it is not always convenient or possible to initialize all the private data members. You may want to omit some of the parameters. In the declaration for the constructor in Listing 16.4, you must provide all seven parameters. You may want to provide the option of creating an object without supplying all its values. There are two ways to do this. The first is to use default arguments for the function. For an illustration, replace the prototype for the constructor in the public section of the class definition with the following statement:

```
Weather( float = 0.0, float = 0.0,      // Constructor
         float = 0.0, float = 0.0,
         float = 0.0, int = 0,
         float = 0.0 );
```

Then declare instances of the class Weather without supplying any arguments:

```
Weather Tuesday, Wednesday  // Declare two new instances
```

The second way to accomplish the same operation is to apply function overloading. You add a default prototype with no arguments and a corresponding constructor declaration. Listing 16.4 presents a partial class definition showing how to add a default constructor with function overloading.

16

Listing 16.4. A partial listing of the modified `Weather` class definition.

```
// Weather class
class Weather
{
public:
     Weather( float, float, float,    // Constructor
              float, float, int, float );
     Weather( void );                 // Default constructor
     void SetValues( float, float,    // Access function
              float, float, float, int, float );
     void Display();                  // Display weather
     ~Weather();                      // Destructor
private:
     :
};
// Utility programs for member functions
Weather::Weather( void )
{
   // Assign initial values to private data
   :
}
// This access function sets private variables
void Weather::SetValues( float thi, // High temperature
        float tlo,                  // Low temperature
        float rain,                 // Inches of rain
        float bp,                   // Barometric pressure
        float rh,                   // Relative humidity
        int wd,                     // Wind direction
        float wv )                  // Wind velocity
{
     high_temperature    = thi;     // Weather statistics data
     low_temperature     = tlo;
```

continues

Listing 16.4. continued

```
    inches_rain         = range( 0.0, 20.0, rain );
    barometric_pressure = range( 27.0, 32.0, bp );
    relative_humidity   = range( 0.0, 100.0, rh );
    wind_direction      = range( 0, 7, wd );
    wind_velocity       = range( 0.0, 200.0, wv );
}
:
:
```

With the class definition in Listing 16.4, you can declare an object either with all its parameters or without any parameters. An access function, `SetValues()`, can be used to establish weather data after the object has been declared. Listing 16.5 shows a program that uses the class with the default constructor.

Listing 16.5. The source listing for WEATHER1.CPP.

```
// WEATHER1.CPP - Illustrates use of a class object with
// the default constructor
#include <iostream.h>
#include "weather.h"
void main()
{
    Weather Today( 77.8, 64.1, 0.0, 31.2, 41.2, 2, 15.3 );
    Weather Yesterday;   // Declare using default constructor
    cout << "\n Display today's Weather\n";
    Today.Display();
    Yesterday.SetValues( 67.3, 45.3, .5, 29.2, 84.0, 4, 11.1 );
    cout << "\n Display Yesterday's Weather\n";
    Yesterday.Display();
}
```

The results are similar to those in Listing 16.3. In this example, the values of the `Yesterday` object were established with the `SetValues()` access function. You can also initialize the values of an operation with an assignment statement, as in

```
Weather Today( 120.8, 84.1, 0.0, 31.2, 41.2, 2, 15.3 );
Weather HottestDay;   // Declare using default constructor
HottestDay = Today;
```

The HottestDay object is assigned the contents of the Today object. You can also initialize an object when you declare it. In the example

```
Weather Tuesday = Weather( 108.8, 80.1, 0.0, 31.2,
                           41.2, 2, 15.3 );
```

the Tuesday object is declared and initialized with the constructor.

Objects and the const Keyword

Like other variables, objects can be read-only. As you remember, if you place the const keyword in front of a variable declaration, it becomes a constant. You can initialize it when you declare it; after that, it becomes read-only. In the example

```
const int i_val = 3;
```

the variable i_val is declared as a constant equal to 3. If you attempt to assign a new value to i_val, you will get a compiler error.

Objects can also be constants. In the following example, the Friday object becomes a constant object as soon as the constructor finishes initializing it:

```
const Weather Friday( 94.3, 40., 0.0, 31.1, 42.1, 3, 6.3 );
```

When a variable is declared as a constant, the C++ compiler has no trouble determining whether an attempt is made to change its value. However, for a class object, it is not always apparent. To make sure that a member function does not modify an object, the compiler will not let you call any member function to operate on a const object. There is an exception. Many times, you have member functions that never modify any members of an object. One familiar example is the Weather::Display() function. All it does is display the contents of an object. If you place the const keyword after the parameter list of a member function, the function becomes a read-only function. The C++ compiler permits you to call a read-only member function for a const object. Here is a partial listing of the Weather class definition, showing how to make a member function into a read-only function:

```
class Weather
{
public:
```

```
     // Public member functions
     :
     void Display() const;     // Read-only member function
private:
     // Private member functions
     :
};
:
// Function displays weather statistics
void Weather::Display() const
{
   // Code to display object
   :
}
```

In the preceding code, the changes required to make a member function read-only are indicated in bold print. Note that the `const` keyword is added to both the prototype and the declaration of the member function. Now you can use the read-only method (member function) with a constant object, as illustrated in the following example:

```
const Weather Friday( 94.3, 40., 0.0, 31.1, 42.1, 3, 6.3 );
cout << "\n Display Weather for Friday\n";
Friday.Display();   // Display is a read-only member function
```

You can also make member functions into read-only member functions if they retrieve the value of a data member. However, if you try to make read-only a member function that modifies any data members, you will get a compiler error. Furthermore, a read-only member function cannot call a member function that is not read-only.

It is good practice to make member functions read-only whenever possible. Read-only member functions are more useful because they can be used with both variable and constant objects.

Arrays of Objects

When you need more than one instance of a class, you can declare multiple objects and give each one a name. Another way is to declare an array of objects. Declaring an array of objects is as simple as declaring an array of `int` data types. For example, the following line declares an array of `Weather` objects:

```
Weather WArray[3];  // Declare a 3-element array of objects
```

Here the default constructor is used to initialize all three array elements. Now you need to store some actual values in the members of each element. You can use the `Weather` class `SetValues()` access function to initialize data members:


```
// Establish values of first object element
WArray[0].SetValues( 90.9, 70., 0.1, 30.1, 80.1, 2, 1.3 );
```

You could establish data member values by using an assignment statement:

```
    WArray[1] = Today;          // Assign values to data members
                                // of the second and third
    WArray[2] = Yesterday;      // object elements
```

You could also initialize the data members of object array elements when you declare the array, as shown in the following statement:

```
// Declare and initialize array of objects
Weather WArray2[3] =
{
    Weather( 90., 74., 0.0, 30.1, 60.1, 3, 1.3 ),
    Weather( 92., 70., 0.0, 30.2, 60.2, 3, 2.4 ),
    Weather( 94., 68., 0.0, 30.3, 60.3, 3, 3.5 )
};
```

In the preceding statement, each of the three array element objects are initialized using the constructor. Once an object array is declared, its elements can be referenced the same way any other array element is referenced. The following example displays the data members for all three array elements:

```
for ( i = 0; i < 3; i++ )
    WArray2[i].Display();
```

Objects within Objects

The member of a class can be another class object, which is referred to as a *member object*. When you use member objects, you are practicing another OOP concept, called composition. *Composition* is the act of building an object "composed" of other objects. For example, you can define a class of weather stations, called `Station`, which will include the class `Weather` as a member. The definition for the `Station` class is placed in the header file station.h (see Listing 16.6) and included in source files that use the class.

Listing 16.6. The source listing for the station.h header file.

```
// station.h - Class definition for a weather station object
#include <string.h>  // Prototype for strncpy() library function
class Station
{
private:
     char Name[20];        // Name of station
     int Longitude;        // Longitude of station in degrees
     int Latitude;         // Latitude of station in degrees
     Weather Statistics;   // Weather class member object

public:
     Station( char *, int, int, float, float, float, float,
              float, int, float );      // Constructor
     Station( void );                   // Default constructor
                                        // Access function
     void SetStation( char *, int, int, int, Weather );
     void Display() const;              // Display weather
     ~Station();                        // Destructor
};
// Utility programs for member functions
// The constructor that is called when a varable is declared
Station::Station( char *SName,          // Station name
                                        // Station location:
                  int SLongitude,       //   Longitude
                  int SLatitude,        //   Latitude
                          // Definition for data object
                  float thi,            // High temperature
                  float tlo,            // Low temperature
                  float rain,           // Inches of rain
                  float bp,             // Barometric pressure
                  float rh,             // Relative humidity
                  int wd,               // Wind direction
                  float wv )            // Wind velocity
```

16

```
     // Member initialization function (after parameter list)
       : Statistics( thi, tlo, rain, bp, rh, wd, wv )
{
     strncpy( Name, SName, 20 ); // Move SName to Name member

     // Use range function to make sure that longitude
     // and latitude values are in valid range
     Longitude = range( 0, 360, SLongitude ); // Station
                                              // Longitude
     Latitude  = range( -90, 90, SLatitude ); // Station Latitude
     cout << "Station Constructor was called\n";
}
// The constructor that is called when a varable is declared
Station::Station( void )     // Default constructor
{
     Name[0]='\0';           // Station name
     Latitude      = 0;
     Longitude =  0;
     cout << "Default Station constructor was called\n";
}
// Function displays Weather data for station
void Station::Display() const
{
     int Lat1, Lon1;
     char *LatDir, *LonDir;
     if ( Latitude < 0 )
     {
          Lat1 = - Latitude;
          LatDir = "South";
     }
     else
     {
          Lat1 = Latitude;
          LatDir = "North";
     }
     if ( Longitude > 180 )
     {
          Lon1 = Longitude - 180;
          LonDir = "East";
     }
```

continues

Listing 16.6. continued

```
    else
    {
         Lon1 = Longitude;
         LonDir = "West";
    }
    cout << "\nWeather Station: " << Name << "\n"
         << "   Location - Latitude: "
         << Lat1 << " degrees " << LatDir << "\n"
         << "              Longitude: "
         << Lon1 << " degrees " <<  LonDir << "\n";
    Statistics.Display();
}
Station::~Station()
{
    cout << "Destructor was called to destroy Station object\n";
}
```

The definition for the `Station` class is just like other class definitions except that it has a private member, named `Statistics`, which is a `Weather` class object. Notice that no arguments are specified. The constructor for `Statistics` is not called until a `Station` object is declared.

A special *member initializer* function is called when a `Station` object is declared, to construct the member object `Statistics` before the `Station` constructor is called. The member initializer is actually a call to the member object's constructor and is specified in a rather unique form. You place a colon (:) after the parameter list of the function declaration of the `Station` constructor. The colon is followed by a call to the member object's constructor, complete with an argument list. Note this example:

```
Station::Station( char *SName, SLongitude, SLatitude,
            float thi, float tlo, float rain, float bp, float rh,
            int wd, float wv )
        : Statistics( thi, tlo, rain, bp, rh, wd, wv )
{
      // Constructor statements
      :
}
```

Note that the parameters in the argument list for the member initializer correspond to the parameters in the class `Station` constructor's parameter list. If you have more than one member initializer, you form a comma-delimited list of member initializers. The following example demonstrates how to specify a list of member initializers:

```
// Class PetShop definition
class PetShop
private:
     int AnimalCount;
     Animal Cat( a );      // Member objects
     Animal Dog( b );
     Animal Bird( c );
⋮
public:
     PetShop( int, int, int, int );
     ⋮
};
// PetShop Class object constructor
PetShop::PetShop( int a, int b, int c, int d )
                : Cat( a ), Dog( b ), Bird( c )
{
   // Code for constructor
   ⋮
}
```

If you omit a member initializer for a member object, the member object's default constructor will be used. Because the definition for the `Weather` class has a default constructor, you could omit the member initializer, as in

```
Station::Station( char *SName, SLongitude, SLatitude,
          float thi, float tlo, float rain, float bp, float rh,
          int wd, float wv )
{
      // Constructor statements
      ⋮
      // Use access function to set values of member object
      Statistics.SetValues( thi, tlo, rain, bp, rh, wd, wv );
}
```

There are two reasons why you probably would not want to do this. First, this method is not as efficient as using the member initializer because you assign values to the data members of the member object twice—values are assigned by both the default constructor and the `SetValues()` function. Second, you might want the member object to be a constant. Remember that a constant object is declared with the `const` keyword. Only an object's constructor can initialize a constant object. The constructor for the `Station` class cannot initialize a constant member object.

If you omit a member initializer for a member object that has no default object, the compiler generates an error.

The `Station` class shown in Listing 16.6 also contains a default constructor, a function to display object contents (`Display`) and a destructor (`~Station`).

Listing 16.7 presents the source listing for STATION.CPP, which declares two instances of the `Station` class and displays their contents. The results of executing STATION.EXE are shown in Listing 16.8.

Listing 16.7. The source listing for STATION.CPP.

```
// STATION.CPP - Demonstrates use of Station class
#include <iostream.h>
#include "weather1.h"
#include "station.h"
void main()
{
     Station NewYork( "New York City",74, 40, 84.2, 78.1, 0.0,
                      31.2, 41.2, 2, 15.3 );
     NewYork.Display();

     Station Dallas( "Dallas", 96, 32, 88.2, 71.3, .5,
                     29.2, 44.0, 4, 11.1 );
     Dallas.Display();
}
```

Take a moment to marvel at the high level of abstraction in the preceding program. All the work is done within the class definition. The class knows how to manipulate the object. As a result, the program logic that uses the class is rather simple. You just declare an object and start using it.

From the results of executing STATION.EXE (see Listing 16.8), you can see when the various constructors were called. The member initializer is first called to initialize the `Statistics` member object. The `Station` class constructor is then called to initialize the `NewYork` object. The `Station` class

Display() member function is called to display the contents of the NewYork object. This Display() function calls the Weather class Display() member function to display the weather statistics. The process is repeated for the Dallas object. Notice that when the program exits, it calls the destructor functions.

Listing 16.8. Results of executing STATION.EXE.

```
Class Weather constructor was called
Station Constructor was called

Weather Station: New York City
   Location - Latitude: 40 degrees North
              Longitude: 74 degrees West
  Weather statistics
Temperature (Degrees Fahrenheit)
  High: 84.2  Low: 78.1
Rain 0 (inches)
Relative humidity: 41.2
Barometric pressure 31.2 (inches mercury)
Wind-  direction: East
       velocity:  15.3(miles per hour)
Class Weather constructor was called
Station Constructor was called

Weather Station: Dallas
  Location - Latitude: 32 Degrees North
             Longitude: 96 degrees West
  Weather statistics
Temperature (Degrees Fahrenheit)
  High: 88.2  Low: 71.3
Rain 0.5 (inches)
Relative humidity: 44
Barometric pressure 29.2 (inches mercury)
Wind-  direction: South
       velocity:  11.1(miles per hour)
Destructor was called to destroy Station object
Class Weather destructor was called
Destructor was called to destroy Station object
Class Weather destructor was called
```

Examples of Class Usage

Earlier in this chapter, you were introduced to the definition of a class named Weather. As you saw more features of classes, code changes were made to the class definition and its member functions. All the changes made to the Weather class have been combined into a single program—WEATHER1.CPP—which is presented in this section. Listing 16.9 is a source listing for the header file weather1.h, which contains the Weather class definition. Listing 16.10 is a source listing for the program that uses the class.

Listing 16.9. The source listing for the weather1.h header file.

```
// weather1.h - Weather class definition
class Weather
{
public:
     Weather( float, float, float,          // Constructor
              float, float, int, float );
     Weather( void );
     void SetValues( float, float, float, // Access function
              float, float, int, float );
     void Display() const;                // Display weather
     ~Weather();                          // Destructor
private:
     float high_temperature;     // Weather statistics data
     float low_temperature;
     float inches_rain;
     float barometric_pressure;
     float relative_humidity;
     int wind_direction;         // 0=N 1=NE 2=E 3=SE
                                 // 4=S 5=SW 6=W 7=NW
     float wind_velocity;
 };
 // Utility programs for member functions
 // Note: function name range is overloaded
 int range (int low, int high, int value)
 {
      return  (value < low) ? low :
              (value > high) ? high : value;
 }
```

16

```
float range (float low, float high, float value)
{
     return  (value < low) ? low :
             (value > high) ? high : value;
}
// The constructor that is called when a varable is declared
Weather::Weather( float thi,     // High temperature
         float tlo,              // Low temperature
         float rain,             // Inches of rain
         float bp,               // Barometric pressure
         float rh,               // Relative humidity
         int wd,                 // Wind direction
         float wv )              // Wind velocity
{
     high_temperature    = thi;  // Weather statistics data
     low_temperature     = tlo;
     inches_rain         = range( 0.0, 20.0, rain );
     barometric_pressure = range( 27.0, 32.0, bp );
     relative_humidity   = range( 0.0, 100.0, rh );
     wind_direction      = range( 0, 7, wd );
     wind_velocity       = range( 0.0, 200.0, wv );
     cout << "Constructor was called\n";
}
// The constructor that is called when a varable is declared
Weather::Weather( void )                 // Default constructor
{
     high_temperature     = 0.0;         // Weather statistics data
     low_temperature      = 0.0;
     inches_rain          = 0.0;
     barometric_pressure  = 27.0;
     relative_humidity    = 0.0;
     wind_direction       = 0;
     wind_velocity        = 0.0;
     cout << "Default constructor was called\n";
}
void Weather::SetValues( float thi,      // High temperature
         float tlo,                      // Low temperature
         float rain,                     // Inches of rain
         float bp,                       // Barometric pressure
         float rh,                       // Relative humidity
         int wd,                         // Wind direction
         float wv )                      // Wind velocity
```

continues

Listing 16.9. continued

```
{
     high_temperature    = thi;         // Weather statistics data
     low_temperature     = tlo;
     inches_rain         = range( 0.0, 20.0, rain );
     barometric_pressure = range( 27.0, 32.0, bp );
     relative_humidity   = range( 0.0, 100.0, rh );
     wind_direction      = range( 0, 7, wd );
     wind_velocity       = range( 0.0, 200.0, wv );
}

// Function displays weather statistics
void Weather::Display() const
{
     char *direction[] =
     { "North", "Northeast", "East", "Southeast",
       "South", "Southwest", "West", "Northwest" };

     cout << "  Weather statistics\n"
          << "Temperature (Degrees Fahrenheit)\n"
          << "  High: " << high_temperature
          << "  Low: "  << low_temperature  << "\n"
          << "Rain "    << inches_rain << " (inches)\n"
          << "Relative humidity: "
          << relative_humidity << "\n"
          << "Barometric pressure "
          << barometric_pressure
          << " (inches mercury)\n"
          << "Wind-  direction: "
          <<    direction[wind_direction] << "\n"
          << "       velocity:  "
          << wind_velocity << "(miles per hour)\n";
}
Weather::~Weather()
{
    cout << "Destructor was called\n";
}
```

The program WEATHER1.CPP demonstrates how to create and use `Weather` objects. You are shown how to initialize an object in the following ways:

- When you declare the object
- With the `SetValues()` member function, also known as an access function
- With an assignment statement

The program shows also how to declare and use constant objects and arrays of objects.

Listing 16.10. The source listing for WEATHER1.CPP.

```
// WEATHER1.CPP - Illustrates use of Weather class
#include <iostream.h>
#include "weather1.h"
void main()
{
     Weather Today( 120.8, 84.1, 0.0, 31.2, 41.2, 2, 15.3 );
     cout << "\n Display today's Weather\n";
     Today.Display();

     // Use access function to initialize object
     Weather Yesterday;     // Declare using default constructor
     Yesterday.SetValues( 67.3, 45.3, .5, 29.2, 84.0, 4, 11.1 );
     cout << "\n Display Yesterday's Weather\n";
     Yesterday.Display();

     // Declare and initialize object
     Weather Tuesday =
             Weather( 98.8, 80.1, 0.0, 30.4, 44.2, 3, 3.1 );
     cout << "\n Display Tuesday's Weather\n";
     Tuesday.Display();

     // Initialize object with assignment statement
     Weather HottestDay;     // Declare using default constructor
     HottestDay = Today;
     cout << "\n Display Weather for hottest day\n";
     HottestDay.Display();
```

continues

Listing 16.10. continued

```
    // Initialize a const object

    const Weather Friday( 94.3, 40., 0.0, 31.1, 42.1, 3, 6.3 );
    cout << "\n Display Weather for Friday\n";
    Friday.Display();

    // Declare array of objects
    Weather WArray[3];      // Declare array of 3 Weather objects
    // Establish values of first object element
    WArray[0].SetValues( 90.9, 70., 0.1, 30.1, 80.1, 2, 1.3 );
    WArray[1] = Today;      // Assign values to data members
                            // of the second and third
    WArray[2] = Yesterday; // object elements
    cout << "\n Display Weather for Arrays\n";
    for ( int i = 0; i < 3; i++ )
         WArray[i].Display();

    // Declare and initialize array of objects
    Weather WArray2[3] =
    {
         Weather ( 90., 74., 0.0, 30.1, 60.1, 3, 1.3 ),
         Weather ( 92., 70., 0.0, 30.2, 60.2, 3, 2.4 ),
         Weather ( 94., 68., 0.0, 30.3, 60.3, 3, 3.5 )
    };
    for ( i = 0; i < 3; i++ )
         WArray2[i].Display();
}
```

What You Have Learned

In this chapter, you learned about classes and objects and were briefly introduced to object-oriented programming (OOP). Specifically, you learned the following:

- How OOP is based on the concepts of abstraction, encapsulation, and class hierarchies

- How to use a class to create a new data type
- How to define data and function members of a class
- What constructors and destructors are and how to create and use them
- How to hide data and why it should be hidden
- How to declare, initialize, and use class objects
- How to create constant objects and read-only functions
- How to create and use arrays of objects
- How, using composition, you can build objects containing objects

Using Memory with Classes

It may be said that his wit shines at the expense of his memory.

—Alain René Lesage
Gil Blas (1735)

In This Chapter

So far, you have learned about classes containing data members that take up a fixed amount of memory during their lifetime. In this chapter, you learn how to change the size of objects dynamically, and you learn some useful techniques to use with dynamically sized objects. Specifically, this chapter covers the following topics:

- Objects and the free store
- Overloading the assignment operator
- The `this` operator

- Dynamic memory allocation for an array of objects
- The copy constructor
- Overloading the new and delete operators

The Free Store and Objects

As you learned in the section "The Free Store—Memory Allocation Operators" in Chapter 11, you can use the new and delete keywords to allocate and deallocate memory. In review, you can allocate a memory block with the new operator:

```
int *iptr;             // Allocate a pointer to an int
int (*array)[];        // Allocate a pointer to an array
struct Bird
{
     char Name[30];
     int  count;
};
Bird *BirdPtr;         // Allocate a pointer to structure Bird

iptr = new int;        // Allocate a block of memory for an int
array = new int[20];   // Allocate a block of memory for an array
BirdPtr = new Bird;    // Assign a block for structure Bird
```

The language element new is not a function because it has no arguments. It is an operator, like + and -. The new operator allocates a pointer of the type specified by the operand to the right of new. If new cannot return a memory block, it returns a null pointer.

You can delete the memory block and free up the memory with the delete operator:

```
delete iptr;
delete array;
delete BirdPtr;
```

Allocating Memory for Member Pointers

Sometimes you are not sure how big to make a member object when you define a class. One solution is to make it large enough to hold the maximum amount of data you will ever need. A better solution is to declare a pointer to the member object when you define the class. Then you can use the `new` and `delete` operators within a member function to dynamically allocate space for the pointer. When you declare a class object, a memory block of the appropriate size will be allocated for the member objects.

In the example presented in Listing 17.1, the `Quotation` class is defined in the header file quote.h. The data members consist of two pointers to character strings. The `Quotation` constructor calls the `strlen()` run-time library function to get the length of the `Auth` string argument. Then the constructor uses the `new` operator to allocate enough memory to hold the string, and assigns it to the `author` data member. Finally, the constructor copies the `Auth` argument strings into the allocated space. The constructor repeats the process for the `quote` member pointer. The destructor frees the allocated space associated with the `author` and `quote` pointers. There is also a member function to store and retrieve values, and one to display the member data.

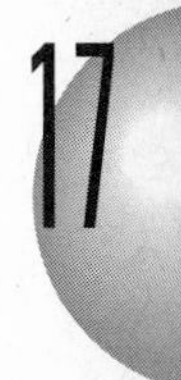

Listing 17.1. The source listing for the quote.h header file.

```
// quote.h - Quotation class used to illustrate dynamic memory
// allocation of data members
#include <string.h>
class Quotation
{
public:
     Quotation( char *, char * );        // Constructor
     Quotation( void );                  // Default constructor
     void Display() const;               // Display quotation
     ~Quotation();                       // Destructor
                                         // Access functions:
     void SetAuthor( char * );           //   Store an author
     void SetQuote( char * );            //   Store a quote
     char *GetAuthor( void ) const;      //   Fetch the author
     char *GetQuote( void ) const;       //   Fetch the quote
```

continues

Listing 17.1. continued

```
private:
     char *author;                          // Author of quotation
     char *quote;                           // Text of quotation
};
// Member functions

// The constructor that is called when a variable is declared
Quotation::Quotation( char * Auth, char *Quotation )
{
    int length;
    length = strlen( Auth );      // Get length of argument
    author = new char[length+1];  // Allocate buffer
                                  // for author name
    strcpy( author, Auth );       // Copy string Auth to author
    length = strlen( Quotation );
    quote  = new char[length+1];  // Allocate buffer for quote
    strcpy( quote, Quotation );
}
// The constructor that is called when a variable is declared
// with no arguments
Quotation::Quotation( void )      // Default constructor
{
    author = NULL;
    quote  = NULL;
}
void Quotation::SetAuthor( char *Auth )     // Initialize Author
{
    int length;
    length = strlen( Auth );      // Get length of argument
    author = new char[length+1];  // Allocate buffer for
                                  // author name
    strcpy( author, Auth );       // Copy string Auth to author
}
void Quotation::SetQuote( char *Quotation ) // Initialize quote
{
    int length;
    length = strlen( Quotation ); // Get length of argument
    quote  = new char[length+1];  // Allocate buffer for quote
    strcpy( quote, Quotation );
}
```

```
char *Quotation::GetAuthor( void ) const
{
    return author;
}
char *Quotation::GetQuote( void ) const
{
    return quote;
}
// Function displays Quotation and author
void Quotation::Display() const
{
     cout << quote << "\n"
          << "                 ---" << author << "\n";
}
Quotation::~Quotation()
{
    delete author;
    delete quote;
}
```


The Quotation class shown in Listing 17.1 was placed in a header file and used by QUOTE.CPP, the program in Listing 17.2, which declares three Quotation objects. The default constructor is used to initialize the third Quotation object so that the data members consist of null pointers.

Listing 17.2. The source listing for QUOTE.CPP.

```
// QUOTE.CPP - Demonstrates use of Quotation class
#include <iostream.h>
#include "quote.h"
void main()
{
     Quotation Ben( "Benjamin Franklin",
             "Some are weatherwise, some are otherwise." );
     Ben.Display();
     Quotation Pat( "Patrick Henry",
             "I am not a Virginian, but an American." );
     Pat.Display();
     Quotation Fred;
}
```

When QUOTE.CPP is compiled, linked, and executed, you get the results shown in Listing 17.3. Figure 17.1 illustrates how the objects are represented in memory.

Listing 17.3. The results of executing QUOTE.EXE.

```
Some are weatherwise, some are otherwise.
                ---Benjamin Franklin
I am not a Virginian, but an American.
                ---Patrick Henry
```

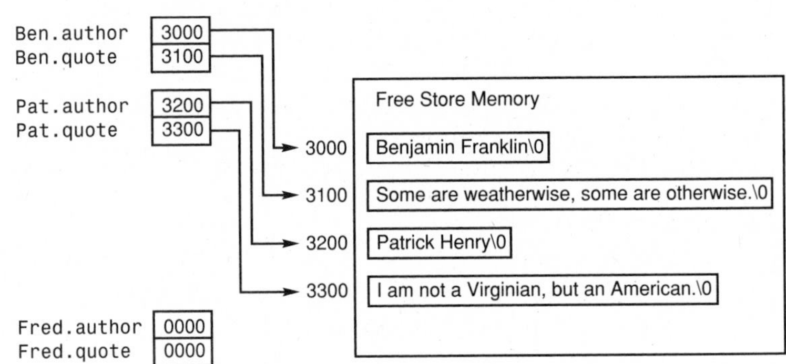

Figure 17.1. Memory representation of* `Quotation` *objects.

In the memory representation, you can see that the two pointers for the `Ben` and `Pat` objects point to the strings in the allocated memory buffers. However, the `Fred` object contains null pointers. If you were to assign a value to it, using the statement

```
Fred = Ben;
```

the contents of the member data for the `Ben` object would be transferred to the member data belonging to the `Fred` object. That means that both objects would point to the same data. If you change the contents of `Fred`, the contents of `Ben` will be changed. If either of the objects is destroyed (the object's destructor is called), the objects for the other pointers may no longer point to valid data. Furthermore, when the second object is destroyed, the `delete` operator is called by the destructor to free the same pointer the second time. Such an operation can produce unpredictable and often disastrous results.

The point is that you cannot use the assignment statement to assign values to one object with values of another object if the first object contains pointer members that point to memory allocated from the free store. There are several ways to get around this problem. You could use the access functions to transfer the member data from `Ben` to `Fred`:

```
Fred.SetAuthor( Ben.GetAuthor() );
Fred.SetQuote( Ben.GetQuote() );
```

Another technique is to overload the assignment operator with a special kind of member function. Then you can safely use the assignment operator to assign one `Quotation` object to another.

Overloading the Assignment Operator

You learned about function overloading in Chapter 12, "Functions." Operators in C++ are treated similarly to functions and can be overloaded. This means that you can supply a special function that is called to perform an assignment operation. In this section, you learn how to overload the assignment operator.

Whenever the compiler is compiling an assignment statement, the compiler generates code to call one of its built-in functions to perform the assignment based on the type of operand. You can supply a special function that is called in place of the built-in function whenever the operand is a `Quotation` type object. The following additional code, printed in bold, can be added to the definition of the `Quotation` class:

```
// Quotation class used to illustrate dynamic memory
// allocation of data members
#include <string.h>
class Quotation
{
public:
     :
     Quotation & operator=( const Quotation & );  // Overload =
private:
     char *author;        // Author of quotation
     char *quote;         // Text of quotation
};
// Member functions
    :
// Overload assignment (=) operator
Quotation & Quotation::operator=( const Quotation &source )
```

```
{
    delete author;
    delete quote;
    SetAuthor( source.author );
    SetQuote( source.quote );
    return *this;
}
```

As you can see, you provide the prototype and member function definition for a function called `operator=()`. The parameter, which is the same type as that of the class, is preceded with the `const` keyword. This designates that the parameter is a constant and cannot be modified by the function.

The function first frees the memory pointed to by the `author` and `quote` pointers. Note that the default constructor sets the values of the pointers to `NULL`. The `delete` operator performs no operation if it is passed a null pointer.

The function next calls the two access functions to assign new values to the strings. The `SetAuthor()` access function allocates a `new` memory buffer and copies into the buffer the string containing the name of the author. The `SetQuote()` function performs the same operation for the `quote` pointer. There is one final mystery—the `return` statement. What is `*this`? You learn about the `this` pointer in the next section.

QUOTE1.CPP, the program in Listing 17.4, uses the `operator=()` member function for the `Quotation` class.

Listing 17.4. The source listing for QUOTE1.CPP.

```
// QUOTE1.CPP - Demonstrates use of overloaded assignment
// operator
#include <iostream.h>
#include "quote.h"
void main()
{
     Quotation Ben( "Benjamin Franklin",
             "A used key is always bright." );
     Ben.Display();
     Quotation Fred;
     Fred = Ben;
     Fred.Display();
}
```

Here is this program's output:

```
A used key is always bright.
                ---Benjamin Franklin
A used key is always bright.
                ---Benjamin Franklin
```

The this Pointer

Now that you have gained a little experience with classes and member functions, you might ask the following question: "You tell me that you use the members without reference to the object that owns them. How do I know which object points to the member?" Good question. When a member function is called, C++ creates a pointer named `this`, which points to the object used to call the member function. The `this` pointer is used only by member functions. For example, when the function `Ben.Display()` is called, `this` points to the object `Ben`. For example, consider the following member function:

```
void Quotation::SetQuote( char *Quotation )    // Initialize quote
{
    int length;
    length = strlen( Quotation ); // Get length of argument
    quote  = new char[length+1];  // Allocate buffer for quote
    strcpy( quote, Quotation );
}
```

Here the data member `quote` is referenced. The following two statements are basically equivalent:

```
quote = new char[length+1];
this->quote = new char[length+1];
```

If you called this statement with

```
Ben.SetQuote( "Lost time is never found again." );
```

both `quote` and `this->quote` would point to the `quote` member for the object `Ben`. Usually, you don't care about the `this` pointer. However, there are times when you need to use `this`. Suppose, for example, that you are comparing two member strings and you want to return the object that is lower in the alphabetic sequence. You can use the following member function:

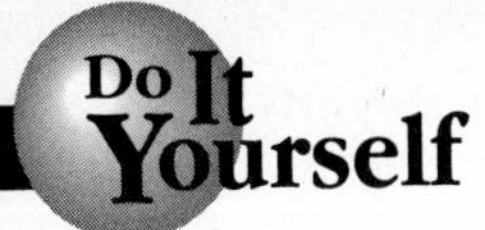


```
// Member function used to compare two authors
Quotation & Quotation::CompareAuthor( Quotation &Q_Object )
{
    // Compare strings
    if ( strcmp( author, Q_Object.author ) < 0 )
           return *this  // Return reference to owner object
    else
           return Q_Object;
}
```

The `strcmp()` library function compares two strings. It returns a negative value if the first string is less than the second string, or a zero if the strings are equal. `strcmp()` returns a positive value if the first string is greater than the second string. For this example, the member function returns a reference to either the object passed as an argument or the object used to call the member function, which is `*this`. The asterisk dereferences the pointer. You use the asterisk because you want to return the object itself. `this` is a pointer to the object; `*this` is the actual address of the object. The following statements illustrate how to call this function:

```
Quotation Quoater;
Quoater = Ben.CompareAuthor( Pat );
```

In the example, the objects `Ben` and `Pat` are compared. A reference to the lower alphabetic sequence is returned and assigned to the `Quoater` object.

In a previous example, the `this` pointer was used with the `return` statement without explanation. Here is the explanation. In C and C++, assignment statements can be chained to do multiple assignments, as in

```
int i, j, k,
i = j = k = 42;
```

Furthermore, the assignment is *right-associative*. This means that the compiler evaluates an assignment expression from right to left. How the preceding statement is evaluated is indicated by the following groups of parentheses:

```
(i = (j = (k = 42)));
```

In other words, `k` is assigned a value, then `j`, and then `i`. The overloaded assignment operator function must behave the same way. To achieve that, you must return the results of the assignment operation. You do this by returning a reference to the object that called the member function. Because the `this` pointer contains the address of this object, you return *this to return a reference to the object. As a result, you can chain assignments together by using the member function. Listing 17.5 illustrates the use of a chain of multiple assignments that takes advantage of the overloaded assignment operator member function which returns *this. Listing 17.5 also uses the Quotation class defined in quote.h. The results of executing QUOTE2.EXE are shown in Listing 17.6.

Listing 17.5. The source listing for QUOTE2.CPP.

```
// QUOTE2.CPP - Illustrates multiple replacements using
// an overloaded assignment operator member function that
// returns object
#include <iostream.h>
#include "quote.h"
void main()
{
     Quotation Benjamin( "Benjamin Franklin",
          "He that's secure is not safe." );
          Quotation Ben[3];
     Benjamin.Display();
     Ben[0] = Ben[1] = Ben[2] = Benjamin;
     Ben[0].SetQuote( "An empty bag cannot stand upright." );
     Ben[1].SetQuote(
            "There never was a good war or a bad peace." );
     Ben[2].SetQuote( "There is no little enemy." );
     for (int i = 0; i < 3; i++ )
            Ben[i].Display();
}
```

Listing 17.6. The results of executing QUOTE2.EXE.

```
He that's secure is not safe.
                ---Benjamin Franklin
An empty bag cannot stand upright.
                ---Benjamin Franklin
There never was a good war or a bad peace.
                ---Benjamin Franklin
There is no little enemy.
                ---Benjamin Franklin
```

17

Figure 17.2 illustrates how the array objects are stored in local memory and how the buffers containing the strings are stored in the free store memory pool.

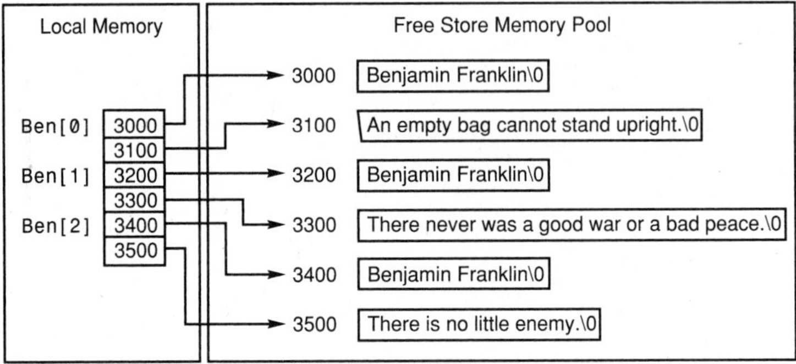

Figure 17.2. *Memory representation of* `Quotation` *objects for QUOTE2.CPP.*

The technique of returning a dereferenced `this` pointer is used to chain `cout` statements:

```
cout << "Population of Canada" << CanadaPopulation << "\n";
```

Support for the insertion operator is provided by overloading the left-shift operator (<<). This overload function returns `*this`, which is the `cout` object. Note that the left-shift operator is *left-associative*.

You can also use the `this` pointer to make sure that the pointer passed as an argument is not the same as the object used to call the member function. Note the following example:

```
// Member function used to compare two authors
Quotation & Quotation::SetValues( Quotation &Other_Object )
{
     if ( this == &Other_Object )
          return;  // Objects are the same
     :
            // Objects are different
}
```

The `this` pointer is a constant pointer. In other words, it was declared internally with the `const` keyword. Its value cannot be changed to point to anything else. If you attempt to change the value, the compiler will generate an error message.

Dynamic Allocation of Arrays of Class Objects

You can dynamically allocate arrays of objects with the new keyword. To do this, you allocate a pointer that has the type of an object and then allocate space for the pointer. In the example

```
Quotation *Ben;
Ben = new Quotation [4];
```

no constructor is called when the pointer is declared. However, when the memory is allocated, the default constructor is called for each of the four elements. You have to initialize each element. You use the following form of the delete operator to free up the memory used by the Ben array:


```
delete [] Ben;  // Correct method
```

You must include both the left and right square brackets. When the compiler encounters [], it generates code that calls the destructor for each of the four object elements before the pointer ben is deleted. If you just free the Ben pointer with the statement

```
delete *Ben;     // Wrong
```

the memory associated with the pointer will be freed, but the memory associated with any pointer members will remain allocated and lost from the free store memory pool. In the case of the Quotation class, this is important because each element contains pointers, and its associated memory blocks must be freed. After calling the destructor for each element, the memory containing the array of objects is freed. Listing 17.7 illustrates how to allocate memory for an array of objects.

Listing 17.7. The source listing for QUOTE3.CPP.

```
// QUOTE3.CPP - Illustrates dynamic object allocation
#include <iostream.h>
#include "quote.h"
int main()
{
     Quotation Benjamin( "Benjamin Franklin",
          "He that's secure is not safe." );
     Quotation *Ben;
     Ben = new Quotation [3];
```

continues

Listing 17.7. continued

```
    if ( Ben == NULL )
    {  // Always make sure that the pointer is valid before
       // using it.
         cout << "Unable to allocate memory\n";
         return 1;
    }
    Benjamin.Display();
    Ben[0] = Ben[1] = Ben[2] = Benjamin;
    Ben[0].SetQuote( "An empty bag cannot stand upright." );
    Ben[1].SetQuote(
           "There never was a good war or a bad peace." );
    Ben[2].SetQuote( "There is no little enemy." );
    for (int i = 0; i < 3; i++ )
           Ben[i].Display();
    delete [] Ben;
    return 0;
}
```

The output from executing QUOTE3.EXE is identical to the output of QUOTE2.EXE (see Listing 17.6). Figure 17.3 illustrates how the array objects and the buffers containing the strings are stored in the free store memory pool. The pointer `Ben` is in local memory.

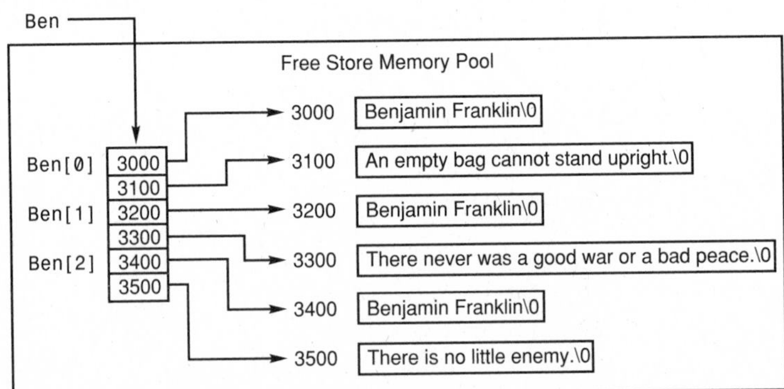

***Figure 17.3.** Memory representation of `Quotation` objects for QUOTE3.CPP.*

The Copy Constructor

The *copy constructor* is a constructor that initializes one object with another object of the same type. This constructor is called whenever you initialize a data object with the contents of another object. The copy constructor simply copies the contents of one object to the object being initialized. A default copy constructor is supplied by the compiler. The copy constructor is used in three cases:

- When you initialize an object, as in the second statement in this example:

  ```
  Quotation Ben("Benjamin Franklin",
                "Remember that time is money.");
  Quotation Ben2( Ben );    // Copy constructor is used
  ```

- When you pass an object by value as an argument to a function, a temporary object is created, and the copy constructor initializes that object with the contents of the actual object. The temporary object is passed as a formal argument in the called function. Remember that when you pass an argument by reference, you pass the address of the argument to the function.

- When a function returns an object from a function, a temporary object is created, and the copy constructor initializes its value with the contents of the return expression object. The temporary object is returned to the calling program. When you return a reference, you return the address of the object.

Whatever the case, if your objects contain data member pointers that point to buffers in the free store, you will probably experience unpredictable and possibly catastrophic results. The reason is that corresponding pointers in both objects point to the same free store buffer. When one object is destroyed, the buffer is freed. The pointer for the other object can be invalid. This is the same problem you experience with the default assignment operator, and the solution is the same.

To solve the problem, you can add to your class a member function that overloads the default copy constructor. Here is the copy constructor for the `Quotation` class:

```
// Quotation class definition
#include <string.h>
```

```
class Quotation
{
public:
     Quotation( char *, char * );        // Constructor
     Quotation( void );                  // Default constructor
     Operator( const Quotation & );      // Copy constructor
:
};
// Member functions
    :
// Copy constructor
Quotation( const Quotation &source )
{
    SetAuthor( source.author );
    SetQuote( source.quote );
}
```

The copy constructor calls the `SetAuthor()` and `SetQuote()` member functions to initialize the object used to call the copy constructor with the values of the object passed as an argument.

Notice that the argument of the copy constructor must be a reference to an object and not the actual object. There are two reasons for this. First, the overhead associated with passing a reference is less than the overhead associated with passing a function by value. Second, and most important, the copy constructor is used when any object is passed by value. If the copy constructor's argument were passed by value, it would get into an infinite recursive loop that would last until the stack was used up and the program crashed.

Notice also that the `const` keyword is specified. As a result, the function cannot modify the argument object.

There are differences between the copy constructor and the assignment operator. The assignment operator operates on an existing object, whereas the copy constructor creates a new object. The assignment operator needs to check for self-modification, but self-modification of the copy constructor is impossible. The assignment operator must return `*this`, whereas the copy constructor returns no value.

The set_new_handler( ) Function

You have already been advised that you should always check the pointer returned by the new operator to make sure that you have a valid pointer before you use it. If there is no more free store memory, new returns a null pointer. There is an alternative to testing the pointer. You can write your own error-handling function, call the set_new_handler() function, and pass it the address of your error-handling function. Then, if the new operator is unable to return a valid pointer, it calls your error-handling function. From then on, you do not have to test the pointer returned by the new operator to make sure that it is valid.

17

When you call the set_new_handler() function, you must include the new.h header file because it contains the function's prototype. Listing 17.8 presents the source listing for NEWTEST.CPP, which illustrates the use of the set_new_handler() function.

Listing 17.8. The source listing for NEWTEST.CPP.

```
// NEWTEST.CPP - Illustrates use of set_new_handler() function
// for setting a user-defined new operator error handler
#include <iostream.h>
#include <new.h>      // Prototype for set_new_handler()
#include <stdlib.h>  // Prototype for exit()
int no_more_memory( size_t size )
{
    cout << "Failure in an attempt to allocate a buffer of "
         << size << " bytes\n"
         << "There is not enough memory left "
         << "in the free store\n";
    exit( 1 ); // Exit from the program
    return 0;  // Return required because handler returns an int
}
void main()
{
     long allocated_memory =0;
    _set_new_handler( no_more_memory ); // Establish error
                                         // handler
     for (;;)  // Loop forever
```

continues

Listing 17.8. continued

```
    {
         char *ptr;
         pst = new char[10000];
         allocated_memory += 10000;
         cout << allocated_memory
              << " bytes of memory has been allocated\n";
    }
}
```

NEWTEST.CPP is a simple program that repetitively allocates memory until it runs out of memory. When that happens, the `new` operator calls the `out_of_memory()` error-handling function. `out_of_memory()` displays and calls the `exit()` run-time library function, and `exit()` exits the program.

The user-supplied error function must have the following form:

```
int error_function_name( size_t size );
```

This function must return an `int` value and have a single argument of type `size_t`. The argument will contain the size of the requested memory block.

The results of executing NEWTEST.EXE are shown in Listing 17.9. This program was compiled with the Small memory model option. For the small memory model, the size of the free store is 64K. The memory allocation failed after it had allocated 60,000 bytes of memory and attempted to allocate another 10K.

Listing 17.9. The results of executing NEWTEST.EXE.

```
10000 bytes of memory have been allocated
20000 bytes of memory have been allocated
30000 bytes of memory have been allocated
40000 bytes of memory have been allocated
50000 bytes of memory have been allocated
60000 bytes of memory have been allocated
Failure in an attempt to allocate a buffer of 10000 bytes
There is not enough memory left in the free store
```

Overloading the new and delete Operators

There are times when you need to create your own custom memory management system. C++ enables you to do this by overloading the `new` and `delete` operators. You just write two new functions, `operator new()` and `operator delete()`. Listing 17.10 is a simple example that illustrates how to overload the `new` and `delete` operators.

Listing 17.10. The source listing for NEWNEW.CPP.

```
// NEWNEW.CPP - Illustrates how to overload new and delete
// operators
#include <iostream.h>
#include <stdlib.h>  // Prototype for calloc()
#include <stddef.h>  // Common run-time library constants
void *operator new( size_t size )
{
     void *ptr;
     ptr = calloc( size ); // Allocate memory block and fill
                           // it with zeros
     if (!ptr)
     {
          cout << "Execution error: Free Store ran "
               << "out of memory\n";
          exit();
     }
     return ptr;
}
void operator delete( void *ptr )
{
     free( ptr );
     ptr = 0;                // Make pointer null
}
void main()
{
    char *buffer;
    buffer = new char[20]; // Allocate zero-filled 20-byte buffer
```

continues

Listing 17.10. continued

```
    // Use the buffer
    :
    delete [] buffer;       // Delete the buffer
}
```

The parameter of the `operator new()` function is of type `size_t`. When the compiler encounters a `new` operator, it determines the size of the requested memory block from evaluating the operand and then passes the block size as a type `size_t` value to the `operator new()` function. This function must have a `size_t` type argument and must return a `void` pointer. The `operator delete()` function must have a `void` pointer parameter and a void return (it returns no value).

In NEWNEW.CPP, the user-supplied `operator_new()` function calls the `calloc()` run-time library function, which allocates a memory block and fills it with zero values. The `operator delete()` function calls the `free()` run-time library function to release a memory block, and assigns the pointer a null value.

You can also overload the `new` and `delete` operators with class-specific member functions. To do this, you include the `operator new()` and `operator delete()` member functions, as shown in the quotenew.h header file in Listing 17.11. The modifications made to the `Quotation` class are in bold print.

Listing 17.11. Overloading the `new` and `delete` operators with additions to the `Quotation` class definition.

```
// quotenew.h - Illustrates how to overload new and delete
// operators for use by a class
#include <iostream.h>
#include <stdlib.h>  // Prototype for calloc()
#include <stddef.h>  // Common run-time library constants
// Quotation class definition
class Quotation
{
public:
     Quotation( char *, char * );        // Constructor
     Quotation( void );                  // Default constructor
     void *operator new( size_t size);
     void *operator delete( void *ptr );
```

```
   :
};
// Member functions
     :

// Overloaded new operator for Quotation class
void *Quotation::operator new ( size_t size )
{
     void *ptr;
     ptr = calloc( size ); // Allocate memory block and fill
                           // it with zeros
     if (!ptr)
     {
          cout << "Execution error: Free Store ran "
               << "out of memory\n";
          exit();
     }
     return ptr;
}
void Quotation::operator delete( void *ptr )
{
     free( ptr );
     ptr = 0;  // Make pointer null
}
```

When the new and delete operators have been overloaded in a class definition, new and delete are used to handle class objects. For example, when the compiler encounters the statement

```
Ben = new Quotation [3];  // Allocate 3 objects
```

the compiler calls the Quotation class operator new() member function to allocate the memory. When the delete operator is called to delete Ben, the compiler calls the Quotation class operator delete() member function to delete the object.

Incidentally, the new operator is called *before* the class constructor is called, and the delete operator is called *after* the destructor is called. For that reason, the operator new() and operator delete() member functions are static functions and cannot call any other member functions. Note that a static function exists for the lifetime of the program. Class member functions—other than operator new() and operator delete()—exist only for the lifetime of an object.

If the new and delete operators are overloaded and you need to use the global new operator, use the global operator as illustrated in this statement:

```
Benjamin = ::new Quotation [6]; // Use global new operator
::delete Benjamin;              // Use global delete operator
```

What You Have Learned

In this chapter, you learned how to use the free store with classes to dynamically allocate the size of a class. Specifically, you learned the following:

- How to use the `new` operator to allocate a memory block for a pointer data member
- How to use the `delete` operator to free a memory block
- What the relationship between objects and the assignment operator is
- When you need to overload the assignment operator and how to do it
- What the `this` pointer is and how to use it to reference the object used to call a member function
- How to use the `new` operator to allocate memory for an array of objects
- What the copy constructor is
- When to overload the copy constructor and how to do it
- How to create an error handler for the `new` operator
- How to overload the `new` and `delete` operators

More on Using Classes

I was gratified to be able to answer promptly, and I did. I said I didn't know.

—Mark Twain
Life on the Mississippi (1883)

In This Chapter

The C++ language is an extremely powerful language. In the last two chapters, you learned how to define and use various simple classes. You learned about public and private class members. You learned about constructors that create objects, and destructors that discard objects. And you learned about many other characteristics of a class. It is not that any of these C++ OOP features are difficult to understand; there are just many things to learn.

It would be beneficial to stop right now and write some programs of your own that define and use classes. Continue writing programs until you understand how to use all the features you have learned so far. It is not just a matter of learning these features; you need to remember them. The best way to do that is to gain experience, and the only way to gain experience is to write some programs. Let your imagination be your guide. Design a class that defines objects of interest to you. If you are interested in stocks and bonds, create a class that defines a stock market. If you like astronomy, create a class having to do with astronomical objects. OK, go write some programs. The book will wait.

Now that you have written some programs of your own, you are probably a little more familiar with classes. It is time to learn even more. In this chapter, you are introduced to more features of classes and objects. Specifically, you learn about the following topics:

- `static` members
- Friend classes and functions
- Operator overloading
- Conversion functions

static Data Members

At times, you may want to set a variable once and have it retain its value for the rest of the program's execution. That is easy—use a `static` variable. But what if you want the variable to be available to objects only, but hidden from the rest of the program? If you use a `private` member variable, its value will be lost when the object is discarded by the destructor. Its value would have to be reinitialized by each object when it is declared. There is a solution to this problem.

C++ enables you to declare a `static` variable with a class. You already know that each object has its own set of data members. C++ handles `static` member variables differently from other member variables. Only one copy of a `static` member variable is allocated. It is shared by all instances of the class. Other than that, the `static` member variable is used the same way any other data member is used by member functions. You can understand this better if you look at an example.

Suppose that you have a portfolio of stocks, bonds, and savings and you want to determine what percentage of your investment is in each category. You can do this by using a `static` data member that maintains your investment total. Listing 18.1 is the source listing for the header file that defines the class `Investment`. Listing 18.2 presents the program INVEST.CPP, which uses the class.

Listing 18.1. The source listing for the invest.h header file.

```
// invest.h - Definition of class Investment
// Investment class is used to illustrate the use of
// a static data member
#include <string.h> // Prototypes of strlen() and strcpy()
#include <iomanip.h>
class Investment
{
public:
     Investment( char *, float );    // Constructor
     void Display() const;           // Display investment data
     ~Investment( void );            // Destructor
private:
     char category[20];              // Investment category
     float amount;                   // Amount invested
     static float total;             // static data member
};
// Member functions
// The constructor that is called when a variable is declared
Investment::Investment( char * cat, float Amt )
{
     strncpy( category, cat, 19 );
     amount = Amt;
     total += Amt;
}
// Function displays investment, amount, and percentage
void Investment::Display() const
{
     cout << setw(10) << category
          << setw(10) << amount
          << setw(12) << amount*100.0 / total << "\n";
}
```

continues

Listing 18.1. continued

```
Investment::~Investment()
{
     total -= amount;
}
```

The `Investment` class contains two private data members plus a `static` private data member named `total`. Figure 18.1 shows the memory storage for the private variables. Notice that there exists only one copy of `total`, which is shared by all three instances of the `Investment` class.

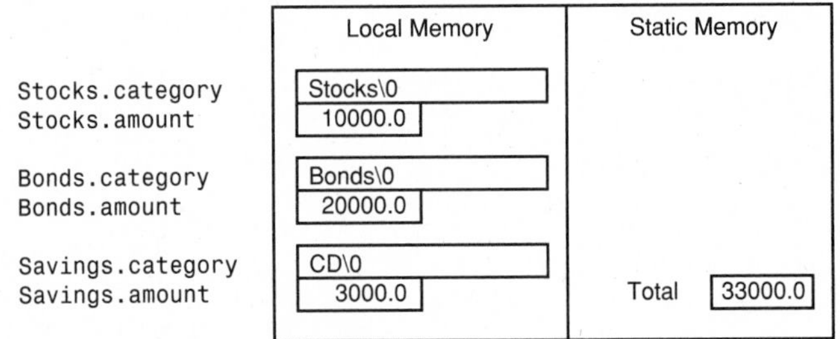

Figure 18.1. *Memory storage of* `Investment` *objects.*

When an `Investment` object is declared, the constructor is called. It adds the argument `Amt` to the `static` member variable `total` and initializes the other data member values. After the three investment category objects have been declared, `total` contains the sum of money invested. When the `Display()` member function is called, it displays the category, amount invested, and percentage of the total amount invested for the category. When the destructor is called, the amount is subtracted from `total`.

You have one problem: you need to initialize `total` to zero. You cannot do this in a constructor because it would be initialized every time an object is declared. What you want is to initialize `total` only once. One way to do that is to initialize the `static` member variable at file scope. This means that you can initialize it outside any function, as shown in Listing 18.2. Other than that, a private `static` data member is treated like any other private data member. That is, you cannot access it outside `Investment`'s member function.

Listing 18.2. The source listing for INVEST.CPP.

```
// INVEST.CPP - Illustrates use of static variables
#include <iostream.h>
#include "invest.h"
float Investment::total = 0.0;

void main()
{
     Investment Stocks( "Stocks", 20000.0 );
     Investment Bonds( "Bonds", 10000.0 );
     Investment Savings( "CD", 3000.0 );
     cout << "     Investment Portfolio\n";
     cout << "Category      Amount  Percentage\n";
     Stocks.Display();
     Bonds.Display();
     Savings.Display();
}
```


Here is the program's output:

```
     Investment Portfolio
Category      Amount  Percentage
    Stocks     20000     60.6061
     Bonds     10000      30.303
        CD      3000     9.09091
```

`static` data members are mainly useful when you want all instances of a class to access or share a common resource.

static Member Functions

Another way to initialize the `static` member variable `total` is to add a `static` member function to initialize it. The `SetTotal()` member function is a `static` member function and can be placed in the `Investment` class (refer to Listing 18.1). Here is how `SetTotal()` will appear:

```
class Investment
{
public:
     :
     static void SetTotal();   // static member function
private:
     :
}
// Member function
:
Investment::Settotal()
{
     total = 0;  // Initialize the total
}
```

You can initialize the `static` private data member before you create any objects by calling the `SetTotal()` `static` member function. You can call the `static` function by prefixing its name with the name of the class and the global resolution operator, as in the following example:

```
main()
{
     Investment::SetTotal();  // Initialize the static member
     :
}
```

This syntax is used to indicate that the operation relates to the class as a whole and not to any specific object. You can use this form before you declare any objects because the `static` member is not dependent on the existence of any objects. The following rules apply to a `static` member function:

- It cannot access any non-`static` data members.
- It cannot call any non-`static` member functions.
- It has no `this` pointer.

All these restrictions make sense because there is not necessarily any object data to reference when a `static` member function is called. If there were any object data, you would have no way of referencing it.

> `static` member functions are mostly used for retrieving or storing any status information that is common to all the information.

Friends

Encapsulation, or data hiding, is one of the major goals of OOP. In support of this goal, C++ makes it difficult to access member data except under the gentle control of member functions. As a result, data is protected from careless misuse, provided classes are properly designed and implemented.

There are times, however, when multiple classes work closely together and need to access each other's private member data. This feature is allowed in OOP and is supported by C++. Therefore, when you have two "friendly" classes and you want one class to be able to access the other's private members, you can designate a friend relationship by using the `friend` keyword. A *friend function* is a nonmember function that is allowed to access the private members of a class. A *friend class* is a class whose member functions can access the private members of another class.

Friend Classes

One class can specify that another class may use its private data members by declaring that the other class is a friend. To do this, you add the following declaration to the class definition:

```
friend class-name
```

This declaration can be placed anywhere in the class definition statement. The following example shows how it works:

```
// ROMEO.CPP - Demonstrates friend class syntax
#include <iostream.h>
class Romeo
{
public:
    friend class Juliet;  // Juliet is Romeo's friend
    Romeo( void );        // Constructor
    ~Romeo( void );       // Destructor
private:
    int data_of_Romeo;
};
Romeo::Romeo( void )
```

```
{
    data_of_Romeo = 1;
}
Romeo::~Romeo( void )
{
    cout << "Value of Romeo's data: " << data_of_Romeo << "\n";
}

class Juliet
{
public:
    void Change( Romeo *r );
};
// Member function
void Juliet::Change( Romeo *r )
{
    r->data_of_Romeo = 2;     // Change Romeo's private data
}

void main()
{
    Romeo rc;
    Juliet jc;
    jc.Change( &rc );         // Change Romeo's private data
}
```

The first thing to note is that the `friend class` statement can be anywhere in the class definition. In other words, it is not influenced by the `public` and `private` statements. The `friend` statement is a one-way reference. This means that one class can proclaim that another class is a friend, and the other class can access its private member data. The class `Juliet` can reference `Romeo`'s private member data. However, `Romeo` cannot reference `Juliet`'s private member data. You could add a `friend class Romeo;` statement to the definition for `class Juliet` to allow both classes to access each other's private member data.

To demonstrate the use of `friend` classes better, this chapter reconsiders the address book application presented in Chapter 16, "Classes." In this chapter, however, the address book application is developed with more of an object-oriented approach. To begin, first consider the address book to be an object. A class named `PhoneBook` is designed that contains the address book as the data, and member functions are used to create and maintain the address book entries. A `PhoneBook` data object contains a linked list of phone book entries. Each entry is defined by a structure named `ADDRESS`.

A friend class named `LinkedList` contains member functions that position the `current` record pointer in the phone book object, and contains a member function to display the current record. `LinkedList` is a friend of the class `PhoneBook`. `LinkedList` is granted the privilege of accessing private member data belonging to `PhoneBook`. Listing 18.3 is a listing for the address1.h header file, which contains the definitions of both classes and their member functions. In addition, address1.h contains the definition of the structure `ADDRESS`.

Listing 18.3. The source listing for the address1.h header file.

```
// address1.h - Address book header file
#include <iostream.h>  // Needed for screen I/O
#include <fstream.h>   // Needed for file I/O
#include <io.h>        // ios: manipulators
#include <fcntl.h>
#include <string.h>    // Prototypes for strlen() and strcpy()
#include <ctype.h>

struct ADDRESS         // Phone book entry definition
{
     char     name[20];
     char     phone[15];
     char     address[23];
     char     city[14];
     char     state[3];
     char     zip[14];
     int      age;
     void     *next;     // One-way linked list pointer
};

class PhoneBook
{
public:
     friend class LinkedList;          // LinkedList is our friend
     PhoneBook( char *filename );      // Constructor
     void add_object( void );          // Add new item
     void change_object( void );       // Edit current item
     void delete_link( void );         // Delete current link
     ~PhoneBook( void );               // Destructor
```

continues

18

Listing 18.3. continued

```
private:
     void get_string( char *message, char *item, int maxsize );
     void get_input( ADDRESS *p );
     void add_link( void );
     ADDRESS *head;        // head points to first object
     ADDRESS *current;     // current points to current object
     char sfilename[50];
};

// Private member functions
//*********************************************************
// get_string() - Inputs string data item
void PhoneBook::get_string( char *message,
                            char *item, int maxsize )
{
     char ch;
     char s[80];
     if ( strlen( item ) > 0 )
     {
          cout << "\nCurrent value for " << message
               << " is: " << item
               << ". Change it (Y/N)?: ";
          cin.seekg( 0L, ios::end );     // Empty input stream
          cin >> ch;
          if ( ch != 'Y' && ch != 'y' )  // Not Y, y
               return;
     }
     cout << "\nEnter " << message << ": "; // Display prompt
     cin.seekg( 0L, ios::end ); // Empty input stream
     cin.get( s, 80 );          // Input string
     s[maxsize-1] = '\0';       // Truncate if max size exceeded
     strcpy( item, s );         // Copy string s to input item
     return;
}
//*********************************************************
// get_input() - Enters data for one entry from keyboard
void PhoneBook::get_input( ADDRESS *p )
{
     cin.seekg( 0L, ios::end );  // Empty input stream
     get_string( "name", p->name, 20 );
     get_string( "phone number", p->phone, 15 );
```

```
    get_string( "address", p->address, 23 );
    get_string( "city", p->city, 13 );
    get_string( "state", p->state, 3 );
    get_string( "ZIP code", p->zip, 14 );
    cout << "\nEnter age: ";
    cin.seekg( 0L, ios::end ); // Empty input stream
    cin >> p->age;
}

// Public member functions
//**************************************************************
// Constructor - Initializes phone book list
// Read address book entries from the file ADDRESS.DAT
PhoneBook::PhoneBook( char *filename )
{
    int size = 1, count = 0;
    ADDRESS *p;
    current = 0;
    head    = 0;
    ifstream fis( filename, ios::binary ¦ ios::nocreate );
    if ( ! fis )
        cout << "Address Book File is not available\n";
    else
    {
        while ( 1 )              // Read forever
        {
            add_link();
            if ( !fis.read( (char*)current,
                sizeof( ADDRESS ) ) )
                 break;          // Exit on end of file
            count++;
            current->next = 0; // Always last link
        }
        delete_link();           // Delete empty link
        cout << "Address Book contains "
            << count << " entries\n";
        strncpy( sfilename, filename, 49 ); // Save filename
        fis.close();
    }
}
```

continues

Listing 18.3. continued

```
//*****************************************************
// add_object() - Adds an address book entry
void PhoneBook::add_object( void )
{
     add_link();
     cout << "\nEnter new address book entry\n";
     get_input( current );
}
//*****************************************************
// change_object() - Changes existing address book entry
void PhoneBook::change_object()
{
     cout << "\nEdit address book entry\n";
     get_input( current );
}
//***********************************************************
// add_link() - Allocates memory block for object and links it
// in list
void PhoneBook::add_link( void )
 // add_link() adds a link to the linked list
{
     ADDRESS *p , *plast;
     // First point to last object in linked list
     p = head;
     plast = p;
     while ( p != NULL )
     {
          plast = p;
          p = (ADDRESS *)p->next;
     }
     p = plast;
     current = new ADDRESS; // Allocate memory block
     if ( current == NULL )
          return;
     memset( (char*)current, 0, sizeof( ADDRESS) );
     if ( p == NULL )
          head = current;
     else
          p->next = current;
 }
```

```
//*****************************************************
// delete_link() - Removes memory block from linked list
void PhoneBook::delete_link()
{
     ADDRESS *ptr, *pdelete, *p, *plast;
     if ( current == NULL )     // Is list empty?
          return;
     pdelete = current;         // Link to delete
     if ( head == current )     // Is current link first link?
     {
          head = (ADDRESS *)current->next; // Point to second
                                           // link (or NULL)
          current = head;
     }
     else
     {
          ptr = (ADDRESS *)pdelete->next; // Next link (or NULL)

          for ( p = head, plast = p;      // Go to previous link
                p != current && p != NULL;
                plast = p, p = (ADDRESS *) p->next );
          current = plast;

          if ( current != NULL )
               current->next = ptr;     // Link last link to next
     }
     delete pdelete;                    // Free memory block
}
//************************************************************
// Destructor
// writefile() - Writes address book entries to file ADDRESS.DAT
PhoneBook::~PhoneBook( )
{
     int     count = 0;
     ADDRESS *p, *plast = NULL;
     ofstream ofs( sfilename, ios::binary );
     if ( !ofs )
          cout << "Unable to write Address Book File\n";
     else
     {
          p = head;
```

continues

Listing 18.3. continued

```
        while ( plast != p && p != NULL )
        {
             ofs.write( (char*)p, sizeof( ADDRESS ) );
             plast = p;
             p =     (ADDRESS *)p->next;  // Go to next link
             count++;
        }
        ofs.close ();
        cout << count
             << " entries written to Address Book File\n";
    }
}

//**********************************************************
// LinkedList class definition
class LinkedList
{
public:
     LinkedList( PhoneBook * );
     void display( void );
     void go_next( void );
     void go_previous( void );
     void go_top( void );
private:
     PhoneBook *PB;     // Point to PhoneBook object
};

// Member functions for class LinkedList
//**********************************************************
LinkedList::LinkedList( PhoneBook *phone )
{
     PB = phone;
}
//**********************************************************
// go_next() - Positions pointer to next link in linked list
void LinkedList::go_next()
{
     ADDRESS *p;
     if ( PB->current != NULL && PB->current->next != NULL )
          PB->current =  (ADDRESS *)PB->current->next;
}
```

```
//*****************************************************
// go_previous() - Positions pointer to previous link
void LinkedList::go_previous()
{
     ADDRESS *p, *plast;
     if ( PB->head == NULL )
     {
          PB->current = NULL;
          return;
     }
     for ( p = PB->head, plast = p;
           p != PB->current && p != NULL;
           plast = p, p = (ADDRESS *) p->next );
     PB->current = plast;
}
//*****************************************************
// go_top() - Positions to header
void LinkedList::go_top()
{
     PB->current = PB->head;
}
//*****************************************************
// display() - Displays an address book entry
void LinkedList::display( )
{
     if ( PB->current == NULL )
          cout << "Nothing to display\n";
     else
     {
          cout << PB->current->name << "\n";
          cout << PB->current->address     << "\n";
          cout << PB->current->city
               << ", "      << PB->current->state
               << " "       << PB->current->zip   << "\n"
               << "Phone: " << PB->current->phone << "\n"
               << "Age:   " << PB->current->age   << "\n";
     }
}
//********* End of LinkedList member functions *********
```

You may remember the ADDRESS structure from Chapter 15, "Structures and Unions." ADDRESS contains the definition of an address book entry that includes the name, phone number, address, and other data. The structure contains also a pointer to the next node of a one-way linked list pointer. As a reminder, this pointer contains the address of the next address book entry (the next ADDRESS object). The private data members for the PhoneBook class consist of the following items:

head	The pointer to the first address book entry in the linked list
current	The pointer to the current address book entry in the linked list
sfilename	A character array used to save the name of the address book file

It is the responsibility of the PhoneBook public member functions to provide a public interface for creating and maintaining the address book. (As you recall, the public interface consists of public members, which can be accessed from outside the class.) The constructor creates an address book object and builds the linked list as it reads entries from a file. You may notice that the file object fis is an instance of the class ifstream and is declared when the file is opened. The object name fis is used to reference the read() and close() member functions of the ifstream class. The destructor writes the address book to the file before it discards the object.

Three public member functions can be called by the user's program to maintain the address book. The add_object() member function adds a new, user-supplied address book entry to the tail of the linked list. This member function calls the add_link() and get_input() functions. The change_object() member function prompts the user to change the contents of the current address book entry. Finally, the delete_link() function deletes the current address book entry from the linked list.

Three private member functions are used by other PhoneBook member functions. The get_string() function is a generalized keyboard input function that prompts the user to type one of the address book entry items. The get_input() function requests input data for the items for an address book entry and calls the get_string() function. The add_link() function allocates memory for a new object and adds it to the linked list.

The constructor for the LinkedList class simply assigns the address of the PhoneBook class object to a pointer named PB. Once a LinkedList object has been declared, its member functions reference PhoneBook's private data members—`head` and `current`—by using the `PB` pointer, as illustrated in Listing 18.3. The `Display()` function displays an address book entry. The `go_next()` and `go_previous()` functions position the `current` address book entry pointer to the next and previous record, respectively. The `go_top()` function positions the `current` pointer to the first address book entry.

Listing 18.4 is the source listing for the program ADDRESS1.CPP, which uses the `PhoneBook` and `LinkedList` classes. Notice that you declare the `PhoneBook` object named `List`. The single parameter is the name of the file named ADDRESS.DAT, which contains the address book data. Next you pass its address as an argument when you declare the `LinkedList` object named `L`.

Listing 18.4. The source listing for ADDRESS1.CPP.

```
// ADDRESS1.CPP - A simple address book application that
// illustrates the use of a friend class. Class LinkedList is a
// friend of class PhoneBook. This program shows how to
// build a one-way linked list.
#include "address1.h"

// Linked list management utilities prototypes
int get_command( void );
void help( void);
void main()
{
     int     cmd;
     PhoneBook List( "ADDRESS.DAT" ); // Declare PhoneBook
                                      // Object List
     LinkedList L( &List );           // Declare LinkedList
                                      // Object L
     help();                          // Display commands
     while ( 1 )                      // Loop forever
     {
          cmd = get_command();        // Input command from user
          switch ( cmd )
          {
               case 0:      // A - Add a record
                    List.add_object();
                    break;
```

continues

Listing 18.4. continued

```
                case 1:     // C - Change entry
                     List.change_object( );
                     break;
                case 2:     // D - Delete current entry
                     List.delete_link();
                     break;
                case 3:     // N - Display Next entry
                     L.go_next();
                     break;
                case 4:     // P - Display Previous entry
                     L.go_previous();
                     break;
                case 5:     // H - Help
                     help();
                     break;
                case 6:     // X - Write data and eXit
                     return;
                default:
                     break;
           }
           L.display();
     }
}
//**********************************************************
// get_command() - Inputs command letter from keyboard
int get_command( )
{
     int ch, cmdno;
     char s[80];
     char  cmds[] = {"ACDNPHX"};
     cout << "\nEnter a command (A, C, D, N, P, H, or X): ";
     cin.seekg( 0L, ios::end ); // Empty input stream
     cin >> s;  // Get character from keyboard
     ch = s[0];
     ch = toupper( (int)s[0] );
     for ( cmdno = 0; cmds[cmdno] && ch != cmds[cmdno]
                     ; cmdno++ );
     return cmdno;
}
//**********************************************************
```

```
// help() - Lists program command help
void help( void )
{
     cout << "   ADDRESS BOOK HELP\n";
     cout << " Enter one of the following commands\n";
     cout << "      A - Add an entry\n";
     cout << "      C - Create an entry\n";
     cout << "      D - Delete an entry\n";
     cout << "      N - Display Next entry\n";
     cout << "      P - Display Previous entry\n";
     cout << "      H - Help\n";
     cout << "      X - Write data and eXit\n\n";
}
```

ADDRESS.CPP contains a command processor that controls which operation it performs. You enter one of the commands, and it calls the public interface functions of the `PhoneBook` and `LinkedList` classes to perform various operations. You can scrutinize entries, change them, or add new ones.

The whole beauty of the `PhoneBook` class is that its implementation is completely invisible to the program that uses it. If you get a very large address book that will not fit in memory, you could change the class to read an entry or a group of entries, one at a time, from a file. The program that uses the class would never know the difference. The public interface remains unchanged. However, there is an interdependence between the `PhoneBook` and `LinkedList` classes. If you change one, you may have to change the other. This is a disadvantage of using friends. A class should not have very many friends because you could end up rewriting large amounts of code when you change a class with many friends.

Listing 18.5 shows sample output from the execution of ADDRESS1.EXE.

Listing 18.5. Sample dialog from the execution of ADDRESS1.EXE.

```
Address Book contains 8 entries
   ADDRESS BOOK HELP
 Enter one of the following commands
     A - Add an entry
     C - Create an entry
```

continues

Listing 18.5. continued

```
     D - Delete an entry
     N - Display Next entry
     P - Display Previous entry
     H - Help
     X - Write data and eXit


Enter a command (A, C, D, N, P, H, or X): P<Enter>
Blue, Howard
2345 55th Street
Muleshoe, TX 78333
Phone: (202)555-2222
Age:   23

Enter a command (A, C, D, N, P, H, or X): P<Enter>
Newton, Issac
4112 Berkshire Street
London, EG 01111
Phone: (222)555-1111
Age:   201

Enter a command (A, C, D, N, P, H, or X): X<Enter>
8 entries written to Address Book File
```

Friend Functions

When you are designing classes, you should examine all your classes to see whether there are some methods that do the same thing in different classes. Instead of coding a member function twice, you will want to code it once and let the various classes share it. In this way, you reduce coding and maintenance costs.

If you want two or more classes to share a function, you can specify that a function is a friend function by prefixing the function prototype in the class definition with the keyword `friend`. In the following example, both the classes `Dog` and `Cat` can call the friend function `Master`:

```
Class Dog
{
private:
     char MasterName1[30];
     :
public:
     :
void friend master( const Dog & d, const Cat & c );
};

Class Cat
{
private:
     char MasterName2[30];
     :
public:
     :
void friend master( const Dog & d, const Cat & c );
};
:

// friend function
void master( const Dog & d, const Cat & c )
{
    if ( !strcmp( d.MasterName1, c.MasterName2 ) );
        cout << "The cat and the dog have different masters\n"
}
```

The run-time function `strcmp()` compares the two strings and returns a nonzero value unless they are equal. The message is then displayed.

Notice that the `master()` friend function prototypes are prefixed with the keyword `friend`. The `master()` function is not a member function of either class. It belongs to no class. It is just an ordinary function except that it is allowed to access private data members. Notice also that the `friend` keyword is not used with the function definition.

Because the `master()` function is a friend of the classes `Dog` and `Cat`, `master()` is allowed to access their private member data. Unless a function needs to access a private member directly, it does not have to be a member or friend function. In a member function, the object is implied, and you can reference member data without the object name. However, in a friend function, you must use the object name to reference its member. In the preceding example, you use `d.MasterName1` to reference the `MasterName1` member of object `d`.

18

A member function has class scope, which means that you can have the same function name in different classes. A friend function has file scope, meaning that no other function in the file can have the same name and signature.

When you use a friend function, you need to pass the object (or objects) as arguments. This is illustrated in the following program fragment:

```
void main()
{
     Dog poodle( ... );
     Cat Siamese( ... );
     master( poodle, Siamese  );
     :
}
```

Friend functions are often used when you do operator overloading. You are introduced to that topic in the next section and afforded the opportunity to be introduced to more friends.

Operator Overloading

In Chapter 17, "Using Memory with Classes," you learned how to overload the simple assignment operator (=). That was an example of *operator overloading*. Of all the operators, the assignment operator is the one that is most frequently overloaded. You learned also how to overload the `new` and `delete` operators. You can overload almost all the C++ operators.

If you did not have any arithmetic operators to work with, you could probably represent an algebraic expression with function calls. For example, you could represent the expression

```
x = a*(b + c)
```

with

```
Store( Multiply( a, Add( b, c )), x );
```

I will leave it to you to interpret this expression. A complicated expression would be almost impossible to interpret. However, most languages incorporate operators that make the representation of algebraic expressions much more readable. That is true for numeric equations. For other data types, you still need to use functions. For example, to concatenate two character strings, you can use the `strcat()` run-time function. C++ provides the power to overload operators so that you can make objects behave more like numeric data types.

Overloading Operators to Support Complex Numbers

It is time to look at an example of operator overloading. Scientific programming languages, such as FORTRAN IV, support overloading of the algebraic operators (+, -, *, and /) and functions to support complex numbers. A complex number consists of the real and imaginary components of the number. C, C++, BASIC, and Pascal do not provide special support for complex numbers. In C, if you were going to use complex variables, you would need to write special library functions to support even the most primitive mathematical operations. In C++, however, you can define a new data type by defining a class.

In the following example, you first call this class `Complex`. You then overload the +, -, *, and / operators. You also add a member function, `Display()`, to display a complex number coordinate pair. The point of the example is to demonstrate how to overload operators. No attempt will be made to explain the theory of complex numbers. Don't be too disappointed, though. If you are interested, your local library should have several excellent books on complex variable theory. Listing 18.6 presents the definition of the class `Complex`.

Listing 18.6. The source listing for the complex.h header file.

```
// complex.h - Complex class used to illustrate dynamic memory
// allocation of data members
#include <iostream.h>
#include <stdlib.h>  // Needed for exit()
class Complex
{
public:
     Complex( float, float );          // Constructor
     Complex( void );                  // Default constructor
     void Display() const;             // Display Complex
                                       // Overloaded operators
```

continues

Listing 18.6. continued

```
     Complex operator +( const Complex & ); // Add two complex
                                            // numbers
     Complex operator -( const Complex & ); // Subtract two
                                            // complex numbers
     Complex operator *( const Complex & ); // Multiply two
                                            // complex numbers
     Complex operator /( const Complex & ); // Divide complex
                                            // number
private:
     float real;         // real component of complex number
     float imaginary;    // imaginary component of Complex
};
// Member functions

// The constructor that is called when a variable is declared
Complex::Complex( float r, float i )
{
     real = r;
     imaginary = i;
}
// The constructor that is called when a variable is declared
// with no arguments
Complex::Complex( void ) // Default constructor
{
    real = 0;
    imaginary = 0;
}
// Function displays Complex number coordinate pair
void Complex::Display() const
{
     cout << real << "  " << imaginary << "i\n";
}
// Overload the addition (+) operator
Complex Complex::operator+( const Complex & cn )
{
    return Complex( cn.real+real, cn.imaginary+imaginary );
}
// Overload the subtraction (-) operator
Complex Complex::operator-( const Complex & cn )
{
    return Complex( cn.real-real, cn.imaginary-imaginary);
```

```
}
// Overload the multiply (*) operator

Complex Complex::operator*( const Complex & cn )
{
    return Complex( ( real * cn.real ) -
                    ( imaginary * cn.imaginary ),
                    ( real * cn.imaginary ) +
                    ( cn.real * imaginary ));
}
// Overload the divide (/) operator
Complex Complex::operator/( const Complex & cn )
{
     float divisor;
     divisor = ( cn.real * cn.real ) +
               ( cn.imaginary * cn.imaginary );
     if ( divisor == 0 )
     {
        cout << "Zero divide was attempted\n";
        exit( 1 );
     }
     return Complex( (( real * cn.real ) +
                      ( imaginary * cn.imaginary )) / divisor,
                     (( cn.real * imaginary ) -
                      ( real * cn.imaginary ))/divisor );
}
```

A `Complex` object is declared with two `float` values. The first is the real component of a complex number, and the second is the imaginary component. When the constructor is called, it stores the parameter values in the two private data members for the object. If you provide no parameters, the data members are initialized to zero.

Notice that the parameters to the overload functions are constant references. When you overload an operator, it is more efficient to pass class objects by reference rather than by value. Furthermore, you should pass `const` object references so that you can pass constant objects to your overload function when you use it.

If both operands of any of the overloaded operators are `Complex` objects, the compiler generates code to call class `Complex` member functions that overload the operator.

The operand to the left of the operator becomes the object for which the operator function is called. The object to the right of the operator becomes the function parameter. For example, consider the following:

```
Complex x( 1.0, 2.0 ), y( 2.0, 3.0 ), z;
z = x * y;
```

In the preceding expression, the `operator*()` function is called for the `Complex` object `x`, and the `Complex` object `y` becomes the parameter, as shown in this equivalent statement:

```
z = x.operator*( y );
```

The `operator*()` function computes the product and returns a `Complex` object containing the results. The `Complex` object `z` is assigned the value of the results.

Listing 18.7 presents a program that uses the `Complex` class to perform arithmetic on complex numbers. Notice that the declaration has two parameters. The first is the real component of the complex number, and the second is the imaginary component.

Listing 18.7. The source listing for COMPLEX.CPP.

```
// COMPLEX.CPP - Illustrates use of the Complex class
#include "complex.h"
void main()
{
     Complex a;                     //  0   0i
     Complex b( 2.0, -3.0 );        //  2  -3i
     Complex c( -2.0, 1.0 );        // -2    i
     Complex d( 1.0, 2.0 );         //  1   2i
     Complex e( 3.0, -4.0 );        //  3  -4i
     Complex f( 2.0, -1.0 );        //  2   -i
     Complex g( 0.0, 5.0  );        //  0   5i

     cout << "(2,-3) + (-2,1) = ";
     a = b + c;
     a.Display();

     cout << "(2,-3) - (1,2)  = ";
     a = b - d;
     a.Display();
```

```
        cout << "(2,-3) * (-2,1) = ";
        a = b * c;
        a.Display();

        cout << "(1,2)/(3,-4) + (2,-1)/(0,5) = ";
        a = d/e + f/g;
        a.Display();
        cout << "(1,1)*(1,1)*(1,1)*(1,1) = ";
        a = Complex( 1, 1 );
        for (int i = 1; i < 4; i++)
            a = a * Complex( 1, 1 );
        a.Display();
}
```

Here are the results of executing COMPLEX.EXE:

```
(2,-3) + (-2,1) = 0  -2i
(2,-3) - (1,2)  = -1  5i
(2,-3) * (-2,1) = -1  8i
(1,2)/(3,-4) + (2,-1)/(0,5) = -0.4  0i
(1,1)*(1,1)*(1,1)*(1,1) = -4  0i
```

18

When Can You Use Operator Overloading?

Operators are most frequently overloaded to support numeric classes. However, this is not a rule. Some programmers overload the + operator to support string concatenation. You can overload any of the operators listed in Table 18.1.

As you see can in Table 18.1, some of the operators are of unary type. When you overload a unary operator, the operator operates on the object used to call it. There are no other parameters passed. For example, the prototype for a member function to overload the ! unary operator for ABC objects is

```
ABC::ABC operator !( void );
```

Several operators, such as the minus sign (-), can be either a unary or binary operator. For negation (-33), the minus sign is a unary operator. For subtraction (3 - 4), the minus sign is a binary operator. You can overload the minus sign or any operator with dual types for either arity. *Arity* is the number of operands the operator operates on (either unary or binary). For

example, you can overload either or both arities of the minus sign operator, as illustrated in the following pair of prototypes that overload the negation and subtraction operators:

```
ABC::ABC operator -( void );
ABC::ABC operator -( const ABC & );
```

Table 18.1. Operators that can be overloaded.

Operator	*Name or Meaning*	*Type*
,	Comma	Comma
!	Logical NOT	Unary
!=	Inequality	Relational
%	Remainder	Arithmetic
%=	Modulus assignment	Assignment
&	Address	Unary
&	Bitwise AND	Bitwise
==	Equality	Relational
&&	Logical AND	Logical
&=	Bitwise AND assignment	Assignment
()	Function call	Primary
type	Type cast	Unary
*	Indirection	Unary
*	Multiplication	Arithmetic
*=	Multiplication assignment	Assignment
+	Addition	Arithmetic
+	Unary plus	Unary
++	Postincrement	Unary
++	Preincrement	Unary
+=	Addition assignment	Assignment
-	Negation	Unary
-	Subtraction	Arithmetic

Operator	*Name or Meaning*	*Type*
`--`	Postdecrement	Unary
`--`	Predecrement	Unary
`-=`	Subtraction assignment	Assignment
`->*`	Dereference pointer to	Class
`/`	Division	Arithmetic
`/=`	Division assignment	Assignment
`:>`	Base operator	Unary
`<`	Less than	Relational
`<<`	Left-shift	Shift
`<<=`	Left-shift assignment	Assignment
`<=`	Less than or equal to	Relational
`=`	Simple assignment	Assignment
`>`	Greater than	Relational
`>=`	Greater than or equal to	Relational
`>>`	Right-shift	Shift
`>>=`	Right-shift assignment	Assignment
`[]`	Array element	Primary
`^`	Bitwise exclusive OR	Bitwise
`^=`	Bitwise exclusive OR assignment	Assignment
`¦`	Bitwise inclusive OR	Bitwise
`¦=`	Bitwise inclusive OR assignment	Assignment
`¦¦`	Logical OR	Logical
`~`	Bitwise complement	Unary
`delete`	Deallocate object	Allocation
`new`	Allocate object	Allocation

Not all operators can be overloaded. You cannot overload the operators listed in Table 18.2.

Table 18.2. Operators that cannot be overloaded.

Operator	*Use*
`.`	Class member operator
`.*`	Pointer-to-member operator
`::`	Scope resolution operator
`?:`	Conditional expression operator
`sizeof`	Size-of operator

The following rules restrict overloading:

- You cannot invent your own operators. You can overload only the operators presented in Table 18.1. In dBASE you can use the `**` operator for exponentiation. You cannot create your own exponentiation operator in C++ by using the `**` operator.
- You cannot change the arity of an operator. (As noted, arity is the number of operands an operator acts on.) If the operator has a binary arity, you can create an overload function that supports only binary operations. For example, the logical NOT operator, `!`, is a unary operator. You cannot overload it to behave like a binary operator for a class object.
- You cannot change the precedence of an operator. (See the section "Precedence" in Chapter 8.) A multiplication operator will always have a higher precedence than an addition operator no matter how many times you overload it. In the following example, the answer will be 9 because the multiplication is performed first:

  ```
  x = 1 + 2 * 4;
  ```

  The only way to change the precedence is to use parentheses to regroup the subexpressions.
- You cannot change the associativity of an operator. (Operator associativity is presented in Table 8.8 in Chapter 8.) When an operand is surrounded by two operators that have the same precedence, the operand is grouped with either the one on the left or the one on the right, depending on the operator's associativity.

For example, the precedence of the addition and subtraction operators is the same, and both have *left-to-right associativity* (also called *left-associativity*). As a result, the following expression is processed from left to right:

```
w = x + y - z;    // (x + y) is evaluated first
```

The following statement, using parentheses for grouping, is processed in the same manner as the preceding statement:

```
w = (x + y) - z; // Control evaluation order with use of ()
```

- You cannot change the way an operator works for built-in data types. For example, you cannot write an overload function that adds integers, because that is a built-in function.
- You can overload any of the operators listed in Table 18.1.
- You cannot overload any of the operators listed in Table 18.2.

Although you can overload an operator, doing so may not necessarily be a good idea. The arithmetic operators are best used with numeric data objects. Furthermore, if the use of an operator makes an expression hard to read and understand, it is better not to use operator overloading. For example, suppose that you overload the < (less than) relational operator to compare two strings. The following statement may be confusing; even though you are comparing two strings, it may appear to some programmers that you are comparing two pointers:

18

```
if ( string1 < string2 )
     :
```

Here is a good guideline: do not use overloading if it makes the program difficult to read or provides for expressions that can be ambiguously interpreted.

Remember that when you overload the + operator, the += operator is not overloaded. If you want += overloaded, you will need to write an `operator +=()` function to overload that operator.

Overloading Operators with Friend Functions

Sometimes you cannot use a member function to overload an operator because it involves different types of objects. Under these circumstances, you can use a friend function to overload an operator. Why would you want to do this? Suppose that you want to add a real number to a complex number, using the following expression:

```
Complex x(3,1), z;
z = x + 3.3
```

You could use a member function to overload the + operator to allow adding a `float` to a complex number, as shown in the following example:

```
class Complex
{
public:
     :
     Complex operator +( const float )
private:
     float real;
     float imaginary;
}
:
// Member functions to overload + operator
Complex Complex::operator +( const float number )
{
   return Complex( real+number, imaginary );
}
```

There is still a problem. The problem is that the complex number would always need to be specified first, as in the preceding example. The reason is that the object which calls the `operator +()` member function is on the left side of the operator. You could tell the other programmers that the rule is, "When you want to add a `float` to a complex number, you always have to specify the complex number on the left side of the operator." But that is a sloppy and unnecessary restriction. People will laugh at anyone who imposes it. There are too many things to remember when you are programming, and you do not need silly restrictions. The solution is to add an additional function to further overload the + operator. This function handles the `float` type on the left side of the expression. To do this, you must use a friend function in this way:

```
class Complex
{
public:
     :
                                   // Add float to complex number
   friend Complex operator +( const float, const Complex & );
```

```
private:
   float real;
   float imaginary;
};
:

// Friend function adds float to complex number
Complex operator +( const float number, const Complex &cn )
{
   return Complex (cn.real + number, cn.imaginary);
}
```

Now that you have overloaded the + operator, you can use it as shown in the following code fragment:

```
Complex y(3,1), x;
x = y + 4.0;
x.Display();
x = 4.0 + y;
x.Display();
```

Incidentally, the results from executing the preceding statements are the same for both the assignment statements:

```
7 1i
7 1i
```

A friend function is commonly used to reverse the order of the operands. Such a function can be used whenever you want to handle two types of objects as operands. However, you do not have that problem when both operands are class objects of the same type. This example uses member functions for operator overloading when both operators are of type `Complex`. However, you could use friend functions for the same purpose, as illustrated in the following example:

```
// Friend function adds two complex numbers
Complex operator +( const Complex &cn1, const Complex &cn2 )
{
   return Complex (cn1.real + cn2.real,
                   cn1.imaginary + cn2.imaginary );
}
```

The preceding friend function is equivalent to the corresponding member function. Notice that the principal difference between the member function approach and the friend function approach is that the friend function has two `Complex` class parameters instead of one. A friend function

18

always requires one more argument than its equivalent member function. The extra argument specifies the object that is used to call the equivalent member function.

As an exercise, write functions that overload all the arithmetic operations (+, -, *, and /) so that they will correctly evaluate the following expressions:

```
Complex a( 3.0 , 2.0 ), b;
b = a + 3.0;
b = 3.0 + a;
b = a - 3.0;
b = 3.0 - a;
b = a * 3.0;
b = 3.0 * a;
b = a / 3.0;
b = 3.0 / a;
```

Any of the functions listed in Table 18.1 can be overloaded with the use of member functions. You can use friend functions to overload all the operators in Table 18.1 except =, (), [], and ->.

Overloading the Insertion (<<) Operator

When the << operator is used with any class ostream object, such as cout, it becomes the insertion operator. The bitwise operator is overloaded for the ostream class for all basic data types. The ostream class contains member functions used to overload the << operator. Each member function converts the values of one of the basic data types into a form that can be displayed, and inserts it into the output stream. There is an ostream class member function for all basic data types. This is the mechanism used by C++ to output information. Note also that cout is an instance of the ostream object and is automatically declared by C++ when a program executes.

You can overload the << operator so that you can use it with the cout object to display the contents of your own object. For example, if you overloaded the << operator to display a Complex object, you can display the complex_number Complex object by using the statement

```
cout << complex_number;
```

To overload the << operator to display the contents of a Complex object, you provide a friend function with the following prototype to the Complex class definition:

```
friend ostream & operator <<( ostream &ost, const Complex &cn );
```

As you can see, this friend function contains two arguments. The first argument must be a reference to an ostream object. The second argument is a reference to a Complex object. Because the first argument is an ostream object, you cannot use a member function. You must use a friend function. Next you create the friend function that overloads the << for the Complex object. Here is a listing of the function:

```
// Friend function that overloads << insertion operator
ostream & operator <<( ostream &ost, const Complex &cn )
{
    ost << cn.real << " " << cn.imaginary << "i ";
    return ost;     // Insertion operator returns ostream object
}
```

18

The reason that you need to use a reference to the ostream object instead of just referring to the cout object is that you might want to refer to other ostream objects, such as cerr, using the same function. (Recall from Chapter 7, "Input and Output," that the cerr object is the standard error channel to which error messages are usually directed.) This function can also be used to direct output to a file. The second argument is also passed as a reference (rather than by value) to save memory and time.

The two float data members, real and imaginary, of the Complex object, as well as the character string containing the imaginary symbol i, are inserted into the output stream.

The function returns a reference to the ostream object. This is done so that insertion operator expressions can be chained together into a single statement. You learned about this technique in Chapter 7, "Input and Output," before you knew anything about classes. Now it is time to reexamine this process. C++ evaluates an output statement from left to right. Once a subexpression (such as cout << value) is evaluated, it returns an ostream object. The returned object becomes the left operand for the next subexpression. The next subexpression is evaluated in the same manner. This process is repeated until the last subexpression has been processed. For example, consider the following statement:

```
cout << "Hello" << 3  << "\n";
```

This statement is evaluated from left to right. The leftmost subexpression (`cout << "Hello"`) is evaluated first. The string `"Hello"` is inserted into the output stream. Then the `cout` object reference is returned, and the expression effectively becomes

```
cout << 3 << "\n";
```

The next subexpression (`cout << 3`) is then evaluated. The integer is converted to ASCII and inserted into the output stream, and the `cout` object is returned. The expression becomes

```
cout << "\n";
```

The process is repeated for the third and last subexpression. That is why returning an `ostream` object allows you to chain `ostream` objects.

Now return your attention to the friend function that overloads the insertion operator for `Complex` objects. Here is an example of code that uses this friend function:

```
Complex a(3.0, 2.0);
cout << "The complex number is: " << a;
```

Here is the output:

```
The complex number is: 3.3 2i
```

The general form of a friend function used to overload the `ostream` insertion operator (<<) for an object named `obj` of a class named `class_name` is

```
ostream & operator<<( ostream & ost, class_name & obj )
{
    ost << ... // Insert object contents to output stream
    return ost;
}
```

Conversion

The C++ language conforms to a group of rules for converting from one basic data type to another (see the section "Data Conversion" in Chapter

11). C++ implicitly performs conversion whenever possible. You can override implicit conversion by using *casts* (see the section "Type Casting" in Chapter 11). In summary, the C++ compiler generates code that performs conversion when data types are different during the following operations:

- A value assignment

  Example: `int i = 3.0;`

- Arithmetic operation

  Example: `i = 3.0 * 4;`

- Passing an argument to a function

  Example: `sin(3);`

- Returning a value from a function

  Example: `int i=pow(3,4);`

You can specify which conversions are performed when you define your C++ classes. You can define the conversion between a class and the basic data types, and between classes.

Using the Constructor to Designate Conversion

If a constructor has only one argument, it is considered to be a *conversion function*. The type of that one argument is used to implicitly designate the type of conversion required. The constructor for the `Complex` class has two arguments. You can turn it into a conversion function by making the second argument a default argument. That will allow it to accept a single argument. Here is the change to the prototype for the `Complex` class constructor that will make it a conversion function:

```
class Complex
{
public:
    Complex( float real, float imaginary = 0 );
    :
```

```
private:
     float real;
     float imaginary;
};
```

With this definition of the constructor, you can specify only the real component of a complex number; the imaginary component is assumed to be 0. Any of the following statements will convert the variable a to (3,0):

```
Complex a( 3.0, 0.0 ); // No conversion
Complex a( 3.0 );      // a.imaginary is set to 0
Complex a( 3 );        // int is converted to float
a = Complex( 3 );      // int is converted to float
a = 3.0;               // Equivalent to a = Complex( 3.0 )
a = 3;                 // int is converted to float
```

Because the + operator was overloaded in the last section, conversion is also implicitly performed during arithmetic:

```
a = a + 4 + Complex( 5,3 );    // int values are converted
                               // to float values
```

By making the second argument a default argument to the specification of the prototype of the class `Complex` constructor, you can call the constructor with a single argument. This allows the constructor to become a conversion function. Then you can perform implicit conversion when passing a single value to a complex number for all basic data types. There is no valid mathematical way to convert a `Complex` data type to any of the basic data types. The allowable implicit conversion modes that are supported for converting values to and from a `Complex` data type are shown in Table 18.3.

Table 18.3. Conversion supported for the `Complex` class.

Type From/To	*Type* `Complex`	`double`	`float`	`int`	`long`
`Complex`	None	No	No	No	No
`double`	Yes	None	Yes	Yes	Yes
`float`	Yes	Yes	None	Yes	Yes
`int`	Yes	Yes	Yes	None	Yes
`long`	Yes	Yes	Yes	Yes	Yes

If you have a class object that can be converted, through special conversion, to a different data type, you can write a member function that "overloads" the casting keywords. This member function is called a *conversion operator*. You can write a conversion to replace any casting keyword. For example, suppose that you have a class, called `Time`, that converts a time from seconds past midnight into hours, minutes, and seconds. The class definition for `Time` is shown in Listing 18.8. The listing provides an example of `long` and `float` conversion operator functions, which are shown in bold print.

Listing 18.8. The source listing for the time.h header file.

```
// time.h - Time class used to illustrate conversion operators
#include <iostream.h>
#include <iomanip.h>
#include <stdlib.h>                     // Needed for exit()
class Time
{
public:
     Time( long );                      // Constructor
     Time( void );                      // Default constructor
     Time operator +( const Time & ); // Add two Time numbers
     Time operator +( const long );    // Add Time to long
                                        // Add long to Time
     friend Time operator +( const long, const Time & );
                                  // Overload insertion operator
     friend ostream & operator <<( ostream &ost, const Time & );
     Time operator -( const Time & ); // Subtract two Times
     operator float() const;     // float conversion operator
     operator long() const;      // long conversion operator
private:
     long seconds;               // seconds past midnight
     int hours;
     int minutes;
     int secs;
     void spm_to_hhmmss();       // Convert seconds to h,m,s
};
// Member functions

// The constructor that is called when a variable is declared
Time::Time( long spm )          // spm = seconds past midnight
```

continues

18

Listing 18.8. continued

```
{
     seconds = spm;
     spm_to_hhmmss();
}
// The constructor that is called when a variable is declared
// with no arguments
Time::Time( void )             // Default constructor
{
    seconds = 0;
    hours = minutes = secs = 0;
}
// Add Time to long number
Time Time::operator +( const long number )
{
    return Time( seconds + number );
}

// float conversion operator
Time::operator float() const
{
    return (float)seconds;
}
// long conversion operator
Time::operator long() const
{
    return seconds;
}

// Add objects
Time Time::operator +( const Time & spm_object )
{
    return Time( spm_object.seconds + seconds );
}
Time Time::operator-( const Time & spm_object )
{
    return Time( spm_object.seconds - seconds );
}
// Convert seconds past midnight to hours, minutes, and seconds
void Time::spm_to_hhmmss()
{
    long temp;
```

```
    hours = seconds / (3600);
    minutes = (seconds - (long)(hours *3600L ))/60;
    secs = seconds - ((hours * 60L )+ minutes )*60;
}
// Friend function that adds long to Time number
Time operator +( const long number, const Time &spm_object )
{
     return Time ( spm_object.seconds + number );
}
// Friend function that overloads << insertion operator
ostream & operator <<( ostream &ost, const Time &spm_object )
{
    ost.fill('0');  // Zero fill
    ost << setw(2) << spm_object.hours     << ":"
        << setw(2) << spm_object.minutes << ":"
        << setw(2) << spm_object.secs;
    return ost;      // Insertion operator returns ostream object
}
```

18

Neither the `operator float()` nor the `operator long()` function takes any arguments, and neither has a return type. These are conversion operators. A conversion operator must be a member function, and it must not be a `static` function. It cannot be a friend function. The `float()` function converts a `Time` object to a `float` data type value. The `long()` function converts a `Time` object to a `long` data type value. Whenever the compiler encounters code that requires a conversion from a `Time` object to a `float` *or* a `long` data type, it uses the `float()` or `long()` member function. The example presented in Listing 18.9 uses the `Time` class and demonstrates the use of the `float()` and `long()` member functions. Again, the statements that are converted with the `float()` and `long()` member functions appear in bold print.

Listing 18.9. The source listing for TIME.CPP.

```
// TIME.CPP - Illustrates use of float() and long() member
// functions
#include "time.h"
void main()
{
     Time seconds = 84000;
```

continues

Listing 18.9. continued

```
    float f;
    long  l;
    cout << seconds << "\n";
    f = seconds;                // Compiler uses float function
                                // for conversion
    f = float( seconds );       // Also converts Time -> f
    f = (float)seconds;         // Also converts Time -> f
    f = a.operator float();     // Converts using explicit call
    cout << f << "\n";          // Displays 84000
    l = seconds;   // Compiler uses long function for conversion
    cout << l << "\n";          // Displays 84000
}
```

This solution to conversion may not always work. Consider the following example:

```
#include "time.h"
Time seconds;
float f, x;
x = seconds + 333   // Compiler error
```

Here the compiler generates an error when it encounters the fourth statement. The error is caused because the compiler detects an ambiguity in the way it can generate code. The compiler determines that it can interpret the statement in two different ways:

```
x = (float)seconds + 333
x = seconds + Time( 333 );
```

When the compiler detects the ambiguity, it has no way of determining which way it should choose, so it generates an error.

You can resolve this ambiguity by removing one of the implicit conversions. Another method is to create a member function to perform the addition operations. Here are some examples:

```
void add( const float );  // Member function to add basic
                          // data type value to Time object
friend Time add( const Time &, Const Time & ); // Add two
                                               // Time objects
```

A third solution is to get rid of the conversion operator altogether and supply your own conversion functions, as in

```
Time long_to_Time( const long );  // Member function
```

which converts a `long` value to a `Time` object.

A fourth solution to eliminate ambiguity is to overload the + operator for all three possible cases. Note the following example:

```
friend Time operator+( const Time &arg1, const Time &arg2 );
friend Time operator+( long arg1, const Time &arg2 );
friend Time operator+( const Time &arg1, long arg2 );
```

This way, the compiler does not have to do any conversion at all. It generates code to call the appropriate function based on the types of arguments.

The best approach is to use conversion operators only when you have a good justification for using them. You can always use constructors with more than one argument and do explicit conversion by using member functions like the `long_to_Time` function just illustrated.

What You Have Learned

In this chapter, you learned more about the use of classes. Specifically, you learned the following:

- How and when to use `static` member data and functions
- What friend classes and friend functions are
- How to rewrite the address book application, using more of an OOP approach
- How to do operator overloading and when to use it
- How to overload the arithmetic and insertion operators
- How to do implicit and explicit conversion between class objects and built-in data types

Inheritance

The best is the enemy of the good.

—Voltaire (François-Marie Arouet)
"Dramatic Art" from *Dictionnaire Philosophique* (1764)

In This Chapter

Ever since humans started programming computers, they have spent time scrounging around for a function that they can use as an alternative to writing one. Programmers do not like "to reinvent wheels." Programming libraries have been around since the early mainframe computers filled large buildings with vacuum tubes, magnetic core memory, and big magnetic tape drives. Entire programming staffs dedicate their working lives to programming and maintaining software function libraries.

All programming languages possess some form of library that a programmer can use to save time in writing and testing a computer program. Using code invented by someone else has several advantages. You don't have to design it, code it, test it, and debug it. You are free to agonize over the code that you *must* design, code, test, and debug.

For the C language, there exist hundreds of commercially available libraries that contain functions to perform almost any imaginable task. All you have to do is call functions supported by a library and link in a precompiled code for the library functions. If a library function fills your needs, there is no problem. You have satisfied your goal of achieving reusability.

Sometimes, though, you find that a function does only a portion of what you need to do. Usually, the source code for a library is not available. That is normally not a problem because all you care about is that the functions in the library solve your problem. However, if you need to change the behavior of a function, you have to change the source code. Even if the source code is available, you modify it to meet your needs. Then you test and debug your modified library function. That substantially diminishes the advantage of using someone else's function. You have expanded the universe of "things that can go wrong in your program." You have more code to test, debug, and maintain. These kinds of things cause schedules to slip. If you do not have the source code, you have two alternatives. You can write the function from scratch, or you can alter your program to conform to the limitations of the function. Unfortunately, you lose the reusability advantage.

Reusable code is a major goal of OOP. This goal is supported by the C++ language through the use of classes, which provide a higher degree of reusability than traditional function libraries. Because classes provide a mechanism for hiding the representation of data through the use of member functions, you have a better integration of data and functionality than you do with a function library.

However, C++ supports an even better technique than the traditional library function code-modification method. C++ enables you to extend classes through the use of *class inheritance*. You can derive new classes from old classes. Starting with an original class, called a *base* class, you can derive a new class that *inherits* the properties of the original class. These properties include the member data definitions and member functions (methods). You can build libraries of classes and either use these classes or derive new classes. Once a base class has been coded, tested, debugged, and included in a class library, you can derive a new class from the base class, knowing confidently that you don't have to retest the original base class when you derive a new class. You just need to design, code, test, debug, and maintain the code in the derived class. Usually, deriving a new class from a base class takes less time than creating the entire class from scratch.

The number of commercially available class libraries has exploded in the last few years. Usually, the source code for the classes in the libraries is supplied with the class library to make it easier for you to derive new classes.

In this chapter, you are introduced to class inheritance. It is an elegant concept that is simple to implement, but the task of designing an optimum class hierarchy can be quite challenging. This chapter covers the following topics:

- What C++ class inheritance is and how to use it
- What a base class is
- How to derive one class from another
- How to use a derived class
- What a member function redefinition is
- What a virtual function is and how to use it
- What multiple inheritance is and how to use it
- What a multiple base class is

19

The Zoo

Before plunging into the details of class inheritance, consider a real-world example of how you might make use of a hierarchy of related classes. Suppose that a zoo manager is overwhelmed with paperwork and assigns you, as zoo programmer, the job of creating a computer program that tracks animals in the zoo. The problem is that there are different types of information required to describe each kind of animal. You could write the program in C, using a structure for each type of data (monkeys, birds, and so on). The problem with that approach is that you will have to write code to support each type of structure. You could create a single structure called `ANIMALS`. All the data that is common to all the animals—such as name, inventory number, and birthday—would fit nicely in the structure. You can store the data that is unique to a specific type of animal, such as `number_of_eggs` laid, in the same class, using unions.

Here is what a simple structure might look like:

```
struct bird
{
     float height;
     float beak_length;
     int   aviary;
     float wingspan;
     int   number_of_eggs;
     char  crown;
};
struct reptile
{
    float length;
    float diameter;
    int   cage_number;
    int   legs;
    char  poisonous;
    int   teeth;
};


struct monkey
{
    float height;
    char  pregnant;
    int   island_number;
    int   number_of_teeth;
    int   tail_length;
    char  fur_condition[20];
};

struct ANIMALS
{
     char species[30];
     char birthday[8];
     char name[30];
     float cost;
```

```
        float weight;
        int type_animal;
        char sex;
        union
        {
             struct bird Bird;
             struct reptile Reptile;
             struct monkey Monkey;
        };
};
```

Each of the structures in the union contains data specific to a category of zoo animal. The definitions of the `bird`, `reptile`, and `monkey` structures contain different data for each type of animal. Do not concern yourself with the actual data—it is not important. All you have to notice is that each of the structures contains data members specific to the animal type.

When you develop code with the `ANIMALS` structure, you have to write special code to handle each type of animal. For example, if you are developing a report that describes the characteristics of each animal in the zoo, you might write code resembling the following program fragment:

```
/* Display animal characteristics */
#include <stdio.h>
#define BIRD    1
#define REPTILE 2
#define MONKEY  3
void main() {};

void animal_report( ANIMALS *a )
{
          char *sex[2] = { "Male", "Female" };
          printf(
               "Species: %s  Name: %s  Cost: %8.2f  Sex: %s\n",
               a->species ,
               a->cost ,
               sex[ a->sex ] );
      switch ( a->type_animal )
      {
      case BIRD:
           /* Display properties of a bird */
           printf(
           "Weight: %6.2f  Height: %6.2f  Beak length: %6.2f",
```

19

```
          a->weight,
          a->Bird.height,
          a->Bird.beak_length );
     printf( "Wingspan %d\n", a->Bird.wingspan );
     printf( "Location: Aviary number: %d \n",
          a->Bird.aviary );
     printf( "Number of eggs laid per season %d",
          a->Bird.number_of_eggs );
     if ( a->Bird.crown == 1 )
          printf ("Comment: A crown is present" );
     :
case REPTILE:
     /* Display reptile characteristics */
     printf(
          "Weight: %6.2f  Length: %6.2f  Diameter: %6.2f\n",
          a->weight,
          a->Reptile.length,
          a->Reptile.diameter );
     printf( "Is the reptile poisonous? " );
          if ( a->Reptile.poisonous == 'Y' )
               printf( "Yes\n" );
          else
               printf( "No\n" );    :
     if ( a->Reptile.legs == 0 )
          printf( "%s is a snake.\n", a->name );
     else
          printf( "%s has %d legs.\n",
               a->name, a->Reptile.legs );
     if ( a->Reptile.teeth > 0 )
          printf( "%s has %d teeth.\n",
               a->name, a->Reptile.teeth );

     printf( "Location: cage number: %d\n",
          a->Reptile.cage_number );
          :
case MONKEY:
     /* Display characteristics of a monkey */
     printf(
     "Weight: %6.2f  Height: %6.2f  Tail length: %6.2f\n",
          a->weight,
          a->Monkey.height,
          a->Monkey.tail_length );
```

```
            if ( a->sex == 1 && a->Monkey.pregnant > 0 )
                printf( "%s is %d weeks pregnant",
                   a->name, a->Monkey.pregnant );
            printf( "Condition of %s's fur: %s\n",
                 a->name, a->Monkey.fur_condition );
            printf( "%s has %d teeth.\n",
                 a->name, a->Monkey.number_of_teeth );
            printf( "Location: Monkey island number: %d\n",
                 a->Monkey.island_number );
              :
        :
      }
};
```

The animal_report() function incorporates code that displays the contents of the union, depending on the type of zoo animal described in the ANIMALS structure. The structure member type_animal is used to specify which code is executed in the switch statement.

There are several disadvantages of implementing the program in C with structures and unions. In the first place, the program can become rather complex if you have many types of animals to process. This makes the code difficult to read. It is also difficult to isolate code that relates to a specific structure member. For example, code that uses the name member is scattered throughout the program. If you need to change the code that processes the name member, you will need to make many changes to the program.

In addition, the code is difficult to maintain. Whenever you add a new type of animal, you will have to add code for the new type everywhere in the program where a switch case is used to handle specific animal types. Then you must recompile the entire program. You will have to test the entire program to make sure that all the other switch cases still operate correctly. This can make the process of adding a new type of animal to the zoo a costly and time-consuming process.

By now, you may be concluding from this example that there is a better way. You are right. The objective of the designers of C++ was to provide one. The "better way" is C++ language class inheritance.

Deriving a Class

Suppose that you decide to use C++ to write the zoo animal tracking application. The first thing you do is write down all the properties of each type of animal. A simplified list is provided in Table 19.1.

Table 19.1. Properties of zoo animals.

Birds	*Reptiles*	*Monkeys*
species	species	species
name	name	name
birthday	birthday	birthday
cost	cost	cost
sex	sex	sex
weight	weight	weight
height	length	height
beak length	diameter	island number
aviary	cage number	number of teeth
wingspan	legs	tail length
number of eggs	poisonous	fur condition
crown	teeth	

Now you determine which properties are common for all types of animals, and you define a class that includes the common properties. This is what is involved in determining the ***class hierarchy***. The base class contains a group of generalized properties common to all the planned derived classes. Figure 19.1 illustrates a class hierarchy with the common properties at the top represented by a "generalized animal." The derived classes in the figure are represented by pictures of animals.

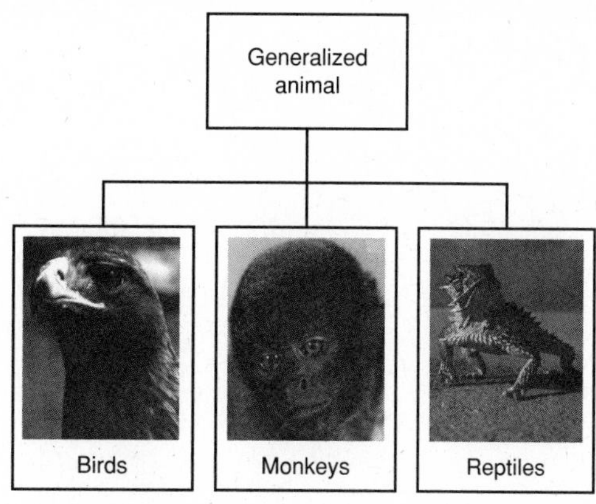

Figure 19.1. Class hierarchy for the* `Animal` *class and derived classes.

The class can be called `Animal`. The data members in `Animal` represent the properties that are common to all three types of animals:

```
class Animal
{
public:
     Animal();
     Animal( char *sp, char *bd, char *nm, float ct,
             float wt, int ta, char sx );
     char *GetSpecies();
private:
     char  species[30];
     char  birthday[8];
     char  name[30];
     float cost;
     float weight;
     char  sex;
};
```

19

The next step is to create classes for each of the three animal types: `bird`, `reptile`, and `monkey`. There are two roads you can travel when you define a structure for the individual animal types. You can make the `Animal` class a member of the new classes. However, that would be an erroneous relationship because a `monkey` class does not contain a generic `Animal` object. The relationship is the other way around—a monkey is a subcategory of the class `Animal`.

The second and correct road to travel is to use *class inheritance*, which compels one class to become a subcategory of another. Here is how to make the class `bird` become a special type of class `Animal`. You define the class `bird` as you would any other class:

```
// Derived class: bird

class bird : public Animal
{
public:
     bird( char *sp, char *bd, char *nm, float ct,
           float wt, char sx ,
           float ht, float bl, int av,
           float ws, int ne, char cn );
     void Print( void ) const;
private:
     float height;
     float beak_length;
     int   aviary;
     float wingspan;
     int   number_of_eggs;
     char  crown;
};
```

The class name (`bird`) is followed by a colon and the keyword `public`, which is followed by the name of the class (`Animal`). As a result, the class `bird` becomes a *derived class*. It is derived from the class `Animal`, which is a *base class*. Incidentally, you can use the `private` keyword. The distinction between the use of `private` and `public` keywords is described later in this chapter.

When you declare a `bird` object, you do not have access to the private members of the class `Animal`. However, you can access any of the base class's public (or protected) members. The `protected` keyword is discussed in the next section. You can call any of the class `Animal` public member functions. This means that the public members of the base class become public members of the derived class. The derived class is said to inherit the public members of the base class. A derived class does not inherit the private members of a base class. Here is an example of a declaration for a bird object:

```
bird Parrot( "Parrot", "12/02/90", "Polly", 535.00, 3.0 .0,
             15.0, .5, 5, 30.0, 0, 1 );
```

The first seven parameters are passed to the class Animal constructor, which establishes values for all the values for the bird objects that are private data members from the class Animal. The remaining parameters are passed to the bird class constructor. The constructors are discussed in more detail in the section "Implementing a Derived Class" later in this chapter.

When a derived class object is declared, the program automatically calls the base class constructor and then the derived class constructor. When the object is destroyed, the program automatically calls the derived class destructor and then the base class destructor.

As noted earlier, the derived class has access to the base class public member functions. For example, the statements

```
char *ptr;
ptr = Parrot.GetSpecies();
cout << ptr;
```

result in the display of the contents of species, which is Parrot. The GetSpecies function returns a pointer to a character string containing the species.

The protected Keyword

You have learned about public data members and private data members. Here is a new one: *protected* members. Usually, a base class uses the protected keyword instead of the private keyword. In other words, the protected keyword is used as a label for a section of class members. This use is like the private keyword because you can access protected members only with public member functions. As you know, derived classes cannot access private members of its base class. However, derived classes can access protected members of its base class. Therefore, derived functions can inherit from the base class any data that is ordinarily hidden from the external world. You can add new member functions to the derived class that access protected data in the base class.

> When you design a class that you plan to use as a base class, use the `protected` keyword in place of the `private` keyword so that the derived class can have access to certain members that cannot be accessed by the external world.

Private Derivation

You can use the `private` keyword when defining a derived class. This technique is called *private derivation*. Note the following example:

```
class ApplePie : private Pie
{
};
```

Here public and protected members of the base class `Pie` become private members of the derived class `ApplePie`. This means that they can be accessed from only the private member functions of the derived class. You can derive a class from a derived class. Note the following example:

```
class ChocolateCake : public Cake
{
};

class GermanChocolateCake : private ChocolateCake
{
};
```

The preceding example is illustrated in Figure 19.2. Note that public and protected members belonging to class `Cake` are inherited by class `ChocolateCake` and class `GermanChocolateCake`. However, private members belonging to class `Cake` are not inherited.

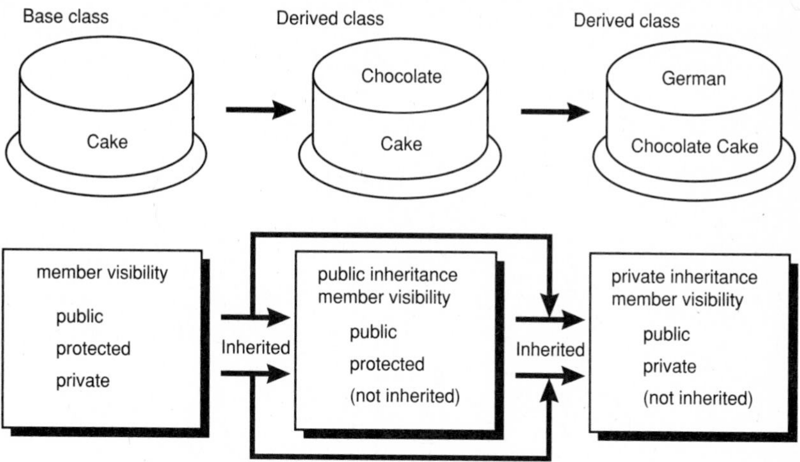

Figure 19.2. *Inherited class member visibility.*

Implementing a Derived Class

Now that you know what data belongs in the base class and in derived classes, you are ready to implement the classes. The constructor for the derived class contains parameters to establish values for both the base and derived data members. The form of the `Animal` base class constructor is

19

```
Animal::Animal( char *sp, char *bd, char *nm, float ct,
                float wt, char sx )
{
     // Establish values for static data members
     :
}
```

Once you have established the constructor for the base class, you can write the constructor for the `bird`, `reptile`, and `monkey` derived classes. Here is the code for the class `bird` constructor:

```
bird::bird( char *sp, char *bd, char *nm,
            float ct, float wt, char sx,
            float ht, float bl, int av,
            float ws, int ne, char cn ) :
           Animal( sp, bd, nm, ct, wt, sx )
```

```
{
    height          = ht;
    beak_length     = bl;
    aviary          = av;
    wingspan        = ws;
    number_of_eggs = ne;
    crown           = cn;
}
```

Notice that a colon separates the constructor function heading from a call statement to the base class (`Animal`) constructor. Notice also how the arguments that correspond to the base class are passed from the derived class to the base class (see Figure 19.3).

```
bird::bird(char*sp, char*bd, char*nm, float ct, float wt, char sx,
    float ht,
    float bl,
    int av,
    float ws,
    int ne,
    char cn ) : Animal (sp, bd, nm, ct, wt, sx)
{
    .
    .
    .
}
```


Figure 19.3. Passing arguments from the derived class to the base class.

There is also a default constructor for the base class, which initializes its private members. And there is a corresponding default constructor for each of the derived classes.

> If you need a constructor for the base class, you must provide a constructor for the derived classes even if you do not have any initialization to perform for the derived class. The reason is that if the derived class has no default constructor, the default constructor for the base class would never be called when you declare a derived class object.

As you learned earlier, the base class constructor is called before the derived class constructor is called. The class Animal constructor establishes the base class private data members. When it returns, the class bird constructor is called to initialize the derived class private data members. There are no destructors, but if there were, the derived class destructor would be called before the base class destructor is called.

The Animal base class contains various access functions used to fetch the contents of its private member data. It contains also the PrintAnimal() function, which displays its private member data. You can use the derived class object name to call a member function of the base class. In the following example, the call to PrintAnimal() calls the base class member function to print the contents of its private members:

```
bird Parrot( "Parrot", "12/02/90", "Polly", 535.00, 3.0 .0,
            15.0, .5, 5, 30.0, 0, 1 );
Parrot.PrintAnimal();
```

All three derived classes have a print function named Print(). This print function displays all the private data relating to a specific type of data, including the data in the base class.

As you can see, the technique required to implement a derived class is relatively simple. The difficult part is in the design of the class hierarchy. Your goal is to increase reusability and reduce maintenance. You can derive as many classes as you like, and you do not have to make any changes to the base class. Furthermore, you can change the *representation* of the data in the Animal base class without affecting any of the objects.

What is meant by representation? Suppose that you want to change the representation of birthday from an eight-character string to a long integer that represents the date as days past December 31, 1900. You can do this without having to change any of the derived classes. Figure 19.4 shows a representation of the class hierarchy for the classes defined in Listing 19.1.

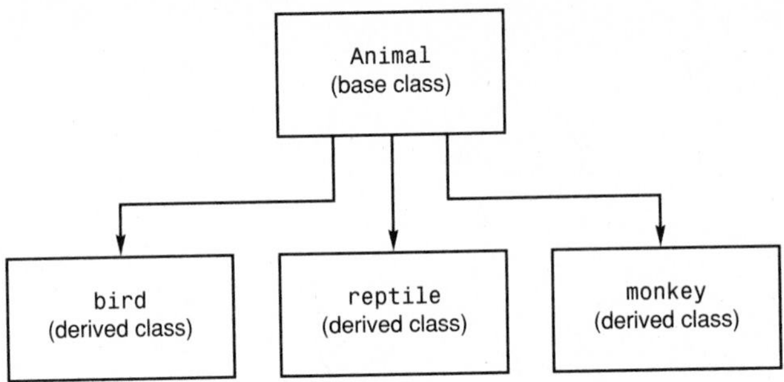

Figure 19.4. Class hierarchy for the zoo application.

Listing 19.1 presents a listing of the zoo.h header file. It contains the definition of the `Animal` base class and three derived classes: `bird`, `reptile`, and `monkey`.

Listing 19.1. The source listing for the zoo.h header file.

```
// zoo.h - Definition of classes Animal, bird, reptile,
// and monkey
#include <string.h>   // Contains prototypes for strncpy()
#include <stdlib.h>   // Contains macros for min/max
#include <iostream.h> // iostream object definition

// Base class Animal

class Animal
{
public:
     Animal();
     Animal( char *sp, char *bd, char *nm, float ct,
             float wt, char sx );
     void SetAnimal( char *sp, char *bd, char *nm, float ct,
             float wt, char sx );
     char *GetSpecies();
     char *GetName();
     char *GetBirthday();
     float GetCost();
     float GetWeight();
     int   GetSex();
     void  PrintAnimal() const;
```

```
private:
     char  species[30];
     char  birthday[8];
     char  name[30];
     float cost;
     float weight;
     char  sex;
};
// Constructor
Animal::Animal( char *sp, char *bd, char *nm, float ct,
            float wt, char sx )
{
    strncpy( species, sp, 29 );
    strncpy( birthday, bd, 8 );
    strncpy( name, nm, 29 );
    cost = ct;
    weight = wt < 0.0 ? 0.0 : wt;
    sex = ( sx == 0 ) ? 0 : (( sx == 1 ) ? 1 : 0);
}
// Default constructor
Animal::Animal()
{
    species[0]   = '\0';
    birthday[0] = '\0';
    name[0]      = '\0';
    cost         = 0.0;
    weight       = 0.0;
    sex          = 0;
}

// Access functions

void Animal::SetAnimal( char *sp, char *bd, char *nm, float ct,
            float wt, char sx )
{
     Animal( sp, bd, nm, ct, wt, sx );
}

char *Animal::GetSpecies()   { return species;  }
char *Animal::GetName()         { return name;  }
char *Animal::GetBirthday()  { return birthday; }
```

continues

Listing 19.1. continued

```
float Animal::GetCost()          { return cost; }
float Animal::GetWeight()      { return weight; }
int      Animal::GetSex()          { return sex; }
// Print Animal object
void Animal::PrintAnimal() const
{
    char *SexNames[2] = { "Male", "Female" };
    cout << "\n-------------- Zoo Animal --------------\n"
         << "Species: "    << species
         << "  Name: "     << name  << "\n"
         << "  Cost: "     << cost
         << "  Sex:  "     << SexNames[ sex ]
         << "  Weight:  "  << weight << "\n";
}
//////////////////// Derived Classes //////////////////////
// Derived class: bird

class bird : public Animal
{
public:
     bird( char *sp, char *bd, char *nm, float ct,
           float wt, char sx ,
           float ht, float bl, int av,
           float ws, int ne, char cn );
     bird();
     void Print( void ) const;
private:
     float height;
     float beak_length;
     int   aviary;
     float wingspan;
     int   number_of_eggs;
     char  crown;
};
// bird constructor
bird::bird( char *sp, char *bd, char *nm, float ct,
            float wt, char sx,
            float ht, float bl, int av,
            float ws, int ne, char cn ) :
         Animal( sp, bd, nm, ct, wt, sx )
```

```
{
    height         = ht;
    beak_length    = bl;
    aviary         = av;
    wingspan       = ws;
    number_of_eggs = ne;
    crown          = cn;
}
bird::bird() : Animal();
{
    height         = 0.0;
    beak_length    = 0.0;
    aviary         = 0;
    wingspan       = 0.0;
    number_of_eggs = 0;
    crown          = 0;
}
void bird::Print() const
{
      PrintAnimal();
      cout << "Beak length: " << beak_length
           << " Wingspan: " << wingspan
           << "    Location: Aviary number: " << aviary << "\n"
           << "Number of eggs laid per season: "
           << number_of_eggs << "\n";
      if ( crown == 1 )
      cout << "Comment: A crown is present\n";
}
////////////////////////////////////////////////////////
// Second derived class: reptile
class reptile: public Animal
{
public:
     reptile( char *sp, char *bd, char *nm, float ct,
             float wt, char sx ,         // Base class members
             float lt, float dr, int cn, // reptile class members
             int ls, char ps, int th );
     reptile();
     void Print( void ) const;
private:
    float length;
    float diameter;
```

continues

Listing 19.1. continued

```
    int   cage_number;
    int   legs;
    char  poisonous;
    int   teeth;
};
// Member functions
// Constructor
reptile::reptile( char *sp, char *bd, char *nm, float ct,
             float wt, char sx ,      // Base class members
             float lt, float dr, int cn,
             int ls, char ps, int th ) :
         Animal( sp, bd, nm, ct, wt, sx )
{
    length         = lt;
    diameter       = dr;
    cage_number    = cn;
    legs           = ls;
    poisonous      = ps;
    teeth          = th;
}
reptile::reptile() : Animal()
{
    length         = 0.0;
    diameter       = 0.0;
    cage_number    = 0;
    legs           = 0;
    poisonous      = 0;
    teeth          = 0;
}
// Member functions
void reptile::Print() const
{
    PrintAnimal();
    cout << "Length: "     << length
         << "  Diameter: " << diameter
         << "      Location: cage number: "
         << cage_number << "\n"
         << "The reptile is ";
    if ( poisonous == 1 )
         cout << "poisonous.\n";
```

```
    else
        cout << "not poisonous\n";
    cout << GetName();
    if ( legs == 0 )
        cout << " is a snake.\n";
    else
        cout << " has " << legs << " legs.\n";
    if ( teeth > 0 )
        cout << "Number of teeth: " <<  teeth << "\n";
}
///////////////////////////////////////////////////////////
// Third derived class: monkey
class monkey : public Animal
{
public:
     monkey( char *sp, char *bd, char *nm, float ct,
             float wt, char sx ,   // Base class members
             float ht,  int in,    // monkey members
             int nt, float tl, char *fc );
     monkey();
     void Print() const;
private:
    float height;
    int   island_number;
    int   number_of_teeth;
    float tail_length;
    char  fur_condition[20];
};
monkey::monkey( char *sp, char *bd, char *nm, float ct,
             float wt, char sx ,   // Base class members
             float ht, int in,     // monkey members
             int nt, float tl, char *fc ) :
        Animal( sp, bd, nm, ct, wt, sx )
{
    height         = ht;
    island_number  = in;
    number_of_teeth= nt;
    tail_length    = tl;
    strncpy ( fur_condition, fc, 19 );
}
```

continues

Listing 19.1. continued

```
monkey::monkey() : Animal()
{
    height            = 0.0;
    island_number     = 0;
    number_of_teeth   = 0;
    tail_length       = 0.0;
    fur_condition[0] = 0;
}
// Access functions
void monkey::Print() const
{
     PrintAnimal();
     cout << "Height: " << height
          << " Tail length: "   << tail_length
          << "\nCondition of "  << GetName()
          << "'s fur: " << fur_condition
          << "\nNumber of teeth " << number_of_teeth
          << "\nLocation: Monkey island number: "
          << island_number << " \n";
}
```

Using Derived Classes

Once you have implemented the derived and base classes, most of the work is done. Now all you have to do is declare objects you need and then print them. Listing 19.2 presents a source listing of the simple program ZOO1.CPP, which uses the derived classes defined in Listing 19.1. You declare an object for a derived class as you would declare any other C++ object. You just specify the parameters that are specific to the type of object being declared. The results of executing ZOO1.EXE are presented in Listing 19.3.

Listing 19.2. The source listing for ZOO1.CPP.

```
// ZOO1.CPP - Illustrates derived classes
#include "zoo.h"
void main()
```

```
{
    monkey Capuchin( "Capuchin Monkey", "10/02/87", "Samuel",
                491.00, 2.1, 0,
                15.25, 3, 28, 16.25, "Good" );
    monkey Marmoset( "Marmoset Monkey", "03/11/89", "Mary",
                565.00, .25, 1,
                6.2, 2, 32, 8.25, "Excellent" );
    bird Macaw( "Hyacinthyne Macaw", "07/15/85", "Mac",
                600.00, .5, 0,
                15.0, .77, 5, 30.0, 0, 1 );
    reptile Cobra( "Indian cobra", "04/04/86", "Mike",
                900.00, 5.2, 1,
                5.1, 4.1, 7, 0, 1, 2 );
     Capuchin.Print();
     Marmoset.Print();
     Macaw.Print();
     Cobra.Print();
}
```

Listing 19.3. The results of executing ZOO1.EXE.

```
-------------- Zoo Animal --------------
Species: Capuchin Monkey      Name: Samuel
  Cost: 491  Sex:  Male  Weight:  2.1
Height: 15.25 Tail length: 16.25
Condition of Samuel's fur: Good
Number of teeth 28
Location: Monkey island number: 3

-------------- Zoo Animal --------------
Species: Marmoset Monkey      Name: Mary
  Cost: 565  Sex:  Female  Weight:  0.25
Height: 6.2 Tail length: 8.25
Condition of Mary's fur: Excellent
Number of teeth 32
Location: Monkey island number: 2
```

continues

Listing 19.3. continued

```
-------------- Zoo Animal --------------
Species: Hyacinthyne Macaw     Name: Mac
  Cost: 600  Sex:  Male  Weight:  0.5
Beak length: 0.77 Wingspan: 30    Location: Aviary number: 5
Number of eggs laid per season: 0
Comment: A crown is present

-------------- Zoo Animal --------------
Species: Indian cobra     Name: Mike
  Cost: 900  Sex:  Female  Weight:  5.2
Length: 5.1  Diameter: 4.1      Location: cage number: 7
The reptile is poisonous.
Mike is a snake.
Number of teeth: 2
```

Extending Inheritance

You can derive a class from a derived class. Any class derived from another derived class inherits the properties of all its ancestors. For example, suppose that you want to derive a new class, named `turtle`, from the `reptile` derived class. Listing 19.4 presents a listing of the zoo-ext.h header file, which contains a definition of the `turtle` class. This class is similar to the class definitions presented earlier, except that the derived class `reptile` constructor is referenced instead of the base class `Animal`. On the assumption that all turtles have four legs, a four-integer value is passed to the `reptile` class constructor. Figure 19.5 shows a representation of the class hierarchy for the zoo application with the `turtle` class added.

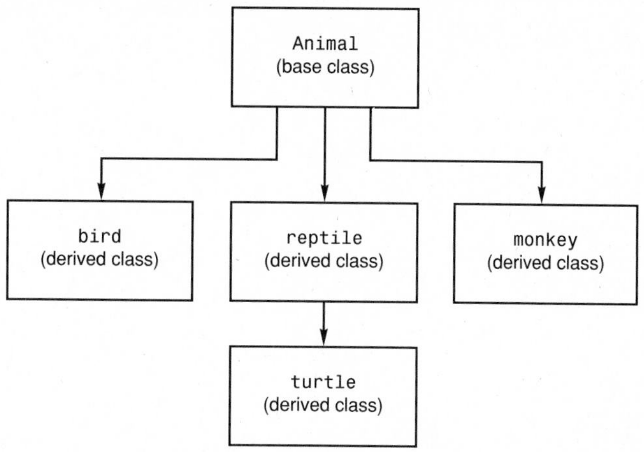

Figure 19.5. *Class hierarchy for the zoo application with the* `turtle` *class added.*

In the `Print()` function, the `reptile` class `Print()` function is called. Notice that the global scope resolution operator is used to reference this function.

Listing 19.4. The source listing for the zoo-ext.h header file.

```
// zoo-ext.h - Illustrates extended inheritance
#include <string.h>   // Contains prototype for strncpy()
#include <iostream.h> // iostream object definition
//
///////////////////////// Derived Classes //////////////////////
// Derived Class: turtle
class turtle : public reptile
{
public:
     turtle( char *sp, char *bd, char *nm, float ct,
             float wt, char sx ,     // Base class members
             float lt, float dr,     // reptile class members
             int cn, char ps, int th,
             char *ts, int ha );     // turtle class members
     void Print( void ) const;
```

continues

19

Listing 19.4. continued

```
private:
     char type_shell[30];
     int habitat;
};
// turtle constructor
turtle::turtle( char *sp, char *bd, char *nm, float ct,
            float wt, char sx ,        // Base class members
            float lt, float dr,        // reptile class members
            int cn, char ps, int th,
            char *ts, int ha ) :       // turtle class members
          reptile( sp, bd, nm, ct, wt, sx, lt, dr, cn, 4,
                  ps, th )
{
     strncpy( type_shell, ts, 29 );
     habitat = ( ha == 0 ) ? 0 : 1;
}
void turtle::Print() const
{
      char *Habitat[] = { "Water", "Terrestrial" };
      reptile::Print();
      cout << "\nType of turtle shell: " << type_shell
           << "   Habitat: " << Habitat[ habitat ] << "\n";
}
```

When you extend any class and add new data members, it is the responsibility of the derived class constructors to initialize the new data members.

Listing 19.5 presents the source listing for the ZOO2.CPP program. This program illustrates the use of the `turtle` class definition to declare `turtle` objects. Notice that both the zoo.h and zoo-ext.h header files are included. Furthermore, when a member function in a derived object has the same name as a function in the base class, any reference to that function name will reference the function in the derived class.

This is just another example of the benefits of C++ classes. Through C++ classes, you are able to extend the `reptile` and `Animal` classes without even touching them.

Listing 19.5. The source listing for ZOO2.CPP.

```
// ZOO2.CPP - Illustrates use of derived class
#include "zoo.h"
#include "zoo-ext.h"
void main()
{
    turtle Tom( "Leatherback Turtle", "10/02/40", "Thomas",
                1491.00, 1001.1, 0,
                80.00, 16.0, 71, 0, 22, "Ridges down back", 0 );
    turtle Jane( "Alligator snapping turtle", "04/04/89", "Jane",
                20.00, 11.2, 1,
                8.1, 6.2, 81, 0, 22, "Smooth shell", 0 );
     Tom.Print();
     Jane.Print();
}
```

Listing 19.6 presents the results of executing ZOO2.EXE.

Listing 19.6. The results of executing ZOO2.EXE.

```
-------------- Zoo Animal --------------
Species: Leatherback Turtle     Name: Thomas
  Cost: 1491  Sex:  Male  Weight:  1001.1
Length: 80  Diameter: 16      Location: cage number: 71
The reptile is not poisonous
Thomas has 4 legs.
Number of teeth: 22
Type of turtle shell: Ridges down back   Habitat: Water

-------------- Zoo Animal --------------
Species: Alligator snapping turtle     Name: Jane
  Cost: 20  Sex:  Female  Weight:  11.2
Length: 8.1  Diameter: 6.2      Location: cage number: 81
The reptile is not poisonous
Jane has 4 legs.
Number of teeth: 22
Type of turtle shell: Smooth shell   Habitat: Water
```

Redefining a Base Class Member Function

In the preceding section, the function `Print()` was *redefined* by a derived function. This is an important concept, as you will see when you learn about virtual functions later in the chapter. In this section, you examine *function redefinition*.

Listing 19.4 showed the member functions for the class `turtle`. One of its member functions is `Print()`. The `turtle` class is derived from the `reptile` class, which also has a function named `Print()`. As indicated in the text, when a member function in a derived class has the same name as a function in the base class, any reference to that function name will reference the function in the derived class. As a result, the `Print()` function for the `turtle` class displays `turtle` objects, and the `Print()` function for the `reptile` class displays `reptile` objects.

Some of the private data members belonging to the class `reptile` are to be displayed by the `Print()` function belonging to the class `turtle`. Because the data members are private, they cannot be directly referenced by the `turtle` class. As a result, the `Print()` member function belonging to the `reptile` class is called from within the `turtle` class `Print()` member function through use of the global resolution operator:

```
reptile::Print();
```

The `bird` and `monkey` classes also have a `Print()` function (refer to Listing 19.1). However, they do not perform redefinition because, like the `reptile` class, they are derived from the base class `Animal`. `Animal` does not contain a `Print()` member function to redefine.

Conversion between Base and Derived Class Objects

The C++ language enables you to implicitly assign a derived class object to its base class object. For example, you can do the following:

```
Animal animal1;       // Base class object declaration
monkey Capuchin( "Capuchin Monkey", "10/02/87", "Samuel",
                 491.00, 2.1, 0,
                 15.25, 3, 28, 16.25, "Good" );
animal1 = Capuchin;   // You can convert monkey object to
                      // animal object
```

C++ implicitly converts the `Capuchin` object to the `animal1` object. It transfers values for data members of the `Capuchin` object that correspond to the members of the `animal1` object. The conversion performed by the preceding assignment statement is shown in Table 19.2.

Table 19.2. Converting a derived object to a base object.

animal1 *Data Members*	=	*Capuchin* *Data Members*
species	←	species
name	←	name
birthday	←	birthday
cost	←	cost
sex	←	sex
weight	←	weight
	(not used)	height
	(not used)	island_number
	(not used)	number_of_teeth
	(not used)	tail_length
	(not used)	fur_condition

C++ does not allow you to convert a base object to a derived object. For example, you cannot do this:

```
Capuchin = animal1;  // Wrong! Cannot convert!
```

There are members in the `Capuchin` object that do not exist in the `animal1` object, as indicated in Table 19.2. If you were allowed to convert an `animal1` object to a `Capuchin` object (base object to a derived object), you would have data members that would not be initialized. This could cause unpredictable results, ranging from garbage being displayed by `turtle::Print` to a crash of the program.

Pointers to a Base Class

You can also implicitly convert a pointer to a derived class object to a pointer to its base class object. Note this example:

```
Animal *baseptr1, *baseptr2; // Pointer to base class object
monkey Capuchin( "Capuchin Monkey", "10/02/87", "Samuel",
                 491.00, 2.1, 0,  // Derived object
                 15.25, 3, 28,
                 16.25, "Good" );
bird Macaw( "Hyacinthyne Macaw", "07/15/85", "Mac",
                 600.00, .5, 0,
                 15.0, .77, 5, 30.0, 0, 1 );
baseptr1 = &Capuchin; // You can convert pointer to monkey
                      // class object to pointer to animal
                      // class object
baseptr2 = &Macaw;
```

As illustrated, you can make a pointer to a base class (`Animal`) point to derived classes (`bird` and `monkey`). When you point to an object by using a pointer to a base class, the type of pointer determines which class member functions you can call. For example, if you use `baseptr1` or `baseptr2`, you can call only `Animal` class member functions:

```
char *nm;
bird *birdptr;              // Pointer to bird object
nm = baseptr1->GetName();   // Animal::GetName is called
baseptr2->Print();          // ERROR: there is no Animal::Print
                            // member function
birdptr = &Macaw;           // Point to a bird object
birdptr->Print();           // bird:Print() is called
```

It is possible to convert a base pointer to a derived pointer. However, you will need to use an explicit cast, as in

```
Animal *ptranimal;               // Pointer to base class
bird   *ptrbird;                 // Pointer to derived class
ptranimal = &Capuchin            // Instance of monkey object
ptrbird = (bird *) ptranimal;    // Allowed but dangerous
```

The compiler allows you to specify the last statement. However, it is dangerous because `ptrbird` will point to a `monkey` class object, and you will refer to invalid data. This generates unpredictable results. If this "feature" is not used properly, it can cause your program to crash.

> There are times when implicit conversion from a derived class object to a base class object will not work properly. For example, if a class has a member that is a pointer pointing to a free store memory buffer, the conversion transfers only the value of the pointer. As a result, the corresponding members in both objects point to the same memory buffer. The consequences of this are unpredictable and can result in a catastrophe. You can solve the problem by overloading the constructor with a single-argument conversion constructor function (see the section "Conversion" in Chapter 18). An example of a conversion function for converting a derived class object to a base class object is provided in the next section.

Dynamic Binding and Virtual Functions

In the last section, you learned that if you use a pointer to a class object and you call a member function, the member function that is called is associated with the type of pointer rather than with the type of object the pointer points to. Here is one more example:

```
reptile *reptile_ptr;          // Pointer to reptile object
turtle Tom("Turtle", ... );    // Declare turtle object
reptile_ptr = &Tom;            // Point to turtle object
reptile_ptr->Print();          // Call reptile::Print()
```

The function called is determined when the program is compiled. This is called *static linking*. It would be nice if the `Print()` function associated with the object `turtle` were called instead of its ancestor's `Print()` function (`reptile::Print`). But because the compiler uses the type of the pointer to determine which function to call, the compiler calls the `reptile::Print` function. The behavior is expected, but it may not suit your needs.

What Are Virtual Functions?

You can use *virtual functions* to alter this behavior so that the function is associated with the object being pointed to. When you call a virtual function through a pointer to a base class, the function belonging to a derived class is called. For example, if the `Print()` function is a virtual function, the following statements result in the execution of the `Print()` function belonging to the `turtle` class:

```
Animal *animal_ptr;          // Pointer to Animal object
turtle Tom("Turtle", ... ); // Declare turtle object
reptile Joe("Snake, ... )    // Declare reptile object
animal_ptr = &Tom;           // Point to turtle object
animal_ptr->Print();         // Print() is virtual function
                             // turtle::Print() is called
animal_ptr = &Joe;           // Point to reptile object
animal_ptr->Print();         // Print() is virtual function
                             // reptile::Print() is called
```

The behavior of virtual member functions is opposite from that of an ordinary member function. You can make a chain of functions with the same name virtual by placing a declaration for the member function in the class definition of the base class and placing the `virtual` keyword in front of the function prototype. The following statements illustrate which code needs to be added to the `Animal` class to convert the `Print()` functions in the derived classes into virtual functions. Add the following declaration to the `Animal` class:

```
class Animal
{
private:
    :
```

```
public:
     :
     virtual void Print() const;
     :
};
```

Next add a dummy `Print()` function definition for the member class:

```
void Animal::Print() const
{
}
```

You do not need to add the `virtual` keyword to the declaration of the `Print()` functions in the derived classes. They automatically become implicitly virtual. That is all you need to do to make the `Print()` function shown in Listing 19.1 into a virtual function.

> *Dynamic binding* is an OOP term which means that the function to be called is determined when the program is executing. This is different from *static binding*, which means that the function to be called is determined when the program is compiled. An ordinary function call is an example of static binding.
>
> You implement dynamic binding in C++ by using virtual functions. The address of the virtual function is determined while code is executing. The address is chosen from a table of virtual function addresses, called a *v-table*, depending on the object being used. The v-table is an array of function pointers for every class that uses a virtual function. Each object contains a hidden pointer to the v-table. When a virtual function is executed for an object, the executing code uses the hidden v-table pointer in the object to determine which virtual function to call. This operation is very efficient and is as fast or faster than executing a `switch` statement that would be required to simulate the same operation in a C program.

Note that only member functions can be virtual functions. Traditional or friend functions cannot be virtual functions.

Using Virtual Functions

It is time to explore a new example. A base class, called `Manufacturer`, contains the name of an item manufactured (`item`) and the manufacturer's price (`cost`). Another class, named `Wholesale`, is derived from the base class. The class `Retail` is derived from `Wholesale`. The `Manufacturer` class definition contains a declaration for the virtual functions `Report()` and `Price()`. The `Report()` and `Price()` member functions in the derived classes become implicit virtual functions. The classes contain also a conversion member function used to properly convert a derived class to a base class. This was done because memory is allocated from the free store to store the `item` name. The assignment operator (=) was also overloaded for the same reason.

Listing 19.7 presents a listing of the definitions of the three classes. Listing 19.8 contains the source listing for PRODUCTS.CPP. Notice that the class definitions are placed in a header file and the member functions are placed in a source file. This is necessary because a header file containing class definitions can be included in several source files in a multiple-file program. Notice also that the `#ifndef` compiler directive is used so that the class definitions are *not* included if the symbolic constant `__Products` exists. The first time the header file is encountered, `__Products` is defined. If the header is included a second time in a source file, its contents are ignored. This technique is commonly used to make sure that a definition is included only once.

Listing 19.7. The source listing for the products.h header file.

```
// products.h - Classes that illustrate use of virtual
// functions
#ifndef __Products
#define __Products

class Manufacturer                   // Base class
{
protected:
    char *item;
    float cost;
public:
    Manufacturer( char *im, float ct);
    Manufacturer( const Manufacturer & mr );
```

```
    Manufacturer( void );
    virtual float Price( void );
    char *GetItem( void );        // Return item
    virtual void Report( void );
    ~Manufacturer( void );
    Manufacturer & operator = ( const Manufacturer & mr );
};
////////////////////// Derived Class ////////////////////////
class Wholesale : public Manufacturer
{
protected:
    char *item;
    float w_markup; // Amount of markup
public:
    Wholesale( char *im, float ct, float w_markup );
    Wholesale( const Wholesale & we );
    Wholesale( void );
    float Price( void );        // Implicitly virtual
    void Report( void );        // Implicitly virtual
    ~Wholesale();
    Wholesale & operator = ( const Wholesale & we );
};

////////////////////// Derived Class ////////////////////////
class Retail : public Wholesale
{
public:
    Retail( char *im, float ct, float w_markup,
           float r_markup );
    Retail( const Retail & r );
    Retail( void );
    float Price( void );        // Implicitly virtual
    void Report( void );        // Implicitly virtual
    ~Retail();
    Retail & operator = ( const Retail & r );
private:
    float r_markup;      // Retail markup
};
#endif
```

19

Notice that the `virtual` keyword is used only for the base class (`Manufacturer`) declaration of `Report()` and `Price()`. The `virtual` keyword is not used with these two functions in either of the derived classes. Notice also in Listing 19.8 that the `Manufacturer` base class contains a dummy member function definition for the virtual member `Report()` function. This dummy function is not usually called. It is called only if you explicitly call it or if one of the derived classes did not have a `Report()` member function.

The virtual member function `Price()` performs valid operations in the base class. It is explicitly called from the `Wholesale::Price()` member function to get the manufacturer's price.

Listing 19.8. The source listing for PRODUCTS.CPP.

```
// PRODUCTS.CPP - Contains member functions for classes
// Manufacturer, Wholesale, and Retail, and illustrates
// use of virtual functions
#include <iostream.h>
#include <string.h>
#include "products.h"

////////////// Member Functions for Manufacturer //////////
Manufacturer::Manufacturer( char *im, float ct )
{
    item = new char [strlen( im ) + 1];
    strcpy( item, im );
    cost = ct;
}
Manufacturer::Manufacturer( const Manufacturer & m )
{
    item = new char [strlen( m.item ) + 1];
    strcpy( item, m.item );
    cost = m.cost;
}
Manufacturer::Manufacturer( void )
{
    item = 0;
    cost = 0.0;
}
float Manufacturer::Price( void )
{
     return cost;
}
```

```
char *Manufacturer::GetItem( void )
{
    return item;
}
void  Manufacturer::Report( void )
{
    cout << "This function is never called\n";
}
Manufacturer::~Manufacturer()
{
    delete item;
    cout << "class Wholesale destructor was called..."
         << " delete item\n";
}
Manufacturer & Manufacturer::operator=( const Manufacturer & m )
{
    if ( this == &m )    // Does object point to itself?
        return *this;    // If so, return it to itself
    delete item;
    item = new char [strlen( m.item ) + 1];
    strcpy( item, m.item );
    cost = m.cost;
    return *this;
}
////////////// Member Functions for Wholesale /////////////
Wholesale::Wholesale( char *im, float ct, float mp )
            : Manufacturer( im, ct )
{
    w_markup = mp;
}
Wholesale::Wholesale( const Wholesale & m )
{
    w_markup = m.w_markup;
}
Wholesale::Wholesale( void )
{
    w_markup = 0;
}
float Wholesale::Price( void )
{
    return Manufacturer::Price() + w_markup;
}
```

19

continues

Listing 19.8. continued

```
void Wholesale::Report( void )
{
    cout << GetItem() << " Wholesale cost: "
         << Price() << "\n";
}
Wholesale::~Wholesale()
{
    cout << "class Wholesale destructor was called..."
         << " nothing to do\n";
}
Wholesale & Wholesale::operator=( const Wholesale & w )
{
    if ( this == &w )  // Does object point to itself?
        return *this;  // If so, return it to itself
    delete item;
    item = new char [strlen( w.item ) + 1];
    strcpy( item, w.item );
    cost = w.cost;
    w_markup = w.w_markup;
    return *this;
}
///////////// Class Retail Member Functions /////////////
Retail::Retail( char *im, float ct, float wm, float rm ) :
       Wholesale( im, ct, wm )
{
    r_markup = rm;
}
Retail::Retail( const Retail & r )
{
    r_markup = r.r_markup;
}
Retail::Retail( void )
{
    r_markup = 0.0;
}
float Retail::Price( void )
{
    return Wholesale::Price() + r_markup;
}
void Retail::Report( void )
```

```
{
    cout << GetItem() << "  Retail price: "
         << Price() << "\n";
}
Retail::~Retail()
{
    cout << "class Retail destructor was called..."
         << " nothing to do\n";
}
Retail & Retail::operator=( const Retail & r )
{
    if ( this == &r )  // Does object point to itself?
        return *this;  // If so, return it to itself
    delete item;
    item = new char [strlen( r.item ) + 1];
    strcpy( item, r.item );
    cost = r.cost;
    w_markup = r.w_markup;
    r_markup = r.r_markup;
    return *this;
}
```

Destructors for the derived classes did not have to be supplied. However, they were supplied to illustrate the order in which destructors are called when an object is destroyed.

19

USEPRODS.CPP, the program in Listing 19.9, illustrates the use of the three classes declared in the products.h header file. In this example, five `Retail` objects are declared. An array of pointers, `ptr[5]`, to the base class is declared, and each element is assigned the address of one of the `Retail` objects. Then the `Retail::Print()` virtual function is called to display the retail price of each object.

Listing 19.9. The source listing for USEPRODS.CPP.

```
// USEPRODS.CPP - Illustrates use of virtual functions
#include <iostream.h>
#include "products.h"  // Contains class definitions
void main()
{
    Retail widget( "Widget", 19.44, 5.44, 12.10 );
```

continues

Listing 19.9. continued

```
    Retail skyhook( "Skyhook", 112.00, 54.34, 91.22 );
    Retail chair( "Chair", 35.00, 14.34, 22.22 );
    Retail table( "Table", 49.00, 12.56, 33.33 );
    Retail lamp( "Lamp", 10.01, 2.34, 5.55 );

    widget.Report();
    skyhook.Report();
    Manufacturer *ptr[5];
    ptr[0] = &widget;
    ptr[1] = &skyhook;
    ptr[2] = &chair;
    ptr[3] = &table;
    ptr[4] = &lamp;
    for ( int i = 0; i < 5; i++ )
        ptr[i]->Report();
}
```

This example contains three files. Before you compile and link this program, you must establish a project file, USEPRODS.MAC. You do this by choosing the New Project command from the Project menu and then adding the files USEPRODS.CPP and PRODUCTS.CPP to the project. Then choose Rebuild All from the Project menu. When you execute USEPRODS.EXE, you should obtain the results presented in Listing 19.10. The retail price should be displayed for each of the `Retail` objects. Each of the destructors displays a message as the object is destroyed. The base class destructor is the only one that performs any useful task. It uses the `delete` operator to free the free store buffer. Notice the order in which the destructors are called as each object is destroyed.

Listing 19.10. The results of executing USEPRODS.EXE.

```
Widget  Retail price: 36.98
Skyhook  Retail price: 257.56
Widget  Retail price: 36.98
Skyhook  Retail price: 257.56
Chair  Retail price: 71.56
Table  Retail price: 94.89
Lamp  Retail price: 17.9
class Retail destructor was called... nothing to do
```

```
class Wholesale destructor was called... nothing to do
class Wholesale destructor was called... delete item
class Retail destructor was called... nothing to do
class Wholesale destructor was called... nothing to do
class Wholesale destructor was called... delete item
class Retail destructor was called... nothing to do
class Wholesale destructor was called... nothing to do
class Wholesale destructor was called... delete item
class Retail destructor was called... nothing to do
class Wholesale destructor was called... nothing to do
class Wholesale destructor was called... delete item
class Retail destructor was called... nothing to do
class Wholesale destructor was called... nothing to do
class Wholesale destructor was called... delete item
```

The OOP term for what you can do with virtual functions is *polymorphism*. Generally, a polymorphic object is one that can assume multiple forms. In OOP, polymorphism is the capability of a single statement to reference many different methods, depending on the object type being operated on. With C++ virtual functions, you can call member functions for an object without designating the type of the object.

19

Pure Virtual Functions

It does not seem very aesthetic to place in the base class a dummy function that is never called. There is a more elegant solution. Instead of placing a dummy `Report()` function in the base class, you can declare a *pure virtual function*.

You do this by placing `= 0` after the prototype for the virtual function in the base class definition, as indicated in the following example:

```
class Manufacturer
{
     :
public:
     virtual void Report() = 0;  // Pure virtual function
     :
}
```

A pure virtual function does not require a function definition, but there is a restriction. If you use a pure virtual function in the class `Manufacturer`, you can never declare any type `Manufacturer` objects. This restriction is imposed to prevent any user program from creating an object with a pure virtual function and then calling that function.

Any class that contains a pure virtual function is called an *abstract class*. You can derive other classes from it, but you cannot create an object from it. However, you can declare pointers to an abstract class. Any class from which you can create an object is sometimes called a *concrete class*. A concrete object is the opposite of an abstract class.

If a class is derived from an abstract class and does not contain a redefinition for a pure virtual function, that class also becomes an abstract class. You cannot declare any instances from it either. It is common to create a class hierarchy with one or more abstract classes at the top and with concrete classes at the bottom. The concrete classes are derived from abstract classes and other concrete classes.

Destructors Revisited

As illustrated in the sample results in Listing 19.10, if destructors are supplied for the base and derived classes, the destructors are called in the reverse order from that of the constructors. In other words, when an object for a derived class is to be destroyed, its destructor is called. Then its base class destructor is called.

However, if you dynamically allocate memory for a derived object and store the address of the object's memory block to a pointer to a base class, and then later delete (`delete`) the memory buffer, only the destructor for the base pointer is called. The derived object's destructor is never called. In the following example, a pointer to the `Manufacturer` base class is declared, a memory block is allocated for the `Retail` class, and a `Retail` object is created:

```
Manufacturer *baseptr;
baseptr = new Retail( "Tuba", 244.01, 84.34, 125.55 );
```

This works properly. You can use the base pointer to call the `Report()` function to print a retail object:

```
baseptr->Report(); // Call virtual function Retail::Report()
```

However, when you apply the `delete` operator to a base class pointer to free the pointer, only the base class destructor is called:

```
delete baseptr;    // Only base class destructor is called
```

This is not a problem for the class defined in Listings 19.7 and 19.8 because the derived class destructors do nothing anyway. But if the derived class performs some important operation, it still will not get called.

The solution to this problem is to make the destructor virtual by placing the `virtual` keyword in front of the base class destructor prototype in the class definition, as in

```
virtual ~Manufacturer();
```

As you know, the names of the base and derived class destructors differ. This does not matter. If the `virtual` keyword precedes the destructor prototype, destructors for all derived classes become implicitly virtual. When the base class destructor is virtual and the `delete` operator is applied, the destructor for the object pointed to is called. In this example, the `Retail` class destructor is called first, the `Wholesale` class destructor is called next, and the `Manufacturer` destructor is called last.

Whenever you design a class that uses virtual functions, you should give it a virtual destructor, even if the base class does not need one. The reason is that one of the derived classes might need a destructor.

Constructors cannot be virtual.

Multiple Inheritance

You have learned about classes derived from a single base class. This type of class derivation is called *single inheritance*. You can also derive a class from more than one base class. This type of class derivation is called *multiple inheritance*. Consider an example of a class definition for a fictitious animal, called the `flyingmonkey` class. It is derived from both the `monkey` and `bird` classes, as shown in the following class definition:

```
class flyingmonkey : public monkey, public bird
{
    :
}
```

Figure 19.6 illustrates multiple class hierarchy, with the class `flyingmonkey` derived from two other classes.

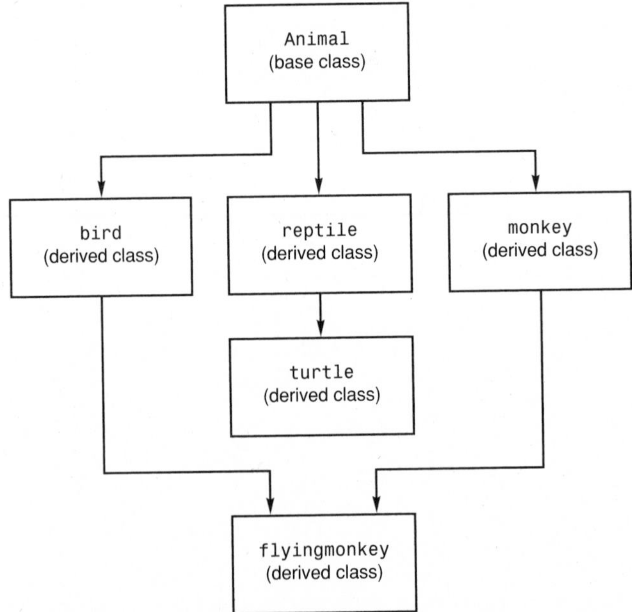

Figure 19.6. *Multiple-inheritance class hierarchy for the zoo application.*

The `flyingmonkey` class inherits members from both `monkey` and `bird` classes. This means that because both `monkey` and `bird` classes are derived from the base class `Animal`, you get two copies of each member of class `Animal`. It becomes more complicated to call access functions from the base class. For example, you cannot directly access the `Animal` class `GetName()` member function:

```
flyingmonkey Pete( ... );    // Declare object Pete
Pete.GetName();              // Ambiguity error
```

The compiler does not know which of the two member functions by the same name to call: `monkey::GetName()` or `bird::GetName()`. To resolve this ambiguity, you can use the following statement to specify which function should be called:

```
Pete.monkey::GetName();      // Correct
```

In this case, it does not really matter because both `GetName()` functions return the same value. The important thing to remember is that you can use the global resolution operator to resolve any ambiguous name references.

You can avoid having two copies of the name, birthday, weight, and other common members by designating that the base class `Animal` is a virtual base class. You do this by placing the `virtual` keyword before the "derived from" class name in the definition of `bird` and `monkey` classes, as shown in the following statements:

```
class bird public virtual Animal
{
    :
}
class monkey public virtual Animal
{
    :
}
```

Now that the `Animal` class has become a virtual base class, only one copy of the members belonging to the base class exists. Any references to the `Animal` class members are unambiguous. For certain types of applications that require multiple inheritance, virtual base classes can prove useful. However, there is a greater processing overhead associated with virtual base classes. You can improve speed performance and program size by avoiding virtual base classes whenever possible.

What You Have Learned

In this chapter, you learned about class inheritance—one of the most important aspects of OOP. It isn't that C++ OOP concepts are incomprehensibly difficult; it's just that there is much to learn. You are now ready to use what you have learned and develop your own application. Perhaps you want to create an inventory of your things. You can create a generalized base class, called Things. You can then derive classes for various categories of things, like VCR tape collection, CDs, books, computer hardware, computer software, and so on. This is just a suggestion. However, the only real way to learn C++ is to work with it.

Specifically, you learned the following:

- Why C++ can provide a better approach for developing an application than C can
- How to implement class inheritance in C++
- How to derive a class from a base class
- How to develop a class hierarchy
- How class members are accessed from derived classes
- What to use the `protected` keyword for
- How to derive a class from another derived class
- How to use member function redefinition
- How to convert between a base class and a derived class
- How to use pointers to a base class
- How to use virtual functions to support polymorphism
- How and when to use virtual destructors
- How to implement multiple inheritance
- How to use a virtual base class

File Input and Output

Let blockheads read what blockheads write.

—Philip Dormer Stanhope, Earl of Chesterfield
Letters to His Son (1750)

In This Chapter

Most programs need to read or write disk files. You haven't yet learned how to do this. The address book application from Chapter 15, "Structures and Unions," is useless if you cannot save your address book entries in a file and retrieve them later. Imagine how useless a spreadsheet or word processor program would be if you could not read or write files. In this chapter, you learn how to use C++ object-oriented file I/O operations. The following topics are covered:

- Opening and closing a file
- Reading and writing information to an open file
- Using techniques for file I/O
- Using random access I/O to sort a file

In addition, you learn about the C language standard and low-level run-time file I/O functions.

Introduction to Files

You have been using keyboard and screen input/output operations with `cin` and `cout` `iostream` class objects and the insertion (<<) and extraction (>>) operators since you wrote your first C++ program in Chapter 4. In Chapter 7, "Input and Output," you looked at object-oriented I/O operations in detail. Techniques for disk file I/O operations are similar to techniques for keyboard and screen I/O operations. The difference is that files must be *opened* before they can be used. After you complete I/O operations on a file, you must close the file. If you don't close it, it closes when you exit your application. It is always best to close a file when you are finished with it. However, when a file I/O object goes out of scope, its destructor is called to close the file.

What *is* a file? A *file* is a space on the disk in which data is written, which can then be referenced by a directory entry. The disk operating system (DOS) maintains the directory and interfaces with your program to read data from the file or write data to it. You call the C++ language object-oriented I/O package, which calls the low-level DOS interface routines to do file I/O operations.

You can write two types of files with C++ stream operation functions: text and binary. A *text file* contains only ASCII characters. Your program source file is an example of a text file. Specifically, an MS-DOS text file consists of lines of data in which each line is terminated with a carriage return and linefeed character. The linefeed character is called a *newline* character and is ASCII character 10. When you write a file in text mode and a newline character is encountered, MS-DOS inserts a carriage-return character (ASCII character 13) before the linefeed in the output stream. When you read a file in text mode, MS-DOS removes the carriage returns from the input stream. In UNIX, a line in a text file is terminated with a linefeed. As a result, UNIX versions of C++ text-file I/O operations do not insert carriage returns in the output stream.

A *binary file* contains bytes filled with any bit pattern. A binary file can be characterized as any file that is not a text file. An executable (.EXE) file is an example of a binary file. When you read or write a file in binary mode, a newline character is treated like any other character—there is no special end-of-line processing.

Binary mode usually stores information more efficiently on the disk because binary files are smaller. This is especially true if you are storing numbers. If you store a 10-digit number in ASCII mode, it takes 10 bytes to store the number, plus additional space to store decimal points and sign characters (+/-). When you store an integer in binary form on disk, it takes only two bytes of disk space and also preserves the precision of floating-point numbers. A floating-point number takes only four bytes of disk space. Suppose that you translate a floating-point number to ASCII format and write the number to a text file. Later you read the text file and convert the ASCII representation of the number back to a floating-point number. You might have a slightly different number because some precision can be lost in the conversion.

Usually, binary files are written to or read from disk faster than text files. In binary mode, the system does not have to examine each character to see whether it is a newline character. Furthermore, it takes time for the computer to do number conversions. You can save considerable computer time if you write an entire floating-point array in binary form. You do not waste time doing any number conversion, which is required if you write a similar array in text form.

The distinction between text and binary files is important in C++ because the two kinds of files are handled by different C++ language I/O functions. For example, text file I/O reads a line from a text file until it reaches the newline character. Binary file I/O reads a block of data from a binary file and uses the low-level file I/O operations.

20

Chapter 7, "Input and Output," referred to input and output *streams.* So far, you have used an *input stream* when referring to input from the keyboard, and an *output stream* when referring to output to the screen. An input stream, however, can come from a disk file, and an output stream can be directed to a disk file. The only difference is that when streams are related to a disk file, they must be opened or created before you can use them or refer to them. The phrase "opening an output stream" means that the file is opened; the phrase "closing an input stream" means that the file is closed.

File I/O Alternatives

Microsoft C/C++ provides several alternatives for doing file I/O operations:

- C++ object-oriented `iostream` class library. You can use this library to create `iostream` objects for I/O operations in C++ programs. You can call the member functions belonging to the objects to do buffered formatted text I/O and unbuffered or binary I/O operations. You can also use insertion and extraction operators to do file I/O.
- ANSI C run-time library stream I/O. This library contains such functions as `fopen()`, `fread()`, `fwrite()`, and `fprintf()` for doing buffered I/O. They are used in C programs but can be used in C++ programs. The functions are presented later in this chapter.
- C language low-level I/O library. This library contains functions such as `open()`, `close()`, `read()`, `write()`, and `lseek()` for performing unbuffered or direct I/O operations. These functions are normally used in C programs but can be used in C++ programs. The functions are presented later in this chapter.
- Microsoft Foundation Classes (MFC) library. This library contains the `CFile` classes, which you can use for disk I/O operations. It is used in C++ programs especially for developing Windows applications.

The iostream Class Hierarchy

Figure 20.1 is a hierarchy diagram of the `iostream` classes. From the figure, you can see the relationships of the various `iostream` classes.

`istream` is the base class from which the input stream classes are derived. It is best suited for text input mode. Your interface with the `istream` class is normally through the predefined `cin` object. The `ifstream` class is used for disk input operations. You can specify that `ifstream` objects process either text or binary files. You can use the various `ios` and `istream` base class member functions and formatting options with `ifstream` objects. When you create an `ifstream` object and specify parameters, a file is opened. When the destructor is called, the file is closed.

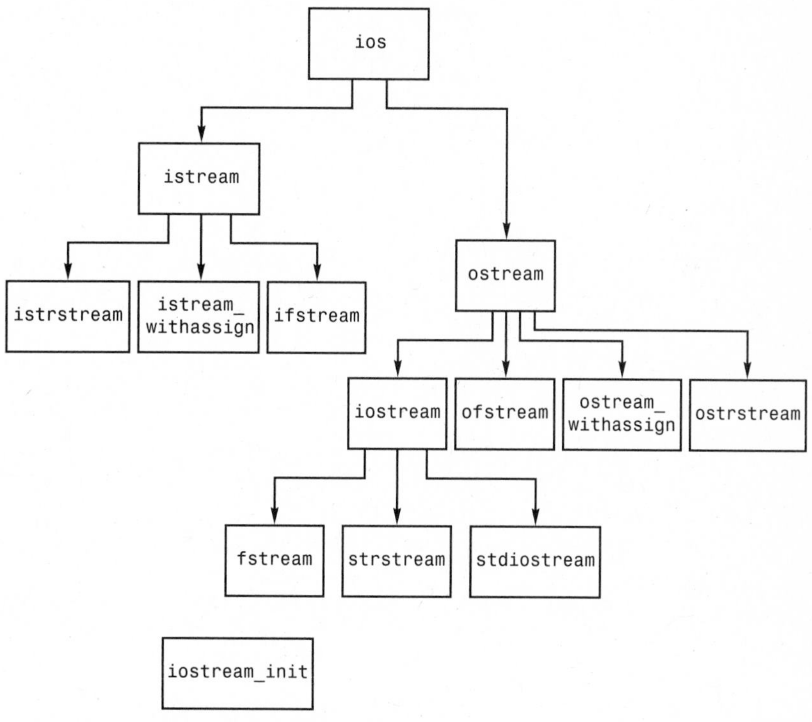

Figure 20.1. *The* `iostream` *class hierarchy.*

`ostream` is the base class from which all the output stream classes are derived. The primary output stream classes are `ostream`, `ofstream`, and `ostrstream`. The `ostream` class supports the predefined objects `cout`, `cerr`, and `clog`. `ostream` objects are used mainly for outputting text in either buffered or unbuffered mode. `ofstream` objects are used to do file output operations. You declare an `ofstream` object if you are planning to write to a disk file. If you supply a filename when you declare an `ofstream` object, the file is opened. You can specify that the file is to be written in binary or text mode. If an `ofstream` object is already declared, you can use the `open()` member function to open the file. When the `ofstream` class destructor is called to destroy the object, the file is closed. In addition, you can use the `close()` member function to close the file. The `ostrstream` object is used to direct a stream to a memory buffer in the same way the `sprintf()` C run-time library function is used.

You use the `iostream` class for both input and output. An `iostream` object is both a source and a destination for a byte stream. The `fstream` class supports both input and output disk file operations. You use `fstream` objects when you want to do simultaneous read and write operations on the same file.

Opening and Closing a File

As noted, you must open a file before you can access it. When you declare an `ifstream` or `ofstream` object and provide a filename, the file opens. You pass the constructor either one or two arguments: the first argument is the name of the file you want opened, and the second argument (if specified) is a type `int` value consisting of one or more file mode settings. You can also declare an `ifstream`, `ofstream`, or `fstream` object without opening a file if you supply no arguments. Then you can use the `open()` member function to open the file. Here are examples of statements that create `ifstream`, `ofstream` and `fstream` class objects:

```
#include <fstream.h>

// Open file c:\\test\\sample.txt to be used as input
ifstream infile( "c:\\test\\sample.txt" );

// Open file c:\\test\\sample.new for output
ofstream ofile( "c:\\test\\sample.new" );

// Open file sample1.txt for input
ifstream ifile;   // Declare ifile object of type ifstream
ifile.open( "c:\\test\\sample1.txt" );

// Open file Hamlet.doc for both input (ios:in) and
// output (ios::out). If file does not exist (ios::nocreate),
// return open failure indication (fifo = 0).
fstream fifo( "Hamlet.doc", ios::nocreate
              ¦ ios::in ¦ ios:: out );
```

```
// Open file money.txt. If it does not exist (ios::nocreate),
// do not create it but return an open failure indication.
ofstream outfile("money.txt", ios::nocreate );
```

The file stream object I/O header file (`#include <fstream.h>`) contains the definitions of the `iostream` classes. You must include this file if you intend to do any input or output operations.

In the first example, the C:\TEST\SAMPLE.TXT file will be opened in read-only mode. Are you wondering why there are two backslash characters (\\) in the example? If you remember, a backslash in a string begins an escape sequence. The second character in this example is `t`. If only one backslash is used, `\t` will be replaced in the string constant with a tab character. Two backslashes, however, will be replaced in the string with a single backslash. Escape sequences are described in the section "C Language Screen Output" in Chapter 7, "Input and Output."

If the name of the object declared (such as `infile`, `ofile`, or `ifile` in the examples) is not equal to zero, the open operation is successful. If the object has a zero value, the open operation is unsuccessful. The objects named `infile` and `ifile` are instances of the class `ifstream`. The object named `ofile` is an instance of the `ofstream` class. The object named `fifo` is an instance of the `fstream` object. These objects are used to reference the opened file for all subsequent file I/O operations. Always test the validity of the object. If the test fails, you must take corrective action, as in

```
ifstream fin( "silly.txt" );
if (!fin)
{
     cout << "I could not open the file";
     exit( 1 ); // Give up
}
```

20

As mentioned, the second parameter is the file mode argument, if it is specified. (The prototypes for the `iostream` constructors contain a default second parameter.) The file mode argument is an `int` value used to specify the type of file I/O operations that will be performed when the file is opened. You can specify one or more file mode settings. Multiple file mode settings are separated with logical OR (¦) operators. There are eight file mode constants (see Table 20.1). They are defined in the `ios` class, and you need to use the global resolution operator to reference them.

Table 20.1. The file mode constants.

Type	*Meaning*
`ios::binary`	Indicates that the file is a binary file. If not specified, text mode is assumed.
`ios::in`	Opens an existing file for reading. By default, reading begins at the beginning of the file. The `ifstream` class member functions that open a file use this file mode as the default. Note that either `ios::in` or `ios::out` (or both) must be specified when opening a file with the `fstream` class.
`ios::out`	Creates a new text file for writing. If the file exists, it is truncated to zero length, and any existing contents are destroyed. Writing begins at the beginning of the file. The `ios::trunc` mode is the default setting when a file is opened with `ios::out`. The `ofstream` member functions that open files use this option as the default.
`ios::ate`	Seeks to the end of the file when the file is successfully opened. This file mode differs from `ios::app` in that with `ios::ate` mode set, you can write data anywhere in the file—you can even overwrite existing data.
`ios::app`	Opens an existing file in append mode. Writing begins at the end of the file. If the file does not exist, it is created. You are allowed to write data only at the end of the file.
`ios::trunc`	Truncates the length of the file to zero if the file exists. This option is the default mode when a file is opened with the `ios::out` mode set.

Type	*Meaning*
`ios::nocreate`	Does not create the file if it does not exist. If the file does not exist, the open operation fails.
`ios::replace`	The open operation fails if the file already exists.

Listing 20.1 provides a sample program, WRITE1.CPP, that demonstrates how to create a file, write a string to the file, and then close the file.

Listing 20.1. The source listing for WRITE1.CPP.

```
// WRITE1.CPP - Illustrates text file I/O
#include <iostream.h>
#include <fstream.h>                         // Needed for file I/O
#include <io.h>                              // ios: manipulators

int main()
{
     ofstream ofile( "d:\\test.new" ); // Open output file
     if ( !ofile )
     {
          cout << "Output file open error\n";
          return 1;
     }
     else
          ofile.write( "Sample File", 11 ).put( '\n' );
          ofile << "More data\n";
     return 0;
}
```

20

Notice that the `ofile` object is used with the `write()` and `put()` member functions belonging to the `ofstream` class. The file is opened, and the output is written to the file with `write()` and `put()`. (These two functions are discussed in the next section.) Then the insertion operator (<<) is used to output more data. When the main program exits, the `ofstream` destructor is called to destroy the `ofile` object. The destructor closes the file and flushes any buffers associated with the file output stream.

When you output anything to a file, the data does not actually go directly to the file. The data is first placed in an internal block of memory called a *buffer*. When the buffer fills with characters, it is written to the disk file. When you are finished with the file, characters can remain in the buffer. The close operation writes to the disk file any characters that might remain in the buffer. This operation is called *flushing*. The `close()` and `flush()` member functions flush a buffer to a file. Here are examples for an `ofstream` object named `ofile`:

```
ofile.close();
ofile.flush();
```

When the `ofile` object goes out of scope, data is flushed to the file, and the file is closed.

After a file is closed, the operating system can use its internal file structure for another file. Because the number of files that can be opened at one time is limited, it is a good practice to close a file when you are finished using it. If you have too many files open at one time, you could exceed the maximum file limit imposed by MS-DOS and cause a file I/O open error to occur. This file limit can be set through the CONFIG.SYS `FILES =` command. (See your MS-DOS manual for more information regarding the maximum number of files.)

Reading and Writing a Text File

In the preceding section, you observed the use of the `write()` and `put()` member functions and the insertion operator in WRITE1.CPP. These output operations write data to a file in text mode. The function `write()` writes a string with a specified length to the file, and `put()` writes a single character. Here is a statement from WRITE1.CPP:

```
ofile.write( "Sample File", 11 ).put( '\n');
```

The `write()` member function has two arguments: the first is a pointer to a string, and the second is the number of characters to output. The `put()` function writes a string, without the null terminator, to the file. As for any `ostream` operations, the operations can be chained together. This is possible because each operation returns an `ostream` object. To chain member functions, you separate the member function calls with a member operator (.).

The `put()` member function is passed a single argument, an `int` type value. A newline escape sequence is output to the file; the newline character is a linefeed (ASCII 10) character. In text mode, when a newline character is encountered in the output stream, a carriage return (ASCII 13) is inserted in front of the linefeed in the output stream.

You can also use any of the `ostream` manipulator functions discussed in Chapter 7 or any of the file I/O operations used with keyboard and screen I/O functions you are familiar with. WRITE2.CPP, the program in Listing 20.2, shows how to use the insertion operator (<<) to output to a file.

Listing 20.2. The source listing for WRITE2.CPP.

```
// WRITE2.CPP - Illustrates text file I/O with numbers
#include <iostream.h>
#include <fstream.h>                      // Needed for file I/O
#include <io.h>                           // ios: manipulators
#include <fcntl.h>
int main()
{
     int i;
     float f;
     ofstream ofile( "d:\\test.new" ); // Open output file
     if ( !ofile )
     {
          cout << "Output file open error\n";
          return 1;
     }
     else
     {
          for ( i = 0, f= 1.0f ; i < 10; i++, f /= (float)i )
          {
               ofile << "i = " << i << "f = " << f << "\n";
          }
     }

     return 0;
}
```

20

Listing 20.3 displays the contents of the output file TEST.NEW, generated by WRITE2.EXE.

Listing 20.3. The contents of the output file TEST.NEW.

```
i = 0f = 1
i = 1f = 1
i = 2f = 0.5
i = 3f = 0.166667
i = 4f = 0.0416667
i = 5f = 0.00833333
i = 6f = 0.00138889
i = 7f = 0.000198413
i = 8f = 2.48016e-005
i = 9f = 2.75573e-006
```

In addition, you can use the extraction operator (>>) to read a text file that contains ASCII representations of numeric values, and convert them to their internal numeric value. In fact, this operation works like its corresponding keyboard operation except that using the extracton operator inputs from a file rather than the keyboard. You can also use the `get()` member function to read data from a file. `get()` can have one or two arguments. If you supply one argument, it is a `char` variable that is read from the file. If you supply two arguments, the first argument is a pointer to a `char` buffer that receives data read from the file. The second argument is the maximum number of bytes read from the file. Note the following example:

```
ifstream ifile( "TEST.TXT" ); // Open file for input
char *buffer[100], c;
ifile.get( buffer, 99 );      // Get next 99 characters
ifile.get( c );               // Read a single character
```

The `get()` member function has a variety of overloaded forms. There are actually three prototypes of the `get()` member functions that are commonly used:

```
ifstream & get( char *string, int n, char delim = '\n' );
istream & get( char & c );    // Read a character to c
int get( void );              // Return a single character
cin >> c;                     // Input a character (c is char)
```

The first form inputs a character string, *string*, with a maximum length of *n* bytes until the delimiter character, *delim*, is encountered. The *delim* argument is a default argument. If not specified (which is the normal form), the default character is a newline character. This means that for the two argument forms of the `get()` member function, characters are read until the newline character is encountered. The newline character is not read. A `NULL` is placed at the end of the character string.

The second form reads only a single character from the file and places it into the character variable `c`. The third form of `get()` extracts a single character from the stream and returns it as an integer value.

More examples of the use of the `get()` function are provided in the following sections.

Techniques for File I/O

There are several ways to perform file I/O. You can read or write a character, a line, or a block of data at a time. The following sections illustrate each of these methods.

Reading and Writing One Character

You can use the `put()` member function to write one character to a file, and the `get()` function to read one character from a file. COPY1.CPP, the program in Listing 20.4, uses these functions to copy one file to another.

Listing 20.4. The source listing for COPY1.CPP.

```
// COPY1.CPP - Illustrates text file copy operation
#include <fstream.h>                    // Needed for file I/O
#include <io.h>                         // ios: manipulators
int main( void )
{
     char c;
```

continues

Listing 20.4. continued

```
    ifstream ifile( "d:\\test.txt", ios::nocreate );  // Open
                                                       // existing file

    if ( !ifile )
         {
         cout << "Input file open error\n";
         return 1;
         }
    ofstream ofile( "d:\\test.new" ); // Open output file
    if ( !ofile )
    {
         ifile.close();
         cout << "Output file open error\n";
         return 1;
    }
    while ( ifile.good() )     // Loop while read is "good"
    {
       ifile.get( c );
       if ( !c )
           break;              // Quit if c is a null character
       ofile.put( c );
    }
    ifile.close();             // File is closed
    ofile.close();             // File is closed
    return 0;
}
```

Both files are opened in text mode because the `ios::binary` file mode is not specified. This means that the end-of-line translations are performed. That doesn't matter, though, because all characters in the input file will be transferred to the output file. The input file is the same one written in the first example, D:\TEST.TXT. It is opened to read because the `ifile` is type `ifstream`. If TEST.TXT does not exist, the constructor returns a null (zero) value, and the object is set to a null value. As a result, an error message is displayed, and the program exits with a return code of 1 to indicate that an error occurred. The output file, D:\TEST.NEW, is opened to write a file when the `ofile` object of type `ofstream` is created. If TEST.NEW does not exist, the program creates it. If the open operation is successful, the program executes a `while` loop.

The `while` statement expression tests the value returned by the `good()` member function. As long as it returns a true (1) value, the read operation is valid, and the loop executes repeatedly. As soon as the end of the file is encountered, the `good()` member function returns a null value. At that time, the `while` loop exits. The body of the `while` statement contains a call to the `get()` member function, which sets the value of its argument to either a character or a zero value. `get()` returns a zero if the input file encounters the end of the file. As a result, the loop is executed repeatedly while there are characters to copy. The program calls the `put()` member function to write the character `c` to the output file.

There is an internal pointer for each file that points to the current position in a file. When a file is opened to read, this pointer is positioned at the beginning of the file. You learn more about positioning the file pointer later in the chapter.

When all the characters have been copied, the loop exits, and the program exits. The `ifstream` and `ofstream` destructors are called to close the input and output files. `main()` returns a zero value to indicate that the copy was successful.

The contents of the input file (TEST.TXT) and the output file (TEST.NEW) are now identical.

Reading and Writing One Line

You can read or write one line at a time instead of a single character. The `get()` member function reads one line of data from a file each time it is called. The `put()` member function writes one line of data each time it is called.

`get()` reads one line of data from the file, beginning at the current file position. The function transfers a line of data to the `char` pointer variable *`string`*. You use the `int` variable *`n`* to specify the size of *`string`*. The function transfers data until one of the following occurs:

- *`n`* – 1 characters are transferred.
- A newline character is reached. The newline character is also transferred.
- The end of the input stream is reached.

The two-argument form of the `get()` function reads lines of data from the input stream. When `get()` reads a line of data, the function does *not* transfer the newline character to the input string. Then `get()` appends a null character (`\0`) to terminate the string. A single-argument `get()` member function can be called to transfer the newline character to the `char` variable `c`.

Another member function, `getline()`, has the same syntax as the two- or three-argument `get()` function. The `getline()` function reads the line of data and then positions the current file pointer to the beginning of the next line of data. In other words, `getline()` skips over the newline character.

The `put()` function transfers the contents of the *`string`* argument to the output file, beginning at the current file position. The terminating null character, `\0`, is not transferred.

One-line-at-a-time I/O is used only with text files. The `get()` member function depends on having a line of text of reasonable length and terminated with a newline character. This type of I/O is useful if you are doing text-related operations, such as processing a text file.

COPY2.CPP, the program in Listing 20.5, copies one file to another with the one-line-at-a-time, two-argument `get()` member function.

Listing 20.5. The source listing for COPY2.CPP.

```
// COPY2.CPP - Illustrates file copy operation one line at a time
#include <iostream.h>
#include <fstream.h>   // Needed for file I/O
#include <io.h>        // ios: manipulators
#include <string.h>    // Prototype for strlen() function
int main( void )
{
     char s[100]; // Allow for lines up to 100 characters
     char c;

     ifstream ifile( "copy3.cpp", ios::nocreate ); // Open
                                             // existing file
     if ( !ifile )
          {
```

```
          cout << "Input file open error\n";
          return 1;
          }
     ofstream ofile( "copy3.new" );        // Open output file
     if ( !ofile )
     {
          ifile.close();
          cout << "Output file open error\n";
          return 1;
     }
     while ( ifile.good() )      // Loop while read is "good"
     {
        ifile.get( s, 100 ).get( c );
        cout << s << "\n";
        if ( ifile.good() )
            ofile.write( s, strlen(s) ).put( c );
     }
     ifile.close();              // File is closed
     ofile.close();              // File is closed
     return 0;
}
```

Both files shown in Listing 20.5 are opened for text mode operations. This means that the end-of-line translations are performed. The input file is the COPY3.CPP program. If COPY3.CPP does not exist, an error message is displayed, and the program exits with an MS-DOS error return code of 1 to indicate that an error occurred. The output file, COPY3.NEW, is opened when the `ofile` object is declared. If COPY3.NEW does not exist, the program creates it. If the file exists, it is overwritten. If the open operation is successful, the program executes the `while` loop.

The `while` condition contains a call to `ifile.good()`, which returns either a 1 or a null value. This condition returns a 1 unless the input file encounters the end of the file, or a disk read error occurs. As a result, the loop is executed while there are lines to copy. To read and write the file, the program calls the following:

- The two-argument `ifile.get()` to read a line of data
- The single-argument `ifile.get()` to read past the newline character into variable `c`

- The `ofile.write()` function to write a line of data
- The `ofile.put()` function to write the newline character (`c`) to the output file

There is an internal pointer for each file that points to the current position in the file. When a file is opened to read, this pointer is positioned at the beginning of the file.

When all the characters have been copied, the loop exits, and the `close()` member function is used to close the input and output files. `close()` does not actually need to be called because when the destructor is called to close the `ofile` and `ifile` objects, the files are closed. The `main()` function returns a zero value to indicate that the copy was successful.

The input file (COPY3.CPP) and the output file (COPY3.NEW) contain identical text after COPY3.EXE executes. Trust me. Better yet, don't trust me. Type the program yourself and run it. Add your innovative modifications to the program, such as displaying lines backward as you copy them.

Reading and Writing a Block of Data

You have seen how to read and write a file one character or one line at a time. You also can read and write an entire block of data in binary or text mode with a single command. Furthermore, you can read or write an array or a structure with one I/O operation. The member functions that perform block I/O operations are `read()` and `write()`. Here are their prototypes:

```
istream& read( char *buffer, int count );
ostream& write( char *buffer, int count );
```

The argument *`count`* is the maximum number of characters to read or write. The argument *`buffer`* is the address of a buffer.

The `gcount()` member function returns the number of bytes that were read (or written) by the previous `iostream` operation. The number returned should be the same number as *`count`* unless an error occurs or the EOF (end of file) is encountered. The `gcount()` member function is used in the program COPY3.CPP (see Listing 20.6) to retrieve the actual number of characters input by the `read()` member function.

The read() and write() functions are the fastest methods of transferring data between memory and a disk file. There are times, however, when efficiency is not as important as other considerations. For example, if your application must count the lines in a file, you will probably process the file a line at a time. Such an application becomes more complex if you use block I/O operations instead of one-line-at-a-time I/O operations.

Listing 20.6 presents COPY3.CPP. This program copies one file to another with the block I/O functions read() and write().

Listing 20.6. The source listing for COPY3.CPP.

```
// COPY3.CPP - Illustrates a block I/O file copy
#include <stdlib.h>
#include <iostream.h>
#include <fstream.h>        // Needed for file I/O
#include <io.h>             // ios: manipulators
#include <fcntl.h>
int main( void )
{
     const BUFSIZE=512;
     char buffer[BUFSIZE]; // Allow for buffers up to 512
                           // characters
     int size;

     ifstream ifile( "copy3.cpp", ios::nocreate ¦ ios::binary );
     if ( !ifile )
          {
          cout << "Input file open error\n";
          return 1;
          }
     ofstream ofile( "copy3.new", ios::binary ); // Open output
                                                 // file
     if ( !ofile )
     {
          ifile.close();
          cout << "Output file open error\n";
          return 1;
     }
     while ( ifile.good() )   // Loop while read is "good"
     {
```

continues

20

Listing 20.6. continued

```
            ifile.read( buffer, BUFSIZE );
            size = ifile.gcount();
            if ( size > 0 )
                ofile.write( buffer, size );
        }
        ifile.close();              // File is closed
        ofile.close();              // File is closed
        return 0;
}
```

In Listing 20.6, both files are opened for binary mode operations. COPY3.CPP is the input file, and COPY3.NEW is the output file. If the open operation is successful, the program executes the `while` loop.

The `while` condition contains a call to the `ifile.good()` member function, which returns a status code as described in the last section. The `while` loop continues until an error occurs or the EOF is encountered. The program calls the `read()` member function to read a block of data, and the `write()` member function to write `size` characters to the output file.

When the last block is encountered, the loop exits. Then the `close()` member function is called to close the input and output files. `main()` returns a zero value to indicate that the copy was successful.

Saving and Retrieving Your Address Book to a Disk File

Now that you know how to read and write files, it is time to revisit your address book application. How do you decide which type of I/O to use? You could use any of the following methods to read and write address book entries:

- One-character-at-a-time I/O
- One-line-at-a-time I/O
- Block I/O

If you want to use your address book entries in another program that processes text files, such as a word processor, you might want to output the entries with one-line-at-a-time I/O. You would write each member of the ADDRESS structure to a file, much like the display() function that displays to the screen.

If you do not need the address book to be in text form, you might choose binary mode I/O. Then you would need to choose between the block iostream member functions read() and write(), and the one-character-at-a-time member functions get() and put(). For the latter two, you would need to use a nested loop. The output loop would repeat for each address book entry, and the inner loop would repeat for each character in the structure. The block I/O method would be much easier. A single block I/O statement would read or write an entire address book entry. You would need only one looping statement.

In the following examples, block I/O is used. You use the write() member function to write your address book entries to a disk file named ADDRESS.DAT. The read() member function is called to read the address book entries.

When the address book application executes, a type PhoneBook object is declared. When the class PhoneBook constructor is called, ADDRESS.DAT is read. And when the program exits, the class PhoneBook destructor is called. It writes the address entries to the ADDRESS.DAT file. Class constructors and destructors that appeared in the address1.h header file in Listing 18.3 in Chapter 18 contained the code for reading and writing the ADDRESS.DAT file. In this section, the code for the class PhoneBook constructor and destructor is discussed, now that you are more familiar with object-oriented file I/O. Listing 20.7 presents the class PhoneBook definition and constructor.

20

Listing 20.7. The header file for the class PhoneBook constructor used in the address book application.

```
// address1.h - Address book header file
#include <iostream.h>   // Needed for screen I/O
#include <fstream.h>    // Needed for file I/O
#include <io.h>         // ios: manipulators
#include <fcntl.h>
#include <string.h>     // Prototypes for strlen() and strcpy()
                        // functions
```

continues

Listing 20.7. continued

```
#include <ctype.h>

struct ADDRESS
{
     char     name[20];
     char     phone[15];
     char     address[23];
     char     city[14];
     char     state[3];
     char     zip[14];
     int      age;
     void     *next;   // One-way linked list pointer
};

class PhoneBook
{
public:
     friend class LinkedList;        // LinkedList is our friend
     PhoneBook( char *filename );    // Constructor
     void add_object( void );        // Add new item

     void change_object( void );     // Edit current item
     void delete_link( void );       // Delete current link

     ~PhoneBook( void );             // Destructor
private:
     void get_string( char *message, char *item , int maxsize );
     void get_input( ADDRESS *p );
     void add_link( void );
     ADDRESS *head;        // head points to first object
     ADDRESS *current;     // current points to current object
};


// Public member functions
//**************************************************************
// Constructor - Initializes phone book list
// Read address book entries from the file ADDRESS.DAT
PhoneBook::PhoneBook( char *filename )
```

```
{
     int size = 1, count = 0;
     ADDRESS *p;
     current = 0;
     head    = 0;
     ifstream fis( filename, ios::binary | ios::nocreate );
     if ( ! fis )
          cout << "Address Book File is not available\n";
     else
     {
          while ( 1 )              // Read forever
          {
               add_link();
               if ( !fis.read( (char*)current,
                    sizeof( ADDRESS ) ) )
                     break;        // Exit on end of file
               count++;
               current->next = 0; // Always last link
          }
          delete_link();           // Delete empty link
          cout << "Address Book contains " << count
               << " entries\n";
          fis.close();
     }
}
```

The constructor attempts to open the ADDRESS.DAT file in read-only binary mode. If the open operation is unsuccessful, the constructor assumes that there are no address book entries, displays a message, and returns. Otherwise, the constructor begins reading address book entries. The `add_link()` function is called to allocate space for a new entry. Then the `read()` member function is called to read the one address book entry from the file into the allocated space. Note that `read()` reads one element that is the size of one address book entry (`ADDRESS` type variable). You continue allocating and reading blocks until you attempt to read a block and encounter the end of the file. In that case, the `read()` member function returns a zero value. The program exits from the `while` loop. You still have an empty allocated link, and the program deletes it by calling the `delete_link()` function.

Listing 20.8 presents the source code for the class `PhoneBook` destructor. The destructor is called right before the program exits. The destructor writes all address book entries to the file ADDRESS.DAT.

20

Listing 20.8. The source listing for the class `PhoneBook` destructor used in the address book application.

```
//*****************************************************
// Destructor for Class PhoneBook - Writes address book
// entries to the file ADDRESS.DAT
PhoneBook::~PhoneBook( void )
{

     int     count = 0;
     ADDRESS *p, *plast = NULL;
     ofstream ofs( "ADDRESS.DAT", ios::binary );
     if ( !ofs )
          cout << "Unable to write Address Book File\n";
     else
     {
          p = head;
          while ( plast != p && p != NULL )
          {
               ofs.write( (char*)p, sizeof( ADDRESS ) );
               plast = p;
               p = (ADDRESS *)p->next;  // Go to next link
               count++;
          }
          ofs.close ();
          cout << count
             << " entries written to Address Book File\n";
     }
}
```

The destructor attempts to open the ADDRESS.DAT file in write-only binary mode. If this operation is unsuccessful, the destructor assumes that the disk is full or that something else is wrong, and takes the easy way out—it gives up and returns. Otherwise, the destructor calls the `go_top()` function to position the address book entry pointer at the top of the linked list (see Listing 18.3 in Chapter 18). Then the destructor writes the current `ADDRESS` structure data block to the file. You continue traversing the linked list and writing blocks until you reach the end of the linked list. When that happens, the `while` condition is no longer true. The `while` statement exits, causing the destructor to close the file and return.

Random File I/O Operations

All file access that has been described so far in this chapter is sequential. You perform *sequential access* by starting with the first byte in the file and continuing until you reach the end of the file. By comparison, *random access* permits you to read data anywhere in a file. When you want to access data in a file in any order other than sequential, use random access I/O operations.

Earlier in this chapter, the *current file position* was referred to. Because you were accessing files in all the examples sequentially, it was not necessary that you understand the current file position (in this discussion, referred to as the *file pointer position*). When you perform random access, however, this file position becomes important.

Positioning the File Pointer

Whenever you read or write information to or from a file, the I/O data transfer operation begins reading or writing data starting at the current file pointer position. When the operation is complete, the file pointer is repositioned after the last byte of data read or written.

Here are some examples of how C++ maintains the file pointer position. When you open a file, the file pointer position is at the beginning of the file, as illustrated in Figure 20.2. For example, the following statement is used to open a file:

```
ifstream afile( "TEXT.TXT", ios::nocreate ¦ ios::binary );
```

20

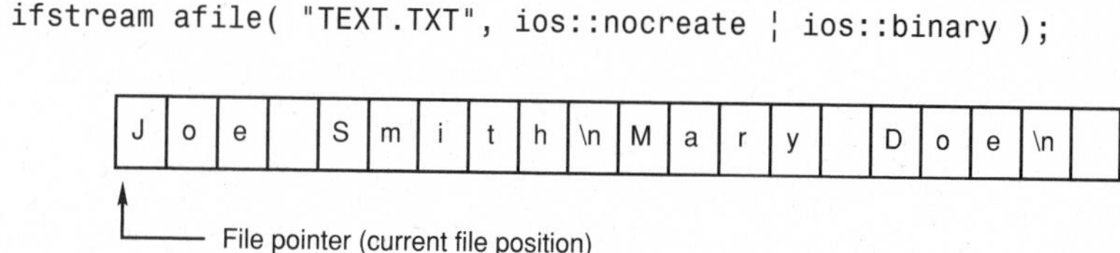

Figure 20.2. *The position of the file pointer when the file is opened.*

After you read a line from the file, using the `getline()` member function, the file pointer is positioned at the character following the newline character, as illustrated in Figure 20.3 and the following example:

```
char buffer[100];
afile.getline( buffer, 99 );
```

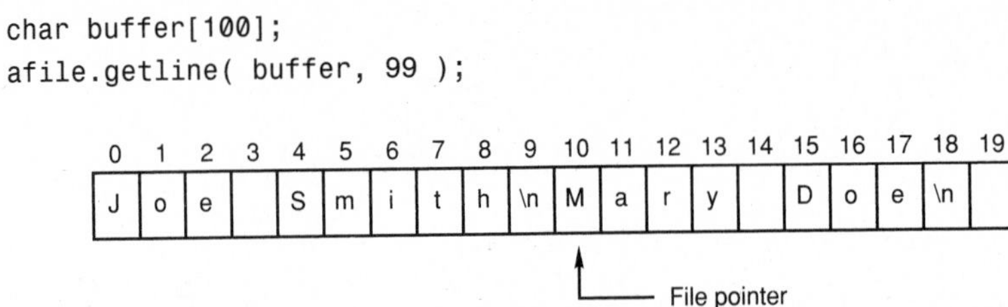

***Figure 20.3.** The position of the file pointer after a read operation.*

When you read the next line, the read operation begins with the `M` in `Mary`. If you open a file in append mode, the file pointer is positioned one byte past the last byte in the file. This fictitious byte is called the end-of-file (EOF) character.

The next section shows you how to use the two member functions that enable you to query and reposition the file pointer when you perform random access file I/O.

Member Functions Used with Random Access File I/O

The functions you use to do random access file I/O are `tellg()` and `seekg()`. Here are their prototypes:

```
#include <iostream.h>
streampos iostream::tellg();
iostream & seekg( streampos offset );
iostream & seekg( streampos offset, int origin );
```

The `tellg()` member function returns a `streampos` type value, which is the position of the file pointer measured in bytes from the beginning of the file. `streampos` is a `typedef` equivalent to a `long` and is defined in iostream.h.

Suppose that the file pointer is positioned as it is in Figure 20.3 and you call `tellg()` with the following statements:

```
char buffer[100];
ifstream afile( "TEXT.TXT", ios::nocreate ¦ ios::binary );
```

```
afile.getline( buffer, 99 );
streampos cfp = afile.tellg();
```

The value of `cfp` will be assigned a value of 10 because the file pointer is positioned at byte number 10. If `tellg()` is not successful, it returns a –1 value; otherwise, `tellg()` returns the file position.

You can reposition the file pointer with the `seekg()` function. The next I/O operation begins at the new location of the file pointer. The first argument is the file pointer, `streampos`, and the second argument is *`offset`*. The third argument is *`origin`*, which indicates the reference point for the repositioning operation. The origin must be one of the following constants: `ios::beg`, `ios::cur`, or `ios::end`. These constants are defined in Table 20.2.

Table 20.2. Constants used with the `seekg()` member function.

Constant	*Meaning*
`ios::cur`	The origin is the current position of the file pointer.
`ios::end`	The origin is the end of the file.
`ios::beg`	The origin is the beginning of the file.

The `seekg()` member function moves the file pointer to a new location that is offset in bytes from the location specified by the origin. The offset can have a positive or negative value. If the value is positive, the file pointer is moved toward the end of the file; if the value is negative, the file pointer is moved toward the beginning of the file. Starting with the example shown in Figure 20.3, you can reposition the file pointer three bytes to the right of its current position with the statement

```
afile.seekg( 3, ios::cur );
```

Figure 20.4 shows the new location of the file pointer.

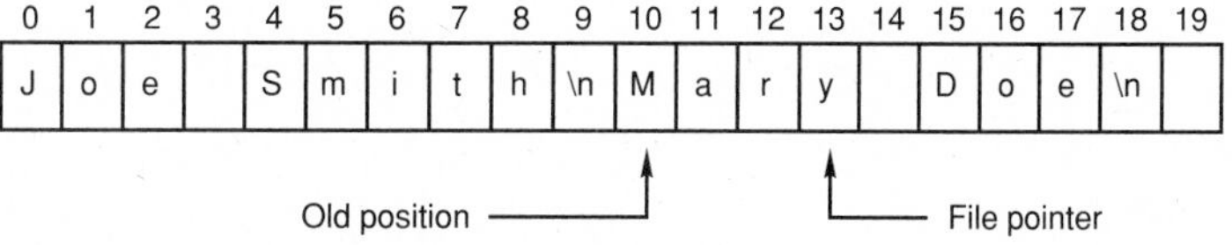

Figure 20.4. *Using `seekg()` with the `ios::cur` constant.*

If you used the `ios::beg` constant, as in

```
afile.seekg( 3, ios::beg );
```

it would reposition the file pointer to the fourth byte in the file, as illustrated in Figure 20.5.

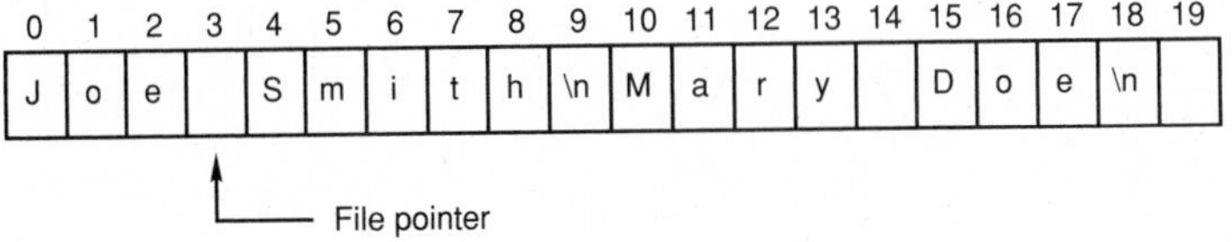

Figure 20.5. *Using* `seekg()` *with the* `ios::beg` *constant.*

As indicated, you can use `seekg()` to reposition the file pointer anywhere in the file. You can even position the pointer beyond the end of the file and effectively extend the file.

If you open a file in text mode, you can get strange and unexpected results because of end-of-line translations. In a text file, the `tellg()` member function is good only for finding the current file pointer position through a zero offset. It is better to open a file in binary mode when you use the `seekg()` or `tellg()` member function.

LSEEK1.CPP, the program in Listing 20.9, illustrates the use of the `seekg()` and `tellg()` member functions.

Listing 20.9. The source listing for LSEEK1.CPP.

```
// LSEEK1.CPP - Illustrates use of seekg() and tellg() functions

#include <stdlib.h>
#include <iostream.h>
#include <fstream.h>        // Needed for file I/O
#include <io.h>             // ios: manipulators

int main()
{
     streampos position;    // tellg() returns streampos value
     char buffer[100];

     ifstream ifile( "d:\\test.txt", ios::nocreate
                    | ios::binary );
```

```
    if ( !ifile )
        {
        cout << "Input file open error\n";
        return 1;
        }

// Position file pointer to beginning of file:
    ifile.seekg( 0L, ios::beg );   // Note: Same as seekg( 0L );
    position = ifile.tellg();
    cout << "Beginning of file position = "
        << position  << "\n";

    ifile.read( buffer, 20 );      // Read 20 characters

// Fetch current position:
    position = ifile.tellg();
    cout << "Current position seek = " << position << "\n";

    ifile.seekg( 10L, ios::cur );  // Move 10 characters forward
// Fetch current position:
    position = ifile.tellg();
    cout << "Current position seek = " << position << "\n";

// Set the end of the file:
    ifile.seekg( 0L, ios::end );
    position = ifile.tellg();
    cout << "Position for end of file = " << position << "\n";
    return 0;
}
```

Listing 20.10 shows the output from executing LSEEK1.EXE.

20

Listing 20.10. The output from executing LSEEK1.EXE.

```
Beginning of file position = 0
Current position seek = 20
Position for end of file = 897
```

You now know how to use the `iostream` member functions that accomplish file pointer positioning and query operations. In the next section, you look at a sample program that uses `seekg()` and `tellg()` to do random access file I/O operations.

Using Random Access I/O for Sorting Operations

Suppose that you want to sort a database which contains too much data to fit in memory. One way to sort the data is to keep a list, in memory, of just the smallest portion of the file needed to do the ordering. This portion is the field used as the key for the sort. You also keep a list of file positions of each data entry in the file. You rearrange the keys and their associated file positions to the desired sort order. Then you use random access read operations to retrieve data entries from the database in that sort order. The original database remains in its original physical order.

This section presents a sample program that uses this technique to sort a file. Assume that, although the database might be large, you have sufficient memory to hold all the index keys.

Specifically, you'll be sorting the file ADDRESS.DAT, which is generated by ADDRESS.EXE, as described in Chapters 15 and 18. First you define the problem: sort the file ADDRESS.DAT in ascending order by name. To accomplish this, you need a design. The following steps provide that design:

1. Read the file and extract the names and file pointers for each address book entry. Build an array containing these names and file pointers.
2. Sort the array, using the run-time library `qsort()` function.
3. Start processing at the beginning of the sorted array. Read from the file the address entry that corresponds to a file pointer array element. Write the entry to a new file by using sequential I/O.
4. Repeat step 3 until all array elements have been processed. The new file will be in alphabetical order by name.

The next step is to figure out what functions you need for the application. Here are some suggestions:

`reader()`	Read input file and build index array
`writer()`	Write sorted data to the new file

`error_exit()` Print the error message and exit

`compare()` Compare two names for `qsort()`

The program will declare two data structures. The `ADDRESS` structure from Chapter 15, "Structures and Unions," includes the name, address, and other members. The second structure is the `INDEX` structure, which contains a `char` array that holds the name, and a `long` member that contains the position of each address book entry in the file ADDRESS.DAT. The name member is the sort key. You declare the `INDEX` structure like this:

```
typedef struct ndx
{
     char     name[20];
     long     position;
} INDEX;
```

The complete SORT2.CPP program is presented in Listing 20.11, which appears later in this chapter. Before examining the complete program, you need to understand its elements. First the program declares a pointer to an array of `INDEX` structures. The input file, ADDRESS.DAT, is then opened. You use the `seekg()` member function to position the file pointer to the end of the file. That way, you can use the `tellg()` function to return the length of the file in bytes.

Then you use the `seekg()` function to position the file pointer to the beginning of the file. You use the length of the file to compute how many entries, `nitems`, are in the file. Now you know how many `INDEX` array elements you need. You use the `new` operator to allocate memory for the array from the free store. These steps are performed with the following statements:

```
ifile.seekg( 0, ios::beg );  // Position to beginning of file
nitems = (int)( size / sizeof( address ) );
index = new INDEX[nitems];
if ( index == NULL )
     error_exit( "Insufficient memory" );
```

Now that the array `index` of `INDEX` structures has been created, the program calls the `reader()` function. First `reader()` declares variables, including an instance of the `ADDRESS` structure. `reader()` reads each address book entry into the instance. The contents of the `name` member and the file position of the entry are stored in an `INDEX` structure element of array `index` with the following statements:

```
index[count].position = infile.tellg();
infile.read( (char *)&entry, sizeof( address ) );
if ( infile.good() )
{
     strcpy( index[count].name, entry.name );
     count++;
}
```

After all the entries have been accessed, the `reader()` function returns control to the calling program.

Next you call the library function `qsort()`, which sorts the array. To the `index` array, you pass the size of each element, the number of elements, and the address of the `compare()` function. `compare()` is a user-supplied function that compares two elements. If the value of the first element is greater than the value of the second element, a positive value is returned. If the first value equals the second, a zero is returned. Otherwise, a negative value is returned. The program will sort the array by name. Therefore, the library function `strcmpi()` is used to compare the `name` members of each element. This function compares the first and second arguments and returns the proper `int` value based on the comparison. The `qsort()` function uses a *quicksort* algorithm to sort the array elements. When this function returns, the array is sorted.

> The quicksort algorithm, sometimes called the *partition-exchange* sorting algorithm, is an efficient procedure for sorting a group of items with a digital computer program. The quicksort algorithm is attributed to the mathematician C. A. R. Hoare.

At this point, the program proceeds to the next step by calling the `writer()` function. `writer()` creates the file ADDRESS.NEW in write mode. Next a `for` loop is executed that repeats for each element in the sorted array, `index`. For each element, the following steps are performed:

1. Reposition the input file, ADDRESS.DAT, to the file position designated by `index[i].position`. This places the file pointer to an address book entry.
2. Read an address book entry.
3. Write the address book entry to the output file, ADDRESS.NEW.
4. Display the name and phone number.

Finally, the input and output files are closed, and the SORT2.EXE program exits. Incidentally, if an error occurs, the `error_exit()` function is called to print an error message and exit.

The new file, ADDRESS.NEW, is sorted in ascending order by name.

Listing 20.11. The source listing for SORT2.CPP.

```
// SORT2.CPP - Sorts the address book file to illustrate
// random access I/O
#include <iostream.h>
#include <string.h>
#include <fstream.h>    // Needed for file I/O
#include <io.h>         // ios: manipulators
#include <fcntl.h>
#include <iomanip.h>
#include <search.h>
#include <stdlib.h>     // Needed for exit() function
// ADDRESS - Address book structure
struct address
{
     char     name[20];
     char     phone[15];
     char     address1[23];
     char     city[14];
     char     state[3];
     char     zip[14];
     int      age;
     struct address *next;  // One-way linked list pointer
};
// INDEX - Structure that holds keys and file positions
struct INDEX
{
     char     name[20];
     streampos     position;
};

int compare( const void *s1, const void *s2 );
const ERROR= 1;
```

continues

Listing 20.11. continued

```
// Prototypes
int reader( ifstream ifile, INDEX index[] );
void error_exit( char *message );
void writer( ifstream ifile, INDEX index[], int count );
void main()
{
     int nitems;
     INDEX *index;

     ifstream ifile( "ADDRESS.DAT",
                     ios::nocreate | ios::binary );
     if ( !ifile  )
          error_exit( "Address Book File is not available\n" );
     else
     {
          // Find maximum size of index. First position to EOF.
          ifile.seekg( 0, ios::end );
          streampos size = ifile.tellg();  // Get length in bytes
          if ( size == 0 )
               error_exit( "Seek error" );
          ifile.seekg( 0, ios::beg );  // Position to beginning
                                       // of file
          nitems = (int)( size / sizeof( address ) );
          index = new INDEX[nitems];
          if ( index == NULL )
               error_exit( "Insufficient memory" );
          cout << "Number of items to sort: " << nitems << "\n";
          // Read index
          nitems = reader( ifile, index );
          // Sort INDEX elements
          qsort( index, nitems, sizeof(INDEX), compare );
          // Write out sorted file
          writer( ifile, index, nitems );
     }
}
//*************************************************************
// compare() - Compares two strings
int compare( const void *s1, const void *s2 )
{
     return strcmpi( ((INDEX *)s1)->name, ((INDEX *)s2)->name );
}
```

```
//*************************************************************
// error_exit() - Prints file error message and exits
void error_exit( char *message )
{
     cout << message << "\n";
     exit( ERROR );
}
//*************************************************************
// reader() - Reads address book entries from the file
// ADDRESS.DAT
int reader( ifstream infile, INDEX index[] )
{
     int count = 0;
     address entry;
     while ( 1 )
     {
          index[count].position = infile.tellg();
          infile.read( (char *)&entry, sizeof( address ) );
          if ( infile.good() )
          {
               strcpy( index[count].name, entry.name );
               count++;
          }
          else
             break;
     }
     cout << "Address Book contains " << count << " entries./n";
     return count;
}

//*************************************************************
// writer() - Writes sorted output to ADDRESS.NEW
void writer( ifstream ifile, INDEX index[], int count )
{
     address entry;
     ifile.seekg( 0, ios::beg );  // Rewind input file
     ofstream fout( "ADDRESS.NEW", ios::binary  );
     if ( !fout )
          error_exit( "Unable to write Address Book File\n" );
     else
```

20

continues

Listing 20.11. continued

```
    {
        cout << "\nSorted Phone Directory\n";
        for ( int i = 0 ; i < count ; i++ )
        {
            ifile.seekg( index[i].position, ios::beg );
            ifile.read ( (char *) &entry, sizeof( address ) );

            fout.write( (char *) &entry, sizeof( address ) );
            cout << setw( 10 ) << index[i].position
                << setw( 20 ) << entry.name
                << setw( 15 ) << entry.phone << "\n";
        }
        cout << count
            << " entries written to Address Book File\n";
    }
}
```

Listing 20.12 shows the output from executing SORT2.EXE. Note that the list is sorted alphabetically by name.

Listing 20.12. The output from executing SORT2.EXE.

```
Number of items to sort: 7
Address Book contains 7 entries.
Sorted Phone Directory
       282     Benjamin, James  (212)334-3365
         0          Blank, Joe  (602) 555-9876
       564        Blue, Howard  (202)555-2222
        94           Doe, Mary  (999)555-5432
       376        Gates, Billy  (202)555-1313
       470       Newton, Issac  (222)555-1111
       188        Records, Bob  (444)555-1234
7 entries written to Address Book File
```

Using the C Language Standard File I/O Run-Time Library Functions

Because C++ is an extension of C, you can still use the C language file I/O run-time library functions to do file I/O. In this discussion, you learn how to use these functions. As you read about these I/O functions, you'll notice how similar many of them are to the C++ I/O functions described earlier in the chapter.

Opening and Closing a File

The `fopen()` function opens a file. You pass this function two arguments: the first is the name of the file you want opened, and the second is a pointer to a string containing *file type* characters. File type characters specify the type of file I/O operations you plan to do. The arguments can be literal string constants or pointers to a string. Note an example:

```
FILE *filep;
if ( (filep = fopen( "c:\\test\\sample.txt", "w" )) == NULL )
     printf( "File open error\n" );
```

The standard file I/O header file (`#include <stdio.h>`) contains the declaration for the structure `FILE` and the prototypes for all the file I/O functions, along with other definitions. You must include this file if you intend to do any input or output operations.

The file type is the second parameter of the `fopen()` function. The file type specifies the type of file I/O operations to be performed when the file is opened. There are six file types, which are described in Table 20.3.

Table 20.3. The six file types.

Type	*Use*
`"r"`	Opens an existing file for reading. Reading begins at the beginning of the file.
`"w"`	Creates a new text file for writing. If the file exists, it is truncated to zero length, destroying any existing contents. Writing begins at the beginning of the file.
`"a"`	Opens an existing file in append mode. Writing begins at the end of the file. If the file does not exist, it is created.
`"r+"`	Opens at the beginning of an existing text file for reading and writing.
`"w+"`	Creates a new text file for reading and writing. If the file exists, it is truncated to zero length.
`"a+"`	Opens an existing file or creates a new file in append mode. You can read data anywhere in the file. However, you can write data only at the end of the file.

The type character contains the disk file types shown in Table 20.3, plus a *mode* type. The mode type can be either `b` for binary mode or `t` for text mode. If the mode type is omitted, text is assumed. For example, the following statement opens a file in binary mode to write:

```
if ( (filep = fopen( "test.abc", "wb" )) == NULL )
     printf( "File open error" );
```

After a file is closed, the operating system can use the instance of the file structure for another file. Because the number of files that can be opened at one time is limited, you should close a file when you are finished using it. If you have too many files open at one time, you could exceed the maximum file limit imposed by MS-DOS and cause a file I/O open error to occur. This file limit can be set with the CONFIG.SYS `FILES =` command. (Your MS-DOS manual provides more information about the maximum number of files.)

Here are prototypes for the `fopen()` and `fclose()` functions:

```
FILE *fopen( const char *filename, const char *type )
int fclose( FILE *filep );
```

The `fopen()` function returns a `FILE` pointer if the operation is successful, and a null value if the operation fails. The `fclose()` function returns a zero if the close operation is successful; otherwise, `fclose()` returns an end-of-file (EOF) character. In MS-DOS, the EOF character is a –1 value.

Reading and Writing a Text File

The `fputs()` and `fputc()` functions write data to a file in text mode. `fputs()` writes a string to the file, and `fputc()` writes a single character. The following lines illustrate the use of these two functions:

```
fputs( "Sample File", filep );
fputc( '\n', filep );
```

The `fputs()` function has two arguments: the first is a pointer to a string, and the second is the file pointer that is used with all other file I/O functions. The `fputs()` function writes a string, without the null terminator, to the file.

The `fputc()` function also is passed two arguments. The first is a `char` type value, and the second is the file pointer. A newline escape sequence is output to the file; the newline character is a linefeed (ASCII 10) character. In text mode, when a newline character is encountered in the output stream, a carriage return (ASCII 13) is inserted in front of the linefeed in the output stream.

Some file I/O function names are similar to the names of keyboard and screen I/O functions you are familiar with, except that an `f` has been added to the beginning of the name. Table 20.4 presents some similar functions.

Table 20.4. A comparison between keyboard/screen I/O functions and file I/O functions.

Keyboard and Screen I/O Functions	*File I/O Functions*
`getchar()`	None
`getc`	`fgetc( FILE *fp )`
`gets( char *s )`	`fgets( FILE *fp, char *s )`

continues

Table 20.4. continued

Keyboard and Screen I/O Functions	*File I/O Functions*
`printf( char *s, ...)`	`fprintf( FILE *fp, char *s, ... )`
`putchar( int ch )`	None
`putc( int ch )`	`fputc( int ch, FILE *fp )`
`puts( char *s )`	`fputs( char *s, FILE *fp )`
`scanf( char *s, ...)`	`fscanf( FILE *fp , char *s, ...)`

At times, you may want to write numeric values to a file while in text mode. To do so, you must convert the numbers—as stored in internal format—to ASCII representations of the number. The `fprintf()` function can be used for this purpose. In fact, `fprintf()` works like the `printf()` function except that `fprintf()` outputs to a file instead of the screen (`stdout`).

You can use the `fscanf()` function to read a text file containing ASCII representations of numeric values and convert them to their internal numeric value. This function works like the `scanf()` function except that `fscanf()` inputs from a file instead of the keyboard (`stdin`).

File I/O Techniques with C Language ANSI I/O

There are several ways to perform file I/O. You can read or write one character, one line, or a block of data at a time. The following sections illustrate these methods.

Reading and Writing One Character

You can use the `fgetc()` function to read one character from a file, and the `fputc()` function to write one character to a file. `fgetc()` reads a single character from the input file, beginning at the current file position, and returns the character as an `int` value. Here are the prototypes of `fgetc()` and `fputc()`:

```
int fgetc( FILE *fp )
fputs( char *s, FILE *fp )
```

Reading and Writing One Line

Instead of reading or writing a single character, you can read or write one line at a time. The `fgets()` function reads one line of data from a file each time it is called. The `fputs()` function writes one line of data each time it is called. The prototypes of these two functions are

```
char *fgets( char *string, int n, FILE *fp );
int fputs( char *string, FILE *fp );
```

The `fgets()` function reads one line of data from the file, beginning at the current file position. The function transfers a line of data to the `char` pointer variable *`string`*. You use the `int` variable *`n`* to specify the size of *`string`*. The function transfers data until one of the following occurs:

- *`n`* – 1 characters are transferred.
- A newline character is reached. The newline character is also transferred.
- The end of the input stream is reached.

The `gets()` function reads lines from the keyboard, and the `fgets()` function reads lines from a file. When `gets()` reads a line of data, it does *not* transfer the newline character to the input string. The `fgets()` function, however, transfers the newline character to the end of the input string. Both functions append a null character (`\0`) to terminate the string.

20

The `fgets()` function returns a pointer to a string if the operation is successful; otherwise, `fgets()` returns a null pointer.

The `fputs()` function transfers the contents of the *`string`* argument to the output file, beginning at the current file position. The terminating null character, `\0`, is not transferred. The function `fputs()` returns a zero if the operation is successful, and a nonzero value (EOF) if it is not successful.

One-line-at-a-time I/O is used only with text files. `fgets()` and `fputs()` depend on having a line of text of reasonable length and terminated with a newline character. (Note that a reasonable length of text is less than 1,000 bytes—usually less than 80 characters.) This type of I/O is used if you are doing text-related operations, such as processing a text file.

Reading and Writing a Block of Data

You have seen how to read and write a file one character or one line at a time. You also can read and write an entire block of data in binary or text mode with a single command. In addition, you can read or write an array or a structure with one I/O operation. The functions that perform block I/O operations are `fread()` and `fwrite()`. Here are their prototypes:

```
size_t fread( void *buffer, size_t size, size_t count, FILE *fp)
size_t fwrite( void *buffer, size_t size, size_t count, FILE *fp)
```

The first mystery to be unveiled is `size_t`, which is a `typedef` name declared in stdio.h. `size_t` is in many of the Microsoft C/C++ 7 run-time library function prototypes and is defined as an `unsigned int`.

The argument *`buffer`* is the address of an element. An element can be a variable, an array, or a structure. The argument *`size`* is an `unsigned int` that defines the size of the element. The argument *`count`* is an `unsigned int` that defines the number of elements to be written or read—with `fwrite()` and `fread()`, respectively. *`fp`* is the `FILE` pointer for a file that is already written.

The `fread()` function returns the number of elements that were actually read. The number returned should be the same number as *`count`* unless an error occurs or the EOF is encountered. The `fwrite()` function returns the number of elements that were written unless an error occurs.

`fread()` and `fwrite()` are the fastest methods of transferring data between memory and a disk file. There are times, though, when efficiency is not as important as other considerations. For example, if your application must count the lines in a file, you will probably want to process the file line by line. Such an application becomes more complex if you use block I/O operations instead of one-line-at-a-time I/O operations.

Low-Level File Input and Output Operations

All the C run-time library I/O functions discussed previously in this chapter are called *standard I/O functions* because they correspond to the ANSI standards. Most C language compilers also support a category of I/O functions called *low-level I/O.* Low-level I/O functions perform I/O operations and take advantage of the computer hardware. They are usually more efficient than standard I/O functions but are not portable. That is, if the code is moved to another type of computer, the low-level functions might not work. Microsoft C/C++ 7—along with DOS, Windows, and OS/2—supports low-level I/O functions, although they might not be supported for certain hardware architectures.

When you perform a low-level file I/O write operation, the data is not buffered and goes directly to the disk file. Standard I/O, however, is buffered. The data is not transferred to disk until the buffer fills, or until `fflush()` or `fclose()` is called. You should not mix standard I/O and low-level I/O operations; use one type or the other.

Low-level I/O functions are more difficult to use but much faster than standard file I/O functions. For that reason, this type of I/O is worth investigating. The following sections cover the three basic low-level file I/O functions: `open()`, `read()`, and `write()`.

Low-Level I/O Header Files

When you are using low-level I/O functions, you need to include the following header files:

```
#include <stdio.h>
#include <fcntl.h>
#include <sys\types.h>
#include <sys\stat.h>
#include <io.h>
```

20

Opening and Closing a File

You must always open a file with the `open()` function before you can use it. Its prototype is

```
int open( char *filename, int oflag [, int pmode] );
```

The first argument is the *filename*. The second argument, *oflag*, is the *open flag*, which is used to determine what kind of file is being opened. You specify the third argument, *pmode*, only if you are creating a new file.

You can specify one or more *oflags*. If more than one is specified, the multiple open flags are separated with logical OR (¦) operators. Note an example:

```
afile = open( "D:\\AFILE.XYZ", O_RDONLY ¦ O_EXCL ¦ O_BINARY );
```

O_RDONLY ¦ O_EXCL ¦ O_BINARY are three *oflags*. The open flags are described in Table 20.5.

Table 20.5. The low-level I/O open flags.

oflag	*Meaning*
O_APPEND	Repositions the file pointer to the end of the file before every write operation.
O_BINARY	Indicates binary mode operation.
O_CREAT	Creates and opens the file for writing. If the file exists, this flag is ignored. The third argument, *pmode*, must be specified and can have one of three values: S_IREAD — Reading permitted S_IWRITE — Writing permitted S_IREAD ¦ S_IWRITE — Both reading and writing permitted
O_EXCL	Returns an error value if the specified file exists when O_CREAT is specified also.
O_RDONLY	Opens the file for reading only. If this flag is specified, neither O_RDWR nor O_WRONLY can be specified.
O_RDWR	Opens the file for reading and writing. If this flag is specified, flags O_RDONLY and O_WRONLY cannot be specified.
O_TEXT	Opens the file in text mode.

oflag	*Meaning*
O_TRUNC	Destroys contents of the file if it exists and truncates the file length to zero. Either O_WRONLY or RDWR must be specified.
O_WRONLY	Opens the file for write only. If this flag is specified, O_RDONLY and O_RDWR cannot be specified.

One of the following three open flags must be specified: O_RDONLY, O_RDWR, or O_WRONLY.

The third argument, *pmode*, is not specified unless O_CREAT is specified. Even then, if the file already exists, the value of *pmode* is ignored. Otherwise, *pmode* is used to specify the read-only permission file attribute, which is established when the file is closed for the first time. This means that you can open a file in read-only mode, write to it, and close the file. The next time it is opened, the read-only attribute is set. There are two possible integer constants that you can specify: S_IREAD and S_IWRITE. These constants are defined in the sys\stat.h header file. In MS-DOS, S_IWRITE has no meaning because you cannot grant write-only permission to a file. When the S_IREAD constant is specified for *pmode*, the file attribute is set to read-only.

The open() function returns an int file handle if the open operation is successful. Otherwise, it returns a –1, which indicates an error.

The close() function is called to close a file. The prototype is

```
int close( int handle );
```

The file with the corresponding *handle* is closed. If a zero is returned, the close was successful. If an error occurs, a –1 is returned.

20

The Low-Level read() Function

The prototype for the low-level read() function is

```
int read( int handle, void* buffer, unsigned int count );
```

The *handle* argument is the associated file handle returned by the open() function. The char pointer *buffer* is the address of the buffer that receives the data. *count* is the maximum number of characters to read. The read() function attempts to read *count* bytes into *buffer* from the file. read() begins reading at the current file position.

The `read()` function returns the actual number of bytes read. The number might be less than *count* if the EOF is encountered during the read operation. If a zero is returned, it is an indication that the file pointer was positioned at the end. If an error occurs, –1 is returned.

If the file is opened in text mode, each occurrence of the carriage return/linefeed sequence is replaced with a single linefeed. Only the single linefeed character is counted in the returned byte count. This also can cause the *count* argument to differ from the return value.

The Low-Level write() Function

The prototype for the low-level `write()` function is

```
int write( int handle, void* buffer, unsigned int count );
```

The *handle* argument is the associated file handle returned by the `open()` function. The *buffer* argument is the address of the buffer containing characters to write. The *count* argument is the number of bytes to write. `write()` begins writing at the current file position. If the file is opened for appending, the operation begins at the end of the file.

`write()` returns the number of bytes that actually were written. The return value is not affected by text end-of-line conversion while in text mode. If an error occurs, a –1 is returned.

Error-Handling and Status Functions

This section describes functions that report the status of an I/O operation. The following functions are discussed:

```
int ferror( FILE *fp );
int feof( FILE *fp );
void clearerr( FILE *fp );
void perror( char *string );
```

The `feof()` function returns a nonzero value if the EOF was encountered as a result of the last read operation. If the EOF was not encountered, `feof()` returns a zero.

Many of the functions return some type of error indication when an error occurs. You don't know, however, exactly what went wrong. The `fread()` function returns the number of bytes read. You do not know if you reached the EOF or experienced a dreadful disk read error. The C language supports several error-handling functions that report error conditions.

The `ferror()` function returns a nonzero value if an error occurs during read or write operations on the specified file. If no error occurs, `ferror()` returns a zero.

If an error occurs, the internal error indicator remains set until you call the `clearerr()` function, which resets the internal error and the EOF indicators. The argument for the `clearerr()` function is the `FILE` pointer, which returns no value. The internal error indicator also is reset if the `fseek()`, `lseek()`, or `rewind()` function is called.

The `perror()` function prints an error message to the `stderr` stream. You provide the function with your own error message. The function displays your error message, followed by a colon and the system error message for the last function call that encountered the error. The system error message is followed by a newline. Note this example:

```
if ( ferror( fp ) )
     perror( "File I/O message occurred" );
```

The preceding statement could print the following message:

```
File I/O message occurred: Too many files open
```

Positioning the File Pointer

20

Whenever you read or write information to or from a file, the I/O data transfer operation begins reading or writing data starting at the current file pointer position. When the operation is complete, the file pointer is repositioned after the last byte of data read or written.

The C run-time library functions for doing random access file I/O are `ftell()`, `fseek()`, `rewind()`, and `lseek()`. Here are the prototypes of the first three functions:

```
#include <stdio.h>
long ftell( FILE *fp );
```

```
int fseek( FILE *fp, long offset, int origin );
void rewind( FILE *fp );
```

The `ftell()` function returns a `long int`, which is the position of the file pointer measured in bytes from the beginning of the file.

The `rewind()` function repositions the file pointer to the beginning of the file. The `fseek()` function repositions the file pointer to a specified position in the file.

The next I/O operation begins at the new location of the file pointer. The `fseek()` function returns –1 if an error is encountered. The first argument, *`fp`*, is the file pointer, and the second argument is *`offset`*. The third argument, *`origin`*, which indicates the reference point for the repositioning operation, must be one of the following constants: `SEEK_CUR`, `SEEK_END`, or `SEEK_SET`. These constants are defined in Table 20.6.

Table 20.6. Constants used with the `fseek()` and `lseek()` functions.

Constant	*Meaning*
`SEEK_CUR`	The origin is the current position of the file pointer.
`SEEK_END`	The origin is the end of the file.
`SEEK_SET`	The origin is the beginning of the file.

The `fseek()` function moves the file pointer to a new location that is offset in bytes from the location specified by the origin. The offset can have a positive or negative value. If the value is positive, the file pointer is moved toward the end of the file; if the value is negative, the file pointer is moved toward the beginning of the file.

Low-Level File Pointer Positioning

The `lseek()` function serves the same purpose for low-level file I/O operations that `fseek()` and `tellg()` serve for standard I/O operations. The `lseek()` function is used to position and query the file pointer position. Its prototype is

```
long lseek( int handle, long offset, int origin )
```

The *handle* argument is the associated file handle returned by the `open()` function. You can reposition the file pointer by using `lseek()`, and the next I/O operation begins at the new location of the file pointer. The `lseek()` function returns –1 if an error is encountered. The third argument, *origin*, indicates the reference point for the repositioning operation. It must be one of the constants defined in Table 20.6.

The `lseek()` function moves the file pointer to a new location that is offset in bytes from the location specified by the origin. The offset can have a positive or negative value. If *offset* is positive, the file pointer is moved toward the end of the file. If *offset* has a negative value, the file pointer is moved toward the beginning of the file.

With `lseek()`, you can reposition the file pointer anywhere in the file. You can even position the pointer beyond the end of the file to extend the file.

You can use the `lseek()` function to find the current file pointer position by specifying an offset of zero and using the current origin. Note this example:

```
cfp = lseek ( fhandle, 0, SEEK_CUR ) /* Get current position */
```

Similarly, you can use `lseek()` with a zero offset to find the length of the file in bytes, as in

```
cfp = lseek ( fhandle, 0, SEEK_END ) /* Get length of file */
```

Summary of the C Run-Time I/O Functions

20

Here is a list of the standard file I/O functions presented in the last part of this chapter:

```
FILE *fopen( const char *filename, const char *type )
int fclose( FILE *filep );
int fgetc( FILE *fp )
char *fgets( char *s, FILE *fp )
int fputc( int ch, FILE *fp )
int fputs( char *s, FILE *fp )
int fprintf( FILE *fp, char *s, ... )
char *fscanf( FILE *fp , char *s, ...)
```

```
size_t fread( void *buffer, size_t size, size_t count, FILE *fp )
size_t fwrite( void *buffer, size_t size, size_t count, FILE *fp )
long ftell( FILE *fp );
int fseek( FILE *fp, long offset, int origin );
void rewind( FILE *fp );
```

Here is a list of the low-level file I/O functions:

```
int open( char *filename, int oflag [, int pmode] );
int close( int handle );
int read( int handle, void* buffer, unsigned int count );
int write( int handle, void* buffer, unsigned int count );
long lseek( int handle, long offset, int origin )
```

Finally, here are the standard file I/O error-processing functions:

```
int ferror( FILE *fp );
int feof( FILE *fp );
void clearerr( FILE *fp );
void perror( char *string );
```

What You Have Learned

In this chapter, you learned how to read from and write to files. Specifically, you learned the following:

- The use of object-oriented file I/O operations
- Techniques for using `iostream` file I/O functions
- The use of random access I/O to sort a file

The chapter also described the standard I/O run-time library functions and the Microsoft C/C++ 7 low-level file I/O functions.

Compiler Directives

A definition is the enclosing a wilderness of ideas within a wall of words.

—Samuel Butler
Higgledy-Piggledy (1912)

In This Chapter

Compiler directives, also called *preprocessor directives*, are commands that control a compiler. They are evaluated by the C/C++ 7 preprocessor before the compiler processes any source code. You have already learned about some compiler directives, such as `#define` and `#include`. In this chapter, you learn more about these directives as well as others:

- `#include`
- `#define`

- `#undef`
- Conditional directives
- `#pragma`

Compiler Directive Syntax

A compiler directive begins with a pound sign (#). The directive can be preceded only by blanks—no other characters—and is followed by the command. Before the development of ANSI standard C, the pound sign had to appear in the first column, and spaces could not separate the pound sign from the command that followed. ANSI C, supported by the Microsoft C/C++ 7 compiler, removed these restrictions. A compiler directive ends with a newline character. The directive is *not* terminated by a semicolon. All three of the following examples are valid ways to use a compiler directive:

```
#include <stdio.h>
# include  <stdio.h>
     #      include <stdio.h>
```

Although you can have spaces, the first example shows the most commonly used style. If you want a compiler directive to extend over several lines, specify a backslash character immediately before the newline character, as in

```
#define VERY_LONG_MACRO "This message will extend over\
two lines."
```

The C/C++ Preprocessor

Now that you have learned the syntax of compiler directives, you are ready to see how they are processed. The C/C++ preprocessor is a subsystem of a compiler system and has its own line-oriented syntax processor that processes the compiler directives. Generally, the C/C++ preprocessor can do the following operations:

- Perform macro substitutions (`#define` directive processing)

- Insert other files into a source file (`#include` directive processing)
- Conditionally control the source code (`#if` and associated directives)

Figure 21.1 illustrates how the C/C++ preprocessor alters a source file by inserting files and performing macro substitutions. The resulting altered source file is then passed to the compiler.

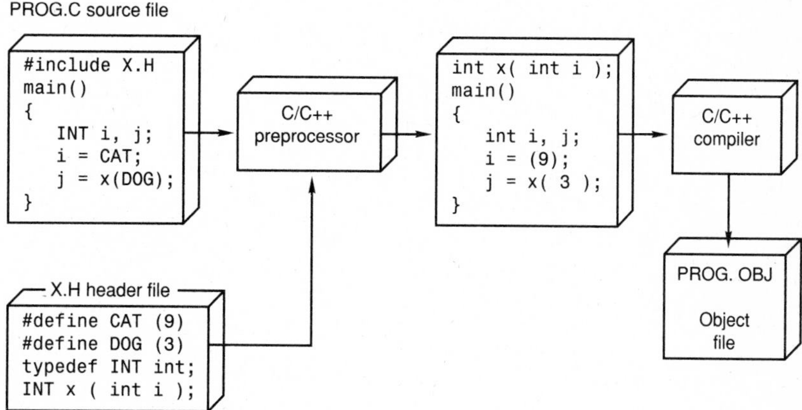

Figure 21.1. *The C/C++ preprocessor alters the source file.*

The #include Directive

The `#include` compiler directive inserts the contents of a specified file into the source file in place of the `#include` directive. The directive can have two forms:

```
#include <filename>
#include "filename"
```

If the filename is enclosed in angle brackets (<>), the preprocessor searches for the file in the *standard directory*. This is the DOS directory in which the C and C++ language include files are stored. Available with all C and C++ compilers, these include files provide definitions, declarations, and constants used by C run-time library functions and C++ class libraries. Microsoft C/C++ 7 contains include files also for Windows API functions and the MFC (Microsoft Foundation Classes) library. The MFC is a complete class library for Windows.

The Microsoft C/C++ 7 preprocessor searches the libraries that you assign with the DOS environment variable named `INCLUDE`. For example, an `INCLUDE` environment variable can be established with the following DOS command:

```
SET INCLUDE= C:\C700\INCLUDE;
```

This DOS `SET` command establishes the `INCLUDE` environment variable, which tells the Microsoft C/C++ compiler that the standard C/C++ include files are in the directory `C:\C700\INCLUDE`. You can also establish environment variables with the **E**nvironment Variables command on the **O**ptions menu in the PWB.

The mechanism for establishing the proper `INCLUDE` environment variable is usually established when you install Microsoft C/C++ 7. The real advantage of using the first form (with the angle brackets) is that you can search multiple standard directories.

In the second form, the filename follows `#include` and is enclosed in double quotation marks. When you use this form, the preprocessor first searches for the file in the same directory in which the source file resides. If the file cannot be found there, the preprocessor searches the standard directory for the file.

The file that is inserted is called the *include* file or *header* file and usually has a filename extension of .h. The filename must be a valid DOS filename and cannot contain wild-card characters. A header file simplifies programming because it traditionally contains macro definitions, data structure definitions, prototypes, and any global data declarations used for communications among source files. The header file's purpose is to provide a place to put statements common to many source files. Header files make initial programming, modifications, and maintenance easier.

A header file can contain multiple `#include` statements. This technique is called *nesting*. It is unusual to use more than two levels when nesting header files, but nesting is supported up to 10 levels, and sometimes multiple levels are useful. For example, you might have a group of header files that you frequently use with an application. You can create a header file named fio.h, which is presented in Listing 21.1.

Listing 21.1. Nesting with the fio.h header file.

```
// fio.h - Contains list of include statements
#include <iostream.h>
#include <string.h>
#include <fstream.h>
#include <io.h>
```


You can include fio.h in your source file, and the preprocessor will insert all five header files in the source file, as in

```
#include <fio.h>
main()
{
    ⋮
}
```

The #define Directive

As a preface to this discussion of the `#define` statement, you should be aware that the use of `#define` to specify a symbolic constant is an antiquated remnant of the C language. C++ uses the `const` qualifier to provide a superior, more powerful method for creating constants. `const` is discussed in the section "The `const` Qualifier" in Chapter 6. `#define` statements are used predominantly in include files shared by C and C++.

The `#define` compiler directive is used for text substitution and function-like macros. You can think of the `#define` statement as a simple find-and-replace operation, like one you might use with a word processor.

Simple Text Replacement

In its simplest form, the `#define` statement is followed by a macro name and the text to be replaced. This text is called the *macro body*. Traditionally, when the macro name is used to define a constant, the name appears in uppercase. This makes it easier for you to distinguish macro names from other program variables. A variable name should be in lowercase and have a macro name that identifies its use. Do not worry about name length because only the first 31 characters are interpreted. The name, however, can have any number of characters, including letters, numbers, and the underscore (_). If the name gets too long, it can get rather silly and diminish readability.

After the preprocessor has processed a `#define` statement, whenever the macro name is encountered in the source code, the preprocessor replaces that name with the macro body. Note this example:

```
#define PI (3.1415926L)
```

Using the `#define` command to define a constant is the most popular form. It is considered bad programming style to use constant values in a source file for two reasons:

- A constant value does not reveal its purpose. A macro name should indicate the purpose of the constant. MAX_SIZE, for example, has more meaning than 749.
- It is easier to change a constant in the `#define` statement than to search and replace every instance of the constant in the source file.

Listing 21.2 illustrates sample code that can be improved with the use of macros.

Listing 21.2. Sample code that uses constant values.

```
func()
{
     int      buf[302];
     for ( i = 0; i <=  301; i++ )
          buf[i] = cfunc( 302 - i );
     for ( i = 302; i >= 0; i-- )
     :    buf[i] = 303 - dfunc( buf[302 - i] );

}
```

The type of code in Listing 21.2 can be messy to change. Suppose that you need to increase the array to 409 elements. First you use a macro to define 409. Then you replace references to 302 with `MAX_SIZE`, 301 with `(MAX SIZE-1)`, and 303 with `(MAX_SIZE+1)`, as shown in Listing 21.3.

Listing 21.3. Sample code that uses macros.

```
#define MAX_SIZE (409)
func()
{
     int      buf[MAX_SIZE];
     for ( i = 0; i < (MAX_SIZE-1); i++ )
          buf[i] = cfunc( MAX_SIZE - i );
     for ( i = MAX_SIZE; i >= 0; i-- )
          buf[i] = (MAX_SIZE+1) - dfunc( buf[MAX_SIZE - i] );
     :
}
```

The code in Listing 21.3 is better. It is always a good idea to enclose the macro body in parentheses so that, if you mistakenly omit an operator, the compiler will catch the bug.

Because preprocessor syntax is different from C/C++ language syntax, programmers have trouble changing languages when they are engaged in coding. Here are two common mistakes:

- You erroneously insert a semicolon at the end of a macro definition.
- You erroneously insert an equal sign (=) between the macro name and macro body.

If you terminate a macro definition with a semicolon by mistake, it will probably create a bug in your code. In the example

```
#define BAD_DEFINE 20;
int bug[ BAD_DEFINE ];
nobug = x_val * BAD_DEFINE;
```

you will get a compiler error on the statement in which `bug` is declared. However, you will get lucky on the statement assigning `nobug` a value. The preprocessor expands this expression to

```
nobug = x_val * 20;;
```

and the extra semicolon is treated by the compiler as a null statement. No problem? This bug could go undetected for years. If you reverse the expression to `nobug = BAD_DEFINE * X_VAL`, the compiler will detect the bug because the expression is expanded to

```
nobug = 20; * X_VAL;
```

Just be careful and *never* terminate a macro expression with a semicolon.

Now assume that you are typing along and you mistakenly enter

```
#define SIZE = 30
```

instead of

```
#define SIZE 30
```

This is a common mistake made by programmers. When the macro is expanded, the `= 30` will replace the macro name. Usually, the compiler detects such an error. There are, however, undetectable cases, such as

```
x_val = SIZE;
```

The preprocessor expands this macro to

```
x_val == 30;
```

The computer interprets this as a perfectly legal expression and continues on its way. Unfortunately, you are left with the task of figuring out why `x_val` is not getting initialized to 30. Again, be careful and never make this mistake.

Macros That Resemble Functions

Another form of macro resembles a function. Like a function, this macro takes arguments. When the macro is used in a program, the arguments in the macro function call in the code to replace the occurrences of the arguments in the macro body with the values supplied in the C/C++ statement. The instance of the macro in the code is then replaced with the macro body. Note the following example:

```
#define ONE (1.0L)
#define TWO (2.0L)
#define PI (3.1415926)
#define COS( x ) = ( sqrt( ONE - pow( sin( x ), TWO ) ) )
:
z = COS( PI );
```

When the preprocessor expands this macro, it will replace `x` in the macro body, used as an argument to the `sin()` function, with 3.1415926. The code seen by the compiler is

```
z = ( sqrt( (1.0L) - pow( sin( (3.1415926) ), (2.0L) ) ) );
```

> Do not place any spaces between the macro name and the first left parenthesis for macros that resemble functions.

For function macros, if you put spaces between the macro name and the first left parenthesis, the preprocessor will think that the left parenthesis begins the expression and is not a macro argument. You can have more than one argument specified in a macro definition, as in

```
#define MULTIPLY( x, y ) ( x * y )
:
z = MULTIPLY( 3, 4 ) + MULTIPLY ( 5, 7 );
```

The Microsoft C/C++ 7 preprocessor translates this to the following:

```
z = (3 * 4) + (5 * 7);
```

The preprocessor does no type checking. The programmer must provide the macro with the correct data type; otherwise, the compiler issues a warning or an error.

The Microsoft C/C++ 7 library implements some run-time library functions as macros. Examples are the `toupper()`, `tolower()`, `isupper()`, `putc()`, and `min()` functions.

Advantages of Using Macros

There are several advantages of using macros instead of functions:

- Macros have no type restriction.
- The preprocessor checks the argument count.
- Macros are faster than functions.

Consider each of these advantages. First, because macros have no type restriction, you can use a macro for different data types without getting an error if you handle the arguments correctly. For instance, the `min()`

function is implemented as a macro and can be used with any data type. The `min()` function is defined as

```
#define min(a,b) (((a) > (b)) ? (a) : (b))
```

Second, the C/C++ preprocessor checks to see whether you have the correct number of arguments specified. If you do not specify a prototype for a function, the compiler does not verify that the number of actual arguments in a function call equals the number of formal arguments in the function. However, it is a good programming practice always to specify prototypes.

Finally, macros execute faster than functions because there is an overhead associated with calling a function. The overhead is the machine language code that the compiler must generate in order to place the arguments on the stack and call the function. The macro code executes faster because the function call setup code is not present and does not need to be executed.

Advantages of Using Functions

Although macros have certain advantages, there are some advantages of using functions:

- Functions do not cause side effects.
- Functions check argument data types.
- Functions are easier to debug.
- Functions do not replicate code unless you use inline functions.

Consider the issue of side effects. For example, look at the `toupper()` macro defined in the ctype.h header file:

```
#define toupper(c) ( (islower(c) ) ? _toupper(c) : c)
#define _toupper(c) ((c) -'A'+'a' )
```

If you use a function that returns a character as an argument to `toupper()`, the function is called twice, as shown in this example:

```
#include <stdlib.h>
#include <ctype.h>
char     fetchc();
main()
{
```

```
:
c = toupper( fetchc() );

}
```

The preprocessor expands this macro to

```
c = ( (( fetchc() & 2) )  ? (( fetchc() ) -'A'+'a' ) : c );
```

Notice that `fetchc()` is called twice. This undesirable side effect will probably cause a problem and is a disadvantage of using macros.

The code for a function takes a certain amount of memory, but the function can be called by many programs. These calls take a negligible amount of memory compared to the memory the function takes. Each time a function-like macro is used, it has approximately the same memory requirements as a function that does the same job. Consequently, if you have many instances of a function-like macro, you use much more memory than if you called a function in place of each instance. For example, if a function used 300 bytes of memory, five instances of a function-like macro would take about 1,500 bytes of memory.

The #undef Directive

The `#undef` directive removes the name of (or "undefines") a `#define` macro from the macro list. Here is the syntax of `#undef`:

```
#undef macro-name
```

The specified *`macro-name`* is undefined. Whenever a `#define` statement is issued, the statement remains in effect for the rest of the source file or until an `#undef` statement is issued. ANSI standard C states that it is illegal to redefine an existing macro name. You must, therefore, use an `#undef` command to remove a name before you can redefine it. For example, if you have the macro `SIZE` defined, you can undefine it with

```
#define SIZE (9)
:
#undef SIZE
```

After the `#undef` is issued, the macro `SIZE` is no longer in the macro list and no longer valid for the rest of the source file.

Conditional Directives

Sometimes when you are developing a program, you want part of the program to be ignored by the compiler. For example, you might have some print statements that you use for debugging. You want those statements to compile when you are ready to test the program, but you don't want the debugging code to appear in the version of the program you deliver to a user.

For another example, you might have a program that runs on different computers and has a small subset of the code that is machine-dependent. One option is to maintain two versions of the program. This is not easy to do, however. It's difficult to keep the versions synchronized, especially if many programmers are making changes. Another option is to use *conditional directives*, conditionally used to skip parts of the code during the compilation process.

Conditional directives are similar to C++'s `if` and `else` statements but are processed by the Microsoft C/C++ 7 preprocessor. Here are the conditional directives:

```
#if macro-condition-expression
#else
#endif
#elif macro-condition-expression
#ifdef macro-name
#ifndef macro-name
```

The *`macro-condition-expression`* must be a constant expression. All macros in the expression are expanded before the expression is evaluated. All constants in the expression are translated to `long int` constants. A *`macro-condition-expression`* evaluates to a true (1) or false (0) value.

For each `#if` directive, there must be a corresponding `#endif` directive. An `#else` directive can be placed between the `#if` and `#endif` statements. The form is

```
#if condition
     code block 1
#else
     code block 2
#endif
```

code block 1 and *code block 2* are blocks of any number of C++ language statements. A code block also can contain preprocessor directives. If the `#if` directive condition evaluates to a true (1) value, *code block 1* is compiled, and *code block 2* is ignored. If the condition evaluates to a false (0) value, *code block 1* is ignored, and *code block 2* is compiled. `#if-#endif` pairs can be nested. `#elif` is a short form of the `#else` directive followed by the `#if` directive.

IF2.CPP, the program in Listing 21.4, illustrates how the conditional statements operate. Because `OPTION` equals 1, the messages `1. Option is true.` and `2. Option is true.` are displayed. Because `DEBUG` is false (0), no debug message is displayed.

Listing 21.4. Examples of conditional directives.

```
// IF2.CPP - Illustrates conditional directives
#define OPTION 1
#define DEBUG 0
#include <iostream.h>
main()
{
     :
#if OPTION
     cout << "1. Option is true.\n";
#else
     cout << "1. Option is false.\n";
#endif                               // if OPTION
     :
#if !OPTION
     cout << "2. Option is false.\n";
     :
#elif OPTION
     cout << "2. Option is true.";
#endif                               // if !OPTION
     :
#if DEBUG
     cout << "Print debug message\n";
#endif                               // if DEBUG

}
```

The #ifdef and #ifndef directives are obsolete. They are not part of the ANSI standard because the new defined operator was adopted. However, the Microsoft C/C++ 7 compiler still supports #ifdef and #ifndef for compatibility. The Microsoft C/C++ 7 header files actually make extensive use of the #ifdef and #ifndef directives. The #ifdef directive operates like the #if directive except that the condition is true (1) if the macro name is defined. Otherwise, the condition evaluates to false (0). In the example

```
#undef MOUSE
#ifdef  MOUSE
     cout << "The mouse exists.";     // Code block
#endif
```

the code block will be ignored because the macro MOUSE is undefined. The #ifndef directive evaluates to true if the macro name does *not* exist. This directive is the opposite of #ifdef. The following example shows how the defined operator can be used for the same purpose:

```
#undef MOUSE
#if defined( MOUSE )
     cout << "The mouse exists.";     // Code block
#endif
```

If a macro name in an #if directive condition does not exist, it evaluates to a zero. This means that you can accomplish the same results without using the defined operator, as illustrated in the following example:

```
#undef MOUSE
#if MOUSE == 0
     cout << "The mouse exists.";     // Code block
#endif
```

The #pragma Directive

The ANSI standards committee recognized the need to establish certain parameters specific to the type of computer on which the C and C++ compilers are implemented. To this end, the committee adopted the #pragma directive. You use the #pragma directive to provide the compiler with machine-specific instructions to perform an action at compile time.

The forms of the #pragma directive supported by Microsoft C/C++ 7 are summarized in Table 21.1. You can get more information regarding a

#pragma from the PWB online Help system or the Microsoft C/C++ 7 documentation. For example, if you have multiple source modules in a project and you want to override the stack-checking compiler option for a single module, you place the following #pragma directive at the beginning of the module:

```
#pragma check_stack (off)
```


Table 21.1. The #pragma directives supported by Microsoft C/C++ 7.

#pragma Directive	*Description*
alloc_text (*list*)	An obsolete #pragma directive that specifies the segment where function definitions will reside.
auto_inline (on ¦ off)	Inhibits the inline expansion of a function.
check_pointer (on ¦ off)	Instructs compiler to turn pointer checking on or off.
check_stack (on ¦ off)	Instructs compiler to turn stack checking on or off.
code_seg (*list*)	Specifies a segment where functions are to be allocated.
comment (*type*, *comment*)	Inserts comment record in object file or executable file.
data_seg (*list*)	Specifies the data segment where data is to be allocated.
function (*function-list*)	Specifies that calls to specified function will be intrinsic (normal).
hdrstop ("*filename*")	Placed at some location in a source file (not a header file). When the preprocessor encounters this #pragma directive, the state of compilation is displayed up to the location of the #pragma statement.
inline_depth (*number*)	Specifies the number of times inline expansion can occur.

continues

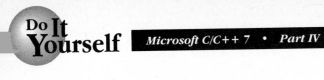

Table 21.1. continued

#pragma *Directive*	*Description*
`inline_recursion (on ¦ off)`	Controls inline expansion of directly or mutually recursive functions.
`init_seg (`*segment*`)`	Specifies the segment that affects the order in which startup code is executed. For example, DLL code needs to defer initialization.
`intrinsic (`*function list*`)`	Indicates that calls to specified functions will be intrinsic instead of having normal function calls for specified functions. An intrinsic function can be inline or have special calling conventions. Run-time library functions, such as `strlen()`, have both inline and normal forms, and the value of the `intrinsic` mode setting determines which form is used.
`linesize (`*number*`)`	Specifies the number of characters per line in a source file.
`loop_opt (on ¦ off)`	Turns on and off loop optimization for selected functions.
`message (`*message*`)`	Sends a specified message to standard output without stopping the compilation.
`native_caller (on ¦ off)`	Turns on or off the option to remove native-code entry points from within source code when p-code functions are called only by other p-code functions.
`optimize (`*list*`, on ¦ off)`	Specifies compiler optimization options.
`pack (1 ¦ 2 ¦ 4)`	Specifies packing alignment for structure types. You can specify 1-, 2-, or 4-byte alignment.
`page (`*pages*`)`	Skips the specified number of pages in source listing.
`pagesize (`*lines*`)`	Specifies the number of lines per page in source listing.

#pragma *Directive*	*Description*
skip (*lines*)	Skips the specified number of lines in source listing.
subtitle ("*subtitle*")	Specifies a subtitle to display below the title for source listing.
title ("*title*")	Specifies a title line to display at the top of each page of source listing.
warning (*specifiers*)	Specifies the compiler warning level for the rest of source file.

What You Have Learned

In this chapter, you learned about compiler directives and the Microsoft C/C++ 7 preprocessor. Specifically, you learned the following:

- How to use header files and how to include them with the #include directive
- How to use the #define directive to define constants and macro functions
- How to use the conditional directives (#if, #else, #endif, #elif, #ifdef, and #ifndef) to control which blocks of source code are compiled
- What the #pragma directive is good for

22

Common Programming Errors

It is one thing to show a man that
he is in error, and another thing
to put him in possession of the truth.

—John Locke
"Essay Concerning Human Understanding" (1690)

In This Chapter

The C++ language is a difficult language to learn—harder than C, BASIC, and dBASE, but not as difficult as assembly language. Even the most experienced programmers in any language rarely create a completely bug-free program on the first try. It is a fairly accepted rule in the computer industry that there is about one bug for every 20 lines of code. This rule usually applies to all computer languages. In January, 1990, the AT&T

telephone network failed because of a bug in a newly delivered C program for an AT&T network switching computer. Telephone service was shut down for hours.

All complex programs usually have bugs. In this chapter, you examine some of the common pitfalls of C and C++ programming. The chapter describes errors that can occur with the following:

- Arrays
- Braces
- Comments
- Functions
- `if-else` statements
- Macros
- Operators and operator precedence
- Pointers
- Semicolons
- Strings
- Switches

C and C++ Pitfalls

Look carefully at the various kinds of commonly made errors listed in Table 22.1. Each of these pitfalls is explained in detail in this chapter.

Table 22.1. Common C and C++ pitfalls.

Category	*Pitfall*
Arrays	Misuse of array indexing
Arrays	Misuse of multidimensional arrays
Arrays	Walking off the end of an array

Category	*Pitfall*
Braces	Unbalanced braces
Comments	Mistakenly nesting comments
Comments	Unbalanced C language comment delimiters (`/*` and `*/`)
Functions	Failure to include the header file for a run-time function
Functions	Failure to check the return value
Functions	Passing an argument *by reference* when passing *by value* is required
`if-else`	Mismatched `if-else` statements
Macros	Mistakenly placing spaces between the macro name and the left parenthesis in a function-like macro
Macros	Omitting parentheses from macro arguments
Macros	Tripping over side effects of macro arguments
Operators	Misuse of increment operator (`++`) and decrement operator (`--`)
Operators	Using an assignment operator (`=`) rather than an equality relational operator (`==`)
Precedence	Failure to consider operator precedence
Pointers	Declaring a pointer with the wrong type
Pointers	Failure to initialize a pointer
Pointers	Forgetting to use the address-of operator (`&`) for pointer assignment
Semicolons	Failure to terminate a statement with a semicolon
Semicolons	Mistakenly inserting a semicolon between the `for` or `while` statement condition and the statement block
Semicolons	Mistakenly inserting a semicolon after a preprocessor directive
Strings	Failure to allocate memory for a string

continues

Table 22.1. continued

Category	*Pitfall*
Strings	Mistakenly using single quotation marks to enclose strings or using double quotation marks to enclose `char` constants
Strings	Omitting the null character as the string terminator
`switch`	Failure to include a `break` statement within a `switch` statement

Array Errors

If you are accustomed to using arrays in other languages, such as BASIC, PASCAL, or dBASE, you might make mistakes because C++'s array syntax differs from that of other languages. Although you have learned the array syntax in C++, you can easily make a mistake when specifying or using arrays. This discussion covers the most common array errors.

Misuse of Array Indexing

Most languages begin indexing arrays from 1. C++, however, begins indexing arrays from 0. The index for the last array element, therefore, is one less than the number of elements. Here is a common mistake that some programmers make:

```
#define MAXELEM (3)
int i, ary[MAXELEM];
for ( i = 1; i <= MAXELEM; i++ )    // Wrong!
     ary[i] = 7;
```

In this example, the `for` loop initializes the array elements beginning at the second `ary` element and ending with the fourth array element. Not only does the first element not get initialized as intended, but memory beyond the limits of the array memory is erroneously overwritten. This error can be difficult to detect. The corrected code is

```
#define MAXELEM (3)
int i, ary[MAXELEM];
for ( i = 0; i < MAXELEM; i++ )      // Correct
     ary[i] = 7;
```

Misuse of Multidimensional Arrays

Programmers familiar with other languages tend to specify incorrectly the multiple dimensions inside a pair of brackets. Note an example:

```
int ary[2,3];          // Wrong!
```


This dimensioning causes an error that is detected by the Microsoft C/C++ compiler. However, for some compilers, this is a perfectly valid statement. The correct form for declaring a multidimensional array is

```
int ary[2][3];         // Correct
```

Walking Off the End of an Array

The C++ language does not prevent you from making array subscript range errors. In the example

```
char ary[4];
ary[99] = 3;           // Wrong!
```

the second statement overwrites data outside the array. C++ makes no attempt to detect this error, so the programmer must be certain that this does not happen.

Errors with Braces

Misplaced or missing braces are a common programming mistake. Programmers sometimes forget to enclose a multiple statement block in braces for an `if` or `while` statement. Because a pair of braces is omitted in the following example, the program loops until the computer is rebooted:

```
int     i = 5, x[6];
while (i > 0)                  // Wrong!
     x[i] = cfunc();
     i--;
```

Here the index `i` does not get decremented. The corrected code is

```
int     i = 5, x[6];
while (i > 0)                  // Correct
{
     x[i] = cfunc();
     i--;
}
```

In this example, the problem is immediately revealed as soon as you enter the loop. Similar missing braces in more complex programs, however, can cause mysterious problems and be difficult to trace.

Programmers often forget to enter the closing brace in a pair of braces. Although the compiler detects this mistake, it is sometimes hard to determine which brace is missing in a complex program. This is an excellent justification for following the programming style guideline #9 presented in the section "Programming Style" in Chapter 2. The brace alignment and statement indentation rule facilitates the hunt for a missing brace.

Comment Errors

Comments are essential to any program and an important component of good programming style. There are two common mistakes that programmers make in specifying C language comments (`/* comment */`): forgetting the closing delimiter and trying to nest comments. You can avoid such problems with antiquated C language comments by replacing them with C++ comments (`// comment`). All text from the double slashes (`//`) to the end of the line is considered part of the comment. C++ comments are also easier to type. A third common mistake can occur, though, when you convert C comments to C++ comments.

Unbalanced Comment Delimiters

One mistake that C programmers make is to forget to include the closing comment delimiter, `*/`. When you edit your source file, be sure to terminate a comment with `*/`.

Attempting to Nest Comments

You cannot nest comments in C. If you attempt to nest a comment, you will get some mysterious compiler error messages. This bug usually occurs when you try to comment out a section of code and forget to consider any comments that might be within that block of code. The phrase *comment out* is used by programmers to indicate that a section of code is enclosed by comment delimiters so that the section is invisible to the compiler. The following is an example of nested comments:

```
/* This is a comment.
    /* This is a nested comment. */
*/
```

Converting from C Comments to C++ Comments

When you convert from C comments to C++ comments, do not forget that C comments can extend over multiple lines. It is not sufficient to replace `/*` with `//` everywhere in the program and then remove all instances of `*/`. In the following example, when you convert the C comment, you must change

```
/* This is a C comment. It
   can extend over several
   lines. */
```

to

```
// This is a C++ comment. C ++ comments
// can extend over several
// lines.
```

Function Errors

Although the C++ language is a compact language with less than 70 keywords, the Microsoft C/C++ run-time library and class libraries have over 600 functions. To avoid errors, you can use the PWB online Help system to check syntax, obtain descriptive information, and find examples of the use of a function. Errors relating to the misuse of functions are not uncommon, however.

Failure to Include the Header File for a Run-Time Function

One of the most common mistakes in using library functions and classes is to forget to include a function's associated header file. Header files must be included because they contain prototypes for functions and constant definitions. If you do not know which header file is required for a run-time function, while you are in the PWB editor, highlight the function or language element name and press F1. The online help will display the syntax of the function as well as its associated header file(s).

The following example shows what can go wrong when you do not supply the header file:

```
#include <iostream.h>
void main()
{
     double x;
     x = pow( (double) 3.0L, (double) 3.0L);  // Compute 3 cubed
     cout << "x = " <<  x << "\n";
}
```

The `pow()` run-time function returns a `double` data type value. If you compile this program, the system gives you an error about a missing prototype. The message informs you that it will return an `int` value. The C++ language is much more restrictive than C. C++ will not allow you to execute this program because there is no prototype for the `pow()` function. To obtain the correct answer, you must include the math.h header file, which contains the prototype for `pow()`.

Failure to Check the Return Value

One error often made by inexperienced programmers is to ignore return values. Many of the class and run-time library functions return a value that must be tested before you proceed. For example, you must test the object created by the `iostream` class when a file is opened so that you can see whether the object is valid before you use it. Consider this example:

```
ifstream ifile( "TEST.TXT" );
if ( !ifile )
{
     cout << "File cannot be opened";
     exit( 1 );
}
```


If the object is `NULL`, you cannot continue because you cannot use that object for file I/O operations. You must perform some type of error recovery.

Another important example is the `new` operator. The pointer returned by the `new` operator must always be tested. Look at this example:

```
char *ptr;
if ( (ptr = new char [ 30000 ] ) == NULL )
{
     cout << "Insufficient memory";
     exit( 1 );
}
```

If there is not enough memory to allocate a buffer, the `new` operator returns a `NULL` pointer. Programs written by professional programmers have crashed when they ran out of memory because the programmers failed to check the return value.

Passing an Argument by Value Instead of by Reference

Some programmers mistakenly pass a variable *by value* instead of *by reference* (the address of the variable). This error is commonly made with the scanf() function. Here is a sample program that does not work correctly:

```
#include <stdio.h>
#include <iostream.h>
void main()
{
     int     i_val, status = 1;
     while ( status == 1 )
     {
          cout << "Enter a number between 1 and 10";
          status = scanf( "%d", i_val );  // Wrong!
          cout << "\nYou entered number "  << i_val;
     }
}
```

The variable i_val is passed by value, but the scanf() function expects the argument to be passed by reference. The scanf() function call statement should be

```
status = scanf( "%d", &i_val );  // Correct
```

When you need to pass a variable by reference, you can use the address-of operator (&), as illustrated in the preceding statement, or you can use a pointer to the variable. The C++ compiler does not catch this bug, so you have to track it down.

Errors with if-else Statements

One common mistake that programmers make in coding a nested if statement is to associate an else statement with the wrong if statement. The else statement is associated with the closest if statement that does not have an else. Here is an example of a nested if-else statement that yields erroneous results:

```
#include <iostream.h>
#include "animal.h"
void animal( int animal, int type )
{
    if ( animal == DOG )
```

```
          if ( type == POODLE )
               groom();
     else
          cout << "Animal is not a dog.";
}
```

This indentation is used only to make the output easier to read. Unfortunately, the indentation is misleading because the `else` statement appears to be associated with the first `if` statement. But the `else` is actually associated with the nearest `if` statement, which is the second `if` statement. Obviously, the programmer intended to have the print statement associated with the first `if` statement. This problem can be corrected with braces:


```
#include <iostream.h>
#include "animal.h"
animal( int animal, int type )
{
     if ( animal == DOG )
     {
          if ( type == POODLE )
               groom();
     }
     else
          cout << "Animal is not a dog.";
}
```

Now the function works correctly. Here is the rule: If you have an `else` statement in a nested `if-else` construct, you must enclose the statement block within braces.

Macro Errors

Preprocessor macros are an extremely useful part of the C++ language. Preprocessor directive syntax differs from C++ language syntax. This can lead to a category of pitfalls that causes unexpected problems.

Invalid Specification of Function-like Macros

When you are specifying a function-like macro with a `#define` directive, be careful not to put a space between the macro name and the argument. In the example

```
#define ADD (a,b) ( a + b )          // Wrong!
int addit( int i, int j )
{
     return ADD(i,j);
}
```

the preprocessor treats the macro `ADD` as a simple macro and equates the macro name to `(a,b) (a + b)`, expanding it to

```
return (a,b) (a + b) ( i + j );
```

When this macro is compiled, it generates several syntax errors. The problem is not always easy to interpret because you never see the expanded statement. You will get a syntax error message similar to `'a': undefined`, which should be a clue to assist you in tracking down the problem.

The best remedy to this problem is prevention. *Never* place a space between the macro and the argument.

Omitting Parentheses from Macro Arguments

Neglecting to enclose macro arguments in parentheses is a mistake of inexperienced programmers. The oversight can cause mysterious and unexpected results. Here is a simple example:

```
// MACRO3.CPP - Illustrates problems caused by not enclosing
// macro body in parentheses
#include <iostream.h>
#define DIVIDE2(a) a/2
void main()
{
     int answer;
     answer = DIVIDE2( 6 + 4 );
     cout << "The answer is: " << answer << "\n";
     answer = DIVIDE2( 4 + 6 );
```

```
    cout << "The answer is: " << answer << "\n";
}
```

The output from this program is

```
The answer is: 8
The answer is: 7
```

This output is not what you would expect and probably not what you intended. The intended answer for both cases is 5. Because parentheses were omitted from the argument, the macro for both cases is expanded to

```
answer = 6 + 4/2;
answer = 4 + 6/2;
```


Because the division operator has a higher precedence than the addition operator, the division is performed before the addition. This is why you should always enclose the macro argument in parentheses. The correct form is

```
#define DIVIDE2(a) ( a/2 )
```

Some programmers recommend that all macro definition arguments be enclosed in parentheses, even simple constant macros.

Tripping Over Side Effects of Macro Arguments

You must be careful when you specify arguments for a function-like macro because you can encounter undesirable side effects. For example, consider the `toupper()` macro defined in the ctype.h header file:

```
#define toupper(c) ( (islower(c)) ? _toupper(c) : c)
#define _toupper(c) ((c) -'A'+'a' )
```

If you use a function that returns a character as an argument to `toupper()`, the function is called twice, as shown in the following example:

```
#include <stdlib.h>
#include <ctype.h>
char fetchc();
main()
{
:
c = toupper( fetchc() );
:
}
```

The preprocessor expands the macro to

```
c =  ( (( fetchc() & 2) )  ? (( fetchc() ) -'A'+'a' ) : c );
```

Notice that `fetchc()` is called twice, which will probably cause a problem. This side effect is a disadvantage of using function-like macros. You can avoid any side effects in this example by using a variable as the argument instead of using a function call, as in

```
#include <stdlib.h>
#include <ctype.h>
char fetchc( void );
main()
{
:
c = fetchc();
c = toupper( c );
:
}
```

Operator Errors

This section describes pitfalls associated with the use of operators and operator precedence. These errors are sometimes difficult to detect because the compiler never catches them. However, if you are aware of the possibility of making such errors, you will probably not make as many.

Misuse of the Increment Operator (++) and the Decrement Operator (--)

Both the increment operator (++) and the decrement operator (--) can cause undesirable side effects if not used correctly. For example, there is no way to predict how the statement

```
int answer, value = 4;
answer = value * value++;
```

will be processed. Either 16 or 20 can be assigned to the answer variable. The value is unpredictable because the C++ language does not specify which operand is processed first. The best approach is to avoid this type of ambiguity by incrementing value either before or after answer is assigned.

Using the Wrong Operator

Another common error is to type the assignment operator (=) rather than the equality relational operator (==). This mistake usually occurs in a decision-making statement. In the example

```
int test = 3;
:
if ( test = 999 )    // Oops, should have used ==
     test999();
```

the statement is obviously supposed to call the function test999 if the variable test equals 999. Unfortunately, = was typed rather than ==, and the variable test was assigned a value of 999. Here is the correct form:

```
int     test = 3;
:
if ( test == 999 ) // Corrected statement
     test999();
```

Failure to Consider Operator Precedence

Programmers do not usually make operator precedence errors when they are using different operators in an arithmetic expression. Note the following example:

```
x = 3*4 + 9*8;
x = 9*( 33 + x);
```

Most experienced programmers know that a multiplication operator (*) has a higher precedence than an addition operator (+). One mistake that beginning programmers make, however, is to ignore precedence at other times. Look at this example:

```
#include <iostream.h>
int cfunc( void );
void main()
{
     int j;
     if ( j = cfunc() == 99 )   // Error
          cout << "cfunc returned" << j << "\n";
}
int cfunc (void)
{
     return 99;
}
```

Unfortunately, `j` is not set to the return value. The problem is that the relational equality operator (==) has a higher precedence than the assignment operator (=). Instead of setting `j` to 99, `j` is set to 1—the result of comparing the value returned by the function `cfunc()` to 99. To obtain the intended result, the statement in error must be corrected by adding parentheses:

```
if ( ( j = cfunc() ) == 99 )   // Correct
```

Always observe the C++ language precedence rules. Table 8.8 in Chapter 8, "Operators and Expressions," lists the precedence of operators.

Pointer Errors

Mistakes in using pointers can be catastrophic because a pointer can change the value of any addressable location. This section presents mistakes that programmers commonly make when using pointers.

Declaring a Pointer with the Wrong Type

The rule is that a pointer must be declared to have the same data type as the data to which it points. Suppose that you declare a pointer to an `int` and then assign the pointer the address of a `double`, as in this example:

```
// POINT3.CPP - Illustrates erroneous results obtained when you
// declare pointer with wrong data type
#include <stdio.h>
void main()
{
     int *ptr;
     float x = 999.0f;
     ptr = &x;
     cout << "*ptr = "
          << *ptr
          << "\n";
     cout << "   x = "
          << x
          << "\n";
```


The example compiles correctly on the C compiler. When you execute the program, you get the following output:

```
*ptr = 0.000000
   x = 999.000000
```

The program interpreted that `ptr` pointed to an `int`, so the value was converted from an `int` to a `float`. The value displayed is incorrect. This is one example of using a pointer to the wrong type—which affects every pointer operation.

Fortunately, the C compiler displays a warning message if you assign the address of one data type to a pointer with another data type.

Remember never to ignore warning messages.

The C++ language will not let you do this. It flags this statement as an error, and the following message is then displayed:

```
...: error C2446: '=' : no conversion
between 'int __near *' and 'float __float * '
```

The fact that C++ does not allow you to make this type of error is another advantage of using C++.

Failure to Initialize Pointer

Never use a pointer that has not been initialized. You don't know where an uninitialized pointer points, and it can wipe out any addressable memory.

The same is true when you uninitialize a pointer. For example, suppose that you allocate memory for a buffer with the `new` operator. After you finish using the memory, you use the `delete` operator to release the memory. At that time, the pointer is uninitialized and no longer points to a valid address. Consider an example:

```
#include <iostream.h>
#include <stdlib.h>
void main()
{
     char *ptr;
     if ( ( ptr = new char [ 2000 ] ) == NULL )
     {
          cout << "Out of memory\n";
          exit( 1 );
     }
     :
    delete ptr;
     :
     *ptr = 1;    // Error! Pointer has been uninitialized!
}
```

After allocated memory has been freed, the pointer is no longer valid. Using a pointer that has been uninitialized is a common error that can be difficult to track down.

Missing the Address-of Operator (&)

Beginning programmers often forget to use the address-of operator (&) when assigning a pointer, as in

```
int i, *ptr;
ptr = i;
```

The preceding statement is invalid because it attempts to store an `int` to a pointer to an `int`. The compiler detects this condition and displays an error message:

```
error C4047: "=" : different levels of indirections
```

This warning should never be ignored. To correct the condition, you must use the address-of operator (&):

```
int i, *ptr;
ptr = &i;
```

The C++ compiler will not let you make this mistake. It flags the statement as an error and displays the following error message:

```
...: error C2446: '=' : no conversion
        between 'int __near *' and 'int '
```


Semicolon Errors

Programmers seem to have trouble coping with the semicolon. This section presents common pitfalls you may encounter when using the semicolon.

Missing Semicolon at the End of a Statement

Programmers often forget to terminate a statement with a semicolon. In most cases, if you omit the semicolon at the end of a line, the compiler catches the error. The error message, however, can be misleading. The compiler treats the line following the one with the missing semicolon as part of the statement associated with the current line. As you gain more experience with the C++ language, you will learn to look for certain kinds of errors when you get a misleading error message. A missing semicolon is one of those errors.

Misplaced Semicolon

If you mistakenly place a semicolon between the `for` or `while` statement condition and the statement block, you will have a problem. This mistake is easy to overlook and sometimes hard to track down. In the example

```
int i, ary[10];
for ( i = 0; i < 10; i++ );        // Error! Misplaced semicolon!
     ary[i] = 1;
```

only `ary[10]` is assigned a value. This is bad because it exceeds the array dimension. The correction is easy after you identify the problem:

```
int i, ary[10];
for ( i = 0; i < 10; i++ )    // Correct
     ary[i] = 1;
```

Terminating a Preprocessor Directive with a Semicolon

Some programmers tend to terminate a macro definition with a semicolon. This mistake creates a bug in your code. Note an example:

```
#define BAD_MACRO 20;
int bug[ BAD_MACRO ];
J = BAD_MACRO + x;
```

You will get a compiler error on the second and third C++ language statements. The statements containing the macros are expanded to

```
int bug = [20;];
J = 20; + x;
```

Because both statements contain a semicolon within the statement, the compiler generates an error for both statements.

String Errors

This section describes several common bugs associated with strings. String errors are commonly made by inexperienced programmers.

Failure to Allocate Memory for a String

Programmers sometimes forget to allocate memory for a string. In the example

```
char *ptr;
strcpy( ptr, "This string will trash memory" );
```

the pointer is declared, but the programmer forgot to allocate memory. The `strcpy()` function copies a string (second argument) to another string (first argument). Unfortunately, the pointer is uninitialized, and unknown memory is overwritten. This error can have unpredictable results. There are two ways to correct it. The first is to allocate a buffer with the `new` operator. The second is to allocate an array rather than a pointer to a `char`, as in

```
char ary[80];
strcpy( ary, "This string will be moved to a valid array" );
```

Confusing Single and Double Quotation Marks

Beginning programmers often use the wrong delimiters for string and `char` constants. Double quotation marks must be used as string constant delimiters, and single quotation marks must be used as delimiters for `char` constants. Consider this example:

```
char answer;
char ch = 'A', bee = 'B', null_char = '\0';  // Correct
char *ptr = "This is a message"              // Correct
char msg[] = "This is a message too."        // Correct
:
if ( answer == "N" )     // Wrong! Should use single
                         // quotation marks!
     cout << "No way\n";
```

The if statement condition incorrectly compares the character string N to a char variable. The test will not work as intended. The statement should be coded as

```
if ( answer == 'N' )     // Correct
     cout << "No way\n";
```

Now the if statement condition correctly compares a char variable to the char constant N.

Be careful to use the correct delimiters when you specify a string or char constant.

Underestimating the Actual Length of a String

The amount of space required to hold a string is the number of characters *plus* the null terminator character. Sometimes programmers forget about the null character when they are reserving space for a string. Note the following example:

```
#include <iostream.h>
#include <string.h>
:
void main()
{
     char *ptr;
     char animal[] = { "Kangaroo" };
     char ary[8];
     int     length;
     length = strlen( animal );  // Return 8
     if ( ( ptr = new char [length] ) == NULL )
     {
          cout << "Out of memory\n";
          exit( 1 );
     }
     strcpy( ptr, animal );    // Error! Too few characters!
     strcpy( ary, animal );    // Error! Too few characters!
}
```

The variable animal is nine bytes long (eight bytes for kangaroo plus the null terminator byte). The strlen() function returns 8, which is the length of the string—not including the null byte. The array ary is dimensioned to eight bytes, and the buffer pointed to by `ptr` is eight bytes. The `strcpy()` function copies the variable `animal` to `ary` and `ptr`. The first `strcpy()` function call overwrites one byte of memory that does not belong in the allocated buffer. The second `strcpy()` overwrites one byte outside the dimension of the array. In both instances, this is a serious error that must be corrected because the outcome is unpredictable. Here is the corrected code:

```
#include <stdio.h>
#include <string.h>
:
void main()
{
     char *ptr;
     char animal[] = { "Kangaroo" };
     char ary[9];           // Correct
     int     length;
     length = strlen( animal );  // Return 8
     if ( ( ptr = new char [length + 1 ] ) == NULL )
     {
          cout << "Out of memory\n";
          exit( 1 );
     }
     strcpy( ptr, animal );   // Works fine
     strcpy( ary, animal );   // Works fine
}
```

22

Switch Errors

Programmers sometimes forget to place a required `break` statement within a `switch` statement. Consider the following `switch` statement:

```
switch ( flag )
{
     case 1:
          cout << "The flag equals 1\n";
          break;
     case 2:
          cout << "The flag equals 2\n";
```

```
        case 3:
             cout << "The flag equals 3\n";
             break;
        default:
             cout << "The flag equals something else 1\n";
             break;
}
```

A `break` statement should have been placed after the `cout` statement following the second `case` label. After the `cout` statement is displayed, the program will execute the statement block associated with the third `case` label. This is a perfectly legal operation, but if you don't want the statements associated with the third `case` statement to be executed, you must include a `break` statement before the third `case` label.

What You Have Learned

In this chapter, you learned some common pitfalls that programmers trip over while developing C++ language programs. This discussion of C++ programming problems should help you do the following:

- Recognize potential pitfalls when you encounter them
- Correct errors when you make them
- Avoid potential pitfalls as you are programming

Debugging

The most powerful cause of error is the war existing between the senses and reason.

—Blaise Pascal
Pensées (1670)

In This Chapter

This chapter presents a discussion of debugging methodology and shows you how to debug programs. The Microsoft C/C++ 7 package contains a powerful CodeView debugger. In this chapter, the following topics are covered:

- Types of debugging errors
- Debugging during design
- Using the Microsoft C/C++ 7 CodeView debugger

Debugging

As indicated in Chapter 22, "Common Programming Errors," it is rare for a computer program to work the first time it is run. The program is likely to contain errors, and the more complex it is, the more bugs it will contain. The errors must be detected, isolated, and corrected. This process is known as *debugging*. Correcting an error is usually the easiest step. Debugging is a skill you develop as you gain more experience. You isolate a bug, correct it, recompile the program, and test it. You repeat this process until a correctly working program emerges.

There are four types of errors: *syntax*, *logic*, *regression*, and *dormant*. These are discussed in the following sections.

Syntax Errors

Syntax errors are the easiest ones to fix because they are detected and isolated by the compiler. Many of the errors discussed in Chapter 22 are syntax errors. The PWB compiler interface makes it easy to correct these errors because they are displayed in the Build Results window. You can use the Next Error (Shift+F3) or Previous Error (Shift+F4) commands on the Project menu to highlight the line containing an error or warning message in the source file. You must correct all the errors before the program will compile correctly. Be sure to correct all warnings before you proceed. Then recompile the program.

Logic Errors

Logic errors, or logic bugs, are harder to isolate because they are not detected by the compiler. The program can compile with no syntax errors or warnings and still yield the wrong results. Don't panic. It is the responsibility of a tester to detect that a bug exists and to report it to the programmer. Then the programmer must find the origin of the bug, isolate it, and correct it. Isolating the problem is usually the most difficult phase of debugging a logic error; however, the correction is easy. The Microsoft C/C++ 7 CodeView debugger can help you with this phase.

Regression Errors

Regression errors are ones you accidentally create in an attempt to correct a logic error. Whenever you correct an error, you must thoroughly test the correction to make sure that it fixes the bug you are correcting and does not result in another error. Regression errors are common, but they are easy to isolate and correct. One law of debugging is that a bug is probably caused by the last code you touched.

Dormant Errors

The most embarrassing errors are *dormant errors*—the ones that stay hidden in the back halls of your program and don't reveal themselves until after you deliver the program to your customers. These bugs are harder to detect, but they are easy to isolate and correct. Customers use *real-world data* in their daily work environments, whereas internal testing organizations usually use contrived data. Many software development companies send out *beta test* versions of a program to a sampling of customers so that the program can be tested with real-world data.

Debugging during Design

Software reliability is built into a program. You can design your program so that it is easier to test, debug, and maintain. Even when you encapsulate methods in a class, the tasks performed by class methods can be divided into subtasks. The logical steps for performing a subtask can be incorporated into a function. It is important that you encapsulate subsets of logic into a function. When you define functional modules, you can design each function so that its variables and data are local. This helps reduce the side effects that result from the interaction of variables in other parts of the program. You can control variable interaction by using passed arguments to communicate between functions. You can reduce the number of arguments by passing a structure of data items.

One of the major advantages of modular design is that your program is easier to debug. The reason is that you can isolate and correct a bug more easily if the interaction between program variables is minimized.

Often programmers write *scaffolding* programs (or software drivers) to test the logic paths of an individual function before it is incorporated into the rest of the program. The scaffolding software is not part of the program and is either discarded or retained for maintenance. Software debugging is simpler if you can debug each function separately.

The best recommendation is that you design your program to be modular. Each module can be coded and tested separately from the rest of the program. Then, if you detect an error, you can easily isolate and correct the error because you will have fewer lines of code to inspect.

The Microsoft C/C++ 7 CodeView Debugger

It is now time to learn to use the Microsoft C/C++ 7 CodeView debugger. You create an application, fix some syntax errors, and use the CodeView debugger to locate a logic error.

The Word Count Program (WC.CPP)

To help you learn debugging, this section shows how to create an application and then debug it. The program, called WC.CPP, counts words, characters, and lines in a text file. WC.CPP contains a single class: `WordCount`. The class contains data members that hold the results, its constructor, and a friend function, which overlays the insertion operator (<<) to display `WordCount` type objects. WC.CPP requests that the user type the name of a file, declares a `WordCount` object, and passes it the filename as an argument. When you declare a `WordCount` object, the constructor performs the following actions:

1. Opens the file in text mode
2. Reads a character
3. If the character is a linefeed, increments the line count

4. If the last character was not whitespace and the current character is whitespace, increments the word counter
5. If the character is not whitespace, increments the character counter
6. Increments the byte counter
7. Repeats steps 2 through 6 unless you reached the end of the file
8. Returns execution control

The bottom line is that a `WordCount` object contains the statistics for a text file. Once you have declared a `WordCount` object, you can print the results by using the insertion operator, as in this example:

```
WordCount wc( "Emerald.doc" );
cout << wc;
```

You first code the program and then compile it. Listings 23.1 through 23.3 present the program, with some bugs added for instructive purposes.

Listing 23.1. A sample program with bugs—the wc.h header file.

```
// wc.h - Definition of WordCount class
class WordCount
{
public:
     unsigned long bytecount;    // Number of bytes
     unsigned long charcount;    // Number of characters
     unsigned long linecount;    // Number of lines
     unsigned long wordcount;    // Number of words

     WordCount( char * filename );
friend ostream & operator << ( ostream &os, WordCount &wc );
};
```

Listing 23.2. A sample program with bugs—the WC.CPP source file.

```
// WC.CPP - Member functions for WordCount class
#include <stdlib.h>
#include <iostream.h>
#include <fstream.h>
```

continues

Listing 23.2. continued

```
#include <io.h>         // ios: manipulators
#include <ctype.h>
#include "wc.h"
//////////////////// WordCount constructor ///////////////////
WordCount::WordCount( char * filename )
{
     unsigned int lastch;
     char ch;
     bytecount = 0;   // Number of bytes
     charcount = 0;   // Number of characters
     linecount = 0;   // Number of lines
     wordcount = 0;   // Number of words
     ifstream fin( filename, ios::nocreate );
     if ( !fin )
     {
          cout << "Input file open error\n";
          return;
     }

     while (  fin.good() )
     {
          fin.get( ch );
          if ( ch = '\n' )      // Error
               linecount++      // Error
          if ( bytecount == 0 && !isgraph( ch ) )
               lastch = ch;
          if ( !isspace( lastch ) && !iscntrl( lastch ) &&
                ( isspace( ch ) ¦¦ iscntrl( ch ) ) ) ) ) // Error
                tordcount++;   // Error
          if ( !isspace(ch) && !iscntrl(ch) )
               charcount++;
          bytecount++;
          lastch = ch;
     }

     if ( linecount == 0 )
               linecount++;
}
////////////////// Overload the insertion operator //////////
ostream & operator << ( ostream &os, WordCount &wc )
{
```

```
    if ( wc.bytecount == 0 )
        os << "Nothing to count!\n";
    else
        os << "Word Count Output\n"
           << "Word count: " << wc.wordcount << "\n"
           << "Line count: " << wc.linecount << "\n"
           << "Characters: " << wc.charcount << "\n"
           << "Characters: (Including whitespace) "
           <<     wc.bytecount << "\n";
    return os;
}
```

The sample program WC-USER, as presented in Listing 23.3, illustrates the use of the `WordCount` class. The WC-USER program inputs a filename and declares a `WordCount` object, `WC`. The `WC` object is then output.

Listing 23.3. A sample program that uses the `WordCount` class.

```
// WC-USER.CPP - Illustrates use of WordCount class
#include <iostream.h>
#include "wc.h"
void main()
{
    char filename[40];
    cout << "\nEnter a filename: ";
    cin >> filename;
    WordCount WC( filename ); // Declare WordCount object
    cout << WC;               // Display WordCount object
}
```

Now you need to build a new project file. Name it WC.MAC and add the files WC.CPP and WC-USER.CPP to the project.

Finding and Fixing Syntax Errors

Choose Rebuild **A**ll command from the **P**roject menu to compile the program. If there are no errors, the program will link and run. The compiler, however, detects three errors.

Now you can use one of the nice PWB features. Select the Next Error command from the Project menu (or press Shift+F3). The PWB editor positions the cursor near the line containing the error. In Figure 23.1, the line following the line containing the first error is highlighted. The following explanation of the error is displayed on the message line:

```
error C2143: syntax error : missing ';' before identifier 'if'
```

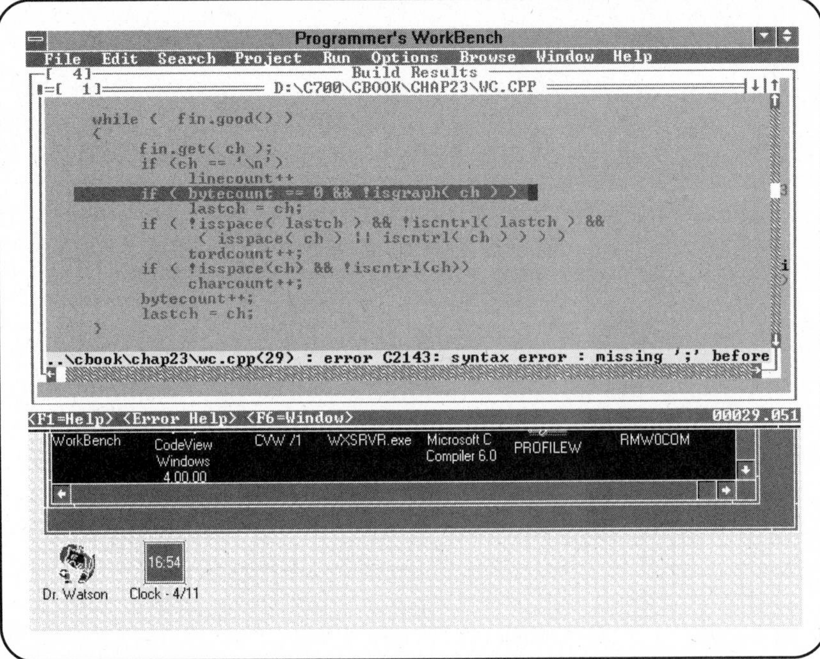

Figure 23.1. The first compiler error in WC.CPP.

The error message might be too long to fit in the message line. You can select the Build Results window and scroll the message to the left to see the rest of it.

As you may have guessed, the line before the highlighted line is not terminated with a semicolon (a common error). You can easily correct the error. The corrected statement is

```
linecount++;    // Correct
```

Press Shift+F3 again to select the next error. The cursor is placed on the line following the line containing the second error (see Figure 23.2). This time, the error message displayed on the message line reveals that there is a missing parenthesis on the line in question. If you count the pairs of parentheses, you can see that there is an extra right parenthesis (the one farthest to the right). Remove the extra parenthesis so that the line looks like this:

```
( isspace( ch ) || iscntrl( ch ) ) )  // Correct
```

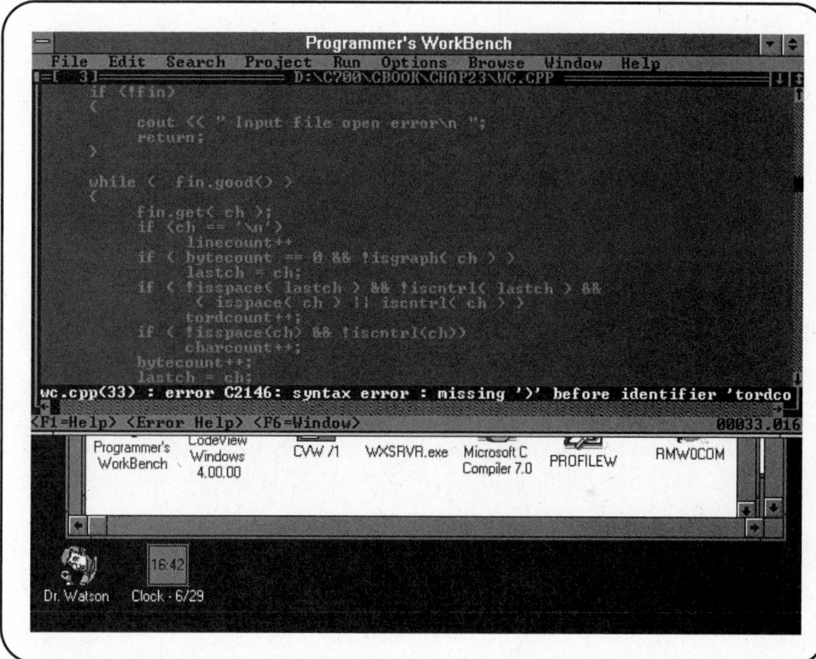

Figure 23.2. The second compiler error in WC.CPP.

If you press Shift+F3 again (or select Next Error from the **Project** menu), you can see that the third error is just an error indicating that the compiler detected errors. Now choose Rebuild **All** from the **Project** menu to try the compile and link operation again. This time, the Build Results dialog box indicates that there are two errors.

Press Shift+F3 one more time, and the line containing the third error is highlighted (see Figure 23.3). The message line indicates that the variable `tordcount` is undeclared. Actually, the variable name `wordcount` was misspelled, and you need to correct it. Change `tordcount` to `wordcount`.

Now that all the compile and link errors have been corrected, you can choose Rebuild **All** from the **Project** menu to try the compile and link operation again. The program compiles correctly, links, and runs. When you are prompted to enter the name of the file, type `WC.CPP` and press Enter. The program reads the file and displays the results. Unfortunately, the results are wrong (see Figure 23.4).

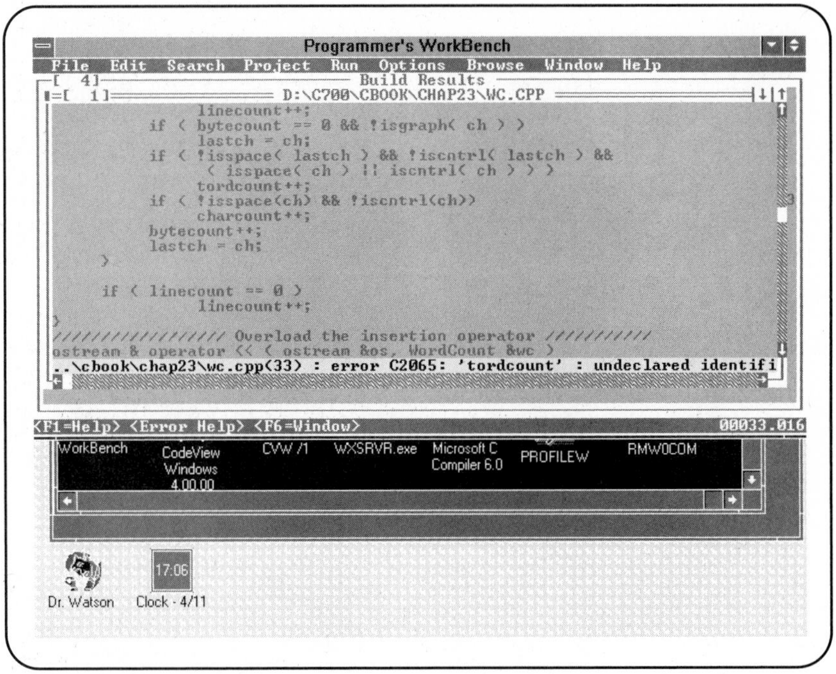

Figure 23.3. *The third compiler error in WC.CPP.*

Using CodeView to Find Logic Errors

Don't worry. You have the Microsoft C/C++ 7 CodeView debugger to help you find the logic bug that lurks somewhere in the program. From the **Run** menu, choose the **D**ebug: WC.exe command.

You are now ready to start a CodeView debugging session. First position the cursor on the following line:

```
WordCount WC( filename ); // Declare WordCount object
```

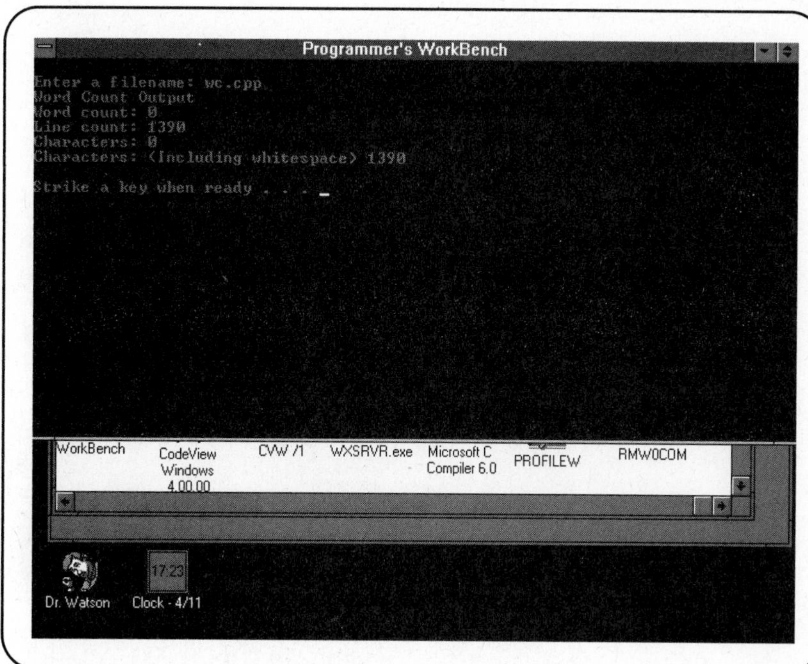

***Figure 23.4.** The results of executing WC.EXE.*

Now either double-click that line or choose the **S**et Breakpoint command from the **D**ata menu. In the dialog box that appears, set the Break at Location radio button. This means that the program will run until the line where the cursor resides is about to be executed, and the program will stop. Next choose the OK push button to set a breakpoint. A *breakpoint* is a point in the program at which the execution pauses and control returns to the debugger. Several types of breakpoints are available. The type used in this example is the one that allows you to designate the line on which program execution pauses. Whatever method you use, the line is displayed in high intensity, as shown in Figure 23.5. When the program is executed, it loads and runs until it reaches the breakpoint. Then the program stops and waits for you to enter another debugger command.

Now press F5 to execute the program. Again, you are prompted to enter the filename. Type `WC.CPP` as before. The program stops executing at the breakpoint. The message `Break at location breakpoint` appears on the message line, and the line to be executed is highlighted. (On my screen, red characters are displayed on a black background.)

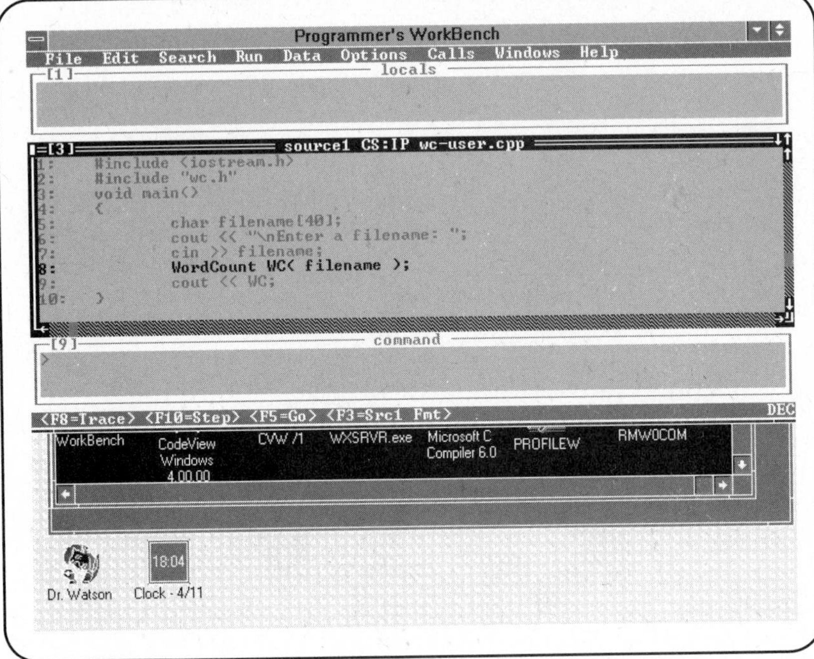

***Figure 23.5.** Setting a breakpoint in the WC.EXE program.*

You now can step through the program one line at a time until you discover what went wrong. Press F8 to single-step. The program executes the `WordCount` statement, and the WC.CPP source file is displayed with the line following the constructor header line highlighted (`WordCount::WordCount`). Single-step through the program (by pressing F8) until the `while` statement is highlighted.

You need to see what the value of the `ch` variable is. It appears in the Locals window. On my screen, the windows are configured so that the Locals window appears at the top of the screen. Scroll the Locals window so that the `ch` variable appears. On my screen, `ch` appears as `ch = 90 'Z'`. (Actually, 90 is just a garbage value because `ch` was declared but never initialized.) Figure 23.6 shows the CodeView screen with the Locals window displaying `ch` and the line containing the `while` statement selected (on my screen, white characters on a black background).

If the Locals window is not visible on your screen, rearrange the windows so that both the Locals window and the program appear on the screen. Press F8 to execute the next source lines of WC.CPP until the cursor is positioned on an `if` statement. Notice that `ch = 47 '\'`. Now press F8 again. Observe that `ch` just changed its value to `\n`, as shown in Figure 23.7.

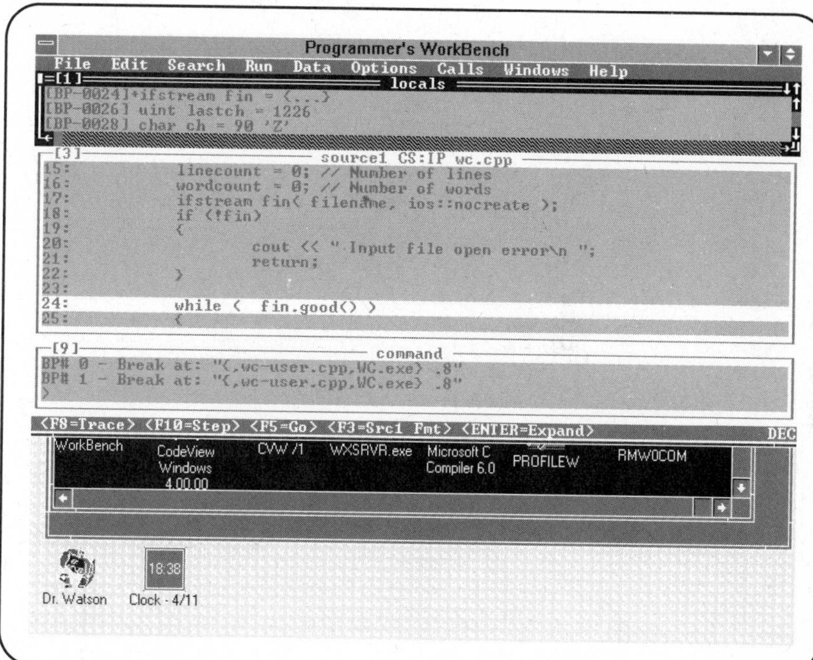

Figure 23.6. *The CodeView screen with the Locals window displayed as WC.EXE is executed.*

Now look at that `if` statement again:

```
if ( ch = '\n' )
```

It is obvious that an assignment operator was used rather than an equality operator (this is another common error). The corrected statement is

```
if ( ch == '\n' )
```

It is time to fix this bug. Exit from CodeView and return to the PWB. Correct the error and choose Rebuild **A**ll from the **P**roject menu. This time, you should get more reasonable results (see Listing 23.4). You need to do some additional testing, but it appears that you have a working program.

Incidentally, you opened this file in text mode, and an end-of-line transformation was performed. This means that all the carriage-return

characters were removed. If you had opened the file in binary mode, the value of `bytecount`, displayed in the last line of Listing 23.4, would be 56 characters larger because this file has 56 lines.

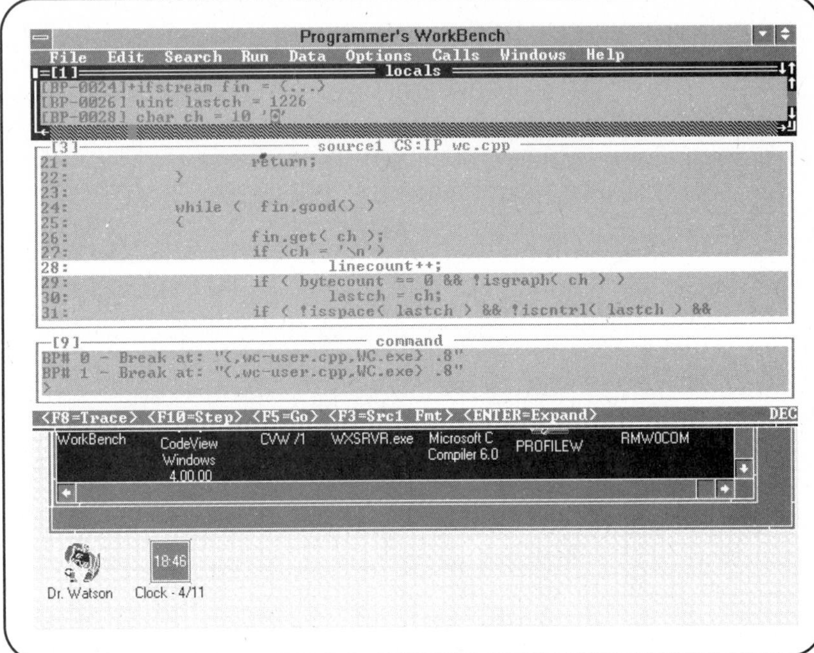

Figure 23.7. *Tracing through WC.EXE.*

Listing 23.4. The results of executing the debugged WC.EXE program.

```
Enter a filename: WC.CPP
Word Count Output
Word count: 218
Line count: 56
Characters: 1400
Characters: (Including whitespace) 1390
```

CodeView's Animation Feature

Now try the animation feature. Choose the **D**ebug: WC.exe command from the **R**un menu. When CodeView executes, choose **A**nimate from the **R**un menu. The debugger slowly executes your program while highlighting each line of code. You can terminate the animation operation by pressing the Esc key or clicking the mouse in the debugging window. Here are the steps for using the animation feature:

- Set a breakpoint as shown in Figure 23.5.
- Press F5. The program executes until it reaches the breakpoint.
- You can display variables and expressions in the Watch window. To add an expression to the Watch window, choose **A**dd Watch from the **D**ata menu, and the Add Watch dialog box appears. The variable name where the cursor is positioned appears in the **E**xpression text box. You can either select that variable or type another variable or expression in the **E**xpression text box. Then choose the OK push button. The expression and its corresponding value appear in the Watch window.
- Choose **A**nimate from the **R**un menu.

You can watch the numbers in the Watch window change as the program executes the `while` loop. As noted, you can stop the animation by pressing Esc or clicking the mouse anywhere on the screen. This feature is useful for isolating an obscure bug. You can also change the speed of the animation with the **T**race Speed command on the **O**ptions menu.

Incidentally, you have been running this program from either the PWB or the CodeView debugger. You can execute WC.CPP from MS-DOS with the following command:

```
D:\>WC
Enter a filename: WC.CPP
Word Count Output
Word count: 218
Line count: 56
Characters: 1400
Characters: (Including whitespace) 1390
```

23

Summary of the CodeView User Interface

CodeView is an extremely powerful debugger. Although it contains more power than most people ever need, many features are available. You can use any of the following methods to interface with CodeView in order to activate its features:

- Keyboard commands and shortcut keys
- CodeView menu system commands
- Commands entered through the Command window
- The mouse

The rest of this chapter summarizes the various features of the CodeView debugger and indicates the methods you use to activate them.

Keyboard Commands and Shortcut Keys

Table 23.1 summarizes the keyboard commands and shortcut keys used with CodeView.

Table 23.1. Keystrokes used with CodeView.

Keystroke(s)	*Use*
F1	Help
Shift+F1	Help table of contents
F2	Toggle the Register window open and closed
F3	Toggle among three source window display formats (**S**ource Window command on **O**ptions menu)
F4	Swap the CodeView screen with the program output screen
F5	Execute program, starting from current position
F6	Move to next window
F7	Execute code until control returns to function selected from the **C**alls menu, and then pause

Keystroke(s)	*Use*
F8	Step through (execute) one line of code
F9	Toggle breakpoint on and off at current line in code
F10	Step through code and skip over function calls
Up arrow	Move cursor up one line
Down arrow	Move cursor down one line
Left arrow	Move cursor left one character
Right arrow	Move cursor right one character
Ctrl+left arrow	Move cursor one word to the left
Ctrl+right arrow	Move cursor one word to the right
Home	Move cursor to beginning of current line
End	Move cursor to end of current line
Page Up	Move cursor up one screen
Page Down	Move cursor down one screen
Ctrl+Page Up	Move cursor left one screen
Ctrl+Page Down	Move cursor right one screen
Ctrl+Home	Move cursor to beginning of window
Ctrl+End	Move cursor to end of window
Shift+F6	Move to previous window
Ctrl+F5	Restore window (Windows menu command)
Ctrl+F7	Move window (Windows menu command)
Ctrl+F8	Size window (Windows menu command)
Ctrl+F9	Minimize window (Windows menu command)
Ctrl+F10	Maximize window (Windows menu command)
Ctrl+F4	Close window (Windows menu command)
Shift+F5	Tile windows (Windows menu command)
Ctrl+F6	Arrange windows

continues

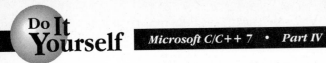

Table 23.1. continued

Keystroke(s)	*Use*
Alt+0	Open or select Help window
Alt+1	Open or select Locals window
Alt+2	Open or select Watch window
Alt+3	Open or select Source window 1
Alt+4	Open or select Source window 2
Alt+5	Open or select Memory window 1
Alt+6	Open or select Memory window 2
Alt+7	Open or select Register window
Alt+8	Open or select 8087 window
Alt+9	Open or select Command window
Alt+F4	Exit (**E**xit command on **F**ile menu)
Alt+F5	Arrange all open windows in an effective layout
Alt+Backspace	Undo last operation (**U**ndo command on **E**dit menu)
Ctrl+Ins	Copy selected text to clipboard (**C**opy command on **E**dit menu)
Shift+Ins	Paste clipboard at cursor location (**P**aste command on **E**dit menu)
Ctrl+\	Search for selected text (**S**earch menu)
Ctrl+/	Repeat last find command (**S**earch menu)
Ctrl+W	Open Add Watch dialog box (**D**ata menu)
Ctrl+U	Open Delete Watch dialog box (**D**ata menu)
Ctrl+Y	Delete expression containing the cursor in the Watch window
Shift+F9	Open Quick Watch dialog box (**D**ata menu)

The CodeView Menu System

This section provides a brief summary of the CodeView menu system. It contains the following menus:

File	Commands that open files and modules, print contents of current window, execute DOS, and exit from CodeView
Edit	Commands that cut, paste, and copy text
Search	Commands that search for patterns, labels, and functions
Run	Commands that execute programs and configure CodeView
Data	Commands that control watch expressions and breakpoints
Options	Commands that set CodeView options
Calls	A list of functions in the program call stack
Windows	Commands that manipulate CodeView windows
Help	Commands that provide help for CodeView

23

The File Menu

The **File** menu contains commands that open files and modules, print window contents, execute the DOS shell, and exit. Table 23.2 summarizes the **File** menu commands.

The Edit Menu

The **Edit** menu contains commands that undo edits, copy selected text to the clipboard, and paste the contents of the clipboard. Table 23.3 summarizes the **Edit** menu commands.

The Search Menu

The **Search** menu provides commands to find text in a source window or locate the definition of a label or function. Table 23.4 summarizes the **Search** menu commands.

The Run Menu

The **Run** menu contains commands that execute program debugging and configure CodeView options. Table 23.5 summarizes the **Run** menu commands.

Table 23.2. The File menu commands.

Command	*Use*
Open Source	Open a source file, an include file, or another text file. A file directory appears from which you choose the file to open.
Open Module	Open source file for a module in the program that is being debugged. A dialog box containing two file lists appears. The first list contains source modules for the program. The second list contains the names of the source files associated with a module. The source file consists of the module itself and included files.
Print	Print all or a portion of the active window.
DOS Shell	Leave CodeView temporarily to execute MS-DOS commands.
Exit	Exit from CodeView.

Table 23.3. The Edit menu commands.

Command	*Use*
Undo	Reverse the last editing change
Copy	Copy the currently selected text to the clipboard
Paste	Insert the clipboard contents at the cursor position

Table 23.4. The Search menu commands.

Command	*Use*
Find	Search for a pattern in the source file
Selected Text	Search for selected text in the source file
Repeat Last Find	Repeat the last text search
Label/Function	Search for a label or function in the program

Table 23.5. The Run menu commands.

Command	*Use*
Restart	Restart the program
Animate	Execute the program in slow motion
Load	Load a program or configure CodeView
Set Runtime Arguments	Set the program's run-time arguments

The Data Menu

The **D**ata menu contains commands that control Watch window operations and breakpoints. Table 23.6 summarizes the **D**ata menu commands.

Table 23.6. The Data menu commands.

Command	*Use*
Add Watch	Add an expression to the Watch window
Delete Watch	Delete an expression from the Watch window
Set Breakpoint	Set a breakpoint in the program
Edit Breakpoints	Modify or remove existing breakpoints
Quick Watch	Display a quick view of an expression

The Options Menu

The Options menu contains commands for configuring the CodeView display and customizing the behavior of CodeView. Table 23.7 summarizes the **O**ptions menu commands.

The Calls Menu

The **C**alls menu shows what functions have been called by your program while it is executing during a debugging session. The list of functions that is displayed in this menu changes to reflect the current status of the stack. You can choose one of the functions displayed in the menu and press the F7 key. The program then executes code until it returns to the selected program. When that happens, the program stops executing and waits for another CodeView command.

Table 23.7. The Options menu commands.

Command	*Use*
Source Window	Set Source window display options
Memory Window	Set Memory window display options
Locals Options	Set Locals window display options
Trace Speed	Set animation speed
Language	Set an expression evaluator
Horizontal Scrollbars	Toggle horizontal scroll bars on windows
Vertical Scrollbars	Toggle vertical scroll bars on windows
Status Bar	Toggle display of the status bar
Colors	Set screen colors
Screen Swap	Toggle screen exchange
Case Sensitivity	Toggle case sensitivity of symbols
32-Bit Registers	Toggle display of 32-bit registers
Native	Toggle display of p-code or machine code

The Windows Menu

The Windows menu contains commands for controlling CodeView windows configuration. Table 23.8 summarizes the Windows menu commands.

Table 23.8. The Windows menu commands.

Command	*Use*
Restore	Restore to full size a window that has been minimized
Move	Initiate process that enables you to use the keyboard to move the current window
Size	Initiate process that enables you to use the keyboard to change the size of the current window
Minimize	Shrink window to an icon

Command	Use
Maximize	Enlarge window to full screen
Close	Close the active window
Tile	Arrange windows to cover screen
Arrange	Arrange windows in an effective debugging layout
Help (Alt+0)	Open or select Help window
Locals (Alt+1)	Open or select Locals window
Watch (Alt+2)	Open or select Watch window
Source 1 (Alt+3)	Open or select Source window 1
Source 2 (Alt+4)	Open or select Source window 2
Memory 1 (Alt+5)	Open or select Memory window 1
Memory 2 (Alt+6)	Open or select Memory window 2
Register (Alt+7)	Open or select Register window
8087 (Alt+8)	Open or select 8087 window
Command (Alt+9)	Open or select Command window
View Output	Swap the CodeView and program screens

The Help Menu

Table 23.9 summarizes the commands you use to access the Help system.

Table 23.9. The Help menu commands.

Command	What Is Displayed
Index	Table of Microsoft Advisor indexes
Contents	Microsoft Advisor contents screen
Topic	Help for current word
Help on Help	Help for Microsoft Advisor
About	CodeView copyright and version number

Command-Window Commands

CodeView provides various debugging commands that you can type in the Command window. Table 23.10 summarizes these commands. The first column shows the command name and, in parentheses, the character(s) you type on the syntax line. Notice a number of nonalphabetic commands at the end of the table.

Table 23.10. The Command-window commands.

Command	*Use*
8087 (7)	Display math coprocessor status
Add Watch (W?)	Add a watch expression
Animate (E)	Execute program in slow motion
Assemble (A)	Assemble instructions
Breakpoint Clear (BC)	Clear the current breakpoint
Breakpoint Disable (BD)	Temporarily disable breakpoint
Breakpoint Enable (BE)	Reenable a breakpoint that has been temporarily disabled
Breakpoint List (BL)	List the breakpoints
Breakpoint Set (BP)	Set a breakpoint
Comment (*)	Make a comment during script
Current Location (.)	Display current program location
Delay (:)	Delay during script
Delete Watch (WC)	Delete a watch expression
Display Expression (?)	Display an expression
Display Global Heap (WDG)	Display Windows global heap
Display Local Heap (WDL)	Display Windows local heap
Display Modules (WDM)	Display Windows modules
Examine Symbols (X)	Search program's symbol table
Global Handle (WGH)	Dereference global memory handle

Command	*Use*
Go (G)	Execute program
Help (H)	Get help
Kill Application (WKA)	Kill Windows application
List Watch (WL)	List watch expressions
Local Handle (WLH)	Dereference local memory handle
Memory Compare (MC)	Compare ranges of memory
Memory Dump (MD)	Dump contents of memory
Memory Enter (ME)	Enter values into memory
Memory Fill (MF)	Fill range of memory with a value
Memory Move (MM)	Move a block of memory from one location in memory to another
Memory Search (MS)	Search within a range of memory for a pattern
Options (O)	Set CodeView options
Pause (")	Pause until a particular keystroke is encountered in a script
Port Input (I)	Read from a hardware port
Port Output (O)	Write to hardware port
Program Step (P)	Step one line or instruction
Quick Watch (??)	Open the Quick Watch dialog box
Quit (Q)	Quit CodeView
Radix (N)	Set radix: hex=16, decimal=10, octal=8
Redirect Input (<)	Read input from a file or device
Redirect Output (>)	Write output to a file or device
Redirect Input/Output (=)	Input and output from device
Redraw (@)	Redraw CodeView screen
Register (R)	Display and modify registers

continues

Table 23.10. continued

Command	*Use*
Restart (L)	Restart program from the beginning
Screen Exchange (\)	View program's output screen
Search (/)	Search text for regular expression
Shell Escape (!)	Run MS-DOS shell or command
Stack Trace (K)	Display stack trace
Tab Set (#)	Set number of spaces per tab
Trace (T)	Trace one line or instruction
Trace Speed (T)	Set animation speed
Unassemble (U)	Disassemble instructions in memory
Use Language (USE)	Switch expression evaluator
View Memory (VM)	Open or set options for Memory window
View Source (VS)	Open or set options for Source window

What You Have Learned

In this chapter, you learned about methods of debugging, and you debugged a sample application. Specifically, you learned how to do the following:

- Identify four types of bugs (syntax errors, logic errors, regression errors, and dormant errors)
- Use the Microsoft C/C++ 7 CodeView debugger

ASCII Code Character Set

ASCII Value Dec	Hex	ASCII Character	ASCII Value Dec	Hex	ASCII Character
000	00	null	007	07	●
001	01	☺	008	08	◘
002	02	☻	009	09	○
003	03	♥	010	0A	■
004	04	♦	011	0B	♂
005	05	♣	012	0C	♀
006	06	♠	013	0D	♪

ASCII Value			ASCII Value		
Dec	Hex	ASCII Character	Dec	Hex	ASCII Character
014	0E	♪♪	048	30	0
015	0F	☼	049	31	1
016	10	►	050	32	2
017	11	◄	051	33	3
018	12	↕	052	34	4
019	13	!!	053	35	5
020	14	¶	054	36	6
021	15	§	055	37	7
022	16	–	056	38	8
023	17	↨	057	39	9
024	18	↑	058	3A	:
025	19	↓	059	3B	;
026	1A	→	060	3C	<
027	1B	←	061	3D	=
028	1C	FS	062	3E	>
029	1D	GS	063	3F	?
030	1E	RS	064	40	@
031	1F	US	065	41	A
032	20	SP	066	42	B
033	21	!	067	43	C
034	22	"	068	44	D
035	23	#	069	45	E
036	24	$	070	46	F
037	25	%	071	47	G
038	26	&	072	48	H
039	27	'	073	49	I
040	28	(	074	4A	J
041	29	)	075	4B	K
042	2A	*	076	4C	L
043	2B	+	077	4D	M
044	2C	,	078	4E	N
045	2D	-	079	4F	O
046	2E	.	080	50	P
047	2F	/	081	51	Q

ASCII Value Dec	Hex	ASCII Character	ASCII Value Dec	Hex	ASCII Character
082	52	R	116	74	t
083	53	S	117	75	u
084	54	T	118	76	v
085	55	U	119	77	w
086	56	V	120	78	x
087	57	W	121	79	y
088	58	X	122	7A	z
089	59	Y	123	7B	{
090	5A	Z	124	7C	¦
091	5B	[	125	7D	}
092	5C	\	126	7E	~
093	5D	]	127	7F	DEL
094	5E	^	128	80	Ç
095	5F	_	129	81	ü
096	60	`	130	82	é
097	61	a	131	83	â
098	62	b	132	84	ä
099	63	c	133	85	à
100	64	d	134	86	å
101	65	e	135	87	ç
102	66	f	136	88	ê
103	67	g	137	89	ë
104	68	h	138	8A	è
105	69	i	139	8B	ï
106	6A	j	140	8C	î
107	6B	k	141	8D	ì
108	6C	l	142	8E	Ä
109	6D	m	143	8F	Å
110	6E	n	144	90	É
111	6F	o	145	91	æ
112	70	p	146	92	Æ
113	71	q	147	93	ô
114	72	r	148	94	ö
115	73	s	149	95	ò

ASCII Value			*ASCII Value*		
Dec	*Hex*	*ASCII Character*	*Dec*	*Hex*	*ASCII Character*
150	96	û	183	B7	╖
151	97	ù	184	B8	╕
152	98	ÿ	185	B9	╣
153	99	Ö	186	BA	║
154	9A	Ü	187	BB	╗
155	9B	¢	188	BC	╝
156	9C	£	189	BD	╜
157	9D	¥	190	BE	╛
158	9E	Pt	191	BF	┐
159	9F	*f*	192	C0	└
160	A0	á	193	C1	┴
161	A1	í	194	C2	┬
162	A2	ó	195	C3	├
163	A3	ú	196	C4	─
164	A4	ñ	197	C5	┼
165	A5	Ñ	198	C6	╞
166	A6	ª	199	C7	╟
167	A7	º	200	C8	╚
168	A8	¿	201	C9	╔
169	A9	⌐	202	CA	╩
170	AA	¬	203	CB	╦
171	AB	½	204	CC	╠
172	AC	¼	205	CD	═
173	AD	¡	206	CE	╬
174	AE	«	207	CF	╧
175	AF	»	208	D0	╨
176	B0	░	209	D1	╤
177	B1	▒	210	D2	╥
178	B2	▓	211	D3	╙
179	B3	│	212	D4	╘
180	B4	┤	213	D5	╒
181	B5	╡	214	D6	╓
182	B6	╢	215	D7	╫

ASCII Value		*ASCII Character*
Dec	*Hex*	
216	D8	╪
217	D9	┘
218	DA	┌
219	DB	█
220	DC	▄
221	DD	▌
222	DE	▐
223	DF	▀
224	E0	α
225	E1	β
226	E2	Γ
227	E3	π
228	E4	Σ
229	E5	σ
230	E6	μ
231	E7	τ
232	E8	Φ
233	E9	θ
234	EA	Ω
235	EB	δ
236	EC	∞
237	ED	ø
238	EE	∈
239	EF	∩
240	F0	≡
241	F1	±
242	F2	≥
243	F3	≤
244	F4	⌠
245	F5	⌡
246	F6	÷
247	F7	≈
248	F8	°
249	F9	•
250	FA	·
251	FB	
252	FC	η
253	FD	^{2}
254	FE	■
255	FF	

Glossary

386 enhanced mode One of the three Windows 3 operating modes running on the 80386 and 80486 microprocessors with access to extended memory and support for non-Windows (DOS) applications. Standard and 386 enhanced modes run in protected mode.

8087 family of math coprocessors Coprocessors that perform high-speed floating and binary-coded decimal (BCD) calculations. This family refers to the 8087, 80287, and 80387 coprocessors. (80486 has a built-in math coprocessor.)

8087 window The CodeView window containing the floating-point math processors display. The 8087 window is empty until 8087 instructions are executed. 8087 math processor emulator registers are also displayed in the 8087 window.

abstract class A class that defines pure virtual functions.

abstraction A technique for hiding the details of a process to focus on the fundamental characteristics.

address A number that specifies a certain section of computer memory.

address range A range bounded by two addresses.

aggregate types Arrays, structures, and unions.

algorithm The organization of a collection of steps that solves a problem.

anonymous variable A variable used to correct a mismatch in type between a function call argument and a referenced parameter. When a function call argument does not match the corresponding type of the referenced parameter, the compiler creates an anonymous variable of the correct type and converts the value of the function call argument to the anonymous variable. The function parameter then references the value of the anonymous variable.

ANSI (American National Standards Institute) An organization responsible for developing voluntary technical national standards.

API (Application Programming Interface) A set of routines and functions providing an interface between an application and the operating system for such operations as file input and output, file management, and graphics output. The Microsoft Windows API is an example.

`argc` An integer designating the number of arguments to be passed to the program from the command line. The traditional name for the first argument of a standard C or C++ `main()` function.

argument A value that is passed to a function. Also called the *actual argument*.

`argv` An array of strings containing command-line arguments. The `argv` argument is passed to the `main()` function when a standard C or C++ language program is executed.

arithmetic conversion An operation that converts numeric values to another type, as in the conversion between integers and floating-point numbers.

arithmetic operator A symbol representing an operator that performs an arithmetic operation on numeric operands.

array A variable that consists of a collection of elements of the same type.

ASCII (American Standard Code for Information Interchange) A commonly accepted set of 255 character codes representing numbers, characters, and special symbols.

automatic variable A temporary variable declared inside a function or statement block and discarded when the function or block exits.

automatic data segment A segment of memory in which local or stack data is stored. See also *DGROUP*.

backslash codes C programming output-formatting codes used with the `printf()` function. Also called *formatting operators*.

base class The original class from which another class is derived.

base name The part of a filename specified before the filename extension.

basic data types The fundamental C and C++ language data types. These are `int`, `char`, `float`, `long`, and `double`.

binary A designation for two-state (on/off) logic. A binary number notational system uses ones and zeros to represent values.

binary file A file that contains values other than text characters. (A binary file is not a text file.) Examples are .EXE, .BMP, and .OBJ files.

binary format A method of disk storage in which data is stored directly from memory to disk without any translation. A numeric number is represented as a binary value in binary format instead of as a series of ASCII numbers.

binary mode A way to access files for which no translations are performed.

binary operator A symbol used to represent an operator that takes two operands.

binary resource file A .RES file output from the resource compiler. .RES files contain compiled data for Windows bitmaps, icons, dialog boxes, and cursor resources.

bit A binary digit or one-eighth of a byte. A bit has a value of either 0 or 1 and is the smallest unit that can be handled by a computer.

bit field A form of structure that permits manipulation of individual bits or groups of bits.

bit-mapped font A font in which each character is represented by an array of bits rather than a set of equations.

bitmap An array of bits representing pixels in a graphics image.

bitwise operator An operator that operates on integer operands one bit at a time. C and C++ language bitwise operators include `&` (AND), ¦ (OR), ^ (exclusive OR), ~ (ones complement), << (left-shift), and >> (right-shift).

block A sequence of statements, enclosed in curly braces, used in definitions and declarations. Also called a *statement block*. A block can refer also to a block of memory.

body The section of a program that contains statements and instructions.

Boolean Data represented as true/false or yes/no values.

breakpoint The designated address where program execution stops.

buffer The portion of computer memory reserved for current data being processed. For example, during input/output operations, this area of memory holds data temporarily.

byte An eight-bit unit for accessing addresses in memory. A byte is the unit of measure for memory and disk space size. One byte contains one ASCII character.

.C The filename extension for a C source file.

case label A constant expression followed by a colon and specified with a `case` statement.

case sensitivity A state that indicates whether an uppercase letter is treated the same as its corresponding lowercase letter. C, C++, and UNIX are case-sensitive. DOS is not.

central processing unit (CPU) The part of a processor where most computer calculations are performed.

char A character data-type variable.

character An alphanumeric symbol. For example, A or 1, B or 2, and so on.

character string A sequence of bytes treated as ASCII characters (letters, numbers, and other symbols). A character string is often enclosed in double quote marks, such as `"string"`.

class A set of elements grouped under a single name. The elements may be of different types. Elements can be member data or member functions. Sections of elements are grouped as private, public, or protected.

class hierarchy A hierarchy of types consisting of a common base class and one or more derived classes.

class inheritance The characteristic of a derived class that enables it to use the public members of its base class. The derived class is said to inherit class members from its base class.

click To press and release quickly one of the mouse buttons while the mouse pointer is pointing to an object on the screen. Usually, you use the left mouse button.

clipboard A temporary storage buffer for text. The clipboard is used to cut, paste, and copy text.

code block Same as a *block* or *statement block*.

code symbol An address of a procedure or function.

comments Program statements that are not executed. In C they are delimited by /* and */, and in C++ they are delimited by //.

compact memory model A memory model that allows one code segment and multiple data segments. This model is not recommended for Windows applications.

compile The process of translating a programming language source into machine code.

compiler A computer program that performs compilation, such as the Microsoft C/C++ 7 compiler.

concrete class A class without pure virtual functions. A concrete class is the opposite of an *abstract class*.

conditional expression A C or C++ language expression that uses ternary operators (?:) to join three operands. If the first operand evaluates to true, the second operand is evaluated. Otherwise, the third operand is evaluated.

constant A value that does not change during execution.

constant expression An expression that evaluates to a constant.

constructor A class member function that is automatically called when an object, which is an instance of the class, is created. A constructor is used to initialize a class object.

control A small window with a simple input/output purpose. Examples are push button controls, edit controls, and static controls.

coprocessor See *8087 family of math coprocessors.*

.CPP The filename extension for a C++ source file.

CPU See *central processing unit (CPU).*

.CUR The filename extension for a cursor resource object.

curly braces Punctuation marks ({}) used as delimiters in programs. In C and C++, they are used to delimit blocks.

cursor A thin blinking line or other representation that indicates the location for typed input or mouse action.

Data type A type of data, such as an `int` (integer) or a `char` (character).

debugger A development tool (program) used to detect bugs. An example is the Microsoft CodeView C/C++ 7 debugger.

declaration A language construct that associates a name with other attributes, such as type or value.

decrement Counting backward in value, as in 7, 6, 5, 4, and so on.

decrement operator The `--` operator, which is used to decrement an expression.

.DEF The filename extension for a module-definition file.

default A condition that is not specified but assumed by a program.

definition A language construct that specifies the interpretation and attributes of a set of identifiers and specifies the memory requirements for an object or function named by the identifier.

destructor A class member function that is automatically called when an object, which is an instance of the class, goes out of scope (is destroyed).

device context Defines the attributes of a device, such as a display or printer. Defines drawing tools and information for a device.

DGROUP A segment that contains local data memory. Also called the automatic data segment. Contains static data, stack, constants, and the local heap.

dialog box An impermanent window that displays program information or prompts for input.

dialog box controls Controls within a dialog box.

dialog script A .DLG file that contains the resource script for a dialog box and all its controls. The dialog script is compiled by the resource compiler to generate a .RES file.

dimension The number of array subscripts.

directive An instruction to the preprocessor to perform some operation on the source code before compilation.

.DLG The filename extension for a dialog resource-script file.

DLL (dynamic linked library) A special library that lets applications share resources and functions.

Double precision A floating-point numeric value that occupies 8 bytes of memory. Double-precision values are accurate to 15–16 significant places.

DPMI A program, called a *server*, that makes extended or expanded memory available to programs. Examples of DPMI servers include the MSDPMI processor for DOS sessions. This server allows programs that take advantage of the 32-bit architecture of the 80386 microprocessor. The Microsoft C/C++ 7 compiler is a 32-bit program. It cannot run under DOS unless MSDPMI is operating but can run in a DOS session under Windows.

drag To move the mouse across the screen while pressing the left mouse button.

dynamic linking Performing a link operation for an application at run time.

editor A software program that originates, edits, and saves text files.

EGA (Enhanced Graphics Adapter) A color video display device that displays 65 colors.

EMM (Expanded Memory Manager) A device driver for controlling expanded memory.

emulator A software math package that simulates the operations of a math coprocessor.

encapsulation A mechanism for hiding the internal workings of a class to support abstraction.

end-of-file marker A code used to signify the end of a file.

environment Program development tools that include a debugger, compiler, editor, and linker.

environment variable A variable stored in a DOS environment table that contains information relating to the software environment. This variable is normally used to store information to assist in the location of files.

EOF A constant symbol that designates the end-of-file marker.

escape character A character, usually a backslash (\), used to signal an escape sequence.

escape sequence A combination of a backslash character (`\`) and another character, used to specify special characters, such as a newline (`\n`) or a tab character (`\t`).

.EXE The filename extension for an executable application file.

executable file A program that contains machine language instructions and is ready to be run by the operating system.

execute To perform instructions in a software program.

expanded memory Memory above 650K that can be used by real-mode programs and controlled through paging by an expanded memory manager.

expression An operand or a combination of operands and operators that yields a single value when evaluated.

extended memory Memory above either 640K or 1M that is made available to protected-mode programs on computers with an 80286 microprocessor or newer. Extended memory is used by Windows in standard or 386 enhanced mode.

extension See *filename extension*.

external level The parts of a C or C++ program that are outside function declarations.

external reference A data item or routine declared in one module but referenced in another.

external variable In C or C++, a variable that is defined outside any function and can be accessed by functions in other source files.

`far` address A four-byte address formed by the segment address (two bytes) and the offset (two bytes) from the beginning of the address.

file handle An integer value returned when a file is opened, and used to reference that file for any I/O operations. A file handle is used with C and C++ language low-level file I/O operations.

file pointer A `long` value that contains the byte address of the current file location. Each time a read, write, or seek operation is performed, the file pointer is repositioned.

filename The name used to reference a file, consisting of a base name and an optional extension. The base name can be followed by a period and a filename extension of up to three characters. In DOS the base name can have up to eight characters.

filename extension An extension to a filename, consisting of up to three characters and preceded by a period. The extension is normally used to represent a file type. For example, the extension .EXE in WORD.EXE indicates that the file is an executable file.

floating point A `float` data type. Also a technique for storing numbers with a decimal point.

font The style and shape of a character in a character set.

formal parameters Variables that receive values passed by a calling program.

format specification A string that is used with the `printf()` and `scanf()` functions and specifies the formatting of variables to display.

friend class A class that can access the private data of the class in which the friend class is declared.

friend function A function that can modify private data for the class in which the function is declared as a friend. A friend function is usually used for function overloading.

function A program code section that enacts a specific task.

function body The statement block that contains a function's local declarations and statements.

function call A statement that passes control to a function.

function declaration The name, return type, and storage class of a function that is to be called. This is also called a *prototype declaration*. Normally, prototype declarations for functions to be called are placed in header files.

function definition The entire function, including the name, formal parameters, declarations, and statement block, and optionally its storage class and return type.

function pointer A pointer to the address of a function.

function prototype See *function declaration*.

global symbol A symbol that is visible throughout an entire program.

global variable A variable that is visible to all sections of a program.

header file A file that usually has an .h filename extension and contains declarations, definitions, and prototypes. A header file, sometimes referred to as an *include* file, is included into source files with the `#include` preprocessor directive.

heap A memory area reserved for memory allocation.

hexadecimal Base-16 numbers represented by the characters 0–F. The letters A–F correspond to the decimal values 10–15, respectively.

hexadecimal system A numeric notational system based on the number 16.

huge memory model A memory model that supports more than one code segment and more than one data segment. Data items can exceed 64K because pointers are all `far` pointers.

I/O (input/output) The exchange of data, such as between the keyboard (an input device) and the terminal screen (an output device). File I/O means reading and writing files.

icon A bitmap resource that represents a small image. An icon displays when an application is minimized.

identifier The name of a variable, constant, macro, function, or data type. An identifier is contrived by the programmer.

include file A file inserted into a source file with a C++ `#include` preprocessor directive.

increment Counting forward in value, such as 6, 7, 8, 9, and so on.

increment operator The `++` operator, which is used to increment an expression.

indirection The process by which a data object is accessed through a pointer instead of through its name.

initialize The process by which a variable is assigned a value when it is declared.

instance A copy of an application that executes separately.

integer A whole number that contains no fractional or decimal part. An integer is represented as a 16-bit binary `int` data type in computers that run DOS and Windows.

keyword A C or C++ language term that has a predefined meaning and provides instructions to the compiler.

kilobyte (K) 1,024 bytes.

label A unique name followed by a colon and placed at the beginning of a C or C++ language statement. A label is used also with the `goto` statement. For a `case` statement, a *case label* is a constant expression followed by a colon.

library A file that contains object modules which are compiled. A linker extracts object modules and includes them in other object modules to build an executable module.

lifetime The period in which a variable or function exists. A local variable or an automatic variable is declared within a function block and exists only when the function is executing. When the function returns, such variables are discarded. A `static` variable exists during the entire execution of a program.

linker A software program that combines object modules to generate an executable module. Object files contain relocatable addresses. Object modules may be user-defined or extracted from a library. The linker loads object modules needed to build the executable file into memory and replaces the relocatable addresses with absolute addresses. The linker continues this process until all external references have been resolved, and then creates an executable module.

linking The operation performed by a linker.

local variable A variable that exists and takes up memory space when the block in which it is declared executes.

loop A program construct that repeats.

low-level language A programming language that is close to machine code. Assembler language is a low-level language.

lvalue An expression that refers to a single memory location. The expression on the left side of an expression must be an lvalue (*l* stands for *l*eft). For example, a variable name is an example of an lvalue.

machine code The native language of a computer, consisting of binary computer instructions a computer interprets to execute a program.

macro A constant or function identifier that is equated to an expression through a `#define` preprocessor directive. The preprocessor substitutes every occurrence of the identifier with the characters to which it is equated before the source file is compiled.

`main()` **function** The function with which program execution begins.

medium memory model A memory model with one data segment and one or more code segments.

megabyte (M) Approximately one million bytes.

member A structure or union element.

member-of operator A dot operator used with the name of a structure and a member to reference the member. An example is `struct.member`.

memory location The address of a procedure or data item.

menu bar The bar at the top of a window and just below the title bar. The menu bar is used to display menus.

module A block of program logic usually organized into a file. Programs can consist of one or more modules.

`near` address A two-byte memory location specified by an offset relative to the beginning of a segment.

newline character A character used to mark the end of a text line. The escape sequence `\n` specifies a newline character.

null character A character, with a zero value (`'\0'`), that marks the end of a string.

null pointer A pointer that points to nothing. It has a value of zero.

.OBJ The filename extension for a program object file.

object code Relocatable machine code created by a compiler.

object file A file that contains object code and has a filename extension of .OBJ. The linker translates object files and object modules from a library into an executable program.

object module An object file that is included in a library.

offset The number of bytes from the beginning of a segment.

OOP (object-orientated programming) A programming model in which modularity is based on the type of the objects and how the projects are related. OOP pertains also to the implementation of a program system that has been subjected to object-oriented analysis and design.

operand A value that is manipulated inside an expression.

operator One or more characters that designate how an operand or operands of an expression are to be operated on. A `+` operator in the expression `1 + 2` designates that the two operands are to be added together.

parameter An identifier, often called a *formal argument*, that receives a value passed to a function. A parameter is used also to refer to command-line arguments.

path A name that specifies the location of a file or directory. A path can contain a drive name, directory names, and a filename.

pointer A variable that contains the address of another variable. A pointer can point to another value in an array or to another data object.

pointer arithmetic Operations that change the value of a pointer. Pointer arithmetic is typically used for array pointers to point to different elements.

polymorphism Having the capability to assume multiple forms. In OOP, polymorphism is the capability of a statement to assume multiple functions, depending on the type of data to be operated on. C++ enables you to specify a family of functions with the same name but different signatures.

`#pragma` An instruction to the compiler to perform some action during compilation. A `#pragma` preprocessor directive is used to specify a `#pragma` statement.

precedence The position of an operator (and its operation) in a precedence table. Operators with higher precedence levels are evaluated before operators with lower precedence levels.

preprocessor A processor that is attached to the compiler and modifies the source code in accordance with directives before the compiler processes the source code.

procedure call An expression that executes statements in another function and uses the value returned from the function as an operand.

protected mode One of the operating modes of the 80286 or 80386 microprocessor. The other mode is *real* mode. The Windows standard and 386 enhanced operating modes run under protected mode.

pseudocode Vernacular language used to indicate the actions you want a program to perform.

pure virtual function A virtual function that requires no function body.

RAM (random access memory) Computer memory.

.RC The filename extension for a resource script file.

real mode One of the operating modes of the 80286 or 80386 microprocessor. The other is *protected* mode. The Windows real operating mode runs in real mode.

recursive process A function that calls itself.

register variable An integer variable placed in a processor register. A program can be faster and smaller with this integer variable.

relational operators Symbols that compare two operands. Examples of relational operators are ==, >=, and <=.

relocatable machine code Code that can be placed in memory at any location and does not contain absolute addresses.

.RES A filename extension for a compiled resource file.

resource A data file that the resource compiler reads and inserts in .EXE or .DLL files. A resource can define such objects as cursors, bitmaps, and icons.

return value A value returned by a function to the calling function.

routine A term for a subroutine, procedure, or function.

run time The time when a program is executing.

run-time library A file containing C or C++ language functions. Functions are added to the application module during the linking process.

scope The portion of a program that can be referred to by name. The scope can be limited to program, source file, function, or block. Visibility of a function or variable.

segment A section of memory that contains code or data. A segment is limited to 64K for 2-byte (`near`) addresses and to 4G (gigabytes) for 4-byte (`far`) addresses. A segment refers also to the starting address of a memory area.

sign The designation of a number as positive or negative.

signature The function argument list. Two functions with the same name have the same signature if their argument lists have the same number of arguments and the arguments are of the same type. Two functions with the same name have different signatures if the functions have a different number of arguments or the types of the arguments differ (or both).

small memory model A memory model with one data segment and one code segment.

source file A text file that contains C or C++ language code.

stack An area of memory in which data can be stored and retrieved in first-in-last-out order. A stack is used to store information for function calls and local variables.

standard error A device to which program errors are directed unless redirected. In DOS the standard error device is the display, and the predefined stream associated with C and C++ language standard error is `stderr`.

standard input The device to which a program reads its input unless redirected. In DOS the standard input device is the keyboard, and the predefined stream associated with C and C++ language standard input is `stdin`.

standard library A library created by the LIB program that contains compiled functions and data. A library is used by a linker to build an executable module.

standard mode A Windows 3 mode that runs on computers with an 80286 or 80386 microprocessor. Standard mode is one of the three Windows 3 modes; the other two are real and 386 enhanced.

standard output A device to which a program sends its output unless redirected. In DOS the standard output device is the display (monitor), and the predefined stream associated with C and C++ language standard output is `stdout`.

static linking The linking of library modules with application modules at link time. The opposite is dynamic linking.

static variable A variable that retains its value for the duration of the execution of a program.

stream A sequence of characters flowing into or out of a program.

stream function A C or C++ language run-time library function that performs stream input and output operations.

string An array of characters terminated with a null character. A null-terminated string.

string constant A string of characters delimited with double quotation characters (`" "`).

structure A set of elements grouped under a single name. The elements may be of different types.

structure pointer A pointer to a structure. When you use a pointer to a structure, structure members can be referenced with a pointer-to operator (->) that separates the pointer name and member name. An example is `ptr->member`.

symbolic constant A name used in place of a constant. A `#define` preprocessor directive or a `const` C++ statement is used to equate a symbolic constant name with a constant expression.

tag A name designated for a union, a structure, or an enumeration.

task A basic unit of scheduling.

terminator A character that ends a string of characters.

ternary operator An operator that takes three operands. The only ternary operator in C and C++ is the conditional operator (`?:`).

text Readable characters, including alphabetic, numeric, and punctuation characters.

text file A file that contains text (ASCII characters).

text format A method of disk storage in which all data is converted to ASCII format.

toggle option A source code instruction that turns a condition either on or off.

twos complement A technique for storing positive and negative values. It involves complementing all the bits and adding 1 to represent a negative number.

type A classification for data. For example, basic data types can be character (`char`), integer (`int` and `long`), floating point (`float`), and `double` type data.

type cast A method of converting one data type to another. For example, to convert an `int` to a `float`, you specify the type cast as the following: `(float) 3`

type checking The process by which a compiler tests to see whether the types of operands of an operator are correct. The C/C++ compiler, using prototypes, can verify that the arguments of a function are the correct type.

type declaration A statement that defines the name and members of a structure or union.

type qualifier The keywords used in declarations to modify data types. Examples are `short`, `long`, `signed`, and `unsigned`.

typedef declaration A declaration that uses a `typedef` keyword to define new data types from existing basic data types.

unary operator An operator with one operand. In C and C++, unary operators are `^`, `~`, `!`, `-`, `++`, `--`, `&`, and `sizeof`.

unlinked dialog box A dialog box activated from an application. Menus activate *linked* dialog boxes.

variable A value that may change during program execution.

virtual function A member function in a base class that you plan to redefine in a derived class.

visibility Refers to areas of a program in which a variable or function can be referenced by name.

whitespace character A set of characters that includes the space, tab, linefeed, newline, and vertical tab characters.

wild card The `?` and `*` characters, which are used to form a pattern for searching for filenames. The `?` wild-card character stands for "any character." The `*` wild-card character means "ignore the rest of the characters in the name." For example, a pattern of `?A*` matches any filename whose second character is `A`.

window A rectangular region on the screen where output is displayed and input is received.

Index

Symbols

A

B

C

D

E

F

J-K

L

M

N

O

P

Q

R

S

T

W

X-Z

Sams—Covering The Latest In Computer And Technical Topics!

Audio

Advanced Digital Audio $39.95
Audio Systems Design and Installation $59.95
Compact Disc Troubleshooting and Repair $24.95
Handbook for Sound Engineers: The New Audio Cyclopedia, 2nd Ed. $99.95
How to Design & Build Loudspeaker & Listening Enclosures $39.95
Introduction to Professional Recording Techniques $29.95
The MIDI Manual $24.95
Modern Recording Techniques, 3rd Ed. $29.95
OP-AMP Circuits and Principles $19.95
Principles of Digital Audio, 2nd Ed. $29.95
Sound Recording Handbook $49.95
Sound System Engineering, 2nd Ed. $49.95

Electricity/Electronics

Active-Filter Cookbook $24.95
Basic Electricity and DC Circuits $29.95
CMOS Cookbook, 2nd Ed. $24.95
Electrical Wiring $19.95
Electricity 1-7, Revised 2nd Ed. $49.95
Electronics 1-7, Revised 2nd Ed. $49.95
How to Read Schematics, 4th Ed. $19.95
IC Op-Amp Cookbook, 3rd Ed. $24.95
IC Timer Cookbook, 2nd Ed. $24.95
RF Circuit Design $24.95
Transformers and Motors $29.95
TTL Cookbook $24.95
Understanding Digital Troubleshooting, 3rd Ed. $24.95
Understanding Solid State Electronics, 5th Ed. $24.95

Games

Master SimCity/SimEarth $19.95
Master Ultima $16.95

Hardware/Technical

First Book of Modem Communications $16.95
First Book of PS/1 .... $16.95
Hard Disk Power with the Jamsa Disk Utilities $39.95
IBM PC Advanced Troubleshooting & Repair $24.95
IBM Personal Computer Troubleshooting & Repair $24.95
Microcomputer Troubleshooting & Repair $24.95
Understanding Fiber Optics $24.95

IBM: Business

10 Minute Guide to PC Tools 7 .... $ 9.95
10 Minute Guide to Q&A 4 .... $ 9.95
First Book of Microsoft Works for the PC $16.95
First Book of Norton Utilities 6 .... $16.95
First Book of PC Tools 7 .... $16.95
First Book of Personal Computing, 2nd Ed. $16.95

IBM: Database

10 Minute Guide to Harvard Graphics 2.3 .... $9.95
Best Book of AutoCAD $34.95
dBASE III Plus Programmer's Reference Guide $24.95
dBASE IV Version 1.1 for the First-Time User $24.95
Everyman's Database Primer Featuring dBASE IV Version 1.1 .... $24.95
First Book of Paradox 3.5 .... $16.95
First Book of PowerPoint for Windows $16.95
Harvard Graphics 2.3 In Business $29.95

IBM: Graphics/Desktop Publishing

10 Minute Guide to Lotus 1-2-3 .... $ 9.95
Best Book of Harvard Graphics $24.95
First Book of Harvard Graphics 2.3 .... $16.95
First Book of PC Paintbrush $16.95
First Book of PFS: First Publisher $16.95

IBM: Spreadsheets/Financial

Best Book of Lotus 1-2-3 Release 3.1 .... $27.95
First Book of Excel 3 for Windows $16.95
First Book of Lotus 1-2-3 Release 2.3 .... $16.95
First Book of Quattro Pro 3 .... $16.95
First Book of Quicken In Business $16.95
Lotus 1-2-3 Release 2.3 In Business $29.95
Lotus 1-2-3: Step-by-Step $24.95
Quattro Pro In Business $29.95

IBM: Word Processing

Best Book of Microsoft Word 5 .... $24.95
Best Book of Microsoft Word for Windows $24.95
Best Book of WordPerfect 5.1 .... $26.95
First Book of Microsoft Word 5.5 .... $16.95
First Book of WordPerfect 5.1 .... $16.95
WordPerfect 5.1: Step-by-Step $24.95

Macintosh/Apple

First Book of Excel 3 for the Mac $16.95
First Book of the Mac $16.95

Operating Systems/Networking

10 Minute Guide to Windows 3 .... $ 9.95
Best Book of DESQview $24.95
Best Book of Microsoft Windows 3 .... $24.95
Best Book of MS-DOS 5 .... $24.95
Business Guide to Local Area Networks $24.95
DOS Batch File Power with the Jamsa Disk Utilities $39.95
Exploring the UNIX System, 2nd Ed. $29.95
First Book of DeskMate $16.95
First Book of Microsoft Windows 3 .... $16.95
First Book of MS-DOS 5 .... $16.95
First Book of UNIX $16.95
Interfacing to the IBM Personal Computer, 2nd Ed. $24.95
The Waite Group's Discovering MS-DOS, 2nd Edition $19.95
The Waite Group's MS-DOS Bible, 4th Ed. $29.95
The Waite Group's MS-DOS Developer's Guide, 2nd Ed. $29.95
The Waite Group's Tricks of the UNIX Masters $29.95
The Waite Group's Understanding MS-DOS, 2nd Ed. $19.95
The Waite Group's UNIX Primer Plus, 2nd Ed. $29.95
The Waite Group's UNIX System V Bible $29.95
Understanding Local Area Networks, 2nd Ed. $24.95
UNIX Applications Programming: Mastering the Shell $29.95
UNIX Networking $29.95
UNIX Shell Programming, Revised Ed. $29.95
UNIX: Step-by-Step $29.95
UNIX System Administration $29.95
UNIX System Security $34.95
UNIX Text Processing $29.95

Professional/Reference

Data Communications, Networks, and Systems $39.95
Handbook of Electronics Tables and Formulas, 6th Ed. $24.95
ISDN, DECnet, and SNA Communications $49.95
Modern Dictionary of Electronics, 6th Ed. $39.95
Reference Data for Engineers: Radio, Electronics, Computer, and Communications, 7th Ed. $99.95

Programming

Advanced C: Tips and Techniques $29.95
C Programmer's Guide to NetBIOS $29.95
C Programmer's Guide to Serial Communications $29.95
Commodore 64 Programmer's Reference Guide $24.95
Developing Windows Applications with Microsoft SDK $29.95
DOS Batch File Power $39.95
Graphical User Interfaces with Turbo C++ $29.95
Learning C++ $39.95
Mastering Turbo Assembler $29.95
Mastering Turbo Pascal, 4th Ed. $29.95
Microsoft Macro Assembly Language Programming $29.95
Microsoft QuickBASIC Programmer's Reference $29.95
Programming in ANSI C $29.95
Programming in C, Revised Ed. $29.95
The Waite Group's BASIC Programming Primer, 2nd Ed. $24.95
The Waite Group's C Programming Using Turbo C++ $29.95
The Waite Group's C: Step-by-Step $29.95
The Waite Group's GW-BASIC Primer Plus $24.95
The Waite Group's Microsoft C Bible, 2nd Ed. $29.95
The Waite Group's Microsoft C Programming for the PC, 2nd Ed. $29.95
The Waite Group's New C Primer Plus $29.95
The Waite Group's Turbo Assembler Bible $29.95
The Waite Group's Turbo C Bible $29.95
The Waite Group's Turbo C Programming for the PC, Revised Ed. $29.95
The Waite Group's Turbo C++Bible $29.95
X Window System Programming $29.95

Radio/Video

Camcorder Survival Guide .... $ 14.95
Radio Handbook, 23rd Ed. $39.95
Radio Operator's License Q&A Manual, 11th Ed. $24.95
Understanding Fiber Optics $24.95
Understanding Telephone Electronics, 3rd Ed. $24.95
VCR Troubleshooting & Repair Guide $19.95
Video Scrambling & Descrambling for Satellite & Cable TV $24.95

For More Information, See Your Local Retailer Or Call Toll Free

1-800-428-5331

All prices are subject to change without notice. Non-U.S. prices may be higher. Printed in the U.S.A.

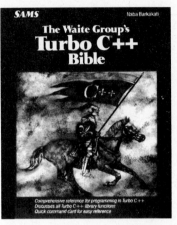

ORDER YOUR SAMPLE PROGRAMS DISKETTE TODAY!

Typing a source file from a listing in a book is no fun. Save yourself hours of grief by ordering the *Do It Yourself Microsoft C/C++ 7* sample programs diskette. On the diskette, you'll find the source code for all the C++ sample programs presented in this book.

Diskettes are available in either 5 1/4" or 3 1/2" format. The cost is $17.00, plus $3.00 for shipping and handling. (California residents, please add 8 1/2% state sales tax.)

Just make a copy of this page, fill in the blanks, and send it with your check, money order, or credit card information to:

Do It Yourself Microsoft C/C++ 7
Sample Programs Diskette
c/o Jeb Long
Software Impressions
P.O. Box 786
La Canada, CA 91011

YES, please send me ______ copies of the *Do It Yourself Microsoft C/C++ 7* Sample Programs Diskette!

@ $17 each = $______

Sales Tax (8 1/2% for California residents ONLY) .... $______

Shipping and Handling .... $ 3.00

Total .... $______

Payment method: Check ______ Money Order ______ Visa ______ MasterCard ______

Card #________________________ Exp. Date ____________

Signature ______________________________

Make check or money order payable to: ***Software Impressions***

Diskette format: **5 1/4"** ______ **3 1/2"** ______

Name: ______________________________

Street address: ______________________________

City: ______________________ State: ____________

ZIP: ____________ Phone (____)____________________

Please allow 2-3 weeks for delivery.

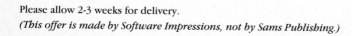

(This offer is made by Software Impressions, not by Sams Publishing.)

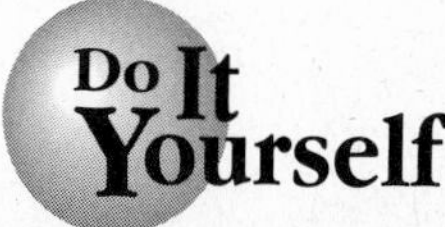